BEGINNING YOUR FAMILY HISTORY

George Pelling

Published by
COUNTRYSIDE BOOKS
in association with
THE FEDERATION OF
FAMILY HISTORY SOCIETIES

First Published by FFHS 1980
Fifth Edition 1990
Reprinted 1992
© George Pelling 1990

Typeset by Acorn Bookwork, Salisbury
Produced through MRM Associates Ltd., Reading
Printed in England

Contents

Figures

Acknowledgements

Acknowledgements for the first four editions are contained in each. The same cover has been used for all editions, except the first; my thanks to Derek Palgrave, who prepared the artwork. I would like to thank the staff of the West Sussex Record Office, where much of my research has been done. The Inventory shown in Figure 16 is reproduced by their kind permission. The reproductions of the census returns in figures 12 and 13 are with the permission of H.M.S.O. for which my thanks. As always, I must express my gratitude to my wife and children for their patience and understanding in allowing me to spend so much time in the service of Family History. My grateful thanks also to the following, for responding so readily to my request for up to date information:

A.J. Camp, Director Society of Genealogists.
General Register Office, St Catherine's House.
General Register Office for Scotland.
Dr C. Kinealy, Administrator, Ulster Historical Foundation.
G.D. Mawlam, Genealogical Society of Utah.
Mrs S. Lumas, Public Record Office.

George Pelling

Introduction

When I talk about my absorbing interest in Family History, the question sometimes arises – "Why do you do it?"

Family History research has been described as a cross between a good detective story and a jig-saw puzzle. Certainly the thrill of the chase is experienced whilst searching and there is great satisfaction when a particularly elusive ancestor is found and put in his allotted place on the Family Tree.

Gradually changing social conditions have given rise to a society in which many people live away from their places of origin and some find it difficult to relate to their present environment. It is a natural step for them to start searching for their "roots" and perhaps explains why family history has become so popular, particularly in America, where it is the most pursued pastime, and there is also great interest in our other former colonies in Canada, Australia and New Zealand. There are, however, many whose families have been in the same area for generations and they obviously have a different motivation. Man has an inherent curiosity about himself and his origins and much contemporary conversation centres around gossip about the family, neighbours and friends.

In 1982 I appeared in a Granada TV series of 5 programmes and in 1985 in a small "slot" on another programme. Following each I received hundreds of letters from all over the North West region, from people of all ages and all walks of life.

Each of us is a product of genetic and environmental influences and by studying our ancestors we can find out more about ourselves. As Don Steel has pointed out in *Discovering Your Family History* ". . . history is not merely a chronicle of past events but an enquiry into the thoughts and actions of people in the past." A closer understanding of our predecessors can be achieved by studying the history of the family, the fundamental social unit, than by the more traditional approaches to national and local history, he justifiably asserts.

Whatever the reason, the veritable explosion of interest in the subject in recent years is remarkable. When the Federation of Family History Societies was founded in 1974, it had less than a dozen members: by 1989 this total had increased to 150, spread across the English speaking world. I little thought, when I wrote the introduction to the First Edition in 1980, that ten years, (and some 70,000 copies), later, I would be writing a Fifth.

The aim of the book remains unchanged, to provide the beginner with the preliminary information necessary to research back to the 16th century; by answering, for each main subject covered, the questions: When? What? Where? How? and Cost? The order in which the subjects are considered will, it is hoped, help keep the cost to a minimum.

The number of ancestors doubles with each generation as you proceed backwards, 4 grandparents, 8 great grandparents and so on, so that 10 generations back (say 300 years) you may have as many as 1,024 ancestors; at

1066 (30 generations) the nominal number would exceed 1,000 million, but, of course, thousands of names would be repeated thousands of times.

Your efforts will be rewarded by finding new relatives and if you follow the steps in this book you should be able to "do-it-yourself". The most rewarding aspect of this fascinating and absorbing pastime, for me, however, was unexpected. Since I set out to find my ancestors I have met many people, and have corresponded with many more, engaged on a similar quest. Although my search was in the past, I found fellowship and friendship in the present. May you be as fortunate.

GEORGE PELLING
March 1990

Figure 1 FAMILY QUESTIONNAIRE FORM

	Your Name	Your Husband's/Wife's Name
Please give full names	....	....
Previous surname(s) where appropriate		
Date/place birth	....	....
Date/place marriage	....	....
Date/place death/burial		....
Occupation	....	....

Your Children's names* 1. .... 2................ 3..........................

Date/place birth	....	....	....
Date/place Marriage	....	....	....
Name of wife/husband	....	....	....
Their children *	1....................	....	....
*(if more than three	2....................	....	....
use additional sheet)	3....................	....	....

	Your father	Your mother (maiden name)
	....	....
Date/place birth/bapt	....	....
Date/place marriage	....	....
Date/place death/bur	....	....
Occupation/Religion	....	....

Your brothers/sisters* 1.................... 2................ 3..........................

Date/place birth/bapt	....	....	....
Date/place marriage	....	....	....
Name wife/husband	....	....	....
Occupation	....	....	....
Their children *	1....................	....	....
	2....................	....	....
	3....................	....	....

	Paternal Grandparents	Maternal Grandparents
Names	....	....
Date place birth/bapt	....	....
Date/place marriage	....	....
Date/place death/bur	....	....
Occupation & Religion	....	....

Any other information...

....

....

Your address ....

....Telephone ....

8

1. The Starting Point – Family Sources

Many excellent Family Histories have been written which are sadly deficient in one respect: very little is known about the author, who assumed, modestly but wrongly, that no one was ever going to be interested in him. The golden rule is to start with yourself and work backwards, generation by generation, proving each step as far as possible by reference to the records available. These will be considered briefly in the following pages.

Do not take a person from the past with your name and try to trace his descendants in the hope that you may be one of them; even if there is a family legend that he is your ancestor. You may find, as you proceed, that your ancestral name several generations back is different from what it is today.

Your first sources are the memories of your immediate family and their treasures lovingly preserved over the years. Talk to all your relatives, in particular to the older generation. If you can tape-record them, do so, and be prepared to jog their memories by asking questions, but mostly listen. If recording is not possible, note what they say and try to persuade them to write down their memories. They will enjoy the experience, you will find the results fascinating reading. Memory fades and needs stimulation, so you may not obtain all the information at once. Ask some more questions after a lapse of time, when they have had the opportunity for further reflection. Your relatives may live far away and you may have to rely upon correspondence, but if your enquiries are vague the replies will be likewise. It is a good idea to send them a questionnaire (see Figure 1) to ensure you get all the essential information but make sure your relative knows who you are and why you need these details. Look for the following: Family Bible; letters; diaries; memorial cards; Birth, Marriage and Death Certificates; Professional Certificates; Birthday Books; Newspaper cuttings (often obituary notices are kept); Samplers (pieces of embroidery worked by young girls to demonstrate proficiency and often framed and displayed); Medals (look at the edge for name, rank and number); Photographs, about which a special word. How many times have you looked at old photos and asked whom do they depict? Try to identify them and write the names lightly on the back. It is possible, although slightly expensive, to re-photograph old faded prints and produce a clear enlarged picture. Good photocopiers will produce reasonable facsimiles.

Sometimes relatives are reluctant to talk about a particular person and there may be a family "skeleton in the cupboard". Be prepared to find illegitimacy, which occurs in nearly every family.

The main source of family information for my maternal grandmother's family, and the inspiration for my starting on the quest for my ancestors was my Aunt Bess, my mother's eldest, unmarried sister, who remembered her great-grandfather, born 1815, and told me the names of his 11 children and 65 grandchildren. It was some years, however, before she told me that she had destroyed her mother's marriage certificate, because the date was less than nine months before her own birth date.

It was 14 years afterwards, in 1984, that I finally located the family bible, or to be accurate that the holder contacted me, via another relative. The moral is obvious, ALL known relatives should be contacted, however remote. My research had not been wasted (research, even that which yields negative information, rarely is), because I was able to prove that one of the entries, (which covered 7 generations from 1765), was inaccurate: confusion having arisen from a marriage of cousins with the same name. So, how had the error occurred? Quite simply, the Bible was not published until 1846, prior entries had been made from memory, which emphasises that ALL sources must be checked for accuracy. Moreover, no one should be accepted as an ancestor, unless and until it is proved beyond all reasonable doubt.

Not everyone is clear about family relationships, particularly cousins, the chart depicted at Figure 2 should enable you to determine any relationship.

Try and find out where your ancestors were buried. Gravestones are an invaluable source for clarifying family relationships and often include information about several generations, which may save you the cost of purchasing birth certificates (see Chapter 5). Stones become worn and the older ones are difficult to read. Record what you can, leaving spaces where words are not clear and indicate where you have made a guess.

e.g. JOHN SMITH(ER?)S died January (?)th 18(53?), Aged 6(5?)

Look for graves in the vicinity bearing the same surname. Families often purchased adjacent plots.

Burial grounds for non-conformists were started in the 17th century and increased in number in the 18th. Public cemeteries were started in London in 1827, but most date from the 1850's or later. Most have well indexed records.

The records for a cemetery still in use will normally be found at the Office at the cemetery. The Register will normally record dates of death and burial, in addition to name, address, occupation and age of the deceased. A grave number will be given, from which the plot can be located from the grave map.

Recognising their unique value, dedicated individuals and public spirited organisations have recorded Monumental Inscriptions and the Society of Genealogists (S.O.G.) has built up a substantial collection. This invaluable work received a tremendous boost in 1978 when the Federation launched an ambitious plan to record all the inscriptions in churchyards and other burial grounds, concentrating first on those most at risk. This ideal target has not yet been fully achieved, but the response from member Societies has been magnificent. Most Societies have appointed a co-ordinator to control the recording of Monumental Inscriptions and other projects. If you are able to help, your local Society would like to hear from you; no expertise is required. Often the results are indexed, which saves valuable searching time, and some have been published.

If the churchyard or burial ground in which your ancestor was buried has been landscaped, or otherwise destroyed, the inscriptions may (should, if after 1906) have been recorded, although often in a disappointingly brief manner. Your local library may have a copy.

Dates on tombstones (like dates in most records) cannot be relied upon as the stone may have been erected years after the first interment; remember also that the stone is a memorial, so all those listed may not be buried there.

Bibliography

Interviewing Elderly Relatives . . ., Eve McLaughlin, FFHS.

Notes on the Recording of Monumental Inscriptions, J. L. Rayment, FFHS.

Family History in Focus, ed. Don Steel and Lawrence Taylor.

Relationships

The chart shown in figure 2 looks daunting but it is essentially very simple, provided you follow the rules step by step. You will know that first cousins have common grandparents; if you did not it can be ascertained from the chart. The key to understanding it is to substitute yourself and your relatives in place of the symbols. For the purposes of this example, (with apologies to the ladies), you are George (since this example is from my mother's family). Place yourself, (George), at GC in column H2. Your mother, Margaret, is C and her father Alfred is CA (your grandfather). Now substitute relatives in columns V1 etc.

V1 (C) is your mother's sister Nora.
V2 (GC) her daughter, Alice, and
V3 (GGC) Janet, the daughter of Alice.

All of the above is illustrated graphically underneath the chart. Reading down column H2, the relationship of George to persons in the V column is stated viz:

n = nephew to Nora.
lc = first cousin to Alice.
lclr = first cousin once removed to Janet.

The principle of the chart is quite simple. George and Alice have common grandparents: Therefore:

Place George at H2 (grandchild)
Place Alice at V2 (grandchild) and

Their relationship is stated where columns H2 and V2 intersect, ie 1c (first cousin). Let us look again at the relationship of George to Alice's daughter, Janet and vice versa – not second cousins, as is commonly supposed.

George is H2 (GC), as before.
Janet is V3 (GGC).

H2 and V3 intersect at 1c1r (first cousin once removed). Logical enough, since Janet is one generation removed from, George's first cousin, Alice. It is of course, Nichola and Janet who are second cousins.

Prince Charles and Princess Diana have a common ancestor, James I of England. He is 11 × GGC and she 10 × GGC: what is their relationship? Extending the chart, he would be in column H13 and she in column V12; they are therefore 11th cousins once removed: if you don't believe me, extend the chart and check it!

Figure 2 RELATIONSHIP CHART

		H	1	2	3	4	5
	CA	→	C	GC	GGC	2 × GGC	3 × GGC
V							
1	C			s	n	gn	ggn	2 × ggn
2	GC			n	1c	1c1r	1c2r	1c3r
3	GGC			gn	1c1r	2c	2c1r	2c2r
4	2 × GGC			ggn	1c2r	2c1r	3c	3c1r
5	3 × GGC			2 × ggn	1c3r	2c2r	3c1r	4c

Key: RELATIONSHIP TO COMMON ANCESTOR (CA): C = CHILD: GC = GRANDCHILD: GGC = GREAT-GRANDCHILD: Number × = Times GREAT (e.g. 3 × GGC = GREAT GREAT GREAT-GRANDCHILD.

Relationship between relatives with a common ancestor: s = sibling (brother or sister): n = nephew/niece: c = cousin: gn = grand-nephew/niece: number r = times removed (e.g. 1c1r = first cousin once removed).

(NB: The chart can be extended indefinitely: cousins will always be on the diagonal from top left to bottom right).

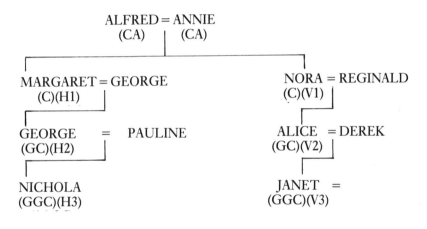

2. Setting Your Sights

Being Selective

Start immediately to fill in a Pedigree Chart (sometimes called a Birth Brief) as far back as you can. A sample chart is shown in Figure 3, which provides spaces for all your ancestors back to your 16 Great-great-grandparents. The most important thing to decide next is which of the possible options you should choose, otherwise you will simply be ancestor collecting with no objective in view. Your choice will be influenced by the data you have immediately available. You may, of course, change your mind later, when you have obtained more material and as you become more familiar with the subject, but you should be aware of the following possibilities at an early stage, since this may influence your approach.

One Name

The researcher collects every reference to a particular surname, wherever and whenever it occurs.

Total Ancestry

Having traced 16 great-great-grandparents, the researcher then looks for their 32 parents, so that every time an ancestor is found he starts looking for two more.

Several Families

The objective is to research a number of families (perhaps those of your 4 grand-parents) in depth, by putting them into their local and historical context, with, perhaps, the ultimate aim of writing a family history.

Seeking Help

The previously stated aim of this book is to show you how to do it yourself, but, however independent and dedicated you may be, you will need help.

Visit your local library, with which you may already be familiar (though perhaps not with the Reference Section of it), where you will find copies of at least some of the material mentioned in the following pages. A list of helpful books appears at the end of this and subsequent chapters. Library books are arranged under code numbers: those listed and most others useful to a Family Historian will be found under code 929. The library notice board should have details of local societies and particulars of any further education classes covering the subject.

Mention has already been made of the Federation of Family History Societies and a current list of member societies is included on the back cover of its magazine *Family History News and Digest*, which is published twice a year.

There is almost certainly a society covering the area in which you live and membership subscriptions are modest (usually £5–£10 per annum). You do not have to be an expert to join; everyone is welcome, especially beginners. Your ancestors may be from a different part of the country and you may feel that your local society is remote from your areas of interest, but most societies produce a quarterly journal, which they exchange with other societies, thus building up a library of material from outside their immediate region. Additionally, most societies hold monthly meetings (except for, perhaps, a summer break) and have speakers on a variety of subjects, national as well as local. Most importantly, you will meet fellow family historians who have experienced the same problems and may be able to help you overcome them. I write from personal experience: in 1973 my employer decided that my services were required in Lancashire. I have no known ancestors north of Felixstowe, but joined the local Society, of which I successively became Treasurer, Projects Co-ordinator, Chairman and Vice-President.

The Federation has an Administrator, whose address is shown on page 77, who will gladly provide a list, upon request. The address of the society secretary may not be close to where you live but do not let that deter you from seeking further information; most societies have more than one meeting venue, some of the larger ones have as many as 11 branches: for example the old county of Lancashire is covered by 4 societies, which between them have no fewer than 20 meeting places.

There are an ever growing number of One Name Societies and individuals who specialise in particular names. To find out whether yours is amongst the thousands now covered, apply to The Registrar, Guild of One Name Studies, Box G, 14 Charterhouse Buildings, Goswell Road, London, EC1M 7BA for a copy of their prospectus.

This is an appropriate point to mention that when writing to anyone, from whom a reply is required, always enclose a stamped, addressed envelope, (of at least A5 size), or if writing to or from overseas send 3 International Reply Coupons, which are obtainable at the Post Office.

Figure 3 **BIRTH BRIEF**

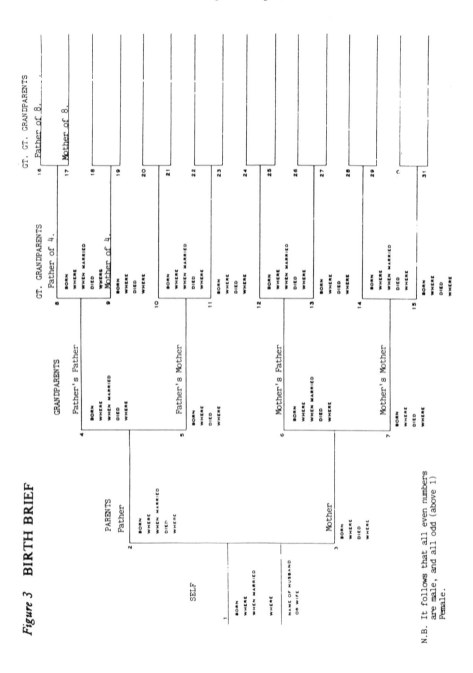

N.B. It follows that all even numbers are male, and all odd (above 1) Female.

Figure 4 FAMILY GROUP SHEET

Chart Number _____

Name _____   Source

Born _____ at _____   _____

Baptised _____ at _____   _____

Married _____ at _____   _____

Died _____ at _____   _____

Buried _____ at _____   _____

Occupation _____   _____

Chart Number _____

Father's name _____   Source

Born _____ at _____   _____

Baptised _____ at _____   _____

Married _____ at _____   _____

Died _____ at _____   _____

Buried _____ at _____   _____

Buried _____ at _____   _____

Occupation _____   _____

Chart Number _____

Mother (maiden name) _____   Source

Born _____ at _____   _____

Baptised _____ at _____   _____

Died _____ at _____   _____

Died _____ at _____   _____

Buried _____ at _____   _____

Occupation _____   _____

Children in order of birth

                                                                             Source   Chart No.

1. _____ born _____ at _____   _____   _____

2. _____ born _____ at _____   _____   _____

3. _____ born _____ at _____   _____   _____

4. _____ born _____ at _____   _____   _____

5. _____ born _____ at _____   _____   _____

6. _____ born _____ at _____   _____   _____

7. _____ born _____ at _____   _____   _____

8. _____ born _____ at _____   _____   _____

9. _____ born _____ at _____   _____   _____

10. _____ born _____ at _____   _____   _____

3. Handling Data

It is obvious that the Pedigree Chart, already considered, only has sufficient space to record the essential basic data:

Birth/baptism, Marriage, Death/burial, with the dates of each. Other information can be included on Family Group Sheets, as illustrated in Figure 4.

You will, however, collect a lot of other material and secondary records will be necessary. No two family historians will ever agree about the best methods of recording additional information, but some generally agreed principles can be stated.

(a) Start recording your information immediately.
(b) Be methodical and be honest. Acknowledge family indiscretions.
(c) Always identify your source and date you made your search.
(d) A research record is as essential as a statement of the results.

List source searched, dates covered and the names for which you have looked, plus place and date of search.

e.g. Parish Register, Rudgwick (Sx), Bapts. Ms. 1760–1812: Burs. 1781–1812. All PELLING entries: BRIDGER, pre 1802. 3/12/ 80 W.Sx.R.O. (Microfilm).

This note illustrates some other recommended practices:

(i) Use capital letters for SURNAMES, particularly vital for families where surnames are also used as christian names.
(ii) (Sx) = Sussex. Place names should indicate the county, in case of duplication elsewhere. For example, you know that the Preston you researched was in Lancashire but it might not be obvious to anyone following, who might have to consider the 10 in other counties.
(iii) Conventional abbreviations (see pages 19–20) have been used in noting the records. This practice should not, however, be extended to the names: the converse also applies, e.g. Jo. found in an archive, should be recorded as such, not as John or Joseph, because that is what you assume it to be.

(e) It is just as important to record negative results. e.g. M.I.s (i.e. Monumental Inscriptions) St. James. Haslingden (Lancs) 23/9/1979; No MUSKIEs.
(f) Whatever system you adopt must be flexible so that additional information can be added, as found. A loose leaf system is therefore recom-

mended and a ring binder larger than A4 will probably be required to accommodate the larger documents you may expect to accumulate.

Opinion is divided regarding the use of index cards; it depends upon what you want the index for and whether it is the best way for you to achieve your retrieval objective. However, the advent of the computer has liberated many family historians from the constraints of card or other paper indexing. Your choice of computer will be governed by your pocket and if (like me) you purchased one for your offspring, without knowing much about it, you are stuck with what you have. If, however, you do not already have one, there is one golden rule to observe before making your choice. First consider the software available and whether it will produce what you require.

(g) Records must be cross referenced. Families should be kept separate, either in distinct sections of the folder, or in separate folders. The same people will occur in both sections and you need to be able to refer easily from one to the other. The following symbols and conventions are those most widely used:

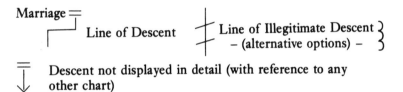

Abbreviations

about, approximately	circa or c.
bachelor	bach.
baptised	bapt.
Bishops Transcripts	BTs
born	b.
buried	bur.
century	cent. (e.g. 18th cent. or C 18)
Codicil	Cod.
Co-heir	Co-h.
Court	Ct.
dated	dat.
daughter	dau.
died	d. or obit.
died childless	d.s.p. or o.s.p.
died unmarried	d. unm.
divorced	div.

educated at	educ.
eldest	eld.
father	f.
grandfather	g.f.
great-grandfather	g-g.f.
heir	h.
infant	inf.
inventory	inv.
junior	jnr.
Letters of Administration	Admon.
licence	lic.
living	liv. (e.g. liv. 1634)
married	m. (or sometimes marr.)
Monumental Inscription	M.I.
of this Parish	o.t.p.
Parish Register	P.R.
Prerogative Court of Canterbury	P.C.C.
Prerogative Court of York	P.C.Y.
Public Record Office	P.R.O.
son	s.
time of	temp. (e.g. temp. Henry V)
widow	wid.
widower	wdr.
wife	w.
Will proved	Will pr.

Charts and Group Sheets are fine for recording data but not for visual display. Eventually, you will probably wish to put your information into Family Tree form, although many competent family historians shirk from doing so because of the severe problems of draughtmanship involved.

The most used (in many cases misused, would be a more accurate description) method is the line pedigree. Most of the pitfalls of confusion and inadequacy of data can be avoided if, once again, certain basic rules are followed.

1. Names of the same generation should be kept at the same level.
2. Lines of descent should be drawn from the marriage symbol; (as shown in Figure 5).
3. Brief narrative information may be added below the name, but the whole purpose and effect of the line pedigree is nullified if it is cluttered with too much detail, which is better recorded elsewhere.

4. Where there is more than one marriage, clearly indicate that fact next to the marriage symbol.

   E.gs: = (1), indicates one or more further marriages.

   = (2), indicates second marriage.

5. Normally record children in strict order of birth, from left to right. However, it may be necessary to depart from this rule, (if so indicate by numbering the children), e.g. where cousins marry, in order not to break the next rule, which should be regarded as inviolate.

6. Never, ever, create confusion by crossing pedigree lines.

7. Record only information which has been verified, which does not mean copying from printed sources, without checking, as far as possible, the original sources. If simply copied, then that should be stated. E.g. (per "title of publication" and its date).

Bibliography

How to Record Your Family Tree, Patrick Palgrave-Moore.

Computers for Family History – An Introduction, David Hawgood.

Figure 5 LINE PEDIGREE

John Pelling = (i)

bur. 15 Feb 1803
Rudgwick (Sx) (aged 67)

John (Jose) Pelling ⌐ Hannah Bridger

bur. 21 Jun 1835 Rudgwick,
    (aged 67)

bapt 17 May 1782 Rudgwick,
m.   20 Apr 1802 Rudgwick
d.   Petworth Workhouse, Sx.
bur. 22 Feb 1860 Rudgwick.

Michael Pelling ⌐ Ann Burfoot

bapt 6 Jun 1818 Rudgwick
d   17 Apr 1861 Ewhurst, Sy.

bapt 13 Jan 1819 Horsham, Sx.
m.   17 Mar 1846 Horsham

Alexander Pelling ⌐ Sarah Jane Penfold

b 10 Jul 1855 Ewhurst
d 23 Nov 1936 Ockley, Sy.

b.   28 Jan 1863 Ifield, Sx.
m.   13 Jan 1895 Dorking, Sy.
d.   2 Dec 1951 Ockley, Sy.

George Alfred Pelling ⌐ Margaret K. Passiful

b 11 Apr 1895 Dorking,
d 22 Mar 1970 Brighton, Sx.

b.   26 Jul 1904 Portslade, Sx.
m.   1 Oct 1932 Portslade
d.   14 Oct 1984 Chichester, Sx.

George Pelling ⌐ Pauline Winifrid Holden

b 25 Jun 1933 Ockley,

b.   30 May 1938 Upminster, Essex
m.   19 Aug 1961 West Blatchington, Sx.

Nichola   **Roger**   **Malcolm David**

b. 16 Oct 1963   b 25 Feb 1965   b 18 Oct 1966 b 1 Jun 1960
Walthamstow   d 25 Feb 1965   Farnborough
London   Orpington(Kt)   (Kent)

4. Who Has Been Here Before Me?

There is only space here to indicate briefly some of the sources available which may be consulted to find out not only what has been done before but also what is being done now.

Genealogists have sometimes spent years researching a family, only to discover that a substantial pedigree already exists. If you find one, however, your task is not over; it has simply been made easier. All printed and manuscript pedigrees should be checked against the original records for authenticity and accuracy and also checked for completeness. Many printed pedigrees were compiled in the nineteenth century when, it is probably true to say, standards of proof were lower than we would consider acceptable today. Some of the pedigrees were prepared for people of standing and "inconvenient" ancestors may have been deliberately omitted. If, however, you approach such pedigrees with the necessary scepticism, invaluable information can be obtained.

Indexes of printed pedigrees are contained in the following books:

The Genealogist's Guide	G. W. Marshall (prior to 1903)
A Genealogical Guide	J. B. Whitmore (1900–1950)
The Genealogist's Guide	G. B. Barrow (1950–1977)

The dates in brackets indicate the dates between which the pedigrees were printed not the dates the pedigrees cover. (E.g. a pedigree from the 16th century to 1890 printed in 1956 would be indexed in Barrow and not in Marshall.)

Burke's Peerage and *Burke's Landed Gentry* contain many printed pedigrees. If you have an ancestor who achieved some distinction in his own field, then he may be listed in *Who Was Who?*, which contains biographical information. More detailed information may be available in *The Dictionary of National Biography*.

The Society of Genealogists, 14 Charterhouse Buildings, Goswell Road, London EC1M 7BA, has a large collection of manuscript pedigrees in its substantial library and there are also many deposited in local libraries and county record offices.

The largest collection of pedigrees is held, however, in the form of Family Group Sheets (approximately 8,000,000), by the Church of Jesus Christ of Latter-day Saints (Mormons), at their main family history library at Salt Lake City, Utah, U.S.A. In addition their International Genealogical Index (IGI), compiled by computer has revolutionised genealogical research in recent years. Books published before the IGI became available suggest that Civil Registration (see next Chapter) is the first record to research. Since, however, registration certificates have to be purchased, it is prudent to consult the IGI first if you are seeking a baptism or marriage before 1875, which is the latest year covered. It should be mentioned that the number of baptisms is much greater than the marriage entries (indexed under both names) and burials are not included except for a minimal number of infants. Marriages known to be included in a printed index elsewhere are not included.

The number of entries, which cover not only England, Scotland, Ireland, Wales, Isle of Man and Channel Islands but also many European countries and America, is staggering; the most recent version, (1988 at the time of writing) containing over 118,000,000 names. The index is on microfiche, small sheets of microfilm about 4 by 6 inches, each containing 16,000 to 17,000 names. The fiche is inserted into a reader, which is very simple to operate. U.K. names are arranged by county, alphabetically by surname, then by given name, and then chronologically, the earliest date being 1538. The lastest technological development, which commenced in 1989 is to transfer the index on to compact disc. When this has been accomplished countrywide (instead of county) searches will be possible.

The Latter-day Saints' Family History libraries in the United Kingdom, of which more than 40 now exist, have the full index. You do not have to be a member of their church to use their libraries, which are freely open to all; no visitor need fear that any attempt to convert them will be made.

Libraries are staffed by volunteers and have restricted opening hours, which should be ascertained when planning a visit.

The Society of Genealogists also has the full index, as do an increasing number of the larger family history societies. Many County Record Offices have the index for their county, which may also be found in the main reference libraries. It must be emphasised that the IGI is an index and, like any other index contains errors. It has been prepared not only from printed sources but also from entries submitted by members of the church and they, like all of us, must be expected to have made some mistakes. All indexes are the tools of genealogical research and not a substitute for it; once an entry is found in any index it should be checked by reference to the original record.

The Latter-day Saints also maintain The Family Registry, another microfiche index, containing names being researched and by whom.

Most Family History Societies have published Registers of their Members' Interests, which show the names being researched, together with their location and dates, and the name and address of the researcher. Some Societies have banded together to produce a larger, Regional Directory, e.g. the North West. Societies usually update their Members' interests between publications of their Register, by printing the names being researched by new members in their journal.

There are also national and international directories, produced annually.

Mention has been made of the Society of Genealogists' Library, which is open to non-members on payment of a fee. The scale, at the time of writing is:

1 hour   £2.50
½ day   £6.00
Day   £8.00

Obviously, if you contemplate using the library on a regular basis, it will be cheaper to join the Society, for which current subscription rates are:

Entrance fee on first joining   £ 7.50
Annual:
  Town members (residing within 25 miles from   £25.00
  Trafalgar Square)
Others (U.K. and overseas)   £16.00
  Reduced rates are available for married couples and students under 25 years of age.

Courses for beginners are run twice yearly, in the spring and the autumn.

The library houses a general slip index of some 3,000,000 names, an index of Chancery and other Court proceedings, with about 4,500,000 references prior to 1800, and has a microfilm collection of nearly 2,500 reels. It also has an extensive collection of printed and typed family histories.

Other contents of this superb library will be described in later Chapters dealing with the subject matter covered.

Opening times: Tuesdays, Fridays and Saturdays: 10 a.m.–6 p.m.
                  Wednesdays and Thursdays: 10 a.m.–8 p.m.

It is closed on Mondays, Bank Holidays and the Friday afternoons and Saturdays, preceding. It is also closed for stocktaking in the week of the first Monday in February.

Bibliography

Burke's Family Index, which is an index of names in:
Burke's Landed Gentry and Burke's Peerage and Baronetage.

Who Was Who?

Dictionary of National Biography.

Unpublished Personal Name Indexes in Record Offices and Libraries, J. S. W. Gibson, FFHS.

National Genealogical Directory.

Genealogical Research Directory, ed. K. A. Johnson and M. R. Smith.

5. Civil Registration

England and Wales

All births, marriages and deaths since 1 July 1837 are supposed to have been registered by the State, but in the earlier years some escaped the net. The country is divided into Registration Districts under the control of a Superintendent Registrar, and Districts are divided into Sub-Districts. Certificates are available from the Registrar only at the time of registration or shortly afterwards; once a register is filled it is sent to the Superintendent Registrar from whom certificates have to be obtained. Usually the indexes of the records (but not the records themselves), which, of course, relate only to events which occurred within that district, may be examined.

(i) Births and deaths are reported to the Registrar by individuals, usually close relatives.
(ii) Marriages:
    Church of England. The officiating clergyman is responsible for notifying the Registrar immediately. Since 1837 two copies of the Anglican marriage registers have been kept by incumbents. When full, one is retained by the Church and the other deposited with the registrar. The register for a small parish in which there are few marriages per year may take years to complete and the Superintendent may, therefore, not have a copy of the register. The record keeping methods in local offices make it difficult to trace a marriage unless the church is known.
    Other Denominations. The Registrar either attends the ceremony or is notified.
    Civil Marriages are registered when they are performed.

If you are sure that your ancestors came from a particular area within a given Registration District then it may be easier, quicker and more convenient to search locally. First obtain an application form and fill it in as far as possible. If you do not know the exact date you are entitled to ask the Registrar to search for a 5-year period. If, for example, you are looking for a birth you think occurred in 1858 you might choose to ask for the years 1856 to 1860 to be searched; if you are certain that it was not before 1858 then you could request a search for the years 1858 to 1862 inclusive. A full (not short) certificate should always be requested; the present cost is £5.50.

Register Offices do not have sufficient staff to undertake indefinite or protracted searches. If such a search is required then a general search in the indexes may be made personally, but it is costly, £13 for any number of successive hours not exceeding six. If you are uncertain whether the entry you have found is the correct one you may ask the staff to verify it by reference to the records. The general search fee covers the cost of 8 verifications: a charge of £2.50 is payable for each subsequent reference checked, unless a certificate is issued from the entry checked, in which case only the certificate fee is charged.

Before undertaking a general search locally, however, you should consider the advantages of making a general search of the National Indexes of births marriages and deaths. Until comparatively recently, there was little choice but to travel to London to consult the indexes, or to get someone to do it for you. Microfilm copies are now available at a number of locations, as shown in the schedule on page 32, in addition to the Family History Centres of the Church of Jesus Christ of Latter-day Saints. Take particular note, however, that most of the local indexes are incomplete.

The full national indexes are housed at St Catherine's House, Kingsway, London, WC8 6JP, (phone 01-242-0262), which can be inspected free of charge and no reader's ticket is required. Opening hours are Monday–Friday 8.30 a.m.–4.30 p.m.

Separate Indexes are kept for Births, Marriages and Deaths. There are four quarterly indexes for each year ending: 31 March, 30 June, 30 September and 31 December. It is important to note that the date in the index is the date of registration NOT the date when the event took place. It may, therefore, be necessary to search the following quarter even when the precise date is known. Thus a birth on December 26 may not have been registered until the first quarter of the following year. The index shows the Registration district, volume and page number. There may be two or more entries for the same name and you may not know in which county the place of registration is located. This can be ascertained from the list in Figure 6. E.g. 8a for the year 1860 is Cheshire. If you are uncertain whether the reference you have found in the index relates to the person you are seeking then the staff will verify it for you within a few days by reference to the records on payment of £3.00. Once you have found the entry which you believe to be the one you want, a simple form must be completed. Unless you can return for the certificate two days or so later you will be asked to self-address an envelope so that it can be posted to you. The cost is the same as locally, £5.50. If you cannot visit St. Catherine's House to make a personal search, certificates may be applied for by post, but only a five year search can be requested and the cost is £15, of which £5 is refunded if the search is unsuccessful. It may therefore be cheaper to pay someone to carry out the personal search for you, if their fee is less than the difference. If, however, you obtain the precise reference, (which consists of Quarter; Year; District; Volume number; Page number), from a microfilm of the indexes, the cost is reduced to £12. Postal applications should not be sent to St Catherine's House but to: General Register Office, Smedley Hydro,

Figure 6 CODES EMPLOYED AT ST. CATHERINE'S HOUSE

ROMAN NUMERALS
1837–1851

ARABIC WITH SMALL LETTER
1852–Aug. 1946

Roman		Arabic	
I	London & Middlesex	1a	London & Middlesex
II	London & Middlesex	1b	London & Middlesex
III	London & Middlesex	1c	London & Middlesex
IV	London & Surrey	1d	London, Kent & Surrey
V	Kent	2a	Kent & Surrey
VI	Beds., Berks., Bucks. & Herts.	2b	Hants & Sussex
VII	Hants. & Sussex	2c	Berks. & Hants.
VIII	Dorset, Hants. & Wilts.	3a	Berks., Bucks., Herts., Middx. & Oxon
IX	Cornwall & Devon		
X	Devon & Somerset	3b	Beds., Cambs., Hunts., Northants. & Suffolk
XI	Glos., Soms. & Warwicks.		
XII	Essex & Suffolk	4a	Essex & Suffolk
XIII	Norfolk & Suffolk	4b	Norfolk
XIV	Cambs., Hunts. & Lincs.	5a	Dorset & Wiltshire
XV	Leics., Northants., Notts. & Rutland	5b	Devonshire
		5c	Cornwall & Soms.
XVI	Oxon., Staffs. & Warwicks.	6a	Glos., Herefords. & Salop.
XVII	Staffordshire	6b	Staffs., Warwicks. & Worcs.
XVIII	Glos., Salop., Staffs., Warwicks. & Worcs.	6c	Warwicks. & Worcestershire
XIX	Cheshire, Derbys. & Flints.	6d	Warwickshire
XX	Lancashire	7a	Leics., Lincs. & Rutland.
XXI	Lancashire & Yorkshire	7b	Derbyshire & Notts.
XXII	Yorkshire	8a	Chesire
XXIII	Yorkshire	8b	Lancashire
XXIV	Durham & Yorkshire	8c	Lancashire
XXV	Cumberland, Lancashire, Northumberland & Westmorland	8d	Lancashire
		8e	Lancashire
XXVI	Brecknocks., Carmarthens., Glams., Herefords., Mons., Pembs., Randors. & Salop.	9a	Yorkshire
		9b	Yorkshire
		9c	Yorkshire
XXVII	Anglesey, Caernarvons., Cardigans, Denbighs., Flints., Merioneths. & Montgomeryshire	9d	Yorkshire
		10a	Durham
		10b	Cumberland, Northumberland & Westmorland
(N.B. As the older volumes (above) are replaced, the Roman numerals are being replaced by Arabic.)		11a	Glamorgan., Monmouth. & Pembrokeshire
		11b	Anglesey, Brecknocks., Denbighs., Flints., Montgomeryshire & Radnorshire

Trafalgar Rd, Southport, Merseyside, PR8 2HH. Remittances from overseas should be by sterling money order.

Figure 7 DATA GIVEN IN BIRTH CERTIFICATES

No.	When and where born	Name if any	Sex	Name and surname of father	Name, surname and maiden name of mother	Occupation of father	Signature, description and residence of informant	When registered	Signature of Registrar	Name entered after Registration

(N.B. Mother's maiden name not shown in indexes prior to September 1911).

It should be noted that a direct ancestor's certificate may not always be the best one to obtain. To explain this statement it is necessary to anticipate slightly the contents of the next Chapter. Census returns may be consulted (free of charge) for the years 1841, 1851, 1861, 1871 and 1881, but it is necessary to know an address. Suppose that your grandfather, Malcolm, had been born in 1866, his sister Nichola in 1863 and his brother David in 1870. The essential information you require (names of parents and mother's maiden name) will be the same on the birth certificates for all three, but by obtaining David's (instead of Malcolm's) you will have an address to check in the 1871 census. The Family is less likely to have moved in the intervening year after 1870 than in the 5 years after 1866 (or in the 5 year period 1861–1866).

Figure 8 DATA GIVEN IN MARRIAGE CERTIFICATES

No.	When married	Names & surnames of each party	Ages	Condition (e.g. Bachelor or Spinster)	Rank or Profession of each party	Residence at time of marriage	Both fathers' names & surnames	Rank or profession of both fathers
Place of marriage and ceremony performed								
Signatures of parties who were married				Signatures of witnesses				

It is easier to find a marriage, and to be certain that you are right, than to find a birth because the names of both spouses are indexed. Look for the less common name first then check with the name of the spouse and, if the references are identical, then you have a match. (N.B. After 1912 the other spouse's name is stated in brackets.)

Figure 9 DATA GIVEN IN DEATH CERTIFICATES

No.	When & where died	Name & surname	Sex	Age (Often only approximate)	Occupation	Cause	Signature description & residence of informant	When registered	Signature of Registrar

Figure 10 **FACSIMILES OF CERTIFICATES ISSUED BY GENERAL REGISTER OFFICE**

CERTIFIED COPY OF AN ENTRY OF BIRTH

The fee for this certificate is 40p.
When application is made by post a
handling fee is payable in addition.

GIVEN AT THE GENERAL REGISTER OFFICE,
SOMERSET HOUSE, LONDON

Application Number 3716

REGISTRATION DISTRICT *Hambledon*

1855. BIRTH in the Sub-district of *Cranley* in the County of *Surrey*

Columns:— 1	2	3	4	5	6	7	8	9	10*
No.	When and where born	Name, if any	Sex	Name and surname of father	Name, surname and maiden surname of mother	Occupation of father	Signature, description and residence of informant	When registered	Signature of registrar	Name entered after registration
291	Tenth July 1855	Alexander	Boy	Michael Pelling	Ann Pelling formerly Burfoot	Labourer	The Mark of Ann Pelling Mother Pottend Street Ewhurst	Twentieth August 1855	Twombell James Rumboll	

CERTIFIED to be a true copy of an entry in the certified copy of a Register of Births in the District above named.
Given at the GENERAL REGISTER OFFICE, SOMERSET HOUSE, LONDON, under the Seal of the said Office, the 30th day of June 1972

This certificate is issued in pursuance of the Births and Deaths Registration Act 1953. Section 34 provides that any certified copy of an entry purporting to be sealed or stamped with the seal of the General Register Office shall be received as evidence of the birth or death to which it relates without any further or other proof of the entry, and no certified copy purporting to have been given in the said Office shall be of any force or effect unless it is sealed or stamped as aforesaid.

BX 886648

CERTIFIED COPY OF AN ENTRY OF MARRIAGE

The fee for this certificate is 40p.
When application is made by post, a
handling fee is payable in addition.

Given at the GENERAL REGISTER OFFICE,
SOMERSET HOUSE, LONDON

Application Number 4675 D

Registration District *Horsham*

1846. Marriage solemnized at *the Church*
in the Parish of *Horsham* in the County of *Sussex*

No.	When married	Name and surname	Age	Condition	Rank or profession	Residence at the time of marriage	Father's name and surname	Rank or profession of father
251	March 17	Michael Pelling	full	Bachelor	Labourer	Horsham	John Pelling	Farmer
		Ann Burfoot	full	Spinster		Horsham	Alexander Burfoot	Farmer

Married in the Parish Church according to the Rites and Ceremonies of the Church of England by Banns by me John F. Haggard, Vicar

This marriage was solemnized between us, Michael Pelling, Ann Burfoot in the presence of us, R. Collins, Elizabeth Burfoot

CERTIFIED to be a true copy of an entry in the certified copy of a Register of Marriages in the District above mentioned.
Given at the GENERAL REGISTER OFFICE, SOMERSET HOUSE, LONDON, under the Seal of the said Office, the 13th day of July 1972

MA 983416

CERTIFIED COPY OF AN ENTRY OF DEATH

GIVEN AT THE GENERAL REGISTER OFFICE,
SOMERSET HOUSE, LONDON

Application Number 5158 D.

REGISTRATION DISTRICT *Hambledon*

1861. DEATH in the Sub-district of *Cranley* in the County of *Surrey*

Columns:— 1	2	3	4	5	6	7	8	9
No.	When and where died	Name and surname	Sex	Age	Occupation	Cause of death	Signature, description and residence of informant	When registered	Signature of registrar
140	Seventeenth April 1861 Pottend Street Ewhurst	Michael Pelling	Male	43 Years	Farm Labourer	Pneumonia 7 days Not certified	Ebenezer Howden In Attendance Cranley Street Cranley	Eighteenth April 1861	Edward Davey Registrar

CERTIFIED to be a true copy of an entry in the certified copy of a Register of Deaths in the District above mentioned.
Given at the GENERAL REGISTER OFFICE, SOMERSET HOUSE, LONDON, under the Seal of the said Office, the 13th day of Sept 19.73

This certificate is issued in pursuance of the Births and Deaths Registration Act 1953. Section 34 provides that any certified copy of an entry purporting to be sealed or stamped with the seal of the General Register Office shall be received as evidence of the birth or death to which it relates without any further or other proof of the entry, and no certified copy purporting to have been given in the said Office shall be of any force or effect unless it is sealed or stamped as aforesaid.

DX 190002

CAUTION:—Any person who (1) falsifies any of the particulars on this certificate, or (2) uses a falsified certificate as true, knowing it to be false, is liable to prosecution.

English death certificates are not very helpful genealogically except perhaps to provide an address for checking in the census returns and to give age at death from which one can compute a birth date. Often the informant is a close relative. N.B. Death Indexes from 1866 onwards give age at death, anyway.

If you do not find the entry that you expect to find at a particular date there are 3 possible reasons.

(a) The date you have is wrong – not uncommon.
  Remedy – Widen your search progressively either side of the date.
  e.g. Believed date 1856: search 1857 and 1855, followed by 1858 and 1854 and so on.

(b) The name is different.
  Remedy – Look for all possible spelling variants. Remember that your ancestor may have been illiterate and the verbal information he gave may have been misheard or misspelt. This happens with common names as well as those more unusual. A researcher in Lancashire has recorded no less than 17 different spellings of Whittaker. The difference may be much greater than a missing or extra letter. One of my grandparent's names was Passiful, which in many records appears as Percival.

(c) It was not registered.
  Remedy – Try alternative records.

The birth and marriage certificates shown in Figure 10 illustrate the point made about names. The birth of ALEXANDER PELLING was registered by his mother, who, it will be seen, made her mark.

The Registrar recorded her maiden name as BIRFETT. The marriage indexes were searched backwards from 1855 for 10 years and forward for 5 (marriages do not always precede births). No marriage between MICHAEL PELLING and ANN BIRFETT was registered. Fortunately, there was only one MICHAEL PELLING who married in the period. The certificate illustrated was obtained and his wife's name proved to be BURFOOT.

The searcher did not know at the time that his Aunt, who never knew her grandparents, had a sampler completed by ANN BURFOOT in 1826. This demonstrates the importance of family information which has already been stressed. It also shows that girls who embroidered samplers including their names were not necessarily literate but may simply have copied or filled in a pattern provided.

The death certificate was important because it provided an address to look for in the 1861 census (see next chapter) without which Michael's birthplace would have been more difficult to find.

Other Indexes Available at St. Catherine's House

(a) Births & Deaths at Sea, 1 July 1837–31 December 1874. (N.B. After 1874 at Registrar General for Shipping & Seamen, Llandaff, Cardiff, Wales.)

(b) Births, marriages and deaths of British Citizens overseas, Consular Returns. From 1 July 1849.

(c) Army returns of Births, marriages and deaths. From 1761.

(d) R.A.F. returns of Births, marriages and deaths. From 1920.

Research in England, (unlike Scotland – see below), has been hampered by access being confined to the indexes; the registers themselves being unavailable.

The system described above is likely to be dramatically changed during the course of the next few years. In January 1990 the Government published a White Paper entitled *Registration: Proposals for change*, setting out its recommendations for reform. Understandably, the Government has become increasingly concerned about the misuse of certificates obtained for various fraudulent purposes. It recommends that records over 75 years old be made available for public inspection in a record library. As it is to be privatised, a charge would be made for access to these. For records less than 75 years old, provision will be made for the issue of non-certified copies of any entries identified from the indexes. However, anyone requiring a certified copy will be required to identify themselves, give an address (which may be checked), state their relationship to the subject of the certificate and the purpose for which it is required.

It will still be possible to purchase certified copies of entries in the indexes over 75 years old, or alternatively non-certified copies.

Channel Islands

No personal Searches may be made.

Jersey

Registration began August 1842.
Superintendent Registrar, States Office, Jersey.
Certificates cost £4 each plus postage, £0.50 U.K., £1 elsewhere. Plus 5 year research charge – Births and deaths £4, marriages £8.

Guernsey and other Islands

Registration of births and deaths commenced 1840. (Sark and Alderney 1925). Anglican marriages 1925. Registrar General, Royal Court House, St Peter Port, Guernsey.
Certificates cost £3.

Microfilm Copies of G.R.O. Indexes

PLACE	LOCATION	B.M.Ds.	YEARS	BOOKING REQUIRED
Birmingham	Central Library		1837–1912	No
Bristol	Central Library	BMs	1866–1912	Yes
		Ds	1866–1937	
Cambridge	C.R.O.		1837–1912	
Huddersfield	Kirklees C.L.		1837–1912	No
Ilford	Redbridge C.L.		1866–1912	
Leeds	Central Library		1837–1980	No
Liverpool	Record Office		1837–1912	
Manchester	Co. Record Office		1837–1912	Yes
Morpeth	Co. Library		1837–1918	
Northallerton	Co. Library		1837–1946	
Portsmouth	Ref. Library	Bs	1866–1912	Yes
St Helens	Century House	BMs	1837–1912	Yes
South Shields	Central Library		1866–1912	
Worcester	Record Office		1837–1912	Yes
York	Central Library		1837–1946	
Aberystwyth	Nat. Library of Wales		1866–1912	Yes
Mold	Library H.Q.		1866–1912	Yes
Swansea	W. Glamorgan R.O.		1837–1912	Yes

Key: C.L. Central Library; R.O. Record Office; W. West; B.M.Ds. Births, Marriages, Deaths.

Isle of Man

Although registration of births was not compulsory until 1878, an Act of 1849 provided that ... 'persons who object to and decline the offices of the Established Church' ... could register births and marriages. The earliest contemporary records therefore date from 1849 but it was also provided that earlier births could be registered, on oath, and the earliest of the 46 recorded under this provision was 1821. Marriages were not centrally registered until 1884. Certificates cost £3, plus search fee, from General Registry, Finch Road, Douglas.

Scotland

Registration did not become compulsory in Scotland until 1855, but Scottish Certificates have always been more detailed.

In addition to the information given on English Certificates, the following is stated:

(i)   Birth. Date and place of parents' marriage (1855 and 1861 onwards). (1855 certificates also state parents' ages and birthplaces.)
(ii) Marriage. Mothers' names.
(iii) Death. Both parents' names.

The Registers of Births, Marriages and Deaths are at New Register House, Edinburgh, where the original registers may be consulted and not just the indexes as in England. The fee is £7.00 per day (but see below). A microfilm copy of the indexes (1855–1920) is held at the Society of Genealogists.

Other Registers Available:
(a)   Marine Register of births and deaths (from 1855).
(b)   Service Records of births, marriages and deaths (from 1881).
(c)   War Registers (from 1899): Deaths:
      1. Boer War (1899–1902).
      Warrant Officers, N.C.O.s and men (Army).
      2. World War I (1914–1919).
      Petty Officers and men (Royal Navy).
      3. World War II (1939–1945).
      Armed forces BUT incomplete.
(d)   Consular Returns: Certified copies of:
      1. Births and deaths (from 1914).
      2. Marriages (from 1917).
(e)   Births, Marriages and Deaths in foreign countries (1860–1965). Compiled on the basis of information supplied.
(f)   Adopted Children Register (from 1930). No entries for persons born before October 1909.
(g)   Air Register of births and deaths (from 1948). Events occurring on aircraft registered in U.K. where deceased or child's father usually resident in Scotland.
(h)   Divorces (from May 1984).

The former queue system has been abandoned, having located the desired index reference, the certificate volumes are delivered to your seat: there is no charge for copying the information. Opening hours 9.30 a.m.–5.30 p.m. Monday–Friday. Certificates cost £5 and there is no extra charge for postal enquiries, if the 5 year search is successful. Otherwise, a charge of £1.60 is made and the balance refunded.

N.B.   Fees for an INCLUSIVE search, which allows access to ALL records
available for consultation are at January (but subject to review in April)
1990:

daily £11; weekly £37; monthly £100; quarterly £200.

Searching in records other than statutory records is conducted in the Search
Rooms, where accommodation is limited. It is advisable to arrive by 9.30 a.m.
to ensure a seat or, if travelling some distance you may write in advance for a
reservation.

Ireland

Registration did not generally begin in Ireland until 1 January 1864. Non
Roman Catholic marriages were, however, registered from 1 April 1845 and
one earlier Marriage Register exists, the German Protestant Church, Dublin
(1806–1837).

Registers of births, marriages and deaths before 31 December 1921 for the
whole country are held at the General Register Office (Oifig an Ard-
Chláraitheora), Joyce House, 8–11 Lombard Street, Dublin 2.

After 31 December 1921, the records for Northern Ireland are separate
(see below). The cost of a Particular Search for any period not exceeding 5
years is £1 but the information supplied must be sufficient to enable an entry
to be positively identified: in the case of a birth the names of both parents,
including the mother's maiden name, are required.

The cost of a certificate (including particular search fee) is £3.00. A
General Search may be made PERSONALLY, on payment of the following
fees:

Births or Deaths: any number of successive hours not exceeding 6: £11.00.
Marriages: any number of successive days not exceeding 6: £11.00.
Other Registers and Records: (N.B. To 31/12/1921 All Ireland: thereafter
    excluding Northern Ireland).
Births and Deaths at Sea (from 1/1/1864).
Consular Returns, Births and deaths abroad (from 1/1/1864).
Births, Deaths and Marriages (Army Act 1879).
Original Certificates of Marriages by Special Licence (Act of 1871).
Original Certificates of Roman Catholic Marriages (1/1/1864–30/9/1881).
Adopted Children (from 10/7/1953).
Certain marriages at Lourdes (Act of 1972).

Northern Ireland

(i.e. Antrim, Armagh, Down, Fermanagh, Londonderry and Tyrone).

Registration of Births and Deaths since 1864 and marriages since 1922 are held at The General Register Office, Oxford House, 49/55 Chichester Street, Belfast, open Monday–Friday 9.30 a.m.–3.30 p.m.

Records of marriages prior to 1922 are held by local Registrars (see also above).

A Particular Search for a specific entry, for a period up to 5 years costs £1.25. Certificates cost £3.75. A PERSONAL General Search costs £4.25 for any period up to 6 successive hours. (N.B. Overseas researchers should note that neither Office holds Emigration Records).

Bibliography

St. Catherine's House, Eve McLaughlin, FFHS.

6. Census Returns

A census has been taken every 10 years since 1801, (except 1941), but it was not until 1841 that the returns had to be preserved. Consequently, for the previous four censuses, only the official statistics generally survive. Occasionally, however, the actual returns did survive, and whilst it is true to say that, generally speaking, the first census of practical use to the genealogist is 1841, you should check to see if you are one of those fortunate researchers whose ancestors lived in an area for which earlier returns have been found. The 1801 census for Winnick with Hulme, of which a brief extract is shown in figure 11, includes a woman aged 92, who was therefore born 1708/9.

In England and Wales, public records are generally available after 30 years but certain records which contain sensitive personal information, including censuses, are subjected to extended closure and do not become available for 100 years. The latest census which can currently be consulted is therefore 1881, (except as detailed below). The 1991 census will become available on the first working day of 1992. In Scotland, however, 1891 is already available.

Unfortunately, almost all Irish censuses up to and including 1891, were destroyed in 1922, but the censuses for 1901 and 1911 may be consulted. Here too, there are exceptions, a few returns survived for 1841 and 1851.

It is easier to describe the later censuses first, 1851 (taken on the night of 30 March), 1861 (7 April), 1871 (2 April), 1881 (3 April), 1891 (5 April) all of which give the following information:

(a) Name of Place, Parish, and whether hamlet, village, town or borough.
(b) Number or name of house and its street or road; some enumerators did not enter the house number but (particularly in rural areas) simply the schedule number, with which it should not be confused.
(c) Names of persons present on Census night (dates as above).
(d) Relationship of each person to the Head of the Household.
(e) Matrimonial status.
(f) Age and sex.
(g) Rank, profession or occupation.
(h) Birthplace (England and Wales by place and county, but generally country only (e.g. Scotland) for those born elsewhere.
(j) Whether blind, deaf or dumb (1871 included whether imbecile, idiot or lunatic).

The 1841 (7 June) census was unfortunately not so informative in several respects; using the letters above:

(b) Very few streets were numbered.
(d) Relationship to the Head of the Household not stated.
(e) Not given.
(f) Ages for those above 15 rounded down to nearest 5 years (e.g. recorded age 45; actual age could be 45, 46, 47, 48 or 49). Ages for those over 60 were often rounded down to the nearest 10 years.
(h) Birthplace simply indicated by "Yes" if born in the same county, "No" if elsewhere in England and Wales. Those born in Scotland, Ireland etc. listed as such.

The marks made by enumerators should be noted:
/ at the end of each household.
/ / at the end of each building.

The exception is the 1851 census in which a line was drawn across the first 4 columns after the end of the building and a shorter line after the household.

The differences between 1841 and 1851 (and later censuses) can be seen from the illustrations in Figure 12 and 13.

Those researchers who have experienced the cramped conditions at the Land Registry building in Portugal Street, London WC2A 1LR, where the microfilmed copies are currently, will be pleased to learn that they are due to be moved, if the necessary preparations are completed to schedule, after Easter 1990 to the Census Room at the Public Record Office, Chancery Lane, WC2A 1LR. Approximately 50 additional microfilm readers are to be provided and there will be a self-service system, which should make research easier and quicker. There is no charge for searching. Admittance is by means of a pass issued for the day, or a Reader's ticket, which permits access to all PRO search rooms. An application form for the latter can be obtained from the Enquiries Desk, but the ticket must be collected personally and proof of identity provided.

Complete holdings of the various censuses for the county will usually be found in the County Record Office or the main county library and many reference libraries have copies for their local area, also on microfilm. Microfilm readers are easy to operate and you will be shown how to use one.

It is necessary to know an address to research a town with reasonable hope of quick success, although if the district in the town is known and this coincides with the sub-districts, you will find these listed on the title page of each index and the amount of searching can be confined. There are street indexes for the larger towns. Enumeration districts vary in size: e.g. Preston (Lancs) 1851: Largest 325 houses with 2,164 inhabitants, smallest 114, with 616.

In rural areas it is possible to research whole villages and the surrounding countryside relatively quickly. Many Societies have started to index the 1851 census for their area and publish the results; over 500 indexes are known to exist.

The biggest and most ambitious project of all, however, commenced in 1988, to index the whole of the 1881 census for England and Wales. The Genealogical Society of Utah (with permission of HMSO) are lending microfilm or photocopies to volunteer transcribers, most of the labour being provided by members of family history societies. The results are transferred to a computer data base. Ultimately, the data will be made available on microfiche, initially arranged by county and then by surname and given name. Obviously, it will be some years before all this dedicated labour comes to fruition.

All details on censuses should be noted including visitors and servants. Families frequently obtained the latter from where their parents lived and a servant's birthplace can, therefore, sometimes provide a clue.

If you cannot find the address bear in mind that the street, name or house numbers may have been changed between the date of the record you have and the date of the census. A local directory (see Chapter 11) may help to solve the problem.

The experienced family historian will not confine himself to one surname but will make a comprehensive search looking for the surnames of married daughters and wives' maiden names. He will also note down the neighbours, not only to provide background information about the environment, but to detect married children living nearby.

The problem of illiteracy runs like a thread through all records and the census is no exception, spelling variants will again be found and ages cannot be relied upon. Some ladies appear to have found the secret of retaining their youth and age less than 10 years between censuses.

Mention was made in the opening paragraph of obtaining information from the censuses for England and Wales after 1881. It is possible but expensive

Figure 11

Extract from Example of rare survival of 1801 census Winnick with Hulme, one of the ten townships of the Parish of Winwick, originally Lancashire, now Cheshire.

Ralph UNSWORTH Sen.	74	Farmer
Nancey UNSWORTH	38	
Ralph UNSWORTH	11	
Peter UNSWORTH	9	
John UNSWORTH	7	
Robt UNSWORTH	4	
Marshall BROWN	19	Servant
Margret Gorst	18	Servant

Figure 12 EXTRACT FROM THE 1841 CENSUS (HO. 107/1092) RUDGWICK, SUSSEX

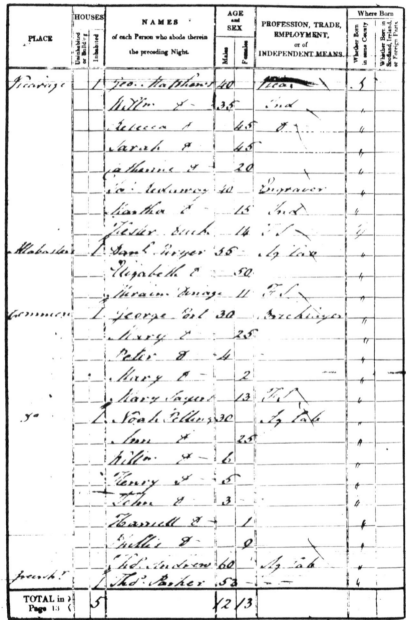

City or Borough of _____

Parish or Township of _Ridgwick_

PLACE	HOUSES		NAMES of each Person who abode therein the preceding Night.	AGE and SEX		PROFESSION, TRADE, EMPLOYMENT, or of INDEPENDENT MEANS.	Where Born	
	Uninhabited or Building	Inhabited		Males	Females		Whether Born in same County	Whether Born in Scotland, Ireland, or Foreign Parts.
Greenhurst continued		1	Sarah Parker		50		✓	
			Mich.l	19			✓	
			John	14			✓	
Tedleigh		1	Ry Lanford	50			✓	
			Mary		50		✓	
			Mary Atherton		7		✓	
		1	Mary Lanford		30	Farming	✓	
			Edward	12			✓	
			Mary		15	F. S.		✓
			Charles Woods	20		Ag Lab	✓	
	2	1	Geo Smith	25			✓	
			Mary		25		✓	
			George	7			✓	
			James	5			✓	
			Mary		3		✓	
			Willm	1			✓	
			Sarah Waller		60	Nurse	✓	
			Willm	9			✓	
	2	1	Jas Shepherd	25		Ag Lab	✓	
			Susan		20		✓	
			Mary		80	Widow	✓	
Vicarage		1	Rich Shermin	40		Ag Lab	✓	
			Hannah		40		✓	
			Sarah Do		9		✓	
			George Do	7			✓	
TOTAL in Page 14		5		13	12			

Figure 13 EXTRACT FROM THE 1851 CENSUS (HO. 107/1648) HORSHAM, SUSSEX

	Name of Street, Place, or Road, and Name or No. of House	Name and Surname of each Person who abode in the house, on the Night of the 30th March, 1851	Relation to Head of Family	Condition
Parish or Township of *Horsham*		Ecclesiastical District of	Borough	City
67	South Street	Matilda Cockburn	Visitor	
		James Dobson	Lodger	U
		William Parker	Lodger	Mar
68	East Street	Frances Sargent	Head	W
69	South Street	Joseph Roberts	Head	Mar
		Elizabeth D°	Wife	Mar
		John D°	Son	U
		Elizabeth D°	Daur	U
70		Michael Keeing	Head	Mar
		Ann D°	Wife	Mar
		Sidney D°	Son	
		Hannah D°	Daur	
		Ann D°	Daur	
		John Sharp	Lodger	Wid
		John Taylor	Lodger	U
		Felix Morgan	Lodger	U
		Stephen Fagan	Lodger	U
		Barnard Fagan	Lodger	U
		Andrew Wood	Lodger	U
4		John Morgan	Lodger	U
Total of Houses	I 3 U B		Total of Persons	

of Horsham		Town of Horsham	Village of	

Age of		Rank, Profession, or Occupation	Where Born	Whether blind or Deaf and Dumb
Males	Females			
	11		Surrey, Richmond	
62		Annuitant	Middlesex, Twickenham	
38		Conductor	Sussex, Worthing	
	63	Pauper Charwoman	Do Framfield	
62		Furniture Dealer (Master)	Do Horsham	
	56		Do Sullington	
26		Furniture Dealer (Journeyman)	Do Horsham	
	24	Dress maker	Do Do	
33		Beer house keeper	Do Rudgwick	
	32		Do Horsham	
4			Do Do	
	2		Do Do	
	6 mo		Do Do	
41		Butcher	Do Nuthurst	
41		Gig Sale	Do Horsham	
45		Hawker	Ireland	
35		Do	Do	
30		Do	Do	
45		Do	Do	
35		Do	Do	
13	7			

and, therefore, advisable only if there is no other possible alternative source. The General Register Office will extract the ages and places of birth of named persons at a specific address for 1891 and 1901 on payment of £16.75 (plus VAT, currently £2.51: N.B. Applications from abroad are not liable to VAT), provided that written permission of the person(s) or a direct descendant is produced and a declaration must be signed that the information will not be used in litigation. An application form (CAS 1/C) can be obtained from St. Catherine's House.

Often overlooked, but valuable in finding out for example whether a non-conformist chapel existed prior to 1851, is the Ecclesiastical Census for that year. Although purely voluntary most places of worship made returns which show name, denomination, place, date of its consecration or erection, space available for worship, the minister or other official, the estimated attendances on 30 March 1851 and the average attendances in the previous year (some figures appear wildly optimistic).

Scottish records are at New Register House, Edinburgh, and the fee for consultation is £5 per day (see however page 35 for 'global' fees covering access to all records).

The censuses for 1901 and 1911, and the survivals of previous returns, for the whole of Ireland are at the National Archives of Ireland, Four Courts, Dublin 7.

Returns for the Channel Islands are available in London and additionally, for Jersey at the Societe Jersiase, The Museum, Pier Rd, St Helier and for Guernsey at Royal Court House, St Peter Port.

The Family History Centres of the Latter-day Saints Church provide a service whereby any of the census reels available for the British Isles may be ordered at a cost of £1.50 per reel, which entitles you to free use of that reel at the library for a month.

Bibliography

Census Returns 1841–1881 on Microfilm: A Directory to Local Holdings, J. S. W. Gibson, FFHS.

Marriage, Census and Other Indexes for Family Historians, J. S. W. Gibson, FFHS.

The Censuses, 1841–1881: Use and Interpretation, Eve McLaughlin, FFHS.

7. Parish Registers, Bishops' Transcripts and Marriage Licences

Significant Dates

The earliest Registers date from 5 September 1538 when Thomas Cromwell, Vicar General to Henry VIII, ordered that every wedding, christening and burial in the Parish should be recorded. The entries were generally on paper and sixty years later in 1598 these Registers were ordered to be copied onto parchment, but the wording of the Act was unfortunate. It was ordered that entries from the old Registers should be copied, "but especially since the first year of Her Majesty's reign". This gave the lazy an excuse to copy only from 1558 and that is why many Registers begin with that year. The 1598 Act approved a provincial constitution of Canterbury of 1597, which provided that, within a month after Easter, transcripts of the Registers for the previous year should be sent to the bishop. The earliest Bishops' Transcripts, therefore, normally date from 1597. When Civil Registration commenced in 1837, many incumbents ceased to send copies, but some conscientious clergy continued to do so for some years afterwards. The importance of Bishops' Transcripts is that they provide a second record, which may have survived when the Parish Register has perished. Even if the Register exists the corresponding B.T. entry should be checked because it sometimes includes additional information.

An unfortunate gap occurs in many Parish Registers during the Commonwealth period 1648–1660. Registers were often not properly maintained and the quality and completeness of the record (if any) varies considerably with the area.

The inexperienced searcher will find some dates in Registers baffling and a short digression is appropriate to consider the dating system, which is a fascinating study in itself.

Charles II left his exile in France on 5 June 1660 and landed at Dover on 25 May. Although having many claims to fame, time travel was not one of them and he could only achieve, what at first appears, a remarkable feat with the aid of the different calendars in use on the Continent and in England.

In England the (Old Style) Julian calendar was still in use whereas most of the Continent had adopted the (New Style) Gregorian calendar in 1582, as had Scotland in 1660. Moreover, the Old Style calendar started the year on 25 March instead of 1 January. England had realised that it was "out of step" which is why some Registers have dates recorded, e.g. 22 February 1722/3 (i.e. 1722 Old Style, 1723 New Style).

The Julian calendar was, by 1751, incorrect by 11 days and Chesterfield's Act, passed in that year, therefore, decreed not only that the following 1 January should be the first day of 1752 but that 2 September should be followed the next day by 14 September. The effect for successive years, therefore was:

> 1750 commenced 25 March 1750–ended 24 March 1750/51
> 1751 commenced 25 March 1751–ended 31 December 1751
> 1752 commenced 1 January 1752–ended 31 December 1752
> (11 September days missing)

Bankers, however, refused to have their year truncated and the financial year due to finish on 25 March was extended by 11 days to 5 April. This anomalous Financial Year continues to this day since no Chancellor since has had the nerve to cut short one of his years.

The next significant date is 25 March 1754, when Hardwicke's Act passed the previous year, came into force. Its stated objective was "An Act for the better prevention of clandestine marriages" and in this it was largely successful. Henceforth, all marriages had to be performed in the Parish Church or designated Parochial Chapelry except those involving Quakers and Jews, who were already keeping satisfactory records. It may surprise you to learn that prior to 1929 marriages could be contracted by boys from the age of 14 and girls from the age of 12. There had for many years been two ways to notify intention to marry, either by Licence or by the publication of Banns. Many clergymen were, however, lax and often married persons from distant parishes, who had not resided in their parishes for the requisite period and apparently without the calling of banns.

The Hardwicke Act ordered that all marriages must be preceded by the calling of Banns or by Licence, that parental consent was required by minors and that registers of banns must be kept. The importance of the banns register should be realised. Occasionally information is given which is not in the marriage register and where the bride and groom were of different parishes the banns were read in both so that there is a record of intended marriages in other parishes, which would otherwise be difficult to find. Note, that banns denote an intention to marry, this does not mean that the marriage necessarily took place, though most did, and it is still necessary to trace the marriage entry.

In 1783 a Stamp Duty of three pence was imposed on every entry recorded in the parish register. Taxation is inevitably followed by evasion, paupers were exempted from the tax and the number of paupers recorded in the registers rose dramatically. Undoubtedly some people avoided the tax by not having their children baptised. Clearly the measure was unsuccessful as a revenue producer and the Act was repealed in 1794.

Rose's Act of 1812 provided for separate registers to be kept for baptisms, marriages and burials respectively on specially printed forms.

Information

Prior to 1754 many registers are a hotch potch. Pages of baptisms may be interspersed with marriages and burials, sometimes pages include all three. The years covered for each record in the register may be different.

Baptisms

Until 1812 entries were on blank leaves. The information given varies from the simple entry of the name of the child, generally (but not always) followed by the name of the father. Some Registers give the name of the mother in addition. The most helpful include the father's occupation and some include places where the parents lived outside the parish and occasionally the date of birth is stated. More rarely details of grand-parents are given. It is a pity that so few scribes were this conscientious.

After 1812, the printed forms provide 8 baptisms per page with columns for: child's christian name, christian names of parents, father's surname, father's occupation and address, and by whom baptised.

Marriages

Until 1753 also on blank pages. From 1754 in a separate printed Register with spaces for: the names of the parties, their status (bachelor, spinster, etc.), their parishes, and the groom's occupation. The entries were signed by both parties, two or more witnesses and the officiating minister. Those who were illiterate made their marks, although there is some evidence that a mark did not always indicate illiteracy. It is, of course, very useful to know whether or not an ancestor could sign his name and the names of witnesses are most important and should always be noted. These were often relatives and may provide a vital clue to family relationships.

It should also be stated whether the marriage was by licence and if an ancestor of yours did obtain a licence to marry you may be fortunate and obtain further information.

The licence itself was presented to the parson and few survive, but the associated allegations, bonds and registers of licences kept in the issuing office are much more likely to be extant and many have been published. The allegation (required until 1823) was a sworn statement that Canon Law had been observed and that there was no legal impediment to the proposed marriage. Two bondsmen were required to lodge securities (from circa 1579) that parents or guardians had given their consent and that there was no present or pending impediment. One bondsman was usually the groom and the other often a relative. The information required varied with the diocese but frequently included, in addition to the groom's and bride's names, their status (i.e. bachelor, widower, spinster or widow), ages (particularly of minors), occupations, places of residence and the church where the marriage was to be celebrated. If therefore the Parish Register indicates marriage by licence then a search should be made for the associated documentation first consulting any indexes available, which should also be searched whenever difficulty is experienced in tracing a marriage. It is a mistake to assume that only gentry obtained licences.

An example will illustrate the value better than description:

> 2 January 1829 Edmund Hills, Hartfield, labourer, 20 (with consent of Wm. Hills, Hartfield, publican) and Mary Anne Pelling, West Hoathly, spinster, 20 (with consent of Thomas Pelling, West Hoathly, labourer, her father).

J. S. W. Gibson's book (see Bibliography) shows, for each county, the licences available, where located and whether published.

Burials

Until 1813 usually only the name is given with the addition of the name of the father in the case of infant burial. Absence of this additional data does not imply an adult burial.

Once again some registers are more informative, stating ages, and sometimes additional detail, such as widow of ....

After 1813 there are eight entries per page with spaces for: name, abode, date of burial, age and officiating minister.

In 1678 an Act was passed to benefit the wool trade requiring that "no corpse of any person (except those who shall die of the plague) shall be buried in any shirt, shift, sheet or shroud .... other than what is made of sheep's wool only".

An affidavit had to be sworn to that effect and penalties were imposed for non-compliance. The Act was not repealed until 1814, but the practice had fallen into disuse long before that date.

Copies of Registers and Indexes

You can save yourself much time and trouble if, before you begin your search, you find out whether the Register has been printed or copied and if so for what period. If it has been then often it will have been indexed and you will be able to extract all entries for the name(s) you want, readily and quickly. Most published works have concentrated, for obvious reasons, on the earliest records for a particular Parish and a convenient stopping point for many was 1812, when, as already described the form in which the Registers were kept was altered. There is, therefore, a period from 1812 to 1837 (when Civil Registration started) when research is less easy.

Marriages are usually the most difficult area of research since many took place in the bride's Parish, and her name will not be known. In the event of parental disapproval, or for some other reason the marriage may not have taken place in either spouses' Parish but elsewhere, theoretically after the required period of residential qualification.

One of the first genealogists to recognise the need for Marriage Indexes was Percival Boyd, who worked on an index for 30 years prior to his death in 1955, his aim being to include every marriage in Parish Registers from 1538 to 1837. His achievement, with aid from a dedicated band of helpers, in indexing perhaps 12%–15% of all marriages with coverage for some 4,200 parishes is remarkable. It is not surprising that the coverage of the index is variable from county to county ranging from almost 100% of Cornish Parishes to only 4% in Staffordshire, and it should be noted that even if a Parish is included in the index the extracts may only be partial. The index is housed in the library of the Society of Genealogists, which also holds the largest collection of copies of Parish Registers.

Recognising the value of Boyd's work, other equally dedicated genealogists have, in recent times, started to compile indexes for counties or areas in which they are particularly interested. The recent Federation booklet (see Bibliography) lists more than 50 indexes in existence and still being compiled and there are a number of others planned. Fees vary from nothing to £5 minimum and the invariable rule is that applications must always be made by letter and be accompanied by a stamped addressed envelope. (N.B. It is unwise to assume the accuracy of indexed data – the actual record should be checked to be certain.)

Where are the Registers and What is the Cost of Research?

Until recently a substantial number were still kept locally in the hands of the incumbent but the Parochial Registers and Records Measure 1978 has led to most of the older Registers now being deposited in the Diocesan Record Offices. The Office in which the records are deposited is usually also the County Record Office but not all Diocesan Registries are under the auspices of local authorities, e.g. The Borthwick Institute, University of York.

Before undertaking a journey to a distant Parish or Record Office there are a number of factors to consider, not least the potential cost. Incumbents still holding registers are legally obliged to permit access, at convenient times, but are entitled to charge a searcher the following fees:

Baptisms, Burials and Marriages before 1837:
Up to one hour £5.00
Each subsequent hour or part thereof £3.50
Post 1837 Marriages . . . . No charge
Furnishing copies of above (for every 72 words) £1.50

It should be emphasised that this scale of charges applies only to researches carried out personally. The incumbent is not obliged to:

(i)   permit the register (or any other record) to be photocopied.
(ii)   supply certificates on postal application.
(iii) make searches on behalf of an enquirer.

If he does research in response to a postal enquiry then he is entitled to charge for his time.

Therefore, whether making a personal search or requesting information by post it is prudent to ascertain how much you will be expected to pay. One way of dealing with the problem of a postal enquiry, and of advantage to both parties, is for the enquirer to state what he is seeking and to enclose a cheque for an amount in words "not exceeding X (whatever you are prepared to spend) pounds", leaving the numerical amount to be filled in by the incumbent.

Care of Archival Material

Parish Registers (and any other original documents which you may wish to consult) are irreplaceable and vulnerable, so always treat them with respect by observing the following rules. Whilst examining records:

(i)   ALWAYS USE PENCIL. Never ink.
(ii)   DO NOT eat, drink, smoke or chew.
(iii) DO NOT rest anything on the document, or run a finger or pencil down it. NEVER attempt to copy by tracing.
(iv)   Turn pages carefully.
(v)   Leave the document as you found it.

Remember you are an ambassador for those who come to research after you, the reception they receive may be coloured by what you have done, or failed to do. One bad impression will last longer than many good ones.

Local Record Offices

A brief introduction is all that can be attempted here. It is essential that all preparatory work be done prior to the visit and that adequate notes are taken with you, plus a folder and notepaper, which should be divided up into appropriate columns if you know in advance the type of record you will be consulting. Record Offices do not have the staff available to deal with detailed enquiries. Some have only limited space available for researchers so do not assume that you can be accommodated. To avoid disappointment, telephone or write first to ascertain:

(i)   Whether the record you want is available.
(ii) Whether it is necessary to book a place and if so whether one is available on the date of your proposed visit.

Many Record Offices publish lists of their holdings of Parish Registers, Bishops Transcripts and other documents; these are invaluable if you anticipate doing a lot of research in a particular area. In many Offices you will not be permitted to take bags and briefcases into the search rooms. Most reference works (e.g. *Discovering your Family History* or *Local Population Studies*) have lists of all the Record Offices throughout the country. There is also a Federation booklet with sketch maps.

Scotland

The old parish registers in Scotland were often badly kept. The majority date from the eighteenth century. There are also a good number for the seventeenth century, but few from the sixteenth; the earliest is 1553. One bonus is that where a baptism is recorded the mother's maiden name is usually stated. Unfortunately there is a dearth of burial or death records. In Scotland there are no County Record Offices and the Registers deposited are at New Register House, Edinburgh, where they may be consulted for a fee of £5.00 per day (but see page 35 for details of "global" fees covering all records).

The Church of the Latter Day Saints is compiling a county index to the old parish registers of baptisms and marriages on microfiche, but it is not likely to be finished for some years. By January 1990 the index covered the counties of Shetland, Orkney, Caithness, Sutherland, Ross and Cromarty, Inverness, Aberdeen, Kincardine, Banff, Moray, Nairn, Angus, Kinross and Clackmannon; and the cities of Aberdeen, Dundee and parts of Glasgow.

Ireland

After the disestablishment of the Church of Ireland an Act of Parliament decreed that its registers were to be deposited at the Four Courts Dublin, which unfortunately was burned in the "troubles" of 1921/2. Only four registers survived the holocaust but some registers had not been deposited and copies had been made of others. The *Handbook* (see Bibliography) lists more than 650 known extant registers by county, stating the earliest year for which baptismal registers are known to exist (the oldest being St. John's, Dublin, 1619). A number have been published. There are similar lists for the Presbyterian Registers (200+, oldest 1674) and Roman Catholic (1,000+, oldest 1690).

Roman Catholic Registers, which mostly remain with the church, are generally of later date, particularly for rural parishes, some of which do not commence until the 1860s. Microfilm copies of pre-1880 registers are held at the National Library Dublin.

The parish graveyard was frequently a common resting place for all denominations and burial entries may well be found in the registers of the established church.

Bibliography

National Index of Parish Registers:
Vol. 1   *General Sources of births, marriages and deaths, before 1837. (Indexed in Vol. 3).*
Vol. 4   *Kent, Surrey and Sussex.*
Vol. 5   *The West Midlands: Gloucestershire, Herefordshire, Oxfordshire, Shropshire, Warwickshire and Worcestershire.*
Vol. 6   *The North Midlands* (Part 1): *Staffordshire.*
Vol. 7   *Cambridgeshire, Norfolk and Suffolk.*
Vol. 8   *Ptl. Berkshire.*
Vol. 11   *North East England* (Part 1): *Durham and Northumberland.*
Vol. 13   *Wales.*

Original Parish Registers in Record Offices and Libraries (Local Population Studies), 5 parts.

Parish Registers, Eve McLaughlin, FFHS.

Bishops' Transcripts and Marriage Licences, Bonds and Affidavits, J. S. W. Gibson, FFHS.

Marriage, Census and Other Indexes for Family Historians, J. S. W. Gibson, FFHS.

Record Offices: How to Find Them, Jeremy Gibson and Pamela Peskett, FFHS.

The Phillimore Atlas and Index of Parish Registers, ed. C. Humphery-Smith.

Genealogical Research in Victorian London) West Surrey F.H.S.
Genealogical Research in Edwardian London) – London Parishes.

Reading Old Handwriting, Eve McLaughlin, FFHS.

How to Read Local Archives, F. G. Emmison.

Scotland

In Search of Scottish Ancestry, G. Hamilton-Edwards.

Introducing . . . Scottish Genealogical Research, D. Whyte.

Scottish Roots, Alwyn Jones.

National Index of Parish Registers:
   Vol. 12 *Sources for Scottish Genealogy and Family History*, D. J. Steel.

Ireland

Handbook on Irish Genealogy, Heraldic Artists Ltd.

8. Other Parish Records

Space does not permit more than a brief reference to some of the additional records which may be found but what Tate describes as "the intimate connection between the parish and the poor" provides a rich source of information often unobtainable elsewhere and providing, perhaps more than any other source, an insight into the way of life of our forebears. Until the Poor Law Reform Act of 1834 the relief of the poor was the responsibility of the Parish and there were many Acts from 1388 onwards, of which the most important were:

(a) 1601 which ordered that the churchwardens and 2 to 4 other substantial householders be nominated yearly as overseers, who were authorised to deal with the relief of the poor, the funds being provided by taxation of the local inhabitants.

Overseers' Accounts may contain details of payment for rent, clothes medical and funeral expenses etc., with the names of recipients.

Churchwardens' Accounts include a wide variety of expenditure and may include payments to the poor and details of bastardy.

Poor Rate Books contain details of those who paid and can amount to a virtual census of the more prosperous parishioners.

John (Jose) Pelling (see figure 5) was not baptised at Rudgwick and his parents were unknown. He was, however, a farmer and thus liable to pay the Poor Rate. Working backwards through the Rate Book it clearly showed the farm passing successively from John to Mary, widow, and to Jose. It also showed that he took over his father-in-law's farm. Since the farms were named it was a simple matter to check their location on the Tithe map for the Parish, which clearly showed that the farms were adjacent, so Jose had married the girl next door. The map also indicated that there were Estate Papers, examination of which provided an unexpected bonus, detailed maps of each farm showing the name and location of each field, its name and acreage. This shows the value of researching the records of a Parish in depth; references were also found in both the Overseers' and Churchwardens' Accounts which shed much light upon the decline in the family's fortunes, as did entries in the Vestry Minutes which chronicle the administration of the Parish and may include, for example, Parish apprenticeships.

(b) 1662 which provided for settlement and removal. The Parish was responsible for those having a legal settlement there, which could be achieved in several ways, of which birth was one. This meant that until 1743/4 (after which a child acquired its mother's place of settlement) it was common practice for vagrant pregnant women to be hastened on from Parish to Parish so that the baby would become the responsibility of another.

Strangers could be removed by order of the Justices and anyone staying temporarily, for example for harvesting, had to have a certificate from his own Parish agreeing to take him back.

Successive Acts almost immobilised the poor so:

(c) The Act of 1696/7 provided that poor persons may enter any Parish provided they possessed a settlement certificate, for which a Federation Vice President has coined the apt phrase "Pauper's Passports". The most iniquitous provision of this Act (not repealed until 1781/2) was that a pauper (and his wife and children) "shall wear upon the shoulder .... a large Roman P together with the first letter of the name of the parish ...."

An ancestor's misfortune can prove of great assistance to the family historian. The pauper was brought before a Magistrate and examined about his origins, parentage, and previous occupations.

These Examination and Removal Orders may survive at the Parish of removal or with the Quarter Sessions Records (usually to be found at the C.R.O.), which are themselves a rich source of genealogical information.

The 1834 Act brought Parishes together into Unions administered by guardians and their records often show payments to paupers to enable them to emigrate. The law relating to settlement was not substantially changed until 1876.

Bibliography

The Parish Chest, W. E. Tate.

Quarter Sessions Records for Family Historians: A Select List, J. S. W. Gibson, FFHS.

Annals of the Poor, Eve McLaughlin, FFHS.

Illegitimacy, Eve McLaughlin, FFHS.

9. Non-Conformist Records The Public Record Office

Many people know that their ancestors were non-conformist (which for the purposes of this chapter embraces all denominations other than the Church of England), and those who do not must always bear the possibility in mind, particularly when researches in relevant C. of E. records have proved unfruitful. Non-conformists do appear in C. of E. Records and the use of born (instead of baptised) and interred (instead of buried) may be an indication of non-conformity.

It cannot be denied that non-conformist research is more difficult. Minority faiths were often persecuted and even in more tolerant times restrictions were placed on their activities. The subject of non-conformity is vast and space is sufficient only to give some indication of the records available.

A commission was appointed in 1837 to consider the state and authenticity of non-parochial registers. It recommended that all records should be sent to the Registrar General and many were surrendered at that time. These have now been transferred to the Public Record Office and microfilmed. The Catholics refused initially, and so did The Society of Friends (Quakers).

One important Register of births surrendered was that kept by Dr. Williams's Library, which was commenced in 1742 by a combined body representing Presbyterians, Baptists and Congregationalists, after concern had been expressed at the failure of many congregations to keep proper records. The importance of Hardwicke's Act has already been stressed and between 1754 and 1836, all marriages, except for those of Quakers and Jews, had to be celebrated by the Church of England in order to be considered legally valid. Monumental Inscriptions are very important for non-conformists since they may in fact be the only record available. It was not until 1880 that non-conformist ministers were given the right to perform burials in C. of E. churchyards. The best known non-conformist burial ground is at Bunhill Fields, which was the main non-conformist burial ground for the London area for more than 200 years. An index is available in the Guildhall Library.

Roman Catholics

Only 79 Catholic Registers were deposited in 1837, (many more have been deposited since), of which Yorkshire accounted for 46, Durham 12 and Northumberland 10. In Lancashire only 1 out of 71 was deposited, and there were none from 16 counties. Those not deposited remained with the Church.

An increasing number are being deposited in Record Offices and the Catholic Record Society has published much valuable material. It should be noted that the Record Society is not a genealogical society, but there is now a Catholic Family History Society, which is a member of the Federation.

Baptists

Baptist records are perhaps the least extensive. 431 chapels (Yorkshire again having the largest number) surrendered registers in 1837, of which there is a complete list in Geoffrey Breed's book (see Bibliography).

United Reformed Church

Formed in 1972 by a union between the Congregational Church of England and Wales and the Presbyterian Church of England. The Presbyterian Historical Society of England combined with the Congregational Historical Society to form the United Reformed Church Historical Society, 86 Tavistock Place, London WC1H 9RT.

The library is open, by arrangement, usually Tuesdays, Thursdays and Fridays: 10.30 a.m.–4 p.m. It is rich in 17th century material and contains more than 6,000 books and 2,500 pamphlets. Prospective visitors are requested to write or phone so that arrangements may be made. Written enquiries are dealt with by volunteer researchers.

(i)   Congregationalists (also called Independents)

No less than 1,278 chapels surrendered Registers in 1837, Yorkshire providing 138, more than twice the total for any other county except London's 77. Some 40 Independent congregations did not accept the 1972 union and they are served by the old Congregational Library, 14 Gordon Square, London WC1H 0AG.

(ii)   Presbyterians and Unitarians

194 Presbyterian registers were deposited (and 6 Unitarian). Lancashire was the leading county with 29 (and 2), nearly double that of the next county Yorkshire 15 (and 3). A number of Registers have been published.

Quakers

The Quakers, founded by George Fox in the mid-17th century, were the most record-conscious of all Non-Conformists. Marriages with non-Quakers were forbidden and there was a very strict ban on cousin relationships. These strictures led to exhaustive enquiries about marriages for which parental consent was always required (until 1883), irrespective of the age of the parties. Three meetings were required before the marriage was contracted and the standard marriage certificate used from 1677 sometimes had as many as 40 witnesses. Before finally handing over all their registers in 1857, digests were made of the entries which date from the early 1600's and include approximately 260,000 births. These are kept at the Library of the Society of Friends, Friends House, Euston Road, London NW1 2BJ.

Indexes available include:

> Marriages in the digest registers (for the greater number of quarterly meetings);
> Journal of Friends Historical Society, Vols. 1–53 (1903–75);
> Deaths recorded in the Annual Monitor (1813–1892);
> Collection of the Sufferings (prior to 1689);
> Dictionary of Quaker Biography.

The library is open (excluding Public Holidays), Monday to Friday, 10 a.m.–5 p.m. Charges at time of writing: Personal searches £2 per hour, Proxy £8 per hour.

Quakers, like certain other denominations, refused to acknowledge months named after heathen gods and used an alternative dating system.

> e.g. 25 March 1737 was 25 1Mo 1737
> and 31 Dec 1737 was 31 10Mo 1737, but from 1752 January became accepted as the first month.

Jews

The Jews were originally expelled from England in 1290. Two principal groups have migrated to Great Britain since the 17th century.

(i)   Sephardic – from Spain, Portugal and Italy.
(ii) Ashkenazi – from Eastern Europe, Bohemia, Germany and Holland.

They have settled quite widely throughout Britain especially in the larger towns and cities, where synagogues were established, records of the congregations are available. Searchers are advised to approach their local synagogue. The Jewish Museum, Woburn House, Upper Woburn Place, London, WC1H 0EP or the Jewish Historical Society, 33 Seymour Place, London, W1H 5AP.

Methodists

It was not the wish of John Wesley (1703–1791) to separate from the Church of England and during his lifetime Methodist chapels were called "Preaching

Figure 11 DIVISIONS OF THE METHODIST CHURCH

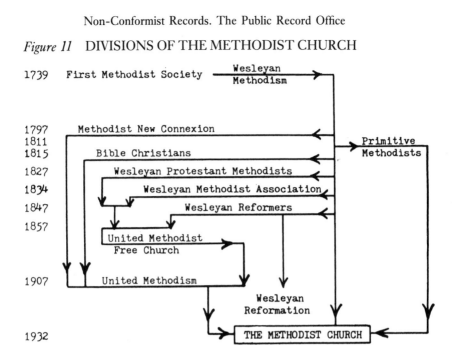

Houses", the parish church being used for baptisms, marriages and burials. The earliest registers date from 1795 when baptisms commenced in some chapels, and burial grounds were also established. Following Wesley's death a number of schisms occurred and Figure 14 shows diagrammatically the divergencies and the eventual reunions.

Number of Registers surrendered (County with most)

Wesleyan Methodists	697 (Yorks. 138)
Primitive Methodists	97 (Yorks. 17)
Methodist New Connexion	48 (Yorks. 15)
Bible Christians	29 (Cornwall 11)

The problem often is to identify to which splinter groups a particular chapel or ancestor belonged. When exploring Methodist records it should be remembered that a man who was, say in 1840, a strong member of the Methodist New Connexion, could have started life as a Wesleyan and been baptised and perhaps married at a completely different chapel. Marriages present a particularly difficult problem. Between 1837 and 1899 many chapels were licensed for marriage only with the presence of a Registrar, who kept the official records. The Chapel record was optional and not always kept.

Public Record Office

The PRO has been mentioned in connection with many of the non-conformist records and it is appropriate to consider it briefly here. The PRO is split between 2 buildings (open 9.30 a.m.–5 p.m. Monday–Friday) and a reader's ticket is required:

(a) Chancery Lane; containing legal records, PCC Wills (see next Chapter), non-conformist registers, and (from 1990) census returns.
(b) Ruskin Avenue, Kew (Richmond); containing mainly Departmental Records, e.g. Military, Naval and Merchant Shipping.

Bibliography

National Index of Parish Registers:
   Vol. 2 *Sources for Non-conformist Genealogy and Family History*, D. J. Steel.
   Vol. 3 *Sources for Roman Catholic and Jewish Genealogy and Family History*, D. J. Steel.

Tracing your Ancestors in the Public Record Office, Jane Cox and Timothy Padfield.

List of Non-parochial Registers and Records in the Custody of the Registrar General, Main Series (Births, Deaths and Marriages).

My Ancestors Were Quakers: How can I find more about them?, E. H. Milligan and M. J. Thomas.

My Ancestor Was Jewish: How can I find out more about him?, ed. Michael Gandy.

My Ancestors Were Baptists: Geoffrey R. Breed.

10. Wills, Letters of Administration and Inventories

"Where there's a will there's a way", is often said in a different context, implying that if you have the determination you will succeed and genealogically speaking it is very apt.

Wills are the truest and most reliable genealogical record available and yet probably the least used. In some cases they are the only firm way of establishing family relationships where two persons of the same name lived in the same neighbourhood at the same time.

We are all familiar with the phrase "last Will and Testament" but a question seldom asked is what is the difference? The answer is simple, a Will was concerned with realty (real estate) and a Testament with personalty (personal property).

Just to confuse the issue, in Scotland the word Testament is always used but it must be appreciated that Scottish (Roman) Law is different from English. In Scotland a man can only alienate, that is freely dispose of, his estate if his wife and children do not survive him. Otherwise he can only dispose of part of it as follows:

WIFE (W) Living	CHILD/CHILDREN (C) Living	Share of Estate	Disposable
Yes	Yes	W. 1/3 C. 1/3	1/3
Yes	No	W. 1/2	1/2
No	Yes	C. 1/2	1/2

This system also originally applied in England but was gradually eroded until, by the end of the 16th century, the old rule applied only in the Province of York (until 1693), Wales (1696) and, strangely, the City of London (1726).

The Statute of Wills 1540 provided that Wills could be made by boys from the age of 14 and girls from the age of 12 (and these ages still apply in Scotland). Anyone could make a Will except: children, lunatics, heretics, apostates, prisoners, slaves and married women. A married woman could not

61

make a Will without her husband's consent until the Married Women's Property Act of 1882 and even that applied only to those married after 1 January 1883.

An English Will is revoked by a subsequent marriage, a Scottish Will is not but if a Scotsman omits to mention unborn children and a child is born after the Will is made, then it is revoked. A holograph Will, entirely in the deceased's handwriting, did not require witnesses (and is still recognised as valid in Scotland). Until 1838 Nuncupative (oral) Wills were valid if there were witnesses.

A Will names a person or persons, the executor(s) (a woman is executrix), to carry out the deceased's (Testator or testatrix) wishes. The executor has to obtain an official document from the Court, the grant of probate, to prove he is the person legally authorised to administer the estate. If the deceased did not make a will then he is said to have died intestate and letters of Administration (usually abbreviated to "Admon.") must be obtained by the next of kin. Sometimes Letters of Administration are granted even when there is a Will because the executor has died or declined to act.

England and Wales

From 11 January 1858, the country was divided into civil probate districts and all Wills proved and Admons granted subsequently are held at the Principal Probate Registry, Somerset House, Strand, London WC2R 1LP. There the indexes may be searched free of charge. Wills may be viewed for 25p so that it is far cheaper to look at the details in a Will than to buy a death certificate. A photocopy of a Will may be obtained for the cost of photocopying.

For postal enquiries, form PR 100 should be obtained, from Somerset House: a 3 year search costs £2.

The annual indexes were printed, for use in the local probate registries. Prior to 1926 the jurisdiction of District registries covered a specific area; subsequently, executors may prove a will, or next of kin obtain letters of Administration, in any registry.

These sets of indexes (to 1928 or later) have now mostly been transferred to county record offices or major libraries, locations given in *Probate Jurisdictions* (see Bibliography). They can too be used as a short cut to finding date of death for most men of any substance dying after 1857.

Prior to 1858 Wills in England had to be proved in the Ecclesiastical Courts (of which there were some 300) and it is the complex system of these which most people find confusing because of the difficulty of determining which Court had jurisdiction. The searcher will not normally know the reason why a Will was proved in a particular court and all courts should be searched. (In the order shown in the flow chart – Figure 15).

Figure 15

FINDING THE APPROPRIATE PROBATE COURT

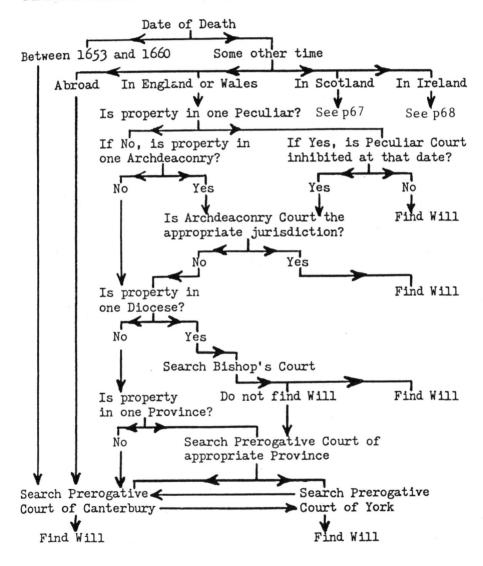

Organisation of the Church of England

The status of an Ecclesiastical Court is related to church administration which is as follows:

(a) The PARISH is the smallest unit having a vicar or rector.
(b) A RURAL DEANERY is an area consisting of a number (not usually more than 12) of parishes headed by a rural dean who is usually minister of one of its parishes.
(c) AN ARCHDEACONRY consists of a number of rural deaneries each in the charge of an archdeacon.
(d) A DIOCESE consists of several archdeaconries over which a bishop has authority.
(e) A PROVINCE is a large area of several Dioceses with the authority vested in an archbishop and until the Archbishopric of Wales was created in 1920 there were only two (Canterbury and York).

Probate Jurisdiction

The Courts of Jurisdiction can now be considered bearing the above hierarchy in mind.

(a) PECULIARS. The smallest probate divisions, which were, by ancient custom, exempt from the Archdeacon's and usually the Bishop's authority. A given Peculiar may consist of:

A single Parish.
Several Parishes, either adjacent or widely separated, which may be even in different counties.
A Manorial Court.
Universities and Colleges (e.g. Oxford and Cambridge).
Certain cities and towns.

At times Peculiar Courts were inhibited (i.e. closed) in which case the next superior Court exercised jurisdiction. Wills were normally proved in Peculiar Courts if the deceased's property was solely within that Peculiar.
(b) RURAL DEANS did not normally exercise probate jurisdiction but in some areas it was customary for them to do so under commission from either the Archdeacon (e.g. Richmond) or from the Bishop (e.g. Diocese of York).
(c) ARCHDEACON'S COURTS. If property was held solely within one Archdeaconry and if the Archdeaconry exercised its jurisdiction (the Bishop claimed jurisdiction over those which did not), then normally the Will was proved in the Court of the Archdeaconry.
(d) BISHOP'S DIOCESAN OR CONSISTORY COURTS.
Granted probates where property was held in more than one archdeaconry but solely within the same diocese. In some dioceses the

Bishop also claimed jurisdiction over the estates of noblemen and clergy within the diocese. A Commissary Court was the name given to a Consistory Court which exercised the jurisdiction of an Archdeacon's Court.

(e) ARCHBISHOP'S COURTS. Granted probate where property was held in more than one diocese. There were 2 Courts:

The Prerogative Court of Canterbury (PCC) which covered all counties not listed under PCY and South Lancashire prior to 1541 and the Prerogative Court of York (PCY) which covered Cheshire, Cumberland, Durham, Lancs., Northumberland, Notts., Westmorland and Yorks.

If property was held in more than one province then Canterbury claimed superior jurisdiction. In the period 1653–1660 all Wills were proved in the PCC. The PCC also had jurisdiction over the estates of those who died overseas. Moreover, executors of people of standing often used a higher court than was necessary.

The PCC is obviously by far the most important Court and indexes to its Wills 1383–1700 have been published. The Society of Genealogists has a card index relating to the period 1750–1800, covering approximately 500,000 Wills. This index is not open to public search but for a modest fee, staff of the Society will check for specific names on request.

Four volumes of this index have been published to date. They deserve a far wider circulation than at present achieved, and this would also help to finance the production of the remaining volumes. All family historians have a vested interest in this project; ask your library if they have copies which cover:

Volume I	Names beginning A–Bh
Volume II	Bi–Ce
Volume III	Ch–G
Volume IV	H–M

PCC Wills are at the Public Record Office and PCY Wills are at The Borthwick Institute, York. Other Wills are to be found at the various County Record Offices. *Probate Jurisdictions* sets out in detail where the Wills for each county in England and Wales are to be found (see Bibliography). Before 1733 the note of probate at the end of a will is in Latin. You can usually pick out the names of testator and executor who proved the will and their relationship, the remainder being legal verbiage of no genealogical relevance.

Inventories

Prior to 1782, when probate or admons. had been granted, several persons were appointed to take a true and perfect inventory of the personal estate. Copies are normally available in the appropriate CRO; some are indexed. Each included all goods moveable and immoveable; clothes, wares, leases

Figure 16 PART OF AN EIGHTEENTH CENTURY INVENTORY

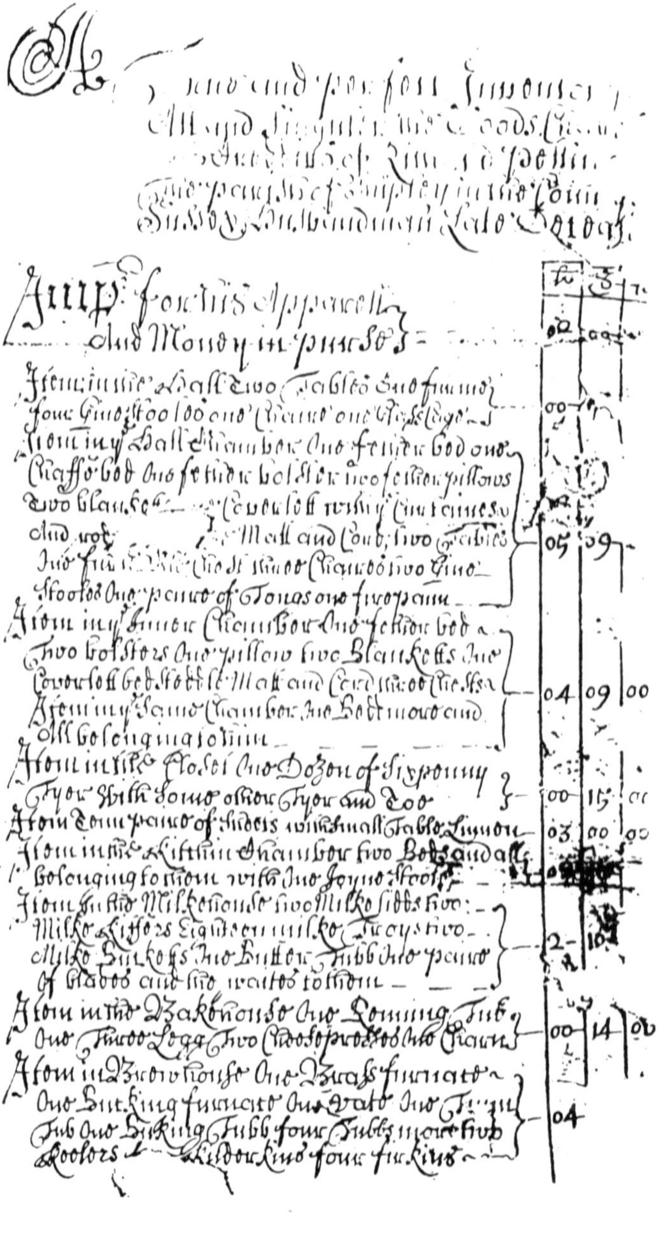

farm stock, cut grass and timber, growing corn, cash rent and debts due. Excluded were lands, hereditaments and wife's paraphernalia (i.e. the clothes fitting to her degree) and in York also her bed and coffer. PCC inventories only survive between 1661 and about 1700.

In many counties the inventory was listed room by room, an example is illustrated and you will quickly realise that no other source is likely to give you such an insight into how your ancestors lived. You may think that you cannot read the example shown, but if you study it for a while you will see that it is: "A true and perfect Inventory, All and Singular the goods chattels and ? creddits of Richard Pelling, the Parish of Shipley in the County of Sussex husbandman" .... and that the first item is .... " for his apparell and money in purse £2.0.0". It then goes on to list the items in each room and given a start I am sure you will be able to decipher most of it.

Scotland

Until 1868 only moveable property could be bequeathed by will. After the Reformation the function of confirming testaments in Scotland (previously exercised by the bishops' courts) was assumed by Commissary Courts set up by royal authority (1566), that of Edinburgh having a local and a national jurisdiction, and the right to confirm the testaments of persons dying out of Scotland but having moveable estate in the country. The jurisdictions of the inferior commissary courts, originally 14 in number but later augmented, covered areas roughly co-terminous with the medieval dioceses. In 1823 the function of confirming testaments was invested in the Sheriff Courts, the commissary court of Edinburgh retaining a local jurisdiction until 1836.

The records of most Sheriff Courts, including their extant commissary records, pass to the Scottish Record Office approximately ten to fifteen years after creation. The Office will advise if records are still in the custody of the appropriate sheriff clerks.

Indexes are available in the Office's Search Rooms at the General Register House, Princes Street, Edinburgh, viz., Indexes to the Commissary Courts' registers of testaments, to 1800, published by Scottish Record Society and also available in many good reference libraries; Index to the personal estates of defuncts, 1827–67 (covering dates varying for different sheriffdoms), which indicate the existence of a confirmed testament in the appropriate Sheriff Court records; certain internal indexes to registers of inventories and confirmations post 1823, transmitted to the Record Office with Sheriff Court Records; the Calendar of Confirmations from 1876 to date.

Ireland

Irish Wills were also proved in diocesan courts, from 1536 to 1858, the Prerogative Court being that of the Archbishop of Armagh. Most Wills were destroyed in 1922 but indexes of 21,000 Wills and Admons. prior to 1800, which survived elsewhere, have been compiled. Copies of most of the indexes of those which were destroyed also survived. Post 1858 Wills have been proved at the Principal Probate Court and are held in the Principal Probate Registry in Dublin.

Wales

All locally proved Welsh Wills prior to 1858 are at the National Library of Wales, Aberystwyth.

Bibliography

A Simplified Guide to Probate Jurisdictions: Where to look for wills, J. S. W. Gibson, FFHS (includes maps; covers whole of British Isles).

The Phillimore Atlas and Index of Parish Registers – also shows probate jurisdictions.

Somerset House Wills from 1858, Eve McLaughlin, FFHS.

Wills before 1858, Eve McLaughlin, FFHS.

Simple Latin for Family Historians, Eve McLaughlin, FFHS.

Latin for Local History. E. A. Goodber.

11. Other Useful Sources

Most of the sources described in the previous chapters will basically provide names, dates and addresses, although more may be gleaned from wills and parish records.

It is important to realise, however, that a recital of names, generation by generation, giving dates of birth, marriage and death, although no doubt interesting as a genealogy, is inadequate as a family history. Do not, I urge you, simply become an ancestor collector. Try and build upon the "skeleton" of the basic information by placing the family events you have discovered into their broader historical context, which will involve investigation of the character and development of the area in which your ancestors lived.

A county history is a good starting point, but much more detail can be obtained from Directories, Newspapers and Magazines, of which libraries usually have a good collection for their locality.

Directories

Local Directories were published from 1780. Generally, a history and topographical description of the district is given and prominent persons and tradesmen are listed. The advertisements are particularly interesting, giving a true flavour of the period.

Newspapers

Having found the date of a birth, marriage or death, a check of the local paper may reveal more details; an obituary notice may contain a potted biography and the report of a funeral details of relatives. Even if the event is not recorded you will find out what were the items making the news which your ancestors may have read (if they could read, which you will probably have noted from other information), or which will have been the subject of gossip and may have influenced their lives or environment. The most comprehensive collection of National and other papers is held by the British Library. Provincial newspapers only included local news from the mid-18th century, and local newspapers only proliferated from the mid-19th century.

Of most use to the Family Historian, and by far the largest, is at Colindale Avenue, Colindale, London NW9 5HE. Open: Monday–Saturday, 10 a.m.–4.45 p.m. The collection consists of daily and weekly newspapers and periodicals: English provincial, Scottish and Irish from about 1700 and London from 1801. Commonwealth and foreign papers are also available.

Prior to visiting, researchers are advised to phone to check whether the material sought is available. Normally, persons under 21 are not admitted.

School and University Records

Often extensive biographical details are included, particularly in the printed University indexes. It is possible to trace several generations where sons of the family attended the same university, as often happened. Schools records may be found at local Record Offices and the Society of Genealogists has an extensive collection for the Public Schools.

Apprentice Indentures

Youths were bound by indentures signed by a parent or guardian and the master to whom they were apprenticed, usually for 5 or 7 years. An example is shown at Figure 17. In 1710 a tax was imposed and central registration followed. The original records are in the P.R.O. Information given includes: Name of Apprentice and Master; father's name (or mother's if she was a widow) until 1760; and often residence.

The Society of Genealogists has an index covering the years 1710–1774.

Taxation

Our ancestors suffered, as we do, from the need of the government to finance its activities. The earliest records are the subsidy rolls, which date from 1290 – of use to family historians between 1524 and 1640, when they provide periodic lists of the wealthier members of the community. Of greater use are the records of the Hearth Tax, which listed virtually all heads of households (with the number of fireplaces, or heated rooms, in their homes), taxing *occupiers* rather than owners. The tax was imposed in 1662 and lasted until 1689, but the records (mostly in the PRO, Chancery Lane) only survive between 1662 and 1674. It was succeeded by the Window Tax, from 1696 to 1851, but this was only on the relatively well-off, and in any case very few records survive.

The most useful tax lists for the 18th and early 19th century are for the Land Tax. Although this was collected from the 1690s, most of the surviving records (in county record offices) are for the period 1780 to 1832, when payment of the tax was a voting qualification. For 1798 only, records for the whole of England and Wales (except Flintshire) are at the PRO (Kew). Names of owners of land and their tenants are given, annually, though occupants of cottages are often un-named.

This Indenture Witnesseth That William Birkett

... doth put himself Apprentice to ... Henry Wynn ...

... to learn ... and with him after the Manner of an Apprentice to serve from the date ... day of Year ... During ...

... unto the full End and Term of ... years ... Therefore from thence next following to be fully complete and ended During which Term the said Apprentice his ... Master faithfully shall serve his secrets keep his lawful commands every where gladly do. He shall do no damage to his said Master nor see it to be done of others but to his Power shall tell or forthwith give warning to his said Master of the same. He shall not waste the Goods of his said Master nor lend them unlawfully to any. He shall not commit fornication nor contract Matrimony within the said Term. He shall not play at Cards or Dice Tables or any other unlawful Games whereby his said Master may have any loss with his own Goods or others during the said Term without licence of his said Master. He shall neither buy nor sell. He shall not haunt Taverns or Playhouses nor absent himself from his said Master's service day or night unlawfully. But in all things as a faithful Apprentice he shall behave himself towards his said Master and all his during the said Term. And the said ... shall teach and instruct or cause to be taught and instructed ...

... And for the true performance of all and every the said Covenants and Agreements either of the said Parties bindeth himself unto the other by these Presents In Witness whereof the Parties above named to these Indentures interchangeably have put their Hands and Seals ... day ... by the Grace of God of the United Kingdom of Great Britain and Ireland QUEEN Defender of the Faith and in the Year of our Lord One Thousand Eight Hundred and Fifty ...

Sealed and delivered ...

William Birkett

John ...

N.B. The Indenture Covenant Article or Contract must bear date the day it is executed and what thing or other thing is given or contracted for with the Clerk or Apprentice must be inserted in Words at Length otherwise the Indenture will be void. The Master or Mistress beside Fifty Pounds and another Penalty and the Apprentice be disabled to follow a trade or be made free.

PENNY

Six Pence

Lowe & Phillips Parchment Manufr Shoe Lane London

Petitions

There are three other major sources for lists of names in the 17th century. Best known are the Protestation Returns, of 1641, when most adult men signed a petition to the King in support of Parliament. A number of county lists have been published. The original lists are in the House of Lords Record Office. About the same time a collection was made in aid of Distressed Protestants in Ireland. This was widely supported, and lists of contributors are in the PRO (Chancery Lane). At the end of the century, a petition of support for William III (following assassination attempts) called the Association Oath Rolls was signed by all office-holders and a great many others; the lists are in the PRO (Chancery Lane).

Army and Naval Records

These are extensive and mainly in the PRO. As might be expected it is easier to trace an officer than other ranks. To trace a soldier successfully it is essential to know his regiment. Of particular interest for the Army is a list of retired officers compiled in 1828, which gives age when commissioned, date of marriage and births of children. The active list 1829–1919 includes, in addition, date and place of birth.

Bibliography

Guide to National and Provincial Directories of England and Wales before 1856, J. E. Norton.
Local Newspapers 1750–1920 – A Select List, J. S. W. Gibson, FFHS.
Alumni Cantabrigiensis, 10 Volumes, J. and J. A. Venn.
Alumni Oxoniensis, 8 Volumes, J. Foster.
Registers of the Universities and Schools of Great Britain and Ireland, P. M. Jacobs.
Land Tax Assessments c1690–c1950, J. S. W. Gibson and D. Mills, FFHS.
The Hearth Tax, Other Later Stuart Tax Lists and The Association Oath Rolls, J. S. W. Gibson, FFHS.
The History of Taxation, B. Sabine.
In Search of Army Ancestry, G. Hamilton-Edwards.
Records of Officers and Soldiers who have served in the British Army, PRO
World War I Army Ancestry, N. Holding, FFHS.
The Location of British Army Records. A National Directory of World War I Sources, N. Holding.
Records of Naval Men, G. Fothergill.
My Ancestor was a Merchant Seaman. How can I find out more about him? C. T. and M. J. Watts.

12. Surnames

"What's in a name? . . ."; contrary to Shakespearian opinion, a great deal. You may have a common name, the derivation of which is fairly obvious, but as your searches progress names will appear on your tree, the origin of which may provoke your curiosity. The more unusual the name the easier research is and you can justifiably make a note of every occurrence of a rare one. Whatever the name it will stem from one of four basic roots:

1. Place.
2. Occupation or Office.
3. Personal (Relationship).
4. Nickname.

Place names are the most numerous, being derived from general places, Hill, Wood, Marsh or particular locations, London, Bedford, York. Originally place names were preceded by various prepositions, which in some cases have become attached: Attwell, Bywater, Underdown, Nash (atten ash). Provoked by an entry in the unreliable guide by Ewen – where my name was equated with that of Pilling, a place in Lancashire, which was clearly nonsense – I traced it to a small hamlet in Sussex, Peelings, which disappeared from the map in the second half of the eighteenth century. Even today, some 700 years after its first appearance there, the name is comparatively rare outside of Sussex, except in neighbouring Surrey.

In my researches I used *The Place Names of Sussex*, one of a series issued by the English Place-Name Society on a county basis, which cover the smallest of places, even farms, an example will show the value:

"Pellingbridge Farm is Pellyngesbregge 1425 Lewes Deeds, Pellyngbrege 1439 (Court Rolls), Pyllyngbregge 1441 (Court Rolls) and is to be associated with Simon de Pelling (1296 Subsidy Rolls), who perhaps came from Peelings in Westham . . ."

The distribution of a particular place surname can be plotted from telephone directories, which may indicate the likely area or origin. Occupational names are sometimes obvious and a common ending is -er. Carter, Forester, Porter and Turner, for example: less obvious, Chaucer (French version of Hosier), Sainter (French saintier – bell founder), Scrimshaw (French scremisseur – fencing master). The clothing industry accounts for some 165 names including, Dyer, Lister, Weaver and there are regional variations of the same process, e.g. Fuller (S. & E.), Walker (W. & N.) and Tucker (S. W.)

Bardsley (see Bibliography), who was the pioneer in the field of surname origins, identified personal names derived not only from fathers (patronymics), but, to the consternation of the Victorians, to whom such names implied illegitimacy (by no means necessarily so), mothers (metronymics). Jackson, Dobson, Williams are obvious forms of the former, whilst the latter includes Annis (from Agnes), Catlin (Catherine), Ibbotson (Isabel) and Margetson (Margaret).

Nicknames fall into many categories: physical characteristics – Redhead, Fairfax, Ballard (bald), Armstrong; moral qualities – Doughty, Noble, Quant (knowledgeable); animals – Farr (bull), Buck, Lovett (wolf-cub); birds – Dove, Swallow, Ruddock (robin); fish – Tench, Trout, Smelt (sardine); oaths etc. – Godber, Mordue, Pardoe.

In England there were no hereditary surnames before the Norman Conquest. They became inherited at any time in the subsequent 300 years, the north was less advanced than the south and in Lancashire and Yorkshire many surnames did not become hereditary much before 1400, and last of all was Wales.

In 1890 Guppy (see Bibliography), reasoning that farmers were the least mobile group counted their number in the Kelly's Directories and classified their names on a geographical basis, thus:

1. General   found in 30–40 Counties.
2. Common   ”   ”   20–29
3. Regional   ”   ”   10–19
4. District   ”   ”   4–9
5. County   ”   ”   2–3
6. Peculiar mostly confined to 1 County.

He found the most popular names to be:
1. Smith; 2. Brown; 3. Taylor; 4. Clark(e); 5. Robinson; 6. Johnson; 7. Wilson; 8. Hall; 9. Green; 10. Wright.

Scottish and Irish names have, as might be expected, their own pecularities.

In some families, surnames of brides are adopted as christian names and where this happens it is invaluable to the researcher.

Bibliography

A Dictionary of English & Welsh Surnames, with special American Instances, C. W. Bardsley.

The Origin of English Surnames, P. H. Reaney.

A Dictionary of British Surnames, P. H. Reaney.

Discovering Surnames, J. W. Freeman.

The Homes of Family Names in Great Britain, H. B. Guppy.

13. Publicising Your Researches

Eventually you will have accumulated sufficient information to present a coherent account of your findings. Do not keep your discoveries to yourself. Someone, somewhere, may be waiting for a vital piece of evidence, which you have. The readily available excuse always is "but I haven't finished yet"; but, if you are an enthusiast you never will!

The easiest way of informing other family historians about your findings is to write an article for the magazine of a Family History Society, editors of which are always looking for suitable material and they will be glad to give advice about presentation. In addition to the results your methods of research may be of interest to others faced with similar problems.

Family History News & Digest, the half-yearly publication of the Federation of Family History Societies, contains a Digest section summarising most articles which have appeared in the Magazines of its members. This, coupled with the exchange of journals between Societies, automatically ensures a wide coverage for your article and you could find yourself, as a result, exchanging information to your mutual benefit (as I have), with a reader in a distant part of the world.

If your forte is the spoken, rather than the written word, you might instead prefer to give an illustrated lecture to a Society located where your ancestors lived. If you do embark on this, thorough preparation is necessary, particularly with the production of visual material, which is essential for any talk lasting longer than twenty minutes.

Most effective, if you have the talent for it, is a tape/slide presentation, in which a slide sequence is accompanied by a commentary and/or additional sound material.

In due course the information accumulated may be far more than can be conveniently summarised within the confines of a single article and a larger publication should be considered. The costs of publication should be weighed against the likely sales; the former may be less than you think and the latter greater. Publications with strong local associations are likely to appeal to libraries. You would, however, be well advised to open a subscription list before committing yourself to much expenditure.

When you have at least three generations of family history recorded you may like to deposit a copy of your research papers in the document collection at the Society of Genealogists. This not only safeguards the information should you mislay your own papers but is a useful way of sharing research.

You may also discover other researches for the same name already in the collection. New additions are recorded in the Society's Journal.

Even if you do not feel able to pursue any of the options outlined above, try to share your researches with others by registering the names you are researching with the appropriate Family History Society and deposit copies of your pedigree charts, but, above all, meet others and share your enthusiasm together.

Family History has enriched my life leading me to new experiences of public speaking, teaching, writing and extensive travel: but for Family History I should never have found myself in a western saloon in the Colorado rocky mountains singing a cockney song to a bunch of cowboys ... but that is another story!

You are warned that this pastime is addictive and may occupy your leisure hours for the rest of your life. May I wish you "good hunting" and who knows, we may find ourselves related.

I originally wrote those last words in 1979, since when for two readers it has proved prophetic.

Bibliography

Projecting Family History; A Guide to Audio-Visual Construction, H. Green.

Biographics. Publish Family History. Inexpensive Ways to Do It Yourself, I. Templeton.

14. Publications of the Federation of Family History Societies

The chapter Bibliographies include works published by the Federation of Family History Societies, which are not generally available in bookshops. A comprehensive list of publications available at January 1990 is shown below; for price list please write (enclosing stamped, addressed envelope, or 3 International Reply Coupons) to the FFHS, Federation Administrator, c/o Benson Room, Birmingham & Midland Institute, Margaret Street, Birmingham B3 3BS.

Family History News and Digest (journal published twice-yearly).

Beginning your Family History.

Current Publications by Member Societies.

Facsimiles of Documents of Use to Family Historians.

The Family Historian's "Enquire Within" (genealogical encyclopaedia).

Forming a One-Name Group.

How to Tackle your Family History (leaflet).

Notes on Recording Monumental Inscriptions.

Register of One-Name Studies.

The Scots Overseas (A Select Bibliography).

World War I Army Ancestry.

Was Your Grandfather a Railwayman?

Location of British Army Records (National Directory of World War I Sources).

More Sources of World War I Ancestry.

Gibson's Guides for Genealogists

Bishops' Transcripts and Marriage Licences, Bonds and Allegations: A guide to their location and indexes.

Census Returns 1841–1881 on Microfilm: A directory to local holdings.

Coroners Records.

The Hearth Tax, Other Later Stuart Tax Lists and the Association Oath Rolls.

Electoral Registers since 1832.

Land Tax Assessments, c.1690–c.1950.

Local Newspapers, 1750–1920: A select list.

Marriage, Census and Other Indexes for Family Historians.

Quarter Sessions Records for Family Historians: A select list.

Record Offices: How to Find Them (with street plans).

A Simplified Guide to Probate Jurisdictions: Where to look for wills.

Unpublished Personal Name Indexes in Record Offices and Libraries.

McLaughlin Guides

Annals of the Poor.

The Censuses, 1841–1881: Use and interpretation.

Illegitimacy Records.

Interviewing Elderly Relatives.

No Time For Family History?

Parish Registers.

Reading Old Handwriting.

St. Catherine's House.

Simple Latin for Family Historians.

Somerset House Wills from 1858.

Wills before 1858.

Index

Index

Public Procurement Law
– the EU directive on public contracts

Simon Evers Hjelmborg, Peter Stig Jakobsen
& Sune Troels Poulsen

Public Procurement Law
– the EU directive on public contracts

DJØF PUBLISHING

Public Procurement Law
– the EU directive on public contracts

1. edition

©2006 by Jurist- og Økonomforbundets Forlag
DJØF-PUBLISHING, Copenhagen

Cover: Morten Højmark
Print: Narayana Press, Gylling
Binding: Jysk Bogbind, Holstebro

Printed in Denmark 2006
ISBN 87-574- 1408-4

DJØF Publishing
17, Lyngbyvej
P.O.B 2702
DK 2100 Copenhagen
Phone: + 45 3913 55 00
Fax: + 45 39135555
e-mail: forlag@djoef.dk
www.djoef.dk-forlag

Preface

This book is intended as an analysis of the new EU Procurement Directive which must be implemented into national law in the Member States before 31 January 2006. The Procurement Directive represents a substantial simplification of the procurement rules in that one directive now acts as replacement of the previous three directives. Moreover, the rules have been brought up to date with the introduction a new procedure, the competitive dialogue, and with rules on the use of *inter alia* framework agreements and electronic auctions. As the new Procurement Directive covers the same area as the previous three directives, it is rather complex for which reason we have found that there was a need to expound on the rules of the new Procurement Directive.

The book presents an overall and systematic analysis of the rules of the new EU Procurement Directive (2004/18/EC). The analyses are based on judgments of the European Court of Justice and the European Commission's communications and the extensive Danish case law, bearing in mind that the new Procurement Directive is based on the principles of the now repealed procurement directives and a number of the previous provisions are re-enacted in the new Procurement Directive.

The book was originally written in Danish. We have found it relevant to translate the book into English since the three previous directives as well as the new Procurement Directive have been transposed directly into Danish law. As a consequence, the rules of the Directive, as set out therein, are directly applicable to Danish law and the extensive Danish case law on the Procurement Directives largely amplifies the analyses of the individual rules of the new Procurement Directive.

The Procurement Directive must be implemented into national law in the individual Member States and, therefore, the rules of the Procurement Directive must be considered in combination with the rules of the individual Member State. However, it is our hope that the analyses of the rules of the Procurement Directive and in particular of Danish case law set out in this book, will also be of interest in other EU Member States.

The book includes information published as of 1 July 2005, and selected subsequently published information. The new EU Utilities Directive (2004/17/EC) is not analysed in this book.

Finally, our thanks and appreciation go to Margot & Thorvald Dreyers Fond, making this English release possible, Marie Heising, our dedicated translator and our devoted student, Sarah Hav Jano, who is responsible for the various indexes.

Contents

18

CHAPTER 1

Aim and principles

1. Aim of the rules

The Procurement Directive[1] is one means by which the EU is seeking to create an internal market with genuine free movement of *inter alia* goods and services and effective competition. The Procurement Directive is intended to create an internal market for *public contracts* and to achieve that aim contracting authorities have to comply with extensive obligations and respect certain requirements in award procedures for public contracts.

In this section the background to the Procurement Directive and its aim are subject to an analysis. Sections 2-4 are an analysis of the sources of law, principles and processes of interpretation to be applied to the analysis of the obligations of contracting authorities. In section 5, the focus is directed towards the rules applicable to public contracts that fall outside the scope of the Procurement Directive.

1.1 Public procurement and the performance
of public works and services

The public sector is responsible for numerous social activities for which it needs to procure goods and services and execute buildings and works. Public procurement can take on a variety of forms, for example purchase of paper cups for a canteen, asphalt works on public roads, construction of schools or computerisation of VAT and tax payments.

Public procurement is motivated by an underlying objective related to the public interest and a public responsibility. The construction of a school is

1. Directive 2004/18/EC of the European Parliament and the Council of 31 March 2004 on the coordination of procedures for the award of public works contracts, public supply contracts and public service contracts hereinafter called the "Procurement Directive".

necessary for the education of pupils which may be an objective of cultural policy, business policy, etc. The construction of an electric power plant may be necessary in order to maintain voltage to the utility network. In the detailed planning of the construction, dimensioning, technology, location, etc. thereof factors such as pollution of the physical environment, competitiveness of domestic undertakings, security and defence, etc. may also be included.

1.1.1 Requirements of the public sector – fulfilled on the basis of contracts
The requirements of the public sector for goods, etc. are predominantly fulfilled by private undertakings on the basis of contracts. Every day the State and public authorities award contracts for the procurement of goods and services and execution of works. The value of the contracts awarded by the State is immense and the contracts account for a substantial share of the output of the individual Member State and of the EU as a whole.[2] The award of public contracts is subject to the EU Procurement Directive.

Traditionally, in procurement procedures contracting authorities – in addition to price and quality – have made a point of awarding the contract to a national undertaking. Therefore, the Procurement Directive is intended primarily to counteract the tendency for contracting authorities to prefer national undertakings and products.

The performance of the public service or works can be entrusted to economic operators, i.e. public or private undertakings. Economic operators may perform engineering or technical works such as the operation of a sewage treatment facility, refuse collection, road maintenance, etc., or they may perform administrative services or healthcare and social services. The performance of such works or services is governed by a contract, the award of which is subject to the Procurement Directive.

1.1.2 Why special rules for the award of public contracts?
The EU Member States are bound by the EC Treaty which aims to create a single market for the free movement of (*inter alia*) goods and services.[3] The single market is based on a prohibition of discrimination against undertakings on grounds of nationality.[4] Further, the Treaty provides that there must be no restrictions on the free movement of goods, services, workers and capital or

---

2. Total public procurement in the EU – i.e. the purchases of goods, services and public works by governments and public utilities – is estimated at about 16% of the Union's GDP or Euro 1,500 billion in 2002.
3. The single market is a means to promote *inter alia* economic development in the EU.
4. Article 12 of the EC Treaty.

on the freedom of establishment.[5] Finally, under the Treaty it is prohibited for public and private undertakings to restrict competition.[6]

It is the realisation that the State – unlike undertakings – is not subject to the discipline of the market forces when purchasing goods or services, which has created the need for introducing rules regulating the award of public contracts. The additional costs of giving preferential treatment to a national undertaking may lead to a budget overrun, a reprimand or similar, but a contracting authority is not, in the same manner as an undertaking, under a threat of bankruptcy if other considerations than optimisation of price and quality are the focus of purchases. A supplementary appropriation or a tax increase can equal out a budget deficit. In *Arkkitehtuuritoimisto Riitta Korhonen Oy*[7] it was expressed as follows:

"… a body acting for profit and itself bearing the risks associated with its activity will not normally become involved in an award procedure on conditions which are not economically justified"[8].

The rationale behind the EU Procurement Directive is the recognition of the fact that the Treaty provisions do not effectively prevent the award of public contracts to national undertakings. The market forces as such, are deemed not to be capable of opening up the national markets for public contracts to international competition. As a consequence, the Procurement Directive is a means to counteract the Member States' predisposition to favour national undertakings in procedures for the award of public contracts by obliging States to use specific procedures for the award of public contracts.[9]

1.1.3 Obligations under the Directive – limited to the award of contract

The Procurement Directive imposes a number of obligations and limitations under which supply, service and works contracts can be awarded. By establishing a very formalised procedure for the award of public contracts, the award procedure becomes more transparent. This serves to limit contracting authorities' scope for discretion in award procedures, and the risk that na-

---

5. Articles 28, 49, 39, 56 and 43 of the EC Treaty.
6. Articles 81, 82 and 86 of the EC Treaty.
7. Judgment of the European Court of Justice of 22 May 2003, case C-18/01, Arkkithetuuritoimisto Riitta Korhonen Oy.
8. Ibid, extract of paragraph 51.
9. At the heart of this obligation is that "any" intention to award a public contract must be advertised at EU level in order that interested undertakings throughout the EU are informed of the possibility for being awarded a public contract. See also chapter 5.3.

tional undertakings are given preferential treatment is thereby reduced. The added transparency promotes more equal terms for economic operators and competition for public contracts is enhanced.

The contracting authority decides *whether* to launch a procedure and *what* to be purchased (in terms of characteristics, performance, quality, etc.). Once the contracting authority has specified its requirements and is ready to find a contracting partner, it is obliged by the Procurement Directive to follow a detailed procedure for the award of the public contract. To that end, the Directive stipulates certain restrictions on *how* a contract can be awarded and to *whom* a contract can be awarded.[10]

Contracting authorities are obliged to apply the procedures set out in the Procurement Directive to the *award* of public contracts. Hence, the obligation to follow the procedures set out in the Directive only applies to the period of time from the decision by the contracting authority to launch a procedure and until the award of the contract has been decided. Moreover, the obligations imposed by the Procurement Directive only apply to the award of contracts to independent economic operators.

Although contracting authorities essentially are free to prepare a specific purchase as they please, the rules of procedure set out in the Procurement Directive nevertheless have a certain bearing on the specification of the object of the contract and the drafting of the contract documents. The provisions of the EC Treaty are also binding on the contracting authorities. For example, the criteria for the award of the contract will have to be linked to the object of the contract.[11] Further limitations stipulate that contact with consultants in the period *before* the launch of the award procedure must be limited, and *after* the award of the public contract the extent to which the contract can be amended without reopening the procedure is restricted.

1.2 Aim of the Procurement Directive
– a single market for public contracts
The Procurement Directive is intended to create a single market for *public contracts* with genuine free movement of goods and services and effective

---

10. Certain contracts are excluded from the scope of the Procurement Directive, see chapter 3 below. See also, for example, judgment of the European Court of Justice of 16 October 2003, case C-252/01, Commission vs. Belgium, concerning a contract the performance of which was subject to special security measures.
11. Judgment of the European Court of Justice of 17 September 2002, case C-513/99, Concordia Bus Finland Oy Ab vs. Helsingin Kaupunki, paragraph 59. See also chapter 4.3 on EU law requirements for the contract specifications.

competition for public contracts.[12] In order to achieve this aim the Directive is also intended to ensure equal treatment of tenderers and transparent award procedures. The means to create a single market for public contracts and to ensure equal treatment and transparent award procedures is the obligation that is imposed by the Procurement Directive to use pre-determined procedures for the award of public contracts. This eliminates the risk that contracting authorities discriminate against economic operators on grounds of nationality and that certain economic operators are given preferential treatment on other grounds, while it also ensures that contracting authorities are not driven by other concerns than economic and objective concerns.

In several judgments the European Court of Justice has pointed out the aim of the Procurement Directive.[13]

1.2.1 Benefits of competition for public contracts

The overriding aim of the Procurement Directive is to create a genuine internal market for public contracts. Public contracts are to be opened up for competition – the contracts are to be subjected to competition to allow undertakings located throughout the EU a genuine chance of being awarded contracts.[14]

In a market with competition for public contracts it is expected that the increased competitive pressure will force existing and potential suppliers to rationalise and improve the efficiency of production, supplier and service networks and administrative procedures in order to offer competitive prices and deliver goods and services at attractive terms. Both society and contracting authorities are expected to gain a number of benefits:

– increased competition is expected to promote advances in technology;
– public authorities are expected to spend less funds on procurement;
– corruption and abuse of power in the process of awarding public contracts are expected to be eliminated through the use of transparent procedures for the award of public contracts.

---

12. Judgment of the European Court of Justice of 27 November 2001, cases C-285/99 and C-286/99, Impresa Lombardini SpA, paragraph 34.
13. Judgments of the European Court of Justice of 16 October 2003 in cases C-244/02, Kauppatalo Hansel Oy vs. Imatran kaupunki, paragraph 32 and C-283/00, Commission vs. Spain, paragraph 73.
14. Judgment of the European Court of Justice of 27 November 2001 in cases C-285/9 and C-286/99, Impresa Lombardini SpA, paragraph 35.

1.2.2 Secondary objective:
  open up to competition and ensure equal treatment

The Procurement Directive is intended to ensure that award procedures for public contracts are *opened up* to *foreign undertakings*, in particular. In the words of the European Court of Justice the aim of the Directive is:

"… to protect the interests of traders established in a Member State who wish to offer goods or services to contracting authorities established in another Member State …".[15]

The *opening-up* of procedures for public contracts is closely linked to the regulation of the EU internal market according to which all trade barriers are carefully assessed under Articles 28 and 49 of the Treaty. In the EU's internal market it is prohibited to discriminate against undertakings on grounds of nationality, and any obstacles (restrictions) to the free movement of (especially) goods and services must be justified by grounds of public policy and be proportional to the objective pursued, taking into account the effect of the obstacle on trade.[16]

A genuine internal market with effective competition for public contracts is only achieved if interested undertakings, in addition to the opportunities for tendering for public contracts, in fact have *equal opportunities* for being awarded these contracts. Interested economic operators' chances of being awarded a public contract are only real, and by inference competition only effective, if the terms – set by the contracting authority – on which economic operators tender are equal. Therefore, in order to ensure equal competitive terms for economic operators, another objective of the Procurement Directive is to ensure *equal treatment* of economic operators by contracting authorities,[17] to the effect that no participant in the competition is given preferential treatment, for example, because of nationality, family relations, the contract-

---

15. Judgment of the European Court of Justice of 3 October 2000, case C-380/98, The Queen vs. H.M. Treasury (University of Cambridge), paragraph 16. See also judgment of the European Court of Justice of 18 June 2002, case C-92/00, Hospital Ingenieure vs. Stadt Wien, paragraphs 43 and 44 and judgment of the European Court of Justice of 27 November 2001 in cases C-285/99 and C-286/99, Impresa Lombardini SpA, paragraph 36.
16. See also chapter 4 on the contract documents and chapter 6 on selection.
17. Recital 2 of the preamble to the Procurement Directive. Judgment of the European Court of Justice of 17 September 2002, case C-513/99, Concordia Bus Finland Oy Ab vs. Helsingin kaupunki, paragraphs 81 and 92 and judgment of the European Court of Justice of 22 June 1993, case C-243/89, Commission vs. Denmark (Great Belt), paragraph 33.

ing authority's prior knowledge of the participant, special knowledge about the proposed contract, etc.[18]

The EU's objective of opening up public contracts to competition and ensuring equal treatment in award procedures implies a number of obligations on the contracting authorities. In the award of public contracts contracting authorities must follow a commercial line of thought comparable to a market in which undertakings compete on the basis of the price, quality, service, etc. of their products and services.[19] Therefore, not only must a public contract *not be awarded* on the basis of discrimination by nationality, preferential treatment, non-objective considerations or arbitrarily,[20] contracting authorities are also under an *explicit obligation* to ensure that the contract is awarded on the basis of objective, reasoned and transparent criteria.[21]

1.2.3 Equal treatment encourages competition

Competition is not about distributing contracts evenly among undertakings within an industry. Indeed, the award of a public contract should take account of the different qualifications of economic operators and the differences in the tenders submitted by them. The underlying objective is to create competition for public contracts and the outcome of the procurement procedure is that (usually) only one economic operator is awarded a contract. It is this uncertainty with respect to the award of the contract which provides the incentive to improve qualifications and to lower prices. The rules are aimed at ensuring equal treatment of tendering undertakings and preventing national favouritism.

This underlying understanding that equal treatment encourages competition is also evident in the selection of the candidates which in a restricted procedure are invited to submit tenders. Any interested economic operator can express its interest in the contract, and the contracting authority is obliged to evaluate all requests. However, when selecting *among the suitable candidates,* the only thing that matters is that the group of tenderers is composed in such a way as to ensure effective competition whereby the contracting authority, presumably, obtains the best tenders or the tenders of the lowest price.[22]

---

18. See also chapter 5 on the procurement procedures and chapter 7 on award.
19. See also section 1.2.5 below on the secondary objective of the Directive of basing the award of contracts on economic considerations.
20. Judgment of the European Court of Justice of 27 November 2001, cases C-285/99 and C-286/99, Impresa Lombardini SpA, paragraphs 44 and 57, concerning the possibilities for eliminating abnormally low tenders.
21. Recital 46 of the preamble to the Procurement Directive. See also chapter 4.
22. See also chapter 6.

The fundamental objective of ensuring competition for public contracts means that any form of cartelisation among tenderers is unacceptable.[23] It would contravene the principle that goes to the root of competition; that undertakings act independently of each other. Furthermore, as a rule, the contracting authority cannot provide one or more undertakings with special information about the procedure.[24] Such "insider" information would shift the individual undertakings' chances of being awarded contracts and thus (partially) deprive the market of its function.[25]

The EU's objective behind the Procurement Directive of opening up public contracts to competition and ensuring equal treatment of candidates and tenderers *has a great influence* on the award procedures. Derived from principles governing,the procedures it has been established that the contracting authority is prohibited from negotiating with the individual tendering undertakings in the period after the opening of the tenders and until the award of the contract has been decided. The reason for the prohibition is that it is difficult to conduct completely transparent negotiations, and it is therefore likely that the tendering undertakings will not be treated equally, cf. the next section.[26]

23. Where tenderers have formed a cartel, the obligation to publish a call for tenders is derogated from. Negotiations may be opened with the individual tenderers directly. See order of the Complaints Board of 7 December 2000, Association of Danish Consulting Engineers vs. Ministry of Culture. An international call for tenders may eliminate the risk of cartelisation among tenderers. It may be possible to avoid an existing cartel by selecting those undertakings that are invited to submit tenders. See order of the Complaints Board, København Lufthavn and ELFO, Documentation 1996.582.
24. See also chapter 6.4 below.
25. On the other hand, another contracting partner cannot be chosen where a dominant undertaking submits the best tender, but own production could be considered as an alternative. Similarly, State aid is not an appropriate ground for excluding a tendering undertaking, unless the aid is unlawful or incompatible. See judgment of the European Court of Justice of 7 December 2000, case C-94/99, ARGE.
26. The Directive affords certain opportunities for awarding contracts on the basis of negotiations in exceptional cases. See chapter 5.2.

1.2.4 Secondary objective: create transparency

The Procurement Directive requires contracting authorities to use special procedures for the award of public contracts.[27] The main features of the procurement procedures prescribed in the Directive are:

– public contracts must be put out to competition;
– only certain pre-determined procedures can be used to award the contract;
– the contract documents must be made public;
– the contract documents must be objective and reasoned;
– economic as well as non-economic criteria can be applied to the evaluation of the tenders.

The obligation to use special procedures is intended to ensure a minimum level of transparency in award procedures for public contracts. By specifying detailed procedural requirements the contracting authority's scope for discretion in the individual stages of the award procedure is limited significantly.[28] The obligations deriving from the Procurement Directive to use special procedures are an instrument in promoting equal treatment of economic operators competing for public contracts, cf. above.[29]

However, transparency of award procedures is an aim on its own. In *University of Cambridge*[30] it was emphasised that the Procurement Directive not only is intended to put an end to discrimination. The Directive also has a more preventive aim in that the mere *risk* of discrimination must be eliminated:

"... the aim of the directives is to avoid ... the risk of preference being given to national tenderers or applicants whenever a contract is awarded by the contracting authorities ...".[31]

27. One key element in procedures for the award of public contracts is that the intention to award a contract must be published at EU level (which obligation cannot be derogated from). See chapter 5.3.
28. See also section 3.3.2 below on the principle of transparency.
29. Judgment of the European Court of Justice of 18 June 2002, case C-92/00, HI vs. Stadt Wien, paragraph 46; order of the European Court of Justice of 16 October 2003, case C-244/02, Kauppatalo Hansel Oy vs. Imatran kaupunki, point 32.
30. Judgment of the European Court of Justice of 3 October 2000, case C-380/98, The Queen vs. H.M. Treasury (University of Cambridge).
31. Ibid, paragraph 17; Judgment of the European Court of Justice of 12 December 2002, case C-470/99, Universale Bau, paragraph 52; judgment of the European Court of Justice of 27 February 2003, case C-373/00, Adolf Truley, paragraph 42.

The transparency achieved by obliging contracting authorities to use set procedures for awarding public contracts improves the economic operators' chances of *predicting* the basis on which the public contract will be awarded. On that account, transparency serves to protect against *arbitrariness* in the award of public contracts, and protection against arbitrary decisions is regarded as a key element in the efforts to encourage, notably, foreign undertakings to conclude public contracts and thus promote competition for public contracts.[32]

The requirement for transparent award procedures is also closely linked to the enforcement of the obligations under the Procurement Directive as transparency enhances the opportunities for verifying whether tenderers have been discriminated against, and whether the principle of equal treatment has been complied with.[33]

*1.2.5 Secondary objective: award of contract based on
    economic considerations*

Another aim of the Procurement Directive is that contracting authorities should base the award of public contracts on economic considerations. The Directive aims to eliminate:

"... the possibility that a body financed or controlled by the State, regional or local authorities or other bodies governed by public law may choose to be guided by considerations other than economic ones ...".[34]

The ensurement of this aim is expected to contribute to the ensuring of equal treatment of economic operators, and thus promoting competition for public contracts. The aim is sought achieved by obliging contracting authorities to base the award of public contracts on objective and economic criteria. If the evaluation of the suitability of the economic operators and of their tenders is focused on the economic aspects, it is comparable to the assessment made by

32. Judgment of the European Court of Justice of 20 September 1988, case C-31/87, Beentjes, paragraph 42; judgment of the European Court of Justice of 27 November 2001, cases C-285/99 and C-286/99, Impresa Lombardini SpA, paragraph 44.
33. Judgment of the European Court of Justice of 18 June 2002, case C-92/00, HI vs. Stadt Wien, paragraph 45; judgment of the European Court of Justice of 27 November 2001, cases C-285/99 and C-286/99, Impresa Lombardini SpA, paragraph 38.
34. Judgment of the European Court of Justice of 1 February 2001, case C-237/99, Commission vs. France, paragraph 42. See also judgment of the European Court of Justice of 27 November 2001, cases C-285/99 and C-286/99, Impresa Lombardini SpA, paragraph 36.

players in a market and, therefore, eliminates discrimination by nationality and preferential treatment. Although at the same time it should be recognised that the rationale behind this aim is probably reflective of economic policies rather than competition concerns.

It is normal and logical for a contracting authority to emphasise the price of the individual tender as well as its overall economic value to the contracting authority, and pursuant to Article 53 of the Procurement Directive the contracting authority is in fact obliged to do so. However, the award of public contracts can also take account of public interests which are not economic in the narrow sense, for example protection of the environment and social considerations.

Evidently, public contracts are intended to fulfil an objective in the public interest and a public responsibility. That being so, non-economic considerations, such as the amount of pollutants discharged from a bus, road system or purification plant, can be taken into account in the preparation and award of public contracts on equal terms with economic interests, such as price, quality, durability, etc. The object and the terms and conditions of the public contract can be specified so as to take account of such non-economic considerations, or non-economic considerations can be laid down as criteria for the award of the public contract.[35]

Economic and non-economic considerations are of diverse nature and the possibility of combining these different considerations somewhat counteracts the aims of transparency and equal treatment in procurement procedures. Nonetheless, the Procurement Directive clearly warrants that non-economic considerations are safe-guarded for in procurement procedures, but the contract documents must be prepared very carefully if the award of a public contract is to be based *inter alia* on the relative compliance with non-economic criteria.[36]

1.2.6 Separate Directive with separate aim: effective enforcement

The rules, and thus the creation of a single market for public contracts, are only likely to be effective if there are measures in place to put an end to infringements of the rules. To that end a Directive has been issued requiring the EU Member States to ensure that the procurement rules are effectively enforced.[37] The aim of the Remedies Directive is to ensure the effective appli-

---

35. For further details see chapter 4.4.
36. See also chapter 4.4.
37. Council Directive 89/665/EEC of 21 December 1989 on the coordination of the laws, regulations and administrative provisions relating to the application of review proce-

cation of the Procurement Directive. The Remedies Directive provides, in particular, that Member States must take measures to ensure that "… decisions taken by the contracting authorities may be reviewed effectively and, in particular, as rapidly as possible …".[38]

1.3 Priority given to opening up competition

The Procurement Directive is reflective of a balancing of the contracting authorities' interest in as flexible procedures as possible against the EU's objective of ensuring competition for public contracts. The result is an obligation on contracting authorities to use special procedures for the award of public contracts. The following sections deal with the actual effects of the obligations laid down in the Procurement Directive.

The prohibition of negotiations with the individual tenderers and the resulting lack of possibility for adjusting the contract documents and the tenders pose problems for the contracting authorities, cf. sections 1.3.1 and 1.3.2 below.[39] In addition, the procurement procedures prolong the award procedure and thereby increase costs. On the other hand, the obligation to use the procurement procedures prescribed in the Directive have certain beneficial effects, cf. section 1.3.3 below.

1.3.1 Prohibition of negotiations

Although the prohibition of negotiations might be well-founded in order to ensure equal treatment of the tendering undertakings, it nevertheless eliminates the flexibility of award procedures which is often necessary in order to optimise the performance/purchase. A contracting authority may, for example, have doubts about which services are capable of satisfying specific public needs. Also, the tendering undertakings may have doubts about, for example, the description, quality or quantity of the products or services which tenders are invited for. Having received the tenders, it may be necessary to adjust the quantity and quality of the services or to seek a reduction in the prices offered. Because of the virtually absolute prohibition of negotiations

---

dures to the award of public supply and public works contracts, hereinafter called "the Remedies Directive".

38. Article 1(1) of the Remedies Directive. See also judgment of the European Court of Justice of 19 June 2003, case C-249/01, Werner Hackermüller, paragraph 22.

39. Negotiations are prohibited in "the open procedure" and "the restricted procedure" and in the last stage of "the competitive dialogue". In exceptional cases it is possible to use "the negotiated procedure". Under the Utilities Directive negotiations with tenderers are possible to greater extent.

with tenderers, it is usually not possible for the contracting authority to adjust the contract documents or discuss the content of tenders with the tenderers in the period from the submission of tenders until the award of the contract.[40]

The prohibition of negotiations may have the effect that the contracting authority does not obtain best value for money thus counteracting one of the principal aims of the Procurement Directive; that enhanced competition for public contracts creates lower prices and innovation, which in turn reduces the costs and improves the quality of public purchases. In this perspective the obligation to use the procedures set out in the Directive in order to limit the contracting authorities' scope for discretion in award procedures, can be deemed to throw out the baby with the bath water since the promotion of competition may reduce the opportunities for obtaining the best and least expensive tender.

However, it is not altogether reasonable to take such a critical view of the Procurement Directive. The background to the Directive was a situation in which public contracts mainly were awarded to national undertakings. In that perspective the obligation to use the procedural rules set out in the Directive can be seen as necessary, bearing in mind that market forces are unlikely to regulate the practices of contracting authorities. In other words "desperate diseases must have desperate remedies".

1.3.2 Considerable foresight required

To the contracting authorities the elaborate requirements set out in the Procurement Directive for the award procedure, including the prohibition of negotiations, have a major impact on the preparation and conduct of the award procedure, in that all decisions in regard to the exact specifications of the object to be purchased and the requirements to be met by the future contracting partner, must be taken before the award procedure is commenced.[41]

The adoption of the most recent Procurement Directive in 2004 is an attempt at accommodating some of the criticism concerning lack of flexibility of award procedures. Contracting authorities can now use the competitive dialogue procedure subject to which they are allowed to negotiate with candidates.[42] Since the use of this procedure derogates from the objectives of the Directive to open up competition for public contracts, ensure equal treatment

40. See also chapter 7.4.
41. The contract notice can be sent before the specifications have been given the final touch, but the content of the contract notice must be in keeping with the specifications.
42. See also chapter 5.2.4 below.

and enhance the transparency of award procedures and thereby reduce the risk that preferential treatment is given to national undertakings, it is subject to certain conditions and limitations.[43]

1.3.3 Time-consuming and expensive?

Procurement procedures conducted in accordance with the EU Procurement Directive can be seen as both time-consuming and expensive. However, in the light of the objective of the Procurement Directive of opening up competition for public contracts, it may be considered of less importance that the obligations to invite tenders for contracts often prolong the award procedure and makes the procedure more expensive.[44]

The Procurement Directive ensures that large public contracts are put out to tender, so that economic operators from all over the EU are given the opportunity to express their interest in the contract, produce evidence of their suitability and possibly submit an actual tender for the contract. Even where applications or tenders are not submitted from foreign undertakings, the mere competition for the public contract often results in considerable price reductions and/or better services. Practise regarding first invitations to tender for a public supply, service or works contract have demonstrated that considerable savings can be made.

In that light, it may be a necessary sacrifice in order to achieve the aims of the Procurement Directive that the obligations to use the procedures of the Directive extend to situations where the contracting authority is demonstrably content with its current business partner or even has a fiduciary relationship with that partner, or the partner has obtained thorough knowledge of the authority's specific needs, requirements, techniques, etc.

---

43. The Procurement Directive provides that the requirements for the object to be purchased can be laid down as performance requirements which allows for a certain flexibility. Furthermore, it is still possible to authorise the submission of variants. See chapter 4.
44. In the Directive allowance has been made for the contracting authorities' interest in speedy award procedures. This is evidenced, in particular, by the time limits to be observed in procurement procedures. Also on other points allowance has been made for the contracting authorities' interests. Article 31 of the Procurement Directive, for example, provides that a contract can be awarded on the basis of negotiations with selected tenderers if special and unforeseen events have given rise thereto. Furthermore, Articles 30 and 31 of the Procurement Directive provides that a contract can be negotiated with selected tenderers if an open or restricted procedure has been held without producing a result. See also chapter 5 below.

In addition to the savings achieved because of the competition for the public contract, use of the procedures of the Directive also requires the contracting authority to define its needs at an early stage and to work out what the main elements of the public contract should be.

The Danish Competition Authority has examined which drawbacks local authorities point to as the most significant. In its report the Authority states that less experienced local authorities say that the Directives are difficult to use. These local authorities call for simpler rules which will make the procurement procedure easier. Local authorities with more experience say that the Directives lack flexibility. These local authorities would like more flexible rules and the opportunities for using new purchasing methods.[45]

Finally, the procedures of the Procurement Directive are factors in ensuring sound public administration, preventing discrimination and eliminating nepotism, all objectives which public contracting authorities are obliged to pursue no matter what.

2. Rules and other sources of law

The Procurement Directive is an important source of law for the analysis of the contracting authority's obligations in procurement procedures. However, the Procurement Directive is not the only basis for this analysis, also other sources of law influence the nature, interpretation and extent of the contracting authority's obligations.

2.1 The Procurement Directive

The Procurement Directive is the primary source of law for the analysis of the obligations that contracting authorities must comply with in the award of contracts for supplies and services. In Denmark the Procurement Directive has been implemented with effect for public contracts concluded after 1 January 2005.[46] The Directive is implemented in its original form. The wording of the Directive is directly applicable forming the basis of the contracting authorities' obligations. Moreover, by virtue of the principle that EU law takes precedence over national law in the event of contradictory provisions of the Directive and national law, the provisions of the Directive reign supreme and

45. Competition Report 2003, p. 296.
46. Executive Order No 937 of 16 September 2004 concerning the procedures for the award of public works contracts, public supply contracts and public service contracts.

must be applied in so far as they are capable of forming the basis for deciding a specific matter.[47]

The Procurement Directive has left a number of choices to the Member States. Denmark[48] has chosen to allow the use of most of the special procurement procedures and types of contracts provided for in the Directive:

– Article 11 on central purchasing bodies,
– Article 19 on reserved contracts,
– Article 29 on the competitive dialogue procedure,
– Article 32 on framework agreements,
– Article 33 on dynamic purchasing systems and
– Article 54 on electronic auctions for supplies and services.[49]

The Procurement Directive is the result of a process that started in 1971, and the rules and obligations prescribed in the Directive should be analysed bearing that in mind, as some of the rules are re-enactments of previous sets of rules whereas other rules are altogether new.[50]

The subject-matter of an individual rule, the legal fact, of the Procurement Directive may not always be clear. The preamble to the Directive and the definitions set out in Article 1 of the Directive are valuable tools aiding the analysis and interpretation of the individual provisions of the Directive. The aim of the Directive and of the individual provisions is stipulated in the preamble to the Directive. Therefore, the preamble is an important source of law for the purpose of interpreting and implying meaning into a specific provision. Article 1 of the Directive contains definitions of many of the terms used in the Directive.

The material concerning the legislative history of the Directive is reflective of the political considerations and objectives behind the Directive, and therefore it may be useful to include the material in the analysis of the Directive and the interpretation of a specific provision. As mentioned above, the

---

47. The principle that EU law takes precedence also applies to judgments from the European Court of Justice on the interpretation of directives.
48. Executive Order No 937 of 16 September 2004 concerning the procedures for the award of public works contracts, public supply contracts and public service contracts, Section 3.
49. Electronic auctions cannot be used to award works contracts. See also recital 14 of the preamble to the Procurement Directive.
50. Judgment of the European Court of Justice of 27 November 2001, cases C-285/99 and C-286/99, Impresa Lombardini SpA, paragraph 50.

procurement rules have been amended successively over a number of years and, therefore, the relevance of the material concerning the legislative history of the individual amendments to the Directive varies, depending on whether a rule is a re-enactment, an amendment or entirely new. But for a specific purpose the material concerning legislative history can be an important source of law.[51]

2.2 The Remedies Directive[52]

The EU has issued a Directive obliging the Member States to ensure that measures for the effective enforcement of the procurement rules are in place.[53] In order to comply with the Remedies Directive a special Complaints Board for Public Procurement has been established in Denmark to review complaints about infringements of the Procurement Directive. The Complaints Board for Public Procurement is empowered to grant complaints suspensive effect, set aside decisions made by contracting authorities and award a complainant damages in the event of a contracting authority's infringement of the procurement rules. The Complaints Board for Public Procurement can refer questions on the interpretation of the Procurement Directive to the European Court of Justice for a preliminary ruling.[54]

2.3 The EC Treaty

The Procurement Directive was adopted on the basis of Articles 47(2), 55 and 95 of the EC Treaty. Pursuant to Articles 2 and 3 of the Treaty the establishment of a single market is a key task for the European Community. The single market is to be attained by removing barriers to the free movement of *inter alia* goods and services between Member States, and the Procurement Directive performs an important role to that end. Against that background the EC Treaty is an important source of procurement law.[55]

The provisions regarding trade barriers on goods and services contained in, for example, Article 28 and Article 49 of the EC Treaty, respectively, are

---

51. Judgment of the European Court of Justice of 7 December 2000, case C-324/98, Telaustria Verlags GmbH and Others.
52. See also section 1.2.6 above and chapter 8 on the aim of the Directive.
53. Council Directive 89/665/EEC of 21 December 1989 on the coordination of the laws, regulations and administrative provisions relating to the application of review procedures to the award of public supply and public works contracts.
54. The Remedies Directive is analysed in chapter 8.
55. The principle that EC law takes precedence also applies to the EC Treaty in so far as the particular rule meets the conditions for being directly applicable.

also aids towards the interpretation of the rules of the directives, in that the aim of the directives likewise is to remove barriers to the freedom to provide services and to trade between Member States.[56] This interpretation based on the aim of the rules has far-reaching implications as will be seen in, for example, chapter 2 on the definition of the term "contracting authority":

"In order to give full effect to the principle of free movement, the term 'contracting authority' must be interpreted in functional terms ..."[57]

The rules on trade barriers in the EC Treaty are directly applicable in parallel with the procedural rules of the Directive. The EC Treaty governs the free movement of *inter alia* goods and services and the EC Treaty and its derived legislation apply directly to contracting authority's actions in the context of award procedures. The prohibition of discrimination on grounds of nationality contained in Article 12 of the Treaty is fundamental to public procurement. Also the provisions on trade barriers in Articles 25, 28 and 49 of the Treaty and legislation originating in the Treaty as well as the principles of, for example, mutual recognition established by the European Court of Justice apply directly.

Discrimination on grounds of nationality is still not uncommon although the significant judgments of the European Court of Justice in this area are likely to have brought this prohibition to the attention of contracting authorities, cf. the following formulation:

"The contractor is obliged to use to the greatest possible extent Danish materials, consumer goods, labour and equipment." [58]

It is an infringement of the rules on trade barriers contained in Article 28 of the Treaty if – in the interest of developing a specific region – a proportion of

---

56. Judgment of the European Court of Justice of 3 October 2000, case C-380/98, University of Cambridge, paragraph 16; judgment of the European Court of Justice of 20 September 1988, case 31/87, Beentjes, paragraph 11.
57. Judgment of the European Court of Justice of 17 December 1998, case C-353/96, Commission vs. Ireland, paragraph 36, comp. 1998.I-8565.
58. Judgment of the European Court of Justice of 22 June 1993, case C-243/89, Commission vs. Denmark (Great Belt), paragraph 4.

the public contracts is reserved for undertakings with production facilities in that area.[59]

It may be a case of indirect discrimination if a public measure consistently works to the disadvantage of foreign undertakings. Also non-transparent approval procedures can amount to indirect discrimination if, for example,

"... the technical specifications selected are so specific and abstruse that, as a rule, only French candidates are able immediately to discern their relevance"[60].

The rules on trade barriers are of particular relevance in three areas.[61]

– To the drafting of the contract documents; for example the wording of the qualifications required of interested undertakings and the demand specifications, etc.[62]
– The evaluation of the suitability of candidates and tenderers and of the tenders submitted must include an evaluation, *in essence,* of the foreign undertakings' qualifications and the properties and qualities of the services offered.
– Moreover, contracting authorities are obliged to recognise qualifications, certificates and approvals obtained or issued abroad which, in essence, equal the national requirements specified in the contract documents.

Public procurement is not tantamount to public regulation and, therefore, a certain modification of the rules of the EC Treaty prohibiting barriers to trade is needed. A public contract is intended to fulfil a specific public requirement. At the same time, the EU has an interest in preventing discrimination on grounds of nationality and in ensuring that undertakings compete on equal

59. Judgment of the European Court of Justice of 11 July 1991, case C-351/88, Laboratori Bruneau, cf. also judgment of the European Court of Justice of 20 March 1990, case C-21/88, Du Pont de Nemours Italiana.
60. Judgment of the European Court of Justice of 26 September 2000, case C-225/98, Commission vs. France, extract of paragraph 81. See also judgment of the European Court of Justice of 16 February 1978, case 61/77, Commission vs. Ireland, concerning the Irish State's imposition of maximum limits for the length and horse power of fishing boats in effect excluding most foreign-based fishing vessels and practically no Irish.
61. The competition rules in Articles 81 and 82 of the EC Treaty and the rules on State aid in Articles 87 and 88 are also applicable to public procurement. See also judgment of the European Court of Justice of 7 December 2000, case C-94/99, ARGE.
62. See also chapter 4 on the basis of the competition and chapter 6 concerning evidence of the required suitability.

terms, but the effects of the individual contract on trade and competition are usually negligible. Further, in order to make the purchase, the technical solutions that are capable of fulfilling the public requirement must be identified. These solutions are not always easily identifiable. As a consequence, in exceptional cases it *may* be necessary to refer to national standards or specific trademarks as examples of the characteristics required of a product or service. However, the requirements for objectivity and individual evaluation of tenders are substantial.[63]

2.4 Acts and executive orders

Denmark has implemented the Procurement Directive by the following acts: promulgation by the Danish parliament of Act on the coordination of the procedures for the award of public works contracts.[64] On the basis of the Act the Ministry of Economic and Business Affairs has issued an Executive Order governing the award of public works contracts, etc.[65] The Executive Order transposes the EU Procurement Directive into Danish law *without changes*.[66] In addition, the Act and the Executive Order govern a few other matters and they contain provisions on the sanctioning of contracting authorities which have infringed the provisions of the Procurement Directive.

The Act on the Complaints Board for Public Procurement is the basis on which procurement rules are enforced.[67] An Executive Order governs the procedure for filing complaints with the Complaints Board for Public Procurement and for the Complaints Board's review of complaints.[68]

---

63. See also judgment of the European Court of Justice of 22 September 1988, case 45/87, Dundalk; and order of the Complaints Board of 11 August 2000, Kirkebjerg A/S vs. County of Ribe.
64. Consolidating Act No 600 of 30 June 1992, as amended by Act No 415 of 31 May 2000 on the Complaints Board for Public Procurement. Act No 338 of May 2005 on Tender Procedures for Public Contracts, on the invitation to tender for building and civil engineering works govern contracts for minor works.
65. Executive Order No 937 of 16 September 2004 on the procedures for the award of public supply contracts, public service contracts and public works contracts.
66. Under the Procurement Directive Member States are afforded certain choices. See also section 2.1 above.
67. Act No 415 of 31 May 2000 on the Complaints Board for Public Procurement, as amended by Act No 338 of May 2005 on Tender Procedures for Public Work Contracts, (the Tender Act) and Act No 306 of 30 April 2003 to amend the Act on the Complaints Board for Public Procurement.
68. Executive Order No 602 of 26 June 2000 on the Complaints Board for Public Procurement.

2.5 Judgments of the European Court of Justice and Danish courts of law

The EU judgments of the European Court of Justice constitute a very important source of law for the analysis of the Procurement Directive and EC law in general. Judgments and orders of the European Court of Justice on the interpretation of the individual provisions of the Directive are binding and applicable to the entire single market, including all contracting authorities.[69] Another aspect to be taken into account when assessing judgments of the European Court of Justice as a source of EC law is that the European Court of Justice, to a wide extent, applies its own interpretation when deciding subsequent cases concerning the Directive, EC rules and fundamental principles.

A small number of the judgments delivered by the European Court of Justice concerns infringement proceedings brought by the European Commission, cf. Article 226 of the EC Treaty. Most of the actions brought before the European Court of Justice are referrals for preliminary rulings under Article 234 of the EC Treaty. Where a preliminary question is referred to the European Court of Justice, the European Court of Justice is asked to clarify the interpretation of specific provisions in directives including other EC rules and principles.

In Denmark judgments of the Danish courts of law on the interpretation of the Directive and Danish law represent an important source of law for determining the obligations of contracting authorities. Judgments arise out of real-life disputes and bring these disputes to closure and a judgment is, therefore, primarily of interest to the parties concerned. In order to reach a decision the court often has to interpret and imply the necessary meaning into the relevant rules and this interpretation is of interest to a wider group in that it is likely to be re-applied when deciding future cases.[70]

2.6 Orders of the Complaints Board for Public Procurement

In Denmark the above-mentioned special administrative complaints board has been set up to review complaints about infringements of the Procurement Directive and the Danish rules. The cases decided by the Complaints Board represent an important source of law for the interpretation of the Procurement Directive in Denmark, *inter alia* because of the large number of decisions which helps to interpret and imply meaning into the procurement rules.

---

69. See also section 4.3 below.
70. See for example judgment of the Western High Court of 14 March 2000, case B-2766-96, IBF Nord A/S vs. Aalborg Local Authority, where expectation damages were awarded in an action for damages.

The Complaints Board for Public Procurement makes decisions on the basis of complaints about infringements of the Procurement Directive.[71] The decisions are first and foremost of interest to the parties concerned. However, in order to reach a decision the Complaints Board must determine the subject-matter of the relevant rule, the legal fact, and herein the Complaints Board is forced to interpret and imply the necessary meaning into the rules, which interpretation is likely to be applied when deciding future complaints.[72]

The Complaints Board is competent to decide whether the procurement rules have been infringed and to impose the sanctions provided for in the Complaints Board Act, cf. chapter 8 below. Disputes arising out of private law fall outside the jurisdiction of the Complaints Board.[73] In Denmark orders of the Complaints Board are of great value as a source of law since the Complaints Board is the principal court of enforcement. This is not changed neither by the fact that certain disputes fall outside the jurisdiction of the Complaints Board, nor by the fact that orders of the Complaints Board can be reversed by the ordinary courts of law.

2.7 The Agreement on Government Procurement (WTO)

Under the auspices of the WTO an agreement on government procurement has been concluded to which the EU is a party. This agreement has no direct effect within the EU and, therefore, cannot form the basis on which a court of law or the Complaints Board decides a dispute. It is the intention of the EU to comply with this agreement and the Procurement Directives are presumed to be in keeping with the agreement. In that light the agreement can be used as a source of law in the application of the procurement rules, and it may contribute to interpreting and implying meaning into the individual provisions.

2.8 Orders and recommendations

The European Commission and the Danish Competition Authority have issued general guidelines explaining and interpreting the procurement rules. The European Commission and the Danish Competition Authority also provide

---

71. Act No 415 of 31 May 2000 on the Complaints Board for Public Procurement, as amended by Act No 338 of May 2005 on Tender Procedures for Public Work Contracts, (the Tender Act) and Act No 306 of 30 April 2003 to amend Act on the Complaints Board for Public Procurement, Section 3, cf. Section 1.
72. Pursuant to Article 234 of the EC Treaty the Complaints Board is empowered to refer preliminary questions to the European Court of Justice.
73. Order of the Complaints Board of 22 March 2002, Johs. Sørensen & Sønner Århus A/S vs. Århus Kommunale Værker.

advice and guidance in specific cases. The general guidelines and the specific "decisions" are merely indicative as neither the European Commission nor the Competition Authority is empowered to issue binding rules or binding decisions. However, the guidelines as well as the decisions are relevant to an analysis of the procurement rules as they derive from authorities with considerable knowledge of the regulation of trade barriers and competition.[74]

3. Fundamental principles

Certain legal principles can be applied to the interpretation of and implication of meaning into the individual rules of the Procurement Directive. The application of general administrative law and EC law must comply with principles of legality, equality and proportionality, and these principles must also be applied in procurement law.

The Procurement Directive forms part of the EU's efforts to create a single market comprising all EU Member States. The background to the Procurement Directive consists of the rules of the EC Treaty on free movement which essentially rest on a prohibition of discrimination of undertakings on grounds of nationality. On the basis of this prohibition the European Court of Justice has established principles of equal treatment and transparency, which are of paramount importance to the interpretation of and implication of meaning into the procurement rules. Indeed, the Procurement Directive contains direct references to certain principles of particular importance in procurement law, cf. below.[75]

3.1 Generally about the application of principles
The application of a principle in a legal context means that the interpretation of and implication of meaning into specific provisions take into account certain overriding considerations. The principles, like the aim of the rules, provide a guide to how a specific provision should be interpreted or which meaning should be implied into the provision. On the other hand, in certain aspects principles, by nature, differ from reflections concerning the aim of the rules

---

74. See also chapter 8.1.3 below.
75. Recital 2 of the preamble to the Procurement Directive and Article 2 of the Procurement Directive.

- in that often they are largely created by the courts of law;
- they are reflective of overriding considerations that apply to various sets of rules and, therefore, do not necessarily have a unique meaning when applied in the context of the Procurement Directive;
- and the substance of the principles evolves continuously through case law.

A principle cannot alone be the basis on which obligations are imposed in connection with the award of contracts, but it may be a benchmark for the interpretation of or implication of meaning into a specific provision.

The principles of equal treatment and transparency are of great importance to the interpretation of and implication of meaning into the provisions of the Procurement Directive in that the European Court of Justice regards them as fundamental to the rules. Moreover, the European Court of Justice has stated that the principles must be applied at all stages of a procedure.[76]

The European Court of Justice has further stated that if the Procurement Directive does not contain specific provisions concerning a particular matter, the fundamental principles of the Community must be applied.[77] The principles of equal treatment and transparency must be regarded as fundamental principles. In combination with the fact that the Directive is a minimum standard directive the principles, in reality, function as a corrective to the specific national rules governing procurement procedures. These rules may be either national law or the contracting authority's own guidelines for the procurement procedure.

3.2 Obligation of equal treatment

Equal treatment of economic operators is fundamental to ensuring competition for public contracts. The European Court of Justice has established equal treatment as a principle that must be applied at all stages of an award procedure for a public contract. The obligation of equal treatment also has a bearing on the contracting authority's conduct before the award procedure is commenced and after it has been concluded, see section 3.2.3 below.

---

76. Judgment of the European Court of Justice of 12 December 2002, case C-470/99, Universale Bau AG, paragraph 93; judgment of the European Court of Justice of 27 November 2001, cases C-285/99 og C-286/99, Impresa Lombardini SpA, paragraph 38.
77. Judgment of the European Court of Justice of 18 June 2002, case C-92/00, HI vs. Stadt Wien, paragraph 42; order of the European Court of Justice of 16 October 2003, case C-244/02, Kauppatalo Hansel Oy vs. Imatran kaupunki, paragraph 31.

3.2.1 A principle of equal treatment in Danish administrative law

Public authorities in Denmark must observe a principle of equal treatment. A principle of equal treatment is fundamental to a society founded on the rule of law since equality before the law ensures the citizens against discretionary decisions by public authorities. A principle of equal treatment does not imply that all matters be treated equally; it implies that comparable matters be treated equally unless there are objective and proportional grounds for not doing so. The principle of equal treatment is largely applied to verify whether specific grounds and the underlying criterion are factually relevant in the specific context, are sufficient basis for determining the outcome of the case and whether the authority has applied the criterion persistently and consistently in the same manner in previous cases.

Essentially, this principle of equal treatment is also applicable to a contracting authority's award of a public contract. By virtue of the principle of equal treatment contracting authorities are obliged, in particular, to take account of only such considerations that are objective keeping in mind the legal basis and field of activity of the contracting authority. In the context of award procedures for public contracts the principle of equal treatment must be modified bearing in mind that the procedure is commenced for the purpose of making a purchase and the procedure usually results in only one undertaking being awarded a contract.

3.2.2 Principle of equal treatment in procurement law

On the basis of the rules of the EC Treaty prohibiting discrimination on grounds of nationality and barriers to trade between Member States, the European Court of Justice has established a principle of equal treatment that must be complied with at all stages of the procurement procedure.[78] The principle of equal treatment is also set out in Article 2 of the Procurement Directive. The obligation of equal treatment reiterates that the contracting authority must ensure that the economic operators compete on equal terms for the public contract.

The analysis of the principle of equal treatment must take account of the background to the adoption of the Procurement Directive. The Directive is rooted in a wish to afford foreign undertakings access to public contracts and in the objective of creating a single market with free movement of *inter alia* goods and services and with effective competition, cf. section 1.2 above.

---

78. Judgment of the European Court of Justice of 12 December 2002, case C-470/99, Universale Bau AG, paragraph 93.

However, the principle of equal treatment does not merely imply a prohibition of discrimination on grounds of nationality, rather it extends to all forms of discrimination of economic operators in procedures for the award of a public contract.[79] Compliance with the principle of equal treatment is particularly important in the three following situations.

- It is of vital importance to competition among undertakings and, hence, to the efficiency of the market that the interested undertakings are afforded the same information about the nature and performance of the contract and the criteria on which they will be selected and the contract awarded and, therefore in this context, equal chances of being awarded the public contract.
- The principle of equal treatment also implies a requirement of consistency in that the transparency of the procurement procedure and thus the equal treatment of candidates and tenderers also require that the suitability of candidates and tenderers and the submitted tenders be evaluated against the pre-determined and common competitive basis. It is, for example, necessary to reject a tender which does not comply with the requirements and conditions laid down in the contract documents. The evaluation of the submitted tenders must be based exclusively on the criteria which are advertised in advance in the contract documents.[80]
- Finally, the same procedure must be applied to the evaluation of the suitability of all the interested candidates and tenderers and of all the tenders, and this procedure must be determined in advance.[81]

If the principle of equal treatment is not complied with in the above situations, and in particular if national undertakings are given preferential treatment, it seems likely that many undertakings would be less interested in ten-

---

79. Judgment of the European Court of Justice of 22 June 1993, case C-243/89, Commission vs. Denmark (Great Belt). See also judgment of the European Court of Justice of 17 March 2005, case T-160/03, AFCon Management Consultants and Others vs. Commission, paragraphs 90 and 91, concerning the obligations of the European Commission in the light of the principle of equal treatment. Order of the Complaints Board of 3 April 2002, Villy Antonsen vs. Aars Local Authority stipulated a requirement that tenders could be submitted by hotels, restaurants, etc. situated within the municipality of Aars.
80. For more details see chapter 7 below.
81. Judgment of the European Court of Justice of 18 October 2001, case C-19/00, SIAC, paragraph 34; judgment of the European Court of Justice of 4 December 2003, case C-448/01, EVN, paragraph 47.

dering for public contracts which would have an adverse effect on effective competition.[82]

The principle of equal treatment has a certain effect on the conduct of the award procedure. As mentioned above, contracting authorities are obliged to organise the award procedure so as to ensure equality of tenderers and that interested undertakings (candidates and tenderers) are treated equally in the course of the award procedure. Therefore, not only must selection criteria and award criteria be *published* in the contract notice or the specifications, they must also, in the evaluation of the tenders, be applied *objectively* and *uniformly* to all tenderers.[83]

Finally, contracting authorities are under a general obligation to ensure all interested undertakings *equal conditions* of competition which obligation goes beyond ensuring equal treatment in the conduct of a specific procedure.[84] A procurement procedure is commenced with the publication of a contract notice on the basis of which economic operators decide whether they will spend time and resources on expressing an interest in the contract and possibly submit a tender. In the interest of guaranteeing equal conditions of competition for candidates and tenderers, on the one hand, and potential tenderers (economic operators which have chosen not to participate in the competition for the specific contract), on the other hand, the contracting authority is under a particular obligation not to make any material amendments to the contract documents in the course of the award procedure.[85] This obligation to ensure equal conditions of competition applies to the formal aspects of a procedure, for example the stipulation of deadlines,[86] and to the content of the contract documents, for example the specification of the object of the contract.

82. Judgment of the European Court of Justice of 4 December 2003, case C-448/01, EVN, paragraph 48.
83. Judgment of the European Court of Justice of 18 October 2001, case C-19/00, SIAC, paragraph 44 (our emphasis). See also judgment of the European Court of Justice of 4 December 2003, case C-448/01, EVN, paragraph 48.
84. Judgment of the European Court of Justice of 25 April 1996, case C-87/94, Commission vs. Belgium (Wallonian buses), paragraph 33.
85. It comes down to a specific evaluation hinging on *inter alia* the type of contract proposed, the contract documents and the chosen procurement procedure. Order of the Complaints Board of 8 August 2003, Eurodan-Huse Vest A/S vs. Sønderborg Andelsboligforening (the Tender Act).
86. Order of the Complaints Board of 21 November 2003, Entreprenørfirmaet Harry Andersen & Søn A/S vs. County of Vejle (the Tender Act) concerning submission of tenders after the final date stipulated in the specifications.

3.2.3 Application of the principle of equal treatment

The procurement law principle of equal treatment is rooted in the EC Treaty.[87] Reference is made to the principle of equal treatment in Article 2 of the Procurement Directive.[88] In that light it is without doubt that the principle of equal treatment must be applied to the interpretation of and implication of meaning into all the provisions of the Procurement Directive.

In terms of time a distinction can be made between the period before, during and after the award procedure. Undoubtedly the principle of equal treatment must be complied with in the period from the decision to launch an award procedure until the decision to award a contract. The principle of equal treatment also matters in the period before the procedure is launched, where it must be ensured that no tenderers are in a position to take or gain an advantage with respect to winning the proposed contract.[89] After the procedure has ended, the principle of equal treatment is applied to determining the extent to which the contract concluded can be amended or extended without a new call for tenders.[90]

The principle of equal treatment is also applicable to areas that fall outside the scope of the Procurement Directive. Since the principle of equal treatment is directly rooted in the EC Treaty, it is not particularly surprising that the principle must be complied with in connection with all purchases covered by the EC Treaty. It is rather more surprising that the European Court of Justice, on the basis of the principle of equal treatment, has outlined certain specific obligations that the contracting authorities must comply with when awarding contracts that fall outside the scope of the Directive.[91]

---

87. Judgment of the European Court of Justice of 22 June 1993, case C-243/89, Commission vs. Denmark (Great Belt); judgment of the European Court of Justice of 27 November 2001, cases C-285/99 and C-286/99, Lombardini, paragraph 37.
88. Article 2 of the Procurement Directive.
89. See chapter 6.4 below about disqualification. See chapter 4.2.4 about access to technical specifications. See also order of the Complaints Board of 30 June 2003, Skanska Danmark A/S vs. Løgstør Local Authority (the Tender Act) in which a consultant prepared two reports and plans for the contracting authority which were not included in the contract documents. But when the consultant subsequently cooperated with one of the tenderers, this cooperation provided that tenderer with a competitive advantage that was deemed to be a violation of the Tender Act.
90. See chapter 3.4.3 below about additional supplies and contracts and chapter 7.6.2 below about changes.
91. See also section 5 below.

3.3 Obligation of transparency

As mentioned several times above, contracting authorities are bound by the prohibition of discrimination on grounds of nationality set out in the EC Treaty. They are obliged to treat candidates and tenderers equally and to ensure that they compete for public contracts on equal terms. However, these obligations are not very functional and it may be difficult to enforce them in the event of infringements, in particular in view of the contracting authorities' scope for discretion in the conduct of the award procedure and bearing in mind that the contracting authorities have all the information, minutes of meetings, etc. in their possession. As a consequence, procedural rules have been laid down in the Procurement Directive.

The obligation of contracting authorities to use special and detailed procedures creates *transparency* and thereby *foreseeability* of award procedures which are essential to ensuring equal treatment of economic operators in the competition for public contracts and to preventing abuse of award procedures to promote unlawful or non-objective interests.[92] Enhanced transparency and thus equal opportunities for being awarded public contracts are expected to arouse economic operators' interest in tendering for contracts in other countries and, as a consequence, promote competition for public contracts. At the same time, enhanced transparency of award procedures for public contracts also has a bearing on the possibilities for verifying whether non-objective or unlawful considerations have been taken into account, whether the principle of equal treatment has been disregarded, thus improving the possibilities for enforcing the procurement rules and ultimately compliance with the rules.

3.3.1 Procedural requirements under the Procurement Directive

The Procurement Directive requires contracting authorities to use special and carefully specified procedures for the award of public contracts. One key element in this regard is that procedures thereby become *transparent*. The obligation of transparency is intended to ensure that as well as providing potential tenderers with the information that a public contract will be awarded, it must also enable potential tenderers to discern the procedure that will be used for the award of the public contract.

One of the principal features in the efforts to ensure transparency is the obligation to *publish* a contract notice. The information to be included in the contract notice and its publication are subject to strict requirements seeing that it is fundamental to the creation of a single market for public contracts

---

92. See also section 1.2.4 above.

that interested economic operators in all EU Member States have access to information about proposed public contracts in good time before the award.[93]

Also the *conduct* of the award procedure must be transparent. The Procurement Directive lists a number of substantive obligations that must be complied with in the conduct of the award procedure although the procedure itself is not regulated in the same level of detail as the requirements for publication. The Procurement Directive prescribes rules on

– which requirements and criteria that can be applied to evaluating candidates/tenderers and their tenders (chapter 4 below);
– which procedures that can be used for the award of a public contract (chapter 5 below):
– which evidence that can be submitted as proof of compliance with requirements and criteria (chapter 6 below); and
– the main features of the procedures for evaluating tenders (chapter 7 below).

3.3.2 Principle of transparency

On the basis of the prohibition of discrimination and the principle of equal treatment of the EC Treaty the European Court of Justice has established the principle of transparency. The principle of transparency supplements the prohibition of discrimination and the principle of equal treatment in that it is intended to ensure that undertakings compete for public contracts on equal terms bearing in mind that the obligation of transparency enables verification that the principle of equal treatment has been complied with.[94]

The principle of transparency must be applied to the preparation as well as the conduct of the award procedure.[95]

Since the principle of transparency is by nature a principle, it lacks cogency, but basically this principle implies that the award procedure must be discernible. According to the European Court of Justice this presumes that

---

93. See also chapter 5.3.
94. Wallonian Buses; judgment of the European Court of Justice of 18 June 2002, case C-92/00, Hospital Ingenieure vs. Stadt Wien, paragraph 45; judgment of the European Court of Justice of 27 November 2001, cases C-285/99 and C-286/99, Impresa Lombardini SpA, paragraph 38; judgment of the European Court of Justice of 12 December 2002, case C-470/99, Universale Bau AG, paragraphs 91, 98 and 99.
95. There is also a requirement that the award procedure be objective, cf. chapter 4 below.

there is a sufficient degree of advertising *at every stage* of the award procedure[96] and that the procedure is foreseeable.

The obligation of transparency was, in substance, amplified in *SIAC*.[97] Pursuant to the Procurement Directive and by virtue of the obligation of equal treatment, a contracting authority is directly obliged to indicate the award criteria in the contract notice or in the specifications, and it follows from the obligation of transparency that the criteria must be stipulated

"... in such a way as to allow all reasonably well-informed and normally diligent tenderers to interpret them in the same way".[98]

Further *SIAC*[99] emphasised that the transparency obligation implies that

"... the adjudicating authority must interpret the award criteria in the same way throughout the entire procedure ...".[100]

Consequently, the award criteria must not be amended during the award procedure.[101] Finally, the obligation of transparency implies that it must be possible to verify that the tenders submitted comply with the requirements.[102]

Failure to prepare and conduct the award procedure in a transparent manner may have the effect that obligations imposed by the Procurement Directive are not complied with. However, it can be difficult for a candidate or a tenderer to prove, for example, that unlawful negotiations have been conducted, that the award criteria were not applied objectively or that non-objective considerations were taken into account. *Virklund Sport A/S vs. Randers Local Authority*[103] shows that the contracting authority has the burden of proof concerning how the award procedure was conducted and in that connection that the successful tender complied with the specifications. To

---

96. Judgment of the European Court of Justice of 12 December 2002, case C-470/99, Universale Bau AG, paragraphs 92 and 93.
97. Judgment of the European Court of Justice of 18 October 2001, case C-19/00, SIAC Construction Ltd.
98. Ibid, paragraph 42.
99. Ibid.
100. Ibid, paragraph 43.
101. Judgment of the European Court of Justice of 4 December 2003, case C-448/01, EVN, paragraph 93.
102. Judgment of the European Court of Justice of 4 December 2003, case C-448/01, EVN, paragraphs 49, 50 and 52.
103. Order of the Complaints Board of 8 October 2004, Virklund Sport A/S vs. Randers Local Authority.

that end the standard of documentation on how the selection and award criteria were applied and the subject of contacts and negotiations, if any, with the tenderers are quite high.[104]

3.3.3 Application of the principle of transparency
The principle of transparency is relevant in the context of interpreting and implying meaning into the individual provisions of the Directive. The principle of transparency only has a residual function in the context of the many aspects of the award procedure which are regulated in minute detail in the Directive. However, where there is doubt as to the interpretation of a provision or where it is necessary to imply meaning into the Directive, the principle of transparency must be applied.[105]

The principle of transparency is derived from the principle of equal treatment and therefore founded in the EC Treaty. Hence, the principle applies to all contracts which are subject to the EC Treaty regardless whether the value thereof is below the thresholds stipulated in the Procurement Directive or whether they are specifically excluded from the scope of the Directive. By means of its case law, the European Court of Justice has established the principle of transparency to the effect that a number of more explicit obligations are emerging, with which the contracting authorities must comply with in the award of public contracts, regardless that they fall outside the scope of the Directive, for more details see section 5 below.

3.4 Effectiveness and the principle of effectiveness
The European Court of Justice has established a principle of effectiveness. The Member States and the law enforcing authorities must apply the principle of effectiveness in two different, yet connected contexts:

- the Procurement Directive and the Remedies Directive and the relevant national rules must be interpreted and applied so as to ensure that the aim of the Directive is effectively achieved;
- measures must be in place to ensure the effective enforcement of the procurement rules guaranteeing that contracting authorities comply with their obligations under the Procurement Directive and the EC Treaty and to pro-

---

104. Order of the Complaints Board of 29 October 1997, Esbjerg Andels Renovationssel- skab A/S vs. Rødding Local Authority.
105. Judgment of the European Court of Justice of 18 June 2002, case C-92/00, HI vs. Stadt Wien, paragraph 42; order of the European Court of Justice of 16 October 2003, case C-244/02, Kauppatalo Hansel Oy vs. Imatran Kaupunki, paragraph 31.

tect the rights of individuals which also contributes to achieving the aim of the Directive.

The guiding principle for the allocation of powers between the EU and the Member States is that the EU lays down the substantive rules which the Member States must comply with – the Procurement Directive and the Remedies Directive. The Member States must implement the Procurement Directive and the Remedies Directive into national law to the effect that the aims of the Directive are achieved.

It is left with the Member States to enforce the EU rules through their administrative systems and the national court structures and to protect the rights of individuals conferred by the EU rules. The European Court of Justice has established a principle that national enforcement rules and procedures must not be less protective of rights deriving from EU law than of those deriving from similar requirements under national law. However, equal treatment does not suffice, the enforcement of rights deriving from EU law must also be *effective*.

By virtue of the principle of effectiveness there is a lower limit on national autonomy in the field of enforcement to the effect that enforcement must not be impossible or excessively difficult. National courts of law and the Complaints Board must apply the principle of effectiveness to assessing whether a national rule undermines or prevents the exercise of rights deriving from EU law or to ensure that these rights are effectively protected.[106] The possibilities for enforcing the Procurement Directive have been reinforced by the Remedies Directive[107] and that Directive, too, must be interpreted by application of the principle of effectiveness.

In particular in regard to the provisions of the Procurement Directive the European Court of Justice will apply the *interpretation* which is best capable of maintaining the full effectiveness of the Directive. As an example, the principle of effectiveness has been applied to define the term "contracting

---

106. Judgment of the European Court of Justice of 24 June 2004, case C-212/02, Commission vs. Austria, paragraphs 22-24.
107. Council Directive 89/665/EEC of 21 December 1989 on the coordination of the laws, regulations and administrative provisions relating to the application of review procedures to the award of public supply and public works contracts.

authority".[108] To ensure the effectiveness of the Procurement Directive specific provisions must be interpreted in the light of the aim of the Directive.[109]

Also the *enforcement* of the procurement rules must take account of the principle of effectiveness. The Remedies Directive must be interpreted so as to ensure the effectiveness of the Directive.[110] Also national enforcement rules must be applied in a manner which ensures their effectiveness. This obligation of effectiveness is intended to ensure that contracting authorities comply with the obligations under the Procurement Directive and the EC Treaty and to protect individuals' rights to damages, for example.

However, the principle of effectiveness lacks cogency and it should be applied so as to take the interests of the contracting authorities into account also. In *Universale Bau*[111] a question was referred to the European Court of Justice concerning the length of the time limit for lodging a complaint about a procurement procedure and the European Court of Justice held that a time limit of 14 days was in keeping with the effective enforcement of the rules.[112]

In the context of enforcement the principle of effectiveness has been applied *inter alia* to assess the possibilities for bringing complaints about the cancellation of a call for tenders,[113] the length of the time limit for instituting proceedings[114] and the introduction of a waiting period between the award decision and the conclusion of the contract.[115]

---

108. Judgment of the European Court of Justice of 16 October 2003, case C-283/00, Commission vs. Spain, paragraph 75; judgment of the European Court of Justice of 12 December 2002, case C-470/99, Universale-Bau AG, paragraphs 57 and 58.

109. Judgment of the European Court of Justice of 12 July 2001, case C-399/98, Ordine degli Architetti delle Province di Milano et Lodi, paragraph 52.

110. Judgment of the European Court of Justice of 18 June 2002, case C-92/00, HI vs. Stadt Wien, paragraph 52; order of the European Court of Justice of 9 April 2003, case C-424/01, CS Communications & Systems Austria GmbH, paragraph 31; judgment of the European Court of Justice of 27 February 2003, case C-327/00, Santex SpA, paragraph 51.

111. Judgment of the European Court of Justice of 12 December 2002, case C-470/99, Universale-Bau AG.

112. In Denmark there is no time limit for lodging complaints. See chapter 8.

113. Judgment of the European Court of Justice of 18 June 2002, case C-92/00, HI vs. Stadt Wien; judgment of the European Court of Justice of 2 June 2005, case C-15/04, Koppensteiner GmbH.

114. Judgment of the European Court of Justice of 27 February 2003, case C-327/00, Santex SpA.

115. Judgment of the European Court of Justice of 24 June 2004, case C-212/02, Commission vs. Austria.

Presumably the practice of the Danish courts of law and the Danish Complaints Board does not fully comply with the principle of effectiveness. It is particularly striking that the legal remedy "interim measures" has not been used since 2000. In the decision whether or not to order a contracting authority to suspend the award procedure, the interest of the contracting authority in completing the purchase carries great weight, but this interest must be balanced against the requirement under EU law of effective enforcement of the rules. Undoubtedly, cessation in the use of this legal remedy would be in contravention of the Remedies Directive and constitute an infringement of the Treaty. However, the Complaints Board is likely to change its practice in the light of *Commission vs. Austria*[116] which establishes that in order to allow the enforcement rules to have practical effect, a reasonable period must elapse between the award decision and the conclusion of the contract as this will increase the opportunities for using interim measures.

The current practice is problematic also in regard to liability in damages. Pursuant to the case law of the Complaints Board a complainant can only be awarded damages if there is a causal link between the contracting authority's infringement of the procurement rules and the financial loss suffered by the complainant. In *M.J. Eriksson A/S vs. Fuglebjerg Local Authority*[117] the contracting authority had made a manifest mistake which decisively distorted competition among the tenderers. Nevertheless, the complainant was not awarded damages on the ground that the complainant's tender should have been rejected as voidable for which reason there was no causal link between the complainant's loss and the infringement committed. By this decision a serious infringement of the procurement rules has no economic repercussions for the contracting authority because of a coincidental circumstance relating to the complainant.

The required high standard of documentation of financial loss and causal link between the loss and the infringement of the procurement rules required of the complainant can be seen as a barrier to the enforcement of the procurement rules in that the economic operators' willingness to file complaints is likely to depend largely on the chances of being awarded damages.[118]

---

116. Judgment of the European Court of Justice of 24 June 2004, case C-212/02, Commission vs. Austria.
117. Order of the Complaints Board of 24 March 2004, M.J. Eriksson A/S vs. Fuglebjerg Local Authority.
118. See also chapter 8.4.

3.5 Proportionality

The principle of proportionality is applicable in EC law in general, according to which all measures must be appropriate, necessary and proportional for achieving the aim they are intended to achieve. The principle of proportionality is relevant to the contracting authority's drafting of the contract documents, determination of requirements for the suitability of tendering undertakings and specifications of requirements for the object of the contract. Only in manifest cases is the application of the principle of proportionality likely to lead to the conclusion that the contracting authority has exceeded its authority, bearing in mind that it is the contracting authority which decides whether a purchase is needed, determines the object of the purchase and the relevant specifications, and allocates the resources required out of the resources available to the contracting authority

4. Application and interpretation of the rules

The starting point for the interpretation of and implication of meaning into the procurement rules is the wording of the individual provisions. This is the premise on which the legislator adopted the set of rules and, therefore, the substance and purpose of the individual rule must be determined primarily on the basis of its wording.[119]

Where the wording can be given different interpretations, other sources of law must be consulted to determine the substance and purpose of the rule. In theory, all the sources of law mentioned in section 2 can be of relevance to the interpretation and implication of meaning into the Procurement Directive, but if the European Court of Justice has delivered a judgment on the interpretation of a specific rule, then that is the interpretation to be given to that particular rule.

If the European Court of Justice has not ruled on the interpretation in issue, then other sources of law must be consulted. Of greatest relevance are the preamble to the Procurement Directive, the definitions set out in Article 1 of the Directive and the material concerning the legislative history due to their obvious connection to the individual provisions of the Directive, and as the purpose of a provision is often explicitly stated in the preamble to the Directive. The EC Treaty, legislative acts and decisions deriving therefrom

---

119. Judgment of the European Court of Justice of 16 October 2003, case C-421/01, Traunfellner, paragraph 27.

constitute the framework for the Procurement Directives and may as such have a bearing upon the purpose of the provisions and, hence, the interpretation of the individual provisions of the Directive. Also the fundamental principles of equal treatment and transparency are obviously relevant, re. section 3 above. Decisions of national courts of law and the Complaints Board for Public Procurement can be taken into account and may be important contributions to the interpretation. Also the WTO rules and administrative orders and recommendations may be of a certain value as sources of law.

4.1 Purposive interpretation of the rules

Sources of law which can be of aid in determining the purpose of a rule are of particular interest since the interpretation of a rule essentially is determined by what the legislator intended with that particular rule.[120] In particular the recitals of the preamble to the Procurement Directive are interesting to the interpretation of the individual provisions of the Directive.

The aim of the Procurement Directive is to create competition for public contracts by affording, in particular, foreign undertakings the opportunities to tender for public contracts, ensuring economic operators equal opportunities for being awarded public contracts, creating transparent award procedures and by making the contracting authorities follow a commercial line of thought when awarding public contracts, cf. section 1.2 above.

Also the context of the rules must be considered as it does not suffice to take account of the objective of creating a single market and ensuring effective competition, etc. Inevitably, the reasons for the procurement procedure must be taken into account; that a public contract is awarded to satisfy a public need. The contracting authority's award decision is largely based on the characteristics, quality and price of the object of the public contract, and thus on obtaining value for money, the best tenders and the best contracting party.[121]

For the purpose of interpreting the individual provisions of the Procurement Directive considerations concerning the aim of the Directive do not necessarily create a uniform picture. It may be necessary to examine the purpose of the individual provisions of the Directive whose wording reflects the legislator's balancing of the objective of ensuring competition against the contracting authority's interest in obtaining best quality at the lowest price.

---

120. Judgment of the European Court of Justice of 27 November 2001, cases C-285/99 and C-286/99, Impresa Lombardini SpA, paragraph 84.
121. See chapter 7 on award criteria.

The interpretation of a specific provision is affected by whether the provision plays a key role in ensuring foreign undertakings the opportunities for being awarded public contracts. Such role is played by the term "contracting authority", which the European Court of Justice has stated must be given a broad interpretation in functional terms.[122] Other provisions of the Directive, on the other hand, are aimed at protecting the interests of the contracting authorities. For example the possibility for allowing the submission of variants is intended as a means to obtain the best quality at the lowest price. The conditions subject to which the negotiated procedure, set out in Articles 30 and 31 of the Directive, can be used are less strict if an open procedure or a restricted procedure has already been conducted without result seeing that the EU's objective of opening up competition for public contracts was achieved by virtue of that open or restricted procedure. Although the contracting authorities' interests carry considerable weight in the interpretation of certain provisions of the Procurement Directive, it should be kept in mind that the fundamental principles of non-discrimination, equal treatment and transparency must always be complied with.[123]

4.2 Balancing of interests

The Procurement Directive or EC law in general does not stipulate any absolute obligations, which contracting authority must always comply with.. The EC law objectives of preventing discrimination on grounds of nationality, opening up competition for public contracts for economic operators, and ensuring equal treatment in and transparency of award procedures for public contracts carry great weight. Nevertheless, each time the Procurement Directive is applicable regard must be had to the object of the contract and to the underlying public need and objective which the contract is intended to satisfy:

– These may be unforeseen and urgent circumstances justifying that some or all of the procedural requirements under the Directive are not complied with;
– it may be necessary to keep a contract secret because of security interests; or

---

122. Judgment of the European Court of Justice of 16 October 2003, case C-283/00, Commission vs. Spain, paragraph 73; judgment of the European Court of Justice of 15 May 2003, case C-214/00, Commission vs. Spain, paragraph 53.
123. Judgment of the European Court of Justice of 16 October 2003, case C-421/01, Traunfellner, paragraph 29.

– it may be necessary to refer to national standards or specific trademarks in the contract specifications.

The possibility of using alternative means more suited to meet the aim of the Directive, and thereby being less restrictive on trade, is a factor in the balancing of the obligations under the Procurement Directive against the objectives in the public interest.

The EU's objective of putting public contracts out to competition probably carries greater weight than the contracting authority's interest in obtaining value for money. On the other hand, once the EU's objectives in opening up the market and ensuring equal treatment of economic operators have been achieved in a specific procurement procedure, the contracting authority enjoys considerable freedom to use the purchase to pursue its own interests.[124]

4.3 Principles of interpretation

The provisions of the Procurement Directive are interpreted conclusively by the European Court of Justice. The European Court of Justice gives the individual provisions of the Directive an *autonomous interpretation* unless the Directive makes express reference to the law of the Member States. A judgment of the European Court of Justice is binding on the Member States, contracting authorities and the national courts of law throughout the EU and, consequently, the interpretation given to a provision of the Directive is uniform throughout the Community.[125]

As mentioned above, the aim of a directive may be essential to the interpretation of a provision therein. The aim of Directive 89/665/EEC,[126] for example, is to ensure that Member States establish effective and rapid procedures to review infringements of the Procurement Directive. This aim may

---

124. See also chapter 4 concerning specification of the object of the contract.
125. Judgment of the European Court of Justice of 27 February 2003, case C-373/00, Adolf Truley GmbH, paragraph 36. See also judgment of the European Court of Justice of 27 November 2001, cases C-285/99 and C-286/99, Impresa Lombardini SpA, paragraph 54; and judgment of the European Court of Justice of 16 October 2003, case C-283/00, Commission vs. Spain, paragraph 79.
126. Council Directive 89/665/EEC of 21 December 1989 on the coordination of the laws, regulations and administrative provisions relating to the application of review procedures to the award of public supply and public works contracts.

warrant that the provisions of that Directive be given an *extensive interpreta-tion* where a literal interpretation would compromise the intended aim.[127]

The Procurement Directive provides for a number of derogations from the obligation to call for tenders in accordance with the provisions of the Directive. Accordingly, Articles 30 and 31 of the Directive provide that in exceptional cases the negotiated procedure can be used. Such a derogation must be *inter-preted strictly* and the burden of proof regarding the existence of the conditions justifying the use of the procedure lies on the contracting authority.[128]

The negotiated procedure can be either with or without publication of a prior contract notice. The publication of a contract notice serves to inform all economic operators throughout the EU that a public contract will be awarded on the basis of negotiations and any economic operator can apply for partici-pation in the negotiations. In the negotiated procedure *without* publication of a contract notice, on the other hand, the contracting authority contacts one or more economic operators directly and negotiates a contract with this or these economic operator(s). The EU's objective of opening up competition for public contracts is only achieved where the first procedure is used and the conditions subject to which this procedure can be used need not be inter-preted as strictly as the conditions for using the latter procedure where no-one besides the economic operators that have been contacted by the contracting authority knows of the possibility for being awarded a public contract.

In recent years there seems to have been an increased focus on ensuring the interests of contracting authorities in procurement procedures. This is substantiated, for example, by the introduction of the competitive dialogue procedure in the Procurement Directive enhancing the opportunities of the contracting authority for obtaining the contract that meets its requirements.

Also in case law, reference is increasingly made to national provisions in the absence of specific provisions in the Procurement Directive concerning the matter in issue.[129] National provisions may be in the form of law or they may be the guidelines determined by the contracting authority for a proce-

---

127. Judgment of the European Court of Justice of 28 October 1999, case C-81/98, Alcatel Austria AG and Others, paragraph 38; and judgment of the European Court of Justice of 19 June 2003, case C-249/01, Werner Hackermüller, paragraph 23.

128. Judgment of the European Court of Justice of 10 April 2003, cases C-20/01 and C-28/01, Commission vs. Germany, paragraph 58.

129. Judgment of the European Court of Justice of 18 June 2002, case C-92/00, HI, para-graph 67; judgment of the European Court of Justice of 19 June 2003, case C-315/01, GAT, paragraph 46; Judgment of the European Court of Justice of 23 January 2003, case C-57/01, Makedoniko Metro, paragraph 61.

dure. Even so, the matter is still subject to some Community regulation in that the fundamental principles must be complied with in all procurement procedures.[130]

5. Contracts that fall outside the scope of the procurement rules[131]

The Procurement Directive lays down certain threshold values.[132] Public contracts of a value below the thresholds stipulated in the Procurement Directive need not be put out to tender in accordance with the procedures set out in the Procurement Directive. Also other public contracts are entirely or partially excluded from the obligations under the Procurement Directive. By virtue of Article 21 of the Directive, public contracts for the categories of services listed in Annex II B to the Directive are only subject to very few obligations. The award of public contracts of a value below the thresholds stipulated in the Directive, and public contracts for the services listed in Annex II B, are not subject to the obligations *deriving from the Procurement Directive* to publish, in advance, the intention to award a contract.

However, any award of public contracts by a contracting authority is subject to the EC Treaty and secondary legislative acts and principles.[133] Of particular relevance in procurement procedures is the prohibition contained in Article 12 of discrimination on grounds of nationality. The rules of the EC Treaty on trade barriers and the obligation linked thereto to recognise the qualifications and approvals of foreign undertakings are also relevant.

The European Court of Justice has inferred from the Treaty that contracting authorities, as a rule, are obliged to apply the principles of equal treatment and transparency to the award of contracts that fall outside the scope of the Procurement Directives. By virtue of these principles, contracting authorities must observe certain obligations when stipulating the terms and conditions of

---

130. Order of the European Court of Justice of 16 October 2003, case C-244/02, Kauppatalo Hansel Oy, paragraphs 31, 33 and 36.
131. Peter Braun, A matter of Principle(s) – The Treatment of Contracts Falling Outside the Scope of the European Public Procurement Directives, 9 Public Procurement Law Review p. 39ff. (2000).
132. See also chapter 3.
133. Contracting authorities may also be bound by national rules, such as Act No 338 of May 2005 on Tender Procedures for Public Work Contracts, on the invitation to tender for building and civil engineering works or Circular No 159 of 17 December 2002 from the Ministry of Finance on the invitation to tender for Government works.

contracts, and they are obliged to pre-determine the procedures for the award of contracts, and not to derogate from these procedures arbitrarily.

5.1 Prohibition of discrimination on grounds of nationality
Contracts awarded by contracting authorities for goods or services are subject to Article 12 of the EC Treaty imposing a general obligation on contracting authorities not to discriminate on grounds of nationality. This obligation of non-discrimination is reflected in the Procurement Directive in that the fundamental obligation not to discriminate against tenderers is emphasised.[134] Generally, the prohibition of discrimination on grounds of nationality is interpreted as an obligation to treat interested undertakings equally, cf. sections 1.2.2 and 3.2.2 above.

The European Court of Justice has implied several obligations into the prohibition of discrimination on grounds of nationality, which obligations contracting authorities must comply with in every award procedure. In *Unitron Scandinavia A/S*[135] the European Court of Justice stated:

"… the principle of non-discrimination on grounds of nationality cannot be interpreted restrictively. It implies, in particular, an obligation of transparency in order to enable the contracting authority to satisfy itself that it has been complied with."[136]

In *Telaustria*[137] the European Court of Justice further stated in regard to the prohibition of discrimination:

"As the Court held in … that principle implies, in particular, an obligation of transparency in order to enable the contracting authority to satisfy itself that the principle has been complied with.[138]

That obligation of transparency which is imposed on the contracting authority consists in ensuring, for the benefit of any potential tenderer, a degree of *advertising* sufficient to

---

134. Article 2 of the Procurement Directive, cf. recital 2 of the preamble to the Procurement Directive.
135. Judgment of the European Court of Justice of 18 November 1999, case C-275/98, Unitron Scandinavia A/S.
136. Ibid, extract of paragraph 31.
137. Judgment of the European Court of Justice of 7 December 2000, case C-324/98, Telaustria.
138. Ibid, extract of paragraph 61. (our emphasis)

enable the services market to be opened up to competition and the impartiality of procurement procedures to be reviewed."[139]

It is presumably because of the fundamental objective of opening up competition for public contracts that contracting authorities' award of contracts that fall outside the scope of the Procurement Directive is subject to certain obligations, irrespective of threshold values. In order to achieve that objective, contracting authorities must comply with the obligation to advertise and obligations of equal treatment and transparency.

Concurrently with the procedural obligations mentioned above, contracting authorities are also bound by the rules on trade barriers set out in the EC Treaty, cf. section 2.3 above. There are no threshold values below which contracting authorities are not subject to the rules on trade barriers set out in the EC Treaty. In *Bent Mousten Vestergaard*[140] the contracting authority had specified that windows and doors for a building should be of a specific make without indicating that other products, too, could be used if they satisfied the requirements laid down. To this the European Court of Justice stated

"It is therefore clear from the case-law that, notwithstanding the fact that a public works contract does not exceed the threshold laid down in Directive 93/37 and does not thus fall within its scope, Article 30 [now Article 28] of the Treaty precludes a contracting authority from including in the contract documents for that contract a clause requiring the use in carrying out the contract of a product of a specified make, without adding the words or equivalent."[141]

The conclusion to be drawn from this case law, is that in award procedures for public contracts all contracting authorities are subject to the following obligations that follow directly from the EC Treaty:

– not to discriminate on grounds of nationality;
– to ensure that the procedure is sufficiently advertised;

139. Ibid, paragraph 62. The word advertising is used in the English language version whereas the French language version uses the word publicité.
140. Order of the European Court of Justice of 3 December 2001, case C-59/00, Bent Mousten Vestergaard vs. Spøttrup Boligselskab.
141. Ibid, paragraph 24. The judgment of the European Court of Justice is cited in judgment of the Western High Court of 8 March 2002, Bent Mousten Vestergaard vs. Spøttrup Boligselskab, Danish weekly law reports 2002.1297 V. In order of the Complaints Board of 27 May 2003, M.J. Eriksson A/S vs. Fuglebjerg Local Authority a requirement that a specific make be used was held to be "objectively reasoned". It is submitted that the order is wrong on this point.

- to treat candidates and tenderers equally;
- to ensure that the procedure is transparent; and
- to comply with the prohibition on trade barriers set out in the EC Treaty.[142]

These obligations apply in particular to the award of public contracts of a value *below* the thresholds stipulated in the Procurement Directive, public contracts for the services listed in Annex II B of the Procurement Directive,[143] concessions[144] and public contracts awarded on the basis of the negotiated procedure *without* publication of a contract notice.[145]

5.2 Extent of the obligations

The extent of the obligations to which contracting authorities are subject for the award of public contracts falling outside the scope of the Procurement Directive is not altogether clear.[146] Particular account should be had of the contracting authorities' interests, bearing in mind that the transaction costs of awarding, notably, small contracts on the basis of a procurement procedure may be excessively large.

From case law it can be deduced that a contracting authority is obliged to *advertise* that a public contract will be awarded. The objective of opening up public contracts for competition inevitably implies that potential candidates and tenderers must be informed of the proposed contract in a way that affords them a genuine chance of expressing their interest in the contract. The obligation under the Procurement Directive to publish a contract notice in the Official Journal does not extend to the situations analysed in this section, but publication in the Official Journal will satisfy the obligation to advertise. Also other forms of advertising are capable of satisfying the obligations, and advertising in the contracting authority's Member State only, may suffice.

Direct contact to more economic operators may be the appropriate means especially where the contract because of its modest value falls outside the

---

142. See also Commission Green Paper of 30 April 2004 on Public-Private Partnerships and Community Law on Public Contracts and Concessions, point 30.
143. Order of the Complaints Board of 14 October 2004, Tolkeservice ApS vs. County of Copenhagen.
144. Order of the Complaints Board of 9 November 1999, More Group Danmark A/S vs. Århus Local Authority.
145. Article 31 of the Procurement Directive; judgment of the European Court of Justice of 10 April 2003, cases C-20/01 and C-28/01, Commission vs. Germany, paragraph 62.
146. The extent of these obligations will probably be determined by the European Court of Justice in the coming years.

scope of the Procurement Directive, and presumably, this procedure satisfies the obligation to advertise the contract.[147] Larger public contracts for the services listed in Annex II B of the Procurement Directive, for example, must probably be properly advertised since these contracts are likely to attract interest from a wider group of potential candidates.

As to the *conduct* of the award procedure, the contracting authority can probably award the contract on the basis of negotiations with selected candidates. Presumably, the contracting authority must ensure – depending on the specific circumstances – that more than one qualified candidate has a genuine chance of being awarded the contract.

147. See also Advocate General Fennelly' Opinion of 18 May 2000, case C-324/98, Telaustria, point 43.

CHAPTER 2

Contracting Authorities

1. The fundamental problem

The State protects a number of interests, public as well as commercial, in carrying out its responsibilities. In connection with these activities, the measures and manner by which the State protects its economic interests may be incompatible with the fundamental principles of the EC Treaty. With the introduction of the Procurement Directive and its precursors, the Community legislature has established that, in the field of public procurement, certain purchases are regarded as public measures with respect to which economic interests incompatible with the Procurement Directive and the EC Treaty cannot be taken into consideration.

1.1 The State's protection of national interests

In several cases the European Court of Justice has given its opinion on the purpose of regulating the purchasing procedures of contracting authorities. In *BFI Holding*[1] and *Mannesmann Anlagenbau Austria and Others*[2] the European Court of Justice explicitly expressed its view on the purpose of the procurement directives as follows:

"… the purpose of coordinating at Community level the procedures for the award of public service contracts is to eliminate barriers to the freedom to provide services and therefore to protect the interests of economic operators established in a Member State who wish to offer goods or services to contracting authorities in another Member State."[3]

---

1. Judgment of the European Court of Justice of 10 November 1998, case C-360/96, Gemeente Arnhem and Rheden vs. BFI Holding.
2. Judgment of the European Court of Justice of 15 January 1998, case C-44/96, Mannesmann Anlagenbau Austria and Others.
3. Judgment of the European Court of Justice of 10 November 1998, case C-360/96, Gemeente Arnhem and Rheden vs. BFI Holding, paragraphs 41-43.

"… the aim of Directive 93/37 [which is] to avoid the risk of preference being given to national tenderers or applicants whenever a contract is awarded by the contracting authorities"[4].

These views are closely linked to the provisions of the EC Treaty on the free movement of goods, freedom to provide services and freedom of establishment and the principles directly deriving from these provisions, such as the principles of equal treatment, non-discrimination, mutual recognition, transparency and proportionality.[5]

The Procurement Directive now stipulates an explicit obligation for the contracting authorities to comply with these principles when making purchases. This is evident from the wording of Article 2:

"Contracting authorities shall treat economic operators equally and non-discriminatorily and shall act in a transparent way."

Both the formal regulation and case law have thus clarified that contracting authorities cannot be guided by separate considerations or interests when launching procurement procedures, but instead have to adhere to the above principles, and in doing so they contribute to the achievement of the aims of the EC Treaty and the Procurement Directive.

1.2 Interpretation in functional terms

The European Court of Justice established already in early case law that when defining the group of bodies that become obligated by the Procurement Directive, the Directive should be interpreted in functional terms. This interpretative principle was formulated by the ECJ in *inter alia Beentjes*[6] as follows:

---

4. Judgment of the European Court of Justice of 15 January 1998, case C-44/96, Mannesmann Anlagenbau Austria and Others, paragraph 33.
5. Recital 2 of the preamble reads: "The award of contracts concluded in the Member States on behalf of the State, regional or local authorities and other bodies governed by public law entities, is subject to the respect of the principles of the Treaty and in particular to the principle of freedom of movement of goods, the principle of freedom of establishment and the principle of freedom to provide services and to the principles deriving therefrom, such as the principle of equal treatment, the principle of non-discrimination, the principle of mutual recognition, the principle of proportionality and the principle of transparency."
6. Judgment of the European Court of Justice of 20 September 1988, case 31/87, Gebroeders Beentjes BV vs. the Netherlands, paragraph 11.

"For the purposes of this provision, the term "the State" must be interpreted in functional terms. The aim of the directive, which is to ensure the effective attainment of freedom of establishment and freedom to provide services in respect of public works contracts, would be jeopardized if the provisions of the directive were to be held to be inapplicable solely because a public works contract is awarded by a body which, although it was set up to carry out tasks entrusted to it by legislation, is not formally a part of the State administration."

In *Ordine*[7] the European Court of Justice applied a similar interpretation to the Procurement Directive:

"Furthermore, the Directive gives definitions of contracting authority' ..., 'works' ... and 'a work' ... The definition given by the Community legislature confirms that those elements are closely related to the aim of the Directive."

1.3 Time for determining status

The appropriate time for determining whether an entity is subject to the Procurement Directive or not, is the date of the commencement of the procurement procedure. As a procedural safeguard the Procurement Directive introduces a system according to which the status of the undertaking is determined at a specific time.

If the conditions for being classified as a contracting authority are met at that point in time, the entity must follow the procedural rules set out in the Procurement Directive as far as the specific purchase is concerned and will in every respect remain subject to the Procurement Directive until the relevant procedure has been completed, even though the procedure, in terms of time, stretches into subsequent financial years in which its status as contracting authority may have changed.[8][9]

However, if the conditions are not met at the specific point in time, but it is foreseeable that they might be met in the future, possibly during the term of the proposed contract, the Procurement Directive does not apply to that specific procurement. This is the basic principle, but it may have to be derogated

---

7. Judgment of the European Court of Justice of 12 July 2001, case C-399/98, Ordine degli Architetti delle Province di Milano et Lodi and Others vs. Comune di Milano, paragraphs 53-54.
8. Judgment of the European Court of Justice of 3 October 2000, case C-380/98, The Queen and H.M. Treasury, ex parte University of Cambridge, paragraph 43.
9. Judgment of the European Court of Justice of 15 May 2003, case C-214/00, Commission vs. Spain, paragraph 54.

from as the anticipated change in status draws nearer and the change seems certain.[10] In *Commission vs. Austria*[11] the Court of Justice stated as follows:

"Even though it is true that for reasons of legal certainty it is, in general, appropriate to consider the contracting authority's possible obligation to arrange a public call for tenders in the light of the circumstances prevailing on the date on which the public contract at issue is awarded, the particular circumstances of this case require the events which took place subsequently to be taken into account."

2. Contracting authorities

This term denotes the bodies which are subject to the Procurement Directive and is defined in Article 1, paragraph 9 of the Procurement Directive. Recital 2 of the preamble to the Procurement Directive reads:

"The award of contracts concluded in the Member States on behalf of the State, regional or local authorities and other bodies governed by public law entities, is subject to the respect of the principles of the Treaty and in particular to the principle of freedom of movement of goods, the principle of freedom of establishment and the principle of freedom to provide services and to the principles deriving therefrom ..."

It appears that there is a certain analogy between the term "contracting authorities" in the Procurement Directive and the term "Member State" in relation to the provisions on free movement and freedom of establishment of the EC Treaty.

2.1 The State, regional or local authorities

Article 1, paragraph 9 provides that "the State, regional or local authorities" are covered by the definition of a contracting authority.

The term *"the State"* not only includes all bodies from the category "the Executive",[12] but in accordance Annex IV to the Procurement Directive on "Central Government Authorities" it also includes bodies from the category

---

10. See the discussion on the significance of future changes in legal status in Advocate General Juliane Kokott's Opinion of 1 March 2005, case C-458/03, Parking Brixen GmbH, points 55-62.
11. Judgment of the European Court of Justice of 10 November 2005, case C-29/04, Commission vs. Austria, paragraph 38.
12. "The Executive" is a term used in paragraph 3 in the Danish constitution to categorise the bodies which enforce the law.

"the Legislature".[13] Annex IV to the Procurement Directive lists national parliaments, all ministries and departments of state with relevant subordinate administrative agencies, which are part of superior/subordinate structures. The State also comprises other government agencies which are not part of superior/subordinate structures, for example because they are required to be politically independent, but are vested with autonomous authority. Finally, all bodies exercising powers that fall within the sphere of "the judiciary",[14] are encompassed by the term *State* as it is used in Procurement Directive.[15] The Annex is probably not exhaustive and is moreover dynamic in that the number of ministries and subordinate authorities continuously changes.

Already in 1988 the European Court of Justice established a generic definition in functional terms of government authorities in *Gebroeders Beentjes*:[16]

"Consequently, a body such as that in question here, whose composition and functions are laid down by legislation and which depends on the authorities for the appointment of its members, the observance of the obligations arising out of its measures and the financing of the public works contracts which it is its task to award, must be regarded as falling within the notion of the State for the purpose of the abovementioned provision, even though it is not part of the State administration in formal terms."

It can be deduced from the judgment that a number of characteristics must be present in order for a body to be categorised as a (government) authority within the meaning of the Procurement Directive, even though the body is not formally integrated into the State administration (in the particular case it was a local land consolidation committee).

In *Commission vs. Belgium*[17] the European Court of Justice held as follows on the issue of whether "Vlaamse Raad" (the Flemish Parliament in the Belgian federal system) was a government authority:

"The same [the term state] is true of the bodies which, in a federal state, exercise those powers at federal level."

13. Term also used in paragraph 3 in the Danish constitution categorising the bodies which legislate.
14. Term used in paragraph 3 in the Danish constitution categorising the bodies which have judicial power.
15. Judgment of the European Court of Justice of 17 September 1998, case C-323/96, Commission vs. Belgium, paragraph 27.
16. Judgment of the European Court of Justice of 20 September 1988, case 31/87, Gebroeders Beentjes BV vs. the Netherlands, paragraph 12.
17. Judgment of the European Court of Justice of 17 September 1998, case C-323/96, Commission vs. Belgium, paragraphs 27-29.

The case is an example of authorities, designated regional authorities in the Procurement Directive, which are vested with legislative powers at the regional level. Regional and local authorities are authorities which have the same responsibilities, but operate at different levels i.e. regional or local level, and encompass regions, municipalities, etc.

It can thus be concluded that the term authority must be given a broad and functional interpretation, thereby encompassing all bodies which are not separate legal persons and which exercise legislative, executive or judicial powers, and the absence of any formal connection to central government is as such irrelevant.

2.2 Bodies governed by public law

In addition to the State and regional and local authorities, also "bodies governed by public law" fall within the term "contracting authorities" within the meaning of Article 1, paragraph 9 of the Procurement Directive. Whether a body is subject to the Procurement Directive comes down to an assessment of whether that particular body satisfies the three *cumulative* conditions set out in Article 1, paragraph 9 of the Procurement Directive.[18] If it does, it will be classified as a *body governed by public law,* notwithstanding that it was established as a private company, and thereby has the same obligations in private law as other private undertakings, which are subject to applicable regulations.[19] It follows that the private law status of an entity cannot affect the classification of that entity as a "body governed by public law" for the purposes of the Procurement Directive since, if this was not the case, the Procurement Directive would be deprived of its intended effectiveness[20] and could not be given a uniform interpretation throughout the EU.[21] Considering the principles of free movement and the natural incentive of securing full compliance with these principles, the term contracting authority, and with that, bodies governed by public law, must be interpreted in functional terms.[22]

---

18. Judgment of the European Court of Justice of 15 January 1998, case C-44/96, Mannesmann Anlagenbau Austria and Others, Paragraph 21.
19. Judgment of the European Court of Justice of 17 December 1998, case C-353/96, Commission vs. Ireland.
20. Judgment of the European Court of Justice of 15 May 2003, case C-214/00, Commission vs. Spain, paragraphs 54-61 and judgment of the European Court of Justice of 13 January 2005, case C-84/03, Commission vs. Spain, paragraphs 27-32.
21. Judgment of the European Court of Justice of 13 January 2005, case C-84/03, Commission vs. Spain, paragraph 27.
22. Judgment of the European Court of Justice of 17 December 1998, case C-353/96, Commission vs. Ireland, paragraph 36.

The predominant aim is the proper functioning of the internal market by opening up competition for certain public contracts and making the procedures transparent.[23] By reference to this aim of the Procurement Directive, the European Court of Justice has stated that the term "body governed by public law" should be interpreted as having a broad meaning.[24]

Most important in the interpretation of whether a body can be classified as a body governed by public law is an analysis of whether, having taken into account all relevant facts and legal issues, it is foreseeable that the body will be guided by other considerations than purely economic ones in a procurement procedure.[25]

In the Procurement Directive[26] bodies governed by public law are defined as follows:

"A 'body governed by public law' means any body:
(a) established for the specific purpose of meeting needs in the general interest, not having an industrial or commercial character;
(b) having a legal personality; and
(c) financed, for the most part, by the State, regional or local authorities, or other bodies governed by public law; or subject to management supervision by those bodies; or having an administrative, managerial or supervisory board, more than half of whose members are appointed by the State, regional or local authorities, or by other bodies governed by public law."

The most distinct difference between, on the one hand, the State and regional and local authorities and, on the other hand, bodies governed by public law, is that the latter must have legal personality and therefore be entities which are legally distinct from the authorities. A body which has legal personality falls outside the definition of the State and regional and local authorities for that mere reason, and is only subject to the Procurement Directive if it satisfies the second and third conditions too.[27]

---

23. See e.g. judgment of the European Court of Justice of 1 February 1999, case C-237/99, Commission vs. France, paragraphs 41-43 and judgment of the European Court of Justice of 15 May 2003, case C-214/00, Commission vs. Spain, paragraph 53.
24. Judgment of the European Court of Justice of 27 February 2003, case C-373/00, Adolf Truley GmbH vs. Bestattung Wien GmbH, paragraph 43.
25. Judgment of the European Court of Justice of 16 October 2003, case C-283/00, Commission vs. Spain, paragraph 92.
26. Article 1, paragraph 9, second indent.
27. Judgment of the European Court of Justice of 17 December 1998, case C-353/96, Commission vs. Ireland, paragraphs 32-33.

The first condition concerning the activities of the body, and the third condition concerning the type of control which can be exercised over the body, serve to define those legal persons which, presumably, are not guided by ordinary market economy considerations and therefore are obliged to observe the provisions of the Procurement Directive when making certain purchases.

A non-exhaustive list[28] of the bodies and categories of bodies governed by public law which satisfy the three conditions of Article 1, paragraph 9 (a), (b) and (c) is set out in Annex III to the Procurement Directive.

2.2.1 First condition – purpose and activities of the body
Numerous undertakings fall outside the definition solely due to the first condition. Only those bodies which are established especially for the purpose of meeting non-industrial and non-commercial needs in the general interest satisfy this indispensable, but insufficient condition. In several cases the European Court of Justice[29] has held that the concept of meeting "needs in the general interest, not having an industrial or commercial character" is a concept of Community law, meaning that it must be given an autonomous and uniform interpretation throughout the EU. The reasons given by the European Court of Justice are that since the Procurement Directive "makes no express reference to the law of the Member States ... [the concept of needs in the general interest] must be given an autonomous and uniform interpretation throughout the Community".[30]

It is immaterial to the assessment of a specific body's status as a body governed by public law, whether the body was *established* for the purpose of meeting needs in the general interest, not having an industrial or commercial

---

28. On several occasions the European Court of Justice has stated that the list is far from exhaustive as the accuracy thereof varies considerably from one Member State to another. The ECJ has thus concluded that if a specific body does not appear in the list, its legal and factual situation must be investigated in each individual case in order to assess whether or not it meets the conditions for being classified as a body governed by public law, cf. *inter alia* judgment of the European Court of Justice of 27 February 2003, case C-373/00, Adolf Truley, paragraph 39, and judgment of the European Court of Justice of 16 October 2003, case C-283/00, Commission vs. Spain, paragraph 77.
29. See e.g. judgment of the European Court of Justice of 27 February 2003, case C-373/00, Adolf Truley GmbH vs. Bestattung Wien GmbH, paragraphs 36-45 and judgment of the European Court of Justice of 16 October 2003, case C-283/00, Commission vs. Spain, paragraph 79.
30. Ibid, paragraph 36.

character, or ensuing, not coinciding with the time of establishment, was entrusted with the obligation to meet needs in the general interests, not having an industrial or commercial character.[31] This is due to concerns relating to the effectiveness of the Procurement Directive since the aim of the Procurement Directive could be easily ignored if activities in the general interest, not having an industrial or commercial character, could be entrusted to an entity not recently established for that purpose, but instead is an existing entity which previously had another purpose. The appropriate time for making the assessment is thus the time of the specific purchase, and if the body at that time carries out activities which meet needs in the general interest, not having an industrial or commercial character, the condition is satisfied.[32]

If a specific body on a lasting basis satisfies needs in the general interest which it is specifically obliged to meet, it is immaterial whether the body in addition to these activities is free to carry out – or does in fact carry out – other types of (industrial or commercial) activities. In *Mannesmann Anlagenbau Austria AG and Others*[33] the European Court of Justice held:

"The condition, laid down in [...] Article 1(b) of the directive, that the body must have been established for the 'specific' purpose of meeting needs in the general interest, not having an industrial or commercial character, does not mean that it should be entrusted only with meeting such needs."

It is also irrelevant in determining whether the body satisfies the condition that the activity meeting needs in the general interest overall only constitutes a relatively small proportion of the activities carried out by the body.[34]

Bodies which only carry out commercial activities, have legal personality under the law pursuant to which they are established, and which are subject to public control (and therefore only satisfy two of the three conditions stipulated in Article 1, paragraph 9 to the effect that they are not bodies governed by public law) must be aware that their status will change affecting all their activities, if they are entrusted with, undertake or subsequent to a

---

31. Judgment of the European Court of Justice of 12 December 2002, case C-470/99, Universale-Bau AG vs. Entsorgungsbetriebe Simmering GmbH, paragraphs 55-59.
32. Judgment of the European Court of Justice of 15 May 2003, case C-214/00, Commission vs. Spain, paragraph 54.
33. Judgment of the European Court of Justice of 15 January 1998, case C-44/96, Mannesmann Anlagenbau Austria and Others vs. Strohal Rotationsdruck GmbH, paragraph 26.
34. Judgment of the European Court of Justice of 15 January 1998, case C-44/96, Mannesmann Anlagenbau Austria and Others vs. Strohal Rotationsdruck GmbH, paragraph 25

procurement procedure are awarded a contractual obligation – for consideration – to perform an activity which meets needs in the general interest, not having an industrial or commercial character, also if this is merely an incidental activity. In such cases it may be expedient to set up a structure where the commercial activities are outside the scope of the Procurement Directive, by establishing a separate legal person which alone is responsible for the non-industrial and non-commercial activities in the general interest.

In *Gemeente Arnhem and Rheden vs. BFI Holding BV* [35] the European Court of Justice stated with respect to the first condition:

"… that the absence of an industrial or commercial character is a criterion intended to clarify the meaning of the term 'needs in the general interest' as used in that provision".

According to the European Court of Justice the first condition must be given an interpretation by which it, from the category "needs in the genral interest", segregates a sub-category concerning needs that fall outside the industrial and commercial area. Accordingly, the mere fact that a specific activity meets needs in the general interest does not rule out that it may also be carried out for industrial and commercial purposes, and in such case the condition is not satisfied.

"… the legislature drew a distinction between needs in the general interest not having an industrial or commercial character and needs in the general interest having an industrial or commercial character" [36].

Needs which are met also by private undertakings and for which competition may be keen are not excluded from the concept of meeting "needs in the general interest, not having an industrial or commercial character". According to the European Court of Justice[37] this is primarily because it is difficult to imagine activities which under no circumstances could be carried out by private undertakings, and a requirement that there should be no private undertakings capable of meeting the needs for which the body in question was set up would therefore be liable to render the term "body governed by public law" meaningless.

35. Judgment of the European Court of Justice of 10 November 1998, case C-360/96, Gemeente Arnhem and Rheden vs. BFI Holding, paragraphs 32-35.
36. Judgment of the European Court of Justice of 10 November 1998, case C-360/96, Gemeente Arnhem and Rheden vs. BFI Holding, paragraph 36.
37. Judgment of the European Court of Justice of 10 November 1998, case C-360/96, Gemeente Arnhem and Rheden vs. BFI Holding, paragraph 44.

The concept of "... needs in the general interest, not having an industrial or commercial character", generally comprises needs which are fullfilled by other means than availability of goods or services in the market place and which, for reasons associated with the general interest, the State or regional or local authorities choose to provide themselves or over which they wish to retain a decisive influence.[38]

The European Court of Justice recognises that while the absence of competition is not an indispensable condition for compliance with the first condition, the existence of competition is not without significance when assessing whether the specific need in the general interest is a need of an industrial or commercial character or not.

"In particular, it must be ascertained whether the body in question carries on its activities in a situation of competition, since the existence of such competition may, as the Court has previously held, be an indication that a need in the general interest has an industrial or commercial character."[39]

The European Court of Justice seems to base this assessment essentially on whether the body not only sells its services or products to the State or regional or local authorities which have established the body, but also offers these products or services to other potential customers in positive competition with private undertakings. In such circumstances the obvious assumption is that the needs in the general interest which the body meets are needs having an industrial or commercial character and, as a result, the first condition is not satisfied.

The principles for assessing which needs can be classified as meeting "needs in the general interest" must be given a broad interpretation and therefore rarely give rise to doubts. Thus activities which are linked to public policy, hygiene and health have been held to be activities of manifest public interest,[40] and activities which "... are likely to give a stimulus to trade and

---

38. See e.g. judgment of the European Court of Justice of 10 November 1998, case C-360/96, Gemeente Arnhem and Rheden vs. BFI Holding BV, paragraphs 50-51 and judgment of the European Court of Justice of 22 May 2003, case C-18/01, Arkkitehtuuritoimisto Riitta Korhonen Oy and Others vs. Varkauden Taitotalo Oy, paragraph 47.
39. Judgment of the European Court of Justice of 22 May 2003, case C-18/01, Arkkitehtuuritoimisto Riitta Korhonen Oy and Others vs. Varkauden Taitotalo Oy, paragraph 49.
40. Judgment of the European Court of Justice of 27 February 2003, case C-373/00, Adolf Truley GmbH vs. Bestattung Wien GmbH, paragraph 51.

the economic and social development of the local authority concerned …"[41] have been regarded as activities meeting needs in the general interest. More surprisingly the European Court of Justice has held that "… activities relating to the organisation of fairs, exhibitions and other similar initiatives meet needs in the general interest" since "The stimulus to trade which results may be considered to fall within the general interest".[42] From these judgments it can be deduced that at least activities which in a broad sense stimulate trade, sales or economic and social development, in principle, can be classified as activities in the general interest and, as a result, the first part of the condition is satisfied.

Hereafter the somewhat more difficult question of whether or not the specific activities are of an industrial or commercial character has to be decided.[43]

For the purpose of assessing whether a specific area of activity meets needs in the general interest the European Court of Justice has stated that a distinction between, on one hand, the activities which in the narrow sense meet needs in the general interest linked, for example, to public policy and, on the other hand, related services which are not linked to public policy cannot be used to determine the classification of the body for procurement purposes if all the services are normally provided by the same undertaking or authority.[44] A body that carries out activities meeting needs in the general interest, even if these activities only account for a small part of its total activities, is overall deemed to meet needs in the general interest as defined in Article 1, paragraph 9 of the Procurement Directive. The same interpretation is applied to the assessment of whether or not the needs are of an industrial or commercial character, cf. in more detail below.

For the specific assessment of whether a body meets "needs in the general interest, not having an industrial or commercial character", all relevant factual

---

41. Judgment of the European Court of Justice of 22 May 2003, case C-18/01, Arkkitehtuu-ritoimisto Riitta Korhonen Oy and Others vs. Varkauden Taitotalo Oy, paragraph 45.
42. Judgment of the European Court of Justice of 10 May 2001 in joined cases C-223/99 and C-260/99, Agorà Srl vs. Ente Autonomo Fiera Internazionale di Milano and Excelsior Snc di Pedrotti Bruna & Co vs. Ente Autonomo Fiera Internazionale di Milano, paragraphs 33-34.
43. Seemingly, there are no cases in which the ECJ has found that a specific body was not a body governed by public law merely because it did not carry out activities meeting needs in the general interest.
44. Judgment of the European Court of Justice of 27 February 2003, case C-373/00, Adolf Truley GmbH vs. Bestattung Wien GmbH, paragraph 54.

and legal circumstances must be taken into account.[45] The European Court of Justice[46] notes the following with respect to the relevant circumstances:

"... relevant legal and factual circumstances, such as those prevailing when the body concerned was formed and the conditions in which it carries on its activity, including, inter alia, lack of competition on the market, the fact that its primary aim is not the making of profits, the fact that it does not bear the risks associated with the activity, and any public financing of the activity in question ...".

In *Arkkitehtuuritoimoisto Riitta Korhonen Oy and Others vs. Varkauden Taitotalo Oy*[47] the European Court of Justice introduced a *rule of presumption* for the distinction between needs in the general interest, not having an industrial or commercial character, and needs in the general interest, having an industrial or commercial character.

"If the body operates in normal market conditions, aims to make a profit, and bears the losses associated with the exercise of its activity, it is unlikely that the needs it aims to meet are not of an industrial or commercial nature."

The parameters for determining whether or not the needs in the general interest are of an industrial or commercial character are (1) whether the body carries out its activities in the general interest in a situation of competition[48] and (2) whether the body operates under normal market conditions[49] and in that respect whether its primary aim is to make a profit, whether it bears the risks associated with the exercise of its activity, and (in particular in situations where the existence of the undertaking is at risk) whether it is financed or is expected to be recapitalised by the relevant authorities. The European Court of Justice has applied this rule of presumption and the steps in earlier case law towards formulating the rule both in preliminary rulings and in direct actions where the European Court of Justice delivers the final judgment.

45. Judgment of the European Court of Justice of 27 February 2003, case C-373/00, Adolf Truley GmbH vs. Bestattung Wien GmbH, paragraph 66.
46. Judgment of the European Court of Justice of 16 October 2003, case C-283/00, Commission vs. Spain, paragraphs 81-82.
47. Judgment of the European Court of Justice of 22 May 2003, case C-18/01, Arkkitehtuuritoimoisto Riitta Korhonen Oy and Others vs. Varkauden Taitotalo Oy, paragraph 51.
48. Ibid, paragraphs 49-50.
49. Ibid, paragraphs 51-55.

In Commission vs. Spain[50] the European Court of Justice was to decide whether a body named SIEPSA, which was a State company created in the form of a commercial public limited company, by decision of the Council of Ministers, should be classified as a body governed by public law by reference to the fact that the specific needs in the general interest, which the company undoubtedly met, were needs that were not of an industrial and commercial character. It was common ground that SIEPSA was established for the specific *purpose* of putting into effect, alone, the programmes and actions provided for in the plan for paying off the costs of and establishing prisons for the purpose of implementing Spain's prison policy. To that end, as its statutes showed, SIEPSA carried out all activities necessary in order to construct, manage and sell Spain's State prison assets. First the ECJ established that the activities met needs in the general interest since they were "… a necessary condition of the exercise of the State's penal powers they are intrinsically linked to public order". The only remaining question was whether the activities were of an industrial or commercial character as it was common ground that the other two conditions were satisfied. With respect to this part of the judgment the ECJ opened with the following comment "… imposition of criminal penalties being one of the rights and powers of the State, there is no market for the goods and services offered by SIEPSA in the planning and establishment of prisons". Then the ECJ concluded that "That company cannot, therefore, be regarded as a body which offers goods or services on a free market in competition with other economic agents". Next the ECJ decided on the argument put forward by Spain that the character of the activities was of minor importance since SIEPSA carried out its activities for the purpose of *making profits,* and established that since those subactivities which can be said to have a commercial character and generate a profit simply were the means employed to attain the main objective - which was assumed to be the implementation of Spain's prison policy – the *main objective* of SIEPSA was not to make a profit. Finally, with respect to determining whether SIEPSA bore an appreciable *risk* in carrying out its activities, the ECJ established that SIEPSA had recorded large losses and that it seemed unlikely that it should have to bear the financial risks bound up with its activities itself, having regard to the fact that they were "… a fundamental constituent of the Spanish State's prison policy, it seems likely that that State, being the sole shareholder, would take all necessary measures to prevent the compulsory liquidation of SIEPSA". In consideration of these circumstances the ECJ found that the needs in the general interest met by SIEPSA were not needs of an industrial or commercial character and therefore, SIEPSA should be classified as a body governed by public law.

In *Agorà and Excelsior Snc di Pedrotti Bruna & Co vs. Ente Autonomo Fiera Internazionale di Milano*[51] the European Court of Justice was to decide whether a body named Ente Autonomo Fiera Internazionale di Milano (hereinafter "Ente Fiera"), converted into a legal person incorporated under private law, should be classified as a body governed by public law. In the proceedings it was established that the second and third conditions were satisfied and therefore the status of the body would depend on whether the specific needs

---

50. Judgment of the European Court of Justice of 16 October 2003, case C-283/00, Commission vs. Spain.
51. Judgment of the European Court of Justice of 10 May 2001 in joined cases C-223/99 and C-260/99, Agorà Srl vs. Ente Autonomo Fiera Internazionale di Milano and Excelsior Snc di Pedrotti Bruna & Co vs. Ente Autonomo Fiera Internazionale di Milano.

which the body met were needs in the general interest, not having an industrial or commercial character. According to the articles of association of Ente Fiera its *objects* were "... to carry on and facilitate any activity concerned with the organisation of fairs and exhibitions and conferences and any other initiative which, by fostering trade relations, promotes the presentation of the production of goods and services and if possible their sale".[52] With respect to competition in the market place the ECJ held that the activity was carried out "... at international level by a number of different operators ... who are in competition with each other".[53] Ente Fiera was not established in order to make profits, but it was managed according to the criteria of performance, efficiency and cost-effectiveness.[54] The ECJ opened by establishing that the activities met needs in the general interest considering the stimulus to trade that was the direct result of the activities. Then, by reference to the facts *that* Ente Fiera's activity was an economic activity in the form of provision of services in an existing competitive market, *that* Ente Fiera, despite being a non-profit making body, was operated on the basis of market economy principles of performance, efficiency and cost-effectiveness and *that* Ente Fiera bore the economic risk of its activities itself, the ECJ[55] established that "... this does not involve needs which the State generally chooses to meet itself or over which it wishes to retain a decisive influence"[56] and concluded that Ente Fiera carried out activities meeting needs in the general interest of an industrial and commercial character, and therefore, Ente Fiera did not satisfy the first condition of the Procurement Directive for being classified as a body governed by public law.

There are no specific requirements for the character of the instrument which enjoins obligations on the body in order to meet the needs in the general interest for which the body was specifically established or is made responsible for subsequently. Therefore, the obligation to meet such needs does not have to be evidenced in articles of association or statutes, but must merely be capable of being objectively ascertained, for example on the basis of a written agreement.[57] It follows that the legal form of the provisions in which the needs are determined is immaterial.[58]

---

52. Ibid paragraph 28.
53. Ibid paragraph 29.
54. Ibid paragraph 30.
55. Ibid, paragraphs 29 and 38-40.
56. Ibid paragraph 41.
57. Judgment of the European Court of Justice of 12 December 2002, case C-470/99, Universale-Bau AG vs. Entsorgungsbetriebe Simmering GmbH, paragraphs 62-63.
58. Judgment of the European Court of Justice of 10 November 1998, case C-360/96, Gemeente Arnhem and Rheden vs. BFI Holding, paragraphs 59-63.

Case law has established that *inter alia* the following activities meet needs in the general interest, not having an industrial or commercial character, and must therefore be given a uniform interpretation throughout the EU:[59]

Printing activities[60] meet needs in the general interest. The body was established in order to produce, on an exclusive basis, official administrative documents, some of which required secrecy or security measures, such as passports, driving licences and identity cards. The character of the activity was neither industrial nor commercial considering that the prices for the printed matter, which the body was required to produce, were fixed by representatives of the government authority, and considering that a control service was responsible for monitoring the printed matter which was subject to security measures. *Forestry*[61] meets needs in the general interest. The body was established in the form of a private company with the objects of carrying out the business of forestry and related activities on a commercial basis and of owning 12 national parks which "… include the provision of recreation, sporting, educational, scientific and cultural facilities". To some extent the reasoning was arrived at by reverse inference as it was decisive of the body's classification as a body governed by public law that it could be characterised as "other public authorities whose public supply contracts are subject to control by the State" which, considering the control the Irish State exercised over the body, was held to be the case.[62]

2.2.2 Second condition – legal personality of the body

There are no requirements for the nature of the provisions establishing the body governed by public law. As a result, the legal form of the body and whether it is established by statute or a measure of private law is immaterial.[63] The European Court of Justice derives this conclusion from the requirement that the term "contracting authority" – of which "bodies governed by public law" are a subset – be given an interpretation in functional terms,

---

59. See e.g. judgment of the European Court of Justice of 16 October 2003, case C-283/00, Commission vs. Spain, paragraph 79.
60. Judgment of the European Court of Justice of 15 January 1998, case C-44/96, Mannesmann Anlagenbau Austria and Others vs. Strohal Rotationsdruck GmbH.
61. Judgment of the European Court of Justice of 17 December 1998, case C-353/96, Commission vs. Ireland.
62. Ibid, paragraphs 3-4 and 34-40. It is noted that the assessment was to be made pursuant to Directive 77/62, Article 1 of which sets out the following definition of the term contracting authorities: "… the State, regional or local authorities and the legal persons governed by public law or, in Member States where the latter are unknown, bodies corresponding thereto as specified in Annex I". In Annex, point VI it is stated with respect to Ireland that "bodies corresponding thereto" are "other public authorities whose public supply contracts are subject to control by the State".
63. Judgment of the European Court of Justice of 10 November 1998, case C-360/96, Gemeente Arnhem and Rheden vs. BFI Holding, paragraphs 59-63.

which requirement precludes that the legal form of the provisions establishing the body be of a specific nature.

The only requirement for legal form is that the body has legal personality.

Whether a specific body has legal personality is a matter of national law and hence not an EU law concept. Decisive in this respect is whether the body has capacity to enter into contracts[64] and to sue and be sued, whereas the legal capacity of the body in terms of, for example, tax law is irrelevant.

2.2.3 Third condition – extent of public influence on the body

The third and last condition of importance to the classification of a body as "governed by public law" within the meaning of the Procurement Directive is that the body, which meets needs in the general interest, not having an industrial or commercial character, and is a person legally distinct from public authorities, is subject to the qualified control of the State or regional or local authorities (public influence) and thus has a "… close dependency on another contracting authority".[65]

In the Procurement Directive public influence can take three different forms which are exhaustively defined in Article 1, paragraph 9:

"… any body … financed, for the most part, by the State, regional or local authorities, or other bodies governed by public law; or subject to management supervision by those bodies; or having an administrative, managerial or supervisory board, more than half of whose members are appointed by the State, regional or local authorities, or by other bodies governed by public law".

2.2.3.1 First indent – for the most part public financing

The first form of public influence is where the body is *financed for the most part* by public authorities. However, not all payments by authorities are encompassed by the word "financed". A distinction needs to be made between, on the one hand, *financing* in the proper sense of the word and, on the other hand, payments for services purchased in a market.

In the first case (proper financing) the first and foremost concern of the authority is to exercise an owner's interests, although the authority needs *not* have ownership interests in the body, in securing the provision of an activity, which it may subsidise by way of payments to a body carrying out activities

---

64. Judgment of the European Court of Justice of 18 November 1999, case C-107/98, Teckal Srl vs. Comune di Viano, paragraphs 49-50.
65. Judgment of the European Court of Justice of 3 October 2000, case C-380/98, The Queen and H.M. Treasury, ex parte University of Cambridge, paragraph 20.

which meet needs in the general interest, not having an industrial or commercial character, and which are not normally capable of being carried out for profit.[66] Furthermore, in a situation where the body suffers a capital loss, etc., the authority typically ensures its restructuring. In the words of the European Court of Justice: Only those payments which "... have the effect of creating or reinforcing a specific relationship of subordination or dependency"[67] may be described as "public financing". At the heart of public financing are those types of payments for which there is no specific consideration since it is usually an unspecified group of people who benefits from the services provided in return for the payments, which payments, therefore, are unlikely to be made by others than authorities. It is the very existence of such uniquely payments to the body in question that determine whether the body has a sufficiently close dependency on public authorities.

In the latter case (payment for services purchased) the authority is a customer on an equal footing with other potential customers demanding the services offered by the body in the market place and pays in return for the services purchased in the same manner as other potential public and private customers. Such payments from authorities are not made uniquely to bodies governed by public law and add nothing to the decision whether the recipient (the body) has a sufficiently close dependency on public authorities. Accordingly, such payments should not be taken into account when assessing whether a body is financed, for the most part, by public authorities.

In the specific case each payment received from public authorities must be assessed individually to determine whether the body is subject to a specific "contractual consideration" for the payment,[68] and if it is, the payment is irrelevant to assessing whether the body is to be classified as "governed by public law". It seems that, as a guide, payments in the form of public financing can be distinguished from payments not in the form of public financing in terms of whether the payments flow from obligations of a *general* nature determined otherwise than by contract, and payments which flow from obligations of a *specific* nature determined by a contract in private law, respectively.

---

66. It may possibly be argued that if and to the extent that the individual activities would be discontinued if the payments from public authorities ceased, such public service activities would be financed by public funds.
67. Judgment of the European Court of Justice of 3 October 2000, case C-380/98, The Queen and H.M. Treasury, ex parte The University of Cambridge, paragraph 21.
68. Judgment of the European Court of Justice of 3 October 2000, case C-380/98, The Queen and H.M. Treasury, ex parte University of Cambridge, paragraph 23.

In *The Queen vs. University of Cambridge*[69] the European Court of Justice was asked to decide whether Cambridge University by virtue of the payments made to it by the Treasury and other education authorities was a body governed by public law seeing that it was common ground that the University satisfied the condition of meeting needs in the general interest, not having an industrial or commercial character and the condition of having legal personality. In the proceedings the European Court of Justice examined a number of payments individually, and stated that payments in the form of grants for *general* research and *general* grants for students who cannot pay the tuition fees themselves are payments which in general finance the activities of Cambridge University and for which there is no specific contractual consideration, hence such payments should be classified as public financing. By contrast, the ECJ found that payments for specific research work and the organisation of specific seminars or conferences constituted payments for specific contractual services provided by the University, which were moreover of a "commercial nature". In that context it was irrelevant to the assessment of the nature of a contractual service whether it happened to coincide with an activity provided in the general interest.

The expression used in the Procurement Directive "financed, for the most part" by *public financing* simply means that more than half (more than 50 %) of total financing is in the nature of *public financing*. Accordingly, where the sum of all payments from private individuals and entities and all payments from public authorities in their capacity as customers is less than the sum of payments from public authorities capable of being classified as *public financing*, the condition is satisfied.[70] Public financing may derive from various public sources and in order for the condition to be satisfied it is not a requirement that it derives from one specific public authority, etc.

Taking into consideration that the composition of the sources of financing may change over time with the effect that for certain periods of time the body may be financed for the most part by *public financing*, whereas it for other periods of time may be financed for the most part by other sources, the European Court of Justice, in the light of this temporal dilemma, has established principles for the classification of a specific body as governed by public law for specific purchases. By reference to principles of legal certainty and predictability and the provisions of the Procurement Directive on indicative notices, the European Court of Justice has stated that the appropriate period for determining the status is 12 months, for which reason a body retains its status as contracting authority "... for 12 months from the beginning of each budgetary year".[71] A body whose status depends on the specific composition

69. Judgment of the European Court of Justice of 3 October 2000, case C-380/98, The Queen and H.M. Treasury, ex parte University of Cambridge.
70. Ibid, paragraphs 27-36.
71. Ibid, paragraph 39.

of the sources of financing must once a year, on the basis of the *budgeted* income it expects to receive in the following financial year, decide whether its status in that year will be that of a body governed by public law.[72]

In *Kruse & Mørk A/S vs. Jetsmark Energiværk A.m.b.a.*[73] the Complaints Board decided, without giving the specific grounds, that the power plant Jetsmark Energiværk A.m.b.a. was not a body governed by public law, but from the reported statements the Board seems to have emphasised that Jetsmark Energiværk A.m.b.a. was entirely privately financed, did not receive any (public or private) grants, and that it was not subject to any type of management supervision/intervention for which reason that part of the condition seemingly was not satisfied.[74]

2.2.3.2 Second indent – subject to management supervision

The second of the three alternative criteria for dependence relates to the extent to which public authorities are able to exercise influence over the activities of the body. With respect to this criterion the European Court of Justice has stated:

"As the Advocate General has observed at point 48 of his Opinion, since management supervision within the meaning of … the Directive constitutes one of the three criteria referred to in that provision, it must give rise to dependence on the public authorities equivalent to that which exists where one of the other alternative criteria is fulfilled, namely where the body in question is financed, for the most part, by the public authorities or where the latter appoint more than half of the members of its managerial organs."[75]

It is immaterial whether public authorities are capable of influencing *procurement decisions directly* since the condition is satisfied merely where the public authorities exercise an *indirect* control.

In *Commission vs. Ireland*[76] the body was subject to the minister's instructions and *inter alia* had to adhere to the Government's policy with respect to forestry, and the minister had powers to supervise the body's economic activities. Against that background the European Court of Justice held:

72. Ibid, paragraph 41.
73. Order of the Complaints Board of 11 August 2003, Kruse & Mørk A/S vs. Jetsmark Energiværk A.m.b.a.
74. In the transcript of the order the Complaints Board for Public Procurement states in a parenthesis: "By contrast, a power plant such as the one concerned appears to be encompassed by the concept of contracting authority set out in the Utilities Directive …"
75. Judgment of the European Court of Justice of 1 February 2001, case C-237/99, Commission vs. France, paragraph 49.
76. Judgment of the European Court of Justice of 17 December 1998, case C-353/96, Commission vs. Ireland, paragraph 39.

"It follows that, while there is indeed no provision expressly to the effect that State control is to extend specifically to the awarding of public supply contracts by [the body], the State may exercise such control, at least indirectly."

In *Commission vs. France*[77] the bodies (SA HLMs) were obliged to include detailed standard clauses in their statutes, and the technical characteristics and cost prices of the construction of new houses were determined by the minister. The minister was further empowered to suspend the managerial organs and appoint a provisional administrator in the event of, for example, serious mismanagement and to dissolve the body and appoint a receiver. In that context the European Court of Justice, by reference to the nature of the public control, held that:

"... the management of SA HLMs is subject to supervision by the public authorities which allows the latter to influence the decisions of the SA HLMs in relation to public contracts".

Further, referring to the Opinion of the Advocate General, the European Court of Justice stated the following interesting *obiter dictum*:[78]

"As the Advocate General observes at point 67 of his Opinion, since the rules of management are very detailed, the mere supervision of compliance with them may in itself lead to significant influence being conferred on the public authorities."

It follows that even where the public control is merely a (rather more passive) supervision of compliance with applicable statutes and where these statutes governing the activities of the body are very detailed, the condition *may* be satisfied.

The control must be exercised in advance of or at the same time as the decisions since control exercised subsequently does not enable the authorities to influence the procurement decisions of the body.[79] It follows that where the only control is a subsequent annual approval of the annual accounts of the body, the condition is not satisfied.[80]

---

77. Judgment of the European Court of Justice of 1 February 2001, case C-237/99, Commission vs. France, paragraph 59.
78. Ibid, paragraph 52.
79. Judgment of the European Court of Justice of 27 February 2003, case C-373/00, Adolf Truley GmbH vs. Bestattung Wien GmbH, paragraph 70.
80. Ibid, paragraph 74.

In *Adolf Truley GmbH vs. Bestattung Wien GmbH* [81] the European Court of Justice went through the other supervisory powers conferred upon the public authority in relation to the body (Bestattung Wien) and concluded that the management of the body was subject to public supervision. The European Court of Justice based this on the following supervisory powers "... its conduct from the point of view of proper accounting, regularity, economy, efficiency and expediency" and also on the possibility of inspecting the body's business premises which together had the effect that "Such powers therefore enable the Kontrollamt actively to control the management of that company."[82]

Satisfaction of the condition therefore hinges on whether the public authority can exercise a control which enables it to influence, at least indirectly, the body's procurement decisions.[83] In the special cases where the activities of a body are meticulously governed by applicable law, more passive supervisory powers may constitute sufficiently qualified influence over the management of the body.

It need not be one and the same public authority, etc. which exercises the control, it merely has to be exercised by authorities, etc. which can be classified as public authorities, etc. within the meaning of the Procurement Directive. Hence, it is decisive whether the public authorities, etc. together can exercise sufficient control over the management of the body.

It is unclear whether management supervision within the meaning of the Procurement Directive merely extends to positive control in the sense that public authorities, etc. alone – and against the wishes of other possible owners of the body – can enforce certain decisions, or whether it also extends to negative control meaning the capacity to block proposed decisions, but not the capacity to enforce other decisions itself. The wording of the provision in Article 1, paragraph 9 of the Procurement Directive seems to dictate that only positive control is encompassed under management supervision to the effect that only the power to enforce decisions and thus obtain the decisive influence constitutes the control required under the Procurement Directive. The following statement by the European Court of Justice appears to support this interpretation:

"As the Advocate General has observed at point 48 of his Opinion, since management supervision within the meaning of ... the Directive constitutes one of the three criteria referred to in that provision, it must give rise to dependence on the public authorities

81. Ibid.
82. Ibid, paragraph 73.
83. It follows that a specific, qualified control cannot be required, as is the case with respect to in-house services, the control of which must be similar to the control exercised over the authority's internal departments. See also section 3 below.

equivalent to that which exists where one of the other alternative criteria is fulfilled, namely where the body in question is financed, for the most part, by the public authorities or where the latter appoint more than half of the members of its managerial organs."[84]

The provision stipulates financed *for the most part* and appointment of the *majority* of members to the managerial board. As the condition of management supervision must be given the same interpretation, the logical assumption is that the condition is only satisfied if the control exercised over the management is decisive.

Furthermore, in circumstances where the control is of a more limited negative nature (right of veto), it cannot be assumed that the body will not follow a strictly economic/commercial procurement policy merely because public authorities, etc. are capable of blocking proposed decisions or *de facto* block proposed decisions, since the counterweight composed of private interests presumably would pursue a commercial procurement policy persistently.

2.2.3.3 Third indent – appointment of majority of board members

The last of the three alternative dependency criteria relates to public authorities' possibilities of exercising a direct influence on all the affairs of the body by virtue of a right to appoint the *majority* of the members of the superior managerial board of the body.

Crucial with respect to this condition is that the appointment of the majority of the members of the managerial board leads to control of the decision-making within the body. Where the managerial board consists of an equal number of members of whom only half are appointed by public authorities, etc., the internal rules on voting on the board, including whether the chairman has the casting vote, etc., are decisive.

Where statutes, articles or rules of procedure stipulate that the managerial board pass decisions by qualified majority only and the members appointed by public authorities form a majority, but not a qualified majority, it is questionable whether this condition really is satisfied, despite the formal compliance therewith. For example the Merger Control Regulation[85] provides that the possibility/risk of control is sufficient in order to establish control, but for the purposes of the Procurement Directive the rules probably only apply where the body is subject to the *de facto* positive control of public authorities, since the aim of the Procurement Directive indeed is to regulate the public influence on the market in connection with procurements.

84. Judgment of the European Court of Justice of 1 February 2001, case C-237/99, Commission vs. France, paragraph 49.
85. Council Regulation (EC) No 139/2004 of 20 January 2004 on the control of concentrations between undertakings.

The Procurement Directive refers to the administrative, managerial and supervisory board. The reason is that the company-law set-up varies from Member State to Member State and the provision is intended to encompass all boards entrusted with the superior management of the body, and in particular with procurement policy.

As the provision is worded, it must be interpreted to mean that the majority of the members of the superior managerial board are *de facto* appointed by the public authorities, etc. It follows that the condition is probably not satisfied during periods of time when the majority is not *de facto* appointed by public authorities, even though they could have been. A right to approve members subsequently is unlikely to satisfy this condition.

It need not be one and the same public authority, etc. which appoints the majority of the members of the managerial board. The provision merely stipulates that the majority be appointed by authorities, etc. which can be classified as public authorities, etc. within the meaning of the Procurement Directive. Hence, whether one single authority can appoint the majority of the members of the managerial board and thus indirectly control the board is not decisive, but rather whether the public authorities, etc. together can appoint the majority and thereby obtain the indirect control of the body.

2.3 Associations of authorities and bodies governed by public law

The final part of Article 1, paragraph 9 of the Procurement Directive defining "contracting authorities" is a residual alternative to the primary term "bodies governed by public law" in that a body cannot simultaneously fall within the ambit of more than one category of contracting authorities described in the Procurement Directive.

It follows that an association consisting of authorities as defined in the Procurement Directive (the State and regional or local authorities) does not, as an association of authorities, separately fall within the scope of the Procurement Directive if the association already is covered by the definition of "contracting authority".[86] The provision is only relevant if the association of authorities does not separately constitute a contracting authority. By far the majority of associations of authorities or bodies governed by public law fall within the scope of the Procurement Directive because they satisfy the criteria defining a contracting authority and must therefore observe the procurement rules when making purchases.

---

86. Judgment of the European Court of Justice of 10 November 1998, case C-360/96, Gemeente Arnhem and Gemeente Rheden vs. BFI Holding BV, paragraph 27.

A group of contracting authorities making purchases together (through a loose association) must obviously comply with the Procurement Directive in so far as the contracts they offer are public contracts that must be put out to tender, even in the event that private undertakings form part of the purchasing association.[87] In this context it must be pointed out that the guiding rule is that each contracting authority in the association is considered a contracting authority within the meaning of the Procurement Directive unless they have delegated the powers to award the contract to a central body, which in such case is considered the contracting authority within the meaning of the Procurement Directive.[88]

3. Connected companies/bodies

A number of public contracts are awarded by public authorities, etc. to bodies which in various ways are linked with the public authorities, etc. Where these contracts are concluded between legally distinct persons, the provisions of the Procurement Directive apply. In *Commission vs. Spain*[89] the European Court of Justice was asked for a decision on whether the procurement directives had been implemented correctly into national law, where the national provisions generally exempted contracts made between bodies governed by public law from the procurement rules. The European Court of Justice found as follows:

"In accordance with [the Procurement Directive], it is sufficient, in principle, if the contract was concluded between a local authority and a person legally distinct from it. The position can be otherwise only in the case where the local authority exercises over the person concerned a control which is similar to that which it exercises over its own departments and, at the same time, that person carries out the essential part of its activities with the controlling local authority or authorities." ... "Consequently, in so far as it excludes, a priori, from the scope of the codified law relations between public authorities, their public bodies and, in a general manner, non-commercial bodies governed by public law, whatever the nature of those relations, the Spanish law at issue in this case constitutes an incorrect transposition of [the Procurement Directive]."

87. See however section 5 below on the possibilities of escaping the procurement obligation through central purchasing bodies.
88. Order of the Complaints Board of 16 December 2004, Brunata A/S vs. Aalborg Boligselskab af 1956 and Others.
89. Judgment of the European Court of Justice of 13 January 2005, case C-84/03, Commission vs. Spain, paragraphs 37-41.

3.1 In-house services

The term "in-house services" refers to those activities which are handled by contracting authorities internally, i.e. activities provided by means of internal resources without contracting with external third parties. It is widely left to the contracting authorities to determine which services they want to provide by means of internal resources and for which services they will award public contracts to third parties. The Procurement Directive is silent in this respect as it is an internal matter for the contracting authorities.

In the Procurement Directive the term "public contracts" is defined as follows:

"'Public contracts' are contracts for pecuniary interest concluded in writing between one or more economic operators and one or more contracting authorities and having as their object the execution of works, the supply of products or the provision of services within the meaning of this Directive."[90]

It appears that a public contract within the meaning of the Procurement Directive *inter alia* must be concluded between a contracting authority and a separate and from the contracting authority legally distinct *economic operator*. For that reason alone, execution of works or production and supply of goods and services by public authorities cannot be categorised as *public contracts* and is not subject to the Procurement Directive in so far as these activities are provided without the purchase of external resources from economic operators.

Under the Procurement Directive a contracting authority is not excluded from being classified as an economic operator. This is due to the broad definition of economic operators in the Procurement Directive.

"The term 'economic operator' shall cover equally the concepts of contractor, supplier and service provider. ... The terms 'contractor', 'supplier' and 'service provider' mean any natural or legal person or public entity or group of such persons and/or bodies which offers on the market, respectively, the execution of works and/or a work, products or services."[91]

It is evident from this definition that the all-important criterion determining whether a legal entity can be characterised as an economic operator is whether it offers products (works, goods or services) on the market. Therefore, a department within the organisational structure of the contracting authority, which also offers products on the market, may be characterised as an

90.   Article 1, paragraph 2 (a).
91.   Article 1, paragraph 8.

economic operator within the meaning of the Procurement Directive.[92] If contracts are concluded with external parties other than the other departments within the legal person and contracting authority to which the department offering the products belongs, products are definitely offered *on the market* and, therefore, the department offering the products constitutes an economic operator within the meaning of the Procurement Directive. It is then crucial to define which departments belong to the same legal person and contracting authority as the department that offers the products, and which departments belong to other (external) contracting authorities, since contracts with this latter contracting authority may fall within the ambit of the Procurement Directive in that they may be considered contracts for pecuniary interest.

Presumably, the State cannot be regarded as one contracting authority within the meaning of the Procurement Directive with the effect that purchases between the individual ministries and agencies, etc. can be categorised as internal provision of services. Organisational dependence is probably the decisive factor in distinguishing one authority from another.[93]

Regional and local authorities must be regarded as separate and independent contracting authorities comprising those departments which are responsible for the regional and local provision of services or works and which do not have distinct legal personality, but form part of an hierarchical system in which they are ultimately subject to the control of the politicians elected to the regional or local authority.

3.1.1 Scope of the in-house rule
The basic principle of the Procurement Directive is that contracts concluded between economic operators and *external* (legally distinct persons) contracting authorities fall within the ambit of the Procurement Directive whether or

---

92. Recital 4 of the preamble reads: "Member States should ensure that the participation of a body governed by public law as a tenderer in a procedure for the award of a public contract does not cause any distortion of competition in relation to private tenderers." See also judgment of the European Court of Justice of 7 December 2000, case C-94/99, ARGE Gewässerschutz, paragraph 28 and judgment of the European Court of Justice of 11 January 2005, case C-26/03, Stadt Halle, RPL Recyclingpark Lochau GmbH vs. Arbeitsgemeinschaft Thermische Restabfall- und Energieverwertungsanlage TREA Leuna, paragraph 45.
93. In Advocate General Kokott's Opinion of 1 March 2005, case C-458/03, Parking Brixen GmbH, emphasis is given to whether in the relationship between two authorities one is unilaterally entitled to give binding directions to the other authority, or at least by virtue of supervisory powers is entitled to control and possibly change decisions made by the other authority, cf. points 66-68.

not the economic operators are contracting authorities themselves, whereas contracts concluded with *internal* (same legal person) departments within the contracting authority, as mentioned, fall outside the ambit of the Procurement Directive. The legal form of the contract is immaterial to the applicability of the Procurement Directive, except that the Procurement Directive only applies to contracts *for pecuniary interest* concluded *in writing*

Where the contracting authority chooses to organise the provision of its services in separate – and from the contracting authority distinct – legal persons, it makes the task of defining the contracts concluded between the contracting authority and the separate legal person difficult.

On the one hand, it may be argued that where an activity is formally separated into an independent legal person distinct from the contracting authority, any contracts concluded between the contracting authority and the separate legal person should be viewed as any other contract concluded between a contracting authority and an economic operator with the implications that this might have under procurement law. On the other hand, it may be argued that the particular structure in which a contracting authority chooses to organise its services, etc. is not a matter which should have any implications under the Procurement Directive as long as there are no third parties involved in the organisation.

Even contracts concluded with a separate legal entity may be in the nature of in-house contracts if the separate legal entity economically and in regard to decision-making depends on the public authority to a degree which is comparable to internal allocation of responsibilities within the authority.[94] To that end, it will have to be assessed whether the contracting authority is capable of exercising a *control* over the formally separate entity and whether the formally separate entity carries out the *essential part* of its activities for its owners.[95]

The Complaints Board for Public Procurement[96] has decided on this issue in a case where Odense Local Authority had set up two companies and subsequently awarded the rights to waste treatment, respectively water supply to these companies without conducting a procurement procedure. The companies were 100 %-owned by Odense Local Authority and the members of the

94. Advocate General Léger, case C-94/99, ARGE, point 50; Advocate General Alber, case sag C-108/98, RI.S.A.N., point 52.
95. Judgment of the European Court of Justice of 18 November 1999, case C-107/98, Teckal Srl vs. Comune di Viano and Azienda Gas-Acqua Consorziale (AGAC) di Reggio Emilia, paragraph 50.
96. Order of the Complaints Board of 11 October 1996, Luis Madsen and Others vs. Odense Local Authority.

companies' boards of directors and management were all either employees of the Authority or appointed by the Authority. The Board held:

"The formation of the companies does not as such trigger the launch of a procurement procedure. Following an overall evaluation, the decision to conclude the main contracts with the two companies and have the services provided by them is found to be an allocation of responsibility for all the services provided by the Authority which - at least for as long as the Authority has the controlling interest in the companies - is not comparable to a public contract."

The Complaints Board, thus, advocates the view that the way in which a contracting authority chooses to organise itself should *not* have repercussions under procurement law, not even in circumstances where a contract is concluded between a contracting authority (Odense Local Authority) and persons which are legally distinct from it (the 100 %-owned companies), provided, however, that the authority has the controlling interest in the companies.

Subsequently, the European Court of Justice[97] has clarified that, as a main rule, the procurement rules apply to contracts awarded by a contracting authority to an institution formally distinct from that contracting authority. The only determining factor is that it is a contract between a contracting authority and a person legally distinct from it. In the specific case a group of local authorities had formed a consortium and subsequently entrusted the heat supply and the management of the heat supply plant to this consortium. Viano Local Authority had entrusted certain responsibilities to the consortium, of which Viano Local Authority was a co-founder, without a prior call for tenders pursuant to the Procurement Directive. The European Court of Justice answered the preliminary question as follows:

"The answer to the question must therefore be that Directive 93/36 is applicable in the case where a contracting authority, such as a local authority, plans to conclude in writing, with an entity which is formally distinct from it and independent of it in regard to decision-making, a contract for pecuniary interest for the supply of products, whether or not that entity is itself a contracting authority."[98]

97. Judgment of the European Court of Justice of 18 November 1999, case C-107/98, Teckal Srl vs. Comune di Viano and Azienda Gas-Acqua Consorziale (AGAC) di Reggio Emilia.
98. Judgment of the European Court of Justice of 18 November 1999, case C-107/98, Teckal Srl vs. Comune di Viano and Azienda Gas-Acqua Consorziale (AGAC) di Reggio Emilia, paragraph 51.

However, the European Court of Justice pointed out that a call for tenders is not required where the institution carrying out the contract has a very close dependency on the contracting authority. The European Court of Justice remarked the following:

"The position can be otherwise only in the case where the local authority exercises over the person concerned a control which is similar to that which it exercises over its own departments and, at the same time, that person carries out the essential part of its activities with the controlling local authority or authorities." [99]

To summarise, the European Court of Justice stresses that where the contracting authority (1) retains a *control* over the separate legal person which is similar to the control it exercises over its own internal departments that are part of superior-subordinate structures, and (2) the separate legal entity *mainly carries out activities for the contracting authority*/-ies which own(s) it, the contracting authority can award contracts to such legally distinct entities, without complying with the procedures of the Procurement Directive..

3.1.2 Control criterion

When assessing whether a *control* is exercised, consideration must be had to whether the separate entity is empowered to make its own commercial decisions, draft its own budget, determine strategies and engage key employees, etc. In this assessment it is relevant to include ownership structure, rights deriving from articles of association to appoint board members, etc. which, directly or indirectly, allows the exercise of a controlling influence. [100]

If the authority is able to exercise a controlling influence over the separate entity, the authority is – due superior-subordinate structure – able to issue binding administrative orders thus, in principle, rendering a contract superfluous. Accordingly, the existence of a formal contract between the authority and the separate entity under such circumstances is not considered a *contract* within the meaning of the Procurement Directive. [101]

---

99. Judgment of the European Court of Justice of 18 November 1999, case C-107/98, Teckal Srl vs. Comune di Viano and Azienda Gas-Acqua Consorziale (AGAC) di Reggio Emilia, paragraph 50.
100. See the explicit regulation set out in the Utilities Directive, Directive No 2004/17, Article 23, cf. Article 2, paragraph 1.
101. See also Advocate General Léger's Opinion, case C-94/99, ARGE Gewässerschutz, point 59.

The *obiter dictum* made by the European Court of Justice in *Teckal*[102] is unclear in so far as the control criterion is concerned as it mentions a control which is similar to that which is exercised over own departments, but it also seems to refer to it in its plural form, which would imply that *more* contracting authorities *simultaneously* can exercise a control over the same entity (legally distinct person) similar to that which they exercise over their own departments.[103]

This view does not seem easily reconcilable with principles of administrative law generally putting into practice a system of superiority/subordination in which a positive *exclusive* control is exercised over the subordinate departments in the form of a right to issue binding administrative orders. It goes without saying that in such a system only one superior department can be authorised to issue binding administrative orders considering the risk that orders issued by two or more superior departments might be contradictory. Referring to the view if the European Court of Justice,[104] the separate entity must be subject to "... enabling the [...] public authority to influence the [separate entity's] decisions. It must be a case of a power of decisive influence over both strategic objectives and significant decisions."

The qualified control upon which the European Court of Justice makes the conclusion of a contract between a contracting authority and a legally distinct person without a prior call for tenders conditional, may be difficult to bring into compliance with national company law subject to which a contracting authority only can exert influence as a shareholder in accordance with the statutory rules on the allocation of competences. An executive in a contracting authority will not often be in a position to instruct the board of directors or management of a 100 %-owned company to carry out an administrative order which is not in the interest of the company, since the board of directors and management, by virtue of company laws, are obliged to pursue only the interests of the company in preference to the interests of others, including those of shareholders. It follows that under national company law it may be difficult to obtain an influence which is similar to the influence that can be exercised over internal departments which by virtue of the superior-subordinate principle must comply with administrative orders whether they are in the interest of the department or not. Indeed Advocate General Kokott advocates a relaxation of this criteria[105] arguing

102. Judgment of the European Court of Justice of 18 November 1999, case C-107/98, Teckal Srl vs. Comune di Viano and Azienda Gas-Acqua Consorziale (AGAC) di Reggio Emilia.
103. The Complaints Board refers to "controlling influence" which *ipso facto* cannot be exerted by more than one contracting authority.
104. Judgment of the European Court of Justice of 13 October 2005, case C-458/03, Parking Brixen GmbH, paragraph 65.
105. Advocate General Kokott's Opinion of 1 March 2005, case C-458/03, Parking Brixen GmbH, point 63-76.

that it will be almost impossible to obtain such a qualified control over limited liability companies governed by private law and, therefore, public authorities would be excluded from using this company structure. By reference to *Stadt Halle*[106] Kokott concludes that it is not decisive whether the authority has the same *formal* possibilities of exercising influence over a semi-public company as it has over its own departments, but instead whether the authority *de facto* at all times and in all areas is able to influence the semi-public company's pursuit of the objectives in the public interest.

By making the following statement in *Stadt Halle*[107] the European Court of Justice placed emphasis on the nature of the overriding objective pursued by the semi-public company:

"In this respect, it must be observed, first, that the relationship between a public authority which is a contracting authority and its own departments is governed by considerations and requirements proper to the pursuit of objectives in the public interest. Any private capital investment in an undertaking, on the other hand, follows considerations proper to private interests and pursues objectives of a different kind."

The European Court of Justice has provided guidelines in *Parking Brixen*[108] as to the legal concept of "control" and the changes herein following a conversion in the legal status of a municipal body to a company limited by shares. In that connection the court stated the following:

"By contrast, Stadtwerke Brixen AG became market-oriented, which renders the municipality's control tenuous. Militating in that direction are:

a) the conversion of Stadtwerke Brixen – a special undertaking of the Gemeinde Brixen – into a company limited by shares (Stadtwerke Brixen AG) and the nature of that type of company;
b) the broadening of its objects, the company having started to work in significant new fields, particularly those of the carriage of persons and goods, as well as information technology and telecommunications. It must be noted that the company retained the wide range of activities previously carried on by the special undertaking, particularly those of water supply and waste water treatment, the supply of heating and energy, waste disposal and road building;

---

106. Judgment of the European Court of Justice of 11 January 2005, case C-26/03, Stadt Halle, RPL Recyclingpark Lochau GmbH vs. Arbeitsgemeinschaft Thermische Restabfall- und Energieverwertungsanlage TREA Leuna.
107. Judgment of the European Court of Justice of 11 January 2005, case C-26/03, Stadt Halle, RPL Recyclingpark Lochau GmbH vs. Arbeitsgemeinschaft Thermische Restabfall- und Energieverwertungsanlage TREA Leuna, paragraph 50.
108. Judgment of the European Court of Justice of 13 October 2005, case C-458/03, Parking Brixen GmbH, paragraphs 67-69.

c) the obligatory opening of the company, in the short term, to other capital;
d) the expansion of the geographical area of the company's activities, to the whole of Italy and abroad;
e) the considerable powers conferred on its Administrative Board, with in practice no management control by the municipality.

In fact, as regards the powers conferred on the Administrative Board, it is clear from the decision of reference that the statutes of Stadtwerke Brixen AG, particularly Article 18 thereof, give the board very broad powers to manage the company, since it has the power to carry out all acts which it considers necessary for the attainment of the company's objective. In addition, the power, under the said Article 18, to provide guarantees up to EUR 5 million or to effect other transactions without the prior authority of the shareholders' meeting shows that the company has broad independence vis-à-vis its shareholders.

The decision of reference also states that the Gemeinde Brixen has the right to appoint the majority of the members of Stadtwerke Brixen AG's Administrative Board. However, the referring court notes that the control exercised by the municipality over Stadtwerke Brixen AG is limited, essentially, to those measures which company law assigns to the majority of shareholders, which considerably attenuates the relationship of dependence which existed between the municipality and the special undertaking Stadtwerke Brixen, in the light, above all, of the broad powers possessed by Stadtwerke Brixen AG's Administrative Board."

Accordingly it must be concluded that the powers accorded to a (sole) shareholder under corporate law is insufficient to constitute "control" under the in-house doctrine, and in the absence of further controlling measures, the separate legal entity in question cannot be awarded public contracts without complying with the Procurement Directive.

Advocate General Kokott[109] concludes in more generic terms that the state of the law provides that there be a relationship between, on the one hand, the need to/prospects of achieving the political objectives in the general interest and, on the other hand, the degree to which influence can be exercised on the semi-public company.

Against this background it must be assumed that the European Court of Justice does not refer to a positive forward-looking *influence* on the management of the company, but rather to a subsequent *control* of whether the company complies with the policy governing the activities of the company, which control may be achieved through legislation (or regulations, etc.) or derive from agreements such as shareholders' agreements or other provisions. Further, it must be assumed that this control should be accompanied by powers

---

109. Advocate General Kokott's Opinion of 1 March 2005, case C-458/03, Parking Brixen GmbH, points 72-73.

to intervene in the event of non-compliance, the nature of which must ensure their effectiveness.

As is emphasised by both the European Court of Justice and the Complaints Board, the control criterion is only one of three cumulative conditions which must be satisfied in order to be comprised by the definition of a body governed by public law in Article 1, paragraph 9 of the Procurement Directive. The second condition that the body has legal personality is obviously satisfied in the context of this discussion, whereas the last condition that the body was established for the specific purpose of meeting needs in the general interest, not having an industrial or commercial character, is immaterial which is explicitly pointed out by the European Court of Justice.[110] It follows that the right to award contracts to separate legal persons without conducting a procurement procedure (which right is not authorised by the Procurement Directive) extends beyond the provision in Article 18 of the Procurement Directive authorising such award of service contracts provided that the legal person to which the right/contract is awarded without conducting a procurement procedure is itself a contracting authority.

The Procurement Directive makes no mention of joint ventures neither within the meaning of the Utilities Directive,[111] nor in the more traditional sense of a company (legally distinct person) characterised by being subject to the *joint control* of at least two contracting authorities. In view of the fact that the European Court of Justice in *Teckal*[112] in principle recognised that more than one contracting authority may share the required control over a company, making the company a joint venture, contracts between such a joint venture (company) and a contracting authority which shares the joint controlling influence over the joint venture may therefore be classified as an in-house transaction exempted from the scope of the Procurement Directive. Furthermore, the individual contracting authority is probably not required to be in a position to exercise a *negative control* enabling it to block decisions in the joint venture company, as the European Court of Justice does not seem to

---

110. Judgment of the European Court of Justice of 18 November 1999, case C-107/98, Teckal Srl vs. Comune di Viano and Azienda Gas-Acqua Consorziale (AGAC) di Reggio Emilia, paragraph 50, in fine.
111. Article 23, paragraph 2 (b). This provision stipulates that the term joint venture means those contracting authorities which together form a separate company which must satisfy certain requirements for dependency on one of the contracting authorities that is part of the joint venture, and it does not refer to the company which carries out the activities.
112. Judgment of the European Court of Justice of 18 November 1999, case C-107/98, Teckal Srl vs. Comune di Viano and Azienda Gas-Acqua Consorziale (AGAC) di Reggio Emilia.

stress the importance of such rights, provided that the joint venture is owned exclusively by contracting authorities.

In *Stadt Halle*[113] the European Court of Justice explicitly established that participation by a private undertaking in such a joint venture company means that all contracts concluded between the joint venture and public authorities are subject to the provisions of the Procurement Directive. In this connection it is immaterial whether the authority holds the controlling influence or whether the private undertaking only has a minority holding with no influence, since the mere presence of private participants inevitably has an effect on the objectives pursued by the semi-public company, as economic interests are the reason why private participants provide know-how and financial resources. In principle, this shift of focus, which is regarded as the inevitable result of participation by private undertakings in semi-public companies, precludes that the authority can exercise a control over the semi-public company similar to that which it exercises over its own departments, even if it is legally possible to establish such a qualified control. In *Coname*[114] the European Court of Justice formulated it as follows:

"In that regard, it must be held that a structure such as that of Padania may not be treated in the same way as a structure through which a municipality or a city manages, on an in-house basis, a public service. As is apparent from the file, Padania is a company open, at least in part, to private capital, which precludes it from being regarded as a structure for the 'in-house' management of a public service on behalf of the municipalities which form part of it."

The reason is, according to the European Court of Justice, that the award of contracts to a semi-public company in which a private undertaking participates without calling for tenders would distort competition in that the private participant(s) having an interest in the semi-public company would gain an advantage over its competitors in procedures for public contracts because of its co-ownership.[115]

113. Judgment of the European Court of Justice of 11 January 2005, case C-26/03, Stadt Halle, RPL Recyclingpark Lochau GmbH vs. Arbeitsgemeinschaft Thermische Restabfall- und Energieverwertungsanlage TREA Leuna

114. Judgment of the European Court of Justice of 21 July 2005, case C-231/03, Consorzio Aziende Metano (Coname) vs. Comune di Cingia dé Botti, paragraph 26.

115. Judgment of the European Court of Justice of 11 January 2005, case C-26/03, Stadt Halle, RPL Recyclingpark Lochau GmbH vs. Arbeitsgemeinschaft Thermische Restabfall- und Energieverwertungsanlage TREA Leuna, paragraph 51.

3.1.3 Activities criterion

The second criterion emphasised by the European Court of Justice is that the legal person *mainly* carries out activities for the local authority/-ies owning it. This criterion seems to take inspiration from the exemption clause in the Utilities Directive[116] concerning affiliated undertakings/joint ventures.

This criterion seems to be of great importance as it is to some degree connected to the question whether the legal person is at all an economic operator within the meaning of the Procurement Directive. As outlined above, an economic operator is defined as a legal person which offers products (works, goods or services) in the market. A separate legal person which *only* carries out activities for one contracting authority that owns and controls it does not offer products in the market and, for that mere reason, a contract awarded to it is not a public contract since the legal person is not an economic operator.

By contrast, a legal person which also offers products to others than the contracting authority owning/controlling it is an economic operator, and contracts concluded with contracting authorities, including the contracting authority owning it, may be subject to the Procurement Directive. Owner/group of owners should probably be interpreted in broad terms including not only the direct owner, but also indirect interests.[117]

The factual circumstances should be taken into account when assessing whether the formally independent entity is legally separate from the contracting authority. If the entity *de facto* carries out a substantial part of its activities for third parties, the dependency on the contracting authority required in order to avoid the calling of tenders does not exist. It follows that in order to avoid the calling of tenders, it is also a requirement that the independent entity *mainly carries out its activities for its owners.*[118]

The interpretation of the terms *mainly* and *activities* has given rise to much debate among the Advocates General of the European Court of Justice in a series of Opinions.[119]

---

116. Directive 2004/17/EC of the European Parliament and of the Council of 31 March 2004 coordinating the procurement procedures of entities operating in the water, energy, transport and postal services sectors, Article 23.

117. In support of this view see Advocate General Stix-Hackl's Opinion, case C-26/03, Stadt Halle, RPL Recyclingpark Lochau GmbH vs. Arbeitsgemeinschaft Thermische Restabfall- und Energieverwertungsanlage TREA Leuna, points 80-82. For the opposite view, see Advocate General Léger's Opinion, case C-94/99, ARGE Gewässerschutz, point 77.

118. Advocate General Léger's Opinion, case C-94/99, ARGE Gewässerschutz, point 73.

119. Advocate General Léger's Opinion, case C-94/99, ARGE Gewässerschutz; Advocate General Stix-Hackl's Opinion, case C-26/03, Stadt Halle, RPL Recyclingpark Lochau

Activities should be defined as only those which are actually carried out, whereas potential activities provided for in the articles of association or elsewhere as well as activities imposed by law or otherwise are irrelevant in this respect.[120]

Linguistically *mainly* simply means more than 50 %. However, this criterion must be assessed bearing in mind that public authorities carry out non-profit making activities, and exclusively to that end provide services that could also be provided by an economic operator. It follows that where the market activities of a separate legal person essentially are in the form of sale of services to others than its owners, these services are not of a nature that exempts them from the procurement rules.

The assessment whether the activities of a legal entity are mainly carried out for the contracting authority/-ies owning it must probably be made in quantitative as well as qualitative terms.[121] To that end the specific area(s) of activity, which is the object of the contract with the owner/group of owners, must be assessed in order to determine whether the activities in this or these area(s) are mainly carried out for the owner/group of owners.

The exact percentage required must come down to a specific assessment and from case law *mainly* cannot be interpreted otherwise than representing more than 50 % in each area of activity. Advocate General Stix-Hackl[122] argues in favour of the need for a flexible and specific assessment, and against that background rejects an analogy with Article 23 of the Utilities Directive setting out a provision, subject to which calls for competition can only be avoided if more than 80 % of the activities are carried out for the

GmbH vs. Arbeitsgemeinschaft Thermische Restabfall- und Energieverwertungsanlage TREA Leuna and Advocate General Kokott's Opinion of 1 March 2005, case C-458/03, Parking Brixen GmbH.

120. Advocate General Stix-Hackl's Opinion, case C-26/03, Stadt Halle, RPL Recyclingpark Lochau GmbH vs. Arbeitsgemeinschaft Thermische Restabfall- und Energieverwertungsanlage TREA Leuna, point 83 and Advocate General Kokott's Opinion of 1 March 2005, case C-458/03, Parking Brixen GmbH, point 81.

121. Advocate General Stix-Hackl's Opinion, case C-26/03, Stadt Halle, RPL Recyclingpark Lochau GmbH vs. Arbeitsgemeinschaft Thermische Restabfall- und Energieverwertungsanlage TREA Leuna, points 88-95 and Advocate General Kokott's Opinion of 1 March 2005, case C-458/03, Parking Brixen GmbH, points 82-85.

122. Advocate General Stix-Hackl's Opinion, case C-26/03, Stadt Halle, RPL Recyclingpark Lochau GmbH vs. Arbeitsgemeinschaft Thermische Restabfall- und Energieverwertungsanlage TREA Leuna, points 79-95, in which the Advocate General in this respect argues that although 80 % of the turnover is derived from the owner/group of owners, that does not alone mean that the activities criterion is satisfied in the particular case. The ECJ did not rule on this point of the Advocate General's Opinion.

owner/group of owners.[123] The reasoning is that the aim is to open up the market for public contracts for competition and that undertakings in this market should be able to compete on equal terms for public contracts. If an undertaking with significant activities in the market were given preference to contracts with its owners (one or more public authorities), the undertaking would thereby gain an advantage that would distort competition in the market. This is a concern that can be taken into account in the assessment.[124]

3.2 Decentralised entities

In certain circumstances a contracting authority can set up itself in several decentralised entities according to function, which autonomously make provisions for and conduct procurement procedures independently of the other divisions of the same contracting authority. The most important effect thereof is that these decentralised entities are regarded as separate contracting authorities under the Procurement Directive, essentially implying that the individual entity's public contracts must be valued separately from the other divisions' public contracts[125] even where contracts concluded by more divisions coincide in terms of time. This is because each division is regarded as a separate contracting authority with the rights and obligations that follow from such status by virtue of the Procurement Directive.

The conditions subject to which a division which organisationally belongs under a contracting authority, despite this organisational affiliation, is deemed sufficiently independent are set out by the Commission's Internal Market Directorate-General in earlier guidelines[126] to a previous version of the current Utilities Directive.[127] In a letter of 27 September 2000[128] to the Perma-

---

123. See Article 23 and recital 32 of the preamble to Directive 2004/17/EC of the European Parliament and of the Council of 31 March 2004 coordinating the procurement procedures of entities operating in the water, energy, transport and postal services sectors.
124. Advocate General Stix-Hackl's Opinion, case C-26/03, Stadt Halle, RPL Recyclingpark Lochau GmbH vs. Arbeitsgemeinschaft Thermische Restabfall- und Energieverwertungsanlage TREA Leuna, point 89.
125. See further below under 3.4.
126. Commission's guidelines of 20 January 1993 entitled: "Policy Guidelines on Contracts awarded by Separate Units of a Contracting Entity under Directive 90/531/EEC ("Utilities")", document CC/92/87.
127. Directive 2004/17/EC of the European Parliament and of the Council of 31 March 2004 coordinating the procurement procedures of entities operating in the water, energy, transport and postal services sectors.
128. The letter was forwarded by the Commission in reply to a complaint sent to the Commission in the wake of orders by the Complaints Board for Public Procurement in ca-

nent Representation of Denmark to the EU these guidelines were also deemed of importance in relation to the now repealed Services Directive.[129]

In the guidelines the Internal Market Directorate-General underlined that a specific assessment would have to be made of whether a particular division can be regarded as a contracting authority independent of the superior contracting authority to which it belongs organisationally, and that this assessment should be based on the following elements:

– is the entity responsible for the procurement procedure, in charge of the conduct thereof and authorised to award the contract;
– does the entity have its own budget and does it provide the financing for the contract;
– is the purchase intended for the entity's own activities or for the activities of more entities or for the contracting authority as a whole; and finally
– does the contracting authority, despite having formally delegated the purchasing competence, seek to exploit its position as a large-scale purchaser to obtain economic advantages.

3.3 Affiliated undertakings

"Affiliated undertakings" is not a term used in the Procurement Directive. The Utilities Directive[130] uses the term "public undertaking". These undertakings are defined as any legal person affiliated to the contracting (utilities) authorities by virtue of a "dominant influence" and, therefore, directly or indirectly affiliated to the contracting (utilities) authority without regard to the undertaking's area of activity, legal form, etc. and is itself a contracting (utilities) authority within the meaning of the Utilities Directive.

By contrast, a company or an undertaking affiliated to a contracting authority is not, because of this affiliation, a contracting authority within the meaning of the Procurement Directive. Only where an undertaking affiliated

ses L.R. Service ApS vs. Bramsnæs Local Authority, Ringsted Local Authority, Sorø Local Authority, Skovbo Local Authority and Solrød Local Authority and can be obtained from the Competition Authority. The orders delivered by the Complaints Board for Public Procurement did not conform to the Commission's understanding of how decentralised entities' purchases should be valued. For a detailed account thereof see chapter 3.4.

129. Council Directive 92/50/EØF of 18 June 1992 relating to the coordination of the procedures for the award of public service contracts.
130. Directive 2004/17/EC of the European Parliament and of the Council of 31 March 2004 coordinating the procurement procedures of entities operating in the water, energy, transport and postal services sectors.

to a contracting authority satisfies the three conditions set out in Article 1, paragraph 9 of the Procurement Directive to the effect that it is classified as a body governed by public law, is it in itself considered to be a contracting authority within the meaning of the Procurement Directive.[131] The assessment must be made separately for each company in the group and the public control/public ownership is only one of several cumulative conditions.[132]

Contracts between contracting authorities and affiliated companies, which may themselves be contracting authorities, are in principle subject to the Procurement Directive. The only exceptions are where the legal person which carries out the activities is not an economic operator within the meaning of the Procurement Directive, or where the legal person carrying out the activities is an economic operator within the meaning of the Procurement Directive, but must be regarded as an internal unit (despite its status as a legally distinct person) of the contracting authority and, therefore, satisfies the dual requirement of control and composition of customers (mainly sales to the contracting authority/-ies owning it) established by the European Court of Justice.

3.4 Privatisations – transition

It is not unusual that contracting authorities conclude long-term contracts concerning an activity which is subsequently divested and at the same time sold in whole or in part. This activity typically represents an important asset to the divested legal person and yields a profit for the contracting authority as the owner, when the entire or part of the ownership interest in the divested company is sold, possibly in connection with a stock market listing.

There are various implications in terms of procurement law of such a set-up.

"Internal" contracts concluded between a contracting authority and its internal department or separated legal entity (fulfilling the in-house requirements) without a tender procedure, will as a main rule "follow" the internal department/controlled subsidiary, if divested during the lifetime of the contract, even though such contracts change nature and become "public contracts" after the sale. This is due to the fact that the appropriate time for assessing whether a call for tenders is required is the time of purchase. From a

---

131. Judgment of the European Court of Justice of 13 January 2005, case C-84/03, Commission vs. Spain, paragraphs 27-32.
132. Judgment of the European Court of Justice of 15 January 1998, case C-44/96, Mannesmann Anlagenbau Austria AG and Others vs. Strohal Rotationsdruck GmbH, paragraphs 37-41.

procurement law perspective this transitional phenomenon is not a serious problem to other market participants that will have to wait for competition to open up until the contract expires and is to be renewed. After the sale it is not self-implied that the wholly or partially divested company is no longer a body governed by public law and hence a contracting authority which is subject to the provisions of the Procurement Directive when making purchases. This should be taken into account in connection with the sale.

However, in certain circumstances the situation may be different. It must be assessed whether the sale and the contract between the divested and wholly or partially sold company and the contracting authority are bound up with each other. In this assessment matters such as the period of time between the conclusion of the contract, the divestment and the sale and, in particular, whether the wholly or partially sold company is capable of performing the contract itself or whether the acquiring undertaking is required to make a considerable indirect contribution may be of relevance. The impact of these matters is stronger the longer the term of the contract concluded without a call for tenders. In *Commission vs. Austria*[133] the European Court of Justice seem to adopt these two criteria as decisive:

It must be borne in mind that the transfer of 49 % of the shares in AbfallgmbH took place shortly after that company was made responsible, exclusively and for an unlimited period, for the collection and treatment of the town of Mödling's waste. Furthermore, AbfallgmbH became operational only after Saubermacher AG took over some of its shares.

If a contracting authority divests a specific area of public activity into a separate legal person immediately after having concluded a long-term contract concerning that particular area of activity, and at the same time sells half of its ownership interest therein to a private undertaking, which is required to contribute to the performance of the contract concluded, the net effect of this construction is that the contracting authority has concluded a contract with an undertaking which is partly owned and controlled by a private undertaking that was not selected as a result of a tender procedure since sale of ownership interests in companies are not as such in the nature of a public contract within the meaning of the Procurement Directive. In such a situation the transactions are overall likely to constitute a circumvention of the Procurement Directive since any private participation in the separate legal person, by virtue of the in-

---

133. Judgment of the European Court of Justice of 10 November 2005, case C-29/04, Commission vs. Austria, paragraph 39.

house rule, makes it impossible for a contracting authority to enter into contracts without a prior call for tenders.[134]

Advocate General Geelhoed touches upon this difficult question in his Opinion in *Commission vs. Austria*[135] in which Mödling local authority (1) on 21 May 1999 decided to outsource activities in the field of waste management to a separate company (separate legal person), (2) on 16 June set up the wholly-owned company AbfallwirtschaftsGmbH, (3) on 25 June 1999 decided to entrust the waste management to AbfallwirtschaftsGmbH, (4) on 15 September 1999 concluded contracts with AbfallwirtschaftsGmbH on the waste management, etc. for an indefinite period, (5) on 1 October 1999 decided to sell 49% of the shares in AbfallwirtschaftsGmbH to a private undertaking, Saubermacher Dienstleistungs Aktiengesellschaft, with which there had been a dialogue on the acquisition of the co-ownership since 25 June 1999, (6) on 6 October 1999 changed the articles of association of AbfallwirtschaftsGmbH to reflect the change in ownership structure and guarantee the local authority the controlling influence over AbfallwirtschaftsGmbH, (7) on 13 October completed the sale of 49% of the share capital to Saubermacher Dienstleistungs Aktiengesellschaft. AbfallwirtschaftsGmbH did not start its activities until 1 December 1999. Initially and in keeping with *Stadt Halle*[136] the Advocate General notes that following the change in ownership structure AbfallwirtschaftsGmbH could no longer be regarded as a company that had an in-house relation with Mödling local authority for which reason it was relevant to determine whether or not the conclusion of the contract and the sale were connected transactions. For that purpose Advocate General cited <u>that</u> already when AbfallwirtschaftsGmbH was set up, Mödling local authority started looking for a private partner, and <u>that</u> through Saubermacher Dienstleistungs Aktiengesellschaft's participation Mödling local authority secured the new company the expertise required in order to operate AbfallwirtschaftsGmbH with a view to making a profit <u>since</u> AbfallwirtschaftsGmbH did not start its activities and did not fulfil its obligations towards Mödling local authority under the contracts on waste management *until after* Saubermacher Dienstleistungs Aktiengesellschaft had become co-owner (and contributed the required expertise to AbfallwirtschaftsGmbH). In this respect the Advocate General stated: "The certainty that AbfallGmbH would gain the contract from the municipality of Mödling made the acquisition of a holding in that undertaking attractive to a private tenderer. However, such forms of external hiving-off in which the hived-off entity is made appealing to private tenderers by means of a contract for an unlimited period acquired in advance by way of a 'dowry' may

---

134. See above under paragraph 3.2 and the judgment of the European Court of Justice of 11 January 2005, case C-26/03, Stadt Halle, RPL Recyclingpark Lochau GmbH vs. Arbeitsgemeinschaft Thermische Restabfall- und Energieverwertungsanlage TREA Leuna.
135. Advocate General Geelhoed's Opinion of 21 April 2005, case C-29/04, Commission vs. Austria.
136. Judgment of the European Court of Justice of 11 January 2005, case C-26/03, Stadt Halle, RPL Recyclingpark Lochau GmbH vs. Arbeitsgemeinschaft Thermische Restabfall- und Energieverwertungsanlage TREA Leuna.

not undermine the effectiveness of Directive 92/50. The directive is also applicable to such arrangements"[137]

4. Other types of influence

Other undertakings, which are not contracting authorities as defined in the Procurement Directive, may nevertheless be subject to the provisions of the Procurement Directive to a limited extent because of various relations that they may have to contracting authorities. In this respect it is immaterial whether they are private or semi-public undertakings.

4.1 Concessionaires

Public *works* concessions are defined as follows in the Procurement Directive:

"'Public works concession' is a contract of the same type as a public works contract except for the fact that the consideration for the works to be carried out consists either solely in the right to exploit the work or in this right together with payment."[138]

It follows from the definition that it is distinctive of concessions that the consideration for the performance is a right to use the work commercially, possibly accompanied by the payment of a small cash purchase price.

In Commission vs. Italy[139] the European Court of Justice was to decide whether a contract awarded for the lottery computerisation system of the Italian Republic was an alleged concession or a combined supply and service contract. The Italian Republic awarded the contract to the consortium Lottomatica without a prior call for tenders on the grounds that it was a concession which was not subject to the procurement directives. The European Court of Justice examined the object of the contract closely and in that respect emphasised that the introduction of the computerised system did not involve a transfer of responsibility to Lottomatica (the concessionaire) for the various activities inherent in the lottery, pointing to the following five characteristics of the contract: "*First*, the lottery collectors continue to be responsible for accepting bets and the function of the concessionaire's terminal is merely to register, automatically check and transmit the data resulting from the steps taken by the person managing the registration point. The technical programme states that the latter must be able, in the event of a mistake being made, to rectify what has been registered and even to cancel a ticket issued

---

137. Advocate General Geelhoed's Opinion of 21 April 2005, case C-29/04, Commission vs. Austria, point 57.
138. Article 1, paragraph 3 of the Procurement Directive.
139. Judgment of the European Court of Justice of 26 April 1994, case C-272/91, Commission vs. Italy.

by the terminal." "*Second*, the draws are carried out by the Draw Committees … which are State bodies, like the Area Committees … which retain responsibility for checking and validating winning tickets." "*Third*, …, it is always the public administration which ultimately approves and pays out prizes." "*Fourth*, the fact that the first point of the technical programme states that the tender also relates to 'everything else that is necessary for the conduct of the lottery' does not justify the conclusion that the concessionaire takes part in the exercise of public authority but merely signifies that he must operate within the bounds of the concession." "*Fifth*, the … argument that the voluntary payments made by players in the lottery constitute a fiscal charge which entails that the concessionaire is taking part in the exercise of public authority is ill-founded." Against that background the European Court of Justice came to the following conclusion:[140] "As shown in paragraphs 7 to 11 of this judgment, the conduct of the lottery is not transferred to the concessionaire whose task is confined to technical activities relating to the setting up and operation of the computerized system. Those activities comprise the supply of services to the public administration and also the supply of certain goods to it."

The rules of the Procurement Directive do not apply to service concessionaires of service concessions as defined in the Procurement Directive[141] since Article 17 thereof provides that the Procurement Directive does not apply to such concessions.

Characteristic of service concessions is that the *commercial risks* involved with the provision of the service pass to the concessionaire. For example the collection of user charges for a service involves the risk that the user charges will not cover the costs of providing/making the service available. This is of no concern to the contracting authority which grants the concession. If the risks involved with the service essentially remain with the contracting authority, the contract will not be in the nature of a concession, but should be categorised as a public service contract with the implications in procurement law that follow from the fact that the contract is a public service contract. In *Parking Brixen*[142] the European Court of Justice clarifies the legal distinction between public service contracts and service concessions with reference to payments, as follows:

---

140. Paragraph 32.
141. Article 1, paragraph 4 of the Procurement Directive: "'Service concession' is a contract of the same type as a public service contract except for the fact that the consideration for the works to be carried out consists either solely in the right to exploit the work or in this right together with payment."
142. Judgment of the European Court of Justice of 13 October 2005, case C-458/03, Parking Brixen GmbH, paragraph 39.

"It follows from that definition that a public service contract within the meaning of that directive involves consideration which is paid directly by the contracting authority to the service provider."

In her opinion in *Parking Brixen*[143] Advocate General Kokott distinguishes service concessions relative to service contracts. Brixen Local Authority had transferred the responsibility for managing two public parking grounds subject to payment to its wholly-owned subsidiary Stadtwerke Brixen AG for a period of nine years without a prior call for tenders. The private parking enterprise operating in the town – Parking Brixen GmbH – appealed against this decision, which gave the Advocate General an opportunity for addressing this distinction among other things. In the terms set out in the management agreement with Brixen Local Authority governing one of the two parking grounds with approx. 200 parking spaces, it was stipulated that the concessionaire – Stadtwerke Brixen AG – in consideration of the right to manage the parking ground should (1) pay an annual amount of € 151,700 to Brixen Local Authority, which amount would be increased proportionate to future increases in the parking charges; (2) employ the local employees already working within the area; (3) assume any and all responsibility for the parking ground, including an obligation to keep it in good state and condition; (4) assume responsibility for the free use of bicycles; and (5) make an area available for a weekly market held in the parking ground. Against that background the Advocate General found that the agreement was a service concession since the commercial risks involved with the management had passed to Stadtwerke Brixen AG in that Stadtwerke Brixen AG in addition to paying its own costs also had to pay an annual amount to Brixen Local Authority based on the parking charges chargeable from the users of the parking ground.

Chapter III of Title III of the Procurement Directive sets out the rules governing contracts awarded by public *works* concessionaires which are *not* contracting authorities themselves.

Under these rules the concessionaire, whether it is a single undertaking or a group of undertakings (consortium), must comply with several of the obligations laid down in the Procurement Directive for the conclusion of *works contracts* with third parties, whereas there are no special obligations with respect to the conclusion of service and supply contracts. *Third parties* are defined as all undertakings which were not part of a consortium established for the purposes of the original competition for the concession and undertakings related to them.[144]

---

143. Advocate General Kokott's Opinion, case C-458/03, Parking Brixen GmbH, points 27-39.
144. Pursuant to Article 63, paragraph 2 of the Procurement Directive "related undertakings" mean: "... undertakings over which the concessionaire can exert a dominant influence, whether directly or indirectly, or any undertaking which can exert a dominant influence on the concessionaire or which, as the concessionaire, is subject to the dominant influence of another undertaking as a result of ownership, financial participation or the rules which govern it. A dominant influence on the part of an undertak-

Notwithstanding that this is not stipulated in the Procurement Directive, presumably these obligations only apply to contracts concluded by the concessionaire in order for it to perform the relevant concession awarded by the contracting authority and not to other contracts concluded for purposes of other projects.

4.2 Recipients of subsidies[145]

Undertakings which conclude certain works contracts[146] with economic operators involving building works for hospitals, sports facilities, recreational and leisure facilities, school and university buildings and buildings used for administrative purposes and which receive direct subsidies from contracting authorities corresponding to more than 50 % of the estimated value of the works contract must comply with the obligations set out in the Procurement Directive for the award of contracts.[147] This is the case whether or not the undertaking is a contracting authority since, if the undertaking is not a contracting authority, the contracting authority granting the subsidies is under an obligation to ensure compliance with the Directive when granting the subsidies.

This obligation also applies to the conclusion of service contracts[148] connected to the above-mentioned works contracts if these service contracts too are directly subsidised by more than 50 % by a contracting authority.

The said undertakings are not directly subject to the Procurement Directive seeing that the Directive prescribes that the *Member States* take the necessary measures to ensure that these undertakings comply with the Procurement Directive when concluding such contracts, except in situations where the contracting authorities themselves conclude the contracts on behalf and account of the undertakings, in which case they are obviously responsible for ensuring compliance with the provisions of the Procurement Directive.

The reason for this provision is that presumably the amount of the subsidies is reflective of the influence which the contracting authority is able to exercise over the conclusion of such contracts. The provision should also be

---

ing is presumed when, directly or indirectly in relation to another undertaking, it (a) holds a majority of the undertaking's subscribed capital; (b) controls a majority of the votes attached to the shares issued by the undertaking; or (c) can appoint more than half of the undertaking's administrative, management or supervisory body."
145. Article 8 of the Procurement Directive.
146. Works contracts covered by Annex 1 of the Directive.
147. If the value of the contract exceeds the threshold for works contracts of € 5,923,000.
148. If the value of the contract exceeds the threshold for service contracts of € 154,000.

seen in the light of the definition of public contracts[149] as the grant of subsidies may be a means to circumvent the Procurement Directive.

4.3 Undertakings granted special or exclusive rights[150]

Undertakings which by a legislative act are granted special or exclusive rights to carry out a public service must comply with the principle of non-discrimination on the basis of nationality[151] in the award of *supply contracts* (goods) concluded for the purposes of providing the public service. By contrast, there is no obligation to observe this principle in the award of works and service contracts.

If the special or exclusive right is granted to an undertaking which is categorised as a contracting authority, it must observe this principle that follows from Article 12 of the EC Treaty in the award of all contracts

4.4 Sale and leaseback schemes

Sales by contracting authorities of various tangible or intangible assets to third parties, contracting authorities or economic operators, are not categorised as public contracts. Only *purchases* made by public authorities of certain works, supplies and services are in the nature of public contracts.

If a specific asset is sold in order to raise capital and then leased back against payment of, for example, periodic leasing charges, the subsequent leasing agreement may constitute a service contract within the meaning of the Procurement Directive to the effect that the contract must be put out to tender. In that case, sale and leaseback schemes are unlikely to attract any interest, as the buyer of a specific asset typically is not interested in acquiring the asset if a leasing agreement is not connected to the sale.

Leasing of land, existing buildings or other real property and rights thereon are exempted from the Procurement Directive as these are services which are excluded from Annex II A to the Procurement Directive.[152] This means that sale and leaseback schemes concerning land, existing buildings and other immovable property and rights thereon fall outside the scope of the

---

149. See chapter 3.
150. Article 3 of the Procurement Directive.
151. The prohibition is set out in Article 12 of the EC Treaty and is therefore directly binding on the Member States.
152. Note 4 to Annex II A to the Directive. In recital 24 of the preamble it is stipulated: "In the context of services, contracts for the acquisition or rental of immovable property or rights to such property have particular characteristics which make the application of public procurement rules inappropriate."

Procurement Directive, whereas leasing of other assets by contracting authorities essentially is subject to the provisions of the Procurement Directive.[153]

5. Central purchasing bodies

In the Procurement Directive central purchasing bodies[154] are defined as:

"A 'central purchasing body' is a contracting authority which:
– acquires supplies and/or services intended for contracting authorities, or
– awards public contracts or concludes framework agreements for works, supplies or services intended for contracting authorities."

In the context of the Procurement Directive it appears that central purchasing bodies are categorised as contracting authorities and are therefore in that capacity subject to the Procurement Directive. It thus follows that private undertakings which do not satisfy the definition of a contracting authority set out in the Procurement Directive cannot be central purchasing bodies within the meaning of the Procurement Directive.

Contracting authorities which purchase works, supplies or services through a central purchasing body as defined in the Procurement Directive are deemed to have complied with the provisions of the Procurement Directive only if the central purchasing body has complied with them.[155] The implication thereof is that the contracting authorities do not have to conduct their own procurement procedures for such purchases provided that the central purchasing body already has conducted a procurement procedure in accordance with the Procurement Directive.

In order for a contracting authority to purchase products through other contracting authorities without a prior call for tenders it is a prerequisite that these other contracting authorities, when they concluded *their* contracts, have

---

153. If a building is converted after a sale and leaseback in accordance with instructions of the contracting authority in its capacity of lessee and user of the building, the main rule is that the conversion is a works contract within the meaning of the Procurement Directive and therefore must be awarded on the basis of a call for tenders if the value of the contract exceeds the threshold, cf. orders of the Complaints Board of 29 January 2002 and 18 July 2002, Ministry of Economic and Business Affairs vs. Farum Local Authority.
154. Article 1, paragraph 10 of the Procurement Directive.
155. Article 11, paragraph 2 of the Procurement Directive.

informed the public[156] as well as the other economic operator(s), with which they contracted, of their intermediate role, and that it is taken into account under the contract that an inknown number of specified contracting authorities may purchase products under the contract. If this condition is not satisfied, a subsequent increase in the number of contracting authorities which purchase products under a specific contract will change the contract to such a material extent that it will be deemed to constitute a new contract, the award of which is subject to a new call for tenders. This is the case regardless whether the value of the individual purchase is so modest that the threshold value is not exceeded since, as a main rule, a change of contracting parties is deemed to be such a material change that it is in reality a new contract.

As the Procurement Directive is worded, contracting authorities which make purchases through a central purchasing body are exposed to the risk of violating the Procurement Directive in connection with a specific purchase, since the contracting authority is only considered to have complied with its obligations under the Procurement Directive if the central purchasing body complied with the obligations under the Procurement Directive when it conducted the procurement procedure and awarded the contract. It will thus have repercussions for the central purchasing body as well as the contracting authorities that make purchases through the central purchasing body, if the central purchasing body does not comply with the provisions of the Procurement Directive in connection with the award of a public contract to an economic operator.

The provisions of the Procurement Directive on the calculation of the value of a purchase extend to such purchases of which a part is purchased through a central purchasing body without the conduction of a procurement procedure and of which another part is purchased directly. For such purchases the total value must be calculated in accordance with the usual principles to the effect that even small purchases in terms of value may have to be put out to tender if there is the prescribed link between these purchases and the purchases made through a central purchasing body.[157]

---

156. In the contract notice published in the Official Journal.
157. See also chapter 3.4 and order of the Complaints Board of 29 September 2003, Unicomputer A/S vs. Greve Local Authority.

Contracts subject to the Procurement Directive

1. Conclusion of contract

The obligations of contracting authorities under the Procurement Directive concern "public contracts". The Procurement Directive defines public contracts as:

"'Public contracts' are contracts for pecuniary interest concluded in writing between one or more economic operators and one or more contracting authorities and having as their object the execution of works, the supply of products or the provision of services within the meaning of this Directive."[1]

In the light of this definition a contracting authority's written agreements with independent undertakings concerning the contracting authority's *purchase and delivery* of supplies or services or concerning the *execution* of works for the authority are subject to the Procurement Directive.[2] Where a contracting authority also meets the definition of an economic operator and submits a tender for a public contract in competition with private economic operators, the preamble to the Procurement Directive emphasises that[3]

"Member States should ensure that the participation of a body governed by public law as a tenderer in a procedure for the award of a public contract does not cause any distortion of competition in relation to private tenderers."

1. Article 1, paragraph 2 (a) of the Procurement Directive.
2. Strictly interpreted this means that oral agreements are not subject to the procurement rules. However, a contracting authority which enters into an oral agreement on a public contract that would otherwise be subject to the procurement rules and which is not subsequently evidenced in writing will probably be found to have circumvented the procurement rules.
3. Recital 4 of the preamble to the Procurement Directive.

1.1 Contracts for pecuniary interest

There must be a binding obligation between two or more parties which are economically independent of each other.[4] The general provisions of national law should be applied to the evaluation of whether a contract is a contract for pecuniary interest.

In contrast thereof are situations, where a public authority subsidises individuals, undertakings or other authorities without consideration. Subsidies are often contingent on the beneficiary performing specific actions or using the money for a specific purpose, but the situation is different from a purchase in that the public authority typically receives nothing by way of a product, service or result of works in return.[5]

At times there may be a situation categorised as something in between a purchase and subsidies. Local authorities may, for example, be obliged to make services such as domestic help available to the citizens or provide them with certain aids. One means by which these obligations can be fulfilled is through the conclusion of framework agreements with several suppliers. The conclusion of such framework agreements is subject to the Procurement Directive. Where the applicable law prescribes that the citizens may choose the supplier and be reimbursed of the costs or part of the costs by the local authority, the agreement between a supplier and a citizen is not subject to the Procurement Directive regardless that part of the payment derives from the local authority since there is no contract for pecuniary interest between the local authority and the supplier.

Certain contracts for pecuniary interest are explicitly exempted from the rules of the Procurement Directive. Among these contracts are public service contracts for the supply of water or heat which is typically supplied by an exclusive rights holder.[6]

1.2 Envisaged or actual purchases

A purchase must have been effected, i.e. a contracting authority is entitled to receive a service, supplies or have works executed. Also, contracts between an economic operator and a contracting authority for services to be delivered directly to the end-users are subject to the Directive. Examples of such contracts are where an economic operator is responsible for domestic help ser-

---

4.   Cf. section 1.4 below.
5.   Cf. section 1.3 below.
6.   See also Article 18 of the Procurement Directive and section 6.3 below.

vices or the provision of aids. Also collection of household refuse is governed by a contract between an economic operator and a contracting authority.

In contrast thereof are contracts subject to which a public authority lets premises, sells properties or used items or sells by-products from public activities (heat, wood chips. etc.).[7]

Actual as well as envisaged purchases are covered by the Procurement Directive. The determining factor is whether the proposed contract governing the purchase is subject to negotiations. The Procurement Directive extends to framework agreements as well as options despite the fact that they are only to be performed/used at some point in the future or perhaps not at all.

1.3 Performance against consideration

The contract for pecuniary interest entails that the economic operator renders a performance (supplies, services or execution of works) and the contracting authority pays an amount of money for the value of the performance.

Essentially, only contracts subject to which the contracting authority pays a usual fee for the performance by way of an economic consideration are subject to the Procurement Directive.

7. Sale, etc. by a public authority can be subject to the Procurement Directive on other grounds. Reference is made to Commission Communication on State aid elements in sales of land and buildings by public authorities, *Official Journal C 209, 10/07/1997, pp. 3-5 in which the Commission points out that it will assume that no state aid is involved where the State or regional or local authorities sell land and buildings through an unconditional bidding procedure accepting the best bid. The conditions for the sale are described in detail by the Commission in the said Communication which is not binding on the authorities. The Commission has made a similar recommendation for the sale of activities (privatisations), cf. Commission's 23rd Annual Report on Competition Policy* (1993), points 402-403, in which the Commission recommends the following procedure to prevent problems relating to State aid in connection with sales of parts of or entire businesses on the market (i.e. not through a stock exchange): "(i) a competitive tender must be held that is open to all comers, transparent and not conditional on the performance of other acts such as the acquisition of assets other than those bid for or the continued operation of certain businesses; (ii) the company must be sold to the highest bidder; and (iii) bidders must be given enough time and information to carry out a proper valuation of the assets as the basis for their bid ... In all cases, there must be no discrimination based on the nationality of prospective buyers ..."

"It follows from that definition that a public service contract within the meaning of that directive involves consideration which is paid directly by the contracting authority to the service provider."[8]

Gifts whereby equipment, for example, is made available to the public authority is not subject to the Procurement Directive. This is seen by way of the definition set out in the Procurement Directive of public contracts which must be "for pecuniary interest".[9] It also follows from the provision in Article 9, paragraph 1 of the Procurement Directive on the calculation of the value of public contracts which

"... shall be based on the total amount payable, net of VAT, as estimated by the contracting authority".

The Procurement Directive also covers certain contracts, so-called concessions, for which the contracting authority does not pay a usual fee; instead the consideration is by way of a right to exploit the works, services or supplies. Public works concessions are governed by a specific Title in the Directive prescribing certain limited obligations for contracting authorities as well as for the concessionaires.[10] Article 17 of the Procurement Directive provides that service concessions are exempted from the procurement rules, but the obligations and principles laid down in the EC Treaty must be observed when awarding the concession and by the concessionaire in procedures for the award of contracts.[11]

1.4 In-house services and own production

A public authority can choose to carry out services or produce supplies itself. Performance by the authority itself, often called in-house services, is not covered by the Procurement Directive. The Procurement Directive does not

---

8. Judgment of the European Court of Justice of 13 October 2005, case C-458/03, Parking Brixen GmbH, paragraph 39.
9. Where an amount is made available for purchasing equipment of a specific make, this condition on which the gift is made means that the public authority does not have a free choice and, as a consequence, the contract is not subject to the Procurement Directive despite the purchase being made on the basis of a contract for pecuniary interest. Where, by contrast, an amount is made available for purchasing generic equipment, the contract to be concluded subsequently is subject to the Procurement Directive.
10. Articles 56-65 of the Procurement Directive. See also chapter 5.7 below.
11. See also Article 17 of the Procurement Directive and section 6.2 below

stipulate a duty to outsource the execution of public works or the provision of public services.

The Procurement Directive only covers contracts concluded with contractors, suppliers or service providers. The Directive uses the general term "economic operator".[12] However, whether there is a duty to comply with the rules of the Procurement Directive is not decided by the term, but instead by whether the holder of the contract is *independent* of the contracting authority. A contract between two *departments* of the same public authority is not subject to the Procurement Directive seeing that the contract to all intents and purposes reflects the internal allocation of responsibilities within the authority.

1.4.1 In-house rule

The in-house rule primarily applies to services, supplies or works provided or carried out by the authority's own employees. If the authority chooses not to carry out works or provide a service or a product itself, the service, etc. can only be left with others in compliance with the rules of the Procurement Directive, regardless whether an economic operator or another public authority is awarded the service. On that account a local authority, for example, cannot without inviting tenders as provided in the Directive leave a service to another local authority.[13]

The in-house rule may also apply where an activity has been divested into a separate legal entity, for example a limited liability company, or where an activity is carried out in a joint venture with other public authorities. In such a situation it is all-important that only contracts which are in actual fact reflective of internal policies within the authority are exempted from the obligation to call for tenders. This distinction should be based on economic as well as legal considerations.

From a legal perspective the distinction is where the authority leaves the provision of a service to a separate legal person.[14] Even contracts concluded with a separate legal entity may be in the nature of in-house contracts if the

---

12. "The term 'economic operator' shall cover equally the concepts of contractor, supplier and service providers. It is used merely in the interest of simplification", Article 1, paragraph 8, second indent of the Procurement Directive.
13. Judgment of the European Court of Justice of 13 January 2005, case C-84/03 Commission vs. Spain, paragraphs 37-41. See however Article 18 of the Directive on service contracts awarded on the basis of an exclusive right and section 6.3 below.
14. Judgment of the European Court of Justice of 18 November 1999, case C-107/98, Teckal Srl vs. Comune di Viano, paragraph 50.

separate legal entity economically and in regard to decision-making depends on the public authority to a degree which is comparable to internal allocation of responsibilities within the authority.[15] To that end, it will have to be assessed whether the contracting authority is capable of exercising a *control* over the formally separate entity and whether the formally separate entity carries out the *main part* of its activities for its owners.[16][17]

1.4.2 Outsourcing and verification tenders

A contracting authority may decide to outsource the provision of services or supplies or the execution of works to economic operators and the contract concluded in that respect is subject to the Procurement Directive. However, quite often it happens that an internal department of the authority submits a tender for the contract that the authority has put out to competition.

A tender submitted by an internal department of the authority is normally called a *verification tender* since the tender is usually intended to serve as a basis for deciding whether the service, etc. should be provided by internal or external sources. Under the Procurement Directive verification tenders are allowed, but in terms of contract law it is not a genuine tender as it does not originate from an independent economic operator.

A verification tender should be regarded as a means for establishing whether there are any cost savings to be gained from outsourcing. If the internal department submits the tender of the lowest price or the most economically advantageous tender, a contract within the meaning of the Procurement Directive will not be concluded, instead the authority cancels the procedure on the ground that it will not lead to the conclusion of a contract with an economic operator. A cancellation on such grounds would normally be considered objectively reasoned.[18]

---

15. Advocate General Léger's Opinion, case C-94/99, ARGE, point 50; Advocate General Alber's Opinion, case C-108/98, RI.S.A.N., point 52.
16. Judgment of the European Court of Justice of 18 November 1999, case C-107/98, Teckal Srl vs. Comune di Viano, paragraph 50.
17. For more details on the legal basis for the in-house rule in chapter 2.3.1 above.
18. If the contracting authority's real aim of the procedure was to motivate its own employees to be more efficient and therefore all along was not counting on selecting an external tenderer, the procedure and the cancellation thereof can probably not be held to have been objective for which reason the contracting authority is likely to incur liability in damages, cf. order of the Complaints Board of 18 September 1998, Danish Association of Consulting Engineers vs. Frederiksberg Local Authority.

In *Danish Association of Consulting Engineers vs. Frederiksberg Local Authority*[19] the Complaints Board established that "A verification tender is not a tender under Community tender legislation but merely a technique for the contracting authority to assess whether it will be appropriate to offer the given assignment for tender. Furthermore, a contracting authority must be able to decide not to award a contract by reference to a verification tender being better than the external tenders, since as a general rule the contracting authority must be free to give up its intention to contract and to decide not to award a contract if the contracting authority does not find the tenders received satisfactory. Consequently, it is not in violation of Community tender legislation for a contracting authority to have its organisation prepare a verification tender."

The submission of a verification tender is not subject to the special procedures set out in the Procurement Directive.[20]

Nor does the Procurement Directive prevent a public authority from taking back responsibility for a service that has been provided by external operators for a period of time. The taking back of responsibility is not subject to the procedures set out in the Procurement Directive.

2. Which contracts are covered by the Directive

The obligations prescribed by the Procurement Directive to apply special procedures cover *public contracts*. Public works contracts, public supplies contracts and public service contracts are regarded as public contracts.[21] Certain contracts are explicitly exempted from the scope of the Procurement Directive.[22]

As the Procurement Directive is a measure in the efforts to create a single market and develop competition for public contracts, a broad interpretation should be applied to determine which contracts are covered by the Procurement Directive. As a consequence, unless a public contract is explicitly exempted in the Procurement Directive, it should be regarded as falling subject to the obligations of the Directive, cf. section 3.6 below.[23]

19. Order of the Complaints Board of 18 September 1998, Danish Association of Consulting Engineers vs. Frederiksberg Local Authority.
20. See also order of the Complaints Board of 27 April 2001, Dansk Transport og Logistik vs. Nykøbing Falster Local Authority.
21. Article1, paragraph2 (b), (c) and (d) of the Procurement Directive.
22. For more details see section 3.6 below.
23. In exceptional cases, it should be possible to establish otherwise that a particular type of contract is not covered by the Directive, cf. judgment of the European

The manner (purchase, rent, leasing, etc.) in which a product or service is transferred from an economic operator to a contracting authority is irrelevant to determining whether a contract is subject to the Procurement Directive. In this regard the scope of the Procurement Directive should also be given a broad interpretation. The key factor in determining whether a contract is subject to the Procurement Directive is that an independent economic operator under a contract executes works or provides supplies or services to a contracting authority to fulfil a requirement with the contracting authority.

2.1 Individual types of contracts

The current Procurement Directive replaces three procurement directives which governed public works contracts, public supply contracts and public service contracts, respectively. The reason for bringing together the three types of contracts in one procurement directive was a wish to simplify legislation. By bringing together all public contracts in one procurement directive, it is emphasised that the conclusion of public contracts is largely subject to the same rules and procedures regardless of the object of the contract. However, considering that the threshold values that must be met before the Procurement Directive becomes applicable are considerably higher for works contracts[24] than for service and supply contracts, it is imperative that public authorities are not able to circumvent the obligation to invite tenders by artificially classifying a public contract as a public works contract.

It is for the contracting authority to define, having assessed its requirements, what it wishes to purchase in a given situation and, hence, what the object of the contract is to be. The Procurement Directive does not contain rules concerning the definition of the object of the contract, but the authority's description of its requirement and, in particular, the object of the contract decides whether a contract is in the nature of a public works contract, a public supply contract or a public service contract.[25]

The definitions given to the three types of contracts in the Procurement Directive are distinctly different. Supply and service contracts are defined according to their content (supplies, services). Works contracts typically cover deliveries as well as provision of services, and they are distinguished

---

Court of Justice of 7 December 2000, case C-324/98, Telaustria Verlags GmbH and Telefonadress GmbH vs. Telekom Austria AG.
24. Article 7 of the Procurement Directive, cf. section 3 below.
25. In the specific procedure it is necessary to identify the object of the contract by reference to the Common Procurement Vocabulary, for more details see chapter 4.2 below.

from supply and service contracts on the basis of the purpose of the contract (fulfilment of the requirement of the public authority).

In the next sections the three types of contracts as defined in the Procurement Directive will be analysed and their characteristics outlined. Contracts *combining* the three types of performance will be analysed in section 2.2 below.

2.1.1 Works contracts

The Procurement Directive defines public works contracts as follows:

> "'Public works contracts' are public contracts having as their object either the execution, or both the design and execution, of works related to one of the activities within the meaning of Annex I or a work, or the realisation, by whatever means, of a work corresponding to the requirements specified by the contracting authority. A 'work' means the outcome of building or civil engineering works taken as a whole which is sufficient of itself to fulfil an economic or technical function."[26]

Works comprise the construction and demolition of buildings, road construction, etc. Also other activities such as installation work or paint work which, taken in isolation, could be characterised as provision of services, are classified as works in the Procurement Directive in so far as they are linked to the construction of a building.[27] Annex I to the Procurement Directive lists the activities which can be categorised as works.

For an activity to be classified as a works within the meaning of the Procurement Directive it is a prerequisite that a set of *works activities* are carried out in order to fulfil an economic or technical function. In the light of the types of activities listed in Annex I to the Procurement Directive a specific activity may or may not be classified as works; for example the construction of a roof structure as opposed to repair and maintenance which will be a service covered by Annex II to the Procurement Directive.[28]

The works activity must fulfil an *economic or technical function*. In this assessment regard is had to the particular public requirement that is fulfilled by for example the provision of infrastructure, construction of residential property or office blocks, etc.

26. Article 1, paragraph 2 (b) of the Procurement Directive.
27. By contrast, where for example wiring is carried out in an existing building, it will be a service covered by Annex II to the Directive.
28. Annex I, class 45.22 to the Procurement Directive compared with Annex II A, category 1.

The definition of a works contract as set out in the Procurement Directive emphasises that it is the *objective* of the contracting authority – the fulfilment of a requirement specified by the authority – which determines whether a specific activity falls within the Procurement Directive. The *means* by which this is achieved is immaterial, cf. the words "by whatever means".

The definition of "public works contracts" is an attempt to extend the Procurement Directive to situations where the *result of the contract* is that works activities are carried out to fulfil an economic or technical function, the result of which is a requirement specified by the contracting authority.

Consequently, a contract concluded on the initiative of and executed and financed by an economic operator which also retains full or partial ownership of the result of the works activity may be in the nature of a public works contract covered by the Procurement Directive.

Contracts for the acquisition or rental of land, existing buildings or other immovable property or rights thereon are exempted from the Procurement Directive regardless that they may be characterised as public *service contracts.*[29] Nor is a private contractor's construction of a building, as a main rule, subject to the Procurement Directive, not even where the building is intended for subsequent letting to a contracting authority.

The definition of works contracts set out in the Procurement Directive is wide-ranging. The European Court of Justice has clarified that the Procurement Directive must be interpreted in such a way so as to ensure that it effectively opens up competition for public works contracts.[30] Also contracts for the acquisition or rental of premises, which are otherwise explicitly exempted from the scope of the Procurement Directive,[31] may be subject to the Directive if new buildings, conversions, extensions, renovation etc. are constructed or carried out in connection with the acquisition or lease. If the role of the contractor really is to finance and execute construction works which from the outset is intended to fulfil the specific requirements of a particular contracting authority, the contract may be subject to the Procurement Directive.[32]

---

29. Article 16 (a) of the Procurement Directive. Contracts for financial services concluded in connection with or prior to or after the contract for the acquisition or rental of land, etc. are covered by the Directive.
30. Judgment of the European Court of Justice of 12 July 2001, case C-399/98, Ordine and Others, paragraph 52.
31. Cf. section 3.6 below.
32. See for example order of the Complaints Board of 30 August 2004, Benny Hansens Tømrer- og Snedkerforretning ApS vs. Vangsgade 6 ApS, in which the Complaints Board by reference to the Tender Act (subject to which works contracts are to be interpreted in accordance with the Procurement Directive) held that the contract be-

As a consequence, a contract may be interpreted differently where the contracting authority has sold, for example, land or buildings with a view to executing works intended to fulfil a requirement with the contracting authority. Likewise, where works are executed to fulfil a requirement specified by the contracting authority and the contract, therefore, is comprised by the definition of a public works contract as set out in the Procurement Directive. In such circumstances the European Court of Justice would be expected to assess the situation in such a way so as to ensure that the Procurement Directive is not deprived of practical effect.[33]

Ordine[34] concerned the Italian system for granting building permits subject to which the landowner pays the municipality for the permit. However, if the landowner executed certain infrastructure or service structure works, concerning for example roads, sewers, schools, churches, etc., the landowner would be granted a reduction in the amount payable. These types of works are typically executed subject to a public works contract. The system in issue was not a typical one in relation to the definition of a public works contract set out in the procurement directive. However, having interpreted the procurement directive and assessed the specific circumstances, the European Court of Justice came to the conclusion that the works were in the nature of "public works" within the meaning of the procurement directive and that, consequently, a contract for the execution thereof could only be awarded in accordance with the procedures laid down in the directive.[35]

A contract remains a works contract even though it, in addition to the execution of works, also comprises design.[36] Execution of works normally involves deliveries of supplies, materials and equipment. Often the contracts

tween Boligselskabet BSB Ølgod, branch 11 and Vangsgade 6 ApS for the acquisition of a property with 20 housing units in reality was a "works contract", despite the fact that Vangsgade 6 ApS had bought the property and subsequently as developer had constructed the housing units and then transferred the property to Boligselskabet BSB Ølgod, branch 11.

33. Judgment of the European Court of Justice of 12 July 2001, case C-399/98, Ordine and Others vs. Comune di Milano, paragraph 55. In the assessment it will carry great weight whether the actual ownership and powers over the result of the works activity belong to the contracting authority or the economic operator. See also section 3.2.3 below on sale and leaseback.

34. Judgment of the European Court of Justice of 12 July 2001, case C-399/98, Ordine and Others vs. Comune di Milano.

35. Ibid, paragraphs 97-99. The European Court of Justice stated as an *obiter dictum* that it was for the local authority to decide whether it wanted to arrange the call for tenders or whether it would leave it to the landowner.

36. Article 1, paragraph 2 (b) of the Procurement Directive.

for these deliveries are concluded by the contractor and, therefore, are not subject to the Procurement Directive. If the products, materials or equipment is provided by the contracting authority, the contracts concluded by the authority to that end must be awarded following the procedures set out in the Procurement Directive, cf. 3.2.1.2 below. The value of supplies, materials or equipment must be included in the calculation of the threshold value of a contract.[37]

2.1.2 Supply contracts

The Procurement Directive defines public supply contracts as follows:

"'Public supply contracts' are public contracts other than those referred to in (b) having as their object the purchase, lease, rental or hire purchase, with or without option to buy, of products."[38]

Within the framework of Article 28 of the EC Treaty regarding the prohibition on barriers to trade, the European Court of Justice has defined supplies as:

"products which can be valued in money and which are capable, as such, of forming the subject of commercial transactions."

According to the case law of the European Court of Justice, products such as agricultural produce, metal ore, machines, electricity, waste, etc. are categorised as supplies. Where a contracting authority, as the contractor, purchases building material or material to be used in connection with the construction of works, such purchases will be in the nature of supply contracts. Furthermore, the value of these contracts must be included in the calculation of the threshold value of the works activity.

2.1.3 Service contracts

The Procurement Directive defines public service contracts as follows:

"'Public service contracts' are public contracts other than public works or supply contracts having as their object the provision of services referred to in Annex II."[39]

---

37. Article 9, paragraph 4 of the Procurement Directive.
38. Article 1, paragraph 2 (c), first indent of the Procurement Directive.
39. Article 1, paragraph 2 (d), first indent of the Procurement Directive.

By the choice of wording this provision extends to those public contracts that cannot be characterised as public works contracts or public supply contracts, respectively.[40]

Public service contracts cover a very varied selection of services of which only some are likely to be of any interest to undertakings located outside the Member State of the contracting authority. Against that background the Procurement Directive classifies services into two groups, A and B.[41] These categories of services are listed in Annex II A and Annex II B to the Procurement Directive.[42]

The classification of a contract as either an A service contract or a B service contract is greatly important in terms of the obligations to which the contracting authority is subject under the Procurement Directive:

The award of contracts which have A services as their object is subject to all the provisions of the Procurement Directive, including the obligation to publish contract notices, etc.[43]

The award of contracts which have B services as their object is solely subject to Article 23 (technical specifications) and Article 35, paragraph 4 (notice to advertise the award of a public contract).[44]

The various categories of services are described in words in Annex II to the Procurement Directive. However, in the light of the very diverse nature of the services comprised by the Procurement Directive it is necessary to specify in more detail which service the contract is for.[45] Hence, in addition to describing the individual service in words, Annex II of the Procurement Directive also refers to the classification of the service in the CPV nomenclature[46] and

---

40. In Article 50(1) of the EC Treaty services are defined as: "Services shall be considered to be 'services' within the meaning of this Treaty where they are normally provided for remuneration, in so far as they are not governed by the provisions relating to freedom of movement for goods, capital and persons."
41. Recital 19 of the preamble to the Procurement Directive.
42. See section 6.2 below on services exempted from Annex II A and Annex II B.
43. Article 20 of the Procurement Directive.
44. Article 21 of the Procurement Directive. The general rules and principles of the EC Treaty also apply to contracts for B services, cf. chapter 1.5 above and Article 2 of the Procurement Directive.
45. The now repealed Services Directive (92/50/EC) also provided that the CPC description of a service was binding on the contracting authority, cf. judgment of the European Court of Justice of 24 September 1998, case C-76/97, Walter Tögel, paragraph 37.
46. The CPV nomenclature is referred to in chapter 4.

the CPC nomenclature.[47] For purposes of describing a particular service as either an A service or a B service the CPV nomenclature should be used. However, where the description of a service in the CPV nomenclature differs from the description in the CPC nomenclature, Annex II to the Procurement Directive provides that the CPC description be used.

In the specific circumstances the service proposed must be analysed to determine whether it falls within the categories listed in Annex II A or Annex II B. An analysis should be based on Annex II A which is an exhaustive list of the services that are categorised as A services. Also, for the purpose of classifying services as either A or B services the contracting authority must look at the facts to determine whether a contract has as its object services that are not of the same type, in which case, the services must be classified as A services, respectively B services.[48]

On the basis of the classification the individual services must be valued to determine whether the contract, in its entirety, is subject to the rules of the Procurement Directive on A services or B services.[49] The main purpose of the contract is irrelevant in this respect.[50]

Basically, the contracting authority decides the types of services to be comprised under one contract. This decision is only likely to be overruled where the grouping of several types of services under one contract merely is intended to have the effect of classifying the contract, as a whole, as a B service.[51]

2.2 Mixed contracts

Public contracts often comprise a combination of works, supplies and services. In order to assess its obligations under the Procurement Directive the contracting authority must classify each of the works, products and services to be provided under the acquisition/contract to determine the relevant threshold value and which rules of the Procurement Directive that must be

47. The UN Central Product Classification.
48. Judgment of the European Court of Justice of 24 September 1998, case C-76/97, Walter Tögel, paragraph 38; judgment of the European Court of Justice of 14 November 2002, case C-411/00, Felix Swoboda GmbH vs. Österreichische National Bank, paragraph 62; order of the Complaints Board of 28 April 2003, Centralforeningen af Taxiforeninger i Danmark vs. County of Vestsjælland.
49. Article 22 of the Procurement Directive.
50. Judgment of the European Court of Justice of 14 November 2002, case C-411/00, Felix Swoboda GmbH vs. Österreichische National Bank, paragraph 49.
51. Judgment of the European Court of Justice of 14 November 2002, case C-411/00, Felix Swoboda GmbH vs. Österreichische National Bank, paragraph 57.

applied to the award of the contract. A contract which covers works, supplies and services must always be classified as *either* a public works contract *or* a public supply contract *or* a public service contract covering all the works, supplies and services under the (combined) contract.

First, the contract must be analysed with a view to establishing whether it comprises the provision or execution of one or more types of works, products or services. This analysis should be based on the definitions set out in the Procurement Directive of public works contracts, public supply contracts and public services contracts, respectively.[52]

Next, in accordance with the Procurement Directive two measures are used for classifying public contracts which combine the execution of works, delivery of supplies and provision of services: *the main purpose* of the contract and *the value* of the individual elements of the contract. A correct classification may determine whether the contract must be awarded in accordance with the procedures set out in the Procurement Directive, since the threshold values for contracts for works, supplies and services are not the same.[53]

2.2.1 Main purpose of the contract

The main purpose determines the classification of a contract for the provision of products or services which also comprises design, installation or works.

In connection with a contract for the *supply of products*, such as machinery or technical plant, it is often necessary to carry out incidental siting or installation operations which may be very costly. In isolation, the siting and installation operations can be characterised as services. However, if the execution thereof is incidental to the supply of products, the contract, as a whole, is considered a supply contract.[54]

Hence, for the purpose of classifying the contract the main purpose of the contract must be distinguished from the services that are incidental thereto.

In connection with the *supply of products,* such as machinery or equipment, execution of works may be necessary. Also for the purpose of classifying a public contract as either a supply contract or a works contract the *main purpose* of the contract must be identified.

---

52. See section 2.1 above.
53. See section 3 below for more details about the threshold values.
54. "A public contract having as its object the supply of products and which also covers, as an incidental matter, siting and installation operation shall be considered to be a 'public supply contract'." Article 1, paragraph 2 (c), second indent of the Procurement Directive.

A contract for the *provision of services* may require the execution of works activities. If the execution of the works is incidental to the provision of the services, the contract, as a whole, is a service contract. The classification of the contract is determined by the main purpose thereof.[55]

A contract for the *construction of a building* may include design work, for example architectural and engineering services, which, in isolation, are services.[56] If an independent economic operator is responsible for the design, the contract must be put out to tender if its value exceeds the threshold value of service contracts as stipulated in the Procurement Directive. If, by contrast, the design is part of the overall works, the contract, as a whole, is a works contract.[57]

In certain situations a contracting authority may be particularly interested in grouping various purchases, thus avoiding the obligation to put the contract out to tender in accordance with the procedures of the Procurement Directive, either because of the specific rules that apply to certain services or the high threshold values that apply to works contracts.

Grouping of, for example, certain services and minor works can be a useful means by which a service contract, which is otherwise subject to a call for tenders, is brought outside the scope of the Procurement Directive provided that the contract, as a whole, can be classified as a works contract and that the total value does not exceed the high threshold values for works contracts. In a similar vein, grouping of certain services can be a useful means by which certain contracts can be brought outside the scope of the Procurement Directive; a service contract which covers services listed in Annex II A as well as services listed in Annex II B, and the value of the Annex II B services exceeds the value of the Annex II A services is not subject to a call for tender under the Procurement Directive, cf. Articles 20-22 of the Procurement Directive. For that reason, the contracting authority may have an interest in grouping an upcoming purchase of Annex II B services with an upcoming purchase of an Annex II A service, thus avoiding a call for tenders for the contract for the Annex II A services. In *Dansk Taxi Forbund vs. County of Vestsjælland*[58] the County had purchased certain *services* (patient transport services) without a prior call for tenders under the EU procurement rules. These services covered (1) emergency ambulance services, (2) transport of lying patients and (3) transport of sitting patients. The value of each of these services separately exceeded the threshold value, but the County regarded the first

---

55. "A public contract having as its object services within the meaning of Annex II and including activities within the meaning of Annex I that are only incidental to the principal object of the contract shall be considered to be a public service contract." Article 1, paragraph 2 (d), third indent of the Procurement Directive.
56. The design may be the responsibility of the contractor.
57. Article 1, paragraph 2 (b) of the Procurement Directive.
58. Order of the Complaints Board of 8 April 2003, Dansk Taxi Forbund vs. County of Vestsjælland.

two services as Annex II B services and only the third service as an Annex II A service, and since the value of the Annex II B services clearly exceeded the value of the Annex II A service, none of the services was put out to tender. In its order the Complaints Board established that each of the three services was an Annex II A service for which reason they should all have been put out to tender in accordance with the EU procurement rules, but added with respect to the grouping of the services under one contract that "for a number of years the defendant has had a contract with Falcks Redningskorps A/S covering all three services and, on the information provided, the decision made by the defendant in 2001 to continue this practice of covering all three services under one contract was founded on objective grounds. Therefore, the defendant would not have contravened [the procurement directive] had it decided to conclude one contract covering all three services and then invited tenders for all three services with a view to awarding one contract covering all of them."[59]

For the purpose of *classifying the contract* and thus determining which threshold value is applicable, contracts such as the above-mentioned must be analysed to identify the main purpose of the contract and the services which are incidental thereto.[60] The object of the contract as defined in the contract documents is an indicator of the main purpose of the contact, as are any other statements made by the contracting authority in that regard in the contract documents. A contract for property management, for example, will be considered a public service contract regardless that the property manager is expected to execute certain works activities. If necessary, the requirement with the contracting authority that led to the decision to award a public contract must be analysed.

In *Gestion Hotelera*[61] a contract covered the management of a casino, the management of a hotel and extensive works activities. The contract could only be awarded to an undertaking that was competent to manage a hotel as well as a casino. The local authority owned the hotel where the casino was to be opened, and the works concerned the conversion of the hotel to accommodate the casino and elevate the hotel to a five-star hotel. The contract documents did not specify the exact works to be carried out and did not contain a provision for remuneration for the works. Overall the European Court of

---

59. See also order of the Complaints Board of 28 April 2003, Centralforeningen af Taxiforeninger i Danmark vs. County of Vestsjælland.
60. Recital 10 of the preamble to the Procurement Directive and Article 1, paragraph 2 (d), third indent of the Procurement Directive.
61. Judgment of the European Court of Justice of 19 April 1994, case C-331/92, Gestion Hotelera international SA vs. Comunidad Autonoma de Canarias, Ayuntamiento de Las Palmas de Gran Canaria and Gran Casino de Las Palmas SA.

Justice found that the works were incidental to the object of the public contract which was considered to be a public service contract.

2.2.2 *Value of the individual elements of the contract*

The value of the individual elements of a contract is used to determine the particular type of service (A services and B services) or whether it is for supplies or services.

A contract for the provision of services by way of siting or installation operations as well as the supply of products must first be distinguished from those supply contracts that cover siting and installation operations, seeing that the main purpose of the contract determines the classification of these contracts.[62]

For other mixed contracts it is necessary to value the services, respectively supplies that are covered by the contract. The value is determined on the basis of the remuneration, excluding VAT, which the contracting authority is likely to have to pay.[63] It can be difficult to value the individual elements of a mixed contract, but the contracting authority must carry out all investigations necessary to procure information on an objective basis, and must, if necessary, consult external consultants.[64] If the value of the services exceeds the value of the supplies, the contract, as a whole, is subject to the rules on public service contracts as set out in the Procurement Directive.[65] If the situation is the opposite, the contract, as a whole, is subject to the rules on public supply contracts as set out in the Procurement Directive.[66]

Public service contracts may cover services that are not of the same nature and thus be a mix of A and B services. The value of the individual services provided under such contracts must be determined. The contract, as a whole, will be subject to the rules applicable to A services or B services, respectively, depending on whether the value of the A services exceeds the value of

---

62. See section 2.2.1 above.
63. See also section 3.4 below on the calculation of the estimated value of a contract.
64. Ability to *prove* that adequate investigations were made in order to determine the estimated value of a contract is particularly relevant if the conclusion to the investigation is that the value of the contract does not exceed the threshold values stipulated in the Procurement Directive, cf. section 4 below.
65. If the service is listed in Annex II B to the Procurement Directive, the entire contract is subject to the limited obligations that apply to these categories of services. If the contract covers A and B services, they must be valued separately to determine whether the contract, as a whole, is subject to the rules applicable to A service or the rules applicable to B services, cf. Article 22 of the Procurement Directive.
66. Article 1, paragraph 2 (d), second indent of the Procurement Directive.

the B services, or vice versa.[67] The classification as either A or B services has a great bearing on the contracting authority's obligations under the Procurement Directive.[68]

A mixed contract which covers supplies as well as Annex II A services and Annex II B services, the values of which are such that the value of the supplies is less than the aggregate value of the A and B services, and the value of the B services is greater than the value of the A services, does not have to be put out to tender under the EU procurement rules at all regardless that the supplies as well as the A services each exceed the applicable threshold values.

2.3 Ownership and financing

The key area to which the Procurement Directive applies is the conclusion of a public contract which may be anyone of three types (works, supplies or services) and subject to which the ownership of the object is transferred to the contracting authority which in return pays a consideration.

In addition, the Procurement Directive applies to certain other contracts, the object of which is financed by the economic operator or subject to which the economic operator retains ownership of the object.

2.3.1 Execution of works

The Procurement Directive applies to works contracts concerning

"... the realisation, by whatever means, of a work corresponding to the requirements specified by the contracting authority".[69]

This provision is intended to ensure that works executed for the benefit of the contracting authority and therefore constituting an alternative to works financed "by normal means" are covered by the Procurement Directive.[70]

In *Ordine*[71] the European Court of Justice interpreted the provision in functional terms. A contract is subject to the Procurement Directive

– if it has as its object the execution of works; and

67. Article 22 of the Procurement Directive.
68. Ibid.
69. Article 1, paragraph 2 (b) of the Procurement Directive.
70. Special rules set out in the Procurement Directive apply to works concessions. See also chapter 5.7 below.
71. Judgment of the European Court of Justice of 12 July 2001, case C-399/98, Ordine and Others, paragraph 52. The judgment concerns the similar provision in Directive 93/37, now repealed.

- this corresponds to a requirement specified by the contracting authority in advance; and
- the work fulfils an economic or technical function.

This definition covers those situations where new buildings are constructed for use by the contracting authority and in accordance with the contracting authority's specified requirements and subsequently transferred or leased to the authority. It also covers those situations where existing buildings are transferred to an economic operator, converted and then leased or sold back to the contracting authority.[72]

Sale and leaseback schemes subject to which a contracting authority sells a property which is then renovated and leased to the contracting authority can take one of two forms. If title to the property in effect remains with the contracting authority, the works are normally executed to fulfil a requirement with the authority.[73] If title effectively is transferred to the new owner, the contract must be assessed in the same light as contracts subject to which a building owned by an economic operator is converted with a view to leasing it to a contracting authority. Decisive in this situation is whether the real purpose of the conversion is to fulfil a requirement with the contracting authority.[74]

If the contract is subject to the procurement rules, the contracting authority can fulfil its obligations in that respect by making sure that the economic operator conducts a tender procedure. Alternatively, the contracting authority must assume the responsibilities of builder and conduct the tender procedure.

2.3.2 Purchase, lease or rental of products

The Procurement Directive classifies contracts as supply contracts whether they have

"… as their object the purchase, lease, rental or hire purchase, with or without option to buy, of products".[75]

By this definition neither the ownership of the product nor the financing of the purchase has any bearing on whether the contract is subject to the Procurement Directive. Whether there is an obligation to invite tenders is deter-

72. See orders of the Complaints Board of 29 January 2002 and 18 July 2002, Ministry of Economic and Business Affairs vs. Farum Local Authority, and chapter 2.4.4 above.
73. Orders of the Complaints Board of 29 January 2002 and 18 July 2002, Ministry of Economic and Business Affairs vs. Farum Local Authority.
74. See section 2.1.1 above.
75. Article 1, paragraph 2 (c) of the Procurement Directive.

mined solely on the basis of whether it is a public contract for supply of products intended to fulfil a requirement or function with the contracting authority.

2.3.3 Provision of services

Pursuant to the Procurement Directive a service contract is a contract the object of which cannot be classified as supplies or works.[76] The Procurement Directive does not contain specific provisions about the financing of service contracts presumably because services, by nature, do not necessarily translate into a physical manifestation. Audit services result in an audit report, architectural services result in drawings, transport services carry the object of the transport to another location, whereas knowledge applied in the creative process and the transport carried out are invisible. The economic operator has no interest in retaining ownership of the result of the service.[77]

Only a few of the provisions of the Procurement Directive concern the financing of services. Service concessions are explicitly exempted from the scope of the Procurement Directive.[78] Service contracts for research and development are exempted from the scope of the Procurement Directive if the benefits of the research and development activity accrue to the economic operator, regardless that the service is remunerated by the contracting authority.[79] The rules on State aid set out in the EC Treaty are relevant in these situations.

2.4 Term of contracts

It is the Commission's view that continuing contracts for services should be put out to competition at regular intervals which has been interpreted to mean every three to five years. In *L.R. Service ApS vs. Ringsted Local Authority*[80] the Complaints Board stated the following in regard to the term of service contracts:

"It must be assumed that the Service Directive allows the deduction of a rule saying that an ongoing service performance covered by the directive must be offered for tender once in a while, e.g. every four years, cf. the principle in [Article 9, paragraph 8 of the Procurement Directive]."

76. Article 1, paragraph 2 (d) of the Procurement Directive.
77. Assuming that a lien cannot be exercised and that there are no copyrights
78. Article 17 of the Procurement Directive.
79. Article 16 (f) of the Procurement Directive, cf. section 6.2 below.
80. Order of the Complaints Board of 28 May 1999, L.R. Service ApS vs. Ringsted Local Authority.

This view is unacceptable for the mere reason that the provision in Article 9, paragraph 8 addresses the situations where the term of a contract goes beyond four years and thus acknowledges, in theory, that this might be the case.

In fact, the Complaints Board has subsequently modified its view in *Supervisory Council for the County of Storstrøm vs. Rønnede Local Authority.*[81]

The case concerned a call for tenders for a so-called function contract concerning road maintenance in the municipality of Rønnede during the period 1 January 2002 till 31 December 2015 with an option for renewal for a further three years, i.e. a term of contract of 14 years possibly prolonged with another three years. The procedure for awarding a function contract was described as a procedure in which the contracting authority, in the contract documents, specifies in detail requirements for the road in terms of functional requirements (such as friction, cracks and evenness). On the basis of the description it was the economic operator's responsibility to choose the processes and materials that would guarantee that these requirements were met. The economic operator's freedom of choice with respect to the composition of materials made it even more attractive for it to develop better/cheaper surfacing, and also, the flexibility guaranteed by way of the economic operator's scope for determining the exact organisation of the works in the long run would optimise the execution of the works from an economic perspective. Tenders were invited on the basis that roads do not have an official service life, but in general municipal roads of that kind were expected to operate for 12 to 15 years. Overall, a function contract of a term corresponding to the average service life of a road could be considered a capital/operating investment concluded with a hand-over. Against this factual background the Complaints Board stated as follows: "Neither the Works Directive nor the other public procurement directives contain any time limitation as to the duration of contracts for ongoing services, and the directives do not allow any conclusions as to mandatory time limitations on duration. On the contrary, in order to pay respect to the public procurement directives, contracting authorities can only conclude long duration contracts in the field of building and construction if this is warranted by technical/financial aspects of the building and construction work in question." The Complaints Board went on to conclude that the term of the contract complied with EU procurement law, although emphasising that it had been taken into account in its consideration that "[Rønnede Local Authority's] reason for concluding the mentioned contract was based on aspects that could also be invoked by other road management bodies".

In the light of the case law the conclusion is that no rules on the permissible term of a contract can be deduced from the Procurement Directive, but considering the aims of the Procurement Directive, a term of more than three to five years should be justified by economic and/or technical circumstances which are not unique to the contracting authority that has awarded the contract.

It has been suggested that Article 81 EC could apply to this end, as long term public contracts could result in foreclosure effects and thereby restrict

81. Order of the Complaints Board of 5 November 2003, Supervisory Council for the County of Storstrøm vs. Rønnede Local Authority.

competition. However, in *Coname*[82] the European Court of Justice seem to have taken the view that concession contracts is not considered as agreements between undertakings for the purposes of Article 81 EC. Similar arguments could possibly be raised in relation to public contracts.

3. Threshold values

Only large contracts must be put out to tender as the Procurement Directive only applies to contracts whose estimated value, excluding VAT, exceeds certain thresholds. The reason for setting threshold values is that although improved opportunities for tendering for public contracts is essential to competition in the EU's single market, excessive formalities should be avoided. Procurement procedures can be very onerous economically and in terms of administration, to which should be added that presumably foreign undertakings are first and foremost interested in large contracts.

3.1 Significance of the threshold values

If the estimated value, excluding VAT, of a contract is below the threshold set for the particular type of contract, the contract can be concluded without applying the procedures set out in the Procurement Directive. If the value of a contract is below the threshold, the contract will not have to be put out to competition under the Procurement Directive. The contract can be awarded to an economic operator of choice.

However, all contracts, of whatever value, are subject to the rules of the EC Treaty which provide that the principles of non-discrimination, equal treatment and transparency must be complied with.[83] [84]

3.2 Individual thresholds[85]

The thresholds for public contracts are indicated in Article 7 of the Procurement Directive in the following amounts:

---

82. Judgment of the European Court of Justice of 21 July 2005, case C-231/03, Consorzio Aziende Metano (Coname) vs. Comune di Cingia dé Botti, paragraph 12.
83. See chapter 1.5 above.
84. See also Article 2 of the Procurement Directive.
85. The thresholds indicated correspond to Commission Regulation (EC) No 1874/2004 of 28 October 2004 amending Directives 2004/17/EC and 2004/18/EC of the European Parliament and of the Council in respect of their application thresholds for the procedures for the award of contracts.

	Government authorities (Annex IV to the Directive)	Other authorities (municipalities, etc.)
Supply contracts	€ 154,000	€ 236,000
– defence, products covered by Annex V to the Directive	€ 154,000	
– defence, products not covered by Annex V to the Directive[86]	€ 236,000	
Service contracts	€ 154,000	€ 236,000
– special services, B services,[87] R&D services[88] and certain telecommunications services.[89]	€ 236,000	€ 236,000
Works contracts	€ 5,923,000	€ 5,923,000

As mentioned above, the threshold amounts are a compromise between the interests in guaranteeing competition in the internal market and in avoiding imposition of excessive formalities on contracting authority's award of contracts. Moreover, the thresholds have been determined in consideration of the EU's obligations towards the WTO.[90]

3.3 Estimated value of the contract

The estimated value of a contract decides whether the contract meets or exceeds the thresholds. The value of the contract is the total amount, excluding VAT, which the contracting authority is likely to pay under the contract.[91] In this amount should be included taxes, if any, delivery costs, transport costs, etc. The contracting authority must carry out thorough market research to

86. Presumably the products explicitly excluded in Annex V are completely exempted from the rules of the Procurement Directive because of their use in the field of defence, cf. Article 10 of the Procurement Directive and Article 296 of the EC Treaty. The tender obligation under this provision thus applies to a category between the products mentioned in Annex V and products in the field of defence.
87. Services covered by Annex II B to the Procurement Directive.
88. See, however, also Article 16 (f) of the Procurement Directive providing that certain R&D contracts are entirely excluded from the scope of the Procurement Directive, see also section 3.6 below.
89. Certain telecommunication services defined in category 5 of Annex II A to the Procurement Directive whose CPV positions correspond to CPC reference numbers 7524, 7525 7526.
90. Recital 7 of the preamble to the Procurement Directive establishes that "... [the WTO Agreement] does not have direct effect. The contracting authorities covered by the Agreement which comply with this Directive and which apply the latter to economic operators of third countries, which are signatories to the Agreement, should therefore be in conformity with the Agreement."
91. Article 9, paragraph 1 of the Procurement Directive.

procure the information necessary for estimating the value of the contract.[92] Especially where the contracting authority concludes that the value of a contract is less than the applicable threshold, it should be able to substantiate that the estimated value was arrived at on objective and sound grounds and that all relevant aspects were taken into account.

The estimate must be based on the proposed contract, including any options and renewals.[93] It may be appropriate to take account of previous experience with similar contracts, recommended prices and rates, consultants' knowledge, etc. Potential tenderers should only be consulted with caution as such consultations may lead to a violation of the principle of equal treatment. The Procurement Directive provides detailed rules on the calculation of the estimated value of public contracts, etc.[94]

3.4 Time of the estimate

The estimated value of a contract must be valid at the time when the contract notice is sent or when the award procedure is commenced.[95] The estimate has an impact on the entire procurement procedure. If it, in the course of a procedure conducted in accordance with the Procurement Directive, becomes apparent that the value does not, as estimated, exceed the thresholds, this is not sufficient ground for not applying the rules of the Procurement Directive. If, by contrast, the contracting authority estimated the value of a contract to be lower than the applicable threshold on the basis of sufficiently objective information, it has no bearing on the obligation to call for tenders that one or more of the tenders submitted are of a value equal to or greater than the threshold.

3.5 Contracts subsidised by more than 50 %

The Procurement Directive applies to certain contracts which are directly subsidised by more than 50 % by the contracting authorities.[96] For contracts which are subsidised to such an extent that they are subject to the Procurement Directive, the contracting authority must, at the time of granting the

---

92. See order of the Complaints Board of 16 December 2003, Bilhuset Randers A/S and Others vs. Sønderhald Local Authority and order of the Complaints Board of 12 December 1996, Entreprenørforeningens Miljøsektion vs. I/S Sønderborg Kraftvarmeværk, where such thorough research had not been carried out.
93. Article 9 of the Procurement Directive.
94. See sections 3.4 and 3.5 below for further details.
95. Article 9, paragraph 2 of the Procurement Directive.
96. Article 8 of the Procurement Directive.

subsidies, take measures to ensure either that the recipient complies with the Procurement Directive or that the contracting authority is allowed to invite tenders and award the contracts on behalf of the recipient.

The reason for this provision is that, presumably, the amount of the subsidies is reflective of the influence which the contracting authority is able to exercise over the conclusion of such contracts.[97] The provision should also be seen in the light of the definition of public contracts, cf. section 3.2 above, as the grant of subsidies may be a means to bypass the Procurement Directive.

Subsidised contracts are only covered by Article 8 of the Procurement Directive if they are connected to certain types of works:

- civil engineering activities, cf. Annex I of the Procurement Directive. The threshold value is € 5,923,000;
- building work for hospitals, facilities intended for sports, recreation and leisure, school and university buildings and buildings for administrative purposes. The threshold value is € 5,923,000;
- service contracts which are connected to the above-mentioned works contracts. The threshold value is € 154,000.

4. Valuation of contracts

The contracting authority is expected to make a reasoned estimate of the value of a contemplated contract in order to determine whether the value of the contract is likely to exceed the applicable threshold and thus trigger a procurement procedure for the award of the contract.

The estimated value of a proposed contract must be calculated by applying certain methods specified in the Procurement Directive[98] and is thus not a matter of pure discretion.

With a view to assessing whether the thresholds will be exceeded, the estimated value of the contract must be realistic since it is for the contracting authority to prove that the estimate was determined on objective grounds and on the basis of sufficient information. This is particularly important in procedures where it emerges subsequently (for example under a continuing service contract) that the estimate was not in keeping with the facts possibly to the effect that the thresholds were exceeded and the contract should have been put out to tender in accordance with the EU procurement rules.

97. In this respect the provision corresponds to the provisions of the Procurement Directive on bodies governed by public law, cf. chapter 2.2 above.
98. Article 9 of the Procurement Directive.

As a main rule, an incorrect estimate only constitutes a violation of the Procurement Directive if it is not based on objective grounds. As a consequence, it is crucial that the estimate is reached on the basis of sufficient and reliable information.[99]

In *Bilhuset Randers A/S and Others vs. Sønderhald Local Authority*[100] Sønderhald Local Authority had concluded a leasing agreement for 15 cars of the make Peugeot for its home care service without a prior call for tenders. The decision only to obtain seven offers and thus not invite tenders in accordance with the procurement rules was a result of the local authority's investigations into the value of the contract. The estimated value had been calculated on the basis of information obtained from Kommune Leasing which had stated: "The assessment whether a contract for the lease of cars for the home care service is to be put out to tender in accordance with the EU procurement rules must be based on the car most commonly used by the home care services, i.e. a Fiat Punto 1.2." The memo set out calculations showing that the value of the lease of 14 Fiat Punto 1.2 would not exceed the threshold value. To that the Complaints Board made the following statement: "... the contracting authority must make a sound pre-assessment of the value of the acquisition. The pre-assessment must be made on the basis of the general price level of the market and may not be made on the basis of the price of a single make." The Complaints Board also pointed out that the price of all the offers submitted, except one, exceeded the thresholds. Against that background the Complaints Board concluded "... a sound pre-assessment would have shown that the value exceeded the tender obligation threshold. Consequently, ... the contract should have been offered for tender under EU law".

The methods of calculation to be applied for estimating the value of the purchase/contract are explained in detail in the following sections. Considering *inter alia* the diverse value added tax (VAT) rates throughout the EU, VAT should not be included in the calculation of the estimated value of the individual contract.[101]

99. Order of the Complaints Board of 12 December 1996, Entreprenørforeningens Miljøsektion vs. I/S Sønderborg Kraftvarmeværk, in which the Complaints Board emphasised the following: the contract offered by the defendant is of such a scale in terms of quantity and financially that the defendant should have procured a much sounder basis for determining whether or not the contract should have been put out to tender under the procurement rules. The Board finds that the basis on which the defendant omitted to invite tenders for the contract is insufficient in that the contract is subject to Council Directive .... since the threshold values are exceeded.

100. Order of the Complaints Board of 16 December 2003, Bilhuset Randers A/S and Others vs. Sønderhald Local Authority.

101. Article 9, paragraph 1 of the Procurement Directive.

4.1 Subdivision – calculation based on total estimated value of the contract
Article 9, paragraph 1 of the Procurement Directive prescribes the following
main rule for calculating the value of a contract:

"The calculation of the estimated value of a public contract shall be based on the total
amount payable, net of VAT, as estimated by the contracting authority. This calculation
shall take account of the estimated total amount, including any form of option and any
renewals of the contract."

It follows that it is *the total amount* which the contracting authority estimates
that it is likely pay under the public contract which must be taken into account.[102] However, not only the value of the individual contract should be
considered, but rather the combined value of the total purchase (project) as a
whole whether or not it results in the conclusion of one or more contracts,
which is a matter that is not separately provided for in the Procurement Directive. Article 9 of the Procurement Directive is intended as a guarantee that
one or more contracts are valued according to uniform and correct principles
regardless of the exact nature, performance, means of funding and term of the
specific contract.

At the time when the contract is concluded, a number of factors are often
uncertain. These uncertainties may concern the quantities in which each of
the products will be required, how long the performance of the contract will
last, whether it will be expedient to expand the project at a later date (options). The value of such factors can be difficult to estimate, but even so, the
contracting authority is obliged to estimate the value of these uncertain factors and include the estimated values in the final estimate of the total value of
the contract. Also out of regard for the contracting authority's capital budget
and in the interest of keeping within borrowing limits, etc., the total value of
the contract should be estimated at a realistic level, to which end various
methods can be used, for example unit prices.[103]

The calculation of the total value of the contract must be timed to coincide
with the time of the purchase, and the estimated value of the contract must be
valid at the time when the contract notice is sent or, in procedures where a

102. Article 9, paragraph 1, second indent continues: "Where the contracting authority
    provides for prizes or payments to candidates or tenderers it shall take them into
    account when calculating the estimated value of the contract." This is most relevant
    in design contests in which it is common to reward the best projects.
103. In the exceptional cases where pricing is not possible, a contract can be awarded on
    the basis of the negotiated procedure with prior publication of a contract notice, cf.
    Article 30, paragraph 1 (b) of the Procurement Directive.

contract notice is not required, at the time when the award procedure is commenced.[104]

4.2 Lots of a single project or more separate projects

Article 9, paragraph 3 of the Procurement Directive stipulates the following general prohibition on splitting a single purchase (project) into separate lots:

"No works project or proposed purchase of a certain quantity of supplies and/or services may be subdivided to prevents its coming within the scope of this Directive."

The issue addressed in that provision is that a project/purchase cannot be subdivided into separate lots with a view to reducing the value of the individual projects to a level which is below the threshold, thereby avoiding the obligation under the Procurement Directive to invite tenders for the project as a whole. Accordingly, the number of contracts linked to a project is immaterial in this respect.

The prohibition serves to underline the main rule that the pivotal factor is whether the contracts are awarded in the context of one single project and that it is the *total value* of the project as a whole, as estimated by the contracting authority, which is the value to be used for determining whether the thresholds are exceeded.

A contract must always be classified as one[105] of the following: a "public works contract",[106] a "public supply contract"[107] or a "public service contract".[108] Hence, a contract must always be classified as one specific type, irrespective of whether it contains elements of both works, supplies and/or services. This classification is based on the principles set out in Article 1, paragraph 2 for mixed contracts. It thus follows that a contract containing elements of all three types of contracts should only be assessed in the light of one set of rules under the Procurement Directive.

Once the various elements of a contract for works, supplies and/or services as a whole has been classified as a works *contract*, a supply *contract* or a service *contract*, respectively and distinguished from any other proposed contracts, the value of the specific *contract* must be estimated on the basis of the principles set out in the Procurement Directive.

---

104. Article 9, paragraph 2 of the Procurement Directive.
105. Unless it is a concession contract.
106. Article 1, paragraph 2(b) of the Procurement Directive.
107. Article 1, paragraph 2 (c) of the Procurement Directive.
108. Article 1, paragraph 2 (d) of the Procurement Directive.

4.2.1 Principles of the Procurement Directive
for defining lots of a single project

For the purpose of calculating the value of a specific purchase the requirement to consider a project as a whole may necessitate the adding up of the values of different acquisitions/contracts and of the values of acquisitions/contracts which are not executed, delivered, performed or awarded at the same time in so far as these acquisitions/contracts are linked to the same project by virtue of their content or in terms of time.[109]

4.2.1.1 Linked by virtue of content

In the calculation of the estimated value of *works contracts* regard must obviously be had to the value of the works themselves. However, the Procurement Directive specifically prescribes that also the estimated value of the products and equipment necessary for executing the works and placed at the contractor's disposal by the contracting authority must be included in the value of the works contract. This is because this equipment and these products are regarded as remuneration paid by other means than payment of purchase price, and as such are elements of economic value under the contract, regardless that the contracting authority *does not purchase* the products and equipment under the specific works contract.[110]

The principle that the value of supplies required for executing works always has to be included in the calculation, even where the supplies are not purchased at the same time does not necessarily apply to contracts for connected *supplies and services*. But it is beyond doubt that for the purpose of calculating the value of a contract, previous purchases as well as scheduled subsequent purchases, should be given a wide interpretation in functional terms.

The Complaints Board[111] has, for example, established that the purchase of computers with standard software was connected to a subsequent purchase of printers from another supplier (partly) on the ground "... that the printers would be used with the computers".

---

109. .See for example order of the Complaints Board of 16 December 2004, Brunata A/S vs. Aalborg Boligselskab af 1956, branch 8 and Others concerning supply contracts and order of the Complaints Board of 17 June 2005, Gladsaxe Local Authority vs. Den selvejende institution Hareskovbo og Ældreboliginstitutionen Hareskovbo II concerning service contracts.
110. Article 9, paragraph 4 of the Procurement Directive.
111. Order of the Complaints Board of 29 September 2003, Unicomputer A/S vs. Greve Local Authority. The Complaints Board based its order *inter alia* on the fact that

4.2.1.2 Time link

If a specific work is divided into separate lots (typically specialist subcontracts) *and* the contracts for these lots are awarded at the same time, the value of all these contracts must be added up to determine whether the threshold for works contracts has been exceeded. If so, each of the contracts connected to the specific work must be put out to tender in accordance with the EU procurement rules, regardless that the value of the individual contract does not exceed the threshold for works contracts.[112]

The same principle applies where a proposed service contract or a contract for similar supplies is awarded in separate lots *at the same time.*[113]

The requirement that the lots be awarded at the same time should probably be interpreted bearing in mind whether the lots are linked by virtue of their content. Accordingly, the construction of a hospital, for example, which as a whole is classified as a works contract and is divided into separate lots (specialist subcontracts) which are not awarded at the same time, but instead concurrently with the progress of the construction, is unlikely not to be regarded as one single project for the purpose of calculating the threshold of the public works contract regardless that the project is divided into separate lots which, in the narrow sense, are not awarded at the same time.[114] See the next section on the definition of one project as opposed to several separate projects.

4.2.2 Factors in delimiting a single project

The term "project" is not defined in the Procurement Directive. With respect to a specific purchase the term project is used in the Procurement Directive to denote a single separate purchase which may consist in works, supplies or services or a mix thereof.

It is the total value of the defined project which is relevant with respect to the thresholds set out in the Procurement Directive. It can be difficult to delimit a project correctly, but certain guiding principles can be deduced from

the printers in issue were paid for, at least in part, by funds from the same pool which Greve Local Authority had earmarked for the acquisition of the printers. The logic of this reasoning is not clear since the authority is free to use its funds as it chooses.

112. Article 9, paragraph 5 (a), first indent of the Procurement Directive.
113. Article 9, paragraph 5 (a), first indent and (b), first indent of the Procurement Directive.
114. Order of the Complaints Board of 17 June 2005, Gladsaxe Local Authority vs. Den selvejende institution Hareskovbo og Ældreboliginstitutionen Hareskovbo II, concerned a similar situation.

case law from the European Court of Justice[115] for assessing whether a series of contracts are lots of a single project.

Factors such as the character or properties (works, supplies or services) of a product, duration in terms of time, geographical reach, the number of contracting authorities and economic operators[116] and same contracting parties all contribute to determining whether contracts are lots of a single project.

In *Commission vs. France*[117] the European Court of Justice was to decide whether France, in contravention of the Directive, had split certain electrification and street lighting works organised *at the same time,* by dividing the works both on a technical basis (separate contracts for electrification and street lighting) and a geographical basis (separate contracts for each joint municipal grouping). At the outset, the European Court of Justice established the following main rule to be applied in the assessment of whether contracts are lots of a single project or several separate projects:[118] "... the question whether there is a work must be assessed in the light of the economic and technical function fulfilled by the electricity supply and street lighting networks in question". Next, the European Court of Justice found that electricity supply and street lighting networks did not fulfil the same economic and technical function on the following grounds:[119] "An electricity supply network is intended, from a technical point of view, to transport the electricity produced by a supplier to individual end consumers; in terms of economics, they must pay the supplier for what they consume." ... "However, a street lighting network is intended, from a technical point of view, to light public places using the electricity provided by the electricity supply network. The authority providing the street lighting assumes the cost itself, but subsequently recovers the amounts spent from the population served, without adjusting the sums demanded according to the benefit derived by the individuals concerned." Against that background the European Court of Justice established that "Accordingly, works on the electricity supply and street lighting networks cannot be considered to constitute lots of a single work artificially split contrary to ... the Directive".[120] Then the European Court of Justice assessed whether each of the two separate works had been artificially split on a geographical basis. In regard to the *electrification works*[121] the European Court of Justice found that France, in contravention of the Directive, had split the works on the basis that electricity supply networks "... taken as a whole, they fulfil one economic and technical function, which consists in the supply and sale to consumers in the *département* of Vendée of electricity produced and supplied by Électricité de France" and on the circumstantial evidence "... that the invitations for tenders for the contested contracts were made at the same time,

---

115. Judgment of the European Court of Justice of 5 October 2000, case C-16/98, Commission vs. France.
116. Ibid, paragraph 42.
117. Judgment of the European Court of Justice of 5 October 2000, case C-16/98, Commission vs. France.
118. Ibid, paragraph 38.
119. Ibid, paragraphs 52-53.
120. Ibid, paragraph 56.
121. Ibid, paragraphs 64-66.

the similarities between the contract notices and the fact that Sydev, the body comprising the joint municipal groupings responsible for electrification within the *département*, initiated and coordinated the contracts within a single geographical area". In regard to the *street lighting works*[122] the European Court of Justice reached the opposite conclusion citing the following: "... unlike electricity supply networks, street lighting networks are, from a technical point of view, not necessarily interdependent, as they can be restricted to built-up areas and no interconnection between them is necessary. Similarly, it is possible, in economic terms, for each of the local entities concerned to assume the financial burden arising from the operation of such a network."

Also the Complaints Board has ruled on this at times difficult question. From the decided cases it can be deduced that the Complaints Board emphasises the following factors in deciding whether contracts are lots of a single project

In *Danish Chamber of Commerce vs. Frederiksberg Local Authority*[123] the Authority had purchased various *supplies* (aids to relieve elderly people's physical pain) without a call for tenders under the EU procurement rules. These aids included five different types of products: (1) breast prostheses, (2) compression stockings, (3) insoles, (4) corsets, etc. and (5) arm and leg prostheses. For each of these products a separate contract had been awarded, none of which was of a value which exceeded the threshold values, but the total value of these contracts was clearly in excess of the threshold values. The Complaints Board found that the products were *similar supplies* having the effect that it was the total value of all the contracts that should be the basis for determining whether the value exceeded the thresholds. The Complaints Board's reasoning was "... [that] the contract documents for all the contracts had been forwarded together, that several suppliers are capable of supplying all the products in question and that other suppliers are capable of supplying most of the products". In *Crocus I/S vs. Århus Port Authority*[124] the Authority had purchased a *work* (conversion of the port's coal terminal into a bulk terminal, i.e. a terminal for feedstuffs, etc.) without a call for tenders under the EU procurement rules. The works included (1) a connection from the conveying system to a warehouse outside the terminal area, (2) environmental improvement measures to the functioning of certain conveying systems in existing buildings, (3) construction of a weighing device in existing buildings, (4) construction of a new storage hall, and (5) construction of a screening plant in an existing building. For each of these works a separate contract had been awarded, none of which was of a value which exceeded the threshold values, but the total value of the contracts was in excess of the threshold values. The Complaints Board held that "the project comprised different building and construction works which had been offered at more or less the same time as a part of an overall project with a joint purpose. The works in question were thus to be considered as a whole ... Since the budgeted cost for the

122. Ibid, paragraphs 67-71.
123. Order of the Complaints Board of 23 June 1995, Danish Chamber of Commerce vs. Frederiksberg Local Authority.
124. Order of the Complaints Board of 23 April 1997, Crocus I/S vs. Århus Port Authority.

works had certainly exceeded the threshold value of the directive for building and construction works, the port authority was obliged to offer the contract for tender on a Community basis." In *L.R. Service ApS vs. Sorø Local Authority*[125] the Authority had purchased several *services* (cleaning of local institutions) without a prior call for tenders. These services comprised (1) cleaning of a local school and (2) cleaning of the town hall. For each of these services a separate contract had been awarded. While the value of the contract for the cleaning of the local school exceeded the threshold values, the value of the contract concerning the town hall was below the thresholds. Obviously the total value of the contracts exceeded the thresholds. The Complaints Board held that the value of the two contracts should *not* be added up since "... the assignment in question concerned a specific performance based on the individual requirements for cleaning at the town hall and ... the Board had not ascertained any attempt at bypassing tender legislation". Further, the Complaints Board held that "... in this case [there is] no obligation to add up the financial value of the municipality's total cleaning requirements ...". In *L.R. Service ApS vs. Bramsnæs Local Authority*[126] the Authority had purchased several *services* (cleaning of local day care centres) without a prior call for tenders. These services comprised cleaning of one local day care centre which employed its own cleaning personnel. For each of these services a separate contract had been awarded, none of which was of a value which exceeded the thresholds, but the total value of the contracts possibly did. The Complaints Board held that "... Community tender legislation, including Article 7, paragraph 4, second last paragraph of the Services Directive, does not have the purpose of having a contracting authority add up the value of its acquired performances of the same nature, including all its cleaning agreements, regardless of the circumstances. Therefore, the EU procurement rules cannot be used to establish a principle subject to which all cleaning contracts awarded by a local authority always must be added up. This interpretation can also be deduced from the wording of Article 7, paragraph 4, second last paragraph of the Services Directive providing that (only) the values of those lots in which a service is "split" should be added up. There is no indication in this case that in its administration of the cleaning work at the day care centres in question the municipality has sought to bypass Community tender legislation." With this decision the Complaints Board introduced a more subjective standard of assessment by finding it decisive that the Authority had not sought to bypass the procurement rules. See also cases L.R. Service ApS vs. Ramsø Local Authority[127] and L.R. Service ApS vs. Ringsted Local Authority for similar decisions.[128] In *Holsted Minibus vs. Næstved Local Authority*[129] the Authority had purchased several *services* (*inter alia* transport of disabled people) following a call for tenders. These services comprised transport of

---

125. Order of the Complaints Board of 21 January 1999, L.R. Service ApS vs. Sorø Local Authority.
126. Order of the Complaints Board of 28 May 1999, L.R. Service ApS vs. Bramsnæs Local Authority.
127. Order of the Complaints Board of 28 May 1999, L.R. Service ApS vs. Ramsø Local Authority.
128. Order of the Complaints Board of 28 May 1999, L.R. Service ApS vs. Ringsted Local Authority.
129. Order of the Complains Board of 21 March 2002, Holsted Minibus rep. by taxicab owner Keld T. Hansen vs. Næstved Local Authority.

disabled pupils to specific education centres along six different pre-defined routes. None of the individual routes (services) was of a value that exceeded the thresholds, but the total value of the services did. The routes were offered for tender at the same time and contracts were awarded to four taxicab owners. The taxicab owner who had been awarded the contract for route no. 6 terminated the contract at the expiry of the trial period. The contract for route no. 6 was then put out to tender among the eight original tenderers for this route and (re)awarded to the same taxicab owner on new terms. The Complaints Board held that the six routes were lots of one single service for which tenders should be invited in accordance with the EU procurement rules – as they had been. The new contract for route no. 6, on the other hand, should not be a added up with the other five routes for which contracts already had been awarded, which meant this contract should not be put out to tender under the EU procurement rules since its value did not exceed the threshold. In *Unicomputer A/S vs. Greve Local Authority*[130] the Authority had purchased several *supplies* (computers with software and printers) without a prior call for tenders under the EU procurement rules. Among these supplies were 283 computers with standard software of a value which exceeded the threshold and a subsequent contract for 28 printers of a value which did not separately exceed the threshold. The total value of the two contracts obviously exceeded the threshold. The contract for the purchase of the 283 computers with standard software was awarded on the basis of a framework agreement concluded between National Procurement Ltd. – Denmark and Jmdata Consult A/S following a procurement procedure conducted by National Procurement, for which reason Greve Local Authority in accordance with the Procurement Directive could award this supply contract without a prior call for tenders under the EU procurement rules. However, the Complaints Board found that the value of this contract should be added to the value of the contract for the purchase of the 28 printers awarded to WidCad ApS citing the following: "... the time when the printers were purchased was very close to the time when the computers were purchased, and that, at least to some extent, the funds came from the same pool, and that the printers would be used with the computers". Against that background the Complaints Board found that regardless that the value of the contract was nowhere near the threshold value, the contract for the 28 printers should have been put out to tender under the EU procurement rules because the value thereof should be added to the value of the contract for the computers despite the fact that this contract was not covered by the Procurement Directive by virtue of National Procurement Ltd. – Denmark's status as a central purchasing body. In *Gladsaxe Local Authority vs. Den selvejende institution Hareskovbo*[131] Havreskovbo had concluded a service contract with THORA Arkitekter A/S for technical consultancy and advice in the form of total consulting services in connection with the renovation of its buildings in stage 2. The renovation was divided into stages. It was common ground that stage 1 was a separate project. Stage 2 (for which the consulting services agreement had been concluded with THORA Arkitekter A/S) was by the Complaints Board seen as a lot of a bigger project comprising stages 2-5. The Complaints Board based this conclusion on several factors: "... the services in stages 2-5 are of a similar nature and can be provided

---

130. Order of the Complaints Board of 29 September 2003, Unicomputer A/S vs. Greve Local Authority.
131. . Order of the Complaints Board of 17 June 2005, Gladsaxe Local Authority vs. Den selvejende institution Hareskovbo og Ældreboliginstitutionen Hareskovbo II.

by the same service provider". ... "Further, the Complaints Board has placed emphasis on the fact that the aim of the renovation in all of stages 2-5 is to provide Havreskovbo with a modern lay-out ..." For the purpose of calculating the threshold value the fact that the service contracts were scheduled to be awarded at different times cannot be interpreted to mean that they were contracts for separate services. The splitting of the renovation into stages was merely done for practical reasons, in particular the wish to keep the number of housing units unchanged throughout the modernisation. Furthermore, each stage was to be commenced immediately after the completion of the previous stage." Against that background the Complaints Board established "... that in terms of time and by virtue of the content, the link between stages 2-5 is such that they are one single project with the effect that has on the calculation of the threshold value. Since it was undisputed that the value of the service contracts for stages 2-5 exceeded the applicable threshold value stipulated in [the Procurement Directive] for 2004, the defendants were obliged to invite tenders for the service contract for stage 2 in accordance with the EU procurement rules.

It is evident from the decided cases that the Complaints Board repeatedly has held that a series of works contracts, respectively supply contracts were lots a single project/purchase, whereas the Complaints Board in only one case has found that a series of service contracts were lots of a single project/purchase which perhaps suggests a more lenient application of the rules in that area.

Further, the Complaints Board has found that by separating into several small units that remain within the same legal person a contracting authority can bring itself outside the scope of the Procurement Directive with the effects that has in procurement law.[132] By in that way splitting identical contracts into several lots which are concluded at the same time by the smaller units and which should otherwise have been added up in order to estimate whether the thresholds were exceeded, the value of identical purchases need not be aggregated.[133]

In *Lyngby-Taarbæk Local Authority vs. Den selvejende almene boligorganisation Carlshøj*[134] various departments within the housing association Carlshøj had purchased a number of *services* (property management services) without a prior call for tenders under the EU procurement rules. These services covered *inter alia* (1) the management of the hous-

---

132. For the more detailed conditions, see chapter 2.3.2 above and Commission Guidelines of 20 January 1993, entitled: "Policy Guidelines on Contracts awarded by Separate Units of a Contracting Entity under Directive 90/531/EEC ('Utilities')", document CC/92/87.
133. See also *inter alia* order of the Complaints Board of 28 May 1999, cases L.R. Service ApS vs. Bramsnæs Local Authority, Ramsø Local Authority and Ringsted Local Authority.
134. Order of the Complaints Board of 17 July 2002, Lyngby-Taarbæk Local Authority vs. Den selvejende almene boligorganisation Carlshøj.

ing association, (2) the administration of a common waiting list and (3) the administration of the common heating account. Each of the departments had under separate contracts purchased the management services and none of the contracts was of value that exceeded the thresholds, but the total value of the contracts did. At the outset, the Complaints Board established that in the assessment of whether the value of the service exceeds the threshold it is "Basically, … only the value of the service assignment to be contracted that is decisive". Next, the Complaints Board found that the value of the individual management services should not be added up since "The four departments of [the housing association] - Departments A, Departments B, Departments C and the heating station – have independent accounts and apart from the heating station independent boards. The service for which [the housing association] has concluded a contract only concerns one of the four departments – Departments B – and it is only that department that will pay for the service. Finally, it is only the board of Departments B that decides to whom the contract is awarded." With respect to the administration of the waiting list the Complaints Board found that "The administration of the waiting list is such that it is a separate service which is not necessarily connected in functional terms to the management of the Departments."[135]

4.2.3 Lots

Although the total value of a specific project exceeds the applicable threshold, certain lots can nevertheless be awarded to economic operators without a prior call for tenders provided that the other contracts linked to the project are put out to competition in accordance with the EU procurement rules.

The Procurement Directive contains provisions providing that certain *lots* do not have to be put out to tender thereby granting contracting authorities a certain measure of freedom to contract with economic operators without a prior call for tender under the EU procurement rules. The value of the lots must be included in the calculation of the total price of the purchase; hence, the provision cannot be used to reduce the total purchase price to the effect that it has a bearing on whether or not the thresholds are met.

The conditions subject to which lots can be awarded without a prior call for tenders depend on whether the contract is for works, supplies or services. Contracting authorities can disregard the procedures of the Procurement Directive for the award of lots of a value which is less than the following cumulative thresholds:

for works:
- € 1 million and not more than 20% of the aggregate value of the lots as a whole;[136] for supplies and services:
- €80,000 and not more than 20% of the aggregate value of the lots as a whole.[137]

135. See also order of the Complaints Board of 25 November 2002, Skousen Husholdningsmaskiner A/S vs. Arbejdernes Andels Boligforening.
136. Article 9, paragraph 5 (a), second indent of the Procurement Directive.

Interesting in this context is whether the high threshold of € 1 million applicable to works contracts only applies to the *works* regardless whether they are lots of a public works contract, supply contract or service contract, or whether the threshold applies to works as well as supplies and services which as a whole are capable of classification as a public works contract in accordance with the principles set out in the Procurement Directive.

The latter construction is probably the one which is most coherent with the Procurement Directive. For the purpose of calculating threshold values, etc., the Procurement Directive as well as the previous, now repealed directives apply the fundamental principle that works, supply and service contracts which, in accordance with the principles set out in the Procurement Directive and established by case law, are lots of a single project, as a whole must be classified as either a public works contract, a public supply contract or a public service contract by virtue of Article 1, paragraph 2 of the Procurement Directive. Therefore, considering that a contract as a whole is always classified as one of three possible types of contracts, it would be odd if the value and mix of the individual elements of the contract were to be assessed separately in order to determine which lots qualify for exemption. Accordingly, it seems to be best in line with the principles of the Procurement Directive that works as well as supplies and services can be exempted as a whole under the rules of the Procurement Directive in so far as the value thereof is below the threshold set for the particular type of contract.

In practice this question usually arises in connection with public works contracts which are put out to tender as turnkey contracts (covering both design and execution), but in respect of which the contracting authority wishes to exempt lots for certain services (such as architectural, engineering or building consultancy services) from the obligation to invite tenders. In these situations the question is whether the applicable threshold for these lots is € 80,000 or € 1 million. According to the above, the applicable threshold would be € 1 million.

Where *all* the services linked to the works contract are awarded in lots without a call for tenders and the value of *all* the design services is below the threshold of € 1 million, the contracting authority may be alleged to have, in reality, included under the public works contract "... execution of works related to one of the activities within the meaning of Annex I ..." without the intention to include the design work under the contract. In that case it is possible that the fact that *all* the (design) service contracts have been awarded in lots without a call for tenders will be considered a circumvention of the Procurement Directive with the effect that these (design) services are to be considered as a separate service contract to which the thresholds applicable to service contracts apply and possibly also the lower thresholds that apply to service contracts awarded in lots.

137. Article 9, paragraph 5 (b), second indent of the Procurement Directive.

4.3 Additional supplies and contracts

Under a continuing contract it quite often becomes necessary to purchase additional products or prolong the term of the contract. This brings to the fore the question of the right to amend/extend the contract without a call for tenders under the EU procurement rules and the question of the value of such amendments to/extensions of the contract. Article 9, paragraph 1 of the Procurement Directive reads as follows (our emphasis):

"The calculation of the estimated value of a public contract shall be based on the total amount payable, net of VAT, as estimated by the contracting authority. This calculation shall take account of the estimated total amount, including *any form of option and any renewals of the contract.*"

It follows that already when the contracting authority values the original contract, it must largely be able to predict how the project will develop. The provision also prescribes a cautious estimate by stipulating that the value of "any renewals" should be included. This wording indicates that to be on the safe side the contracting authority should base its estimate on a worst-case scenario.

4.3.1 Anticipated supplies and contracts, including options.

Where the contracting authority anticipates, already when determining the scope of the contract, that the contract may develop into a larger order subsequently, the contracting authority should describe this in the contract documents, for example by providing for options for renewals of or additions to the original contract. The contracting authority should not shy away from the use of options seeing that they are "free" in the sense that it is for the contracting authority to decide whether or not to exercise them.

The benefit of extensive use of options/reservations for and descriptions of possible renewals is that these subsequent additions will not be subject to separate calls for tenders. The contracting authority is free to conclude these contracts with the economic operator that was awarded the original contract, but not with other economic operators, even where the value, taken in isolation, exceeds the original threshold due to the fact that these additional contracts already were put out to competition in the original procedure.

The backdrop, however, is that the value of the options must be included in the estimated value of the (main) contract whether or not they are exercised by the contracting authority.

It is crucial that the additions to/renewals of the original contract were provided for in the original competition for the contract, so that potential candidates/tenderers had the opportunity to take that into account in their tenders.[138] As a consequence, a mere reference in the contract to a right to "renegotiate" or similar does not suffice.[139]

In *L.R. Service ApS vs. Skovbo Local Authority*[140] the Authority had awarded an original cleaning contract for the cleaning of various local premises and institutions to ISS. The contract expired in 1997. The contract could be renewed, but did not specify the exact extent, quality, price etc. to be offered under a renewed contract. The Complaints Board held that it was a new contract, and not an anticipated renewal of the original contract, with the effect that it had to be put out to tender under the EU procurement rules because the value of the new contract exceeded the thresholds.

It follows from the above decision that an option for renewal of a contract must be specified in the contract in terms of scope (content and time) and price (possibly merely as a percentage increase or similar) as (neither) options for additions or renewals can be negotiated freely.

4.3.2 Unforeseen supplies and contracts

In the interest of eliminating the risk of circumvention of the rules, contracts for additional services and supplies can only be awarded while keeping within very narrow limits. If the award of contracts for additional services or supplies were without restrictions, the obligations of the Procurement Directive could be circumvented by limiting the value of the original contract to an amount just below the threshold and then successively increase the value of the contract with contracts for additional services concurrently with the progress of the project.

In *L.R. Service ApS vs. Ringsted Local Authority*[141] the Authority had awarded an open-ended cleaning contract for the cleaning of various local institutions to ISS. The contract predated the coming into force of the Service Directive in Denmark. At some point during the term of the contract, and after the coming into force of the Service Directive, the Authority opened a new institution and the cleaning of this institution was added to the existing contract with ISS. The value of this addition to the contract did not exceed the threshold, but the total value of the contract with ISS did. The Complaints Board stated that in

138. In the case that the original contract was awarded on the basis of a procurement procedure under EU law.
139. As to the possibility for awarding a contract for repetitive works or services to the original contracting party without a new call for tenders see Article 31, paragraph 4 (b) of the Procurement Directive.
140. Order of the Complaints Board of 8 June 1998, L.R. Service ApS vs. Skovbo Local Authority.
141. Order of the Complaints Board of 28 May 1999, L.R. Service ApS vs. Ringsted Local Authority.

special circumstances such an addition need not be put out to tender under the EU procurement rules. The special circumstances that the Complaints Board relied upon were that
"Where a public authority has awarded a cleaning contract to a cleaning company following a call for tenders, it often happens that the authority's cleaning requirements change
during the term of the contract, for example because of an increase in the area to be
cleaned following the opening of a new institution. In such cases the authority cannot be
subject to an absolute obligation to invite tenders for the cleaning of the new institution. If
the value of the cleaning is far below the threshold value stipulated in the Service Directive
and only represents a relatively modest share of the value of the overall cleaning carried
out by the cleaning company, it seems reasonable that the cleaning company undertakes
the cleaning of the new institution against a proportional increase in the remuneration due
to it to the effect that the cleaning of the new institution will be covered under the contract
that will be put out to tender when the existing contract expires."

This decision shows that there is some limited scope, which is not authorised
by the Directive, for adding new and unforeseen services to a continuing
contract provided that the value of these services does not separately exceed
the threshold; the value of these services is modest relative to the total value
of the contract; and provided that the addition is not subject to actual negotiations, but is implemented on the same terms that apply to the original service
provided under the contract, which is merely amended to reflect a proportional increase in the remuneration.

However, the Procurement Directive does provide that certain additional
supplies, works or services which become necessary during the term of the
contract because of unforeseen events can be exempted from a call for tenders. Pursuant to these provisions a contract can be awarded on the basis of
the negotiated procedure without prior publication of a contract notice,[142]
provided that the contract for the additional supplies, services or works is
concluded with the original supplier or contractor and on the below conditions applicable to works and services and supplies, respectively.

For works and services:
– when such additional works or services cannot be technically or economically separated from the original contract without major inconvenience to the contracting authorities; or
– when such works or services, although separable from the performance of the original
  contract, are strictly necessary for its completion;[143]
– provided that the aggregate value of the contract awarded for additional works or services does not exceed 50% of the amount of the original contract.

142. For more details about this "procedure" see chapter 5.2.5.
143. Article 31, paragraph 4 (a) of the Procurement Directive.

For supplies:
- when such additional deliveries are intended as either a partial replacement of normal supplies or installations or as the extension of existing supplies or installations; or
- where a change of supplier would oblige the contracting authority to acquire material having different technical characteristics which would result in incompatibility or disproportionate technical difficulties in operation and maintenance;
- provided that the length of such additions or extensions does not exceed three years.

In the light of the above conditions it is clear that the possibilities for making unforeseen purchases under an existing contract without a call for tender are limited in number and scope under the Procurement Directive.

4.3.3 Contracting authorities' possibilities for joining existing contracts

A contracting authority can*not* join a contract already concluded between another contracting authority and an economic operator for a specific purchase without a prior call for tenders whether or not the value of the purchase contemplated by the new contracting authority separately exceeds the threshold. This is because a change of the parties to a contract is considered an amendment of the original contract of such an essential nature that it is in reality a new contract which may be subject to a call for tenders. This is not the case where the original contracting authority satisfies the conditions of a central purchasing body in the context of the specific contract.[144]

4.3.4 Contracting authorities' possibilities for replacing the economic operator

The predominant main rule is that the economic operator, which has been awarded a public contract on the basis of a procurement procedure, can only be replaced following a new procurement procedure conducted in accordance with the Procurement Directive.

Nevertheless, unforeseen situations may arise, for example where the economic operator suspends payments or is declared bankrupt by order of a court and, as a consequence, discontinues its supplies to the contracting authority without notice.

In such a situation the contracting authority can buy in without calling for tenders in the period (corresponding to a normal tender procedure period) until a new contract has been awarded to another economic operator on the basis of a new call for tenders.

---

144. For more details on central purchasing bodies see chapter 2.5 above.

Alternatively, the contracting authority can transfer the rights and obligations under the (breached) contract to a third party (another economic operator) without a prior call for tenders provided that the following conditions are satisfied:

1. the terms of the contract remain unchanged;
2. the situation has emerged due to extraordinary events beyond the control of the contracting authority (bankruptcy) making the change inevitable;
3. the situation arose through no fault of the contracting authority, for example by not having evaluated the tenderers' economic and financial standingwith the necessary care when selecting the original economic operators; and
4. it is not a case of circumvention; the original contract was not awarded with the intention of transferring it subsequently without a call for tenders.

5. Valuation of special types of contracts

In normal circumstances a public contract consists in the delivery of a performance (works, supply or service) to a contracting authority which in return pays a pecuniary remuneration. The consideration is mutual; the contracting authority takes over all rights to the works, supply or service and the remuneration is in the nature of payment of a price.

There are, however, many types of contracts which depart from this classic example for which reason the Procurement Directive prescribes various rules for calculating the value of a contract

- where the seller retains ownership of the works, supply or service (lease agreements);
- where a series of supply or services contracts having the same object are awarded (successive contracts);
- where the quantity is not determined in advance; and
- where the value is calculated otherwise than by indicating a price or the price is not indicated in advance.

5.1 Contracts relating to the leasing, hire, rental or hire purchase of **products**[145]

The Procurement Directive sets out special rules for calculating the value of contracts relating to the leasing of products, i.e. contracts subject to which the economic operator retains ownership of the object of the contract (the prod-

---

145. Article 9, paragraph 6 of the Procurement Directive.

uct). The Procurement Directive does not set out special rules for calculating the value of contracts relating to the rental or hire of *works or services* because such contracts are not usually concluded in practice or they are excluded from the scope of the Procurement Directive.[146]

Whether these contracts include an option to buy the product does not affect the applicability of the special rules for calculating their value.[147]

In Commission vs. Italy[148] the European Court of Justice decided on the definition of an alleged concession vis-à-vis a mixed supply and service contract granted for the lottery computerisation system of the Italian Republic. The Italian Republic had granted the contract to the consortium Lottomatica without a prior call for tenders on the grounds that the contract was a concession which was not subject to the procurement directives. The European Court of Justice examined the contract and pointed out that the implementation of the computerisation system did not involve any transfer of responsibility to the consortium Lottomatica for the various activities inherent in the lottery for which reason it was a public contract which was subject to the procurement directives. With respect to contracts for certain supplies the European Court of Justice stated:[149] "Contrary to the position of the Italian Government, it is irrelevant in that connection that the system in question does not become the property of the administration until the end of the contractual relationship with the successful tenderer and that the 'price', for that supply takes the form of an annual payment in proportion to the revenue. As the Advocate General rightly stated in point 40 of his Opinion, the fact that Article 2 of Directive 88/295 extended the scope of the Directive to 'contracts ... involving the purchase, lease, rental or hire purchase, with or without option to buy, of products' is a reflection of the Community legislature's wish to bring within the scope of the Directive the supply of products which do not necessarily become the property of the public administration and for which the consideration is fixed in abstract terms."

For the purpose of calculating the value of a leasing contract, the Procurement Directive makes a distinction between fixed term leasing contracts and leasing contracts *without* a fixed term.

With regard to fixed term leasing contracts of a term of less than or equal to 12 months, the value of the contract is deemed to be the estimated aggregate value of the individual deliveries to be made during the term of the con-

---

146. Please note that recital 24 of the preamble to the Procurement Directive reads as follows: "In the context of services, contracts for the acquisition or rental of immovable property or rights to such property have particular characteristics which make the application of public procurement rules inappropriate." See also note 4 to Annex II A to the Procurement Directive.
147. Article 9, paragraph 6 of the Procurement Directive.
148. Judgment of the European Court of Justice of 26 April 1994, case C-272/91, Commission vs. Italy.
149. Ibid, paragraphs 24-25.

tract. If the term of the contract is greater than 12 months, the method for calculating the value of the contract is the same, but any estimated residual value of the object of the contract must be added to that amount.[150]

With regard to leasing contracts of supplies *without* a fixed term or the term of which cannot be defined, the value of the contract is deemed to be the estimated monthly value multiplied by 48 whether or not the term of the contract is expected to be greater than four years.[151]

5.2 Successive supply or service contracts

Contracts of a short term can be awarded to fulfil a contracting authority's recurring requirements for supplies of *products* or performance of *services*.

The key element of this provision is that the contracts "are regular in nature" or "intended to be renewed within a given period". For the assessment of whether several contracts form one single separate purchase to the effect that the value of the individual contracts must be added up, regard must be had to whether the contracts are intended to meet the same requirement or fulfil the same function with the contracting authority.[152]

If several contracts are considered to be "successive", it has no bearing on that assessment that the contracts are awarded to different economic operators. If the aggregate value of the contracts equals or exceeds the threshold value of the Procurement Directive, each of these contracts must be put out to tender.

Provided that the contracting authority does not seek to bypass the rules of the Procurement Directive on the calculation of the value of a contract and any consequent obligation to invite tenders for the contracts, it is ultimately the decision of the contracting authority whether short-term or long-term contracts with one or more economic operators are most appropriate bearing in mind its commercial and administrative considerations and choices.[153]

The value of each of these short-term contracts must be added to the value of contracts *of the same type* awarded by the contracting authority during either the preceding 12 months or the most recent financial year for which accounts have been closed, adjusted for expected changes in quantity or value. Alterna-

---

150. Article 9, paragraph 6 (a) of the Procurement Directive.
151. Article 9, paragraph 6 (b) of the Procurement Directive.
152. For more details see section 4.2 on the assessment of whether the contracts are lots of a single project or more separate projects and Article 9, paragraph 5 (b), first indent of the Procurement Directive on the award of contracts for similar supplies in lots.
153. To the contracting authority *framework agreement* may be an alternative to successive contracts.

tively, the contracting authority can base the value on the total value of the successive contracts that it contemplates awarding during the coming 12 months or during the term of the contract if that is greater than 12 months.[154]

The contracting authority is free to choose either the backward-looking or the forward-looking method as long as the method is not chosen with the intention of excluding the contract from the scope of the Procurement Directive and thereby avoid the obligation to invite tenders in accordance with the EU procurement rules.[155]

The provision on the calculation of the value of successive contracts extends to contracts *"of the same type"* which presumably means that the supplies of products or the performance of services provided under the contract must be of the same category.[156] Also, concluded contracts must, presumably, be of the same type.

5.3 Framework agreements and dynamic purchasing systems[157]

A framework agreement is an agreement which entitles – but does not oblige[158] – the contracting authority to enter into a number of contracts without calling for tenders under the EU procurement rules. The European Court of Justice[159] refers to a framework agreement in the following manner:

"… framework agreement turns into a whole the various contracts which it governs …"

The advantage of concluding a framework agreement is that the contracting authority for a term of four years[160] has a contract with an economic operator concerning the economic operator's execution of specific works or provision of specific supplies or services which does not oblige the contracting author-

---

154. Article 9, paragraph 7 (a) and (b) of the Procurement Directive.
155. Article 9, paragraph 7, last indent of the Procurement Directive.
156. See for example Annex II of the Procurement Directive listing A and B services and categories thereof.
157. See chapter 5.5.1.
158. However, the contracting authority can indicate, in the framework agreement, that it undertakes to meet all its requirements for the relevant product (works, supplies, services) from the economic operator(s) with which the framework agreement is concluded, but in the absence of such an indication the contracting authority is free to purchase products covered under the framework agreement from a third party. However, in so far as the contract exceeds the threshold values, it must be awarded through one of the procedures set out in the Procurement Directive.
159. Judgment of the European Court of Justice of 4 May 1995, case C-79/94, Commission vs. Greece, paragraph 15.
160. Article 32, paragraph 2, in fine of the Procurement Directive.

ity to quantify, in advance, the purchases envisaged under the framework agreement, whereas, depending on the terms of the contract, the economic operator is liable to perform specific orders made under the framework agreement.[161]

Regardless of the value of the individual order placed under a framework agreement, it does not have to be put out to tender under the EU procurement rules, provided that it can be comprised under the framework agreement. However, where parallel framework agreements have been concluded with more economic operators regarding the same products, tenders must be invited from these economic operators, where the framework agreement do not establish all the terms of the concrete contract. For more details see Article 32 of the Procurement Directive.

Dynamic purchasing systems are entirely electronic purchasing processes for standardised products (works, supplies and services) generally available in the market. Any economic operator which satisfies the selection criteria and has submitted an indicative tender which complies with the contract documents must be admitted to the system. Under normal circumstances a system cannot last for more than four years.[162]

It is characteristic of both framework agreements and dynamic purchasing systems that the total value of contracts to be concluded under the agreement or the system is not known in advance, which makes it difficult to calculate the estimated value of the agreement/system objectively in accordance with the rules of the Procurement Directive. The Procurement Directive only sets out these guidelines for the contracting authority's estimate:

"With regard to framework agreements and dynamic purchasing systems, the value to be taken into consideration shall be the maximum estimated value net of VAT of all the contracts envisaged for the total term of the framework agreement or the dynamic purchasing system."[163]

It follows that the maximum value for the entire term of the framework agreement or purchasing system, which term must be advertised and limited in time, must be calculated. In accordance with the main principle, options for

---

161. Contracts which contain terms that are substantial amendments to the terms of the framework agreement cannot be concluded under a framework agreement, cf. Article 9, paragraph 2, third indent of the Procurement Directive and the principles set out in order of the Complaints Board of 2 July 1998, Danish Association of Consulting Engineers vs. Københavns Lufthavne A/S.
162. Article 33 of the Procurement Directive.
163. Article 9, paragraph 9 of the Procurement Directive.

renewals of the agreement/system must be taken into account in the calculation.[164]

5.4 *Service* contracts for special or non-specified remuneration

Like contracts relating to the leasing, hire, rental or hire purchase of products, *service* contracts are of a continuing nature for which the remuneration is usually paid as and when the service is provided. As a consequence, the estimated value should be calculated so as to take account of this time dimension since it is unusual for such contracts to indicate a total price for the service. For the purpose of calculating the estimated value of public service contracts[165] which do *not* indicate a total price, a distinction is made between fixed-term contracts and contracts without a fixed term.

In the case of fixed-term service contracts of a term which is equal to or less than 48 months, the value of the contract corresponds to the total value of the contract for the *full* known term.[166]

In the case of service contracts *without* a fixed term or contracts of a term greater than 48 months, the value of the contract is deemed to be the monthly value multiplied by 48 whether or not the contract, at the time of the conclusion, is intended to last for more than four years.[167]

Finally, the Procurement Directive lists which elements of contracts for specific services such as banking and insurance services and certain design services that must be included in the calculation of the value of these contracts.

For *insurance services*[168] the value is the sum of the premium payable and other forms of remuneration.

For *banking and other financial services*[169] the value is the sum of fees, commissions, interest and other forms of remuneration.

For *design contracts*[170] the value is the sum of fees, commission payable and other forms of remuneration.

164. Article 9, paragraph 1 of the Procurement Directive.
165. Article 9, paragraph 8 of the Procurement Directive.
166. Article 9, paragraph 8 (b)(i) of the Procurement Directive.
167. Article 9, paragraph 8(b)(ii) of the Procurement Directive.
168. Article 9, paragraph 8(a)(i) of the Procurement Directive.
169. Article 9, paragraph 8(a)(ii) of the Procurement Directive.
170. Article 9, paragraph 8(a)(iii) of the Procurement Directive.

6. Excluded contracts

A number of contracts are because of their content excluded from the Procurement Directive. The provisions of the Procurement Directive on excluded contracts must be interpreted strictly since they constitute a departure from the EU's fundamental interest in opening up markets to in particular foreign undertakings and competition for public contracts.

However, such a strict interpretation is not valid for contracts which are subject to another set of procedural rules.[171] Nor should it be applied to contracts which are exempted from the Procurement Directive in view of the effective competition in the particular sector.[172]

Contracting authorities may be subject to obligations, other than those imposed by the Procurement Directive, for the award of contracts which are excluded from the scope of the Procurement Directive. In connection with any conclusion of a contract the contracting authority is bound by the EC Treaty and is therefore obliged to observe the principles of non-discrimination, equal treatment and transparency, cf. chapter 1.5 above.[173] They may also be required to follow national or international rules of procedure.

6.1 Defence, secrecy and interests of security

Public contracts awarded by contracting authorities in the field of defence are subject to the Procurement Directive.[174] Pursuant to Article 296 of the EC Treaty contracts in the field of defence can only be excluded from the scope of the Procurement Directive for relevant, specific and proportional reasons. Annex V to the Procurement Directive on the calculation of the threshold values for procurement in the field of defence gives some indication of which categories of products would qualify as sufficient reason: explosives, toxic products, armoured wagons, machinery, telecommunication equipment, orthopaedic appliances, etc.

The derogation contained in Article 296 of the Treaty cannot be relied upon to exclude contracts for civil equipment or civil equipment for specific military purposes, not even where the equipment is procured directly by the defence ministries of the Member States.

---

171. Article 12 of the Procurement Directive on contracts within the utilities sectors.
172. Article 13 of the Procurement Directive concerning the field of telecommunications.
173. See also Article 2 of the Procurement Directive.
174. Article 10 of the Procurement Directive.

The European Court of Justice[175] has laid down narrow limits within which contracts in the field of procurement can be excluded by reference to the derogation. The Commission[176] has summarised the case law as follows:

"– its use does not constitute a general, automatic exemption, but should be justified case by case. States thus have the possibility of secrecy regarding information which would undermine their security and the option of invoking an exemption to internal market rules for the arms trade. They are also obliged to assess whether or not each individual contract is covered by the derogation;
– use by states of national derogation measures is justified only if it is necessary for achieving the objective of safeguarding the essential security interests invoked;
– the burden of proof lies with a Member State that intends to make use of the derogation;
– such proof is to be supplied, if necessary, to the national courts or, where appropriate, the Court of Justice, to which the Commission may refer the matter in the performance of its duties as guardian of the Treaty."

As a consequence, reliance upon the derogation is conditional on an assessment of the nature of each individual contract by the contracting authority.

Article 14 of the Procurement Directive contains a provision on secret contracts and contracts requiring special security measures. It is for the individual Member State to assess whether the protection of national security, state secrets or other essential interests of that Member State requires that a contract be excluded from the Procurement Directive by virtue of Article 14. It is likely that such a case would be brought before the Complaints Board for a review of whether the conditions were satisfied and the European Court of Justice may be asked to give its interpretation. However, the Member State's scope for discretion within the limits of Article 14 is wide and the Member State's duty to reason its discretion is obviously limited.

In *Commission vs. Belgium*[177] Belgium had failed to invite tenders for a contract to perform services involving coastal surveillance by means of aerial photography. The contract

---

175. See *inter alia* judgment of the European Court of Justice of 15 May 1986, case 222/84, Marguerite Johnston vs. Chief Constable of the Royal Ulster Constabulatory and judgment of the European Court of Justice of 16 September 1999, case C-414/97, Commission vs. Spain.
176. Commission Green Paper on Defence Procurement of 23 September 2004, COM 2004, 608, point 3.1.
177. Judgment of the European Court of Justice of 16 October 2003, case C-252/01, Commission vs. Belgium. See also press release from the Commission of 8 July 2004, IP/04/875 »Commission decides to refer Italy to Court over supply of helicopters«.

mainly concerned the provision of regular surveillance by means of aerial photography of the chain of dunes and beaches on the Belgian coast and the processing of the data obtained. The contract would be awarded to an economic operator that fulfilled the following conditions: "(a) possession of a military security certificate; (b) possession of a licence from the aviation authorities to engage in aviation activity; (c) possession of the requisite know-how, technology and equipment; (d) the above three elements to be in the possession of a single undertaking; (e) sufficient financial capacity to be able to provide services annually to the value of some BEF 80,000,000." These requirements were justified by the interest in protecting the security of Belgium's national installations and of the installations of international organisations within its territory, such as NATO for which reason "... all aerial photography in Belgium must be submitted to the Belgian security services for checking and possible censoring, unless the undertaking concerned possesses a military security certificate ...". The European Court of Justice held that "It is therefore for the Belgian authorities to lay down the security measures necessary for the protection of such installations" and thus acknowledged that certain measures were necessary. The European Court of Justice did not address the extent of these measures, but stated with respect to the requirement for a military security certificate that "Obtention of a military security certificate does not, therefore, constitute a merely administrative formality but requires that certain operational conditions be met by the certified undertaking. Furthermore, it means that the undertaking continues to meet security requirements in subsequent operations." Against that background the European Court of Justice concluded that "... execution of the services under the contract in issue must be accompanied by special security measures ... including the obtention by the undertaking providing the service of a military security certificate". The Commission's view that the condition that the tendering undertaking possesses a military security certificate constituted a particular authorisation that the contracting undertaking can require of tenderers and candidates by virtue of Article 46, second indent of the procurement directive, rather than a special security measure was thus dismissed.

The judgment shows that the Member States enjoy considerable freedom to determine the nature of special security measures. Essentially, the European Court of Justice examined the procedures for obtaining a certificate and whether the authority follows these procedures consistently.

6.2 Service concessions and specific exclusions

The Procurement Directive does not apply to service concessions contracts by virtue of Article 17 of the Procurement Directive.[178]

Characteristic of service concessions is that the *commercial risks* involved with the provision of the service pass to the concessionaire. For example the

---

178. Article 1, paragraph 4 of the Procurement Directive: "'Service concession' is a contract of the same type as a public service contract except for the fact that the consideration for the works to be carried out consists either solely in the right to exploit the work or in this right together with payment."

collection of user charges for a service involves the risk that the user charges will not cover the costs of providing/making the service available. This is of no concern to the contracting authority which grants the concession. If the risks involved with the service essentially remain with the contracting authority, the contract will not be in the nature of a concession, but should be categorised as a public service contract with the implications in procurement law that follow from the fact that the contract is a public service contract. In *Parking Brixen*[179] the European Court of Justice clarifies the legal distinction between public service contracts and service concessions with reference to payments, as follows:

"It follows from that definition that a public service contract within the meaning of that directive involves consideration which is paid directly by the contracting authority to the service provider."

In her opinion in *Parking Brixen*[180] Advocate General Kokott distinguishes service concessions relative to service contracts. Brixen Local Authority had transferred the responsibility for managing two public parking grounds subject to payment to its wholly-owned subsidiary Stadtwerke Brixen AG for a period of nine years without a prior call for tenders. The private parking enterprise operating in the town – Parking Brixen GmbH – appealed against this decision, which gave the Advocate General an opportunity for addressing this distinction among other things. In the terms set out in the management agreement with Brixen Local Authority governing one of the two parking grounds with approx. 200 parking spaces, it was stipulated that the concessionaire – Stadtwerke Brixen AG – in consideration of the right to manage the parking ground should (1) pay an annual amount of € 151,700 to Brixen Local Authority, which amount would be increased proportionate to future increases in the parking charges; (2) employ the local employees already working within the area; (3) assume any and all responsibility for the parking ground, including an obligation to keep it in good state and condition; (4) assume responsibility for the free use of bicycles; and (5) make an area available for a weekly market held in the parking ground. Against that background the Advocate General found that the agreement was a service concession since the commercial risks involved with the management had passed to Stadtwerke Brixen AG in that Stadtwerke Brixen AG in addition to paying its own costs also had to pay an annual amount to Brixen Local Authority based on the parking charges chargeable from the users of the parking ground.

However, Articles 43 and 49 of the EC Treaty set out certain obligations to ensure transparency in the award of concessions. This is a principle estab-

---

179. Judgment of the European Court of Justice of 13 October 2005, case C-458/03, Parking Brixen GmbH, paragraph 39.
180. Advocate General Kokott's Opinion, case C-458/03, Parking Brixen GmbH, points 27-39.

lished by the European Court of Justice in several cases.[181] Making the following statement in *Coname,*[182] the European Court of Justice laid down specific guidelines for which obligations relating to transparency that derive directly from primary legislation:[183]

"In that regard, it must be pointed out that, in so far as the concession in question may also be of interest to an undertaking located in a Member State other than the Member State of the Comune di Cingia de' Botti, the award, in the absence of any transparency, of that concession to an undertaking located in the latter Member State amounts to a difference in treatment to the detriment of the undertaking located in the other Member States [...]

In the absence of any transparency, the latter undertaking has no real opportunity of expressing its interest in obtaining that concession.

Unless it is justified by objective circumstances, such a difference in treatment, which, by excluding all undertakings located in another Member State, operates mainly to the detriment of the latter undertakings, amounts to indirect discrimination on the basis of nationality, prohibited under Articles 43 EC and 49 EC."

Against that background the European Court of Justice came to the following conclusion with respect to the transparency obligation:[184]

"In those circumstances, it is for the referring court to satisfy itself that the award of the concession by the Comune di Cingia de' Botti to Padania complies with transparency requirements which, without necessarily implying an obligation to hold an invitation to tender, are, in particular, such as to ensure that an undertaking located in the territory of a Member State other than that of the Italian Republic can have access to appropriate information regarding that concession before it is awarded, so that, if that undertaking had so wished, it would have been in a position to express its interest in obtaining that concession."

The European Court of Justice thus established that for the award of a concession the transparency obligations under Articles 43 and 49 of the EC

181. Judgment of the European Court of Justice of 21 July 2005, case C-231/03, Consorzio Aziende Metano (Coname) vs. Comune di Cingia dé Botti; order of the European Court of Justice of 30 May 2002, case C-358/00, Buchhändler-Vereinigung GmbH vs. Saur Verlag GmbH & Co. KG, Die Deutsche Bibliothek and judgment of the European Court of Justice of 7 December 2000, case C-324/98, Telaustria Verlags GmbH and Telefonadress GmbH vs. Telekom Austria AG.
182. Judgment of the European Court of Justice of 21 July 2005, case C-231/03, Consorzio Aziende Metano (Coname) vs. Comune di Cingia dé Botti.
183. Ibid, paragraphs 17-19.
184. Ibid, paragraph 21.

Treaty imply an *active* measure enabling foreign undertakings to express interests, except where objective circumstances justify discrimination.

One objective circumstance mentioned by the European Court of Justice is where the value of the contract is so modest that it is unlikely to be of any interest to foreign undertakings.[185] The thresholds set out in Article 7 of the Procurement Directive are probably indicative in this respect. The European Court of Justice does not preclude that it may constitute an objective circumstance if the contracting authority is capable of exercising a qualified control over the concessionaire, but rules out that this was the situation in the specific case since the authority's holding represented less than 1% of the share capital, and because the group of owners included private interests, there was for that reason alone no in-house relation between the authority and the concessionaire.[186]

In *Parking Brixen*,[187] the European Court of Justice gave further guidance to the application of Articles 43 and 49 of the EC Treaty in the area of services concession contracts and the consequences of its judgment in *Coname:*[188]

"It is for the concession-granting public authority to evaluate, subject to review by the competent courts, the appropriateness of the detailed arrangements of the call for tenders to the particularities of the public service concession in question. However, a complete lack of any call for competition in the case of the award of a public service concession such as that at issue in the main proceedings does not comply with the requirements of Articles 43 EC and 49 EC any more than with the principles of equal treatment, non-discrimination and transparency."

In relation to services concessions the European Court of Justice seem to indicate that Articles 43 EC and 49 EC dictates that a services concession granting authority is obligated to announce – internationally – its intention to grant a concession and – in case that more than one interested economic operator demonstrates its interest in the concession – put in place a procedure for the selection of economic operators and the award of the services concession contract, which procedure must comply with the principles of equal

---

185. Ibid, paragraph 20.
186. Ibid, paragraphs 23-26.
187. Judgment of the European Court of Justice of 13 October 2005, case C-458/03, Parking Brixen GmbH, paragraph 50.
188. Judgment of the European Court of Justice of 21 July 2005, case C-231/03, Consorzio Aziende Metano (Coname) vs. Comune di Cingia dé Botti.

treatment, non-discrimination and transparency, unless objective circumstances allow for a different approach.

Certain public *service* contracts are explicitly excluded from the scope of the Procurement Directive. The public *service* contracts excluded are contracts for:

"(a) the acquisition or rental, by whatever financial means, of land, existing buildings or other immovable property or concerning rights thereon; nevertheless, financial service contracts concluded at the same time as, before or after the contract of acquisition or rental, in whatever form, shall be subject to this Directive;

(b) the acquisition, development, production or co-production of programme material intended for broadcasting by broadcasters and contracts for broadcasting time;

(c) arbitration and conciliation services;

(d) financial services in connection with the issue, sale, purchase or transfer of securities or other financial instruments, in particular transactions by the contracting authorities to raise money or capital, and central bank services;

(e) employment contracts;

(f) research and development services other than those where the benefits accrue exclusively to the contracting authority for its use in the conduct of its own affairs, on condition that the service provided is wholly remunerated by the contracting authority."[189]

This list of services is remarkable in that the services excluded under (b) and (e) are services which would be categorised as "Other services" in Annex II B, category 27 to the Procurement Directive and, therefore, be explicitly exempted from the limited obligations that apply to contracts for Annex II B services were they subject to the Procurement Directive.

The direct effect of the fact that these services fall entirely outside the scope of the Procurement Directive is that contracts for these services are not regulated by the Procurement Directive at all, regardless of their value.

The indirect effect of the fact that these services fall entirely outside the scope of the Procurement Directive must be that the value of these services should never be included in the calculation of the value of a mixed contract, including these services, to estimate whether it exceeds the threshold. By contrast, the full value of the services listed in Annex II B must be included in the calculation of the total value of a contract.

The exclusion of contracts for financial services has caused some confusion. General borrowing, long-term or short-term, by a contracting authority is subject to the provisions of the Procurement Directive for the mere reason that Article 9, paragraph 8 (a)(ii) of the Directive exactly defines how the

189. Article 16 of the Procurement Directive.

value of these contracts should be calculated. Therefore, the exclusion, which should be interpreted strictly, only covers the following transactions: emissions (issues), purchase, sale and transfer of securities (shares and bonds, etc.) and other financial instruments (futures, swaps and other instruments which are traded in authorised markets).

Consequently, contracting authorities can, for example, buy financial services in connection with the issue of bonds in the name of the contracting authority (borrower) (however not in connection with borrowings based on a back bond issue in the name of the lender since the basis is not relevant to the borrower), buy and sell shares or bonds and make various transfers of custody accounts, etc. without a prior call for tender under the EU procurement rules.

6.3 Exclusive rights[190]

As a supplementary provision to the in-house rule,[191] the exclusion set out in Article 18 of the Procurement Directive ensures that public responsibilities can be allocated sensibly among various contracting authorities without a call for tenders under the Procurement Directive. The provision only authorises the award of exclusive rights to provide *services* and does not apply to works or supply contracts. The provision is worded as follows:

"This Directive shall not apply to public service contracts awarded by a contracting authority to another contracting authority or to an association of contracting authorities on the basis of an exclusive right which they enjoy pursuant to a published law, regulation or administrative provision which is compatible with the Treaty."

Under this provision several contracting authorities can cooperate on the provision of a variety of public services, such as joint tax administration for several local authorities, etc., and transfer the responsibility for carrying out tax assessments, etc. to this joint tax administration without a prior call for tenders under the Procurement Directive, regardless whether the individual local authority holds an ownership interest in the joint unit.

However, a series of conditions must be met before contracts can be excluded under this provision.

---

190. Articles 18 and 3 of the Procurement Directive.
191. For more details see chapter 2.3.1 above.

First, the party performing the service (for example the tax administration) must be a contracting authority *itself*[192] and as such be subject to the Procurement Directive for the award of its own public contracts.[193]

Second, the service must be performed on the basis of an exclusive right. As a consequence, a contracting authority that wishes to make use of this provision cannot award the right to perform the same service to more than one party, thus excluding any form of competition for the provision of the service. An exclusive right can, of course, be limited in terms of scope, geography and time in effect allowing more "exclusive rights" to be awarded, but the individual services must be carefully defined so that the service providers are not able to compete for the provision of the services.

Third, the exclusive right must be *awarded* pursuant to a published law or published administrative provisions. The requirement for publication is a logical consequence of the general principles of transparency in public administration. Law and administrative provisions must be interpreted in broad terms including any public measure comparable to a provision whereby a contracting authority regulates a certain matter for an unspecified number of citizens who are bound by that provision. Whether the award of an exclusive right to perform a service pursuant to law constitutes a *public contract* within the meaning of the Procurement Directive is uncertain, and the question is probably purely academic as the award, even if it were deemed to constitute a public contract for pecuniary interest, by virtue of Article 18 would *not* be subject to the Procurement Directive, provided that all the conditions are met.

Fourth, the laws or administrative provisions pursuant to which the exclusive right is awarded to the contracting authority must be compatible with the Treaty. This condition serves as a safety device to prevent abuse of the exclusive rights provision to, for example, discriminate on grounds of nationality or to prevent that the provision of the service on the basis of the exclusive right is subject to conditions that are contrary to the provisions of the Treaty, in which context notably excess remuneration for providing the service would be contrary to Article 87(1) EC,[194] in so far as Article 86(2) EC does not

---

192. See also chapter 2.2 above.
193. See judgment of the European Court of Justice of 10 November 1998, case C-360/96, Gemeente Arnhem and Gemeente Rheden vs. BFI Holding BV, in which the European Court of Justice established that the term contracting authority should be given the same interpretation in regard to the provision on exclusive rights.
194. Judgment of the European Court of Justice of 24 July 2003, case C-280/00, Altmark Trans GmbH, Regierungspräsidium Magdeburg vs. Nahverkehrsgesellschaft Altmark GmbH.

apply to the activities. Also, Article 86 EC, cf. Articles 81 and 82 EC, are of relevance to the provision of the service.

Article 3 of the Procurement Directive dictates that undertakings which pursuant to a legislative provision have been awarded special or exclusive rights to provide a public service must observe the principle of non-discrimination on grounds of nationality[195] in the award of *supply* contracts necessary for performing the public service obligations, whereas there is no requirement that this principle be observed with respect to the award of works and service contracts in the Procurement Directive itself.

If the special or exclusive right is awarded to an undertaking which is a contracting authority, Article 12 of the EC Treaty requires that the above principle be observed in the award of all contracts.

6.4 Telecommunications sector[196]

The telecommunications sector has been liberalised to a degree which means that undertakings operate at arm's length as a result of the situation of effective competition in this market, for which reason the Utilities Directive[197] provides that this sector is no longer governed by the now repealed utilities directive.

To prevent that telecommunication companies which satisfy the definition of a contracting authority as set out in the Procurement Directive fall subject to the Procurement Directive because of the deregulation under the Utilities Directive, Article 13 of the Procurement Directive contains the following exclusion:[198]

"This Directive shall not apply to public contracts for the principal purpose of permitting the contracting authorities to provide or exploit public telecommunications networks or to provide to the public one or more telecommunications services."

---

195. The principle of non-discrimination is set out in Article 12 of the EC Treaty and is therefore directly binding on the Member States.
196. Article 13 of the Procurement Directive.
197. Directive 2004/17/EC of the European Parliament and of the Council of 31 March 2004 coordinating the procurement procedures of entities operating in the water, energy, transport and postal services sectors.
198. For the reasons for the deregulation, see recitals 5-8 of the preamble to the Utilities Directive and recital 21 of the preamble to the Procurement Directive.

6.5 Contracts awarded pursuant to international rules[199]

Under the Procurement Directive certain international rules on public procurement are given priority over the rules of the Procurement Directive which are thus only of a secondary nature. Generally, this is based on the assumption that the relevant international rules regulate the procedure for awarding public contracts. The Procurement Directive mentions three examples of international rules taking precedence of the rules of the Procurement Directive.

First, international agreements concluded between an EU Member State and one or more third countries (non-EU Member States) for supplies or works intended for the joint implementation or exploitation of a work by the signatory States (the countries bound by the international agreement, the EU Member State as well as the third country) or a service intended for the joint implementation or execution of project by the signatory States take precedence of contracts concluded pursuant to the Procurement Directive. The specific agreement must comply with the EC Treaty, and all public contracts awarded under the international set of rules must be communicated to the Commission.

Second, the Procurement Directive is secondary to international agreements relating to contracting authorities' award of public contracts to undertakings located within or outside the EU concerning the stationing of troops (under the auspices of the UN, for example). Non-application of the procedural rules of the Procurement Directive is not conditional on the conformity of the international agreement with the EC Treaty.

Third, the Procurement Directive ranks after the particular public procurement procedures of international organisations. It is, obviously, a condition that the Member State invoking the procurement procedures of an international organisation is a member of that particular organisation. The supremacy of the particular procedures of the international organisation is not conditional on compliance with the EC Treaty. One example of particular procedural rules for public procurement implemented by an international organisation is the WTO Agreement,[200] "the aim of which is to establish a multilateral framework of balanced rights and obligations relating to public contracts with a view to achieving the liberalisation and expansion of world trade".[201] The WTO Agreement does not have any direct effect on contract-

---

199. Article 15 of the Procurement Directive.
200. Agreement establishing the WTO, Annex 4b, on Government Procurement.
201. Recital 7 of the preamble to the Procurement Directive.

ing authorities, but contracting authorities covered by the WTO Agreement which comply with and apply the Procurement Directive to economic operators of third countries which are signatories to the WTO Agreement are considered to be in conformity with the WTO Agreement in that its provisions are covered under the rules of the Procurement Directive.[202]

6.6 Reserved contracts[203]

The Procurement Directive provides that sheltered workshops can be given preferential treatment in procedures for the award of public works contracts, supply contracts and service contracts.

The reason is that employment and occupation are considered key areas of policy in guaranteeing equal opportunities for all and contribute to integration in society.

Public procurement is an appropriate means for advancing the significant and efficient contribution of sheltered workshops and sheltered employment programmes towards the integration or reintegration of people with *disabilities* into the labour market.

However, in view of the fact that these workshops are not usually able to obtain contracts under normal conditions of competition, the Procurement Directive provides that the right to *participate* in award procedures for public contracts can be reserved for *sheltered workshops*. Alternatively, the contracting authority can reserve the *performance* of public contracts to the context of *sheltered employment programmes* on the condition that the *majority* of the employees are handicapped persons who, by reason of the nature or the seriousness of their disabilities, cannot carry on occupations under normal conditions.

Reservation of contracts for special groups of people is only conditional on the requirement that the contract notice sets out the relevant information.

6.7 Contracts in "excluded sectors"[204]

Public contracts awarded by contracting authorities for *activities exercised within* the energy (gas, heat, electricity),[205] water,[206] transport services[207] and

---

202. Recital 7, second indent of the preamble to the Procurement Directive.
203. Article 19 of the Procurement Directive and recital 28 of the preamble to the Procurement Directive.
204. Article 12 of the Procurement Directive where reference is made to Directive 2004/17/EC of the European Parliament and of the Council of 31 March 2004 coordinating the procurement procedures of entities operating in the water, energy, transport and postal services sectors.

postal services[208] sectors and within exploration for and extraction of energy[209] and the provision of airports and maritime and inland ports or other terminal facilities[210] are covered by the Utilities Directive.[211] [212] As a consequence, the Procurement Directive does not apply to these public contracts.

The decisive and not easily definable criterion is thus whether the contract is awarded for *activities exercised within* the utilities sector, since a contracting authority's purchases of products (works, supplies or services) which are not used for the exercise of these activities are covered by the Procurement Directive in so far as the contracting authority is among the contracting entities, as defined in the Utilities Directive, that are categorised as contracting authorities under the Procurement Directive and therefore are subject to the Procurement Directive.

To that end it is generally assumed that the expression "in the exercise of activities" should be given a broad interpretation. Contracts for the cleaning of administrative offices, training of staff and delivery of IT systems are all awarded in the exercise of the utilities activity even though they are not related to the production. All contracts, interpreted broadly, which a utility is forced to award for the purpose of carrying out its utilities activities as an independent undertaking are deemed to be awarded in *the exercise of* these activities. As a consequence, only contracts concerning entirely separate areas of activity are not covered by the Utilities Directive and are, therefore, subject to the Procurement Directive.

In Strabag & Kostmann vs. Austria[213] the European Court of Justice held that Österreichische Bundesbahnen (the Austrian federal railways which under federal law are responsible for the carriage of persons and goods and for the construction and maintenance of the infrastructures necessary for that purpose and which are wholly-owned by the Aus-

---

205. As defined in Article 3 of the Utilities Directive.
206. As defined in Article 4 of the Utilities Directive.
207. As defined in Article 5 of the Utilities Directive.
208. As defined in Article 6 of the Utilities Directive.
209. As defined in Article 7 (a) of the Utilities Directive.
210. As defined in Article 7(b) of the Utilities Directive.
211. Directive 2004/17/EC of the European Parliament and of the Council of 31 March 2004 coordinating the procurement procedures of entities operating in the water, energy, transport and postal services sectors.
212. However, contracts awarded by contracting authorities in the context of their service activities for maritime, coastal or river transport are covered by the Procurement Directive.
213. Judgment of the European Court of Justice of 16 June 2005 in joined cases C-462/03 and C-463/03, Strabag AG vs. Austria and Kostmann GmbH vs. Austria.

trian State and a utility within the meaning of Article 5 of the Utilities Directive[214]) could award contracts for the construction of railway bridges and works, works involving excavation, earthworks, levelling and concreting and the construction of shafts, tunnels, etc. pursuant to the Utilities Directive if the contracts were awarded in the exercise of the utilities activities. Therefore, the expressions "provision" and "operation" of networks providing a service to the public in the field of transport by railway which constitute the activities that fall within the sectors covered by the Utilities Directive do not limit the scope for applying the Directive to all contracts awarded by the utility provided, however, that the contracts are awarded in the exercise of activities falling within the relevant utility service.

Finally, the Procurement Directive does not apply to the particular public contracts that are explicitly excluded from the scope of the Utilities Directive. These are:[215]

1. bus transport services to the public;[216]
2. contracts awarded for purposes of resale or lease to third parties;[217]
3. contracts awarded by certain contracting entities for the purchase of water and for the supply of energy or of fuels for the production of energy;[218] and
4. contracts concerning utilities activities exposed to ordinary competition in the Member State where the contracting authority is established and where the procedures for establishing this have been complied with.[219]

214. Directive 2004/17/EC of the European Parliament and of the Council of 31 March 2004 coordinating the procurement procedures of entities operating in the water, energy, transport and postal services sectors.
215. A special interim provision applies to postal services providing that the Procurement Directive may apply to certain postal services if a Member States chooses to postpone the transposition of the Utilities Directive for these contracting entities for a longer period of time.
216. Article 5, paragraph 2 of the Utilities Directive. The Directive makes reference to Article 2, paragraph 4 of the now repealed Utilities Directive stipulating: "The provision of bus transport services to the public shall not be considered to be a relevant activity within the meaning of paragraph 2 (c) where other entities are free to provide those services, either in general or in a particular geographical area, under the same condition as the contracting entities."
217. Article 19 of the Utilities Directive.
218. Article 26 of the Utilities Directive.
219. Article 30 of the Utilities Directive.

CHAPTER 4

The Contract Documents

1. Basis for public procurement

The contract documents describe the purchase; the required technical, economic and legal standards are specified therein and a draft contract is prepared entailing this information. Also the procedures selected for completing the procurement and awarding the public contract are set out in the contract documents. Since the contract documents are the basis on which the economic operators submit their tenders, the choices and specifications made and described therein by the contracting authority are pivotal to obtaining the most economically advantageous contract or supplies at the lowest price. Hence, the contract documents make up the basis on which a public contract is awarded. The contract documents are also the key element in the assessment of whether a contracting authority has violated applicable rules and complied with fundamental principles.

1.1 Significance of the contract documents for the procedure

The procurement rules provide that contact between the contracting authority and tenderers in the period from the submission of tenders until the award of the contract be limited (prohibition on negotiations).[1] This restriction is considered essential to the ensurement of transparency in the award procedure and thus the ensurement of equal treatment of economic operators in competitive tendering for public contracts. To the contracting authority this means that all the technical, economic and legal aspects involved with the award of the contract, which will govern the parties' rights and obligations in connection with the subsequent supply of goods, execution of works or provision of

---

1. In "the open procedure" and "the restricted procedure" negotiations are prohibited. See chapter 7 for more details.

a service, must be determined prior to advertising the contract notice (*up-front rule*).[2] The implication for the economic operators of the prohibition on negotiations is that they must submit final and binding tenders on the basis of the contract notice and the specifications, and they cannot subsequently amend or negotiate their tenders (*last-shot rule*).

The Procurement Directive covers a wide array of public contracts (purchase of supplies, execution of works and provision of services). Also, the procurement requirements of public authorities vary greatly. Finally, for economic or other reasons different authorities have different priorities. Bearing that in mind, the conclusion of public contracts and the prior selection and award are based on a very comprehensive list of criteria, specially picked out to ensure that the contract awarded is the one that best satisfies the specific requirements of the public authority. Due to the diverse nature of public contracts the analyses below will only set out the broad guidelines for preparing the contract documents.

1.2 Chapter outline

Contracting authorities have considerable freedom to make a number of procurement decisions ranging from what to buy, whether to base the purchase on price or quality to whether social and environmental considerations should be taken into account. However, in making provisions for the procurement and preparing the contract documents the contracting authority must observe the rules on non-discrimination and prohibition of trade barriers of the EC Treaty and comply with the fundamental principles of equal treatment and transparency. Further, the provisions of the Procurement Directive must be complied with, and particularly Article 23 of Directive on technical specifications is important in relation to the drafting of the contract documents.

The obligations of the contracting authority under the Procurement Directive and the EC Treaty are analysed in sections 2 and 3. Section 4 reviews the possibilities of basing the award of public contracts on *inter alia* non-economic criteria. Section 5 provides an outline of the differences between the criteria used for identifying the winning economic operator and other criteria specified by the contracting authority in the contract documents.

---

2. This must be advertised in the contract notice or stipulated in the specifications.

2. General requirements for the contract documents

The European Court of Justice and the Danish Complaints Board for Public Procurement have established various general requirements for the contract documents to serve as the basis for assessing whether the principles of equal treatment and transparency are complied with in a specific procedure. The general requirements for the contract documents are analysed in this section.

2.1 Transparency

Transparency in the award of public contracts is pivotal to achieving equal treatment of economic operators and thus effective competition for public contracts.[3] The contract documents are the primary source of information for economic operators; advertising the proposed public contract, specifying the object of the contract, the requirements and obligations for the performance of the contract and the procedure for the award of the contract. From the contract documents the economic operators derive the information necessary to determine whether the contract is of interest to them. Having made that decision, the economic operators must decide whether to prepare a tender. To that end it is essential that the contract documents are transparent, thus enabling the economic operators to predict and comprehend which requirements and obligations they must satisfy in the competitive procedure for the contract and the subsequent performance thereof.[4]

The requirement for transparent contract documents is closely linked to the EU's interest in opening up and ensuring equal treatment in competitions for public contracts.[5] This correlation between transparent award criteria and equal treatment in competitions is specified in the preamble to the Procurement Directive:

"To ensure compliance with the principle of equal treatment in the award of contracts, it is appropriate to lay down an obligation – established by case-law – to ensure the necessary transparency to enable all tenderers to be reasonably informed of the criteria and arrangements which will be applied to identify the most economically advantageous tender. It is therefore the responsibility of contracting authorities to indicate the criteria for the award

---

3. See also section 1.3.3 above.
4. Recital 36 of the preamble to the Procurement Directive.
5. See also section 1.2 above. Order of the Complaints Board of 27 November 2002, AON Danmark A/S vs. Odense Local Authority.

of the contract and the relative weighting given to each of those criteria in sufficient time for tenderers to be aware of them when preparing their tenders.'"[6]

The requirement of prior publication of a contract notice set out in the Procurement Directive is intended to ensure the transparency of the contract documents. Inevitably, before tendering for a contract, potential tenderers need to be informed that a public contract will be awarded. All information necessary for evaluating the suitability of the interested undertakings and the tenders submitted must appear in the contract documents[7] and the contracting authorities are obliged to *publish* this information in the contract documents.[8] Transparency is sought further enhanced by the obligation to use standard forms for the publication of a contract notice for the award of a public contract.[9] The fundamental nature of this aspect of the transparency obligation is finally witnessed by the fact that a similar obligation applies to the conclusion of public contracts which fall outside the scope of the Procurement Directive.[10]

Another factor which is fundamental to ensuring that procurement procedures for public contracts are transparent is that the contract documents in open and restricted procedures are *pre-determined.* The obligation to pre-determine the contract documents is even more important in view of the requirement that equal treatment of tenderers must be *ensured throughout the procedure* thus requiring transparency of the contract documents and of the procedure.[11] To ensure equal treatment of the tenderers, the contract documents must form the basis for all stages of the procedure and for the award of the contract.

Furthermore, the evaluation must be based *solely* on *the contract documents,* and the selected criteria must be interpreted in the same way through-

---

6. Recital 46 of the preamble to the Directive, second indent, first and second sentences. Transparency is also essential to the effective *enforcement* of the procurement rules. The contract documents are key to a subsequent assessment of whether the contracting authority complied with the procurement rules, cf. chapter 8.

7. The requirements for the contract documents are determined by the type of procedure: open or restricted procedure or negotiated procedure. See also Annex VII to the Procurement Directive.

8. The information must be specified in the contract notice or the additional documents. See chapter 5.3 below.

9. Annex VIII to the Procurement Directive, cf. Commission Directive No 2001/78/EC of 13 September 2001. See also section 3.2.2 below on the use of the CPV nomenclature.

10. See also chapter 1.5.

11. Order of the Complaints Board of 28 May 2003, Bilhuset Ringsted ApS and Others vs. Ringsted Local Authority.

out the award procedure.[12] Discounts, additional services, etc. can only be considered in the evaluation if the contract documents make provisions relating thereto. In the following orders such provisions had not been made:

- Offer of a discount if contractor awarded more contracts with the contracting authority.[13]
- Savings achieved from a contractor's offer to complete the contract earlier than scheduled in the contract documents.[14]
- Offer of a discount if payments were made every quarter and not once a year as provided in the contract documents.[15]

The words and phrases used in the contract documents will be carefully examined. If, for example, the contracting authority has defined materials as "non-rusting metal", tenders in which "rust-proof metal" is used must be rejected regardless that the contracting authority subsequently states that the latter description was what the contracting authority intended.[16]

If additional documentation and criteria are taken into consideration, it is likely to jeopardise the transparency of the contract documents giving rise to serious concerns of unequal treatment of tenderers.[17] Any additional information to the contract documents sent to interested undertakings must be identical and received by all interested parties at the same time.[18] Also failure to use, for example, a calculation method set out in the contract documents puts the transparency of the procedure at risk and will lead to its cancellation.[19] Likewise in the interest of ensuring transparency in the award of the contract and thus equal treatment of tenderers, the scope for negotiations with the

---

12. Judgment of the European Court of Justice of 18 October 2001, case C-19/00, SIAC Construction Ltd., paragraph 43.
13. Order of the Complaints Board of 14 October 2003, KK-Ventilation A/S vs. County of Vejle; order of the Complaints Board of 27 May 2003, M.J. Eriksson A/S vs. Fuglebjerg Local Authority.
14. Order of the Complaints Board of 13 may 2004, Bravida Danmark A/S vs. Rødovre almennyttige Boligselskab.
15. Order of the Complaints Board of 30 September 2004, Colas Danmark A/S vs. Videbæk Local Authority.
16. Order of the Complaints Board of 20 February 2004, Miri Stål A/S vs. Esbjerg Local Authority.
17. Judgment of the European Court of Justice of 4 December 2003, case C-448/01, EVN AG, paragraph 93.
18. See also chapter 5.3.
19. Order of the Complaints Board of 13 January 2004, E. Pihl og Søn A/S vs. Hadsund Local Authority.

tenderers is very limited in the period from the opening of the tenders till the contract is awarded, and any contact between the contracting authority and a tenderer must be documented.[20]

2.2 Objectivity

A core concern behind the procurement rules is the opening-up of competition for public contracts and the putting into place of effective control measures to ensure that tenderers are not discriminated against on grounds of nationality; that non-objective considerations are not taken into account and that tenderers are not otherwise discriminated against in the award procedure. Equal treatment of tenderers, transparency of the award procedure and, by inference, the possibilities of checking the procedure are improved if the procurement procedure is conducted on the basis of objective criteria. Characteristically, objective criteria are verifiable and unambiguous (height, length, depth, etc.) unlike subjective and qualitative criteria, the meaning of which is capable of interpretation.[21]

The Procurement Directive reflects that much effort has been devoted to ensuring that procedures, selection of qualified candidates and the award of public contracts are based on objective grounds. Especially the obligation to determine, to the extent possible, the technical specifications of the object of the public contract by reference to published standards helps ensure the objectivity of the criteria. About the award the preamble to the Procurement Directive reads:

"Contracts should be awarded on the basis of objective criteria which ensure compliance with the principles of transparency, non-discrimination and equal treatment and which guarantee that tenders are assessed in conditions of effective competition."[22]

The Procurement Directive further defines the requirement of objective award criteria as follows:

"The determination of these criteria depends on the object of the contract since they must allow the level of performance offered by each tender to be assessed in the light of the object of the contract, as defined in the technical specifications, and the value for money of each tender to be measured.

20. Order of the Complaints Board of 15 December 1999, Lifeline ApS vs. Dansk Hunderegister. See also chapter 7.6.
21. See also section 4.5.2 below on the requirement that the criteria must not confer an unrestricted freedom of choice on the contracting authority.
22. Recital 46 of the preamble, first indent, first sentence.

In order to guarantee equal treatment, the criteria for the award of the contract should enable tenders to be compared and assessed objectively."[23]

To that end, the award criteria must be selected so as to permit verification of the accuracy of the information provided by the tenderers.[24] In *SIAC*[25] the European Court of Justice specified that all tenderers must be treated equally in procurement procedures and, therefore, it is a requirement that objectivity (and transparency) is guaranteed throughout the (entire) procedure.[26] Also in the evaluation of the tenders the award criteria must be applied objectively and uniformly.[27]

In several cases the Complaints Board for Public Procurement has found that the specifications did not comply with the requirements of objectivity. Contract documents which are not clear may render it very difficult to assess whether a tender departs from the specifications or contains reservations of a scale which should lead to its rejection.[28]

In *Banverket vs. Nordjyske Jernbaner A/S*[29] a sub-criterion was formulated as follows: "6) Further measures proposed by the tenderers and which comply with/support the performance requirements and will be evaluated favourably." The Complaints Board found that this criterion was so vague that it was not suitable for awarding a public contract.

In *Uniqsoft 1998 ApS vs. Odense Local Authority*[30] it was stated that the contracting authority would thus focus *in particular* on a number of specific criteria. The contracting authority had thus disregarded its obligation to determine sub-criteria to the award criterion "the most economically advantageous tender" in the contract documents.

The requirement of objectivity is not always absolute. For example for the construction of a building, it may be appropriate to lay down aesthetic criteria

---

23. Recital 46 of the preamble to the Directive, third indent, third sentence and forth indent, first sentence.
24. Judgment of the European Court of Justice of 4 December 2003, case C-448/01, EVN AG, paragraphs 49, 50 and 52.
25. Judgment of the European Court of Justice of 18 October 2001, case C-19/00, SIAC Construction Ltd.
26. Ibid, paragraph 45.
27. Ibid, paragraph 44; judgment of the European Court of Justice of 4 December 2003, case C-448/01, EVN AG, paragraph 48.
28. Order of the Complaints Board of 6 February 2003, Hedeselskabet Miljø og Energi A/S vs. Løkken-Vrå Local Authority (the Danish Tender Act).
29. Order of the Complaints Board of 21 June 2004, Banverket vs. Nordjyske Jernbaner A/S.
30. Order of the Complaints Board of 2 may 2000, Uniqsoft 1998 ApS vs. Odense Local Authority

which inevitably entail a certain measure of subjectivity. An independent jury appointed to evaluate the tenders submitted may serve to maintain objectivity.[31] Also the possibility of basing the award of public contracts on *inter alia* non-economic criteria may affect the objectivity of the award procedure seeing that non-economic criteria are likely to be less objective. However, the main reason why the objectivity may be affected in such procedures is the necessity to compare tenders for compliance with somewhat incomparable criteria: economic criteria, such as price and quality, with non-economic criteria, such as the usability of a product, the level of discharge of harmful substances, etc.

Although the contracting authority enjoys considerable freedom to determine the object of the contract and draft the contract documents and, as a consequence, may base the evaluation of the tenders submitted on *inter alia* non-objective criteria, such as aesthetics, the contracting authority must nevertheless respect the natural link between the object of the contract and the selection and award criteria. It thus follows that the award criteria must enable the contracting authority to identify the best tender on objective grounds.

2.3 Written procedures

The contract documents must be in writing.[32] This requirement is intended to substantiate the basis on which the contract is awarded. It is particularly important that the contract documents are in writing because of their (often very high) level of detail. To guarantee equal treatment it is also a requirement that any additional information is supplied to the tenderers in writing.[33]

If, in exceptional cases, the tenderers are contacted after the submission of tenders, but before the award of the contract, it is advisable to make this contact in writing so that the content thereof can be proved later.

2.4 Clear, precise and sufficient description

The information imparted to an economic operator regarding the object of the contract and the requirements, criteria, conditions and procedures for its award must be sufficiently precise to enable the economic operator to grasp the technical, economic and legal aspects of the contract and prepare a tender.[34]

---

31. Title IV of the Procurement Directive sets out the provisions governing design contests (Articles 66-74), cf. chapter 5.4.1 below.
32. Articles 39 and 40 of the Procurement Directive, cf. Article 42.
33. Article 39, paragraph 2 and Article 40, paragraph 4 of the Procurement Directive.
34. Recital 29 of the preamble to the Procurement Directive, last sentence. Judgment of the European Court of Justice of 14 October 2004, case C-340/02, Commission vs.

Information on the object of the contract, etc. must be clear and precise in order that the economic operator is able to comprehend the uncertainties involved with the contract and dares run the financial risk of preparing a tender. In *Eiland Electric A/S vs. County of Vestsjælland*[35] it was found that lack of clarity opens up for random discrimination among the tenderers. The requirements for clarity and precision are closely linked to the EU's interest in opening up competition for public contracts. Pursuant to a Regulation by the Commission contracting authorities are obliged to describe the object of the contract by reference to the Common Procurement Vocabulary (CPV).[36]

The requirements for clarity and precision must furthermore be assessed bearing in mind that a tender is binding on the economic operator for a fixed period of time, and that the tender is the basis on which a possible future contract is concluded. An economic operator only submits a tender if the operator is able to comprehend the risks involved with a possible future contract. If the contract documents are unclear, it is likely that the contracting authority will receive tenders which are "too expensive" as the tenderers are uncertain of what to perform.[37] Another consideration to be taken into account when determining the required level of clarity and precision in the description of the object, etc..is that if a tender, submitted by an economic operator, is not clearly formulated or contains reservations about certain aspects of the contract documents, the contracting authority can, and given certain circumstances is obliged to, reject the tender for that reason alone.[38]

The exact level of the requirements for clarity and precision depends on the specific circumstances; in particular whether specific requirements to the object of the contract have been laid down or a functional description is set

---

France, paragraph 34; order of the Complaints Board of 11 October 2004, Iver C. Weilbach og Co. A/S vs. National Survey and Cadastre; order of the Complaints Board of 11 August 2000, Kirkebjerg A/S vs. County of Ribe; order of the Complaints Board of 8 August 2000, Visma Logistics ASA vs. County of Copenhagen; order of the Complaints Board of 27 June 2000, Deponering af Problem-affald ApS vs. I/S Vestforbrænding.

35. Order of the Complaints Board of 24 October 2001, Eiland Electric A/S vs. County of Vestsjælland.

36. Commission Regulation (EC) No 2151/2003 of 16 December 2003 amending Regulation (EC) No 2195/2002 of the European Parliament and of the Council on the Common Procurement Vocabulary (CPV). See also section 3.2.2 below.

37. There is for example a duty to report, but it is not specified whether this should be done daily, weekly, monthly or annually.

38. See also chapter 7.3. There is limited scope for clarification of vaguely phrased contract documents in connection with the evaluation of the tenders.

out, cf. section 3 below. However, for certain types of contracts the description of the object must specify the minimum requirements the object is to satisfy, for example where it is to operate together with an already existing installation.[39] In order to ensure equal treatment of the existing supplier and the other economic operators in such a procedure, it is necessary to procure and publish sufficient information on the existing installation to guarantee the smooth installation and operation of the new purchase. Such information may concern materials, properties, technical interfaces, dimensions, etc., and it may be necessary to allow inspection and examination of the existing installation.[40]

The requirement for a clear description excludes neither the possibility of specifying the technical specifications as functional requirements nor the possibility of allowing variants in which the tenderers can demonstrate creativity, cf. the following section. However, in the interest of ensuring transparency of the procedure tenderers are not permitted to make reservations with respect to *all* elements of a contract.[41]

3. The object of the contract and the specifications

The contract documents must have as their aim to provide the economic operators with a complete basis on which to prepare their tenders. The documents must be available when the contract notice is published or at the latest when the more detailed specifications are submitted (up-front rule). The key to understanding the level of detail required in the specifications is that in the open procedure and the restricted procedure the economic operators are only allowed one opportunity for submitting tenders, since subsequent contact or actual negotiations between the contracting authorities and the economic operators only are permitted to a very limited extent (last-shot rule).[42]

---

39. See also chapter 6.6 on disqualification.
40. Order of the Complaints Board of 27 September 2000, Svend B. Thomsen vs. Blåvandshuk Local Authority; order of the Complaints Board of 21 June 2000, Arriva Danmark A/S vs. Hovedstadsområdets Trafikselskab; order of the Complaints Board of 18 March 1999, Seghers Better Technology Group vs. I/S Amagerforbrændingen (the Utilities Directive); order of the Complaints Board of 25 October 1995, Siemens A/S vs. Esbjerg Local Authority.
41. Order of the Complaints Board of 2 May 2001, Forlaget Magnus A/S vs. Customs and Tax Authority.
42. See also chapter 7 below.

The contracting authority should draw up the specifications on the basis of the object of the proposed contract. The contract documents must contain a description of the object of the proposed contract, cf. section 3.1 below.

The specifications should reflect which features of the proposed contract the contracting authority regards as essential (properties, performance, durability, delivery time, reliability of delivery, funding, technical, financial and economic risks, etc.). For that purpose the authorities must decide whether these essential features should be laid down as specific requirements or whether the tenderers should be allowed a certain measure of flexibility in the drafting of tenders, thus permitting them to demonstrate creativity, cf. sections 3.2-3.5 below.[43]

The possibilities of submitting variants are analysed in section 3.6 below.

The contracting authority can also choose to lay down non-economic criteria for the award of the contract, which also must be determined in advance. The possibilities of laying down non-economic criteria are dealt with separately in section 4 below.

3.1 Description of the object of the contract

It is of paramount importance that the object of the contract and the requirements and criteria it must satisfy are specified in such a way that the focus is on meeting the contracting authority's specific need and the underlying objective in the public interest. How the need is satisfied also depends on the economic resources allocated to that end. It follows that also contracting authorities have a fundamental interest in obtaining the best value for money for their purchases and the satisfaction of a need or the objective in the public interest. The correlation between the object of the contract, the specific need, the underlying public interest and the allocated economic means dictates which requirements and criteria the contracting authority will base the conclusion of a contract, the selection of qualified undertakings and the award of the contract conditional on.

---

43. Also the type of contract is a factor in determining the level of influence the "contractor" is able to exert over the project, organisation and advice are for example features of a turnkey contract. Order of the Complaints Board of 11 June 1999, H. Hoffmann og Sønner A/S and Others vs. Aalborg Lufthavn AmbA (the Utilities Directive), in which case the Complaints Board emphasised that the call for tenders was for "a turnkey contract for works which had to comply with functional requirements". In that light, a 71% acreage increase compared to the building programme was accepted.

3.1.1 Extensive freedom of choice

In the context of the procurement rules a contracting authority has full powers to manage its own economic funds and decides exclusively whether to make a purchase. An authority pursues an objective in the public interest (such as defence, education, cleaning, etc.) which may require the performance of various activities or the purchase of goods or services. If the means to fulfil the objective in the public interest is the conclusion of a contract with an economic operator for the supply of the required goods or service or execution of works, the procurement rules come into play.[44]

Within the bounds of the decision to make a specific purchase, and obviously keeping within the budgetary framework, the contracting authority has extensive freedom to choose what to buy and to determine the requirements for the properties, quality, price, etc. of the object of the purchase. The procurement rules leave the contracting authority with an extensive freedom of choice to determine how to achieve the objective in the public interest, and in setting out the requirements for the object of the contract, price can be given priority over properties and quality – or vice versa. Also other objectives in the public interest may be included in the decision to award a public contract, such as environmental or social objectives.[45]

When the authority has made its decision, the object of the contract must be described: execution of sewerage work, supply of work tables, land surveying, etc. Furthermore, information on whether it is a framework agreement, on the place of delivery and execution, etc. must be provided, cf. also section 3.3 below on the technical specifications of the contract.[46]

3.1.2 Supplementary requirements

Another consideration to take into account in procurement procedures is whether it should be possible to expand the contract (options) at a later date, and it may also be necessary to lay down various supplementary requirements. Any options under the contract or supplementary requirements must be set out in the contract documents.

An option may, for example, be for a quantitative increase of the contract or an extension of a contemplated building. Or a contract may be scheduled

---

44. A contracting authority may charge an internal department with the supply, etc., cf. chapter 3.1 above.
45. See also section 4 below on the limits, as derived from the EC Treaty and the Directive, within which such criteria can be used.
46. See Annex VII A to the Procurement Directive on the information to be included in the contract notice, point 6.

for a term of four years with the possibility of one or more renewals for, for example, a further year or two.

Further, it may be necessary for a contracting authority to lay down certain requirements for the service to be provided in connection with the object of the contract. For example for the delivery of power units for a district heating plant it is an essential concern to the contracting authority that engine break-downs, if any, are remedied promptly. If the contract is for the delivery of a service, such as ambulance services, the size of the force which the supplier proposes to have on stand-by at all times is a major concern. It may also be necessary to specify which competences are required of the supplier's employees, the maximum period of waiting before the service is delivered, guidelines as to fee levels, etc.

Over a long period of time a public contract is often one of a series of public contracts. This is for example the case with bus services which are subject to frequent calls for tenders. Many other public contracts, such as refuse collection, may have to be considered in a wider context and it may be necessary to lay down supplementary requirements to be met by the supplier. The contracting authority may, for example, require the new supplier to purchase existing facilities, take over buildings, equipment and employees, etc.

In the contract documents the contracting authority may also provide information on public obligations relating to taxes, duties, environmental protection, working conditions, etc.[47]

3.2 European law requirements not deriving from the Procurement Directive

Needless to say that in drawing up the contract documents the contracting authority must comply with the Procurement Directive. But the contracting authority is also obliged to comply with the EC Treaty, secondary provisions and an abundance of case law. The following is merely a summary.[48]

3.2.1 Significance of fundamental EC law

The prohibitions of barriers to trade in EU's internal market set out in the EC Treaty are relevant to public procurement. The prohibitions are primarily obligations on the Member States to implement legislation which does not impede or hamper cross-border trade in goods (Article 28) and services (Arti-

---

47. Article 27 of the Procurement Directive.
48. See also Catherine Barnard, The Substantive Law of the EU: The Four Freedoms, Oxford University Press, 2004.

cle 49). However, these obligations on the Member States extend beyond that, in that all public authorities in the Member States are bound thereby and in that they extend to all government activities, including the award of public contracts.[49]

For the purposes of drawing up the contract documents the prohibitions of trade barriers set out in the EC Treaty are particularly relevant to:

– the specification of the requirements for the object of the contract
– both economic criteria (properties, material, quality, competences, etc.)
– and non-economic criteria (environmental and social concerns)

– the specification of the requirements for the performance of the contract
– the specification of the requirements for compliance with certain standards
– the specification of the requirements for evidence and proof
– and, in particular, to the contracting authority's conduct of the procurement procedure and evaluation of the evidence submitted as proof of compliance with the specified requirements.

The Treaty not only prohibits all kinds of discrimination of manufacturers or service providers established in other Member States. The Treaty also prohibits any restriction which is liable to impede or cause inconvenience to the activities of a service provider established in another Member State or render these activities less advantageous.[50]

Whether a criterion laid down in the contract documents is contrary to the Treaty provisions on trade barriers depends first of all on whether the criterion is intended to or has the effect of impeding or hampering cross-border trade in goods and services. Even if this is deemed to be the case, the criterion may nevertheless be maintained provided that it is not liable to discriminate on grounds of nationality[51] and satisfies three other requirements:

– it is justified for reasons of overriding general interest
– it is of a nature that guarantees the achievement of the intended aim

---

49. The provisions of the EC Treaty also apply to areas that fall outside the scope of the Procurement Directive, cf. chapter 1.5.
50. Judgment of the European Court of Justice of 3 October 2000, case C-58/98, Corsten, paragraph 33.
51. If the criterion is liable to discriminate on grounds of nationality, it may, in exceptional cases, be maintained by virtue of Articles 30, 45 and 46 of the EC Treaty and in compliance with the principle of proportionality.

– it does not go beyond that which is necessary in order to achieve that aim.[52]

Based on the principle of proportionality, the European Court of Justice has established a number of explicit obligations that contracting authorities must comply with. At the heart of these obligations is an analysis, to be carried out by the contracting authority, of whether, taking into account its restrictive effects, the criterion is *appropriate* and *proportional* to guaranteeing the underlying public interest.[53]

Of particular importance in award procedures is the obligation on the contracting authority *actively* to evaluate whether foreign qualifications and the accompanying documentation are equivalent to the requirements set out in the contract documents. By virtue of the EC Treaty contracting authorities are obliged:

– to evaluate whether a product offered or a service provider already complies with the properties/qualifications required, for example because it complies with requirements in the country of domicile;
– to include approvals and authorisations granted by other Member States in the evaluation of whether a foreign product or a foreign service provider complies with the requirements;
– to recognise approvals/certificates issued in other countries if the content thereof guarantees achievement of the objective which underlies the criterion set out in the contract documents;
– to lay down a procedure for evaluating the properties of products offered, or the qualifications of service providers, which is reasonably swift, transparant and not expensive and according to which rejections are reasoned and can be subjected to review.

In several judgments the European Court of Justice has held that criteria laid down by Danish authorities in the contract documents were incompatible with the provisions of the EC Treaty. The most well-known case is the judgment in the Great Belt case where a "Danish content clause" was held to be

---

52. Judgment of the European Court of Justice of 3 October 2000, case C-58/98, Corsten, paragraph 35, cf. paragraph 39.
53. Judgment of the European Court of Justice of 13 November 2003, case C-42/02, Diana Elisabeth Lindman, paragraph 25.

an infringement of the EC Treaty.[54] In an order concerning the purchase of windows it was held to be incompatible with Article 28 of the EC Treaty to specify that windows for a building should be of a particular make.[55]

3.2.2 CPV – the Common Procurement Vocabulary

It is a fundamental requirement that contracting authorities describe the object put out to tender in clear and precise terms, cf. section 2.4 above. This specification may be in the form of words, drawings, etc., but the use of words, in particular, may give rise to questions, uncertainties and misunderstandings.

An EU Regulation has introduced a common classification system for public contracts.[56] The Common Procurement Vocabulary is comprehensive and categorises goods, works and services in minute details. The CPV is intended as a common reference nomenclature to ensure that goods, works and services are described in uniform terms in all EU Member States. The CPV is a key feature in the EU efforts to develop competition in the field of public contracts.[57]

In the contract notice the contracting authority must refer to the CPV reference number which is nearest to the object of the purchase.[58] By requiring that reference be made to the CPV, which is available in all the official EU languages, a substantial Community language barrier is eliminated, and, hence, a serious barrier to opening up competition in the field of public contracts for participation by foreign economic operators is gone.[59]

3.3 Specifically about the technical specifications

The contracting authority determines the characteristics and quality requirements of the product, service or works. The requirements must be specified so as to guarantee that the contract is capable of fulfilling the intended objective.

---

54. Judgment of the European Court of Justice of 22 June 1993, case C-243/89, Commission vs. Denmark (Great Belt case), paragraph 23.
55. Order of the European Court of Justice of 3 December 2001, case C-59/00, Bent Mousten Vestergaard.
56. Commission Regulation (EC) No 2151/2003 of 16 December 2003 amending Regulation No 2195/2002 of 5 November 2002 of the European Parliament and the Council (EC) on the Common Procurement Vocabulary (CPV).
57. Recital 36 of the preamble to the Procurement Directive.
58. Annex VII A to the Procurement Directive, point 6.
59. A number of different nomenclatures are used: CPV, NACE and CPC. In Article 1, paragraph 14, second indent of the Procurement Directive is set out which nomenclatures take precedence in the event of varying interpretations.

Requirements may be specified in regard to chemical, physical and technical characteristics, length, weight and height, choice and durability of material, degradability and reusability of material, etc.

3.3.1 General requirements
The technical specifications of the object to be purchased must be set out in the contract documents.[60] The technical specifications should be defined so as to take into account the overriding aim of the Procurement Directive of equal treatment and competition for public contracts.

"Technical specifications shall afford equal access for tenderers and not have the effect of creating unjustified obstacles to the opening up of public procurement to competition."[61]

Also the principles of equal treatment and transparency must be respected.

3.3.2 Technical specifications or performance requirements
The characteristics and quality of the product, service or works are essential to the award of a public contract in that satisfaction of the specific need in the public interest depends thereon. The provision on technical specifications as formulated in the Procurement Directive reflects the efforts made to balance the interest of contracting authorities in making sure they will get a workable solution and, therefore, allowing flexibility with respect to the technical solutions to be applied, against the dual interests of economic operators in presenting various technical solutions and competing on equal terms. Therefore, the Directive affords contracting authorities the *possibility of choosing* whether they want to lay down detailed technical specifications or merely prefer to set out performance or functional requirements.[62]

If the contracting authority, in the contract documents, chooses to refer to technical specifications in terms of published standards, it knows the content of the tenders in advance. The drawback is that such specifications are invariable.

By only setting out the performance or functional requirements for the object of the contract, the emphasis is on the output to be achieved under the contract and not on the technicalities. For the purchase of a pump, for example, the focus may be on capacity rather than on materials, type, etc. The award of a contract for the construction of a swimming pool may hinge on

---

60. Article 23, paragraph 1 of the Procurement Directive. The contract documents are the contract notice, the specifications or additional documents.
61. Article 23, paragraph 2 of the Procurement Directive.
62. Article 23, paragraph 3 of the Procurement Directive.

whether it can be used for Olympic competitions, and for the award of a cleaning contract the decisive factor may be that the result of the performance under the contract is clean premises, etc. rather than the number of hours used, types of cleaning products, etc.

In *Colas Danmark A/S vs. Videbæk Local Authority*[63] the contractor took over the maintenance of the entire local road system for a period of 15 years.

In *Virklund Sport A/S vs. Randers Local Authority*[64] concerning a contract for a mobile ice rink the freezing capacity requirements for the facility were only specified in terms of the size of the ice rink and the maximum temperatures and wind speed at which the facility should be operational.

In *Bladt Industriens vs. Storebælt A/S*[65] a turnkey contract was awarded for the design and construction of an automotive platform for inspection and maintenance of the West Bridge across the Great Belt on the basis of specifications providing that the equipment should have a life of at least 25 years and constructions at least 50 years.

By laying down performance requirements the private sector is invited to be creative and the contracting party is left with much wider options for the performance of the contract. A contracting authority may opt for a combination of specifications and performance requirements to ensure that certain requirements are complied with and that the object of the contract can be used as intended.

The Procurement Directive only provides that performance or functional requirements

"… must be sufficiently precise to allow tenderers to determine the object of the contract and to allow contracting authorities to award the contract".[66]

This is not a particularly restrictive requirement.[67]

63. Order of the Complaints Board of 30 September 2004, Colas Danmark A/S vs. Videbæk Local Authority.
64. Order of the Complaints Board of 8 October 2004, Virklund Sport A/S vs. Randers Local Authority.
65. Order of the Complaints Board of 7 June 2005, Bladt Industries A/S vs. Storebælt A/S.
66. Article 23, paragraph 3 (b) of the Procurement Directive.
67. Variants may spur the economic operators' creativity even more, cf. section 3.6 below. The Directive authorises the use of procedures especially suitable for identifying possible solutions to specific needs and the award of a contract. See chapter 5.2.4 for details about the competitive dialogue procedure, chapter 5.2.5 for "the negotiated procedure" and chapter 5.4.1 for design contests.

3.3.3 Specification of objective criteria

The Procurement Directive provides that technical specifications must be listed in a certain order of preference. First and foremost specifications must be objective, cf. also section 2.2 above. Annex VI is a definition of what is to be understood by a technical specification. The core of this definition is that the criteria specified must be objective and quantifiable in order to prevent discrimination on grounds of nationality and ensure equal treatment of the economic operators.

Only *exceptionally* in circumstances where it is not possible to specify the object of the contract on the basis of objective criteria, can reference be made to a specific trademark, make, origin, production process, etc.[68] Such reference must be accompanied by the words "or equivalent".

In *Georg Berg A/S vs. Køge Local Authority*[69] it was required that "Rockwoll Uncoated laminar roof liners" be used. The Complaints Board found that this constituted a violation for the mere reason that it was not accompanied by the words "or equivalent". It also constituted a violation in that it would have been possible to use precise and intelligible specifications to describe the desired insulation material without mentioning a reference product.

In *Mariendal El-Teknik A/S vs. County of Nordjylland*[70] the technical specifications only made reference to specific trademarks. The Complaints Board found that this constituted a violation of the obligation to provide an objective description and specification of the object of the contract, especially so in the light of the fact that "concise, precise and readily understandable" technical specifications were submitted before the Complaints Board.

The contracting authority is obliged to examine the quality of a product tendered for to determine whether it meets the requirements stipulated.

3.3.4 Standards

To the widest extent possible technical standards must be identified and defined by reference to published standards. In the Procurement Directive a standard is defined as:

---

68. Article 23, paragraph 8 of the Procurement Directive.
69. Order of the Complaints Board of 5 August 2003, Georg Berg A/S vs. Køge Local Authority.
70. Order of the Complaints Board of 12 April 2005, Mariendal El-Teknik A/S vs. County of Nordjylland.

"a technical specification approved by a recognised standardising body for repeated and continuous application …".[71]

References to published standards in the contract documents are likely to contribute greatly to the creation of transparent technical specifications.

In *BN Produkter Danmark A/S vs. Odense Renovationsselskab A/S,*[72] however, it was the reference to a standard which made the contract documents non-transparent. The contracting entity had required that waste containers be made of *glass fibre* and further that the containers should comply with a standard for waste containers made of *plastic.*

The Procurement Directive provides that published standards must be applied in a specific order of preference to the effect that "national standards transposing *European* standards", etc. take precedence. Only where appropriate European standards, etc. do not exist, can reference be made to *national* standards, etc. and only provided that they are accompanied by the words "or equivalent".[73]

The reason for this prioritisation of standards is that a reference to national standards as a criterion for awarding a contract may constitute a serious barrier to trade seeing that often it will only be the economic operators of the Member State of the contracting authority which will be able to document that their products, etc. are certified according to that standard.[74] Reference to European standards transposed by the Member States, in contrast, ensures a common and known basis for all economic operators on which to prepare tenders. It follows that the obligation to use European standards is essential in order to guarantee objective specifications and, hence, equal treatment of economic operators tendering for public contracts.

3.3.5 Innovation

It is for the contracting authority to decide whether it prefers products or services with known and proven features or whether it requires products or services with improved characteristics, performance levels, materials, etc. in

---

71. Annex VI to the Procurement Directive.
72. Order of the Complaints Board of 2 September 2004, BN Produkter Danmark A/S vs. Odense Renovationsselskab A/S.
73. Article 23, paragraph 3 (a).
74. Judgment of the European Court of Justice of 22 September 1988, case 45/87, Commission vs. Ireland (Dundalk).

which case the contracting authority moves into less well-evidenced and partially uncharted territory.[75]

With respect to all contracts, including contracts performed for purposes of testing, research and development, the technical specifications of the object to be purchased must be determined. The exact nature of these specifications depends on the specific object and, frequently, there will not be any applicable published standards, for example where tenders are invited for an innovative product or service. However, this does not alter the fundamental obligation to specify as clearly and unambiguously as possible which product, service or works the award of the contract is for, cf. section 2.4 above.

3.3.6 Certification, documentation and mutual recognition requirement

The *means by which* the economic operator must prove compliance of its product, service or works with the technical specifications and equivalence with the standards referred to are specified in the contract documents. The exact documentation and certification requirements depend on the product, service or works to be purchased; equipment for oil drilling platforms and equipment for dental treatment may both be classified as "goods", but serve different functions and presumably have to comply with different requirements and documentation standards than contracts for emergency services or accounting services, for example.

Documents, etc. may be issued by public or private bodies and also the producer can submit its own internal technical evidence. While the main rule is that the contracting authority defines which documentation it requires, the Directive does prescribe certain restrictions in this respect.

The Procurement Directive imposes an obligation on contracting authorities to evaluate the technical standard, quality and characteristics even of tenders that do not meet the requirements defined by the contracting authority for proof of compliance with the technical specifications and standards. This obligation on the contracting authorities is derived from the general requirement for mutual recognition originating in EC law. Accordingly, a tender must be considered and cannot be rejected:

---

75. The Procurement Directive stipulates special rules for contracts performed for the purposes of research, testing and development which on certain conditions can be awarded after negotiations. Article 30, paragraph 1 (d) and Article 31, paragraph 2 (a) of the Procurement Directive.

"… once the tenderer proves in his tender to the satisfaction of the contracting authority, by whatever appropriate means, that the solutions which he proposes satisfy in an equivalent manner the requirements defined by the technical standards".[76]

Thus, while it is still the contracting authority which, in accordance with the provisions of the Directive, lays down the requirements for the object to be purchased, the Directive nevertheless provides that the compliance of a tender with the specifications may be proved by *other means* than those referred to by the contracting authority. The documentation is intended to ensure that the products tendered for comply with the specifications laid down by the contracting authority, and to that end it is of the utmost importance that the documentation proves to the satisfaction of the contracting authority that the specifications are complied with. In the light of the importance of this documentation to the contracting authority, the Directive stipulates that documents issued by a "recognised body" would be an "appropriate means" to prove compliance.[77]

If the specifications are set out in terms of performance or functional requirements, the tenderer must in an equivalent manner:

"... prove to the satisfaction of the contracting authority and by any appropriate means that the work, product or service in compliance with the standard meets the performance or functional requirements of the contracting authority".[78]

In many cases it is not possible to refer to a standard which exactly meets the performance or functional requirements prescribed by the contracting authority. Even so, a tender cannot be rejected merely on grounds that compliance with the requirement is proved by means of a reference to a product certified to a published standard, etc. if the standard, etc. addresses the performance and functional requirements prescribed by the contracting authority.[79]

3.3.7 Quality management systems

Contracting authorities can require that candidates and tenderers be certified to specific quality standards, such as ISO. While such certification of an economic operator has no direct bearing on the specific purchase, it will nevertheless be significant to the evaluation of whether the economic operator can be expected to provide the right service of the required quality on time. Qual-

76. Article 23, paragraph 4, cf. paragraph 7 of the Procurement Directive.
77. Article 23, paragraphs 4 and 5, cf. paragraph 7 of the Procurement Directive.
78. Article 23, paragraph 5, second indent of the Procurement Directive.
79. Article 23, paragraph 5, first indent of the Procurement Directive.

ity certification requirements are common with respect to both public and private contracts.

The Procurement Directive does not limit contracting authorities' possibilities for requiring candidates and tenderers to be certified to certain quality standards. However, if such a requirement is made, the Procurement Directive imposes a number of obligations on the contracting authority.[80] The contracting authority must refer to quality management systems that are based on European standards. The contracting authority is also obliged to recognise certificates issued by bodies established in other Member States, and it must evaluate any type of evidence submitted by a candidate or tenderer of compliance with quality assurance measures equivalent to those required in the contract documents.

3.3.8 Accessibility criteria for people with disabilities, etc.

The Procurement Directive provides that whenever possible contracting authorities should lay down the technical specifications so as to take into account accessibility criteria for people with disabilities or design for all users.[81] This provision can only be interpreted as a policy statement and it is the individual contracting authority which determines the requirements to be met by the object to be purchased. Accessibility criteria for people with disabilities can be included in the contract documents and laid down as a requirement in the technical specifications, cf. section 4 below.

3.4 Commercial and economic aspects

The contracting authority is obliged to include economic criteria in the basis on which the contract is awarded. Article 53 of the Procurement Directive provides that the award of a public contract be based on one of two criteria: Either "the lowest price only" or the "most economically advantageous tender" from the point of view of the contracting authority in which case the price of the tender must be among the evaluation criteria. The obligation to lay down economic criteria does not exclude the possibility of including non-economic criteria in the basis on which the contract is awarded, cf. section 4 below.

The obligation to lay down economic criteria is consistent with the obligation to award public contracts on the basis of a competition between interested economic operators, and to guarantee effective competition it is neces-

---

80. Article 49 of the Procurement Directive.
81. Article 23, paragraph 1 of the Procurement Directive and recital 29 of the preamble to the Procurement Directive.

sary for the contracting authority to follow a commercial line of thought.[82] Typically, the obligation to lay down economic criteria is not a major concern. Evidently, when making a purchase, the contracting authority concentrates on the price of the purchase, keeping within the budgetary framework and best value for the available funds.

A contracting authority would be expected to make estimates of cash flow and total costs before calling for tenders. Obviously the price of the product, service or works is a weighty factor in the evaluation of the tenders submitted, but it is nevertheless only one component in the calculation of the costs of the purchase. All elements involved with the purchase, such as transport, training, safety equipment, pollution control, disposal, etc., may pose an expense for the authority. A major share of the total costs of acquiring rolling stock, for example, would be linked with service, maintenance, wearing parts and spare parts.

The funds to finance the purchase may be provided for in the budget, a loan may be raised, or a leasing contract or a concession may be concluded, etc. This is also stipulated in the contract documents as are choice of currency, time and means of payment.

In the contract documents the contracting authority may specify the economic resources available and also the price it is willing to pay for the product, service or works. However, usually these figures are not disclosed to the tenderers, and the price of the contract is one of the competitive elements that the award is based upon.[83]

3.5 Contract

Usually a draft of the contract to be concluded between the contracting authority and the successful tenderer is included among the contract documents. The draft contract sets out various technical, economic and legal details. The designation 'draft' contract should not be taken literally; the details set out in the contract are generally formulated as requirements or conditions which are not open for competition or negotiation, cf. section 5 below. This should be borne in mind while at the same time remembering that any reservations made by a tenderer or irregularities of the tender compared to the requirements or condi-

---

82. See also chapter 1.2 above.
83. Order of the Complaints Board of 8 October 1997, Danish Council of Practising Architects: In that case one essential element was that the contracting authority had stipulated a financial framework and it therefore became necessary to evaluate whether the projects submitted could be cut back without violating the principle of equal treatment and the prohibition on negotiations.

tions specified in the contract documents are likely to oblige the contracting authority to reject the tender.

It is a feature of procurement law that the contracting authority is not free to choose its contracting party, but must select one on the basis of the tenders submitted and the pre-determined and advertised award criteria.[84] The contract is, therefore, concluded on the basis of the contract documents and the successful tender without any scope for amendments, negotiations, etc.[85] As a consequence, the parties' rights and obligations under the contract, such as the terms of delivery, payment, passing of risk, performance, guarantees, etc., must have been thought through before the drawing up of the contract documents, in which connection it must also be determined which elements should be open for competition, cf. section 5 below.

For the purposes of preparing a tender it is of great importance to understand the characteristics of procurement law. Under Danish law an offer is binding on the offeror until it is either accepted or rejected by the contractor. Usually the contract documents stipulate a tender validity period which the tenderers must respect. As mentioned above, it is not possible to amend the tender or conduct actual negotiations.

The draft contract is an important part of the contract documents. Since the contracting authority prepares the draft contract it is, from a business perspective, allowed an unusual and more one-sided opportunity for safeguarding its own interests than would be the case if the contract were subject to negotiations.[86] In terms of procurement law contract documents in which essential legal issues, such as passing of risk, guarantee, payment of interest, price adjustments, penalty, etc., are not mentioned, by way of a draft contract, will more often than not be considered deficient.[87]

The exact content of the contract is only limited by the contracting authority's requests and the draftsman's knowledge of the specific object and type of contract. It is customary to set out rights and obligations, but it is also possible to include elements targeting cooperation, economic incentives for early

---

84. This is the case where the open procedure, the restricted procedure and to some extent the competitive dialogue procedure are used.
85. See also chapter 7.
86. Order of the Complaints Board of 26 August 2004, Per Aarsleff A/S vs. Amager Strandpark I/S for payment of preparations for winter.
87. Order of the Complaints Board of 21 March 2002, Holsted minibus rep. by taxicab owner Keld T. Hansen vs. Næstved Local Authority: a four months' trial period was consistent with the Service Directive, now repealed.

and correct performance, particular mechanisms for solving difficulties of interpretation and disputes, etc.[88]

3.6 Variants[89]

The presumption of the Procurement Directive is that the contracting authorities have knowledge of the technical solutions available on the market.[90] It thus follows that by defining the exact technical specifications of the object to be purchased and by specifying performance and functional requirements the contracting authority can draft the contract documents so as to achieve the requested quality and properties, cf. section 3.3 above.

However, a contracting authority may be interested in allowing economic operators to submit tenders which are based, in whole or in part, on other solutions than those proposed by the contracting authority. In many situations the economic operators are likely to have better knowledge of possible solutions, durability of materials, etc. than both the contracting authority and the consultant(s). The Procurement Directive provides that the contracting authorities can authorise submission of variants, which must be indicated in the contract notice.[91] By authorising variants the contracting authority relies on the tenderers' creativity and market knowledge and hence obtains a broader basis on which to make its decision.

Submission of variants can only be authorised in procedures where the public contract is awarded on the basis of the award criterion "the most economically advantageous tender". In the interest of ensuring equal treatment of tenderers and consistency in the evaluation of the tenders submitted the award criterion "the most economically advantageous tender" must be applied to the evaluation of the regular tenders as well as the variants.[92]

Variants not only concern the technical solutions. In theory, variants can be authorised with regard to all elements of the contract. One example is the use of environmentally acceptable materials; to that end variants may serve as a basis for comparing a conventional solution and an environmentally sound

---

88. See also chapter 5.3 on partnering contracts.
89. See also chapter 7.5 on the treatment of regular tenders and variants in procedures for the award of contracts.
90. External consultants can be engaged to help prepare the procedure.
91. Article 24, paragraphs 1 and 2 of the Procurement Directive, cf. Annex VII to the Procurement Directive.
92. Order of the Complaints Board of 9 June 2004, Per Aarsleff A/S vs. County of Funen and Odense Local Authority.

solution.[93] Variants may also be invited with respect to the funding to the effect that instead of paying for the supply of products or the construction of buildings in a traditional manner, the consideration may, for example, be by way of the award of a concession contract.

In procedures where variants are authorised, tenderers cannot submit more tenders which differ on price *only*. A tenderer must optimise its tender, and submission of a number of tenders differing in terms of price to be opened in a certain order would in reality mean that the price could be negotiated. Nor would submission of tenders that differ on price be consistent with the requirement for finality of tenders.[94]

It is the contracting authority which makes a purchase and conducts a procedure for the purpose of awarding a contract to a supplier. Therefore, variants can only be authorised if the contracting authority specifies *minimum requirements* to be met by the variants.[95] The minimum requirements must be linked to the object to be purchased to ensure a certain basis of comparison for the submitted tenders and variants and to the effect that the rules of the Procurement Directive are not bypassed. The object of the contract must be identifiable to enable the tenderers to prepare tenders and the contract to be awarded, which may be facilitated by defining precise technical specifications, performance requirements or both. The contracting authority is largely free to determine whichever minimum requirements it wishes as long as they are clear, unambiguous and, to the extent possible, objective.[96]

The minimum requirements must be set out in the contract documents or the contract notice. It follows from the obligation to ensure transparency of the procedure and equal treatment of tenderers that this is the only means by

---

93. Guidelines from the Competition Authority and the Environmental Protection Agency: Green Procurement – guidelines into the possibilities of taking environmental considerations into account in procurement procedures, 2002, p. 9.

94. If the tenderer indicates that a tender is a variant, the contracting authority is obliged to assess whether that is really the case. Order of the Complaints Board of 14 October 2003, KK-Ventilation A/S vs. County of Vejle (the Danish Tender Act).

95. Article 24, paragraph 3 of the Procurement Directive; order of the Complaints Board of 21 June 2004, Banverket vs. Nordjyske Jernbaner A/S (the Utilities Directive); order of the Complaints Board of 23 February 2001, Kæmpes Taxi and Nordfyns Busser rep. by Hans Kæmpe vs. Søndersø Local Authority.

96. Order of the Complaints Board of 14 September 1998, Danish Chamber of Commerce vs. Statistics Denmark; order of the Complaints Board of 18 November 1996, European Metro Group vs. Ørestadsselskabet I/S, which order was upheld by judgment of the Eastern High Court of 16 September 2002 in case no. B-104-97 (3rd div.), European Metrogroup vs. Ørestadsselskabet.

which tenderers can be informed of the minimum requirements.[97] Having
established that a variant meets the specified minimum requirements, it is to
be decided whether to award the contract on the basis of the variant (or the
regular tender).[98] This decision is based on the award criterion the "most
economically advantageous tender" and the same sub-criteria that apply to
the evaluation of the other submitted tenders.

4. Non-economic criteria – social and environmental considera-tions[99] [100]

The possibilities for including non-economic considerations in procurement
procedures are examined in this section. Particular emphasis is on the possibilities of basing the award of a public contract on non-economic criteria, cf.
sections 4.4 and 4.5 below.[101]

4.1 Contracting authorities and non-economic considerations
Public authorities are responsible for important public duties and pursue important public objectives, such as education of children and young people,
protection of public health, maintenance of a legal system, refuse collection
and waste treatment and many more. In order to achieve these objectives
public authorities need to make purchases.

In connection with the purchase of specific supplies, services or works the
contracting authority needs to take certain concerns into consideration (price,

---

97. Judgment of the European Court of Justice of 16 October 2003, case C-421/01,
Traunfellner, paragraph 29.
98. Order of the Complaints Board of 31 August 1998, Miri Stål A/S vs. Ringsted Local
Authority.
99. Joël Arnould, Secondary Policies in Public Procurement: The Innovations of the New
Directive, 13 Public Procurement Law Review 2004, pp. 187 ff.
100. Commission Working Paper of 18 August 2004: Buying Green! A handbook on
environmental public procurement, SEC (2004) 1050; Interpretative Communication
of the Commission of 15 October 2001 on the Community law applicable to public
procurement and the possibilities for integrating social considerations into public procurement, COM(2001)0566; Interpretative Communication of the Commission of 5
July 2001 on the Community law applicable to public procurement and the possibilities for integrating environmental considerations into public procurement,
COM(2001)0274. The Communications date back to 2001 and were thus issued before the judgment of the European Court of Justice of 17 September 2002 in case C-
513/99, Concordia Oy AB.
101. See also chapter 7.2.6 on sub-criteria for the award of contracts.

quality, delivery time, reliability of supply, etc.) in order to best satisfy the need in question. In addition, the authority is typically keen to protect and guarantee social and environmental objectives. Social and environmental objectives are considered non-economic interests in that these interests are unlikely to be protected by the market. However, the protection of these interests is of great public concern and may be the direct responsibility of the authorities, for example a local authority, or perhaps simply consistent with the overall public policy. In preparing a procedure the contracting authority can seek to promote such non-economic interests.

The term *environmental considerations* refers to, for example, the public interest in avoiding, to the extent possible, the use, discharge, emission, etc. of substances that are likely to seriously distort the equilibrium in nature or present a serious threat to human health, or the public interest in counteracting the negative effects of such discharge, etc.[102] The public interest in the use of energy generated by renewable sources of energy (such as the sun, wind and water) is also an environmental consideration.[103]

The term *social considerations* refers to the public interest in guaranteeing vulnerable persons access to the job market for example by giving certain groups of people priority to certain jobs. The public interest in guaranteeing workers' rights and working conditions, for example equal treatment, working hours and minimum pay, is also a social consideration.

4.2 Public contracts and non-economic considerations

This section sets out some overall reflections on the possibilities of taking economic and non-economic considerations into account in procurement procedures.

4.2.1 Economic considerations

Evidently the economic value of a tender to the contracting authority must be taken into consideration when awarding a public contract: the costs of the purchase, total costs, quality, delivery time, etc. These considerations are consistent with the aim of the Procurement Directive: contracting authorities must base the award of contracts on cost-effective concerns and they must pretend to operate on market terms.

---

102. Judgment of the European Court of Justice of 17 September 2002, case C-513/99, Concordia Oy AB.
103. Judgment of the European Court of Justice of 4 December 2003, case C-448/01, EVN AG; judgment of the European Court of Justice of 13 March 2001, case C-379/98, PreussenElektra.

Undoubtedly a contracting authority *can* base the award of a public contract on economic considerations *only*. In so doing the contracting authority does not entirely preclude that other objectives, especially environmental objectives, may be pursued since protection of the environment, even from a narrow economic perspective, may represent an economic advantage to the contracting authority. By requiring compliance with environmental criteria the contracting authority may gain a direct economic advantage from the object purchased, for example by taking into account the costs of maintenance, waste treatment or recycling.

4.2.2 Legislation and non-economic considerations

In each of the EU Member States the public interest in protecting environmental and social concerns has prompted extensive legislative activity. The State's protection of environmental and social concerns by means of national *regulation* does not generally conflict with the EU's interest in creating an internal market in that the protected interests are indeed non-economic. The specific regulation, as drafted by the Member State, may be inconsistent with the prohibition of discrimination on grounds of nationality of Article 12 of the EC Treaty, the prohibition of trade barriers of *inter alia* Articles 28 and 49 of the Treaty or not be in keeping with the requirements set out in the Provision of Information Directive.[104]

At the EU level several legislative acts have been adopted for the purpose of harmonising the legislation of the Member States in these areas. National legislation, as amended by EU directives, imposes obligations on public authorities to be observed *inter alia* in connection with procedures for the award of public contracts. In addition, "recommendations" have been issued concerning the protection of the environment and the pursuit of social objectives which a contracting authority may take into account when awarding public contracts.

4.2.3 Procurement and non-economic considerations

Contracting authorities differ from private contractors in that they are part of the public sector. It is the responsibility of contracting authorities to protect public interests, and it may therefore be sensible and expedient if a contracting authority in procurement procedures, where factors such as price, quality,

---

104. Directive 98/34/EC of the European Parliament and of the Council of 22 June 1998 laying down a procedure for the provision of information in the field of technical standards and regulation.

delivery time, etc. are important, also pays attention to other public policy concerns than those directly linked to the object about to be purchased.

Contracting authorities in Denmark may take non-economic interests into consideration in procurement procedures. The scope for integrating non-economic interests may seem somewhat "erratic" and to the tendering under-taking it may be felt like an extraordinary coercive measure. Despite this, there is no doubt that a contracting authority can lawfully base the award of a contract on *inter alia* secondary, non-economic criteria, such as environmental and social objectives, provided that these criteria are *objective* and linked to the object of the procurement.

However, under the Procurement Directive the protection of non-economic interests is not without problems. Primarily because the contracting authority's focus in procurement procedures lies on economic concerns, and the Directive prescribes a direct obligation to base the award of a public contract on economic criteria, cf. section 4.5.5 below. The focus of attention on economic interests does not seem easily reconcilable with the pursuit of non-economic objectives. Indeed two different objectives are sought achieved in the award of public contracts.[105]

In combination with the fact that it is difficult to quantify and guarantee the objectivity of social and environmental considerations, there is a risk that non-objective or even illicit interests are taken into account while at the same time making the control thereof difficult. Finally, on several occasions the protection of non-economic interests has tended towards favouring undertakings or individuals from the same Member State as the contracting authority.

4.3 The three stages of a procurement and non-economic considerations

There is no doubt that also under EU rules can social and environmental considerations be taken into account in procedures for the award of a public contract. Already in a Green Paper from 1996 did the Commission state that the purchasing power of the public sector could be an important means to control the practices of economic operators.[106]

The reasoning is that because of its *scale* a purchasing policy aimed at furthering protection of the environment or guaranteeing the protection of

---

105. Recital 46, third indent of the preamble to the Procurement Directive reads: "The determination of these criteria depends on the object of the contract since they must allow the level of performance offered by each tender to be assessed in the light of the object of the contract, as defined in the technical specifications, and the value for money of each tender to be measured."
106. Commission Green Paper on Public Procurement, 1996.

social interests can impact considerably on undertakings' behaviour and thus contribute greatly to furthering environmental protection and guaranteeing the protection of social concerns.

It has been difficult to find common ground with respect to the means by which these interests could be protected. A difference of opinion which lasted until the *Concordia* judgment by the European Court of Justice[107] and the adoption of the Procurement Directive. The Commission very staunchly insisted on separating the economic considerations linked to the *award* of a contract from the environmental and social objectives that are pursued.

The integration of non-economic interests in procurement procedures has necessitated a division of the procedure into three stages:

–   *The preparation of the contract documents*, including definition of the object of the contract, definition of technical specifications and determination of terms (conditions) for the performance
–   *The award*, conduct of the procedure as provided in the Directive and selection of a contracting party on the basis of pre-determined criteria.
–   *The performance*, materialisation of the object of the contract by way of delivery of supplies, provision of services or execution of works, in which connection the terms (conditions) for the performance are relevant.

Only the award stage is covered by the Procurement Directive. The Directive meticulously sets out how a contracting authority gets from the stage where the object of the contract is defined and conditions determined, to the stage where a contracting party has been selected and a contract can be concluded. The Directive does not address the preparatory and performance stages and in these respects the contracting authority is only bound by the rules and principles of the EC Treaty.

As a first point it will be analysed how non-economic considerations can play a role in defining the object and the technical specification, cf. section 4.3.1. Then there will be an analysis of how non-economic considerations can be laid down as requirements for the performance, cf. section 4.3.2. Finally, it is briefly mentioned that non-economic objectives can be laid down as criteria for variants, cf. section 4.3.3. The possibilities for basing the award of a contract on *inter alia* non-economic criteria are analysed in sections 4.4 and 4.5.

---

107. Judgment of the European Court of Justice of 17 September 2002, case C-513/99, Concordia Oy AB.

4.3.1 The object and the technical specifications

Provided that the provisions of free movement stipulated in the EC Treaty are respected, the margin for defining the requirements to be met by the object of the contract is wide, cf. section 3.1 above. In *Concordia*[108] the Attorney-General expressed it as follows:

"In general, any administration which so wishes can, in defining the goods or services which it intends to purchase, choose the products and services which correspond with its pre-occupations for the protection of the environment."[109]

Environmental and social considerations may be elements which contribute to *defining the object of the contract*. Indeed the object of the purchase may be required in order to fulfil an environmental objective (purification plant, filters for power plants, measuring equipment, etc.) or a social objective (construction of a sheltered workshop, audible warnings at traffic lights, language services, etc.).

The specifications may stipulate environmental and social requirements as a measure of the *quality of the object of the contract*.[110] Houses, for example, may be projected with the aim of ensuring low future energy consumption. This may influence the location of the buildings, choice of materials, window areas, sources of heat, etc. There may be requirements with respect to health and hygiene, broad doorways ensuring easy entry, signs for the blind, etc.

For a service, such as for example public bus transport, performance of the transport is the main service under the contract. As a measure of the quality of the main service and the costs involved with the contract it is relevant to look at the durability of the busses, their fuel consumption, etc. Other quality aspects are the emissions of harmful substances from the busses, the possibilities for reusing the individual parts of the busses, etc. Another example is cleaning contracts which may require that the products used are naturally degradable.

Also for the *execution* of construction work or a service, e.g. refuse collection, the contracting authority can determine requirements. Such requirements may concern energy consumption, waste management, noise, time of collection, etc.

---

108. Ibid.
109. Ibid, paragraph 79.
110. Environmental characteristics and environmental performance are explicitly given as examples of technical specifications in Article 23, paragraph 3, cf. paragraph 6 of the Procurement Directive and Annex VI to the Procurement Directive.

It is not clear to which extent requirements can be made with respect to *production methods*. If and to the extent that the choice of production method has a bearing on the quality of the end-result, the object of the contract, there is no doubt that requirements can be specified for the production method. For example where the only way to eliminate pesticide residues in vegetables completely is by using organic production methods, a requirement that such production methods be used is justified. It is more questionable in circumstances where the production method has no bearing on the quality of the end-result. Presumably, however, a contracting authority can legally require that certain production processes be applied, including the use of organic production methods, even where they are not believed to have any *quantifiable* effect on the quality and properties of the end-result. However, a requirement like that is conditional on the contracting authority being able to verify that an offered product is in fact produced by the required production method.[111]

4.3.2 Terms and conditions for the performance

Contracting authorities enjoy considerable latitude in laying down terms and conditions for the performance of a public contract. The Commission regards this as one of the principal means by which social and environmental considerations can be taken into account. By making the award of a public contract conditional on compliance with social and environmental requirements the contracting authority is able to ensure that social and environmental objectives are achieved whether the works is executed, the service provided or the product supplied by a public or a private supplier.

The Procurement Directive contains a provision on the "conditions for the performance of contracts":

"Contracting authorities may lay down special conditions relating to the performance of a contract, provided that these are compatible with Community law and are indicated in the contract notice or in the specifications. The conditions governing the performance of a contract may, in particular, concern social and environmental considerations."[112]

The award of the public contract is the conclusion of the contracting process. The performance of the public contract is *not* covered by the obligations set

111. See also section 4.5.2 below regarding the requirement that selection criteria be objective and section 4.5.5 below on the possibilities for verifying whether the requirements have been complied with.
112. Article 26 of the Procurement Directive.

out in the Procurement Directive, and therefore, the requirements specified need not be directly linked to the object of the contract; it is suffice if they are relevant to the contracting authority's pursuit of objective public policy concerns, such as protection of the environment or social interests.

Against that background it is possible to determine requirements and conditions for, for example, working environment, equal treatment, ethical standards and rights for vulnerable groups of persons, for example the long-term unemployed. The *Guidelines on social considerations*[113] issued by the Danish Competition Authority highlights three aims to be achieved by social clauses:

– To prevent – e.g. by implementing overall measures in the undertaking to prevent illness and physical and mental burn out.
– To maintain – by launching initiatives securing employees' continued employment with the undertaking – e.g. after long absence due to illness.
– To integrate – by accommodating the undertaking to people who are not on the labour market, e.g. groups such as the long-term unemployed, people on rehabilitation benefits, ethnic minorities, etc.[114]

Requirements which are either linked to the object of the contract or to the contracting authority should not give cause for concern, provided that they are founded in consistent and published public policies and are not examples of random discrimination.

In the assessment of whether a requirement is objective and relevant to the specific purchase, account will be had of whether the contracting authority has a defined strategy for achieving the particular non-economic objective, and it must be required that it can be verified that the objective is achieved.

The scope for including social and environmental considerations is wide as long as the economic operators are not discriminated against on grounds of nationality and the requirements do not in any way constitute indirect barriers to trade between the EU Member States.

4.3.3 Non-economic interests and variants

Neither the EC Treaty nor the Procurement Directive requires that public contracts be awarded exclusively on the basis of economic criteria. Although environmental and social considerations, taken in isolation, often have the effect of increasing costs, thus leading to a higher price than what would be

---

113. Guidelines from the Competition Authority: Social considerations in public procurement – guidelines into the possibilities for including social considerations in procurement procedures, 2004.
114. Ibid, p. 9.

achievable were these considerations not taken into account, it is for the contracting authority to decide how to spend its resources. Environmental and social considerations pose no problems to the competition or equal treatment of economic operators seeing that interested undertakings submit tenders on the same basis.

Indeed because environmental and social considerations may increase costs, the contracting authority may want to know which additional costs are incidental to these considerations. One method of identifying these additional costs is to allow the submission of variants.[115] By choosing this procedure tenderers are asked to submit one tender based on traditional solutions and one or more tenders in which certain defined social and/or environmental considerations are taken into account.[116]

4.4 Generally about award on the basis of non-economic criteria

Previously it was unclear whether contracts could be awarded on the basis of *inter alia* non-economic criteria. It is now clear that they can.

Presumably the aim of the Procurement Directive of opening up public contracts for competition was a very weighty factor in the Commission's reluctance to accept integration of environmental and social considerations into the basis on which public contracts are awarded. It is possible to point to three reasons for the Commission's reluctance.

– If the award is based on criteria that are not linked to the object of the contract, for example the *tenderer's* general policy concerning the disabled, equal treatment, etc., it may defeat the aim of the Directive: equal competition for public contracts is likely to be jeopardised if it is taken into account whether, for example, the overall behaviour of an undertaking is socially responsible.[117]
– If the contracting authority can evaluate tenders on the basis of the more non-economic advantages they offer, it will, viewed separately and from a short-term perspective, result in increased costs compared to the costs of the sole attainment of the specific objective in the public interest.

---

115. See also section 3.6 above
116. The award of the contract is to be made on the basis of the criteria laid down, which criteria must be ranked in order of priority and weighed against each other.
117. Violation of environmental or social legislation may in the specific case cause an undertaking to be excluded from a procurement procedure. See chapter 6 below.

– Finally, there is a risk that non-economic considerations may lead to lack of transparency in the award of contracts since different criteria (economic and non-economic) must be balanced against each other.

4.4.1 Authority to integrate non-economic criteria

Contracting authorities have always been free to choose the award criteria provided that they served to identify the tender most economically advantageous to the contracting authority.[118] This freedom has now been extended to non-economic criteria. Therefore in principle, it is now possible to award a public contract on the basis of *inter alia* which tender best satisfies non-economic criteria, or non-economic criteria may be given no role whatsoever in the competition for public contracts. In *Concordia*[119] the Advocate General expressed it as follows:

"As public authorities have by definition a duty to serve the public interest, that interest must be able to guide them when they enter into a public contract."[120]

Or in more explicit terms: it would be altogether wrong if it was not possible to base the award of a public contract for the acquisition of buses, for example, on the degree to which they pollute or produce noise.

The statutory authority is explained below.

4.4.1.1 The EC Treaty

The European Economic Community, which Denmark joined in 1972, has been transformed into a European community and a European union. In the course of the transformation a number of new areas of policy, including social policy and environmental policy, have become areas of Community policy.

These new areas of policy are not new to the Member States as they have traditionally been responsible for social policy and the protection of the environment. What is new is that the EU acts as caretaker of these areas.

Environmental policy is a top EU priority being one of objectives of the EU as stipulated in Article 2 of the EC Treaty:

---

118. Judgment of the European Court of Justice of 20 September 1988, case 31/87, Gebroeders Beentjes BV.
119. Judgment of the European Court of Justice of 17 September 2002, case C-513/99, Concordia Oy AB.
120. Ibid, paragraph 93.

"Economic progress and social cohesion, and a high level of protection and improvement of the quality of the environment, are complementary pillars of sustainable development and are at the heart of the process of European integration."

This is explicitly expressed in Article 6 of the EC Treaty:

"Environmental protection requirements must be integrated into the definition of an implementation of the Community policies and activities referred to in Article 3, in particular with a view to promoting sustainable development."[121]

Pursuant to the provision in Article 6 of the EC Treaty the following general statement on the protection of the environment is inserted in the Procurement Directive:

"This Directive therefore clarifies how the contracting authorities may contribute to the protection of the environment and the promotion of sustainable development, whilst ensuring the possibility of obtaining the best value for money for their contracts."[122]

Also the integration of social considerations is given a high priority within the EU. Article 2 of the EC Treaty provides that some of the aims of the Community are to promote a high-level of employment and of social protection, equality between men and women and economic and social cohesion

4.4.1.2 The European Court of Justice
The foundation on which the Procurement Directive opens up the possibility for integrating non-economic interests in procurement procedures is found in *Concordia.*[123] The judgment concerned the city of Helsinki's call for tenders for a contract concerning the provision of buses based *inter alia* on the level of noise produced by the buses and their emission of certain harmful substances. The European Court of Justice made it clear that the provision on the award criterion "the most economically advantageous tender" in the then applicable directive:

"... cannot be interpreted as meaning that each of the award criteria used by the contracting authority to identify the economically most advantageous tender must necessarily be of

121. See also recital 5 of the preamble to the Procurement Directive, first sentence. Articles 174 ff of the EC Treaty set out guidelines for an environmental policy for the Community.
122. Recital 5 of the preamble to the Procurement Directive, second sentence.
123. Judgment of the European Court of Justice of 17 September 2002, case C-513/99, Concordia Oy AB.

a purely economic nature. It cannot be excluded that factors which are not purely economic may influence the value of a tender from the point of view of the contracting authority."[124]

The judgment thus established that conditions concerning the protection of the environment could be integrated into the award criterion in identifying the most economically advantageous tender.

4.4.1.3 The Procurement Directive

It is now explicitly provided in the Procurement Directive that environmental and social considerations can be integrated into the award criteria for a public contract.[125] In specific terms this means that the regulation of contracting authorities' award of public contracts is not merely focused on market entry, equal terms of competition and economic considerations. Accordingly, it is beyond doubt that contracting authorities can take account of social and environmental public policy concerns in award procedures for public contracts.

4.4.2 Economic and non-economic value of the criteria
to the contracting authority

Traditionally it has been the understanding that if the award criterion "the most economically advantageous tender" was chosen, then only criteria capable of identifying an increase in the economic value of the tenders submitted could be used. On that account it might be assumed that non-economic criteria likewise only can be integrated if they are of an economic value to the contracting authority. This is not the case.

4.4.2.1 Must non-economic criteria be of economic value?

Firstly, it is not a requirement that social or environmental considerations integrated into the basis for the award must afford the contracting authority *an economic value linked to the contract*. Secondly, it is neither a requirement that the social or environmental public policy concerns pursued are of an *economic* value to the contracting authority. They merely have to be of *value to the contracting authority*, but not necessarily an economic one.[126]

124. Ibid, paragraph 55. See also judgment of the European Court of Justice of 4 December 2003, case C-448/01, EVN AG, paragraph 34 concerning an award criterion requiring the supply of electricity produced by means of renewable sources of energy.
125. Recitals 1, 5 and 44 of the preamble to the Procurement Directive and Article 53 of the Procurement Directive.
126. It follows from recital 46 of the preamble to the Procurement Directive, third indent that award criteria must be determined to "… allow the level of performance offered by each tender to be assessed in the light of the object of the contract, as defined in

In other words and in the context of *Concordia*,[127] it is still legitimate to evaluate tenders submitted in the light of the economic advantages they offer the authorities and which are linked to the town's bus service, but it is also legitimate to award a public contract to the tender which offers advantages to the town overall, for example a reduction in the level of pollution and noise in the town.

4.4.2.2 Award criterion or condition

As stipulated above under 4.3.2, non-economic objectives can be achieved by laying down terms and conditions for the performance of the public contract to ensure that the public policy concerns are pursued even where the public contract or the public responsibility is awarded to an economic operator. There are, in fact, advantages to be gained from integrating environmental and social considerations in the award decision. By integrating environmental considerations into the award criterion more environmental value for money is achieved. The level of pollution caused by the object to be purchased becomes a competitive parameter

As for social considerations there may be a public interest in promoting the integration of certain groups of people into the job markets, groups such as refugees, the long-term unemployed, people with reduced working capacity, etc.

The objective of ensuring employment for these groups of people may be laid down *as conditions*, but appropriately set up, there is nothing to prevent the local authority from inviting competitive tenders from its contractors to determine who is best able to handle this responsibility. Obviously, the price of a purchase carries heavy weight, but social responsibility and social duties are also serious concerns and the use of social criteria as award parameters may be instrumental in making private tenderers more active, thus enabling contracting authorities to make use of their creativity to achieve integration.

4.4.3 Weighting of economic and non-economic criteria[128]

In principle a social or environmental criterion can be given whatever weight is desired. In EVN[129] the award of a contract for the supply of electricity was

---

the technical specifications, and the value for money of each tender to be measured", cf. also section 4.5.5 below.

127. Judgment of the European Court of Justice of 17 September 2002, case C-513/99, Concordia Oy AB. See also section 4.4.1.2 above.

128. See also chapter 7.2.7 on the weighting of criteria.

conditional on two criteria: the net price per kWh – with a weighting of 55% - and energy produced from renewable sources of energy – with a weighting of 45%. In regard to this the European Court of Justice stated:

"... provided that they comply with the requirements of Community law, contracting authorities are free not only to choose the criteria for awarding the contract but also to determine the weighting of such criteria, provided that the weighting enables an overall evaluation to be made of the criteria applied in order to identify the most economically advantageous tender".[130]

Article 53 of the Procurement Directive provides that a contracting authority must specify in advance the weighting given to each of the chosen criteria.[131]

However, taking into account that within the framework of the Directive non-economic criteria are secondary to economic criteria, they cannot be given a weighting of more than 50% in the award decision.

4.5 Specifically about non-economic criteria in the award
The European Court of Justice[132] and the Commission have laid down, in the Procurement Directive, a number of conditions to be satisfied by non-economic criteria applied to the award of a public contract:

- the criteria must be linked to the object of the contract;
- the criteria must not confer an unrestricted freedom of choice on the contracting authority;
- the criteria must be expressly mentioned in the contract documents or the contract notice;
- the criteria must comply with all the fundamental principles of Community law, including in particular the principle of non-discrimination; and
- the criteria chosen must be capable of identifying the most economically advantageous tender.

129. Judgment of the European Court of Justice of 4 December 2003, case C-448/01, EVN AG.
130. Ibid, paragraph 39.
131. See also 5.3.3 below and chapter 7.
132. Judgment of the European Court of Justice of 4 December 2003, case C-448/01, EVN AG, paragraphs 33 and 37; judgment of the European Court of Justice of 17 September 2002, case C-513/99, Concordia Oy AB, paragraphs 59, 64 and 69.

4.5.1 Criteria must be linked to the object of the contract
Pursuant to Article 53, paragraph 1 of the Procurement Directive the criteria must be:

"… linked to the object of the public contract in question …".

The reason for the requirement that the criteria be linked to the object of the contract is that a contract is to be awarded and a winner has to be found among the tenderers. The opportunities for the tenderers to submit the most economically advantageous tender for the contract would not be equal if the award was based on criteria which are irrelevant to the object of the contract.[133] It follows that if a concern is merely of a more general interest to *the particular contracting authority*, it can only be laid down as a contract term.

Furthermore, environmental and social criteria must be objective. The objectivity is *inter alia* determined by whether there is a published and consistently applied policy for the particular area.[134] Objective environmental criteria may, for example, be requirements which are intended to reduce the emission of harmful substances into the environment from the object of the contract when put to use or in connection with the performance of works, a service contract, etc. Another example is an evaluation based on whether energy is produced from renewable sources of energy.

A tenderer's *general* ability to protect the environment or *general* attitude to social concerns cannot be taken into consideration in the award of a public contract. An undertaking's ability to undertake social obligations can only be taken into consideration in the selection of qualified applicants if and to the extent that it proves the undertaking's ability to perform a specific contract.[135]

In *EVN*[136] the European Court of Justice held that it would constitute discrimination among the tenderers in contravention of the Directive if the award of an electricity supply contract is based on the overall percentage of the tenderer's capacity which originated from renewable sources of energy.[137]

---

133. Judgment of the European Court of Justice of 4 December 2003, case C-448/01, EVN AG, paragraph 66.
134. See also the list of terms and conditions in section 4.3.2 above.
135. Judgment of the European Court of Justice of 4 December 2003, case C-448/01, EVN AG, paragraph 66.
136. Ibid.
137. Ibid, paragraph 66.

4.5.2 Criteria must not confer an unrestricted freedom
of choice on the contracting authority

This condition is fundamental in procurement law in that it is reflective of the concern that within the authority's scope for discretion in awarding a public contract non-objective and discriminatory interests may be taken into consideration.[138]

Under the Procurement Directive and the EC Treaty the contracting authority is free to apply its economic resources as it chooses in determining the requirements for the object of the contract, and it may choose to emphasise the characteristics, quality, price, environmental friendliness, etc. of the object. To that end the contracting authority is free to choose the criteria for awarding the contract.[139]

For many years the European Court of Justice has pointed out that criteria for awarding a contract must be objective.[140] The worry is that if a criterion cannot be assessed objectively it opens up the possibility for arbitrary choice and thus an obvious risk of discrimination among the tenderers, which is indeed what the Procurement Directive is intended to prevent.[141]

The Procurement Directive sets out an explicit provision on the objectivity of criteria as a condition for laying down non-economic criteria:

"In order to guarantee equal treatment, the criteria for the award of the contract should enable tenders to be compared and assessed objectively. If these conditions are fulfilled, economic and qualitative criteria for the award of the contract, such as meeting environmental requirements, may enable the contracting authority to meet the needs of the public concerned, as expressed in the specifications of the contract. Under the same conditions, a contracting authority may use criteria aiming to meet social requirements, in response in particular to the needs – defined in the specifications of the contract – of particularly disadvantaged groups of people to which those receiving/using the works, supplies or services which are the object of the contract belong."[142]

Once the object of the contract has been determined, the requirements that it is to meet must be specified objectively. Further, insofar as possible, reference should be made to a published standard, cf. section 3 above.

---

138. Ibid, paragraph 37.
139. See also section 4.4.1 above.
140. Judgment of the European Court of Justice of 20 September 1988, case 31/87, Bentjees, paragraph 37. See also section 2.2 above.
141. See also section 2.2 above.
142. Recital 46 of the preamble to the Procurement Directive, fourth sentence.

The main reason why the integration of environmental and social considerations may nevertheless seem complicated is that

- approved standards for social and environmental objectives;
- relevant certification systems; or
- criteria which unambiguously define which environmental or social objectives are more beneficial to society than others

only are available on a very modest scale.

However, despite the difficulty in laying down technical specifications, the contract documents must still be transparent and the selected conditions and criteria must be objective and published, cf. also section 4.5.5 below.

4.5.3 Criteria must be expressly mentioned in the contract documents
This condition is a reflection of the fundamental requirement for transparency which is one of the main aims of the Procurement Directive as it creates the basis for ensuring equal treatment of tenderers and thus effective competition for public contracts.[143]

4.5.4 Criteria must comply with all the fundamental principles of Community
    Law, including in particular the Principle of Non-Discrimination
This condition shows that the Procurement Directive is evidence of the EU's interest in creating an internal market without barriers to cross-border business activities. It may for example constitute a technical barrier in contravention of the rules of the Treaty if energy produced by wind mills is preferred to energy produced from other renewable sources of energy since certain countries that have prioritised wind mills would have an advantage.

The requirements to be satisfied by the object must not be worded so as to, directly or indirectly, restrict trade between the EU Member States, cf. section 3.2 above. However, even where a requirement is worded in that way, it may nevertheless be permitted if justified by reasons that are objective and sufficient to offset the restrictive effects of the requirement.[144]

---

143. See also chapter 1.
144. Judgment of the European Court of Justice of 17 September 2002, case C-513/99, Concordia Oy AB.

The fundamental principles of EU law, notably the principles of equal treatment and transparency, must be observed when awarding a public contract.[145]

4.5.5 Criteria must be capable of identifying the most economically advantageous tender[146]

The criteria chosen as the basis for the award of a public contract must be intended to and *capable* of identifying the tender which is most economically advantageous to the contracting authority. This requirement is closely linked to the principles of equal treatment and transparency and also calls for a certain level of objectivity of the award criteria. The Procurement Directive sets out the following guidelines with respect to the award criteria:

"Where the contracting authorities choose to award a contract to the most economically advantageous tender, they shall assess the tenders in order to determine which one offers the best value for money. In order to do this, they shall determine the economic and quality criteria which, taken as a whole, must make it possible to determine the most economically advantageous tender for the contracting authority. The determination of these criteria depends on the object of the contract since they must allow the level of performance offered by each tender to be assessed in the light of the object of the contract as defined in the technical specifications, and the value for money of each tender to be measured."[147]

The criteria must enable the contracting authority to verify that the tenders submitted satisfy the requirements. If this verification is not possible, any tenderer might simply profess to have complied with the requirements laid down and such a possibility is against the principle of equal treatment of tenderers.

The Commission's concern that the equal treatment of tenderers would be compromised if a contract could be awarded on the basis of non-economic criteria was confirmed by the *EVN* case[148] concerning the purchase of electricity produced from renewable sources. The problem with electricity is that it is not always possible to determine where the consumed current is actually produced, and a requirement that the electricity be produced from renewable sources of energy is thus nothing more than an empty gesture. Lack of a basis

---

145. See also section 2 above and chapter 1.3.
146. See also chapter 7.2.6 in which award on the basis of non-economic criteria is analysed.
147. Recital 46 of the preamble to the Procurement Directive, third indent.
148. Judgment of the European Court of Justice of 4 December 2003, case C-448/01, EVN AG.

for verification easily jeopardises the equal treatment of tenderers in the award of public contracts since a tenderer may allege that the energy it supplies is produced from renewable sources of energy despite not having incurred the large expenses usually involved therewith. This problem is expected to be solved in part by the implementation of a system of certificates of origin.[149]

In the abovementioned case the authority had made it known that it neither would nor could verify whether the electricity supplied was actually produced from renewable sources of energy.[150] To this the European Court of Justice held that the procurement rules, and especially the principles of transparency and equal treatment, had been disregarded:

"Objective and transparent evaluation of the various tenders depends on the contracting authority, relying on the information and proof provided by the tenderers, being able to verify effectively whether the tenders submitted by those tenderers meet the award criteria."[151]

It practically goes without saying that the only way to ensure tenderers equal chances of being awarded a contract is if the contracting authority is able to verify how they comply relatively with the criteria chosen and a winner can be found on that basis.

4.6 Selection of Qualified Undertakings

It is undoubtedly acceptable and relevant to focus attention on whether an undertaking is qualified to perform the contract for which tenders are invited, cf. chapter 6 below. If the award of a contract is based on *inter alia* non-economic criteria, then the ability to perform and pursue such objectives can also be taken into account in the evaluation of the undertaking's capabilities.

Furthermore, it should be possible to verify that an undertaking is capable of complying with the conditions/requirements laid down for the performance of a specific contract. Nevertheless, the Procurement Directive only provides that the technical and professional ability can be evaluated in the light of the object of the contract.

---

149. Judgment of the European Court of Justice of 13 March 2001, case C-379/98, PreussenElektra, paragraph 80.
150. Judgment of the European Court of Justice of 4 December 2003, case C-448/01, EVN AG.
151. Ibid, paragraph 50.

Where the non-economic criteria are closely linked to the object of the contract, it seems reasonable to require documentation witnessing that the tenderer has the required ability to comply with these secondary requirements. In any case, the contracting authority must be able to include appropriate provisions regulating a breach of contract in the contract.

4.7 Specifically about small and medium-sized enterprises
On the following pages is an analysis of the possibilities for promoting the chances of small and medium-sized enterprises (SMEs) of being awarded public contracts or lots thereof. Particular emphasis is on the possibilities of subdividing a public contract and of making use of subcontractors.

4.7.1 Subdivision of a public contract
The execution of works, provision of services or purchase of similar supplies may be carried out under one contract or several contracts may be awarded, possibly to more separate economic operators. Based on the relevant conditions, qualifications and interests it is for the contracting authority to decide whether to subdivide a contract.

However, when contemplating the subdivision of a public contract, it must be remembered that the value of several contracts concerning a project, which in terms of time and object are connected, must be aggregated in order to calculate the threshold value, and that it is prohibited to subdivide a contract merely for the purposes of preventing it from meeting the threshold values of the Procurement Directive.[152]

A contract may be subdivided for economic reasons linked to the specific object to be purchased. A supplies contract may, for example, be awarded for a short term if the supplier's capability to supply the agreed products is uncertain. A contract covering all deliveries may be awarded for reasons of reliability of delivery or in order to charge one economic operator with the coordination of different activities.

Another reason for subdividing a contract may be to boost the financial interests of small enterprises which are more likely to tender for small contracts on their own than to take part in cooperation (joint venture/consortium) allowing them to tender for large contracts. The European Parliament submitted a proposal recommending that this objective be explicitly encouraged in the Procurement Directive.[153] Although it is not mentioned in the final Direc-

---

152. Article 9 of the Procurement Directive. See also chapter 3.4.
153. Recommendation of 19 June 2003 at the second reading, proposal for Article 6A.

tive, a contracting authority can presumably legitimately subdivide a contract, even though the reason is not connected to its own economic interests, but instead to boosting the financial interests of small enterprises.

In the award of contracts it is prohibited to discriminate, be it directly or indirectly, on grounds of nationality. A public contract which is subdivided is of less value and thus generally less appealing to foreign undertakings. This is, however, balanced out by the greater interest the reduced size of the public contract is expected to attract from smaller, including foreign, undertakings which would not otherwise have been in a position to tender for the contract.

4.7.2 Subcontractors

An economic operator may either carry out all elements of the contract itself or subcontract parts of or the entire contract to other economic operators. It is for the economic operators to decide how they wish to make use of their factors of production, and they may, for example, choose to employ qualified staff or they may have capabilities at their disposal by virtue of a contract with other economic operators (subcontractors). In tendering for a public contract it is essentially left with the economic operator to decide whether it will make use of subcontractors for the performance of the contract.[154]

It is of key importance to the contracting authority that the contract is performed at the agreed time and in accordance with the agreed quality. If products or services are acquired or works executed under a contract with one economic operator, this economic operator will as the main contractor be liable towards the contracting authority for the correct performance of the contract, even though some or all parts of the contract are carried out by other economic operators.

The quality and delivery reliability of a service or product may depend on the undertaking which supplies it. A contracting authority may therefore want to know which undertakings, apart from the contracting party, that will be responsible for the delivery/performance.[155] In the contract documents it may be stated that the tenderer must:

---

154. See also chapter 6.2 below on the evaluation of the economic operator's relationship with subcontractors and the subcontractors' capabilities.
155. For purposes of assessing capabilities and selecting participants an economic operator may rely on the resources of other undertakings to prove economic and financial standing, cf. Article 47, paragraph 2 and Article 48, paragraph 3 of the Procurement Directive. See also chapter 6.2 for proof of abilities.

"… indicate in his tender any share of the contract he may intend to subcontract to third parties and any proposed subcontractors".[156]

This provision improves the possibilities for checking, prior to awarding a contract, whether the future contracting partner is likely to make use of sufficient skills in order to perform the contract. Since the word "proposed" and not the word "chosen" is used in the provision, the economic operators are left with a certain freedom with respect to the final choice of subcontractors.[157]

Contracting authorities cannot prevent the use of subcontractors in general. On the other hand, contracting authorities have a legitimate interest in proof that a candidate or tenderer intending to use the resources of other undertakings for the performance of a public contract does actually have these resources at its disposal if and when it is awarded the contract.[158] It thus follows that if a candidate or tenderer in its application or tender indicates that it intends to use subcontractors for the performance of a public contract, the contracting authority may require proof that the subcontractor does have the technological or economic capacities laid down in the contract documents and that the candidate/tenderer does in fact have the subcontractor's capacities at its disposal.[159]

For administrative reasons a contracting authority can stipulate in the contract documents that *replacement* of subcontractors is not possible after the deadline for submitting tenders.[160] However, in the absence of such explicit provision in the contract documents a tenderer is entitled to replace subcontractors after the deadline for submitting tenders. There may be a pressing practical need for replacing subcontractors, for example a subcontractor's liquidation or bankruptcy, cooperation difficulties or for other reasons emerged subsequent to the submission of the tender. It may also be in the interest of the contracting authority to allow changes in order to avoid that an otherwise qualified tenderer withdraws from the competition. In the decision whether or not to allow a subcontractor to be replaced, it is essential that the replacement does not work to the advantage of one tenderer and thus distorts the equal treatment of tenderers and on that account competition. Conse-

156. Article 25 of the Procurement Directive.
157. Cf. Commission Communication, SEC/2003/0366 final version, p. 10.
158. Order of the Complaints Board of June 2004, A/S Analycen vs. County of Vestsjælland and Others.
159. Judgment of the European Court of Justice of 18 March 2004, case C-314/01, Siemens AG Österreich, ARGE Telekom & Partner, paragraph 46.
160. Judgment of the European Court of Justice of 23 January 2003, case C-57/01, Makedoniko Metro.

quently, presumably only subcontractors which do not carry out essential parts of the contract can be replaced. Whether or not this is the case depends on an evaluation of the effect that the replacement has on the tender in technical and economic terms. Legitimately it must be possible for the contracting authority to require that any replacement of subcontractors be submitted to it for prior approval and that the new subcontractors have the required capacities laid down in the contract documents.

A contracting authority may have an interest in advancing the possibilities of small enterprises for being awarded public contracts. The Procurement Directive contains a specific provision on concessions subject to which the concessionaire may be required to use subcontractors for work representing a specified value of the contract.[161]

5. Competition criteria and fixed terms[162]

Before drafting the contract documents the contracting authority must consider how the purchase and the underlying public requirement are best and most effectively achieved through the procurement procedure. To that end the contract must be broken down into its various elements in order to identify:

– the criteria by which the tenderers will compete and which will be used to identify the successful tender (competition criteria);
– and the requirements and conditions subject to which the tender must be drafted and will be evaluated (fixed terms).

The contracting authority must select the criteria to be used for identifying the successful tender which will be the basis on which the contract is awarded.[163] The criteria on which the tenderers compete and which will be used to identify the successful tender, hence, constituting the basis on which the contract is awarded, should be criteria which are linked to those aspects of the object of the contract which the contracting authority seeks to *optimise*. All criteria of economic relevance may be included in the competition and, in addition to price, factors such as durability, performance, delivery times,

---

161. Article 60 of the Procurement Directive. The provision is a re-enactment of Article 3, paragraph 2 of the repealed Works Directive.
162. See also chapter 7 analysing the award criteria.
163. The criteria for selecting qualified undertakings must be determined in advance. See also chapter 6 below.

environmental properties (for example emission of harmful substances), design, etc. may contribute to identifying the best possible contract, cf. section 5.3 below. On the other hand, price can be used as the only competitive parameter for identifying the best tender, thereby limiting the effect of optimisation through competition in the award of the contract.[164]

5.1 No freedom of choice in the award

A distinctive feature of the procurement rules is that the contracting authorities have limited scope for discretion in the award of a contract. Only exceptionally do the contracting authorities choose their contracting parties. In fact, any interested undertaking must be allowed the opportunity to tender for a public contract, and the contract must be awarded to the tenderer which is capable of performing the contract and, evaluated on the basis of the contract documents, has submitted the best tender[165] unless there are objective and sufficient reasons for cancelling the procurement procedure.[166]

The requirement that tenders submitted be evaluated exclusively on the basis of the contract documents significantly limits the contracting authorities' discretionary scope for choosing the tender they prefer. The requirement that the evaluation be made exclusively on the basis of the contract documents increases the transparency of the award procedure and thus improves the equal treatment of the economic operators. On the other hand, at this stage the contracting authorities have no opportunities for optimising the purchase.

The obligation to evaluate the tenders solely on the basis of the contract documents is closely linked to the prohibition on negotiations with the tenderers in the period from the opening of the tenders until the award decision is made. Since the contract documents, as a main rule, is the *only* basis for evaluating the tenders submitted and awarding the contract, the contracting authority must prepare these documents very carefully.[167]

Also the award criteria must be very carefully worded; if a tenderer is qualified and the tender complies with the requirements, terms and conditions

---

164. Order of the Complaints Board of 13 May 2004, Bravida Danmark A/S vs. Rødovre almennyttige Boligselskab (the Tender Act) on the installation of central heating in 597 semi-detached houses and a kindergarten.
165. Under the Procurement Directive two alternative criteria are allowed: the lowest price only or the tender which is most economically advantageous to the contracting authority, Article 53.
166. See chapter 7.8 below.
167. See chapter 7.6 below on the possibilities for clarification of technical points of a tender.

laid down in the contract documents, the award criteria will determine which tender will form the basis for the contract to be awarded.

5.2 Award after selection

The tenders submitted are evaluated in two stages.

- In the selection stage the qualifications of the tendering undertakings are evaluated. The contract documents constitute the basis for evaluating whether a tendering undertaking has the required qualifications, staff, capital, etc. likely to be necessary for the correct and timely performance of the contract.[168]
- In the award stage the qualified undertakings' tenders are evaluated. The evaluation is made on the basis of the award criteria published in the contract documents, for example price, quality, service, etc.[169]

The selection of tenderers and the award of contract are two separate decisions. Different rules apply to each of them under the Directive, and the main rule is that the criteria applied to the evaluation in one stage cannot be applied to the evaluation in the other.[170] In a number of cases the Complaints Board for Public Procurement has established that it is in breach with the procurement rules to base the award of a contract on *inter alia* an undertaking's qualifications.

The reasoning is that the contracting authority is free to determine which capacities, and the specific nature thereof, it requires of the economic operator which is to be its future contracting partner. As a result, if an economic operator satisfies the requirements, it means that in principle the contracting authority has approved it as a future contracting partner, and all tenders submitted by economic operators which satisfy the requirements must be evaluated on equal terms.

It is not always possible to make a complete distinction between selection and award criteria. Firstly, it is possible that the same criterion can be used in both stages. Secondly, for the award of a service contract long and wide ex-

---

168. See also chapter 6 on the selection of candidates for the competition.
169. See also chapter 7 on the award of orders and conclusion of a contract.
170. In the judgment of 19 June 2003, case C-315/01, GAT, concerning the supply of products, the European Court of Justice found that a "mere reference list" was not capable of identifying the most economically advantageous tender.

perience with the provision of the specific service may be a relevant crite-rion.[171]

5.3 The award – the object, conditions and competition criteria

The contract documents must specify the technical, economic and legal ele-ments of the contract. A further distinction must be made between, on the one hand, the minimum requirements for the contract (fixed terms) and, on the other hand, those criteria that are open for competition among the tendering undertakings (competition criteria). The terms of the contract as well as the competition criteria must *be linked* to the object of the contract which the contracting authority proposes to award.[172]

5.3.1 Open and fixed elements of the contract

The authority chooses which elements of the contract that are open to, respec-tively excluded from competition. However, not all the economic aspects of a contract can be excluded from competition, cf. section 5.3.3 below.[173]

In the light of the proposed contract it is entirely for the contracting au-thority to determine which elements are to be open to competition and which are not, but various elements relating to the object of the contract are often not open to competition. These may be terms governing the passing of risk, interest payment in the event of delay, warranty period, etc.

For the performance of a contract it may be necessary to require the con-tracting party to acquire Real property (purification plant, office building, workshop, etc.) or equipment (busses, machines, etc.) before executing the contract. Or the contracting party may be required to sell premises and/or machinery at the expiry of the contract. Such elements of the contract are normally in the nature of fixed terms.

5.3.2 The object

A contracting authority may choose to determine all details regarding the object of the contract itself. To that end detailed technical specifications may be drawn up and reference may be made to published standards. Finally, tendering undertakings may be precluded from submitting variants. In this

---

171. See also chapter 7.2.8 on the distinction between selection and award criteria. See also order of the Complaints Board of 14 October 2004, SK Tolkeservice ApS vs. County of Copenhagen.
172. See also sections 4.4 and 4.5 above on non-economic criteria.
173. All tenders must comply with the fixed terms. See also chapter 7.4 on rejection of tenders.

situation tenderers will only be able to compete on the economic aspects of the tenders.

On the other hand, a contracting authority may allow the tendering authorities to propose other technical solutions than the one envisaged by the authority. This is possible where the contracting authority only specifies functional requirements or allows variants to be submitted. In such procedures the competition among the tenderers concern the constituent parts, properties and quality of the proposed technical solutions as well as the economic aspects of the tenders.

5.3.3 Competition criteria[174]

The Procurement Directive provides that the contracting authorities must award a contract on the basis of one of the following two criteria:

- the most economically advantageous tender from the point of view of the contracting authority specifying various sub-criteria,
- or the lowest price only.[175]

By requiring the contracting authority to base the award of a contract on one of the two specified criteria, the contracting authority is forced to always take into account the value for money to the authority of the individual tender. If the price or total costs of a tender are lower than those of other tenders, this will add positively to its chances in the competition (except if the tender is abnormally low), but this relative advantage of one tender may be cancelled out by advantages of other tenders relating to elements such as properties, quality, environmental considerations, etc.

If the authority wishes to base the award of a contract on factors other than price, the criteria "the most economically advantageous tender" must be used. This might be the case in procedures where the award of the contract is based on the compliance with certain functional requirements, where variants may be submitted or in design contests. If the criteria "the lowest price only" is chosen, the contracting authority must lay down in advance all the technical, legal and economic elements – except the price – of the contract.

If the criteria "the most economically advantageous tender" is chosen, the contracting authority must lay down sub-criteria. These sub-criteria must be linked to the object of the contract as defined in the contract documents and must be appropriate to identify the relative value for money of each tender in

---

174. This section only briefly outlines the situation. See chapter 7.2 for a thorough analysis.
175. Article 53 of the Procurement Directive, cf. chapter 7 below.

the light of the proposed contract.[176] The Procurement Directive provides that the contracting authority must specify in the contract notice or the contract documents "the relative weighting which it gives to each of the criteria chosen ".[177] However, this obligation to specify the weighting of each criterion is not absolute, cf. chapter 7 for more details. If sub-criteria have not been specified, the tenders submitted can only be evaluated on the basis of the price indicated in the tender.

5.3.4 Other conditions

In procedures for the award of a public contract the contracting authority may take account of environmental and social considerations, cf. section 4 above. Environmental considerations may for example be the reason for the acquisition of a sewage treatment plant and social considerations may be the reason for setting up a sheltered workshop. Furthermore environmental and social objectives may be integrated into the object of the contract to the effect that a product, for example, must be made of recyclable material (environmental considerations) or a school must be constructed to allow access for wheelchair users (social considerations). Finally, environmental and social considerations can be laid down as criteria for the award of a public contract.

Moreover, the contracting authority may require that environmental and social objectives be pursued under the contract. This may translate into certain obligations being imposed on the contracting party in connection with the performance of the contract, cf. section 4.3.2 above.

A contracting authority can legitimately pursue an objective in the public interest in connection with the award of a public contract even where the objective is not directly linked to the specific purchase and it involves additional costs for the authority. For the performance of a contract the contracting party may, for example, be required to employ long-term unemployed, train apprentices, leave part of the performance under the contract to sheltered workshops, etc. The contracting party may also be required to take measures to protect the marine environment against pollution, to introduce a higher standard for health and safety at work than that required by law, etc.

Such elements of the contract can only be regarded as secondary obligations and should under normal circumstances be in the nature of fixed terms. Contract terms which are not directly linked to the object of the contract must be specified in the contract documents or the contract notice.

---

176. See also recital 46 of the preamble to the Procurement Directive, 3rd indent.
177. Article 53, paragraph 2 of the Procurement Directive.

CHAPTER 5

The Procurement Procedures

1. Set procedures and duty of publication

Contracting authorities must use one of the procedures prescribed in the Procurement Directive for the award of a contract and publish its intention to award a public contract.

1.1 Which procedures can be used?
The Procurement Directive gives the contracting authorities a choice between the following procedures:[1]

- open procedure
- restricted procedure
- competitive dialogue procedure[2]
- negotiated procedure
- design contest

Since the contracting authorities are required to use set procedures, the economic operators are able to predict the course of action in procedures for the award of a public contract.

A contracting authority is free to choose between the open procedure and the restricted procedure whereas the use of the competitive dialogue procedure and the negotiated procedure is subject to certain conditions specified in

1. Articles 28-34 and 66-74 (design contests for services) of the Procurement Directive. Framework agreements, dynamic purchasing systems or electronic auctions are superstructures of some of the procurement procedures, cf. section 5 below.
2. Pursuant to Article 29 of the Procurement Directive the individual Member State can provide that the contracting authority may make use of "the competitive dialogue procedure".

the Procurement Directive.[3] The limited discretion for choosing among all the various procedures goes to the root of the aim of creating transparency and ensuring that tenderers are not discriminated against, but compete on equal terms for public contracts. The justification for the main rule that either the open procedure or the restricted procedure be used is that they are the procedures which limit the contracting authorities' scope for discretion or negotiations in the award of a contract most extensively, thus ensuring transparency of the award procedure and, by inference, equal treatment of the tenderers.

1.2 Why the requirement for prior publication?

A contract notice must be published prior to the award of a public contract in which the contracting authority specifies the procedure chosen for the award of the proposed contract.[4] Prior publication of a contract notice is an essential precondition of transparency in award procedures for public contracts and thus also of the competition between economic operators and of the possibilities for enforcing the procurement rules. It is, therefore, a key feature of the Procurement Directive.[5] The notice serves to inform all economic operators throughout the EU of the call for tenders for the proposed public contract. This allows all economic operators the opportunity to make inquiries with the contracting authority, express interest in the contract, receive additional documents and information and, depending on the procurement procedure, submit a tender.

1.3 Outline of the chapter

This chapter has the following chronology: the procurement procedures are analysed in section 2; the requirements for publication are analysed in section 3; certain special procurement procedures: design contests, electronic auctions and dynamic purchasing systems are discussed in section 4; and finally section 5 discusses certain special types of contracts: framework agreements, concessions and partnerships.

---

3. The contracting authority may also choose a design contest, but this procedure is only used within certain areas. See also section 4.1 below.
4. When the negotiated procedure without publication of a contract notice is used, as provided in Article 31 of the Procurement Directive, a contract notice is obviously not published, but pursuant to Article 35, paragraph 4 of the Procurement Directive a notice of the award of the contract and the reason(s) for using this procedure must be published, cf. Article 36 and Annex VII A of the Procurement Directive.
5. See also chapter 1.3.3 on the transparency requirements.

2. The individual procurement procedures

In this section the four main types of procurement procedures, open procedure, restricted procedure, competitive dialogue procedure and negotiated procedure, are described and analysed.[6] All the procurement procedures have a number of features in common:

- The contracting authority publishes a contract notice (or contacts individual economic operators directly).
- Interested economic operators apply for participation in the procedure and submit evidence of their suitability (the candidates).
- From the candidates the contracting authority selects a group of suitable economic operators (the tenderers). (In the open procedure all interested economic operators can submit a tender).
- The contract documents are forwarded to the selected tenderers inviting them in writing to submit tenders.
    - As an alternative, in exceptional cases only, the contracting authority may open a dialogue with a group of suitable candidates to define the technical and/or legal and/or financial aspects of the contract.
- The selected tenderers submit their tenders.
- The final tenders are evaluated.
    - As an alternative, in exceptional cases only, the contracting authority may enter into negotiations with the tenderers on the technical, legal or financial aspects of the contract.
- The contracting authority decides on the award of the contract.
- A contract is concluded with the successful tenderer.

In the analysis of the individual procedure particular emphasis will be on its specific characteristics.

The section opens with some overall comments about choice of procurement procedure.

2.1 Generally about choice of procedure

A contracting authority must use one of the procedures set out in the Procurement Directive for the award of a contract which by virtue of its content and value is subject to the Directive.[7] Since the restricted procedure guarantees a sufficient level of competition and since the open procedure is often impractical, it is left to the contracting authorities to choose freely between these two procedures.

---

6.   Design contests are analysed in section 4.1 below.
7.   See chapter 3 above.

The negotiated procedure and the competitive dialogue procedure can only be used if the contracting authority complies with certain conditions specified in the Procurement Directive. These procedures can only be used in exceptional cases as they involve a greater risk of failure to comply with the principle of transparency and, hence, do not, to the same level as the open procedure and the restricted procedure, guarantee equal treatment and competition. In these two procedures the contracting authority may enter into a dialogue or negotiations with the individual tenderers, and since it is difficult to conduct a completely transparent dialogue or completely transparent negotiations, the likelihood that tenderers will be discriminated against or that non-objective criteria will be taken into consideration is greater when these procedures are used.[8]

The provisions of the Procurement Directive on the possibilities of using the negotiated procedure and the competitive dialogue procedure should be interpreted strictly. The Directive provides that the two procedures can be used in the specific cases expressly referred to therein where the particular nature of the contract requires a close contact between the authority and the economic operators.[9] At the same time it is evident that the close contact, the dialogue or the negotiations, is capable of compromising the aim of the Directive to the effect that the market for public contracts is not opened up and does not guarantee equal competitive terms to the same degree as is the case when the open procedure and the restricted procedure are used. As a consequence, the cases in which a specific procurement procedure can be used are fewer, the less likely that particular procedure is to guarantee equal competition. A strict interpretation seems particularly obvious with respect to the use of the negotiated procedure without prior publication of a contract notice.[10] The European Court of Justice has made the following statement in regard to this procurement procedure:

"The risk of a breach of the principle of non-discrimination is particularly high where a contracting authority decides not to put a particular contract out to tender."[11]

The procedure to be used must be chosen at the latest at the time when the contracting authority decides to launch a procedure to conclude a contract.[12]

---

8. See also section 2.5 below and chapter 7.6 on negotiations
9. Article 28 of the Procurement Directive, cf. Articles 29, 30 and 31.
10. Article 31 of the Procurement Directive.
11. Judgment of the European Court of Justice of 10 April 2003, cases C-20/01 and C-28/01, Commission vs. Germany, paragraph 63.

It is then that the contracting authority must assess whether the contract must be put out to tender. It is also the circumstances at that point in time which decide whether such exceptional events have occurred that for example the negotiated procedure can be used.[13]

The procedure chosen by the contracting authority must be used until a decision to award the contract has been made.[14] Even though another procedure, other than the one chosen, could be used for the award of the contract, the authority is obliged to maintain its choice in view of the fact that it has been published in the contract notice. This gives the economic operators an idea of how the award procedure will be conducted, which the contracting authority cannot arbitrarily depart from.

In exceptional circumstances, events occurred subsequently can justify that the contracting authority departs from the open procedure or the restricted procedure and instead awards the contract on the basis of the negotiated procedure. The contracting authority must state the reasons why the award procedure was changed. The negotiated procedure may, for example, be used where the tenders submitted are irregular[15] or where no tenders are submitted.[16]

2.2 Open procedure

In the open procedure any economic operator can submit a tender.[17] In theory the open procedure should therefore secure the highest level of competition. However, since all interested economic operators can submit tenders, but usually only one is awarded the contract, the use of the open procedure may pose problems from a practical perspective. Where a large number of tenders are submitted, the contracting authority may have to allocate a lot of time and considerable expense to the evaluation. For all, but one of the tenderers, the

---

12. See also Article 9, paragraph 2 of the Procurement Directive, on the calculation of threshold values, cf. chapter 3 above.
13. See for example Article 31, paragraph 1 (c) of the Procurement Directive on unforeseeable events.
14. Judgment of the European Court of Justice of 25 April 1996, case C-87/94, Commission vs. Belgium (The Wallonian buses).
15. In this situation use of the negotiated procedure *with* publication of a contract notice may be justified, cf. Article 30, paragraph 1 (a) of the Procurement Directive.
16. In this situation use of the negotiated procedure *without* publication of a contract notice may be justified, cf. Article 31, paragraph 1 (a) of the Procurement Directive.
17. Article 1, paragraph 11 (a).

costs of preparing the tender are wasted.[18] Therefore, for the purchase of, for example, standardised products or services it may, for the above reasons, be expedient to conclude framework agreements with more economic operators subject to which a small group of undertakings compete for the individual contract.[19] It is also difficult to protect the confidential information in the contract documents in that the documents, in principle, may be obtained by any economic operator. In order to reduce the number of tenders submitted thus making the procedure more manageable and to protect confidential information in the contract documents, the contracting authority should consider using the restricted procedure instead, cf. the next section.

Once the interested undertakings have submitted evidence of their qualifications and their tenders, the tenderer's qualifications[20] and the tenders submitted are evaluated.[21]

2.3 Restricted procedure

In the restricted procedure the economic operators express their interest in the contract on the basis of the contract notice. The suitability of the interested economic operators is then evaluated on the basis of the criteria determined in the contract documents (for further details see chapter 6 below).

It is distinctive of the restricted procedure that the contracting authority can limit the number of undertakings that are invited to submit tenders.[22] The contracting authority must evaluate the suitability of all interested undertakings and then select those undertakings that will be invited to submit tenders.[23] This is reflected in the wording of the Directive stipulating that the contracting authorities simultaneously and in writing

"… invite the selected candidates to submit their tenders …".[24]

The minimum number of candidates (at least five) and, at the contracting authority's option, the maximum number of candidates must be indicated.[25]

---

18. In the context of a framework agreement, agreements can be concluded with more economic operators.
19. See also section 5.1 below on framework agreements.
20. See also chapter 6.
21. See also chapter 7.
22. Article 1, paragraph 11 (b) of the Procurement Directive.
23. See also chapter 6.7 on the specific procedure.
24. Article 40, paragraph 1 of the Procurement Directive.
25. Article 44, paragraph 3, first indent of the Procurement Directive.

Usually the number of candidates that will be selected is indicated within a range of for example 5-8. The selection must be made on the basis of objective and non-discriminatory criteria set out in the contract notice.[26] At least five candidates must be invited to submit tenders.[27] If the number of suitable candidates is below the pre-determined minimum number, the contracting authority may nevertheless continue the procedure by inviting the remaining candidates to submit tenders.[28]

The contract documents are forwarded to the selected candidates with an invitation to submit tenders, which tenders form the basis on which the contract is awarded.[29]

2.4 Competitive dialogue[30] [31]

In the open procedure and the restricted procedure negotiations between the contracting authority and the tenderers are almost entirely prohibited. This has been viewed as an obstacle to the contracting authorities' chances of obtaining best value for money in that use of the economic operator's expertise in certain situations is necessary to achieve the best technical, economic and legal solution to a specific need in the public interest.[32] Until now negotiations have only been permitted if the conditions for using the negotiated procedure were satisfied, cf. section 2.5 below. Under the present Procure-

---

26. Article 44, paragraph 3, first indent of the Procurement Directive. Judgment of the European Court of Justice of 12 December 2002, case C-470/99, Universale Bau, paragraph 84. See also chapter 6 on selection.
27. Article 44, paragraph 3, second indent of the Procurement Directive. In its judgment of 26 September 2000 in case C-225/98, Commission vs. France, the European Court of Justice found that it was a violation of the Directive to indicate that a *maximum* number of five would be selected.
28. Article 44, paragraph 3, third indent of the Procurement Directive.
29. The deadlines are analysed in section 5.3 below. See also chapter 7 on the award of contract.
30. Kai Krüger, Ban-On-Negotiation in Tender Procedures: Undermining Best Value for Money? 4 Journal of Public Procurement, 2004, pp. 397ff. Steen Treumer, Competitive dialogue, 13 Public Procurement Law Review, 2004, pp. 178ff. Adian Brown, The Impact of the New Procurement Directive on Large Public Infrastructure Projects: Competitive Dialogue or Better the Devil you Know?, 13 Public Procurement law Review, 2004, pp. 160ff.
31. Article 29 of the Procurement Directive provides that it is for the individual Member State to decide whether it will allow contracting authorities to use the competitive dialogue procedure.
32. See also section 5.3 below on public-private partnerships

ment Directive contracting authorities can use the competitive dialogue procedure subject to certain specific conditions.

The competitive dialogue procedure is distinctive in that after the selection of a limited number of suitable candidates (at least three) it provides for an additional stage in the award procedure during which the contracting authority can discuss all aspects of the contract with a selected group of interested candidates (the dialogue stage).[33] Once the contracting authority has identified the solution capable of satisfying its needs and of constituting a basis for submitting tenders, the dialogue is concluded. The participants are then invited to submit tenders on the basis of the solution reached and specified during the dialogue (the tender stage).

2.4.1 Cases justifying the use of this procedure

The competitive dialogue procedure can be used for particularly complex projects where it is not possible to award a contract on the basis of the open procedure or the restricted procedure. A project is considered to be "particularly complex" where the contracting authorities

- "are not objectively able to define the technical means in accordance with Article 23(3)(b), (c) or (d), capable of satisfying their needs or objectives, and/or
- are not objectively able to specify the legal and/or financial make-up of a project".[34]

It is not clear in which situations these conditions are met. The basis for the assessment should be the needs of the contracting authority and the purpose of the project, and where it is not possible, on that basis, to define the technical specifications, for example in terms of functional performance, or make provisions for the legal/financial structure of the project up front, the conditions are probably met. Projects in which new technology or new methods are applied, or involving public/private partnerships, are probably likely to comply with the conditions too.[35]

The use of the competitive dialogue procedure is conditional on the contracting authorities proving that they

"… without this being due to any fault on their part, find it objectively impossible to define the means of satisfying their needs or of assessing what the market can offer in the way of

---

33. Article 29, paragraph 3 of the Procurement Directive.
34. Article 1, paragraph 11 (c), second indent of the Procurement Directive.
35. Adian Brown, The Impact of the New Procurement Directive on Large Public Infrastructure Projects: Competitive Dialogue or Better the Devil you Know?, 13 Public Procurement law Review, 2004, pp. 160ff.

240

technical solutions and/or financial/legal solutions. This situation may arise in particular with the implementation of important integrated transport infrastructure projects, large computer networks or projects involving complex and structured financing the financial and legal make-up of which cannot be defined in advance."[36]

The three examples are indicative of the cases in which this procedure can be used. For example a project of a nature which is such that it is not possible to pre-determine the total price of it or specify the contract to a sufficiently detailed level may satisfy the conditions subject to which the competitive dialogue procedure can be used.[37] It thus follows that presumably the cases justifying the use of this procedure largely overlap with the cases justifying the use of the negotiated procedure *with* publication of a contract notice.[38]

The possibilities for opening a dialogue serve the interests of the contracting authorities since by allowing the use of a dialogue, the risk that the economic operators are discriminated against and that non-objective interests are protected is increased, thereby thwarting one of the aims of the Directive. As a consequence, the contracting authorities are subject to heavy requirements and must prove to be faced with a genuine complex problem reflected in the wording that they must be "*objectively not able*"[39] to define conditions and solutions in advance. Among other things the contracting authority must be able to prove that there are no precedents and that it will be unreasonably costly and time-consuming to carry out the examinations necessary in order to prepare the contract specifications.

"*Without this being due to any fault on their part*"[40] suggests that there may be a difference between experienced contracting authorities and not experienced contracting authorities. In the Commission's proposal for a procurement directive, the competitive dialogue procedure could also be used in cases where it was impossible for the contracting authority "to define the tools likely to meet their needs or assess what the contract can offer in

36. Recital 31 of the preamble to the Directive, cf. also Article 29 of the Procurement Directive.
37. Contracts on public-private partnerships may be awarded on the basis of "the competitive dialogue procedure"; Commission Green Paper of 30 April 2004 on Public-Private Partnerships and Community Law on Public Contracts and Concessions (Com(2004) 327 final), points 25 and 26
38. Article 30, paragraph 1 (b) and (c) of the Procurement Directive. See also Adian Brown, The Impact of the New Procurement Directive on Large Public Infrastructure Projects: Competitive Dialogue or Better the Devil you Know?, 13 Public Procurement law Review, 2004, pp. 160ff.
39. Recital 31of the preamble to the Procurement Directive.
40. Recital 31 of the preamble to the Procurement Directive.

terms of technical or financial solutions without this being attributable to a lack of information or deficiencies on their part".[41] The change of wording has caused some uncertainty with respect to the legal position.

The contracting authority must make sure that participants are not discriminated against. It must thus be ensured that all participants receive the same information.[42] The contracting authority must also in advance indicate how the dialogue will be conducted.

In practice the duty to ensure equal treatment of participants is of a different nature in the dialogue stage than in the tender stage. In the dialogue stage the authority can discuss all aspects of the contract, i.e. technical, legal and financial matters, with the selected candidates. The dialogue will be conducted in writing and at meetings with the candidates. In the tender stage, by contrast, there is essentially no contact or negotiations between the contracting authority and the tenderers. This main rule has been materially relaxed by the provision that tenders may be specified, clarified and fine-tuned, cf. below.

2.4.2 Dialogue stage

The dialogue is conducted on the basis of a contract notice in which the contracting authority indicates its needs and requirements. The information to be included in the contract notice is set out in Annex VII to the Procurement Directive. All economic operators may express their interest in participating in the dialogue and from among the suitable candidates the contracting authority chooses a minimum number, at least three, with which a dialogue is opened.[43] This selection is paramount. Since the contracting authority is uncertain of the specific object to be purchased, choosing suitable and innovative business partners for the dialogue stage is key to obtaining the best solutions while at the same time bearing in mind that the future contracting party must be found among the selected candidates.

By allowing the contracting authorities to use the selected economic operators' expertise, the dialogue is intended to identify and define the solution(s) which are capable of meeting the contracting authority's specific needs.[44]

The dialogue is conducted simultaneously with the individual candidates; the contracting authority clarifies its needs and requirements (on the basis of

---

41. COM(2000)275, recital 18 of the preamble to the Procurement Directive.
42. Article 29, paragraph 3, second indent of the Procurement Directive.
43. Article 29, paragraph 3, second indent of the Procurement Directive, cf. Article 44.
44. Article 29, paragraphs 3 and 5 of the Procurement Directive, cf. Article 1, paragraph 11 (c).

the specifications in the contract documents) and the individual candidate elaborates on the solution it proposes. Any technical, financial or legal aspect of the contract may be discussed in this stage.

It can be indicated in advance that the dialogue can take place over the course of several stages. At the end of each stage a deselection takes place so that the dialogue in the next stage is conducted on the basis of a reduced number of solutions. The deselection is made on the basis of the award criteria chosen in advance and laid down in the contract documents. If it transpires during the discussions that a proposed solution does not satisfy the needs and requirements of the contracting authority, the dialogue with that candidate can be ended, and this candidate will subsequently not be invited to submit a tender.[45]

A dialogue that takes place in several stages can be very useful in that while the contracting authority receives a large number of solutions, it is also able to reduce the often very time and cost-consuming work involved with evaluation and dialogue on the basis of comprehensive contract documents and documentation requirements.[46] The solutions submitted must be evaluated, compared and can be presented to the participants, cf. also section 2.4.4 below on confidentiality.

The dialogue is ended when the contracting authority has identified the solution(s) capable of fulfilling its requirements. It is in keeping with the procedure that the contracting authority selects one solution as the preferred solution, or it may be that only one solution is appropriate. A common solution may be prepared provided that the candidates agree thereto, cf. below. The contracting authority formally declares the dialogue concluded, informs the candidates and asks the selected candidates to submit tenders.

2.4.3 Tender stage

Also the final tenders are submitted simultaneously on the basis of the individual candidates' proposed solutions specified during the dialogue.[47] If only one solution is chosen, it is in keeping with the Procurement Directive that only this solution forms the basis for the submission of a tender and that the contracting authority invites the candidate to submit a tender. However, this does not provide a basis for competition in the tender stage and the contracting authority may, therefore, want to base the submission of tenders on more

---

45. If a candidate has submitted several proposals for a solution, the dialogue continues concerning the solutions that have not been deselected.
46. Recital 41 of the preamble to the Procurement Directive.
47. Article 29, paragraph 6, first indent of the Procurement Directive.

solutions and, accordingly, invite more candidates to submit tenders. This would also be more in keeping with the aim of the Directive to ensure competition in the tender stage.[48]

In a draft of the Procurement Directive it was suggested that the contracting authority on the basis of the dialogue and the proposed solutions composed the project that would be best capable of meeting the need in the public interest (so-called "cherry picking"). This would largely guarantee the equal treatment of economic operators and was expected to optimise the public procurement. The proposal was, however, changed to the existing set-up of simultaneity since it was likely to reveal too many of the individual candidates' financial and technical business secrets.

By guaranteeing the confidentiality of the proposed solutions it is expected that candidates are more willing to present innovative ideas and creative solutions. There is, however, one obvious drawback of this set-up: if the contracting authority prefers one solution to the others, then competition is practically eliminated in the tender stage.[49] But also in this situation it may be in the interest of the contracting authority to invite more candidates to submit tenders seeing that the preferred solution may prove so expensive that another solution will have to be chosen.

The Procurement Directive provides that the contracting authority can prepare a common solution on the basis of the dialogue to form the basis for the candidates' submission of tenders. A common solution requires that the candidates have agreed to the disclosure of their solutions and other confidential information.[50]

After submission of tenders it is possible to clarify and specify the tenders:

"These tenders may be clarified, specified and fine-tuned at the request of the contracting authority. However, such clarification, specification or fine-tuning or additional information may not involve changes to the basic features of the tender or the call for tender, variations in which are likely to distort competition or have a discriminatory effect."[51]

---

48. See also Article 44, paragraph 4 of the Procurement Directive.
49. *De facto* equal treatment of candidates and effective competition for the public contract would require that the contracting authority, after the dialogue had ended, determined the specifications of the object of the purchase and then invited all the candidates to submit tenders. As the rules are currently worded, this is not possible, unless the candidates agree hereto, re. below.
50. Article 29, paragraph 3 of the Procurement Directive.
51. Article 29, paragraph 6, second indent of the Procurement Directive.

It is not specified what is meant by "basic features". It must be determined on the basis of the description of the object of the contract and the specifications laid down by the contracting authority, in which it will also be indicated which legal and economic aspects are open for negotiations and which are not.[52]

In principle, any aspect of a tender can be clarified and specified as long as it does not involve such changes to the basic features of the tender or call for tenders which are likely to distort competition or have a discriminatory effect. This provision leaves the technical, economic and financial aspects of a contract open for negotiations. However, in the interest of ensuring equal treatment of the tenderers any additional information which has a bearing on the economic aspects of the tender must be limited. Since the dialogue is ended before tenders are submitted, it is presumably only possible to make clarifications and specifications of a negligible character.

The contract is awarded on the basis of the criterion "the most economically advantageous tender". This limited choice of criteria is appropriate seeing that the successful project is found on the basis of other factors than price. The sub-criteria must be indicated in the contract documents and only these sub-criteria can be applied.

Also the successful tenderer may be asked to clarify aspects of its tender.[53] This provision allows certain changes to be made to the successful project without having to recommence the procedure. However, fundamental aspects of the tender or the call for tenders cannot be changed:

"However, this procedure must not be used in such a way as to restrict or distort competition, particularly by altering any fundamental aspects of the offers, or by imposing substantial new requirements on the successful tenderer, or by involving any tenderer other than the one selected as the most economically advantageous."[54]

The possibilities for negotiating with the successful tenderer is interesting from a practical perspective although the bounds within which the technical and economic aspects of a project or of the contract can be changed in this stage are ill-defined.

---

52. See also chapter 4.
53. Article 29, paragraph 7, second indent of the Procurement Directive.
54. Recital 31, fourth sentence, of the preamble to the Procurement Directive.

2.4.4 Confidentiality

The competitive dialogue procedure involves the risk that information on the participants' technical or financial business secrets, drawings, tests, etc. is disclosed to competitors. Article 6 of the Procurement Directive is a general provision prescribing that tenderers can demand that confidential information be kept confidential. In Article 29 on the competitive dialogue procedure it is stressed that

"Contracting authorities may not reveal to the other participants solutions proposed or other confidential information communicated by a candidate participating in the dialogue without his/her agreement."[55]

There is no simple solution to the problem posed by confidential information. Since the contracting authority must open a dialogue with at least three candidates, a comparison of the proposed solutions is unavoidable, and to improve specific proposals it may be necessary to present candidates with the technical solutions proposed by other participants. Disclosure of a proposed solution to the other participants in the dialogue is, however, conditional on the prior consent of the candidate that has submitted the proposal.[56]

2.5 Negotiated procedure[57]

The Procurement Directive prescribes that in certain cases contracts can be concluded by normal means whereby the contracting authority contacts one or more economic operators and negotiates the specific contents and conditions of the contract.[58] The Procurement Directive defines the negotiated procedure as:

"... those procedures whereby the contracting authorities consult the economic operators of their choice and negotiate the terms of contract with one or more of these".[59]

---

55. Article 29, paragraph 3, third indent of the Procurement Directive.
56. Article 29, paragraph 3, third indent of the Procurement Directive.
57. Kai Krüger, Ban-On-Negotiation in Tender Procedures: Undermining Best Value for Money? 4 Journal of Public Procurement, 2004, pp. 397ff. Adian Brown, The Impact of the New Procurement Directive on Large Public Infrastructure Projects: Competitive Dialogue or Better the Devil you Know?, 13 Public Procurement law Review, 2004, pp. 160ff.
58. Articles 30 and 31 of the Procurement Directive.
59. Article 1, paragraph 11, fourth indent of the Procurement Directive.

Negotiations with selected economic operators can be conducted in one of two ways:

- *After* prior publication of a contract notice where the procedure is similar to a restricted procedure until the submission of tenders. After the final date for submitting tenders the contracting authority opens negotiations with the tenderers on the technical, financial and economic aspects of the public contract.
- *Without* prior publication of a contract notice where one or more economic operators are contacted directly and the contract is then negotiated with this or these economic operators.

Until tenders are submitted, the negotiated procedure with prior publication of a contract notice is similar to the restricted procedure. However, in this procedure the submission of tenders sparks negotiations between the contracting authority and the tenderers aimed at identifying the most competitive tender and the best solution.

2.5.1 Negotiations only in exceptional circumstances

Award of contracts on the basis of prior negotiations is less transparent than award of contracts based on the open procedure and the restricted procedure. As a consequence, this procedure is less suited for promoting the aim of the Procurement Directive to ensure equal treatment of economic tenderers. The Procurement Directive limits the use of the negotiated procedure for the award of contracts to:

"… the specific cases and circumstances referred to expressly in Articles 30 and 31 …".[60]

Since the use of the negotiated procedure to a certain extent is a derogation from one of the main aims of the Procurement Directive, Articles 30 and 31 of the Directive, and the cases and circumstances referred to therein, must be *interpreted strictly.*[61] In practice it is often difficult to establish the existence of the cases and circumstances referred to in Articles 30 and 31 as the Directive does not prescribe a maximum financial threshold for the efforts to be

---

60. Article 28 of the Procurement Directive. See also judgment of the European Court of Justice of 3 May 1994, case C-328/92, Commission vs. Spain, paragraph 12.
61. Judgment of the European Court of Justice of 10 April 2003, cases C-20/01 and C-28/01, Commission vs. Germany, paragraph 58; judgment of the European Court of Justice of 17 November 1993, case C-71/92, Commission vs. Spain, paragraph 36.

made by the contracting authorities in overcoming the difficulties, e.g. in determining the technical specifications of a contract.

Pursuant to the Procurement Directive a contract can only be awarded on the basis of negotiations in the specific circumstances mentioned in Articles 30 and 31.[62] The *burden of proving* compliance with the conditions for awarding a contract on the basis of negotiations lies with the contracting authority.[63] The conditions must be satisfied at the time when the contract award procedure is commenced, see chapter 3 above. At this time the contracting authority should also secure proof of compliance with the conditions.

There are two types of negotiated procedure: with or without prior publication of a contract notice.[64] In the light of the aims of the Procurement Directive of market access, equal treatment and competition, the significance of the two procedures is hugely different. The publication of a contract notice serves to inform economic operators throughout the EU of the possibility of being awarded a contract and they may contact the contracting authority and express their interest in the contract. The negotiated procedure *with* prior publication of a contract notice is in reality a restricted procedure with a right and an obligation to negotiate with the selected tenderers. As such, the selection of qualified candidates must follow the procedures set out in the Directive.[65] By contrast, where the procedure *without* prior publication of a contract notice is used, the economic operators do not know that a contract is being offered until the procedure is completed, a contract awarded, and this information made public.[66]

This significant difference in the level to which the aims of the Procurement Directive are guaranteed must influence the interpretation of the conditions subject to which the negotiated procedure with, respectively without prior publication of a contract notice can be used. The conditions for using this procedure *with* prior publication of a contract notice must be interpreted less strictly than the conditions for using the procedure *without* prior publica-

---

62. Under the Utilities Directive the use of the negotiated procedure is not restricted provided that a contract notice is published, Directive 2004/17/EC of the European Parliament and of the Council of 31 March 2004 coordinating the procedures of entities operating in the water, energy, transport and postal services sectors, Article 40, paragraph 2.

63. Judgment of the European Court of Justice of 10 April 2003, cases C-20/01 and C-28/01, Commission vs. Germany, paragraph 58; judgment of the European Court of Justice of 14 September 2004, case C-385/02, Commission vs. Italy, paragraph 19.

64. Articles 30 and 31 of the Procurement Directive.

65. See also chapter 6.

66. See also section 3.5 below on the obligation to advertise the award of a contract.

tion of a contract notice. This viewpoint finds support in the fact that pursuant to the Utilities Directive the negotiated procedure *with* prior publication of a contract notice can be used on an equal footing with the open procedure and the restricted procedure.

2.5.2 Negotiations with prior publication of a contract notice

Common to the situations where this procedure can be used is that the open procedure and the restricted procedure are not suited for the award of the contract, notably because the contracting authority cannot determine the contract specifications and therefore needs to discuss the contract with suitable candidates. Also tenderers' difficulties in preparing tenders, which comply with the specifications, may justify the use of this procedure.

2.5.2.1 Procedural requirements

Pursuant to the Procurement Directive the negotiated procedure with prior publication of a contract notice can only be used subject to compliance with various requirements:[67]

- a contract notice must be published which must contain the information specified in Annex VII A to the Directive;
- a number of suitable candidates must be selected in accordance with Articles 44-52 of the Procurement Directive;
- negotiations must be conducted with at least three candidates, provided that there are three suitable candidates;[68]
- if the procedure is used in continuation of an open procedure or a restricted procedure, the original procedure must be cancelled and the tenderers notified that the original procedure has ended.

2.5.2.2 Irregular and unacceptable tenders

Irregular tenders.[69] As this condition is worded, it is linked to the contract documents. Tenders may be irregular if they do not comply with language requirements; if they are not submitted in time or are not accompanied by proof of suitability; or if they do not comply with the substantive requirements, for example because they contain reservations or otherwise depart from the contract documents.

---

67. Article 30 of the Procurement Directive.
68. Article 44, paragraph 3 of the Procurement Directive.
69. Article 30, paragraph 1 (a) of the Procurement Directive.

In the interest of ensuring equal treatment and transparency in public procurement procedures, a public contract cannot be awarded on the basis of tenders with these types of irregularities. On the other hand, out of consideration for the contracting authority a new call for tenders under the open or restricted procedure is not required.

Tenders unacceptable under national provisions.[70] As this condition is worded, it covers tenders which for reasons not connected to the requirements specified in the contract documents cannot form the basis for the award of a contract.

Effective competition not achievable. However, the negotiated procedure can only be used if the number of tenders left after deselection of the irregular and unacceptable tenders is not sufficient to ensure effective competition for the public contract.[71] It is thus not possible to cancel an open procedure or a restricted procedure merely because some tenders are irregular or unacceptable. A cancellation in such circumstances would contravene the principle of equal treatment of tenderers in that a deselected tenderer would be given another chance compared to the tenderers which have submitted tenders that conform to the requirements.

Pursuant to Article 30 of the Directive negotiations can be commenced *without* prior publication of a contract notice provided:

- that all tenderers from the original procedure are included;
- if they satisfy the suitability requirements;
- and comply with the procedural requirements, such as timely submission of tenders;
- and that the original terms of the contract documents are not substantially altered.[72] This last condition is intended to safeguard the interests of the economic operators which were potential tenderers in the original procedure.

Only one tender conforms to the requirements. Presumably, negotiations can be commenced with only one tenderer. In such circumstances it would be

---

70. Article 30, paragraph 1 (a) of the Procurement Directive.
71. Article 44, paragraph 3, second indent of the Procurement Directive, contrast with Article 44, paragraph 3, third indent.
72. Order of the Complaints Board of 14 September 2001, Judex A/S vs. County of Århus.

justified to cancel the original procedure,[73] and the lack of competition in the tender stage in combination with the publication of a new contract notice probably satisfies the conditions subject to which the negotiated procedure with prior publication of a contract notice can be used.

2.5.2.3 Prior overall pricing not possible[74]

This derogation is linked to the nature and scope of the supplies, services or works and the uncertainties with respect to the nature and seriousness of the risks involved therewith. Such uncertainties may, for example, arise where a site for building works is geologically unstable or because archaeological studies have to be carried out.[75]

By contrast, this derogation cannot be relied upon where the nature and scope of the supplies, services or works can be safely predicted, but the contracting authority is uncertain of the price, for example because a complex financial or legal structure has been set up.[76]

2.5.2.4 Not possible to establish contract with sufficient precision[77]

This derogation is linked to the nature of the supplies, services or works and the contracting authority's possibilities for specifying them with sufficient precision to permit the award of the contract on the basis of the contract documents without opening negotiations with the tenderers. In considering whether the negotiated procedure can be used in this situation account should be had to whether the specifications can be determined in terms of performance or functional requirements.[78]

The Procurement Directive lists three types of contracts for which the negotiated procedure with prior publication of a contract notice can be used:

– financial services (insurance, banking and investment services),
– intellectual services eg. the design of works.

73. Judgment of the European Court of Justice of 16 September 1999, case C-27/98, Metalmeccanica Fracasso SpA and Others, paragraph 33, cf. paragraph 25.
74. Article 30, paragraph 1 (b) of the Procurement Directive.
75. Commission Green Paper of 30 April 2004 on Public-Private Partnerships and Community law Public Contracts and Concessions, Com (2004)327 final, point 24.
76. Ibid.
77. Article 30, paragraph 1 (c) of the Procurement Directive.
78. Article 23 of the Procurement Directive.

Particularly complex contracts[79] may due to the similarity with the above mentioned contracts be awarded by relying on this derogation. Also partnering contracts for *public works*[80] may fall subject to this provision.

2.5.2.5 Works contracts performed solely for research[81]

The negotiated procedure may be used for the award of a works contract the sole purpose of which is research, testing or development. The procedure cannot be used if the sole aim is to support the research and development efforts of the economic operator.

2.5.3 Negotiations without prior publication of a contract notice

This procedure can be used in various situations. The interests pursued by the contracting authority can be of such a serious nature that the conclusion of a contract cannot await the conduct of a procurement procedure, not even an accelerated procedure. A call for tenders is for example pointless for contracts for which it is certain that there is only one possible tenderer. A call for tenders is for example unnecessary where the aim of opening up public contracts for competition was achieved at an earlier stage in the contract conclusion procedure or by other means.

The negotiated procedure *without* prior publication of a contract notice is, on the one hand, a necessary loophole through which contracting authorities can get round their obligations under the Procurement Directive. On the other hand, the cases in which this procedure can be used must be interpreted strictly in view of the fact that negotiations *without* prior publication of a contract notice is a manifest contradiction of the fundamental objective of the Procurement Directive; to open up public contracts for competition.

2.5.3.1 Procedural requirements

Even where a contract can be awarded lawfully on the basis of the negotiated procedure *without* prior publication of a contract notice,[82] the contracting

---

79. As defined in Article 1, paragraph 11(c), second indent of the Procurement Directive, cf. also section 2.4 above.
80. As defined in Article 1, paragraph 2 of the Procurement Directive, cf. also section 5.3 below.
81. Article 30, paragraph 1 (d) of the Procurement Directive. See also section 2.5.3.5 below on supply contracts. Pursuant to Article 16 (f) service contracts in this area fall outside the scope of the Directive. See also chapter 3.2.
82. Article 31 of the Procurement Directive.

authority must still comply with certain obligations under the Directive. By virtue of the principle of equal treatment the contracting authority must:

– ensure competition for the contract. Whenever possible more economic operators must be contacted. Whether this is possible, in terms of time or for reasons linked to the object of the contract, depends on the specific circumstances;
– apply the grounds for exclusion set out in Article 45, paragraph 1;
– publish a notice of the award of the contract indicating *inter alia* the reasons why this procedure was chosen;[83]
– prepare a report setting out *inter alia* the circumstances justifying the use of this procedure. The report must be communicated to the Commission upon request.[84]

2.5.3.2 No suitable tenders or no tenders[85]

No suitable tenders. As this condition is worded, it is linked to the interests of the contracting authority. The tender must be *unsuitable* for other reasons than mere non-compliance with the requirements and conditions specified in the contract documents. Tenders proposing a solution or a contract which clearly does not satisfy the needs of the contracting authority, and the underlying objective, as described in the contract documents fall within this category. The same is true of tenders which are extraneous to the proposed contract and thus altogether unsuitable for fulfilling the requirements of the contracting authority.

This interpretation of the suitability requirement is in accordance with the inherent requirement in the principle of proportionality that means must be suitable for achieving the intended objective. The negotiated procedure without prior publication of a contract notice is to be seen as a narrow derogation which supports the strict interpretation of unsuitable tenders in this chapter.[86] Accordingly, this derogation cannot be relied upon if the prices of the tenders submitted are too high, the prices indicated are abnormally low or if the tenders in one or more areas depart from the requirements or conditions specified in the contract documents.

If no tenders are submitted, it is first of all easy to verify and, second, the conclusion is clear: Article 31 of the Procurement Directive authorises that

---

83. Article 35 of the Procurement Directive, cf. Annex VII A to the Directive.
84. Article 43 of the Procurement Directive.
85. Article 31, paragraph 1 (a) of the Procurement Directive.
86. Commission public procurement guidelines for supply contracts, point 3.3.2.

selected economic operators can be contacted and that a contract can be negotiated with these operators.

Where the tenders submitted are unsuitable or no tenders are submitted,
negotiations can be commenced with selected economic operators after the
original call for tenders has been formally cancelled and the tenderers, if any,
have been informed thereof.[87] During the negotiations the original terms of
the contract cannot be substantially changed and on that account it is necessary to evaluate any changes to the contract to determine whether they are
likely to attract potential tenderers.[88] It should, furthermore, be kept in mind
that the cases justifying the use of this procedure are very limited which reflects on the degree of changes permitted in the contract.[89]

Effective competition not achievable. The negotiated procedure can only be
used if the number of tenders left after deselection of the irregular and unacceptable tenders is not sufficient to ensure effective competition for the public
contract.[90] It is thus not possible to cancel an open procedure or a restricted
procedure merely because some tenders are not suitable. A cancellation in
such circumstances would contravene the principle of equal treatment of
tenderers in that a deselected tenderer would be given another chance compared to the tenderers that have submitted tenders that conform to the requirements.

No pre-qualified candidates or only one pre-qualified candidate. Sometimes it becomes evident already in the selection stage that there are no candidates which comply with the selection criteria. A situation in which only
one candidate is pre-qualified is unacceptable to the contracting authority.
Although this situation is somewhat similar to the situation where only one
tender complies with the requirements specified, the contracting authority is
disadvantaged even more and it can only hope that the candidate submits a
tender which complies with the requirements and is economically acceptable.

This situation is not addressed in the Procurement Directive. Since Articles 30 and 31 are to be given a strict interpretation, the contracting authority
only has two options. Either it can cancel the call for tenders and recommence an open procedure or a restricted procedure. Or it can continue the
procedure, and if the tender turns out to be irregular or unsuitable or is not

---

87. Article 43 of the Procurement Directive provides that a report be prepared and
    presented to the Commission upon request.
88. See also section 2.5.5 below.
89. See also 2.5.3.4 below.
90. Article 44, paragraph 3, second indent of the Procurement Directive, contrast with
    Article 44, paragraph 3, third indent.

submitted at all, the negotiated procedure can be used. However, there is a strong case for arguing that already at the time when the contracting authority becomes aware that only one candidate will be pre-qualified, and thus only one tender submitted, it can decide to use the negotiated procedure with prior publication of a contract notice, cf. section 5.2.2.2 above.

2.5.3.3 Only one particular economic operator[91]

Two conditions must be satisfied in order to rely on this derogation. A contract can only be awarded to one particular economic operator if justified for technical or artistic reasons or reasons connected with the protection of exclusive rights, and these reasons prove that only one particular supplier can perform the contract.[92]

In Commission vs. Italy[93] a contract for the construction of a rapid transit highway was subsequently supplemented by 12 projects, all of which were awarded to the original contractor without a call for tenders. The European Court of Justice did not find that it had been proved that the technical, logistics and coordination difficulties cited in combination with the fact that more public contracts had been awarded concerning the same overall project made it absolutely necessary to award the supplementary contracts to the original contractor.[94]

On objective grounds it must be ruled out that other economic operators are able to supply the product or service or execute the works. There are no geographic or economic limits to this assessment and also potential suppliers must be ruled out.

In *Commission vs. Germany*[95] the town of Braunschweig had awarded a contract for residual waste disposal by thermal processing for a term of 30 years. The European Court of Justice recognised that in theory protection of the environment could constitute a technical reason, but did not find that it had been proved that the choice of thermal waste processing made it necessary to award the contract to one particular service provider.[96]

---

91. Article 31, paragraph 1 (b) of the Procurement Directive.
92. Judgment of the European Court of Justice of 18 May 1995, case C-57/94, Commission vs. Italy (Ascoli-Mare rapid transit highway), paragraph 24.
93. Ibid.
94. Ibid, paragraph 12.
95. Judgment of the European Court of Justice of 10 April 2003, cases C-20/01 and C-28/01, Commission vs. Germany.
96. Ibid, paragraph 64. See also judgment of the European Court of Justice of 28 March 1995, case C-324/93, Evans Medical Ltd and Macfarlan Smith Ltd., para-

Exclusive rights to provide a service may justify reliance on this derogation,[97] but the mere existence of exclusive rights, such as patents, is not sufficient reason for relying on this derogation; at the same time it must be proved that there are no other suppliers which can perform the proposed contract.[98] For pharmaceutical products this condition is only satisfied where there is no competition in the market. Even where this condition is satisfied with respect to one or perhaps more products, it does not justify that all pharmaceutical products are purchased without a call for tenders.[99]

If technical or artistic reasons are cited as justification for awarding a contract to one particular supplier, the standard of proof is high. For example, a claim that works are complex and difficult is not sufficient proof that the contract can only be awarded to one particular contractor.[100]

In *Commission vs. Greece*[101] concerning the construction of conveyor belts for a thermal-electricity generation plant the European Court of Justice held that it had not been sufficiently satisfied that "Neither the particular characteristics of the product to be transported, nor the instability of the subsoil and the need to attach the system of conveyor belts to the existing one proves, by itself, that that consortium of companies was the only contractor in the Community with the necessary expertise to carry out the works in question."[102]

2.5.3.4 Strictly necessary for reasons of extreme urgency[103]

Three cumulative conditions must be satisfied for the award of a contract based on this provision.[104] Firstly, the contracting authority could not have foreseen the circumstances that brought about the need for concluding the

---

graph 44, on supply reliability and security measures in connection with the supply of narcotic drugs for therapeutic purposes.
97. Article 18 of the Procurement Directive.
98. Judgment of the European Court of Justice of 3 May 1994, case C-328/92, Commission vs. Spain, paragraph 17.
99. Judgment of the European Court of Justice of 3 May 1994, case C-328/92, Commission vs. Spain, paragraph 17.
100. Judgment of the European Court of Justice of 14 September 2004, case C-385/02, Commission vs. Italy, paragraph 21, construction of an overflow basin to hold flood waters.
101. Judgment of the European Court of Justice of 2 June 2005, case C-394/02, Commission vs. Greece.
102. Ibid, paragraph 36.
103. Article 31, paragraph 1 (c) of the Procurement Directive.
104. Judgment of the European Court of Justice of 2 June 2005, case C-394/02, Commission vs. Greece, paragraph 40.

particular contract. These circumstances must not in any event be attributable to the contracting authority.[105]

Secondly, the circumstances must be similar to events of force majeure, such as pollution caused by pipeline ruptures or other unexpected spills, earthquakes or floods.[106] It follows that the need to make the public procurement must be acute. In addition the reasons must be of extreme urgency typically involving public health, public security, the lives and health of human beings and animals, the environment, etc. Economic concerns, such as payment of rent until the construction of a building is finished, measures to avert job losses, etc. cannot be categorised as reasons of extreme urgency.

Thirdly, there must be a causal link between the unforeseen event and the extreme urgency of concluding a public contract brought about by the event.

In *Commission vs. Germany*[107] concerning the dredging of the river EMS to enable a new ship from the shipyard Meyer-Werft to be delivered to the buyer at the agreed time, the conditions were held not to have been satisfied. The alleged unforeseen event was that the relevant authority initially had refused the dredging for ecological reasons. To this the European Court of Justice stated: "The possibility that a body which must approve a project might, before expiry of the period laid down for this purpose, raise objections for reasons which it is entitled to put forward is, consequently, something which is foreseeable in plan approval procedure."[108]

In *Commission vs. Italy*[109] concerning the construction and erection of an avalanche defence, the conditions were held not to have been satisfied. The contracting authority had long been aware of the need for constructing an avalanche defence and it would have been possible to comply with the time limits stipulated in the Directive.

In *Commission vs. Spain*[110] concerning an extension of a university in Madrid the contracting authority tried to prove to the European Court of Justice that a growing number of students and the intake of new students were unforeseen events.

---

105. Judgment of the European Court of Justice of 14 September 2004, case C-385/02, Commission vs. Italy, paragraph 26, construction of an overflow basin to hold flood waters.
106. Commission public procurement guidelines for works contracts, point 3.3.2.
107. Judgment of the European Court of Justice of 28 March 1996, case C-318/94, Commission vs. Germany.
108. Ibid, paragraph 18. See also judgment of the European Court of Justice of 2 June 2005, case C-394/02, Commission vs. Greece.
109. Judgment of the European Court of Justice of 2 August 1993, case C-107/92, Commission vs. Italy, paragraphs 12 and 13.
110. Judgment of the European Court of Justice of 18 March 1992, case C-24/91, Commission vs. Spain.

This derogation can only be relied upon to award public contracts if the provision of supplies or services or the execution of works cannot await the completion of a procurement procedure, not even an accelerated procedure.[111]

2.5.3.5 Supply contracts for experimentation[112]

This derogation relates to research, development, experimentation and specially manufactured products. The contract must be awarded for the purpose of satisfying a need with the contracting authority. To that end the contracting authority can enter into a close cooperation with an economic operator for example with a view to testing new types of material, methods of production, areas of application, etc. This derogation cannot be relied upon to cover the economic operator's costs of the research and development work, acquisition of laboratory equipment, etc., which are not related to a specific purchase.

An economic operator may derive considerable advantages from cooperation with a contracting authority on research and development, etc. and may in that connection have an interest in producing a marketable product. This derogation cannot be relied upon for the award of public contracts which are intended to secure the economic operator a basis for establishing the commercial viability of a product.

2.5.3.6 Commodity market[113]

Reliance on this derogation is conditional on the existence of a recognised market for the relevant products and that the products are in actual fact purchased on that market.

2.5.3.7 Supplies purchased on particularly advantageous terms[114]

This derogation allows for the fact that in special circumstances purchases may be made on particularly advantageous terms, for example in connection with a bankruptcy clearance sale.

This derogation can only be relied upon for the purchase of supplies and only in connection with the definite winding-up of a business or in connection with a forced sale. Accordingly, this derogation cannot be relied upon in situations where a contracting authority receives a particularly advantageous

---

111. Judgment of the European Court of Justice of 3 May 1994, case C-328/92, Commission vs. Spain, paragraph 18.
112. Article 31, paragraph 2 (a) of the Procurement Directive.
113. Article 31, paragraph 2 (c) of the Procurement Directive.
114. Article 31, paragraph 2 (d) of the Procurement Directive.

tender, for example because the economic operator has excess supplies or needs to sell its stocks.

Furthermore, the supplies must be purchased on "particularly advantageous terms". It is not clear which price difference meets this requirement, i.e. what is the measure of a "particularly advantageous" purchase. In any case the standard against which this is measured should be the normal market price and not official list prices taking into account the customary practice within several industries of granting sizeable discounts on the list prices (30-50%).

2.5.3.8 Service contracts following a design contest[115]

Design contests can be organised for plan and design works.[116] Where a design contest has been held and a successful candidate found, the contracting authority can award a service contract for the plan and design works for which the design contest was organised to the successful candidate without a call for tenders.[117]

The contract can only be awarded without a call for tenders if the contracting authority in the contract documents has anticipated that a subsequent public contract would be awarded and if the conditions of the contest provide that the contracting authority is required to award the contract to the successful candidate. If there is more than one successful candidate, all of them must be invited to negotiate before the public contract is awarded.

This derogation can only be relied upon if there is a relevant link between the contest and the public contract which follows the contest. In *Commission vs. France*[118] it was emphasised "that there must be a direct functional link between the contest and the contract concerned".[119]

The contract must be awarded on the basis of the successful design, but there is scope for negotiating adjustments and amendments within the bounds of the contract documents and the successful design.

---

115. Article 31, paragraph 3 of the Procurement Directive. See also section 4.1 below on design contests.
116. Article 1, paragraph 11 (e).
117. Judgment of the European Court of Justice of 14 October 2004, case C-340/02, Commission vs. France.
118. Ibid.
119. Ibid, paragraph 41, cf. paragraphs 38 and 39. In order of the Complaints Board of 8 April 2005, Danish Association of Architetural Firms vs. Danish Defence Construction Service concerning the award of a contract for technical advice and assistance concerning the fitting of a new auditorium for the army's military academy, it was held that there was a relevant link between the contest and the subsequent contract.

2.5.3.9 Additional supplies, works or services

In a few cases the Procurement Directive allows contracts for certain additional deliveries linked to a public contract already awarded to be concluded without a call for tenders.

For *supplies contracts*[120] a call for tenders for contracts for additional deliveries can only be avoided if a change of supplier would result in *technical* incompatibility or disproportionate *technical* difficulties in operation and maintenance. In *Humus/Genplast ApS vs. Den selvejende virksomhed Århus Renholdningsselskab*[121] concerning the purchase of waste containers, the court was not satisfied that a change of supplier would meet the conditions subject to which a call for tenders could be avoided.

Technical difficulties are clearly the primary reason why this derogation can be relied upon, but presumably, economic considerations can be taken into account as well in the assessment of whether the technical difficulties are disproportionate. Additional contracts can only be awarded for a term of three years.

For *public works and service contracts*[122] the additional contracts must have been brought about by *unforeseen* circumstances and be *necessary* for the performance of the original works. Furthermore, the additional contract must be awarded to the original contractor. Finally, it is a requirement for awarding the additional contract to the original contractor that for technical or economic reasons a separation of the additional works or services from the original contract will cause major inconvenience.[123] The value of additional contracts awarded by virtue of this derogation cannot exceed 50% of the value of the original contract.

2.5.3.10 Options for additions to a basic project[124]

This derogation can be relied upon where it is provided and stipulated in the contract documents inviting tenders for a public works or a public service contract that it may be necessary to expand the scope of the proposed contract.

---

120. Article 31, paragraph 2 (b) of the Procurement Directive.
121. Judgment of the Western High Court of 3 May 2001, case B-1447-99, Humus/Genplast ApS vs. Den Selvejende Virksomhed Århus Renholdningsselskab.
122. Article 31, paragraph 4 (a) of the Procurement Directive.
123. The Procurement Directive provides a limited scope for awarding an additional contract to the original contractor even where it is possible to separate the additional and the original contracts.
124. Article 31, paragraph 4 (b) of the Procurement Directive.

The award of a contract by reliance on this derogation is subject to certain conditions. The original contract must have been awarded on the basis of the open procedure or the restricted procedure. The new contract, the addition, can only be awarded to the economic operator that was awarded the original contract. The addition must be in conformity with a basic project thus limiting the scope and nature of changes to the project. The negotiations for the new contract must be commenced within three years of the *conclusion* of the original contract.[125]

Despite these conditions this derogation is of great practical importance where the contracting authority is not certain of the ultimate scale of a public contract

2.5.4 How to conduct a negotiated procedure

A negotiated procedure must be conducted in compliance with the fundamental principles of equal treatment, transparency, objectivity and non-discrimination.[126] These principles have been applied to decide a number of cases and on the basis thereof it is possible to establish certain rules which are independent of whether the negotiations are conducted with or without prior publication of a contract notice. These rules may, however, have to be modified in light of the specific circumstances that justify the use of the negotiated procedure *without* prior publication of a contract notice.

Advertising. The basic principle is that all economic operators must be provided with the same information and afforded the same opportunities for expressing their interest in entering into negotiations.[127] Publication of a contract notice provides a common basis which must be followed up with supplementary specifications, documents or information.[128] After the pre-qualification additional information may be sent to the selected economic operators provided that the principle of equal treatment is complied with.[129]

---

125. Judgment of the European Court of Justice of 14 September 2004, case C-385/02, Commission vs. Italy, paragraphs 30-39.
126. Article 2 of the Procurement Directive on non-discrimination.
127. This is emphasised in Article 30, paragraph 3, but also the principle of equal treatment must be complied with in all negotiated procedures, cf. section 1.5 above. Where individual economic operators are contacted directly *without* prior publication of a contract notice, there is obviously no requirement for general access to information. For such a procedure the contracting authority must strive to contact several economic operators.
128. Where a contract notice is not advertised, information on the contract conditions must be sent to the selected economic operators directly.
129. Article 30, paragraph 3 of the Procurement Directive.

Pre-scheduled course of negotiations.[130] The contracting authority schedules and specifies, in advance, the course of the negotiations in the contract documents. The contract documents must set out a procedure for the conduct of the negotiations until it has been deceided which tender is to form the basis for the award of the contract. Against *inter alia* that background there is a duty to fixate time limits for the submission of tenders.

In order to ensure compliance with the principles of equal treatment and transparency, the contracting authority must adhere strictly to the course it has set out for the negotiations.[131] The participants in the negotiations must be treated equally with respect to information, deadlines for submitting adjusted tenders and the issues negotiated during the individual stages.[132]

Contracting authority in charge of negotiations. The contracting authority schedules and is in charge of the negotiations conducted on the basis of the tenders submitted from the pre-qualified undertakings. It is often expedient to prepare an agenda for the negotiations which may serve as documentary evidence. The contracting authority is under an obligation to state the grounds on which undertakings have been short listed (deselected) and the contract awarded. Detailed minutes must be prepared enabling the contracting authority to prove which issues have been negotiated and thus compliance with the requirements for transparency and equal treatment.

A tenderer cannot on its own initiative change the pre-scheduled procedure. For example, where a deselected tenderer on its own initiative forwards a new or adjusted tender, the contracting authority must reject this tender.[133] In contrast, in the course of the negotiations the contracting authority can request the remaining tenderers to prepare new or adjusted tenders which will provide the basis of the negotiations to be conducted.

Pre-qualification. The procedure is opened with a pre-qualification stage in which a number of qualified economic operators are *selected* and from among them at least three are invited to submit tenders. The selection criteria and the number of economic operators invited to participate in the negotiations must be specified in the contract documents.

Negotiations. Based on the tenders submitted, negotiations are commenced with each economic operator. The tenders submitted are the starting

---

130. Order of the Complaints Board of 4 November 2003, Bombardier Transportation Denmark A/S vs. Lokalbanen A/S.
131. Judgment of the Eastern High Court of 16 September 2002, case (3rd division) no. B-104-97, European Metro Group vs. Ørestadsselskabet I/S.
132. Order of the Complaints Board of 9 March 1999, Technicomm A/S vs. DSB.
133. Ibid.

point for the negotiations and the issues discussed therefore vary. At the same time the negotiations must be capable of ensuring equal treatment. The outcome of the negotiations is of great financial importance to the economic operators financially in that the negotiations gradually reduce the number of tenderers, which inevitably means deselection of some tenderers, and usually result in only one economic operator being awarded a contract. To ensure equal treatment of the tenderers the negotiations must be objective, targeted at the economic and financial implications and genuine, and the contracting authority must point to specific advantages and shortcomings of the tenders. Having reviewed the tenders once, the contracting authority can make recommendations for adjustments of the tenders.

The contracting authority is entitled, but also obliged to negotiate with the selected tenderers. A tenderer that submits a tender which complies with the specifications is entitled to negotiate and consequently to submit at least one adjusted tender.

Negotiations in stages. The negotiations can be scheduled in stages in which the number of tenders on which the negotiations are based is gradually reduced, and thus also the number of economic operators invited to submit tenders (short listing).[134] The deselection of tenders at the end of each stage of the negotiations is determined by the selection criteria ranked in order of priority in the contract documents. The contracting authority may be wise to schedule the negotiations in stages in that it permits the contracting authority to invite a broad selection of tenders, while at the same time enabling it to reduce the time and expense involved with the negotiations.[135] The contracting authority must strive to ensure that the number of remaining economic operators in the last stage of the negotiations is sufficient for genuine competition for the public contract.[136] Presumably, it suffices if only two tenderers are invited to submit final, adjusted tenders.

Confidentiality. During the negotiations the contracting authority compares the tenders submitted. The economic operators will be requested to adjust their tenders on specific points. Shortcomings of a tender in terms of for example technology, price, etc. can be pointed out in the course of the negotiations. In the interest of guaranteeing the confidentiality of the tenders

---

134. Article 30, paragraph 4 of the Procurement Directive, cf. Article 44, paragraph 4.
135. Recital 41 of the preamble to the Procurement Directive.
136. Article 44, paragraph 4 of the Procurement Directive.

the contracting authority cannot while negotiating with one tenderer disclose the other tenderers' proposals for technological solutions, prices, etc.[137]

Final tender. The negotiations are closed with an invitation to the remaining tenderers to submit final, adjusted tenders within a specified time. The contract is awarded to the tenderer which has submitted the tender which is most economically advantageous to the contracting authority evaluated on the basis of the award criteria specified in the contract documents.

Negotiations after award. Negotiations can also be conducted with the successful tenderer. Such negotiations may be necessary as well as useful for final clarification of the technical, economic and legal aspects of the contract, including final decisions on the financing of the project, use of subcontractors, etc. The scope for such negotiations depends on the nature of the object/project. The time schedule, technical features, methods, risk allocation, etc. are in many cases adjusted, provided that negotiations on such adjustments were envisaged in the contract documents and that they do not involve features regarding which the contracting authority has made mandatory requirements in the contract documents.

2.5.5 What can be negotiated?

The contracting authority conducts a procurement procedure with a view to concluding a contract (for supply of products, provision of a service or execution of works). Within the overall framework defined by the contracting authority's needs and the specifications in the contract documents, negotiations are intended to adjust submitted tenders to the requirements determined by the contracting authority in the contract documents.[138]

In theory, all technical, commercial and legal aspects and conditions of a contract can be negotiated; the object of the contract can be modified and the terms and conditions of the contract can be altered. However, the basis on which the call for tenders was made must essentially remain the same, and the objectives of competition for public contracts and equal treatment of economic operators limit the opportunities for negotiations somewhat.[139] The contracting authority contacts the economic operators because it contemplates purchasing a specific product. This product, the object of the contract, is described in the contract documents and this description constitutes the frame-

---

137. Article 6 of the Procurement Directive; order of the Complaints Board of 14 September 2001, Judex A/S vs. County of Århus.
138. Article 30, paragraph 2 of the Procurement Directive.
139. Order of the Complaints Board of 9 March 1999, Technicomm A/S vs. Danish Railways.

work for the negotiations with the economic operators. [140] Where the contracting authority has chosen to award a contract on the basis of "the most economically advantageous tender" specifying various sub-criteria, these criteria serve to deselect tenderers and select the successful tender. Where the contracting authority has chosen the award criterion "the lowest price only", only this criterion can be applied.

It is not possible to define the exact bounds within which negotiations can be conducted. On the one hand, negotiations are, by nature, likely to lead to adjustments, and through negotiations the contracting authority's opportunities for achieving a useful end-result are increased. Also the nature of the project is important when determining whether the bounds of negotiations have been exceeded. [141] On the other hand, equal treatment of economic operators is a serious concern, and especially the need to ensure equal treatment of potential tenderers requires that negotiations be conducted within certain bounds. On that account, negotiations cannot have the effect of *changing substantial aspects* of the tender: the described object and the specifications. In the event of *substantial changes* the call for tenders must be cancelled and a new procedure launched. However, within these limits there is often ample scope for adjusting technical, economic and legal aspects without altering the fundamentals of the project.

In *Højgaard og Schultz A/S and Others vs. Ørestadsselskabet I/S (the Utilities Directive)*[142] concerning the mini metro in Copenhagen the Complaints Board assessed the technical merits, economic implications and the overall impact of the changes on the project as a whole. The Complaints Board did not find that the bounds of negotiations had been exceeded. The Complaints Board placed particular emphasis on the fact "that the changes stipulated do not lead to the inclusion of new elements in the project requiring new technical solutions or substantially changed methods of execution than those applicable to the original project, and that the changes do not impact to any significant extent on the period of execution."[143]

The tenders submitted may vary from or contain reservations about the contract documents. Where the variations or reservations do not concern manda-

---

140. In the contract notice, the specifications and any additional documents.
141. Order of the Complaints Board of 11 June 1999, H. Hoffmann og Sønner ApS vs. Aalborg Lufthavn AmbA (restricted procedure under the Utilities Directive).
142. Order of the Complaints Board of 3 December 1998, Højgaard og Schultz A/S and Others vs. Ørestadsselskabet I/S (the Utilities Directive).
143. The procedure was a negotiated procedure under the Utilities Directive subject to which this procedure can be chosen as an alternative to the open procedure and the restricted procedure.

tory elements of the contract documents, the contracting authority is *neither entitled nor obliged* to reject the tenders, which are merely to be regarded as a starting point for the subsequent negotiations.[144] Indeed, the nature of the negotiations is such that all aspects of the contract must be discussed. However, a contracting authority can stipulate in the contract documents that certain requirements are mandatory (minimum requirements). Any technical, economic or legal aspect can be in the nature of a mandatory requirement (choice of material, dimensions, period of execution, guarantee period, etc.), and the contracting authority can specify in the contract documents that a tender that varies from or contains reservations about mandatory requirements will be rejected forthwith.[145] An interpretation of the contract documents will decide which aspects are mandatory.

Mandatory requirements in the contract documents have a certain impact on the evaluation and the negotiations. By virtue of the principles of equal treatment and transparency tenders which, having been evaluated, are deemed to be irregular or to contain reservations about mandatory aspects must be rejected forthwith.[146] Furthermore, negotiations prior to the award of a contract, and subsequent changes, must respect those aspects of the contract documents which the contracting authority has chosen to make mandatory.[147]

3. Publication

The Procurement Directive imposes several obligations with respect to publication in connection with the award of a public contract.

A public contract can only be awarded after prior publication of a contract notice, cf. sections 3.1 and 3.2.[148]

---

144. Order of the Complaints Board of 4 November 2003, Bombardier Transportation Denmark A/S vs. Lokalbanen A/S.
145. Order of the Complaints Board of 4 November 2003, Bombardier Transportation Denmark A/S vs. Lokalbanen A/S.
146. See chapter 7.4.3 below.
147. Judgment of the Court of First Instance of 28 November 2002, case T-40/01, Scan Office, paragraph 76, cf. paragraph 80.
148. The obligation to publish a contract notice can only be avoided in the exceptional cases where the contract can be awarded on the basis of the negotiated procedure *without* prior publication of a contract notice. The conditions subject to which this procedure can be used are set out in Article 31 of the Procurement Directive. See also section 2.5 above.

Only in exceptional cases does the contract notice constitute a sufficient basis for preparing a tender, and therefore, tenderers need additional information, which is often very comprehensive, and need to be given the opportunity for clarifying unclear issues, cf. section 3.3.

The contracting authority can also publish a prior information notice which indicates the contemplated purchases in the coming year and their estimated value, cf. section 3.4.

Publication of a contract notice is required for all awards of public contracts under the Procurement Directive.[149] Furthermore, candidates and tenderers must be informed directly of the award of the contract or, where appropriate, the cancellation of the procurement procedure. Finally, a detailed report on the progress of the procedure must be prepared, cf. section 3.5.

3.1 The contract notice

At the root of the Procurement Directive is the view that market access and competition for public contracts on equal terms only are achievable through transparent procedures for the award of contracts. The obligation on contracting authorities to publish a contract notice prior to awarding a public contract is a core element in the efforts to ensure transparency. Economic operators throughout the EU are thereby notified that the award of a public contract is proposed and they may contact the contracting authority, express their interest in the contract and provide evidence of their suitability.[150]

The contract notice is a cornerstone of the Procurement Directive since it represents the main source of information concerning when a public contract will be awarded. Based on the information in the contract notice the economic operators decide whether a specific public contract is sufficiently interesting to them to allocate the time and resources necessary for expressing their interest in an invitation to tender, requesting the specifications and any additional information and preparing the evidence required, applying for participation in the procedure and/or submitting a tender. For the award of certain contracts the contract notice is the only basis for preparing tenders.

The contract notice must contain specific information listed in Annex VII A to the Procurement Directive, including the level of standards and personal

---

149. Article 35 of the Procurement Directive, cf. Annex VII A to the Directive.
150. There are also certain requirements for the information to be published, cf. Annex VII A to the Procurement Directive. There is also a *general* obligation to formulate the information "… in such a way as to allow all reasonably well-informed tenderers of normal diligence to interpret them in the same way", cf. judgment of the European Court of Justice of 4 December 2003, case C-448/01, EVN, paragraph 57.

situation required of the economic operators and the evidence to be submitted as proof thereof.[151]

The information forwarded for publication must be set out in a standard format.[152] The use of standard forms makes it easier to access the information and thus contributes to greater transparency in award procedures for public contracts.

The contracting authority chooses the language in which the contract notice is published. The notice is sent to the Commission for publication in the Official Journal. A summary of the notice is published in the other official Community languages.[153]

3.2 Time limits linked to the contract notice

The Procurement Directive provides that a certain time (number of days) must lapse from when the contract notice is sent till the final date for receipt of applications for participation in the procedure and submission of tenders, respectively. The general rule is that in fixing the time limits account must be had of the complexity of the contract and the time required by the economic operators for drawing up applications, respectively tenders.[154]

3.2.1 Generally about time limits

The time limits fixed in the Procurement Directive is intended to balance the contracting authorities' interest in a speedy award procedure against the Community interest in ensuring that the economic operators are allowed sufficient time to provide evidence of their suitability and prepare tenders. The time limits are only intended to protect candidates and tenderers against too many arbitrary and subjective decisions on the part of the contracting authorities and should, therefore, be viewed as safeguards ensuring a minimum level of market access and competition. A contracting authority is therefore free to prolong the time limits.

The minimum time limits fixed according to the Procurement Directive begin to run from *the contracting authority's dispatch* of the contract no-

---

151. Annex VII A, point 17 to the Procurement Directive.
152. Annex VIII to the Procurement Directive, cf. Commission Directive 2001/78/EC of 13 September 2001 on the use of standard forms in the publication of public contract notices.
153. Article 36, paragraph 1 of the Procurement Directive, see also Annex VIII to the Procurement Directive.
154. Article 38, paragraph 1 of the Procurement Directive.

tice.[155] The contracting authority must be able to supply proof of the date of dispatch.[156] The Commission publishes the notices in the Official Journal and the Community pays the expenses incurred in that connection. The Commission sends the contracting authority a confirmation of the publication.[157]

The Commission is obliged to publish the contract notices.[158] The time limits are

- 12 days after dispatch;
- 5 days after dispatch if the notice is forwarded by electronic means;
- 5 days after dispatch where the contracting authority uses the accelerated procedure.

The contracting authorities are under an obligation to await the expiry of certain time limits in the individual stages of the procedure (time limit for receipt of applications for participation, time limit for receipt of tenders).[159] The length of the time limits depends on the procurement procedure chosen, cf. section 3.2.2 below.

The time limits can be shortened if the contracting authority complies with certain obligations:[160]

- The time limits reflect the time needed by the Commission for publication. The time limits may be shortened by 7 days if the notices are transmitted to the Commission by electronic means.[161]
- The time limits reflect the time needed by the economic operators to provide evidence of their suitability and prepare tenders. The time limits can be reduced by another 5 days where unrestricted and full direct access by electronic means is offered to the contract documents and any supplementary document.[162] In contrast, where an on-site visit is required or the specifications only can be inspected at one address, the time limits must be extended.[163]
- Publication of a prior information notice provides the economic operators with information on the nature and scale of the purchases anticipated by the contracting authority

---

155. Article 38 of the Procurement Directive.
156. Article 36, paragraph 7 of the Procurement Directive.
157. Article 36, paragraph 8 of the Procurement Directive.
158. Article 36 of the Procurement Directive.
159. Article 38 of the Procurement Directive.
160. Recitals 33 and 36 of the preamble to the Procurement Directive.
161. Article 38, paragraph 5 of the Procurement Directive.
162. Article 38, paragraph 6 of the Procurement Directive.
163. Article 38, paragraph 7 of the Procurement Directive.

well in advance of the call for tenders for the actual contract. The time limits for receipt of tenders can therefore by shortened to 36 days.[164]

In scheduling the procedure for the contract conclusion the contracting authority must allow the successful tenderer sufficient time for obtaining the required public licences before the start of the contract period.[165]

3.2.2 Individual time limits

Open procedure. The time limit for receipt of tenders is 52 days. The time limit can be shortened to 36 days if a prior information notice is published. The time limit can be shortened by another 7 days if the notice is forwarded by electronic means. The time limit can be shortened by another 5 days if unrestricted and full direct access by electronic means is offered to the contract documents. The time limit cannot be shortened to less than 22 days. The time limit must be extended if an on-site inspection is required.

Restricted procedure, competitive dialogue and negotiated procedure with prior publication of a contract notice.
– The time limit for receipt of requests to participate is 37 days. The time limit can be shortened by 7 days if the notice is forwarded by electronic means.
– The time limit for receipt of tenders is 40 days. The time limit can be shortened to 36 days if a prior information notice is published. The time limit can be shortened by another 7 days if the notice is forwarded by electronic means. The time limit can be shortened by another 5 days if unrestricted and full direct access by electronic means is offered to the contract documents. The time limit cannot be shortened to less than 22 days. The time limit must be extended if an on-site inspection is required.

Supplementary information. The *specifications to the contract documents,* the descriptive document and any supporting documents must be transmitted to the interested undertakings (in the open procedure) and the selected candidates (in the restricted procedure, technical dialogue and negotiated procedure with prior publication of a contract notice) to allow them to prepare

---

164. Article 38, paragraph 4 of the Procurement Directive, cf. Article 35, paragraph 1.
165. Order of the Complaints Board of 22 November 2004, Dansk Restproduktionshånd-tering A.m.b.a. vs. Århus Local Authority.

tenders.[166] The requirements that the tenders must meet, as stipulated by the contracting authority, need not be indicated in both the contract notice and the supplementary specifications.[167] Usually the requirements do not appear in both documents, as the specifications tend to include far more details than the contract notice. However, where a requirement is mentioned in both documents, it must be formulated in identical terms in order to comply with the requirement for transparency.

– In the open procedure the contracting authority must forward the specifications and supplementary documents within 6 days of the receipt of a request.[168]
– In the restricted procedure, competitive dialogue and negotiated procedure with prior publication of a contract notice the Directive provides that the specifications, etc. be forwarded together with the invitation to submit a tender, participate in the dialogue or negotiate. The invitation must indicate the time limit for receipt of tenders, the documents to be enclosed with the tender, the award criteria and the weighting given to each of them, etc.[169]

Any other additional information to the specifications or supplementary documents must be sent not less than 6 days before the final date for receipt of tenders.[170] In the event that it becomes necessary to publish additional information at a later date, it would be appropriate, in the open procedure, to publish a brief notice in the Official Journal setting out this information and information that the time for submitting tenders has been extended. In the restricted procedure the selected tenderers are notified by letter.

---

166. Article 40, paragraph 2 of the Procurement Directive. Alternatively the specifications can be made accessible by electronic means.
167. Order of the Complaints Board of 22 November 2004, Dansk Restproduktionshåndtering A.m.b.a. vs. Århus Local Authority.
168. Article 39, paragraph 1 of the Procurement Directive.
169. Article 40, paragraph 2 of the Procurement Directive, cf. Article 40, paragraph. 5. In the competitive dialogue procedure a dialogue is first opened with the candidates and information on the time limit for receipt of tenders must only be given when the dialogue is ended.
170. Article 39, paragraph 2 and Article 40, paragraph 4 of the Procurement Directive.

3.2.3 Accelerated procedure

In the event of urgency contracts can be awarded subject to shorter time limits.[171] The contracting authority must be able to prove that the circumstances are such that it is necessary to use accelerated procedures.[172] This may be the case, for example, where the existing supplier breaches the contract and therefore is "chucked out". It may also be the case where the supplier is wound up. The key factor is that the urgency must have been caused by external events, and inadequate planning or lack of prudence on the contracting authority's part does not justify the use of the accelerated procedure.[173] The contracting authority must be able to provide evidence of the events justifying use of the accelerated procedure.

In the restricted procedure and the negotiated procedure[174] the time limits can be shortened:

- the time limit for receipt of requests can be shortened to 15 days running from the date of the contracting authority's dispatch of the contract notice;
- the time limit can be shortened further to 10 days if the notice is transmitted by electronic means;
- the time limit for receipt of tenders can be shortened to 10 days;
- the time limit for transmitting supplementary information can be shortened to 4 days prior to the final date for receipt of tenders.[175]

3.3 Supplementary information and questions sessions

The contracting authority specifies, in the contract documents, the requirements to be met, the object of the contract and in the specifications lays down

---

171. Article 38, paragraph 8 of the Procurement Directive.
172. Under Articles 30 and 31 of the Procurement Directive special needs may justify the award of a contract on the basis of "the negotiated procedure", cf. section 2.5 above.
173. Judgment of the European Court of Justice of 18 March 1992, case C-24/91, Commission vs. Spain; order of the Complaints Board of 11 March 2005, MT Højgaard A/S vs. Frederiksberg Boligfond, the contracting authority had failed to observe the obligation to invite tenders in accordance with the Procurement Directive; order of the Complaints Board of 23 January 1996, Danish Council of Practising Architects vs. Glostrup Local Authority, the need to prepare a local plan did not justify use of the accelerated procedure for the award of a total consulting services contract for the extension of a school.
174. The competitive dialogue procedure cannot be conducted as an accelerated procedure.
175. Article 40, paragraph 4 of the Procurement Directive.

the technical, economic and legal terms and conditions of the contract and the procedure for the award of the contract, cf. chapter 4 above. The specifications are sent to those economic operators which request receipt thereof (open procedure) or to those candidates which are considered suitable and invited to submit tenders (restricted procedure), enter into a dialogue (competitive dialogue procedure) or negotiate (negotiated procedure with prior publication of a contract notice).

In order to ensure equal treatment of the economic operators and thus competition for the public contract it is of paramount importance that all tenderers or candidates receive the same information at the same time. The contract documents should be drafted and published with a view thereto. The contract documents may indicate how uncertainties and questions regarding the contract documents are clarified. If it becomes necessary to add additional information to the contract documents, the contracting authority must make sure that all tenderers or candidates receive the same information at the same time.[176] One means by which equal treatment can be achieved is by pre-establishing a procedure in which clarification of uncertainties and the answering of questions can be dealt with. If questions sessions are organised all tenderers and candidates must be invited to participate. Drafting and circulation of written minutes may be a factor in ensuring a common basis for preparing tenders, the dialogue and the negotiations. In *Arkitektgruppen Aarhus K/S and Stærmose & Isager Arkitektfirma K/S vs. Hinnerup Local Authority*[177] the contracting authority had indicated at a questions sessions that two-storey houses would be considered irregular, but nevertheless chose a project based on houses with two storeys. In so doing the contracting authority discriminated against tenderers in contravention of the Procurement Directive.

Contracting authorities that organise joint questions sessions in procedures with only a few tenderers run the risk of concerted practice. They may therefore consider organising separate questions sessions which in turn calls into question the equal treatment of tenderers and the transparency of these sessions. Such problems can be overcome by preparing minutes of the meetings and transmit consolidated, detailed minutes in an anonymous form to all the tenderers.

176. Order of the Complaints Board of 15 December 1999, Lifeline I/S vs. Dansk Hunderegister.
177. Order of the Complaints Board of 9 October 1997, Arkitektgruppen Aarhus K/S and Stærmose & Isager Arkitektfirma K/S vs. Hinnerup Local Authority.

3.4 Prior information notice

The procedural rules set out in the Procurement Directive may be seen by a contracting authority as causing an unwanted delay of a planned project and, for that reason, the authority may be keen to shorten the time between the decision to conduct a procurement procedure and the award of the public contract. To that end the contracting authority may consider using the accelerated procedure[178] or the negotiated procedure *without* prior publication of a contract notice,[179] but the conditions subject to which these procedures can be used must be interpreted strictly and are only exceptionally satisfied.

The reason for stipulating minimum requirements for the time that must lapse between the dispatch of the contract notice and the final date for receipt of requests for participation in the procedure, respectively tenders, is to open up competition for public contracts to economic operators throughout the EU. It may be worthwhile for the contracting authority either to allow longer time and/or inform the economic operators of proposed future contracts well in advance of the call for tenders for these contracts. This serves to improve competition for public contracts, but presumably also improves the possibilities of the contracting authority for achieving best value for money.

By publishing a prior information notice on proposed contracts it is possible to reduce the time limits applicable in the procedures for the individual contracts, cf. section 3.2 above.[180] However, time limits can only be shortened if the prior information notice is dispatched at least 52 days before the dispatch of the contract notice advertising the contract for which the shortened time limits will be used.

Furthermore, the shortened time limits can only be used provided that the prior information notice includes specific information.[181]

– Concerning contracts or framework agreements on supplies or service contracts covered by Annex II A to the Procurement Directive, the individual notice must *inter alia* include information on the individual product areas or categories of services and the estimated total value of the con-

---

178. Article 38, paragraph 8 of the Procurement Directive.
179. Article 31 of the Procurement Directive. See also section 2.5 above.
180. Article 35, paragraph 1 of the Procurement Directive, cf. Article 38, paragraph 4.
181. Article 38, paragraph 4, third indent of the Procurement Directive provides that the prior information notice must include all the information required for the contract notice in Annex VII A, insofar as the information is known at the time of the publication. Annex VII A to the Procurement Directive specifies the information to be included in the prior information notice.

tracts or framework agreements within each product area/category of services which the contracting authority intends to award over the following 12 months. The notice must be sent to the Commission as soon as possible after the beginning of the budgetary year.

– Where works contracts or framework agreements on works are concerned, the essential characteristics of the individual contract or framework agreement must be included as well as the value thereof. Considering that works contracts are often in the nature of one-time purchases, publication must be made as soon as possible after approval of the building programme.[182]

The Procurement Directive establishes certain threshold values for the use of prior information notices.[183] Since publication of a prior information notice is only compulsory where the contracting authority wishes to reduce the time limits, the threshold values are merely an indicator to the contracting authorities and their consultants of when it may be useful to publish a prior information notice out of consideration for the economic operators and themselves.[184]

As an alternative to the publication of a prior information notice, the contracting authority can create a "buyer profile" on the Internet. The identity of the contracting authority is disclosed in the buyer profile and information may be provided on the nature, frequency, amount, etc. of the contracts. Information may also be provided on ongoing invitations to tender, scheduled purchases, contracts concluded, procedures cancelled and any useful general information, such as the contracting authority's address.[185] If the contracting authority wishes to create a buyer profile, it must publish its intention in a prior notice.[186]

Within the limits of the buyer profile, information is given on the expected award of supplies, services or works contracts.

182. Article 35, paragraph 1 of the Procurement Directive.
183. For supply and service contracts: € 750,000, for works contracts: € 5.923.000.
184. Judgment of the European Court of Justice of 26 September 2000, case C-225/98, Commission vs. France, paragraph 38.
185. Annex VIII, point 2.b to the Procurement Directive.
186. Article 36, paragraph 5, third indent of the Procurement Directive, cf. Annex VIII, point 1.a.

3.5 Reports and notices[187]

The economic operators and the Commission are interested in information on how a procurement procedure was conducted, whether an award decision was made and, if so, the reasons for the decision. This information is intended to provide a basis for controlling whether the procurement rules were complied with and thus also a basis for using means of enforcement.

Any award of a public contract under the Procurement Directive must be advertised in a notice.[188] The contracting authority sends a notice of the results of the award procedure to the Commission no later than 48 days after the award of the public contract.[189] The Commission publishes the notice in the Official Journal no later than 12 days after the date on which it was dispatched by the contracting authority. The notice must include information on *inter alia* the nature and extent of the contract, price, name and address of the successful tenderer, name and address of the body responsible for appeal, etc.[190]

Candidates and tenderers must be informed as soon as possible of decisions reached concerning the conclusion of an award procedure.[191] In terms of content the only information required is that a contract has been awarded, a framework agreement concluded or that admittance to a dynamic purchasing system has been granted. If the procedure is concluded otherwise, for example because it is cancelled, the decision to cancel must be reasoned. Unsuccessful candidates or tenderers can request reasons for the contracting authority's decisions, cf. chapter 7.9 below for more detail.[192] The information is usually given in writing, but the contracting authority is only required to do so upon request from an economic operator.

Finally, the contracting authority is under an obligation to draw up a report on every public contract, framework agreement or establishment of a dynamic purchasing system. In the report the contracting authority must set out the reasons for decisions made in the course of the procedure.[193] Among other things the report must include the names of the unsuccessful candidates and tenderers,

---

187. See also chapter 7.9 on duty to notify reasons.
188. Article 35, paragraph 4 of the Procurement Directive.
189. Conclusion of contracts based on a framework agreement need not be notified to the Commission separately and contracts concluded on the basis of a dynamic purchasing system can be notified on a quarterly basis. Article 35, paragraph 4, second and third indents of the Procurement Directive.
190. The information required is listed in Annex VII A to the Procurement Directive.
191. Article 41, paragraph 1 of the Procurement Directive.
192. Article 41, paragraph 2 of the Procurement Directive.
193. Article 43 of the Procurement Directive.

the name of the successful tenderer, the reasons for selecting its tender, etc. Upon request the report must be communicated to the Commission.

4. Special procurement procedures

Public contracts are awarded on the basis of a contracting authority's call for tenders and an economic operator's tender submitted in reply thereto. This is basically how the open procedure, restricted procedure, technical dialogue procedure and negotiated procedure are conducted. Several contracts are not easy to conclude on the basis of this traditional call for/submission of tenders procedure

4.1 Design contests

A contracting authority may need inspiration with respect to the technical or artistic features or the planning of a contemplated contract. For example where it contemplates developing new urban areas, a transport system, processing of personal data, but also the construction of a museum or an educational institution may require careful deliberations.[194] To this end the authority can embark on cooperation with consultants (on the basis of a contract) with a view to drafting the contract documents, or it can open a technical dialogue. The Procurement Directive also provides that the authority can organise a design contest.[195] The Procurement Directive defines design contests as follows:

"'Design contests' means those procedures which enable the contracting authority to acquire, mainly in the fields of town and country planning, architecture and engineering or data processing, a plan or design selected by a jury after being put out to competition with or without the award of prizes."[196]

A design contest may lead to the award of prizes/payments to participants and the winner may be awarded a service contract for the performance of the

---

194. Order of the Complaints Board of 9 March 1998, Danish Association of Consulting Engineers vs. Ledøje-Smørum Local Authority concerning total consulting services (architect, engineer and landscape architect) for the construction of a new library/arts centre and planning of a town park.
195. Title IV, Articles 66-74, of the Procurement Directive sets out special rules for design contests for services.
196. Article 1, paragraph 11, fifth indent of the Procurement Directive.

successful project.[197] The rules on design contests set out in the Procurement Directive must be followed where the value of prizes or payments to participants exceed the threshold or where the value of the service contract awarded, as a result of the contest, exceeds the threshold.[198] These rules provide the contracting authorities with considerable freedom to choose how to organise the design contest. This freedom also extends to the situation where it is anticipated that the contest will determine the award of a contract.[199]

Presumably, the absence of detailed regulation in the area of design contests is attributable to the assumption that the publication of a contest notice and the involvement of experts in the evaluation are sufficient guarantees that the contracting authority can neither discriminate against or treat contestants unequally nor base the contest on non-objective considerations. Also the reasons for organising the design contest suggest that the contracting authority concentrates on the actual result of the contest rather than on giving preferential treatment to one particular economic operator.

Design contests must comply with a few requirements for substance and form. All design contests must be advertised in a contest notice. The notice must include the information specified in Annex VII D to the Directive, including the criteria for selecting participants and the criteria for evaluating the projects.[200] The criteria for selecting participants must be clear and non-discriminatory.[201] It is compulsory to publish a notice announcing the design contest. When a contest has been decided, the results of the contest must be made public.[202]

A design contest can be organised as an open contest in which all economic operators can enter their projects. Or a contest can be organised as closed contest for which the contracting authority selects the participants from among the interested economic operators on the basis of the criteria specified in the contest notice. One or more undertakings can be selected in advance for participation in the contest.[203] The number of candidates invited

---

197. Article 67, paragraph 2 of the Procurement Directive.
198. Article 67 of the Procurement Directive.
199. See also section 2.5.3.8 above on the use of "the negotiated procedure" following a design contest.
200. Article 70 of the Procurement Directive.
201. Article 72 of the Procurement Directive.
202. Articles 69 and 70 and Annex VII D to the Procurement Directive.
203. Order of the Complaints Board of 6 September 1999, Danish Association of Consulting Engineers vs. Ministry of Culture; order of the Complaints Board of 12 July 2001, Danish Council of Practising Architects vs. Ministry of Culture.

to participate in the contest must be sufficient to guarantee genuine competition.[204]

The autonomy of the jury is all-important in order to guarantee equal treatment of participants, that projects submitted are evaluated on objective grounds and to prevent that non-objective interests are pursued. First, it is of the utmost importance to ensure that the members of the jury are independent of the selected participants.[205] Further, it must be ensured that information on the projects submitted is not disclosed to the members of the jury before the final date for submitting projects.[206] Finally, it is vital that the identity of the participants is kept anonymous until the plans and projects have been evaluated and the jury has reached its final opinion or decision.[207]

It may be necessary to clarify aspects of the submitted projects and the members of the jury may put questions to the participants. In order to guarantee the equal treatment of the participants the questions must be recorded in interim minutes.[208] It may be useful to lay down in advance a procedure for the answering of questions whereby anonymity is maintained. Complete minutes must be drawn up on the dialogue between the participants and the members of the jury.[209]

4.2 Electronic auctions[210]
A procedure can be concluded by an electronic auction.[211] Electronic auctions can be used for contracts for, for example, computers, electricity, engineering services, car leasing, mobile telephony, maintenance services, temp services, etc.

Electronic auctions can be used in the open procedure, the restricted procedure and the negotiated procedure *with* publication of a contract notice[212] Electronic auctions can also be used in connection with a dynamic purchasing system or on the reopening of competition, which takes place where several

---

204. Article 72 of the Procurement Directive.
205. Article 73 of the Procurement Directive.
206. Article 71 of the Procurement Directive.
207. Article 74, paragraph 4 of the Procurement Directive.
208. Article 74, paragraphs 3 and 5 of the Procurement Directive.
209. Article 74, paragraph 6 of the Procurement Directive.
210. Article 54 of the Procurement Directive provides that the individual Member State can choose whether it will allow contracting authorities to use "electronic auctions".
211. Article 54 of the Procurement Directive and recital 14 of the preamble to the Procurement Directive.
212. Article 54, paragraph 2 of the Procurement Directive.

framework agreements have been concluded, cf. section 5.1 below.[213] The Procurement Directive defines an electronic auction as follows.

"An 'electronic auction' is a repetitive process involving an electronic device for the presentation of new prices, revised downwards, and/or new values concerning certain elements of tenders, which occurs after an initial full evaluation of the tenders, enabling them to be ranked using automatic evaluation methods."[214]

Electronic auctions are an automated, quantified and objective procedure capable of identifying the tender which offers the lowest price or is most economically advantageous to the contracting authority. The use of electronic auctions may therefore be characterised as perfect competition. However, those stages of the procedure that precede the auction do contain elements of subjectivity. It is therefore emphasised in the Procurement Directive that:

"Contracting authorities may not have improper recourse to electronic auctions nor may they use them in such a way as to prevent, restrict or distort competition or to change the subject-matter of the contract, as put up for tender in the published contract notice and defined in the specifications."[215]

In the interest of ensuring equal treatment and transparency in award procedures for public contracts, the Procurement Directive sets out certain conditions for the use of electronic auctions.

– Where a procedure is to be concluded by an electronic auction, it must be stated in the contract notice.
– Information must be given in advance on the progress of the electronic auction and on whether it will be closed at a specific date, after a certain time has elapsed, or when no new prices or values are received.[216]
– Certain specific information must be included in the specifications.
– The exact specifications of the object of the public contract must be determined.
– Only features which are quantifiable can be made the subject of an electronic auction which must be capable of automatic processing by electronic means without allowing the contracting authority the opportunity to evaluate the features.

213. Article 54, paragraph 2 of the Procurement Directive.
214. Article 1, paragraph 7 of the Procurement Directive.
215. Article 54, paragraph 8, second indent of the Procurement Directive.
216. Article 54, paragraph 7 of the Procurement Directive.

— Throughout the auction no information whatsoever may be disclosed about the identities of the tenderers, cf. below on auction in successive phases.

Until the award of the contract the procedure is conducted in accordance with the chosen procurement procedure. The suitability of the tenderers must be evaluated in accordance with the specifications.[217] Also the tenders submitted must be evaluated to determine whether they comply with the specifications or contain variations, reservations, etc.[218]

A tenderer which is found suitable as a contracting party and whose tender is admissible, and therefore in theory capable of constituting the basis for a contract, can participate in the electronic auction.[219] The auction can concern prices as well as other aspects that are quantifiable and for which an objective value can be expressed. The tenderers are invited to submit new prices/new values. If the award criterion "the most economically advantageous tender" is used, the invitation must be accompanied by the full evaluation of the relevant tenderer's tender. The invitation must also state the mathematical formula to be used in the auction for ranking the tenders on the basis of the prices and values.[220]

The auction can take place in successive phases. Before submitting new prices or values, it is essential that the tenderer is informed of the relative ranking of its tender, and the contracting authority is obliged to communicate this information. Provided that this is stated in the specifications, the contracting authority can also communicate information on the prices or values of other tenders and the number of remaining tenderers.

The submission of tenders is often concentrated towards the time when the auction is expected to close. To allow other tenderers the time to consider and submit a new tender it is considered appropriate to prescribe an automatic prolongation of the auction (for example by five minutes) if a tender is submitted less than x number of minutes before the expected time of closing. Subsequently, it may be necessary to review the successful tender manually to evaluate whether it is abnormally low.[221]

217. See also chapter 6.
218. See also chapter 7.
219. Article 54, paragraph 4 of the Procurement Directive.
220. Article 54, paragraph 5 of the Procurement Directive.
221. Article 55 of the Procurement Directive, cf. chapter 7.4.1.

In order to avoid cartelisation among the tenderers, the Procurement Directive explicitly stipulates that the contracting authority "in no case" may disclose the identities of tenderers during any phase of the auction.[222]

4.3 Dynamic purchasing systems[223]

In connection with the setting-up of a dynamic purchasing system the contracting authority draws up a list of potential suppliers of specific types of products or services.[224] A dynamic purchasing system is established in the context of the open procedure and the procedure is conducted in the same manner as for the award of other public contracts, until the time of the actual award of the individual contracts.[225] A dynamic purchasing system is defined as follows in the Procurement Directive:

"A 'dynamic purchasing system' is a completely electronic process for making commonly used purchases, the characteristics of which, as generally available on the market, meet the requirements of the contracting authority, which is limited in duration and open throughout its validity to any economic operator which satisfies the selection criteria and has submitted an indicative tender that complies with the specifications."[226]

The list is dynamic in that any economic operator is eligible for admission to the system throughout the entire validity period provided that it satisfies the selection criteria and submits an indicative tender that complies with the contract specifications.[227] The advantages to the contracting authorities are that they are afforded a particularly broad range of tenders to select from thereby enhancing competition for the public contract.[228] To the economic operators a dynamic purchasing system can be seen as a preliminary stage in the compe-

222. Article 54, paragraph 6 of the Directive.
223. Article 52 of the Procurement Directive provides that the individual Member State can choose whether it will allow contracting authorities to use "dynamic purchasing systems".
224. See also Article 52 of the Procurement Directive, cf. chapter 6 below.
225. See also chapter 6 below on the selection of qualified undertakings and chapter 7 below on the evaluation of tenders submitted.
226. Article 1, paragraph 6 of the Procurement Directive.
227. Article 33, paragraph 4 of the Procurement Directive.
228. Recital 13 of the preamble to the Procurement Directive. There are considerable similarities with framework agreements, cf. section 5.1 below. The significant differences are that a dynamic purchasing system is open to new suppliers throughout its validity and that competition for the individual contract can be intensified successively.

tition for a public contract. Economic operators participating in the system cannot be billed any charges for their participation.[229]

A dynamic purchasing system is set up by publication of a contract notice indicating the nature of the purchases envisaged under the system as well as the electronic equipment and technical arrangements that the system is based on.[230] Full and unrestricted access must be offered to the specifications and all additional documents throughout the validity period of the system. At the setting-up of the dynamic purchasing system any economic operator can submit evidence of its suitability for admission into the system, which evidence will be evaluated by the contracting authority on the basis of the specifications.

In order to be admitted to the system an economic operator must also submit an indicative tender. The tender must comply with the specifications laid down in the contract documents. The purpose of the indicative tender is to determine whether the economic operator is capable of complying with the specifications for the object of the contract. The economic operators may improve their indicative tenders at any time. This encourages competition, but does not seem to serve any practical purpose, cf. the next paragraph.

Every public contract must be put out to competition, but where a dynamic purchasing system has been established, the individual contract is put out to tender through a simplified procedure. With a notice of at least 15 days a simplified contract notice is published inviting all economic operators to apply for admittance to the dynamic purchasing system.[231] If new economic operators submit evidence of their suitability and an indicative tender in reply to this notice, the evidence and the tender must be evaluated before the invitation to tender for the actual contract can proceed.[232] It is only then that all tenderers admitted to the system are invited to tender for the specific contract.

The contract is awarded on the basis of the award criteria that were specified when the dynamic purchasing system was set up. The award criteria may be clarified in the invitation to submit tenders.

---

229. Article 33, paragraph 7, third indent of the Procurement Directive.
230. Article 33, paragraph 3 of the Procurement Directive.
231. See also Annex VII A to the Procurement Directive.
232. Article 33, paragraph 5 of the Procurement Directive.

5. Special types of contracts

A public contract governs the economic operator's provision of supplies or services or execution of works, and in return the contracting authority normally pays a consideration.

Contracting authorities can conclude contracts to be performed at a later date and of which the exact extent is not determined. Such contracts are termed "framework agreements". The conclusion of framework agreements follows the procedures set out in the Directive in all stages until the award of the contract. However, since framework agreements concern the conclusion of future contracts, the Procurement Directive stipulates special rules for framework agreements, cf. section 5.1 below.[233]

Contracting authorities can also conclude contracts for which payment of a price is not the only consideration, but also a right to exploit the object of the contract financially. Such contracts are termed "concessions". Concessions granted to execute works are covered by special rules set out in the Directive, cf. section 5.2 below.[234]

Contracting authorities may prefer to embark on closer cooperation with an economic operator. Such close cooperation is termed a partnership, cf. section 5.3 below.

5.1 Framework agreements and framework contracts[235]

A contract may set out agreed detailed provisions on quantities, prices and delivery times or certain flexibility may be agreed in one or more areas. A contract which is flexible in terms of quantity, prices or delivery times can be characterised as a framework contract.

In the following framework agreements are distinguished from framework contracts since only framework agreements are subject to the special rules set out in the Procurement Directive. A framework agreement is different from a framework contract in that the economic operator can have no legitimate expectations of minimum sales under the framework agreement. The differ-

---

233. Article 32 of the Procurement Directive, cf. Article 1, paragraph 5 and recital 11 of the preamble to the Procurement Directive.
234. Title III, Chapter I, Articles 56-65, of the Procurement Directive. Article 17 of the Procurement Directive provides that service concessions are exempted from the rules of the Directive.
235. Pursuant to Article 32 of the Procurement Directive it is for the individual Member State to decide whether it will allow contracting authorities to conclude framework agreements.

ence is obvious where a framework agreement is concluded with more economic operators for the supply of the same products or services. Against that
background a framework agreement can be characterised as a standing offer.[236] The Directive defines framework agreements as follows:

"A 'framework agreement' is an agreement between one or more contracting authorities
and one or more economic operators, the purpose of which is to establish the terms governing contracts to be awarded during a given period, in particular with regard to price and,
where appropriate, the quantity envisaged."[237]

Framework agreements are used for purchasing a large variety of supplies,
services or execution of works, for example purchase of furniture or electricity, maintenance of buildings or green areas, consultancy, etc.[238] By using
framework agreements considerable flexibility is achieved in the award of
public contracts, and they may involve huge savings in time and resources.[239]

Framework agreements are concluded following the rules of procedure set
out in the Procurement Directive. The contracting authority is free to choose
the open procedure or the restricted procedure for awarding the framework
agreement, whereas the negotiated procedure only can be used where specific
reasons so justify.[240] A framework agreement forms the basis for concluding
a number of subsequent contracts for the provision of the services covered by
the agreement. The principal difference compared to ordinary contracts is that
the individual contracts for delivery under the framework agreement are concluded at a later date.[241]

---

236. For the calculation of the threshold values of framework agreements see chapter
3.5.3 above.
237. Article 1, paragraph 5 of the Procurement Directive.
238. See for example judgment of the European Court of Justice of 4 December 2003,
case C-448/01, EVN AG, concerning a framework agreement for electricity; judgment of the Court of First Instance of 25 February 2003, case T-4/01, Renco SpA
vs. Council of the European Union concerning general renovation and maintenance
work of the Council buildings; order of the Complaints Board of 14 October 2004,
SK Tolke Service ApS vs. County of Copenhagen concerning a framework agreement for interpretation services; order of the Complaints Board of 2 July 1998,
Danish Association of Consulting Engineers vs. Københavns Lufthavne A/S concerning a framework agreement for technical consultancy and assistance.
239. Central purchasing bodies, such as Statens og Kommunernes Indkøbscentral (National Procurement Ltd. – Denmark), conclude numerous framework agreements.
See also chapter 2.5 above.
240. Article 32, paragraph 2 of the Procurement Directive.
241. Article 32, paragraph 2 of the Procurement Directive.

The subsequent conclusion of the individual contracts under a framework agreement awarded in accordance with the procedures set out in the Directive is not subject to a new call for tenders.[242] This flexible and informal procedure for concluding a contract for specific deliveries can be used even where the value of the individual delivery exceeds the thresholds stipulated in the Directive. However, contracts for supplies, services or works of *a different type* than those covered by the framework agreement cannot be concluded without a call for tenders. The same is true of contracts with *other suppliers* of the products covered by the framework agreement in so far as the value of the products exceeds the relevant threshold.[243]

Where a framework agreement is concluded with one single economic operator, this economic operator can be consulted on an informal basis for the purpose of concluding a contract for delivery. The individual contract is concluded on the basis of the terms laid down in the framework agreement. Whereas the agreement can be *supplemented* in writing, it is not possible to make substantial amendments to the terms of the agreement or the object of the contract.[244] Where it becomes necessary to make substantial amendments, new tenders must be invited in accordance with the rules of the Directive.

Framework agreements can also be concluded with more economic operators, the number of which must be at least three.[245] Where framework agreements are concluded with more economic operators concerning delivery of the same supplies or services, the contracting authority consults one of the economic operators with a view to agreeing the delivery of supplies or services in accordance with the terms laid down in the framework agreement. Heavy demands are made of an economic operator which is party to a framework agreement along with other operators in that the agreement requires it to have personnel and resources available at day's notice, but provides no guarantees that it will ever be awarded a contract with the contracting authority. One solution is that the supplier makes sure that it may use subcontractors.

---

242. Article 32, paragraph 2, second indent of the Procurement Directive and recital 11 of the preamble to the Procurement Directive.
243. Order of the Complaints Board of 29 September 2003, Unicomputer A/S vs. Greve Local Authority concerning the purchase of printers not through a framework agreement on the purchase of printers, etc.
244. Article 32, paragraph 3, first indent of the Procurement Directive, cf. Article 32, paragraph 2, third indent.
245. Article 32, paragraph 4 of the Procurement Directive

Where not all the terms are laid down in the framework agreement, tenders for the individual contracts are invited from the parties to the framework agreement. It thus follows that where a framework agreement is concluded with more economic operators, it is possible to supplement or amend the economic terms on which the individual contract is to be based. It is also possible to make minor modifications to the object of the contract.[246] The contracting authority prepares specifications setting out the new terms and sends them to those economic operators that are parties to the framework agreements exclusively.[247]

A framework agreement can only be concluded for a maximum term of four years. The limited term of framework agreements is reflective of the need to balance the flexibility which the use of framework agreements affords contracting authorities, especially where the object can be modified by inviting tenders from those economic operators which are already parties to the framework agreements, against the requirement of equal treatment of tenderers, notably those that are not parties to framework agreements. Contracts concluded under framework agreements may extend beyond the four-year term of the framework agreement, for example where they are concluded towards the end of the term. However, the procurement rules must not be circumvented.[248]

A framework agreement can only go beyond the term of four years if the purpose of the agreement makes this necessary. A longer term may for example be required where the underlying services are linked to a project of more than four years' duration.

5.2 Concessions[249]

A public contract concerns the execution of works, the supply of products or the provision of services.[250] The consideration received in return is usually payment of a fee, a price. A contracting authority can decide to leave the financing of the public contract to the contracting party which as considera-

---

246. Article 32, paragraph 4 of the Procurement Directive, cf. Article 32, paragraph 2, third indent and recital 11 of the preamble to the Procurement Directive.
247. Article 32, paragraph 4 of the Procurement Directive, cf. Article 32, paragraph 2, second indent.
248. Article 32, paragraph 2, fifth indent of the Procurement Directive.
249. See also the Commission's Interpretative Notice of 12 April 2000 on concessions under Community law. The Notice is only partially applicable seeing that Articles 17 and 56-65 of the Procurement Directive set out provisions on the award of concessions.
250. Article 1, paragraph 2 (a) of the Procurement Directive.

tion is granted the right to exploit the work, service or product financially, possibly together with payment of a fee. In return, the contracting party is responsible for the operation and maintenance and bears the financial risks related thereto.

It is not always clear in advance whether a concession or an ordinary contract will be awarded in that it may be subject to negotiations, cf. section 2.4 on the competitive dialogue procedure and section 2.5 on the negotiated procedure. This is, for example, the case where the negotiations concern the allocation of the economic and financial risks and return. To that end the contracting authority must ensure that the contract does not change nature in the course of the negotiations to the effect that the chosen procurement procedure no longer can be used.[251]

5.2.1 Public works concessions

Contracting authorities require the execution of a variety of different works. Among these are the construction of libraries, purification plants, motorways, bridges, airports, etc.

The execution of the works is frequently left with an economic operator. If also the financing and subsequent operation of the building or plant are left with the economic operator, the contract may be a concession contract. A concession is defined as follows:

"'Public works concession' is a contract of the same type as a public works contract except for the fact that the consideration for the works to be carried out consists either solely in the right to exploit the work or in this right together with payment."[252]

What characterises a concession is that the consideration for the works consists of a right to *exploit* the works. Whether the contract is a concession or a contract against normal consideration depends on the economic aspects of the contract. Inherent in the right to exploit the works lies that the economic operator bears the financial risk involved with the operation thereof. The economic operator is not required to bear the full financial risk since payments in addition to the right to exploit may depend on the profit yielded.

---

251. Commission Green Paper of 30 April 2004 on Public-Private Partnerships and Community Law on Public Contracts and Concessions (Com(2004) 327 final), point 34.
252. Article 1, paragraph 3 of the Procurement Directive.

5.2.2 Award of the concession

Special rules apply to works concessions of a value equal to or greater than €
5,923,000.[253] The main obligation is that contracting authorities must publish
a notice advertising the concession. The information to be indicated in the
notice is listed in Annex VII C to the Procurement Directive.[254]

The criteria that will be applied to selecting candidates and awarding the
contract must be indicated in the notice. In the selection and the award the
contracting authority must respect the rules and principles of the EC
Treaty.[255] In the interest of equal treatment and transparency in award procedures the procedure used for the selection and the award must be determined
in advance as must the time the procedure is expected to take.

According to the Commission, award of a concession contract is conditional on the satisfaction of the following conditions:[256]

– existence of specific rules for selecting the private partner;
– appropriate advertising of the concession offered and of the selection rules
  enabling verification that the procedure has been objective throughout;
– genuine competition among the potentially interested operators and/or the
  operators that are capable of performing the works proposed;
– compliance with the principle of equal treatment of all candidates
  throughout the procedure; and
– the award being made on the basis of objective and non-discriminatory
  criteria.

The Procurement Directive contains a special provision on the possibilities of
awarding public contracts for provision of additional services or execution of
additional works without a call for tenders.[257]

The Procurement Directive also prescribes special rules for concessionaires' award of contracts, notably a duty to publish a contract notice where
the concessionaire wishes to award a contract to a third party.[258]

---

253. Articles 56 and 63 of the Procurement Directive.
254. Article 58 of the Procurement Directive.
255. See also chapter 1.5 above.
256. Commission Green Paper of 30 April 2004 on Public-Private Partnerships and Com-
     munity Law on Public Contracts and Concessions (Com(2004) 327 final), point 30.
257. Article 61 of the Procurement Directive.
258. Articles 62-64 of the Procurement Directive.

5.2.3 Service concessions

Service concessions are explicitly exempted from the scope of the Procurement Directive.[259] This does not mean that contracting authorities have unlimited freedom of choice when awarding service concessions, in particular, they must observe the rules of the EC Treaty and the fundamental principles established by the European Court of Justice.[260]

5.3 Public/Private partnerships[261]

Contracting authorities may opt for closer cooperation with an economic operator on, for example, construction, maintenance or operation of infrastructures and the financing thereof. Also services, such as waste treatment, energy supply, local education administration, etc., can be provided by way of partnering

The reasons for embarking on closer cooperation may be that the contracting authority requires assistance in financing, that it wishes to share the risk involved with a project, or that it does not wish to be responsible for the operation and maintenance of an infrastructure itself.

In terms of procurement law partnering poses certain peculiar problems deriving from the fact that the contracting authority normally selects its partner at a time when only the general features of the project are known and at which time the selected partner is awarded a number of contracts that would otherwise have had to be put out to competition. Moreover, partnering contracts are often of a very long term, 25-30 years are not uncommon. The following sections merely outline the problems in brief.

5.3.1 Partnering – what and why

The procedures described in the Procurement Directive presume that the contracting authority – possibly together with consultants – draws up the contract documents. The authority is assumed to have (gained) complete knowledge of how to satisfy a specific need of having, for example, works

---

259. Article 17 of the Procurement Directive, cf. Article 1, paragraph 4.
260. See also section 5.2.2 above. See also chapter 1.5. Reference is also made to Commission Green Paper of 30 April 2004 on Public-Private Partnerships and Community Law on Public Contracts and Concessions (Com(2004) 327 final), point 29f.
261. Commission Green Paper of 30 April 2004 on Public-Private Partnerships and Community Law on Public Contracts and Concessions (Com(2004) 327 final). Adian Brown, The Impact of the New Procurement Directive on Large Public Infrastructure Projects: Competitive Dialogue or Better the Devil you Know?, 13 Public Procurement law Review, 2004, pp. 160ff.

executed, including the technical and economic solutions available and viable. The market operators (the contractors) are not consulted in the planning process and preparation of the procedure; they submit tenders on the basis of the documents drawn up by the authority.

It may be necessary to consult the economic operators already in the planning process. The introduction of the technical dialogue procedure is reflective of the realisation that it may be necessary for the contracting authority to open a dialogue with the market operators with a view to devising the best solution to a specific need.[262] Also the negotiated procedure *with* publication of a contract notice is useful where it is impossible to price a project or where the technical specifications of the contract cannot be laid down in the contract documents.[263]

Another way of making use of economic operators' knowledge in the early stages of a project is through "partnering".[264] There is, however, the significant difference, as implied by the use of the word "partnering", that a contract is concluded with one single economic operator already in the proposal stages of a project, i.e. when a building programme, project description, quantity indications, etc. are available.

By entering into a contract with an economic operator already at this early stage the contracting authority is able to take advantage of the economic operator's technical and economic knowledge of designing and projecting a building, the risks involved and the opportunities for making savings on the construction. The advantages to the contractor are that its know-how is not at risk of being disclosed to competitors and it benefits financially from its own proposals for technical and economic solutions, improvements and modifications seeing that the contract usually contains an incentive clause.

5.3.2 Procurement law reflections

The procurement rules are founded in contract law. If the value of the contract exceeds the threshold values stipulated in the Directive, cooperation between a contracting authority and an economic operator can only occur on the basis of the procedures of the Procurement Directive. Tenders must be invited allowing the economic operators to compete for the contract on objective terms. The tenders must be binding with respect to price and the cooperation must be

---

262. Article 29 of the Procurement Directive. See also section 2.4 above.
263. Article 30 of the Procurement Directive. See also section 2.5 above.
264. Not uniquely referred to as partnering.

founded in a contract which can only be changed, expanded or modified within narrow limits without a new call for tenders.

A partnering contract can be concluded in accordance with the rules of the Procurement Directive where a building project, for example, is at such an advanced stage of planning that it makes sense for the contractor to offer a price. It must be possible to put a price on the services required for completing the construction works which necessitates the availability of a relatively unambiguous description of the components of the project. On that basis a contract and a partnering agreement can be concluded.

The open procedure or the restricted procedure must be used for awarding the contract unless the specific conditions subject to which the competitive dialogue procedure or the negotiated procedure can be used are satisfied. Where a partner has been selected following one of the procedures provided for in the Procurement Directive, any subsequent contracts for construction, maintenance, operation, etc. can be awarded to that partner without other procedures, provided that the limits of the project as described in the contract documents are not exceeded.

Partnering at even earlier stages of a project is difficult within the framework of the Procurement Directive, in essence because the project is not at a level of finality which enables competition on an objective basis. Such type of partnering would therefore resemble negotiations with the individual economic operators; a procedure which can only be used in exceptional cases under the Procurement Directive, cf. section 2.5 above.[265]

---

265. Under the Utilities Directive the use of the negotiated procedure *with* prior publication of a contract notice is unlimited.

CHAPTER 6

Selection of Participants
– Pre-Qualification

1. Selection of suitable undertakings

A crucial stage in a procurement procedure is the selection of suppliers, service providers or contractors who are allowed to submit tenders. The competition for the proposed contract takes place among these parties. However, before launching the competition the contracting authority must make sure that only tenderers *suitable* to perform the contract submit tenders.

1.1 The underlying considerations

From the point of view of the contracting authority selection of suitable tenderers is indispensable. It is customary that a purchaser verifies that a potential future supplier is capable of supplying the product, providing the service or executing the proposed works since conclusion of a contract with a non-suitable supplier will not satisfy the purpose for which the contracting authority conducts the procedure in the first place. However, unlike other purchasers, contracting authorities covered by the Procurement Directive are obliged to base this verification of suitability on separate criteria whereas private purchasers may perform an evaluation of both suitability and the tenders submitted at the same time.

Although the interests of a contracting authority in ensuring suitability of tenderers are equally legitimate, the Procurement Directive imposes various restrictions on the contracting authorities both with respect to the criteria for verifying suitability and the evidence they can request in support thereof. Indeed one of the aims of the Procurement Directive is to ensure that suppliers, service providers and contractors from all EU Member States are allowed the possibility to tender for proposed contracts; hence contracting authorities must not prevent the achievement of this intended aim in the selection of suitable tenderers or otherwise. Thereby, the Procurement Directive sets out the framework within which the contracting authority can make its selection – defining the criteria which the contracting authority can make the selection upon and the evidence that the contracting authority can request in respect of compliance with the individual selection criteria. Another aim of the Procurement Directive is to enable contracting authorities to exclude, within the above framework, potential non-suitable suppliers

1.2 Rules on exclusion and selection

Articles 44-52 of the Procurement Directive set out the rules for exclusion and selection of potential tenderers. These rules are complemented by the provisions of the EC Treaty, in particular the provisions in Article 28 on the free movement of goods and in Article 29 on the free movement of services and the principle of the right of establishment in Article 43.

Compared to the previous Directives on the purchase of goods and services and execution of works, the provisions of the Procurement Directive are more detailed and thus more copious. The Procurement Directive is intended to spell out the contracting authorities' possibilities and obligations towards excluding and selecting potential tenderers. Case law from the European Court of Justice settling previously unclear and undecided issues, concerning in particular the type of documents and evidence that can be requested, has been widely incorporated into the rules. However, the detailed provisions in Articles 44-52 have prejudiced another aim of the Procurement Directive: simplification of the rules.

1.3 The principles

In addition to the relatively detailed provisions of the Procurement Directive, the principles of equal treatment, non-discrimination, mutual recognition, proportionality and transparency remain applicable to procurement procedures. In reality these principles have merely been crystallised into the specific rules contained in Articles 44-52 of the Procurement Directive and ideally the five principles of equal treatment, etc. would largely have sufficed. However, in practice it is rather convenient that these principles have been clarified in the context of the Procurement Directive in that they help ensure effective competition among suitable tenderers.

The principle of proportionality is embodied directly in Article 44, paragraph 2, second indent. On the basis of the proposed contract the contracting authorities must determine the required suitability criteria, which criteria must be related and proportionate to the object of the contract. This principle must be observed with respect to both the qualitative criteria and the evidence required from the potential tenderers. Such a proportionality assessment leaves the contracting authority with considerable room for discretion. As a consequence, the application of the principle of proportionality to the determination of selection criteria only has the effect of preventing contracting authorities from demanding very substantial evidence, which is already governed to a certain extent by Articles 47-52 of the Procurement Directive, and making excessive demands with respect to technical and economic abilities.

The principles of non-discrimination and mutual recognition guarantee that all qualitatively suitable economic operators in the EU can be selected to submit bids. The selection criteria must not be determined or administered so as to exclude or reject economic operators merely because they are established in another EU Member State. The principle of equal treatment entails that, for example, deadlines and documentation requirements must be the same for all.

Further, the contracting authority must ensure that the selection criteria, required evidence, etc. are sufficiently clear to comply with the principle of transparency.

1.4 Exclusion and selection criteria in certain procedures

Exclusion of potential tenderers is an important element of all procurement procedures, as is determination of selection criteria. However, a contracting authority is unlikely to bother about laying down selection criteria for procedures where the contract is awarded on the basis of the negotiated procedure without prior publication of a contract notice, cf. Article 31. In these cases the contracting authority typically evaluates whether the relevant supplier is suitable (and its situation or circumstances not such that may (or must) lead to exclusion, cf. below) already while assessing the possibilities for using this procedure. Also procedures for the award of service contracts which have as their object the services listed in Annex II B are not governed by the provisions of *inter alia* Articles 44-52, cf. Article 21, for the same reasons as mentioned above regarding the negotiated procedure without prior publication of a contract notice. However, the contracting authority is not prevented from laying down criteria similar to those set out in Articles 44-52 also for the award of service contracts which have as their object the services listed in Annex II B.

1.5 Publication of grounds for exclusion and selection criteria

It follows from Article 36 and Annex VII A to the Procurement Directive that contracting authorities are obliged to specify the chosen selection criteria and non-mandatory grounds for exclusion in the contract notice. This allows potential tenderers to ascertain straight away whether they will be admitted to submit tenders. Information on the exact evidence and documents required must be published in the contract notice or the contract documents, cf. Article 47, paragraph 4 and Article 48, paragraph 6 of the Procurement Directive.

Publication of the chosen selection criteria (and the non-mandatory grounds for exclusion) is necessary to guarantee equal treatment and transparency.[1]

2. Grounds for exclusion

The economic operators' own circumstances may lead to exclusion from the procedure.

2.1 Mandatory and non-mandatory grounds for exclusion

The grounds for exclusion are listed in Article 45 of the Procurement Directive. A distinction is made between mandatory and non-mandatory grounds for exclusion, the first being governed by Article 45, paragraph 1 and the latter by Article 45, paragraph 2. It follows that whereas the contracting authorities of the EU Member States are obliged to exclude potential tenderers from a procedure if their situation is such as described in Article 45, paragraph 1, economic operators whose situation is such as described in Article 45, paragraph 2 can only be excluded if the contracting authority has specified explicitly in the contract notice that such a situation constitutes a ground for exclusion.

2.2 Mandatory grounds for exclusion

Article 45, paragraph 1 provides that candidates or tenderers must be excluded from procurement procedures if they have been convicted by final judgment of one of a list of offences. These are a) participation in a criminal organisation, b) corruption, c) fraud and d) money laundering. Although these grounds for exclusion usually are of only little interest to the contracting authority, it has nevertheless been decided to specify in the Procurement Directive that candidates and tenderers convicted of such offences are excluded from participation in procurement procedures.

---

1. Judgment of 12 December 2002 by the European Court of Justice, case C-470/99, Universale-Bau.

As Article 45, paragraph 1 is worded this is an exclusion in perpetuity from the time of conviction by final judgment. It appears that the Procurement Directive does not contain a provision of whether and, if so, when such a candidate or tenderer may be forgiven and readmitted to participation in procurement procedures.

Where proceedings are conducted against a candidate or a tenderer for corruption, for example, the contracting authority cannot exclude the concerned undertaking from a procedure until a final judgment has been delivered. The requirement for conviction by final judgment inevitably implies that appeal courts have been heard and that all possibilities of appeal have been exhausted or the tenderer or candidate has waived further appeals prior to the end of the period allowed for appeal.

The four offences listed above which oblige the contracting authority to exclude candidates or tenderers are rooted in Community acts. It is, therefore, not by virtue of the Procurement Directive that a conviction for fraud under Danish national law is a mandatory ground for exclusion of a candidate or tenderer.

Paragraph 5 of the contract notice sets out a similar obligation of exclusion in the event of criminal offences.

Article 45, paragraph 1, third sentence of the Procurement Directive stipulates that Member States in their national law can implement provisions according to which candidates and tenderers convicted of corruption, for example, can be admitted to participation in procurement procedures provided that this is justified for reasons of overriding general interest. This provision has not been implemented into Danish law.

Contracting authorities may exclude a candidate or a tenderer if they obtain knowledge, by whatever means, that a conviction by final judgment has been delivered in respect of one of the offences mentioned in Article 45, paragraph 1.

However, the contracting authority usually requires evidence as provided in Article 45, paragraph 1, fourth indent, cf. paragraph 3, in the form of a certificate of criminal record. If such certificates are not issued in the Member State where the undertaking is established, the contracting authority must accept a statement issued by a notary or an administrative authority.

2.3 Non-mandatory grounds for exclusion

Contracting authorities can exclude candidates and tenderers from participation in procurement procedures if the situation of the candidate or tenderer is as described in Article 45, paragraph 2 (a)-(d).

Paragraph 2 (a) lists tenderers which are bankrupt, being wound up, whose affairs are being administered by the court, which have entered into an arrangement with creditors or have suspended their business activities.

In paragraph 2 (b) are listed the situations where a potential tenderer or candidate is the subject of proceedings for a declaration of bankruptcy, for an order for compulsory winding up or administration by the court or of an arrangement with creditors. In these situations there is no order of bankruptcy, winding-up, etc., but merely a petition for such order. This provision appears to be too far-reaching in so far as it extends to petitions filed by others than the tenderer. Petitions for bankruptcy, etc. are usually dealt with swiftly under national law and, therefore, there does not seem to be any reason for excluding a tenderer from participation in a procurement procedure on the sole ground that a petition in bankruptcy, etc. has been filed. It is, for example, possible to prevent a petition in bankruptcy filed by a creditor leading to an actual order of bankruptcy.

Furthermore, a contracting authority can exclude candidates and tenderers convicted of a criminal offence which raises doubts about the candidate's or tenderer's professional conduct, cf. paragraph 2 (c). It is a requirement that the judgment is enforceable. It is also a requirement that there is a conviction for a criminal offence under national law. The requirement that the judgment must raise doubts about the tenderer's or candidate's professional conduct leaves the contracting authorities, which have chosen this ground for exclusion, considerable room for discretion.

Contracting authorities can also exclude candidates and tenderers which have been guilty of grave professional misconduct. It is a requirement that the contacting authority can prove such professional misconduct. In practice one means by which this can be demonstrated is by way of an arbitration award concerning defective works. Another means of proof is where a supplier previously has provided the contracting authority with a flawed service. As it is not a requirement under Article 45, paragraph 2 (d) that the professional misconduct be demonstrated by means of an enforceable judgment or an arbitration award, etc., the contracting authority can refer to its own assessments as proof of grave professional misconduct.

Candidates and tenderers which have not fulfilled obligations relating to the payment of social security contributions can be excluded, cf. Article 45, paragraph 2 (e), as can candidates and tenderers which have not fulfilled obligations relating to the payment of taxes, cf. Article 45, paragraph 2 (f).[2] However, where the payment obligations are being challenged before the authorities or the courts of law, it will probably not be possible to exclude the candidate or tenderer from participation in the procurement procedure.

Finally, contracting authorities can exclude candidates and tenderers which are guilty of serious misrepresentation in supplying information to the contracting authority, cf. Article 45, paragraph 2 (g). The requirement of serious misrepresentation seems to imply that the contracting authority must prove that the candidate or tenderer knew that the information supplied was a misrepresentation and that the misrepresentations were made in order to be admitted to the procedure.

Candidates and tenderers can prove that their situation is not such which justifies exclusion by submitting a certificate which attests thereto issued by the competent administrative authority. In Denmark a certificate covering the cases specified in Article 45, paragraph 2 (a), (b), (e) and (f) is issued by the Commerce and Companies Agency. For obvious reasons a certificate cannot be produced regarding the other grounds for exclusion, set out in Article 45, paragraph 2 (d) and (g), as they are based on the contracting authorities' own experience in dealings with the candidate. Candidates and tenderers established in Member States which do not issue such certificates can instead issue a declaration themselves in which they declare that their situation is not such which justifies exclusion. Such declarations must be made before a notary or other public authority.

It is the explicit main rule that Article 45, paragraph 2 exhaustively sets out the grounds for exclusion. However, in extraordinary circumstances the contracting authority can exclude candidates and tenderers on other grounds. Such exclusion must be founded on objective, relevant and specific grounds. Accordingly, if he contracting authority is able to prove that there is a not remote risk that the candidate or tenderer will take extraneous interests into consideration in performing the contract, it may in the specific circumstances justify exclusion.[3] Furthermore, with reference to bad experience with an

---

2. The Danish Consolidated Act No. 336 of 13 May 1997 limiting debtors' possibilities of participating in public procurement procedures.
3. Order of the Complaints Board of 17 September 1999, Dansk Fjernvarmes Decentrale Kraft/Varme-selskab A.m.b.a. and Others vs. Danish Energy Authority.

undertaking the contracting authority can choose not to pre-qualify that undertaking provided that the grounds for exclusion are reasoned.[4]

2.4 Exclusion for non-compliance with minimum requirements

The grounds for exclusion set out in Article 45 relate to the situation of the candidates or tenderers. In addition, the drafting of the tender or request for pre-qualification may result in exclusion in circumstances where the contracting authority has laid down explicit minimum requirements that have not been complied with. These requirements may be for language, use of tables, maximum number of pages, etc.[5] See also chapter 7.3.3.

2.5 Suitability to pursue the professional activity

Under Article 46 of the Procurement Directive contracting authorities can request documentation that candidates and tenderers are enrolled on professional registers or possess the necessary authorisations. The documentation must prove enrolment on professional registers in the Member State where the candidate or tenderer is established, cf. Annex IX to the Procurement Directive. Also the authorisation must be issued in the country of origin.[6]

2.6 Legal form

It follows from Article 4, paragraph 1 of the Procurement Directive that contracting authorities cannot reject – exclude – candidates or tenderers on the ground that under the law of the country of the contracting authority a supplier of the proposed service is required to be either a natural or a legal person. This provision serves to underline the principle of mutual recognition. Neither can a group of candidates or tenderers be required by the contracting authority to assume a specific legal form as a condition for participation in the procedure. This follows from Article 4, paragraph 2 of the Procurement Directive.

However, once a group of candidates or tenderers is awarded the contract, the contracting authority can require of them to assume a specific legal form. The contracting authority must prove that such change is necessary. A re-

---

4. Order of the Complaints Board of 23 March 2004, Tolkeservice rep. by Aso Hamid vs. County of Viborg.
5. Order of the Complaints Board of 6 August 2001 Oxford Research A/S vs. Faaborg Local Authority
6. Order of the Complaints Board of 6 June 2000, Ernst & Young State-Authorised Public Accountants vs. Diocesan Authority of Funen.

quirement for a specific legal form should always be clearly described in the contract documents.

It is only rarely relevant to require that a chosen supplier assumes a specific legal form, but may be so for the provision of services. One example is where a contracting authority charges a service provider with the management of considerable economic funds, the return on which accrues to the contracting authority. The amount of the return will depend on the legal form of the entity to which the economic funds are transferred in that it is the legal form of the entity which decides whether the amount is taxable or not. Inevitably, in order to be able to compare the tenders submitted, it may be necessary for the contracting authority to require a specific legal form.

3.Generally about the selection criteria

Typically, contracting authorities are keen to ensure that they only receive tenders from undertakings suitable to supply the service or product or execute the works. Consequently, the contracting authorities determine criteria on economic and financial standing and professional ability which the interested economic operators must comply with in order for their tenders to be permitted and evaluated.

3.1 Nature of the selection criteria
The selection criteria are set out in Articles 47-52 of the Procurement Directive. The selection criteria are only intended to uncover which candidates and tenderers are suitable to deliver. Thus, in principle there is no element of relativity connected to the selection criteria and more often than not there will be several suitable candidates and tenderers. The award criteria, in contrast, serve to compare the tenders submitted in order to find the successful candidate. In a procedure for the award of a service contract a criterion such as "relevant experience" is appropriate for finding potential suitable tenderers, but usually not for awarding the proposed contract.[7]

---

7. Order of the Complaints Board of 27 September 2000, Svend B. Thomsen A/S vs. Blåvandshuk Local Authority.

3.2 The Procurement Directive sets out an exhaustive list of selection criteria

Article 44, paragraph 1 provides that only the selection criteria defined by the framework set out in Articles 47-52 are available to contracting authorities. This excludes the possibility of laying down criteria that entail discrimination against candidates or tenderers established in other Member States.[8]

Although Articles 47-52 exhaustively set out the selection criteria available to contracting authorities, the scope for laying down the specific criteria within the framework defined by the Procurement Directive is nevertheless wide. In the majority of procedures it is necessary for the contracting authority to stress the exact requirements it will be looking for. In particular with respect to requirements for experience and technical ability which are not always clear, but must be specified.

3.3 Minimum levels

The contracting authority may choose to indicate minimum levels of ability in the contract notice or the contract documents. The Procurement Directive explicitly provides that any specification of minimum levels must respect the principle of proportionality, cf. Article 44, paragraph 2, first indent: *"The contracting authorities may require candidates and tenderers to meet minimum capacity levels in accordance with Articles 47 and 48."*

The extent of the information referred to in Articles 47 and 48 and the minimum levels of ability required for a specific contract must be related and proportionate to the object of the contract. One such minimum requirement may be that the equity of the candidate or tenderer is of a certain amount, for example at least DKK 5 million, or that the candidate or tenderer has already carried out similar works or services a minimum number of times.

4. Economic and financial standing

To ensure that the suppliers that are selected as the result of a procurement procedure are indeed able to perform the contract, it is almost always appropriate for the contracting authorities to safeguard against awarding the contract to undertakings of insufficient economic standing.

---

8. Judgment of the European Court of Justice of 3 June 1992, case C-360/89, Commission vs. Italy.

4.1 Reasons for the criteria for sufficient economic and financial standing

The reason why contracting authorities can require a certain economic and financial standing of candidates and tenderers, and that such requirements can be considered relevant in the context of proposed contracts, is that the contracting authority risks not having the proposed service delivered at all if the contract is awarded to a tenderer of insufficient standing. To the contracting authority the implication of such default on the part of the successful tenderer entails a reopening of the competition. On the other hand, contracting authorities are obviously obliged not to lay down disproportionate criteria for the economic standing of tenderers. Proportionality must be observed; the criteria for financial and economic standing must be in line with the amount of capital required for the proposed contract to the effect that the criteria are softened where less capital is required. Entry into the market for supplies to contracting authorities, which are subject to the Procurement Directive, would be unfairly and unintentionally restricted if this was not the case. However, contracting authorities enjoy considerable latitude in determining the criteria for economic and financial standing.

The evaluation of the financial and economic standing of candidates and tenderers is not limited to a few areas, but includes, for example, equity as well as cash situation. Also threatening or latent risks may be considered in the evaluation of economic and financial standing. If, for example, the notes to submitted accounts reveal that proceedings are being conducted against the candidate or tenderer for payment of a substantial claim which cannot be honoured, the contracting authority may exclude that candidate or tenderer.

For the purposes of selecting the potential suppliers on the basis of economic and financial selection criteria, provision of security by way of a bank guarantee or similar instrument is not a genuine alternative to compliance with proportionate criteria for economic and financial standing. The performance of the real debtor cannot be guaranteed through a bank guarantee or similar instrument. However, provision of security from the supplier subsequently awarded the contract may typically provide an incentive for performing the contract. Therefore, the Procurement Directive does not provide that compliance with the criteria for economic and financial standing can be met by provision of security. Where a tender is submitted by a subsidiary, it may, however, be necessary to examine whether the parent company has made any undertakings with respect to the obligations of the subsidiary.

The information on the economic and financial standing of candidates or tenderers may indirectly play a role in the evaluation and verification of information submitted by the candidate or tenderer regarding previous experience. This is because the contracting authority can require separate proof of economic and financial standing in the form of a statement of turnover in the area covered by the contract.

4.2 Proof of economic and financial standing
Article 47, paragraph 1 lists the evidence and documents by which candidates or tenderers can prove their economic and financial standing and compliance with any minimum requirements laid down by the contracting authority, cf. Article 4, paragraph 2.

4.2.1 Statements from banks and insurance companies[9]
Statements from banks and insurance companies usually show that the undertaking is eligible for a loan and thus creditworthy. The statements may set out specific information, such as the limits of overdrafts or similar credit facilities. Article 47, paragraph 1 (a) does not specify the exact information of such bank statements and, consequently, they must be appropriate as evidence of compliance with the specific information or minimum requirements determined by the contracting authority.

Article 47, paragraph 1 (a) further provides that proof of relevant indemnity insurance can be required. Typically this proof will be by way of the relevant insurance policy. Notwithstanding the wording of Article 47, paragraph 1 (a) prescribing submission of either bank statements or proof of relevant indemnity insurance, nothing seems to prevent the contracting authority from requiring production of both bank statements and proof of relevant indemnity insurance and the candidate or tenderer can probably submit both documents. Under national law certain services can only be provided subject to indemnity insurance. The contracting authority may, nevertheless, have a legitimate interest in securing proof that the insurance has indeed been taken out, and also the extent of the insurance coverage may be relevant. The contracting authority must observe the principle of proportionality also in this respect. Hence a ruling by the Complaints Board for Public Procurement establishing that for the award of a contract for accounting services, the contracting authority could not require a copy of the indemnity insurance of one of the tendering accounting firms but should have accepted a declaration

9.   Statements from banks, cf. Article 47, paragraph 1 (a).

from the insurance company to the effect that the accounting firm was covered by proper indemnity insurance.[10]

4.2.2 Accounts[11]

Usually the contracting authority requires that candidates or tenderers submit their latest accounts. The accounts include a profit and loss account and a balance sheet which explain or at least provide an indication of the candidate's or tenderer's financial standing. To Article 47, paragraph 1 (b) is added the sentence "where publication of the balance-sheet is required under the law of the country in which the economic operator is established". This addition probably means, cf. Article 47, paragraph 4, that contracting authorities only can require this evidence from candidates and tenderers established in countries where balance sheets (accounts) must be made public. From other candidates and tenderers the contracting authority will have to settle for other documents to prove the undertaking's financial position, cf. Article 47, paragraph 5

4.2.3 Statements of turnover[12]

Also statements of turnover are frequently demanded from potential candidates or tenderers. Only statements for the last three financial years can be demanded. It is a further requirement that it be for the "financial years available" meaning only accounts which have been audited and presented. Furthermore, the contracting authorities cannot reject candidates or tenderers merely on the ground that this requirement has not been complied with if the candidate or tenderer was established within the last three financial years. For obvious reasons the candidate or tenderer cannot submit statements of turnover in years preceding its establishment.[13]

4.3 Evaluation of submitted proof of economic and financial standing

If the contracting authority has not stipulated minimum requirements for, for example, equity, cash resources, relevant turnover, etc., its possibilities of excluding candidates and tenderers will often be limited to exclusion of those

10. Order of the Complaints Board of 6 June 2000, Ernst & Young State-Authorised Public Accountants vs. Diocesan Authority of Funen.
11. Balance sheets or extracts from the balance sheets, cf. Article 47, paragraph 1 (b).
12. Statement of the overall turnover and of turnover in the area covered by the contract, cf. Article 47, paragraph 1 (c).
13. Order of the Complaints Board of 3 January 2002, AC Trafik rep. by Anders Bødker Christiansen vs. County of Frederiksborg.

which, for example, have negative equity, are dependent on future and uncertain capital injections for sufficient cash flow or only sporadically have a relevant turnover, cf. however section 4.5 below. Article 47, paragraph 4 sets out that contracting authorities should specify, in the contract notice or the invitation to tender, which requirements for evidence and documents they have chosen and which other evidence and documents must be provided. This obligation ensures that tenderers do not submit other evidence and documents than those required for proving compliance with the selection criteria for economic and financial standing.

4.4 Proof by other means than those requested

Although the contracting authority, in the contract documents, has specified the required evidence and documents, it may nevertheless be obliged to admit tenders from a candidate or tenderer which proves its economic and financial standing by other means if "for a valid reason, the economic operator is unable to provide" the requested documents, cf. Article 47, paragraph 5. A valid reason would typically be that the documents requested are not obtainable in the country where the candidate or tenderer is established. However, there seems to be other situations where it would be appropriate to accept other types of evidence. For example, circumstances where the contracting authority requires evidence of relevant professional indemnity insurance, but such insurance is not compulsory by law and the candidate or tenderer has opted for self-insurance may qualify as a valid reason. A self-insured candidate or tenderer would have to prove that it controls funds of an amount comparable to insurance protection. The specific proof to be provided in this respect is also determined by the contracting authority which has a natural interest in safeguarding against financially unsound business partners. The requirements must be laid down taking into due consideration the principle of proportionality.

4.5 Control of third party's economic and financial capacities

A candidate or tenderer which alone does not meet the criteria for economic and financial standing cannot be excluded by the contracting authority if the candidate or tenderer proves to have the resources required of other legal or natural persons at its disposal, cf. Article 47, paragraph 2.[14] In practice it will

---

14. Judgment of the European Court of Justice of 2 December 1999, case C-176/98, Holst Italia Spa vs. Commune di Cagliari; judgment of the European Court of Justice of 14 April 1994, case 389/92, Ballast Nedam Group NV vs. Belgium; judgment of the European Court of Justice of 18 December 1997, case C-5/97, Ballast Nedam NV vs. Belgium.

often be a subsidiary which provides proof of economic and financial standing in the form of undertakings from a parent company with greater shoulders financially.

4.6 Groups of candidates and tenderers

Similarly groups, such as consortia, can refer to their aggregate economic and financial capacity and to the capacities of other natural and legal persons provided that these legal persons have undertaken a commitment to that effect and such commitment is proved to the contracting authorities, cf. Article 47, paragraph 3 (and Article 4). This means of complying with economic and financial selection criteria by reference to the capacities of other entities opens up competition and is established by case law of the European Court of Justice.[15]

In the individual case the contracting authorities must evaluate and determine whether the chosen selection criteria for economic and financial standing have been complied with, and the evaluation cannot be deferred until the tenders have been submitted and are ready for assessment.[16]

5. Technical and professional ability

Depending on the proposed contract, it is necessary for the contracting authority to secure competition among the potential suppliers which have the professional ability to perform the contact.

5.1 Publication of requirements for proof of technical and professional ability

Article 48 of the Procurement Directive sets out a relatively comprehensive list of evidence that can be requested by the contracting authority as proof of the candidates' or tenderers' ability to comply with the technical and professional selection criteria. Article 48, paragraph 6 provides that the contracting authority specifies, in the contract notice or the invitation to tender, which documents and evidence must be provided. According to Article 48, paragraph 1, the evaluation of the documents and evidence submitted as proof of

15. Judgment of the European Court of Justice of 2 December 1999, case C-176/98, Holst Italia Spa vs. Comune di Cagliari.
16. Order of the Complaints Board of 30 May 1996 A/S Iver Pedersen vs. I/S Reno Syd and order of the Complaints Board of 1 March 1999, Enemærke & Petersen A/S vs. Fællesorganisationens Boligforening, Slagelse.

technical and professional ability concerns both an assessment and a verification of the documentation. This paragraph addresses, at least to some extent, the common problem encountered in procurement procedures; that, in particular, reference lists of works carried out or deliveries effected previously frequently are inflated without any real possibility of verification for the contracting authority. Furthermore, since experience with similar supplies is often a requirement, and rightly so, it may prove very important that references can be crosschecked. The exact evidence that can be requested by contracting authorities depends on whether the contract is for works, purchase of products or a service.

5.2 Reference lists

Evidence to be provided of relevant experience by means of reference lists is governed by Article 48, paragraph 2 (a). With respect to works, a list of (all) works carried out over the past five years can be requested. With respect to supplies and services, a list of the principal deliveries effected and the main services provided in the past three years can be requested.

The reference list of works must be accompanied by certificates of satisfactory execution of, as a minimum, the most important works. The certificates must also indicate the value, date and site of the works and, obviously, whether the works were carried out according to the rules of the trade and properly completed. The authorities that issue these certificates may submit the certificates to the contracting authority directly.

References included on the reference list of deliveries effected and services provided must be confirmed by the purchasers. If the purchaser was a contracting authority, it must issue a certificate. If the purchaser was a private entity, it must certify the reference list or issue a declaration (of the correctness of the list with respect to the particular delivery or service).

5.3 Professional ability

In order to determine whether candidates and tenderers are suitable, the contracting authority wants to be reassured that they possess sufficient professional competences. Whereas the reference lists refer to the past, the request for information on the competences that will be applied to the performance of the contract looks to the future.

Article 48, paragraph 2 (b) provides that information can be requested on the technicians and technical bodies involved. Candidates and tenderers can refer to their own employees or to consultants and subcontractors, cf. section 5.11. It is underlined that information can be requested on those responsible for quality control especially.

Furthermore, pursuant to Article 48, paragraph 2 (e) information can be requested with respect to the educational and professional qualifications of the service provider or contractor (but not of the supplier).

Finally, service providers and contractors can be requested to produce a statement of the average annual manpower and the number of managerial staff for the last three years, cf. Article 48, paragraph 2 (g). Such statements cannot be requested of suppliers of products.

5.4 Technical facilities, etc.

For the award of supply and service contracts the contracting authority can request descriptions of the technical facilities and measures used by the supplier or service provider for ensuring quality, cf. Article 48, paragraph 2 (c). Descriptions of study and research facilities can also be requested. However, in light of the obligation to observe the principle of proportionality, cf. Article 44, paragraph 2, the contracting authorities must exercise restraint with respect to the number of requests.

Also statements of a) the tools, b) the plant and c) the equipment available to the service provider or contractor for carrying out works under a contract awarded can be requested. This follows from Article 48, paragraph 2 (h). Despite this, the contracting authority cannot require that such equipment, etc. is available to the candidate or tenderer already at the time of the assessment of compliance with the selection criteria or at the time of submission of tenders. Frequently it is necessary for the successful tenderer to acquire additional machinery and equipment for the performance of the contract and in such case paragraph 2 (h) only obliges the candidate or tenderer to state which equipment will be used should it be awarded the contract.[17]

5.5 Complex products and services

Article 48, paragraph 2 (d) provides that a check can be carried out to determine whether the candidate or tenderer is able to comply with the technical and professional requirements for the supply of products or provision of services which are complex or serve a special purpose (for example special IT services). To that end the contracting authority can carry out a check on the supplier's production capacity or the service provider's technical capacity and, if necessary, on the undertaking's means of study and research and quality control measures. Again, it is underlined that the principle of proportional-

---

17. Order of the Complaints Board of 27 June 2000, Deponering af Problem-affald ApS vs. I/S Vestforbrænding and Others.

ity embodied in Article 44, paragraph 2 entails that such control only be requested if and to the extent that the type and nature of the products or the
services so warrant.

5.6 Samples, etc.

In procedures for the award of supply contracts, the contracting authority can
request that samples, descriptions and/or photographs be supplied as evidence
of compliance with the selection criteria, cf. Article 48, paragraph 2 (j). The
authenticity of such evidence must be certified if the contracting authority so
requests.

5.7 Certificates attesting the conformity of products to certain specifications or standards

Article 48, paragraph 2 (j) enables a contracting authority launching a procedure for the award of a supply contract to request certificates issued by official quality control institutes attesting that the products, which will be supplied subsequently, conform to certain standards or specifications.

5.8 Quality standards

Article 49 regulates the situations where the contracting authority – lawfully
– requests the production of certificates issued by independent bodies attesting the compliance of the candidate or tenderer with certain quality standards.
If such standards are based on the relevant European standard series, the
certificates must be issued by bodies which conform to the European standard
series concerning certification. The contracting authority must recognise
equivalent certificates from bodies established in other Member States. The
contracting authority must also accept other evidence of equivalent quality
assurance measures.

5.9 Environmental matters

In procedures for the award of works and service contracts the contracting
authority can request information from candidates and tenderers on the quality management measures they are planning to apply in the performance of
the contract. Furthermore, Article 50 of the Procurement Directive provides
that where the contracting authority requests certificates, reference must be
made to the Community Eco-Management and Audit Scheme (EMAS) or to
environmental management standards based on the relevant European or
international standards, and the certificates must be certified by bodies con-
forming to the relevant EU provisions or other European or international

standards concerning certification. Also equivalent certificates must be recognised and other evidence accepted.

5.10 Information on subcontracting

In procedures for the award of service contracts the contracting authority can require an indication of the proportion of the contract, if any, which the candidate or tenderer intends to subcontract, cf. Article 48, paragraph 2 (i). Where the candidate or tenderer intends to subcontract parts of a service contract, it must prove, by the same means as listed above, that the proposed subcontractors have the technical and professional ability required for performing the relevant parts of the contract. A contracting authority cannot prevent candidates and tenderers from subcontracting parts of a contract, but it can require evidence of the subcontractor's relevant economic and technical capacities. Any replacement of subcontractors by the main contractor always requires the acceptance of the contracting authority. Such acceptance is self-evident in some cases, for example in the event of bankruptcy. In other situations the contracting authority may accept replacement of the subcontractor only on the condition that it does not perform a quantitative or qualitative part of the contract. Furthermore, the contracting authority can preclude subcontracting for the performance of essential parts of the contract.[18]

Moreover, subcontracting is linked to the provision in Article 48, paragraph 3 mentioned below.

5.11 Use of resources belonging to others

In all procurement procedures the tenderer can rely on the professional and technical capacities of other natural or legal persons on the explicit assumption that the tenderer proves to the contracting authority that it will have at its disposal the resources necessary for compliance with the criteria laid down by the contracting authority. In practice the tenderer must produce evidence of such third parties' undertaking to place the necessary resources at the disposal of the tenderer. Reference is also made to section 4.5 above.

5.12 Requirements with respect to skills, efficiency, etc.

For supply contracts requiring siting or installation work and for service and works contracts the contracting authority can evaluate the tenderer's ability

---

18. Judgment of the European Court of Justice of 18 March 2004, case C-314/01, Siemens AG and ARGE vs. Hauptverband der österreichischen Sozialversicherungsträger paragraph 45.

on the basis of information on skills, efficiency, experience and reliability, cf. Article 48, paragraph 5. Such an evaluation requires that the contracting authority specifies the exact information it requests in order to select suitable suppliers. While references, to a certain extent, show experience, it is, depending on the circumstances, somewhat more difficult to evaluate skills, efficiency and reliability objectively. At some level it is possible to prove compliance with these requirements by producing curricula vitae and diplomas for the relevant employees.

6. Disqualification

To ensure that candidates and tenderers submit their tenders on equal competitive terms, the contracting authority is under an obligation to exclude undertakings that have or are likely to have a competitive advantage.

6.1 Disqualification in procurement procedures
The obligation to observe the principle of equal treatment in procurement procedures requires contracting authorities to make sure that their situation or circumstances do not have the effect of bettering one or more potential suppliers' chances of being awarded the contract in comparison to other potential suppliers. Such better position can arise out of a number of situations. One example worth mentioning initially is where the contracting authority in a procurement procedure allows extra time or provides additional information to one potential supplier to the effect that its chances of submitting a successful tender are improved. The principle of equal treatment prescribes that all candidates and tenderers must be subject to the same deadlines and given the same information at the same time.

It thus follows that the meaning of the term qualification used in the context of procurement is not the same as the meaning conferred upon it in, for example, the Danish Public Administration Act or the Danish Administration of Justice Act. The provisions of Part 2 of the Public Administration Act provide that a civil servant must not be involved in cases in which his impartiality might be challenged for specific reasons. The provisions of the Administration of Justice Act confer a similar meaning. Qualification in procurement procedures, in contrast, concerns whether the contracting authority was entitled to admit one or more candidates or tenderers to the procedure following concerns of violation of the principle of equal treatment. If it turns out that the principle of equal treatment was violated because one or more tenderers were disqualified, then such tenderer(s) must be excluded from the procedure and thus from being awarded the contract.

In addition to the principle of disqualification applied in procurement law, the general rules of Danish law applies, and thus also the rules on disqualification set out in Part 2 of the Public Administration Act.

6.2 Disqualification pursuant to the preparation of the procedure

A potential supplier which – against or for no consideration – has assisted in preparing the procedure, and for example made decisions with respect to the type of procedure, the scheduling of the procedure, deadlines, etc. cannot participate in the procedure as a potential supplier. The same applies to potential suppliers which have assisted in drawing up, in particular, the specifications.[19]

However, a potential tenderer is not disqualified from participating merely because it has contributed to the preparation of the procedure. The influence must be substantial – the supplier must have left one or more fingerprints on the contract documents.[20]

On the other hand, potential suppliers that have previously supplied the same or comparable services to the contracting authority are not for that reason alone excluded from participation.[21]

Having said that, it is clear that in fixing deadlines and describing volumes and other facts pertaining to, in particular, complex or bulky purchases, the contracting authority must strive to cancel out the logical advantage which

---

19. Order of the Complaints Board of 23 August 1995, B4 ApS vs. Holbæk Local Authority.
20. Order of the Complaints Board of 8 January 1997, Danish Chamber of Commerce vs. Rigshospitalet.
21. Order of the Complaints Board of 7 July 1995, Valles Trans-Media Byudstyr and Udendørsreklamer K/S vs. City of Copenhagen. Judgment of the European Court of Justice of 3 March 2005, cases C-21/03 and C-34/03 Fabricom, in which Belgian law was held incompatible with the procurement rules as undertakings instructed to carry out research, experiments, studies or development in connection with public works, supplies or services were excluded from procurement procedures, without allowing these undertakings the opportunity to prove that their particular circumstances were not capable of distorting competition. It was also held that the contracting authority cannot wait until the evaluation of tenders before it rejects a tender as disqualified, it must communicate its decision to disqualify to the relevant tenderer in reasonable time before the evaluation of tenders and the award decision.

the former supplier has over the other potential suppliers.[22] In many cases such considerations translate into, for example, deadlines for the submission of tenders being extended to allow other suppliers sufficient time to get acquainted with the area. Furthermore, the contracting authority must exercise extra care to ensure transparency of the procedure.

6.3 Disqualification of the contracting authority

Where the contracting authority itself submits a tender or where a connected party of the contracting authority submits a tender, the contracting authority must carefully consider whether the principle of equal treatment is complied with.

A potential supplier is not disqualified merely because it receives, albeit very substantial, state aid.[23]

By the same token, submission of tenders by the contracting authority as well as connected parties of the contracting authority does not automatically violate the principle of equal treatment.[24] The same applies to tenders submitted by, for example, joint local authority undertakings in which the contracting authority participates.[25]

The terminology used in respect to the contracting authority's own tender is somewhat confusing as the term used under Danish law is verification tender. This is the term used in the Ministry of Finance's Circular on Procurement and Outsourcing of Government Services and Works. The contracting authorities' primary purpose of submitting a verification tender is to signal to the tenderers that the contract will not be awarded to any of them if a comparison of the verification tender and the external tenders shows that no advantages will be gained from having the delivery effected or the service provided by an external supplier. See also sections 3.1.4 and 2.3.1.

The contracting authority can only participate in the procedure as a potential supplier provided that the principle of equal treatment is observed. To this end the contracting authority must demonstrate that there are Chinese walls be-

---

22. Order of the Complaints Board of 25 October 1995, Siemens A/S vs. Esbjerg Local Authority and Order of the Complaints Board of 26 April 1996, E. Pihl & Søn A/S vs. I/S Avedøre Kloakværk.
23. Judgment of the European Court of Justice of 7 December 2000, case C-94/99.
24. Order of the Complaints Board of 30 January 2001, Dansk Transport og Logistik vs. Haderslev Local Authority and order of the Complaints Board of 27 April 2001, Dansk Transport og Logistik vs. Nykøbing Falster Local Authority.
25. Order of the Complaints Board of 11 October 1996, Luis Madsen and Others vs. Odense Local Authority.

tween the contracting department and the tendering department. One prerequisite of compliance with the principle of equal treatment would be *de facto* organisational separation of, as a minimum, the decisions regarding the contracting authority's role as tenderer. An own tender prepared by external consultants would probably not be acceptable in that ultimately, the contracting authority is always responsible for the content, etc. of such tender. Further, the contracting authority would surely not be able to use the negotiated procedure for awarding a contract for which the contracting authority submits an own tender. To ensure equal treatment and avoid disqualification, the department with the contracting authority which is to submit the tender can have no influence on the drafting of the contract documents or otherwise be given an advantage, for example by receiving the contract documents, etc. before other potential tenderers. Inescapably, however, the contracting authority will have certain advantages, such as knowledge, over the other potential suppliers.

6.4 Disqualification of and due to consultants

Where the contracting authority entrusts a consultant with a task, that consultant gains knowledge and a clear idea of the contracting authority's preferences. Contracting authorities make use of external consultants to varying degrees. These external consultants have other clients and often have the capacity to submit their own tenders, typically for services, but also for works contracts. Therefore, disqualification on account of consultants may arise in many ways.

A consultant which has assisted the contracting authority in drafting the contract documents or drawing up the specifications is excluded from submitting a tender. However, if the consultancy has been in the form of preliminary studies, the outcome of which can be imparted to all tenderers in the contract documents, it will not constitute a ground for disqualification. It is pivotal whether the consultant influenced the preparation of the procedure, and in particular the specifications.[26] Consultants which assist the contracting authority in the course of the procedure are obviously excluded from submitting tenders. This would be the case even if the consultant prepares the tender in a entirely separate department or company as the likelihood that information is disclosed, directly or indirectly, from the consultancy section to the tendering section seems too great.[27]

---

26. Order of the Complaints Board of 13 June 1996, Danish Association of Consulting Engineers vs. Roskilde Local Authority.
27. Order of the Complaints Board of 13 January 2004, E. Pihl & Søn A/S vs. Hadsund Local Authority.

A peculiar situation in terms of qualification arises where a consultant ad-
vises the contracting authority as well as one or more tenderers for purposes of
the same procurement. In this particular situation the tenderer which used the
consultant would be excluded from participation in the procedure. However, it
appears from case law, at least in Denmark, that even such double consultancy
is not tantamount to disqualification if the contracting authority can prove that
the consultant in question has established clear guidelines regarding which
employees assist the contracting authority and which assist the tenderer. Danish
case law has thus established that double consultancy is permitted, except
where the consultancy regards the same specialist area (for example environmental matters) and encompasses the evaluation of the tenders submitted.[28]
There seems to be strong cause for criticism of such a lax application of the
principle of equal treatment to double consultancy. In this context it should be
borne in mind that many, notably, large procedures are conducted by consultants on both sides and perhaps because the consultant is indeed a consultant
and not a contracting authority, qualification may be a secondary consideration
only. The concerns, for example with respect to the processing of information,
seem to be so numerous that it can be required of a contracting authority which
admits tenderers, advised by the same consultants as itself, that the authority, as
a minimum, should have made sure on beforehand and verifiably that other
tenderers will not be placed at a competitive disadvantage with respect to information, deadlines, requirements and criteria.

Case law also shows that some contracting authorities have interpreted the
issue of disqualification too rigorously.[29] Accordingly, too much caution on
the part of the contracting authority may also constitute a violation. The contracting authority must and can only reject those tenderers which are eligible
for disqualification.

6.5 Onus of proof in connection with qualification concerns

It is the contracting authority which is liable under the Procurement Directive
and thus responsible for compliance with the principle of equal treatment. If
the contracting authority finds that a candidate or tenderer should be excluded

---

28. Unreported judgment of the High Court of 16 September 2002, European Metro
    Group vs. Ørestadsselskabet I/S (appeal of order of the Complaints Board of 18
    November 1996). Upheld by judgment of the Supreme Court of 31 March 2005.
29. Order of the Complaints Board of 13 June 1996, Danish Association of Consulting
    Engineers vs. Roskilde Local Authority.

because of disqualification, it must exclude that candidate or tenderer.[30] If a potential tenderer finds that the contracting authority was wrong in not excluding another tenderer, it is in principle for that tenderer to prove that the principle of equal treatment was violated because this latter tenderer was not disqualified. There are, however, situations where the violation is so palpable that the onus of proof rests with the contracting authority. For example where there is evidence of oral communication between the contracting authority and one tenderer, it is for the contracting authority to prove which information was given to the tenderer.[31] The same rule applies where individuals with the contracting authority who have been involved with the procedure subsequently become employed by or attached to a tenderer.[32]

A contracting authority which has provided a potential or current tenderer with information on the specifications, etc. of the purchase has placed the tenderer in an awkward position. If it is written information, the tenderer can return it without opening and reading it. If it is oral information, the tenderer may have to publish it. If not, the tenderer runs the risk of being disqualified at a later stage.

7. Principles for limiting the number of tenderers

As a means to avert the application of excessive resources and very lengthy procurement procedures, the contracting authority may limit the number of undertakings invited to submit tenders.

7.1 Scope

Article 44, paragraph 3 specifies the contracting authorities' scope for limiting the number of tenderers. For practical reasons and in consideration of the use of resources it is often necessary to limit the number of undertakings invited to negotiate or conduct a dialogue, especially in the negotiated procedure with publication of a contract notice and in the competitive dialogue procedure. Accordingly, in the restricted procedure, the negotiated procedure

---

30. Order of the Complaints Board of 18 May 1995, Henning Larsens Tegnestue vs. Ministry of Culture.
31. Order of the Complaints Board of 7 August 2003, KAS Transport rep. by Kim Schrøder vs. Århus Local Authority
32. Order of the Complaints Board of 19 February 2001, Zeland Care A/S vs. Frederikshavn Local Authority and order of the Complaints Board of 15 December 1999, Lifeline ApS vs. Dansk Hunderegister.

with publication of a contract notice and the competitive dialogue procedure the contracting authority is permitted to limit the number of undertakings that will be pre-qualified to submit tenders. For obvious reasons the number of tenderers cannot be limited in the open procedure where the contracting authority must accept tenders from all tenderers which comply with the selection criteria and which cannot be rejected on relevant grounds for exclusion. In the exceptional cases where the contracting authority can use the negotiated procedure without publication of a contract notice it is irrelevant to limit the number for the sole reason that only the undertaking identified as a potential supplier is invited to negotiate.

In the restricted procedure the minimum number of candidates is five. In the negotiated procedure with publication of a contract notice and in the competitive dialogue procedure the minimum number is three. However, it is emphasised in the Procurement Directive that the contracting authority must make sure that the number of candidates and tenderers is sufficient to ensure genuine competition. This specification seems to be of particular relevance in markets where perhaps more potential suppliers are owned, in whole or in part, by the same group but officially tender on their own behalves. In order to ensure genuine competition in such procedures it makes sense to stipulate a higher minimum number than prescribed in the Procurement Directive.

Article 44, paragraph 3 further prescribes that contracting authorities may stipulate a maximum number of candidates, but not in the open procedure for the above reasons.

Contracting authorities which intend to invite a minimum and a maximum number of candidates must indicate that decision in the contract notice

7.2 Ways to limit the number of pre-qualified undertakings

Pursuant to Article 44, paragraph 3 the contracting authority must indicate in the contract notice the objective and non-discriminatory criteria or rules it intends to apply if it wishes to limit the number of undertakings selected for pre-qualification in circumstances where more undertakings comply with the selection criteria and cannot be rejected on any of the grounds for exclusion. In this respect the contracting authority must obviously observe the principles of equal treatment, non-discrimination, mutual recognition, proportionality and transparency.

Having said that, it should be kept in mind that the contracting authority is looking to make a purchase. If a large number of undertakings request pre-qualification, the contracting authority has an obvious and legitimate interest in making sure that the supposedly most suitable candidates are invited to tender. The contracting authority is not obliged to draw lots and must therefore determine which candidates are most suitable for the specific purchase on the basis of the specific selection criteria and the evidence submitted by the candidates as proof of compliance with the criteria without making any evaluation with respect to the award of the contract (tenders are not yet submitted at that stage of the procedure where it is possible to limit the number of tenderers). Consequently, it is for the contracting authority to make an overall assessment on the basis of the chosen selection criteria.[33] Alternatively, lots can probably be drawn where it is impossible to reduce the number of candidates having assessed the competitive situation or on the basis of the selection criteria.

The contracting authority may also take into consideration the need to ensure genuine competition. If several candidates are linked to each other, for example by way of cross ownership, etc., the intensity of competition will perhaps be less strong than if there were no links between the candidates. The contracting authority may take this into account.

Within the framework described above it is widely left to the discretion of the contracting authority to determine how many candidates it wishes to pre-qualify. Administration and available resources are often the reasons why a contracting authority wishes to limit the number of undertakings selected for pre-qualification. Also time issues may play a role.

If the contracting authority has developed evaluation models for selecting candidates, such evaluation models must also be published.

8. Other issues relevant to pre-qualification

A brief account is given below of some other issues of relevance to the pre-qualification

8.1 Confidentiality
Information and evidence submitted by candidates and tenderers in order to become pre-qualified must be kept confidential, cf. Article 6 of the Procurement Directive. It is not sufficient reason for not complying with the selection criteria that a candidate considers the information requested confidential. As a rule, potential tenderers which consider the contracting authority a possible

---

33. Order of the Complaints Board of 9 October 1996, El-installatørernes Landsforening and Others vs. Københavns Lufthavne A/S and judgment of the European Court of Justice of 12 December 2002, case C-470/99 Universale Bau.

competitor will have to refrain from participation in the procedure. Exceptionally, however, the contracting authority may, in order to ensure genuine competition for the proposed contract, be obliged to take measures guaranteeing that certain information is only reviewed by selected independent consultants who will confirm to the contracting authorities whether or not the chosen selection criteria are complied with.

8.2 Assignability
An undertaking which has been pre-qualified cannot assign this pre-qualification to another undertaking. Only if the contracting authority explicitly consents thereto can the pre-qualification be assigned. The contracting authority's scope for giving such consent seems to be limited to undertakings which subsequent to pre-qualification have demerged or otherwise are split. In all other cases the contracting authority would be deemed not to have verified whether the assigned undertaking complied with the chosen selection criteria subject to which it might could or should have been excluded from the procedure.[34] For the sake of clarity, it should be borne in mind that the above does not exclude the use of subcontractors.

8.3 Reservations
Apart from the reservation with respect to subsequent acquisition of the required operating equipment to perform an awarded contract, candidates and tenderers which reserve compliance with the chosen selection criteria must be rejected. The evidence submitted must be such that allows the contracting authority to verify beyond doubt whether or not the selection criteria are complied with. However, reservations in regard to, for example, the contracting authority's draft contract should be considered in connection with the evaluation of the tenders and are irrelevant to the pre-qualification.

8.4 Selection criteria vis-à-vis award criteria
In procedures where the award criterion is the economically most advantageous tender on the basis of specified sub-criteria, such sub-criteria must be appropriate to identify the best tender. The overriding main rule is that selection criteria cannot be reused as award criteria. The selection criteria can only

---

34. Order of the Complaints Board of 10 May 2002, Ementor Danmark A/S vs. County of Århus; judgment of the European Court of Justice of 23 January 2003, case C-57/01, Makedoniko Metro and Michaniki AE vs. Elliniko Dimosio.

be used to pick out the suitable potential suppliers. There is an abundance of case law on the mix-up of selection and award criteria.[35]

8.5 Grounds for refusal of pre-qualification

Article 41 of the Procurement Directive contains a general provision to the effect that the contracting authority must inform candidates of "decisions" reached during the procedure. It follows that the contracting authority must inform candidates which are deemed not to have provided evidence of compliance with the chosen selection criteria or which are rejected for the chosen grounds for exclusion of such decision.

Article 41, paragraph 2 further provides that the contracting authority must inform candidates which are not pre-qualified as quickly as possible and in all circumstances within a period of 15 days of the reasons for their rejection. The degree to which such reasons must be specified depends on the particular circumstances. At least the contracting authority must indicate on which exact points the candidate did not provide evidence of compliance with the selection criteria or on which points the candidate's situation caused it to be excluded. Considering that it is a purchase and not an administrative decision, the reasons for the rejection need not be elaborate.[36]

The reason why contracting authorities must inform candidates of the grounds for their decision is, of course, to allow rejected candidates to assess whether to file a complaint – in Denmark with the Complaints Board for Public Procurement.

35. Order of the Complaints Board of 23 January 1996, Praktiserende Arkitekters råd vs. Glostrup Local Authority; order of the Complaints Board of 30 May 1996, A/S Iver Pedersen vs. I/S Reno Syd; order of the Complaints Board of 14 September 1998, Danish Chamber of Commerce vs. Statistics Denmark; order of the Complaints Board of 1 March 1999, Enemærke & Petersen A/S vs. Fællesorganisationens Boligforening, Slagelse; order of the Complaints Board of 16 July 1999, Vognmandsforretning Holst Sørensen A/S vs. I/S Affaldsselskabet Vendsyssel Øst; order of the Complaints Board of 28 December 1999, Skjorte Grossisten A/S vs. Post Danmark; order of the Complaints Board of 2 May 2000, Uniqsoft 1998 ApS vs. Odense Local Authority and order of the Complaints Board of 23 February 2001, Kæmpes Taxi and Nordfyns Busser vs. Søndersø Local Authority.
36. Order of the Complaints Board of 9 October 1996, El-installatørernes Landsforening and Others vs. Københavns Lufthavne A/S.

8.6 Additional documents and information

Contracting authorities can demand that candidates requesting pre-qualification submit documents and information to supplement or clarify the evidence already submitted, cf. Article 51 of the Procurement Directive.

8.7 Lists and certification of pre-approved suppliers.

Article 52 of the Procurement Directive provides that Member States can introduce official lists of pre-approved suppliers or certification to that effect by relevant bodies. Such lists and certification systems must be adapted to the provisions of Article 45, paragraphs 1 and 2 (a)-(d) and (g), Article 46, Article 47, paragraphs 1, 4 and 5, Article 48, paragraphs 1, 2, 5 and 6, Article 49 and possibly Article 50 of the Procurement Directive.

CHAPTER 7

Award of Orders and Conclusion of Contract

1. Choices binding for the award

In this chapter the focus is on the competitive parameters that form the basis for the award of the contract and on matters with respect to the conclusion of the contract with the successful tenderer.

1.1 The competitive parameters

In every procurement procedure the competitive parameter chosen and published by the contracting authority is key to the award of the proposed contract. This is true for both the contracting authority and for the tenderers. Is it the lowest price only or are there other parameters, such as service, quality, etc.?

As a consequence, choosing the competitive parameter requires careful consideration on the part of the contracting authority which must also ensure that the chosen parameter is clear to the tenderers. However, unlike purchase decisions by private undertakings, the contracting authority is not free to choose whichever competitive parameter it prefers. One of the most significant differences between a contracting authority which is subject to the Procurement Directive and a private purchaser is that only the latter can base its choice of supplier essentially on aspects such as previous positive experience with a certain supplier and, hence, a feeling of security with respect to that supplier. By contrast, a contracting authority which is subject to the Directive must accept that as its future contracting party it must select the supplier which submits the best tender as assessed in the light of the competitive parameters chosen, and the only security achieved by the contracting authority is that which stems from the choice and application of the selection criteria, cf. chapter 6.

Articles 53-55 of the Directive set out the rules concerning award of contracts. But also recitals 46-47 of the preamble are important in this respect.

Overall it may be said that with the implementation of the Directive it has become increasingly possible to take non-economic criteria into consideration in the award of contracts, including environmental and social requirements, but at the same time the contracting authority is required to specify the weighting which it gives to the criteria chosen.

1.2 The principles

The principles of equal treatment, non-discrimination, mutual recognition, proportionality and transparency are all of great importance to the award of contracts in procurement procedures.

The most important principle in this respect is probably the principle of transparency. The principle is first and foremost intended to ensure that the award criteria chosen are clear and applied unambiguously by the contracting authority. The award criteria must therefore be described exhaustively, and the contracting authority cannot base the award of a contract on supplementary criteria or interpretations which have not been disclosed to the tenderers. There is an abundance of case law involving the principle of transparency and award criteria.[1]

The transparency principle also serves to ensure that there is no doubt as to which documentation the contracting authority requires for the evaluation of the tenders.

Finally, the transparency principle applies to the rules, such as time limits, which the contracting authority intends to follow in the procurement procedure, notably in the negotiated procedure.

Obviously, the principle of equal treatment too is crucial to the award of orders. If the tenders submitted are evaluated on the basis of a model, this model must be applied consistently to the evaluation of all tenders. The deadlines for submitting variants in the negotiated procedures must be the same

---

1. Order of the Complaints Board of 14 December 2000, Renoflex vs. I/S Vestforbrænding concerning the evaluation model; order of the Complaints Board of 2 May 2001, Forlaget Magnus A/S vs. Customs & Tax concerning the possibilities for making reservations vis-à-vis all elements of the contract; order of the Complaints Board of 24 October 2001, Eiland Electric A/S vs. County of Vestsjælland concerning the evaluation model; order of the Complaints Board of 28 December 1999, Skjortegrossisten vs. Post Danmark concerning the use of a system of scores in connection with the award criteria; order of the Complaints Board of 10 February 1997, Dafeta Trans ApS vs. Lynette Fællesskabet I/S on the weighting model.

for all tenderers and any additional information from the contracting authority to the tenderers must be provided to all of them at the same time and by the same means, etc. The principle of equal treatment is the common thread that runs through the Directive, and by far the majority of decisions concerning violation of the procurement rules refer to violation of the principle of equal treatment (and the principle of transparency) regardless whether a specific provision of the Directive (too) has been violated.[2]

1.3 Published information is the basis

By virtue of the principle of equal treatment and the principle of transparency, the contracting authority is bound by the award criteria and the procedures specified in the contract notice (or contract documents) in the evaluation of the tenders and the conduct of the procedure.

Where the contracting authority has chosen the most economically advantageous tender as the main award criterion and duly specified various sub-criteria, the contracting authority can neither add more sub-criteria nor omit to take one or more of the sub-criteria into consideration in the evaluation of the tenders. As a consequence, before choosing and advertising the main award criterion and sub-criteria for procedures where the main award criterion is the most economically advantageous tender, the contracting authority must carefully consider which are most appropriate for the purpose. Similarly, the contracting authority cannot change the weighting given to or the order of importance of the sub-criteria. Nor can the contracting authority use evaluation models which are not reflective of the chosen main award criterion or the sub-criteria in procedures where the most economically advantageous tender is chosen.[3]

The contracting authority is bound by the tender procedure described in the contract documents and must observe all its own rules for the procedure as specified in the contract documents vis-à-vis all tenderers. In return, the contracting authority enjoys considerable latitude in laying down the rules of the procedure, such as the use of diagrams, time limits, submission of information, etc. One key element in this respect is that the contracting authority

---

2. Order of the Complaints Board of 9 February 2000, Danish Council of Practising Architects vs. Ministry of Foreign Affairs concerning violation as a result of failure to negotiate with all tenderers in a negotiated procedure.
3. Order of the Complaints Board of 24 October 2001, Eiland Electric A/S vs. County of Vestsjælland and order of the Complaints Board of 2 April 2002, ISS Danmark A/S vs. H:S Rigshospitalet. See chapter 4.4 for more detail on non-economic considerations as the basis for the award of contracts.

no later than the publication of the award criterion must specify the manner in which the tenderers are required to submit information. This is particularly relevant in procedures where the main award criterion is the most economically advantageous tender accompanied by several sub-criteria. Before making any advertisement it is imperative that the contracting authority has thought through and prepared diagrams for the tenderers to complete and possibly enclose with the documentation, which will provide the contracting authority with the information necessary to carry out an objective evaluation of the tenders.

If the contracting authority, in the contract documents, has specified that reservations to a draft contract enclosed with the contract documents are not accepted, it must act upon such statement and reject tenders setting out such reservations. In a similar vein, tenders with reservations with respect to other elements of the contract documents must be rejected. Contracting authorities cannot depart from or ease the terms and conditions specified, not even where this has, from the contracting authority's perspective, the unfortunate consequence that tenders from one or more presumably good suppliers must be rejected. It is, therefore, necessary for the suppliers to allocate the resources required for a thorough examination of the contract documents prepared by the contracting authority and to comply with the requirements for completion of diagrams, enclosure of documentation, etc. to prevent that, for example, reservations have to be made in the tenders.

Experience shows that particularly in large and complex procedures suppliers use questions sessions or the negotiations in the negotiated procedure to point to elements of the contract documents which the contracting authority wishes to modify in whole or in part. This is possible within certain limits. The contracting authority can amplify the information specified in the contract documents concerning the proposed service, supply or works, cf. also section 6.1. The contracting authority can also specify the type of equipment that must be used. However, the contracting authority cannot change the essential features of the proposed service, supply or works without launching a new call for tenders. Case law shows that this limit is not easily reached.[4]

Often contracting authorities take a too optimistic view of own resources available for conducting a tender procedure. As a consequence, once the invitation to tender is published, the contracting authority may encounter practical problems in duly observing the time frame specified in the contract

---

4. Order of the Complaints Board of 18 November 1996, European Metro Group vs. Ørestadsselskabet.

documents. In such circumstances the contracting authority may postpone deadlines slightly, but does not have unlimited scope therefore. The reason is that certain potential suppliers may have selected not to apply for pre-qualification or to submit a tender in the light of the resources available to it before the stipulated deadline, cf. also section 3.2 on the importance of the deadline for submitting tenders. If other and later deadlines are then accepted under the procedure, these potential suppliers may with certain legitimacy be able to contend that the terms of the procurement are not in keeping with the principle of equal treatment. Contracting authorities must therefore be realistic when laying down the time frame for the conduct of a procurement procedure, and it is often the case that those contracting authorities that are sensible enough to realise this already when drafting the contract documents and allow plenty of time for the individual stages usually avoid postponing deadlines and, hence, avoid justified criticism.

2. Award criteria

It is the contracting authority which lays down the award criteria according to which the competition for the proposed contract is determined.

2.1 Economic criteria

Whether the contracting authority chooses the lowest price or the most economically advantageous tender as the main award criterion, there is no denying that the award criteria set out in the Directive are economic. In other words, in each procedure the contract is awarded on the basis of economic parameters. This is evident where the lowest price is chosen as the main award criterion, but the same is true where the main award criterion is the most economically advantageous tender despite the specification of sub-criteria. Overall, the contract is awarded to the tender which is most advantageous from an economic perspective.

In the contract notice the contracting authority must specify whether it has chosen the lowest price or the most economically advantageous tender as the main award criterion, cf. Article 36 of the Directive, cf. Annex VII. If the most economically advantageous tender is chosen as the main award criterion, the contracting authority must also specify, in the contract notice or alternatively in the contract documents, or in the competitive dialogue procedure in the descriptive document, the additional criteria for selecting the most economically advantageous tender (specifying the weighting given to each of them, or alternatively ranking them in order of importance), cf. Article 53, paragraph 2.

Generally award criteria must be objective, cf. chapter 4.2.2. This ensures compliance with the principles of transparency, non-discrimination and equal treatment and guarantees that the tenders are assessed and the contract awarded in conditions of effective competition, cf. recital 46 of the preamble to the Directive. The requirement for transparency necessitates that the main award criterion and, where this is the most economically advantageous tender, the sub-criteria be clearly specified. If the award criteria are not clear, submission of an advantageous tender depends on chance exclusively and it is not possible to evaluate the tenders objectively and fairly.[5]

All elements of the award criteria must be suitable for identifying the best tender. This means, first, that it must be possible to determine the relative merits of each sub-criterion in order of making them suitable for competion i.e. price, quality, service, etc. and, second, that the criteria must be determined in the light of the object of the contract. It is not surprising that the contract must be awarded on the basis of criteria which are determined in the light of the object of the contract as there are good reasons for not including irrelevant competitive parameters in the award decision. It follows that, collectively, the award criteria must be suitable for awarding the contract.

The requirements for clarity and objectivity are so restrictive that contracting authorities must be sure to use the exact wording of the Directive in specifying the chosen award criterion: either "the lowest price" or "the most economically advantageous tender". Case law has established that contracting authorities can use neither synonyms nor paraphrases.[6]

2.3 Choice between two criteria

Article 53, paragraph 1 of the Directive provides that the contracting authority must choose either "the most economically advantageous tender" or "the lowest price only".[7]

---

5. Order of the Complaints Board of 16 May 2000, Dansk Transport og Logistik vs. I/S Reno Syd in which the contracting authority was found to have violated the rules by stipulating that it would assess the tenders on the basis of an "overall evaluation" of an incomplete list of parameters.

6. Order of the Complaints Board of 2 May 2000, Uniqsoft 1998 ApS vs. Odense Local Authority in which the contracting authority was found to have violated procurement rules by specifying the award criterion as "the most advantageous solution".

7. Order of the Complaints Board of 23 September 2004, Sammenslutningen af Glatførebekæmpende Vognmænd i Nordjyllands Amt ApS vs. County of Nordjylland.

The contracting authorities are free to choose between these two main award criteria, whether the contract is for the purchase of supplies, services or works. As a main rule this choice is also available irrespective of the type of procedure chosen: open procedure, restricted procedure and negotiated procedure. By contrast, in the competitive dialogue procedure the contract can only be awarded on the basis of the most economically advantageous tender, cf. Article 29, paragraph 1 of the Directive. The choice is also available for electronic auctions, cf. Article 54 of the Directive.

If the contracting authority wishes to receive variants, it must choose the most economically advantageous tender as the main award criterion, cf. Article 24, paragraph 1 of the Directive.

Case law has established that Member States cannot require the contracting authorities to use "the lowest price only" as the only possible award criteria for certain contracts.[8]

2.4 The lowest price only

Where "the lowest price only" is chosen as the main award criterion, the proposed contract is awarded on the basis of one, and only one, competitive parameter; price. Other things being equal, this award procedure is, on the one hand, simpler to the contracting authorities than procedures based on the award criterion "the most economically advantageous tender", and tenderers, on the other hand, are left with a greater degree of certainty that the scope for discretion available to the contracting authority with respect to the sub-criteria linked to the most economically advantageous tender has no impact on the award.

In procedures where the lowest price is the main award criterion it is still possible to evaluate the price on the basis of various elements, such as the price itself, service, spare parts, etc. But the contracting authority cannot put a price on particular advantages of a tender and deduct this price from the price of the tender.[9]

However, the lowest price is usually only chosen as the main award criterion for contracts concerning products or services which are straightforward, or where the proposed supplies, service or works are indeed very thoroughly described in the contract documents and accompanied by various minimum requirements and contract terms. This guarantees the contracting authority the

8. Judgment of the European Court of Justice of 7 October 2004, case C-247/02, Sintesi SpA vs. Autorita per la Vigilanza Sui Lavori Pubblici.
9. Order of the Complaints Board of 13 May 2004, Bravida Danmark A/S vs. Rødovre Almennyttige Boligselskab (pursuant to the Danish Tender Act).

required level of quality, service, etc. stipulated by the contracting authority, for example corresponding to 7 out of 10, to the effect that any adjustments in price, quality, etc. only can be in upwards direction and effectively "for free" as the award is based entirely on price.

In quite a lot of procedures the contracting authority realises that it is rather difficult to create a competitive situation of any value on the basis of the main award criterion the most economically advantageous tender; either it proves impossible to determine other sub-criteria than price or there is no basis for quantifying the sub-criteria for which reason a true evaluation cannot be carried out. Where this is the situation, the contracting authority must usually choose the lowest price as the main award criterion. The example shows how important it is that the contracting authority has given full consideration to the award stage before advertising the call for tenders.

Where the sole basis for the award of a contract is the price, the pricing of reservations become pivotal. This too requires that the contracting authority specify, for example, which elements cannot be made subject to reservations to ensure the broadest possible basis for comparing the tenders submitted.[10] See also section 4.3.

2.5 The tender most advantageous to the contracting authority

Where the contracting authority chooses the most economically advantageous tender as the main award criterion, the award of the proposed contract must be based on "various criteria" determined by the contracting authority and linked to the object of the contract, cf. Article 53, paragraph 1 (a) of the Directive. By choosing the most economically advantageous tender the contracting authority has a much wider basis on which to evaluate the tenders. Although the Directive does not expressly prohibit that price be chosen as the sole sub-criterion to identify the most economically advantageous tender, the wording of Article 53, paragraph 1 (a) that "various criteria" be determined seems to indicate that this is not possible. If price is nevertheless chosen as the only sub-criterion, use of the competitive dialogue procedure and admission of variants are probably precluded. Price must be, and is in practice

---

10. Order of the Complaints Board of 8 August 2000, Visma Logistics ASA vs. County of Copenhagen; order of the Complaints Board of 24 October 2001, Eiland Electric A/S vs. County of Vestsjælland concerning the price of reservations with respect to daily penalties; order of the Complaints Board of 12 August 2003, Skanska Danmark A/S vs. Vejle Local Authority in which it was established that a contracting authority must not place a tenderer which has priced reservations in a better position than tenderers which have not made reservations.

without exception, included as one of several sub-criteria. Sub-criteria must be specified.[11]

Article 53, paragraph 1 is supplemented by recital 46 to the Directive requiring the contracting authorities to describe in clear terms the sub-criteria it has chosen to identify the most economically advantageous tender. It is further stressed that the sub-criteria must be linked to the object of the contract allowing the level of performance offered by each tender to be assessed in the light of the object of the contract as defined in the technical specifications and the value for money of each tender to be measured. In other words, the sub-criteria chosen must be objective.

Where the contracting authority has chosen the most economically advantageous tender as the main award criterion and specified various sub-criteria for the identification thereof, the contracting authority is obviously required to evaluate the tenders on the basis of these sub-criteria. To this end the contracting authority should carefully consider which documentation is needed with respect to each sub-criteria in order to be able to evaluate the tenders.

2.6 Sub-criteria[12]

As mentioned above, the sub-criteria must be linked to the object of the contract and be objective. The Directive does not stipulate a minimum or maximum number of sub-criteria. In practice, an often staggering number of sub-criteria[13] are often specified, sometimes as secondary requirements to the individual sub-criterion.

The sub-criteria must be described in clear terms so that tenderers know the standard by which they will be measured. Obviously, sub-criteria other than those specified in the contract documents cannot be taken into consideration in the evaluation.[14] Furthermore, sub-criteria must be unequivocal and, consequently, expressions such as "overall impression", "contracting

11. Order of the Complaints Board of 10 March 2004, Brd. Thybo A/S vs. Arbejdernes Andelsboligforening af 1938. The Complaints Board declared a procedure under the Tender Act void because the contracting entity had not specified sub-criteria despite having chosen "the most economically advantageous tender" as the award criterion.
12. See also chapter 4.4, in particular 4.4.5 on non-economic criteria.
13. Order of the Complaints Board of 4 November 2003, Bombardier Transportation A/S vs. Lokalbanen I/S, 26 sub-criteria.
14. Order of the Complaints Board of 6 May 2004, Sereno Nordic A/S vs. County of Vejle.

authority's discretion", etc. cannot be used.[15] It is the predominant main rule that sub-criteria must be objective to ensure that the evaluation of the tenders on the basis of the sub-criteria is not left to the unlimited discretion of the contracting authority. Finally, the sub-criteria must be clear.[16]

The contracting authority cannot merely state that it has chosen the most economically advantageous tender as the award criterion. Despite the list of acceptable sub-criteria in Article 53, paragraph 1 (a), the exact sub-criteria must be communicated to the tenderers in writing in the contract docu-ments.[17] Occasionally in procedures where various sub-criteria have been determined in order to identify the most economically advantageous tender, despite the contracting authority's reasonable efforts to specify the individual sub-criteria, it may be necessary to expand on these criteria by providing for additional technical evaluations. In such a situation the contracting authority walks a tightrope in trying to ensure that only elements inherent in the chosen sub-criteria are taken into consideration. If a specialist external firm is hired to carry out these evaluations, the contracting authority will be less exposed to criticism.[18]

It goes without saying that the contracting authority must analyse the sub-criteria consistently throughout the procedure and thus also when evaluating the tenders. If a contracting authority realises that one of the specified sub-criteria is unlawful, it can probably continue the procedure by sending out a corrective statement without cancelling and reopening the procedure. How-ever, the contracting authority should be cautious, and it is probably only possible if the concerning sub-criterion is to be given a low weighting and is not essential. If subsequent review procedures conclude that a sub-criterion is unlawful, the contracting authority will not be able to continue the procedure, but must cancel it.[19]

---

15. Order of the Complaints Board of 9 July 2004, H.O. Service A/S vs. Boligforenin-gen 32 (concerned the Danish Tender Act).
16. Order of the Complaints Board of 21 June 2004, Banverket vs. Nordjydske Jernba-ner A/S.
17. Judgment of the European Court of Justice of 26 September 2002, case C-225/98 Calais, a general reference to the French law on public contracts was held to be a violation of the previous Works Directive with respect to award parameters.
18. Judgment of the European Court of Justice of 18 October 2001, case C-19/00 SIAC Construction.
19. Judgment of the European Court of Justice of 4 December 2003, case C-448/01 EVN AG vs. Austria: "Community legislation on public procurement requires the contracting authority to cancel an invitation to tender where it transpires in review proceedings under Article 1 of Directive 89/665 that a decision relating to one of the

Article 53, paragraph 1 (a) of the Directive sets out a non-exhaustive list of sub-criteria; quality, price, technical merit, aesthetic and functional characteristics, environmental characteristics, running costs, cost-effectiveness, after-sales service and technical assistance, delivery date and delivery period or period of completion.[20]

The most important award criteria are price and quality.

Whereas, in particular, the sub-criterion price is straightforward and indisputably objective, a sub-criterion such as aesthetics is a lot more difficult to assess, and the contract documents must set out secondary criteria for evaluating the aesthetic characteristics to ensure that the evaluation is not performed discretionarily. The same is true of a sub-criterion such as design that may involve functional characteristics as well as individual taste. Also with respect to this criterion is it necessary to stipulate secondary criteria for the evaluation to prevent that it is made on a discretionary basis.

Historically, the use of environmental characteristics as sub-criteria, as described in detail in chapter 4.4, has given rise to much uncertainty. This is because many obvious, and from a social perspective sensible, environmental requirements have been hard to reconcile with the requirement for coherence with the object of the contract. They are, moreover, likely to increase the price of the tender and as such cannot be said to contribute in identifying the most economically advantageous tender. Against that background, compliance with specific environmental requirements has often and legitimately been specified as minimum requirements in the contract documents, or in any case in the contract.

Since environmental characteristics are now specified as a lawful award criterion in Article 53, paragraph 1(a) of the Directive, environmental considerations can be taken into account in procurement procedures. However, as stated in recital 46 of the preamble to the Directive, it is a requirement that the criteria allow the tenders to be compared and assessed objectively, which in practice translates into a specification, in the contract documents, of the environmental characteristics providing tenderers with exact information on the parameters used for assessing the environmental characteristics. A sub-criterion may for example be used to lay down criteria for the protection of the environment by requiring the use of certain types of engines or particle

---

award criteria laid down by that authority is unlawful and it is therefore annulled by the review body."

20. Recital 46 of the preamble to the Directive provides that sub-criteria may be in the form of social requirements, cf. chapter 4.4.

filters for lorries (emission and noise requirements).[21] Moreover, such environmental criteria can be specified even where the contracting authority knows in advance that certain potential tenderers will not be able to submit tenders without changing or replacing their equipment. A sub-criterion requiring the supply of electricity produced from renewable sources of energy is lawful.[22]

Requirements for health and safety at work are usually stipulated by law, but health and safety requirement which are bound up with the proposed supplies, service or works can also lawfully be used as sub-criteria.[23]

The above provisions on environmental requirements are also true of social requirements. Hence, social requirements too can be used as sub-criteria. Recital 46 of the preamble to the Directive provides that social requirements aiming to meet needs of, in particular, disadvantaged groups of people can be used.

In the light of the basic aim of identifying the most economically advantageous tender and that the sub-criteria must be linked to the object of the proposed contract, environmental and social requirements can probably only be given a certain maximum weighting. It seems unlikely that environmental and social requirements and any other non-economic criteria can be given an aggregate weighting of more than 50 %.

2.7 Weighting and order of importance

Where the contracting authority has chosen the most economically advantageous tender as the main award criterion and determined the sub-criteria to be used for identifying this tender, the contracting authority must advertise the relative weighting given to each sub-criterion, cf. Article 53, paragraph 2, first indent of the Directive, for example price 60 %, quality 30 % and environmental characteristics 10 %. This obligation to give weightings to sub-criteria is logical and necessary for the compliance with the principles of equal treatment and transparency; if after having opened the tenders the contracting authority, at its discretion, were allowed to change or at that point in time indicate the weightings given, it would impact decisively on which tenderer would be awarded the contract. The tenderer must be informed of the

---

21. Judgment of the European Court of Justice of 17 September 2002, case C-513/1999 Concordia Bus Finland OY.
22. Judgment of the European Court of Justice of 4 December 2003, case C-448/01 Engvag vs. Austria.
23. Order of the Complaints Board of 27 September 2000, Svend B. Thomsen vs. Blåvandshuk Local Authority.

weightings given to the individual sub-criterion so that they may prepare their tenders in accordance therewith.

In principle a contracting authority can give a sub-criterion whatever weighting it chooses; in the above example price might as well have been given a weighting of 40%, quality 40% and environmental characteristics 20 %. As mentioned, it is essential that the tenderers are informed of the weightings when the chosen sub-criteria are advertised, see also recital 46 of the preamble to the Directive.

In procedures where the contracting authority specifies relatively many sub-criteria, the relative weightings impact significantly on the award of the contract. In such procedures it may often work to the advantage of the contracting authority to stipulate minimum requirements in alternative to the award criteria with the lowest weightings and instead specify fewer sub-criteria which often intensifies competition and definitely makes the evaluation easier.

Article 53, paragraph 2, second indent of the Directive provides that the weightings can be expressed by providing for a range with an appropriate maximum spread. At first glance, this provision is surprising in view of the importance of weightings for the award of the contract and in view of the fact that the weightings must be determined at the latest at the time of the evaluation. Therefore, presumably the range within which the weightings can be expressed must be relatively narrow. Weightings expressed within a range are probably used most appropriately for the award of contracts that require a certain degree of flexibility because of their complexity or unforeseen proposals for solutions.

Only in exceptional cases can the contracting authority omit giving weightings to the sub-criteria chosen. Weighting can only be omitted in cases where the contracting authority is able to demonstrate that it is not possible. It is for the contracting authority to prove that this is the case. The above-mentioned possibility for expressing relative weightings within a range, cf. Article 53, paragraph 2, second indent of the Directive, limits the cases in which the contracting authority can justify not giving weightings to sub-criteria. If the contracting authority can demonstrate that weighting is not possible, it must instead list the sub-criteria in descending order of importance. This serves to ensure a degree of transparency, with respect to which elements will be stressed in the evaluation, which allows the tenderers some opportunity for taking this into account in their tenders. Ranking of sub-criteria is more useful when the number of sub-criteria is small, than when it is large. From a practical point of view it does not seem feasible that a very large number of sub-criteria are equally important and, therefore, the contracting authority must list them in order of importance.[24] Failure to rank or ill-considered ranking may in theory lead to absurd evaluation results. If price, for example, is ranked low, the contracting authority must be prepared to pay an excessive price for quality and service given a high ranking.[25]

Where weighting is not possible, the contracting authority must pay special attention to the order in which the sub-criteria are listed in the contract documents. For example, where the object of the contract is described in much detail in the contract documents, presumably criteria concerning functionality and aesthetics cannot be given a high ranking. If this is nevertheless the case, the contracting authority must ensure that this ranking is clear to all tenderers.[26]

2.8 Sub-criteria vis-à-vis selection criteria

Whereas selection criteria are chosen and used to identify qualified tenderers, sub-criteria in procedures where the award criterion is the most economically advantageous tender are used to assess and compare the competitiveness of the tenders. As a consequence, the sub-criteria have no bearing upon the suitability of the tenderers, for example in the form of references concerning work of a similar character. The sub-criteria must provide a basis for comparing the tenders submitted.

Much EU and Danish case law shows that contracting authorities often mix up selection and award criteria and thus do not comply with their obligations under procurement law.[27]

---

24. Order of the Complaints Board of 4 November 2003, Bombardier Transportation vs. Lokalbanen A/S, in which the contracting authority was criticised for not having listed 26 sub-criteria in order of importance.
25. Order of the Complaints Board of 9 August 2002, Kommuners Revision vs. National Labour Market Authority.
26. Order of the Complaints Board of 11 March 2005, MT Højgaard A/S vs. Frederiksberg Boligfond.
27. Judgment of the European Court of Justice of 19 June 2003, case C-315/01 GAT vs. Österreichische Autobahnen Und Schnellstrassen AG; judgment of the European Court of Justice of 20 September 1988, case 31/87, G. Beentjes vs. the Netherlands; order of the Complaints Board of 23 January 1996, Danish Council of Practising Architects vs. Glostrup Local Authority; order of the Complaints Board of 30 May 1996, A/S Iver Pedersen vs. I/S Reno Syd; order of the Complaints Board of 14 September 1998, Danish Chamber of Commerce vs. Statistics Denmark; order of the Complaints Board of 1 March 1999, Enemærke og Petersen A/S vs. Fællesorganisationens Boligforening, Slagelse; order of the Complaints Board of 16 July 1999, Vognmandsforretning Holst Sørensen vs. I/S Affaldsselskabet Vendsyssel Øst; order

2.9 Evaluation models and points allocation

Concurrently with the relative weighting of the chosen sub-criteria, the contracting authority must also lay down a system for allocating points that will enable it to evaluate and, hence, rank the individual tenders within each sub-criteria. Such a system is necessary as it is evident that the relative weighting cannot be used for allocating points. The contracting authority may for example use a scale of 0 to 10 to evaluate the individual tenders on the basis of each sub-criterion. Having assessed the individual tender on the basis of each sub-criterion, the point given to it is multiplied by the weighting of the sub-criterion. The figures are then added together and the weighted scores of each tender are compared. If the contracting authority chooses to use a scale of 1 to 5 or a scale of 0 to 15, instead of the scale of 0 to 10, the final evaluation of the tenders is often somewhat different and may therefore be decisive of the award of the contract. It thus follows that the system for allocating points must be objective and the individual points must be described. In practice, contracting authorities sometimes choose to define a model tender with points allocated to each sub-criterion. Such models may contain non-linear scales for allocating points depending on whether the tenders are superior or inferior to the model tender.

The chosen sub-criteria and the relative weighting given to each of them must be respected. Therefore, the systems for allocating points must be set up and used in compliance therewith. It is a violation of the principle of equal treatment and the principle of transparency if the actual effect of the system is that the sub-criteria are weighted differently than advertised by the contracting authority in the contract notice or contract documents. From case law there are a number of examples of contracting authorities which, inadvertently or as a result of loss of control, have set up and used systems the actual effect of which was a different weighting than the one that should have been used.[28]

of the Complaints Board of 28 December 1999, Skjortegrossisten vs. Post Danmark A/S; order of the Complaints Board of 2 May 2000, Uniqsoft 1998 ApS vs. Odense Local Authority; order of the Complaints Board of 23 February 2001, Kæmpes Taxi and Nordfyns busser vs. Søndersø Local Authority; order of the Complaints Board of 11 March 2005, MT Højgaard A/S vs. Frederiksberg Boligfond (use of "project organisation" as a sub-criterion not allowed).

28. Order of the Complaints Board of 10 February 1997, Dafeta Trans ApS vs. Lynettefællesskabet I/S; order of the Complaints Board of 29 October 1997, Esbjerg Renovationsselskab vs. Rødding Local Authority; order of the Complaints Board of 28 December 1999, Skjortegrossisten vs. Post Danmark; order of the Complaints Board of 24 October 2001, Eiland Electric A/S vs. County of Vestsjælland; order of the Complaints Board of 2 March 2005, Pumpex A/S vs. Hedensted Local Au-

If a contracting authority has specified and advertised an evaluation model in the contract documents, it is required to use this evaluation model. If it turns out that the evaluation model creates unforeseen problems, the contracting authority must cancel the procedure. By contrast, if the contracting authority, before or after receipt of the tenders, works out an evaluation model which is not disclosed to the tenderers, the contracting authority may choose not to use this evaluation model if it turns out that use thereof would result in either unequal treatment of the tenderers or an evaluation which is objectively unacceptable to the contracting authority. In that case the contracting authority may conduct the procedure either by using a different evaluation model or without using an evaluation model at all.[29]

Furthermore, in connection with the actual allocation of points the contracting authority should not modify the system or give scores which are outside the chosen scales.[30]

Where works contracts are put out to tender, both as specialist subcontracts and as one turnkey contract, the contracting authority must evaluate the tenders as they are submitted if the contracting authority has not provided for other measures in the contract documents. If the contracting authority wishes to include its own additional costs of awarding various specialist subcontracts, instead of one turnkey contract, in the evaluation, it must specify this in the contract documents.[31]

3. Submission and receipt of tenders

The submission and receipt of tenders must also meet certain requirements as to form.

thority (the effect of the chosen evaluation model was that even very large differences in the price of the tenders, which had been given a weighting of 40%, was cancelled out by relatively small differences in the other sub-criteria, pursuant to the Tender Act).

29. Order of the Complaints Board of 13 January 2004, E. Pihl & Søn A/S vs. Hadsund Local Authority.
30. Order of the Complaints Board of 30 September 2004, Colas Danmark A/S vs. Videbæk Local Authority.
31. Order of the Complaints Board of 30 November 2004, mason Finn F. Hansen vs. Boligselskabet Vendersbo (pursuant to the Tender Act).

3.1 Submission of tenders – means of transmission

In the contract documents the contracting authority must specify whether tenders should be transmitted by post, by fax or by electronic means, cf. Article 42, paragraph 5 of the Directive, cf. paragraph 1. It thus follows that tenders must be submitted in writing. The contracting authority is free to choose the means of written communication. However, Article 42, paragraph 2 of the Directive provides that the chosen means of communication must be generally available and thus not restrict potential tenderers' access to the tendering procedure. Often the contracting authority encloses a bid schedule with the contract documents. These are forms with pre-printed text describing the chosen award criterion and with boxes to be filled, possibly with room for additional text, which the tenderers can or often must use. Usually the contracting authority requires a certain number of copies of the tender.

The contracting authority may specify that various means of communication be used in a certain order for the submission of tenders. In numerous procedures the use of electronic means may be worthwhile, notably in those procedures where the tenderers are required to review and complete very detailed bid schedules. Obviously, the contracting authority can stipulate that it will not accept handwritten tenders.

If the contracting authority chooses to receive the tenders electronically, Article 42, paragraph 5 specifically provides that the information regarding the specifications necessary for the electronic submission of tenders, including encryption, must be available to the tenderers. Furthermore, devices for the electronic receipt of tenders must conform to the requirements of Annex X to the Directive. These requirements prescribe that electronic signatures must comply with national provisions on electronic signatures, that it must be possible to determine precisely the exact time and date of the receipt of tenders and that it must be ensured that no-one can access the data transmitted to the contracting authority before the expiry of the time-limit for submitting tenders.[32]

If a submitted tender does not comply with the specifications stipulated by the contracting authority with respect to means, use of bid schedules, language or otherwise, the contracting authority can and must reject the tender.

The procedure for transmitting tenders should be thoroughly described in the contract documents. The division and person to whom the tender should be addressed, that the tender should be forwarded in a sealed envelope and

---

32. The rules set out in Article 54 apply to electronic auctions. The rules set out in Article 42 also apply to design contests, cf. Article 71 of the Directive.

how the envelope should be labelled should be clearly specified. For reasons of confidentiality and the timing of the opening of tenders, etc., tenders should only be transmitted by fax in exceptional cases.

3.2 Significance of deadlines and effect of opening

The contracting authority must specify the final date and time for receipt of tenders. In open procedures the final date for submitting tenders must be stipulated in the contract notice, cf. Article 36 of the Directive, cf. Annex VII, points 12 (a) and 13. In the restricted procedure, negotiated procedure and the competitive dialogue procedure the date, time and place for receipt and opening of tenders are set out in the contract documents.

In the open procedure the persons authorised to be present at the opening of tenders must be named; in order to guarantee that tenders as well as the identity and number of tenderers are kept confidential, tenderers should not be included among them.[33] Case law has established that in the open procedure the contracting authority must fill out the relevant box of the contract notice with the names of the persons who are authorised to be present and cannot omit to do so on grounds that either everybody or nobody besides the contracting authority itself is authorised to be present at the opening of tenders.

The contracting authority opens the tenders submitted at the expiry of the deadline for receipt of tenders. The contracting authority should draw up a list of tenders submitted and the identity of tenderers. Only tenders received within the time stated can and must be evaluated. To ensure compliance with the principle of equal treatment and for reasons of general administrative law, even a delay of only a few minutes in submitting an entire or parts of a tender must lead to its rejection.[34] Also in the negotiated procedure where each tenderer often submits more than one tender, the deadlines for submitting tenders, as specified by the contracting authority, must be observed. If they are not, the tenders must be rejected.

After the final date for receipt of tenders, the tenders become fixed. In the open procedure and the restricted procedure changes cannot be made to the tenders after this time. The same is true of tenders having been submitted in the competitive dialogue procedure. Having received the tenders, the contracting authority is entitled and obliged to review all tenders submitted

---

33. Pursuant to section 7 of the Danish Tender Act tenderers are entitled to be present at the opening of tenders.
34. Order of the Complaints Board of 21 November 2003, Entreprenørfirmaet Harry Andersen & Søn A/S vs. Vejle Local Authority.

timely in order to verify the conformity of the tenders and evaluate them subsequently.

The mere observance of the deadline may act as a competitive parameter, in particular in large and complex procedures where the tenderers must review countless contract documents, etc. and obtain and calculate prices before submitting their tenders. Advertised deadlines can only be postponed for objective reasons since several potential tenderers may have opted not to request pre-qualification or not to participate in the procedure because they believed it would have been impossible for them to prepare a satisfactory tender before the original final date. In practice, this means that only circumstances which in no way whatsoever are related to the affairs of the tenderers can justify an extension of the time for submitting tenders. An extension of the time for reasons of, for example, a considerably improved competition because more tenderers would be able to participate is likely to be a violation of the principle of equal treatment.

In the negotiated procedure in which more tenders are often submitted, compliance with the principle of equal treatment must be ensured also with respect to subsequent deadlines for submitting tenders. As a consequence, all tenderers that participate in a negotiated procedure must be granted the same deadlines. Furthermore, the confidentiality obligations that must be observed in connection with the first tender must also be observed in connection with the second tender, the third tender, etc. Case law seems to have established compliance with the principle of equal treatment if all tenderers are allowed the same time even where this does not lead to the same final date for all tenderers.[35]

The tenderers cannot provide additional information to the tenders after the final date.[36]

If the contracting authority submits own tenders, it too must observe the deadline.

Normally, the final date for the submission of tenders coincides with the start of the tender validity period stipulated by the contracting authority, usually 3 to 6 months.

---

35. Order of the Complaints Board of 18 November 1996, European Metro Group vs. Ørestadsselskabet I/S.
36. Judgment of the European Court of Justice of 25 April 1996, case C-87/94 Commission vs. Belgium concerning Société Regionale Wallonne du Transport.

3.3 Confidentiality of tenders

Contracting authorities must ensure that tenders are kept and treated confidentially, cf. Article 6 of the Directive. The provision expressly stipulates that the contracting authority must not disclose information which the tenderers have forwarded to it and designated as confidential. This is particularly the case with respect to technical and trade secrets and "confidential aspects" of tenders.

A whole new dimension is added to the confidentiality obligation in the very large procedures where large consultancy firms are employed to advise, justly or unjustly, either several tenderers or a tenderer and the contracting authority, see also chapter 6. In these procedures the contracting authority is required to have laid down in advance detailed procedures for observing the confidentiality necessary.

4. Rejection of tenders

In a number of situations the contracting authority is either entitled or obliged to reject tenders submitted. These situations are examined below. Further, the contracting authority may be obliged to adjust tenders submitted in order of being able to evaluate them.

4.1 Abnormally low tenders

Article 55 of the Directive contains a provision on abnormally low tenders. As a first point it must be emphasised that contracting authorities are never obliged, but only entitled to reject tenders that appear to be abnormally low. Rejection may be in the interest of the contracting authority taking into account the uncertainty connected to the performance by a supplier which has offered a price that is considerably lower than the market price, or in any event, a price which is lower than the costs of the performance.

Where a contracting authority, for such reasons, wishes to reject a tender that seems abnormally low, it must follow the procedure set out in Article 55 of the Directive. The Article provides that the contracting authority request, in writing, details on the constituent elements of the tender. These details may relate in particular to methods chosen, exceptionally favourable conditions for the execution of the work or supply of the service and the originality of the work, supplies or services proposed. In other words, before rejecting a tender that appears to be abnormally low, the contracting authority must consult the tenderer. Where the tenderer is able to prove that it will not suffer a loss if it is awarded the proposed contract, there does not seem to be a basis on which the contracting authority can reject the tender on the ground that it is abnormally low and therefore more favourable to the contracting authority than envisaged feasible at the launch of the procurement procedure.

Cases concerning abnormally low tenders are surprisingly numerous involving tenders submitted by suppliers as well as tenders submitted by the contracting authority itself.[37]

Case law has established that whereas contracting authorities may use predetermined methods of calculation for classifying tenders as abnormally low, they should be allowed to revise such calculations if it turns out that they were too pessimistic about the possibilities for receiving economically favourable tenders. In order to be able to evaluate whether the tenders are abnormally low the contracting authority may require, in the contract documents, that the individual prices be accounted for and broken down into prices for the individual constituent elements, and the calculations specified, to give the contracting authority an idea of how the offered price was arrived at. Although such requirements are specified in the contract documents, the contracting authority must nevertheless request information from the tenderer before rejecting its tender, cf. Article 55 of the Directive. A tender may also be rejected if the price thereof is not satisfactorily accounted for.

4.2 Irregular tenders

A contracting authority is always entitled to reject tenders which deviate from the contracting authority's invitation to tender, irrespective of the extent and nature of the deviation and whether it is designated "reservation" and may be priced.[38] If it is a fundamental element of the contract that deviates from the contracting authority's specifications, the contracting authority is obliged to

---

37. Order of the Complaints Board of 8 March 1999, Danish Association of Consulting Engineers vs. Nykøbing Falster Local Authority; order of the Complaints Board of 30 January 2001, DTL vs. Haderslev Local Authority; judgment of the European Court of Justice of 22 June 1989, case C-103/88 Fratelli Costanzo Spa vs. Comune de Milano; judgment of the European Court of Justice of 16 October 1997, case C-304/96 Hera Spa vs. Unita Sanitaria Locale; judgment of the European Court of Justice of 27 November 2001, cases C-285/99 and C-286/99 Impresa Lombardini vs. ANAS; order of the Complaints Board of 9 March 1999, Technicomm A/S vs. DSB.
38. Order of the Complaints Board of 29 April 2003, Lindpro A/S vs. Jørgen Mortensen & Sønner ApS.

reject the tender. In *Visma Logistics ASA*[39] the Complaints Board made the following statement in regard to irregular tenders:

"… it makes no difference whether or not the deviation is termed a reservation. If a deviation concerns one or several basic elements, the EU principle of equality dictates that the contracting authority is obliged not to consider the tender in question. If a deviation does not concern a basic element, the contracting authority has the right – but no obligation – to consider the tender, which means that the contracting authority does not violate the principle of equality by not considering the tender, but that – on the other hand – the contracting authority does not violate the principle of equality either if it chooses to consider the tender."

Where the contracting authority has laid down specific requirements for the drafting of the tenders, non-compliance with such requirements is essentially in the nature of a deviation from fundamental aspects and, hence, the contracting authority is obliged to reject such tenders.[40]

If the contracting authority decides not to reject an irregular tender, the deviation must be priced. See section 7.4.3 below on pricing.

Only in procedures where variants are permitted, can the tenderers submit tenders that deviate materially from the invitation to tender. Variants are discussed below in section 7.5.

Tenders that do not conform to the fundamental requirements set out in the specifications in the contract documents must be rejected.[41]

Direct or indirect reservations made by the tenderer in its tender may make a tender irregular. Reservations are examined below in section 7.4.3.

4.3 Reservations

As often as not tenderers make reservations with respect to one or more aspects of the contract documents. Reservations may concern everything from compliance with the minimum requirements stipulated in the technical specifications to acceptance of the contracting authority's draft contract. In this context it does not matter whether the tenderer designates a deviation from

---

39. Order of the Complaints Board of 8 August 2000, Visma Logistics ASA vs. County of Copenhagen.
40. Order of the Complaints Board of 7 June 2004, A/S Analyccen vs. County of Vestsjælland.
41. Order of the Complaints Board of 20 February 2004, Miri Stål A/S vs. Esbjerg Local Authority, establishing that specifications were to be taken literally; order of the Complaints Board of 2 September 2004, BN Produkter Danmark A/S vs. Odense Renovationsselskab A/S, establishing that the contracting authority should have rejected tenders that were not accompanied by the required documentation.

the contract documents a "reservation". The contracting authority may regard all deviations which are not expressly permitted in the contract documents as irregular with the implication that the tender may be rejected.

Tenderers often formulate the compliance with certain aspects of the contract documents somewhat cryptically/vaguely. Contracting authorities should pay heed to such wordings in tenders in which the tenderers have not commented directly on specific parts of the contract documents, since they often conceal reservations on the part of the tenderers. It is for the tenderer to make sure that the wording of the tender is clear and unambiguous and where this is not the case, the contracting authority may regard it as a reservation that may lead to the tender being rejected.[42]

Overall, it is thus clear in which situations the contracting authority is *entitled* to reject tenders as irregular. It is more interesting to identify the situations in which the contracting authority is *obliged* to reject a tender. As mentioned above, it is ultimately determined by whether the deviation/reservation relates to a so-called "fundamental aspect" of the contract documents.

A fundamental aspect is an element that may have a significant impact on the competition. It may, however, be exceedingly difficult to determine whether a specific reservation will have such an impact.[43] Presumably, the tenderer would not have submitted a tender or would have submitted a tender of a higher price had it not made the relevant reservation. In both instances the competition is clearly and significantly affected. At any rate, all reservations concerning the price stipulated and reservations generally requiring that the tenderer's terms of delivery be applied should be regarded as reservations with respect to fundamental aspects. The same is true of wordings the scope of which, in significant areas, is uncertain. By contrast, if the wording of the contract documents is unclear, any reservations with respect thereto cannot be deemed to constitute reservations with respect to fundamental aspects and in

---

42. Judgment of the Eastern High Court of 7 December 2004, case B-156803, 8th division, Lindpro A/S vs. Jørgen Mortensen og Sønner ApS (pursuant to the Tender Act).
43. Order of the Complaints Board of 26 August 2004, Per Aarsleff A/S vs. Amager Strandpark I/S, in which a reservation concerning preparations for winter was held to be a deviation from fundamental aspects of the contract documents, whereas a reservation with respect to price adjustment of works to be carried out more than 12 months after the date of the tender was not held to be such a deviation. Order of the complaints board of 26 November 2004, E. Pihl & Søn A/S vs. Danish Prison and Probation Service in which a reservation concerning the time schedule was held to concern a fundamental aspect.

such circumstances the contracting authority is not entitled to reject a tender which includes reservations.[44]

In several cases the Complaints Board has found that the number of minor deviations and reservations in aggregate affect the competition to an extent that forces the contracting authority to reject the tender. In *Visma Logistics ASA*[45] the Complaints Board made the following statement in regard to cumulative reservations and deviations:

"Several non-basic elements in a tender may – in the circumstances – together make up a basic element, which means that the contracting authority is obliged not to consider tenders that deviate from them all. It is a prerequisite that reservations and deviations concerned can be characterised as actual deviations from the tender."

As mentioned, where a reservation concerns fundamental aspects, the contracting authority is obliged to reject the tender. Failure to do so is a manifest violation of the principle of equal treatment and may lead to cancellation of the entire procedure.

Where a tender deviates from a non-fundamental aspect of the contract documents (and only in such cases), the contracting authority can, as an alternative to rejection, choose to put a price on the deviation. In *Skanska Danmark A/S*,[46] which was decided pursuant to the Danish Tender Act, the Complaints Board made the following statement in regard to pricing:

"... the pricing of reservations must be made in such a way that the tenderer who made reservations is not thus placed in a better position than tenderers who have not made reservations. The Complaints Board added the following comment: a) Pricing must be made in such a way as to make it certain that the work which the priced reservation concerns can be carried out for the priced amount. If such reliable pricing is not possible, the contracting authority must not consider the tender in question. b) Pricing must be made on the basis of the information contained in the contract documents and may not be made on the basis of any knowledge that the contracting authority may have to the effect that the scope of the work will be smaller than that stated in the contract documents, since a tenderer who has made reservations would otherwise be placed in a better position than the tenderer who has

---

44. Order of the Complaints Board of 26 November 2004, E. Pihl & Søn A/S vs. Danish Prison and Probation Service; the provisions in the contract documents on preparations for winter were unclear for which reason the tenderer's reservations with respect to preparations for winter were not deemed to concern fundamental aspects and warrant rejection.
45. Order of the Complaints Board of 8 August 2000, Visma Logistics ASA vs. County of Copenhagen.
46. Order of the Complaints Board of 12 August 2003, Skanska Danmark A/S vs. Vejle Local Authority.

not made reservations, and who has thus had to include the work in question in his tender in accordance with the information contained in the contract documents."

It is important to be aware that when the contracting authority puts a price on a reservation, it is not to protect the interests of the tenderer that submitted the reservation, but instead to protect the interests of the other tenderers in accordance with the principle of equal treatment.[47]

The contracting authority cannot omit to price reservations, not even standard reservations which are normally waived when the contract is concluded.[48]

The pricing should be determined on an objective and transparent basis not taking into account the information provided by the tenderer in the tender on for example hourly price of extra work since the tenderer cannot with any certainty say that it will be able to maintain the prices stipulated. This also applies to works with respect to which the tenderer has made reservations. The pricing must be genuine and enable a comparison of the tenders submitted.[49]

Obviously, the contracting authority can omit to price reservations made by all tenderers as the reservations will not affect the competition.[50]

It is not uncommon that the contracting authority, in the contract documents, specifies which reservations it will accept and which reservations, typically concerning price and delivery terms, it will not accept and which will, therefore, lead to rejection of the tender.

In *Forlaget Magnus A/S*[51] the contracting authority had stipulated that it would accept reservations with respect to all provisions of the draft contract. The Complaints Board found that this was contrary to the procurement rules as it had the effect of rendering unclear what was offered for tender.

Incidentally, it is not possible to price all reservations. For example, how does a contracting authority price a reservation that a time limit might be slightly

---

47. Order of the Complaints Board of 15 August 2003, Bravida Danmark A/S vs. Statens Forsknings- og Uddannelsesbygninger.
48. Order of the Complaints Board of 9 June 2004, Per Aarsleff A/S vs. County of Funen and Odense Local Authority.
49. Order of the Complaints Board of 26 August 2004, Per Aarsleff A/S vs. Amager Strandpark I/S (concerning pricing of reservations with respect to preparations for winter, which were otherwise deemed to constitute a deviation from fundamental aspects of the contract documents to the effect that the tender should be rejected).
50. Order of the Complaints Board of 8 November 2000, H. Friedmann og Søn A/S vs. Ministry of Research and Information Technology.
51. Order of the Complaints Board of 2 May 2001, Forlaget Magnus A/S vs. Customs and Tax Authority.

exceeded? As a rule, such a tender must be rejected. For clarification of technical matters after the award decision see section 6.1 below.

Indeed because tenders are subject to negotiations in the negotiated procedure, reservations may be made with respect to all provisions of the contract documents, draft contract, etc.[52] However, if the contracting authority expressly states that certain reservations are not accepted, failure to comply with such statement, will lead to rejection of the tender, even in the negotiated procedure.[53]

5. Variants

Basically, a tender must comply with all the requirements specified in the contract documents. However, in procedures where the award criterion is the most economically advantageous tender, Article 24, paragraph 1 of the Directive provides that the contracting authority can authorise the submission of so-called "variants".

It follows from Article 24, paragraph 2 of the Directive that the contracting authority must indicate in the contract notice whether or not variants are authorised. If variants are authorised, the contracting must specify, in the contract documents, the minimum requirements to be met by the variants.[54]

If the contracting authority, due to an error, has not expressly authorised the submission of variants in the contract notice, it can only take such tenders into consideration if it has specified minimum requirements.[55]

In procedures where variants are not authorised, tenderers can only submit one tender. Furthermore, in procedures where variants are authorised, a tenderer's submission of both an ordinary tender and a variant is conditional on an express authority to this effect in the contract documents.

See also chapter 4.3.5 for more details about variants.

---

52. Order of the Complaints Board of 18 November 1996, European Metro Group vs. Øresundsselskabet I/S
53. Order of Complaints Board 4 November 2003, Bombardier Transportation A/S vs. Lokalbanen I/S
54. Order of the Complaints Board of 18 November 1996, European Metro Group vs. I/S Ørestadsselskabet and order of the Complaints Board of 21 June 2004, Banverket vs. Nordjydske Jernbaner A/S. See also chapter 4.3.5.
55. Judgment of the European Court of Justice of 16 October 2003, case C-421/01, Traunfellner GmbH vs. Österreichische Autobahnen Und Schnellstrassen-finanzierungs-AG, paragraphs 27 and 33.

6. Information, amendments and negotiations with tenderers

In practice the contracting authority only has limited scope for settling unclear points with undertakings participating in the procedure. Similarly, although depending on the procedure, the undertakings only have limited scope for discussions, of notably the tender, with the contracting authority.

6.1 Contact between the tenderers and the contracting authority

In the period prior to the expiry of the time for submitting tenders tenderers usually need to clarify certain points in the contract documents. It follows from Article 39, paragraph 2 of the Directive that the tenderers can ask questions of the contracting authority about the contract documents. The contracting authority must answer such requests not later than six days before the expiry of the time for submitting tenders, in the restricted procedure it is four days, cf. Article 40, paragraph 4.

In practice, one or more meetings are often arranged, at least in the more complex procedures, to give the tenderers the opportunity to put oral questions to the contracting authority and maybe even be given a tour of the relevant buildings, etc.

It is important that the contracting authority ensures compliance with the principle of equal treatment and the prohibition on negotiations in connection with these meetings and in replying to questions. All questions should therefore be answered in writing in order that all undertakings, which have asked for the contract documents, receive the question in writing (in an anonymous form) and the same answer. For practical reasons questions and answers are compiled in documents distributed to tenderers at regular intervals.

If the tenderer after the deadline for submitting written questions become aware of unclear points in the contract documents, the tenderer should specify in the tender on which assumptions it is prepared. Provided that the contract documents are actually unclear, such comments would not be regarded as a reservation that may lead to rejection of the tender, but the contracting authority may be required to price the comment if the tenderer has understood the contract documents differently than intended by the contracting authority.

It is for the contracting authority to prove which information it has given to the individual tenderers. Where the contracting authority communicates orally with one or more tenderers, it is also for the contracting authority to prove that a specific piece of information was *not* disclosed to a tenderer.[56] As a consequence, the contracting authority should not answer questions over the phone or meet with tenderers, but should instead ask them to forward any questions they might have in writing.

After the final date for submitting tenders, but before the award decision is made, clarification of other matters may be necessary, i.e. the tenderers' tender. It is the tenderer's responsibility that the tender is understandable and unambiguous. On that account, the contracting authority is entitled and obliged to disregard tenders which are unclear in essential areas. Questions from the contracting authority to the tenderer on the understanding of the fundamental aspects of a tender are a violation of the principle of equal treatment.[57] The contracting authority must therefore have a clear idea of which elements are fundamental aspects of the tender, which is not always an easy task.

If the lack of clarity concerns aspects which are not fundamental to the tender, the contracting authority is entitled to ask questions of the tenderer – a so-called technical clarification.[58] Obviously, it is for the contracting authority to make sure that the request does not turn into negotiations, which are against the prohibition on negotiations. As a consequence, the tenderer must not be allowed to amend its tender.

When the award decision has been communicated to the tenderers, the contracting authority again has a somewhat wider scope for additional technical clarification with the successful tenderer before the final contract is concluded. In *H. Hoffmann og Sønner A/S and Others*[59] the Complaints Board made the following statement in regard to negotiations with the successful tenderer:

"By virtue of the principle of equal treatment established under EU procurement rules a contracting authority cannot negotiate fundamental aspects of a proposed contract with tenderers in the period from the receipt of tenders and until the award decision has been communicated to a tenderer since such fundamental aspects cannot be amended without jeopardising the equal treatment of all tenderers. The specific contact between the defen-

56. Order of the Complaints Board of 7 August 2003, KAS Transport rep. by Kim Schrøder vs. Århus Local Authority.
57. Order of the Complaints Board of 24 October 2001, Eiland Electric A/S vs. County of Vestsjælland.
58. Order of the Complaints Board of 15 August 2003, Bravida Danmark A/S vs. Statens Forsknings- og Uddannelsesbygninger.
59. Order of the Complaints Board of 11 June 1999, H. Hoffmann og Sønner A/S and Others vs. Aalborg Lufthavn Amba.

dant's technical adviser and the successful tenderer in this procedure was established after the defendant had decided to award the contract to the successful tenderer and informed the company thereof. Furthermore, the contact did not aim at changing the contract documents or the tender, but was merely intended to, on the one hand, point out to the tenderer that the points in question were covered by the tenderer's tender and thus covered by the price of the tender and, on the other hand, that the geotechnical conditions at the airport had to be clarified before signing of the contract. Contact between the defendant and the successful tenderer at the time in question and with the purpose in question did not violate the principle of equal treatment."

6.2 Changes to the contract documents after receipt of tenders

Even in the period from the launch of a tender procedure, but before receipt of tenders, the contracting authority can only make minor corrections and non-fundamental changes to the contract documents. Fundamental changes, such as a change of award criterion or sub-criteria, etc., require that the ongoing procedure be cancelled. This is because some potential tenderers may have elected not to participate in the procedure because of the "error". Notwithstanding that these tenderers at the time of the correction/change in theory still would be able to participate, the time elapsed would place them at a competitive disadvantage in contravention of the principle of equal treatment.

As mentioned above, the contracting authority can provide answers to questions from tenderers and other additional information to the contract documents until six days before the final date for submission of tenders (four days in the restricted procedure). Furthermore, at the latest as of this date the contracting authority is prohibited from making changes to the contract documents. After the expiry of the above "deadlines", the only option available to the contracting authority if changes to the contract documents become indispensable is to cancel the procedure. It goes without saying that the contracting authority cannot change the contract documents after receipt of tenders, whether the changes concern fundamental aspects or not.[60]

6.3 Changes to tenders submitted after the final date

Above it is stated that a contracting authority is obliged to reject tenders submitted after the final date for receipt. In a similar vein the contracting authority cannot allow a tenderer to make changes to its tender after the final date, let alone the date of opening.[61] The contracting authority must inform the

---

60. Judgment of the European Court of Justice of 25 April 1996, case C-87/94, Commission vs. Belgium.
61. Judgment of the European Court of Justice of 25 April 1996, case C-87/94, Commission vs. Belgium.

tenderer in unmistakable terms that the changes will not be taken into consideration and that the tender will be evaluated exclusively on the information included in the tender received at the final date. It thus follows that changes to a submitted tender must be received by the contracting authority before the final date for submission; under the general law of contract changes to tenders received by the contracting authority before the final date must be taken into consideration even where they have the effect of increasing the price of the tender.

Presumably, the contracting authority may allow a tenderer to change elements of the tender which are of secondary importance and which will definitely not affect the evaluation thereof.

7. Award of order and conclusion of contract

Having evaluated the tenders on the basis of the chosen award criterion, the contracting authority awards the proposed contract. Then the contract between the contracting authority and the successful tenderer is concluded.

7.1 Based on the contract documents and the successful tender

After the final date for submission of tenders, the contracting authority starts the evaluation of the tenders submitted. It is important that the contracting authority proceeds methodically. In the open procedure the contracting authority must first select the participants on the basis of the selection criteria, cf. chapter 6.

First and foremost, in the evaluation of the tenders the contracting authority must verify that the tenders comply with any requirements as to form stipulated by the contracting authority in the contract documents, such as language requirements, maximum number of pages, media, number of copies, etc. Tenders that do not satisfy the requirements as to form must be rejected forthwith. This may seem a bit rigid, but contracting authorities should ponder over the necessity and appropriateness of these requirements before the contract documents are advertised and forwarded to the tenderers.

Also the evaluation of the tenders as such should be as systematic as possible to prevent arbitrary decisions and ensure transparency. To this end, it may be useful to develop, in advance, a model for the evaluation guaranteeing that all tenders are assessed on the same basis. As mentioned above in section 2.7, a system for allocating points may be helpful. Of course the contracting authority must also verify that the tenders submitted satisfy the requirements stipulated in the contract documents with respect to the proposed service, supplies or works. It is for the contracting authority to prove that the tenderers, notably the successful tenderer, satisfy these requirements.[62]

Once the successful tenderer has been identified, this is communicated to the tenderers, see further details in section 9.2. The contracting authority and the successful tenderer may negotiate adjustments of the contract which, individually and collectively, can only translate into slight changes to the specifications in the contract documents.

7.2 Grace Period – Interval after Award Decision

The basic rule is that a draft contract must be included among the contract documents. This draft contract must set out the main terms and conditions of delivery. If that were not the case, it would be too uncertain what tenders were invited for. In the contract documents the contracting authority can specify with respect to which provisions reservations can be made and which requirements are mandatory. However, the contracting authority cannot allow that reservations be made with respect to all provisions of the draft contract.[63] Presumably, it is only possible to exclude a draft contract entirely from the contract documents for the award of contracts for very elementary supplies

Since the tenderer cannot require that the individual provisions of the contract be negotiated in the period after the award decision, in theory nothing prevents the contracting authority from forwarding the contract for signing by the successful tenderer at the same time as or shortly after the tenderer is informed of the award decision. Indeed neither the Procurement Directives nor the Remedies Directives stipulate a grace period from the award decision until the conclusion of the contract. However, the European Court of Justice has stated[64] that legal protection of the other tenderers against arbitrary decisions on the part of the contracting authority requires both an obligation to inform tenderers directly of the award decision and an obligation to do so in sufficient time for tenderers to examine the validity of the award decision under the procurement rules so that they may file a complaint. In this context, the European Court of Justice emphasises in particular the possibility for applying for interim measures to suspend the procurement procedure and thus prevent the conclusion of the contract.

---

62. Order of the Complaints Board of 8 October 2004, Virklund Sport A/S vs. Randers Local Authority (pursuant to the Danish Tender Act).
63. Order of the Complaints Board of 2 May 2001, Forlaget Magnus A/S vs. Customs and Tax Authority.
64. Judgment of the European Court of Justice of 24 June 2004, case C-212/02, Commission vs. Austria, paragraphs 21-23.

The judgment is of particular interest from a Danish perspective. Firstly, it clarifies the question of the legality of the much used practice in Danish procurement law of concluding the contract at the same time as or shortly after the award decision. Secondly, it renews the focus on the great reluctance of the Complaints Board to grant interim measures and thereby prevent a contracting authority from concluding the contract with the successful tenderer while the procurement proceedings are pending. The restrictive practice of the Complaints Board in this area can probably not be maintained as the Complaints Board, like the contracting authority, is under an obligation to ensure that the tenderers are genuinely protected against arbitrary and unlawful award decisions. It would lack any sense if the Complaint Board's refusal to grant interim measures ultimately deprived the grace period of its function as a means to avert an unlawful conclusion of contract

The European Court of Justice does not give any indication as to the length of time that should elapse from the award decision has been communicated to the other tenderers till the contract can be concluded. The length of the grace period probably depends on the complexity of the procedure, but should not be expected to be less than 14 days in any circumstances.

8. Cancellation

Circumstances may arise or be verified in the course of a procurement procedure entitling the contracting authority to cancel the competition.

8.1 Only objective grounds

It follows from Article 41, paragraph 1 of the Directive that the contracting authority among other things must state the reasons why it has decided *not* to award a contract for which there has been a call for tenders. In consideration of the principle of equal treatment and the above-mentioned Article, the general assumption has been that the contracting authority cannot at its own discretion cancel an ongoing procedure. There must be objective grounds therefore.

In case *Metalmeccanica*[65] the European Court of Justice held that serious or exceptional circumstances are not required for a decision not to award a

---

65. Judgment of the European Court of Justice of 16 September 1999, case C-27/98, Metalmeccanica Fracasso SpA, Leitschutz Handels- und Montage GmbH vs. Amt der Salzburger Landesregierung für den Bundesminister für wirtschaftliche Angelegenheiten, paragraph 25.

contract or not to recommence a procurement procedure always provided, however, that the contracting authority complies with the fundamental principles of Community law on equal treatment, etc.[66] It follows that the contracting authority has extensive powers to cancel an ongoing procedure. It seems that only non-objective grounds, such as to avoid awarding the contract to a specific supplier, would prevent the contracting authority from cancelling a procedure. It is insignificant whether the reason for the cancellation is due to an error committed by the contracting authority.[67] A frequent reason why a contracting authority properly cancels a procedure is (the likely) violation of the principle of equal treatment.

The contracting authority can cancel a procedure even after informing the tenderers of the award decision, if objective grounds justify the cancellation.[68] It is, however, possible that the announcement of the award of the contract to a specific tenderer under contract law will be deemed an acceptance of the tender, thus exposing the contracting authority to liability in damages.

In *Milana A/S*[69] the Complaints Board found that the contracting authority could not legitimately cancel a procedure merely because of a calculation error in all the tenders submitted. Pursuant to the contract documents the tenderers were bound by the overall price of the tenders and, therefore, the contracting authority would have to evaluate the tenders on that basis.

In *Højgaard & Schultz A/S*[70] the Complaints Board found that the actual purpose of the contracting authority's cancellation of an ongoing procedure was a wish to mitigate the effects of a complaint brought before the Complaints Board. The Complaints Board stated that that was not an objective ground and that, consequently, the cancellation was a violation of the procurement rules. The matter was brought before the High Court[71] which found that the main reason for cancelling the procedure was that it was defective and that

---

66. Order of the European Court of Justice of 16 October 2003, case C-244/02, Kauppatalo Hansel Oy vs. Imatran Kaupunki, paragraph 36.
67. Order of the European Court of Justice of 16 October 2003, case C-244/02, Kauppatalo Hansel Oy vs. Imatran Kaupunki, paragraph 36.
68. Order of the Complaints Board of 22 March 2002, Johs. Sørensen & Sønner Århus A/S vs. Århus Kommunale Værker.
69. Order of the Complaints Board of 12 August 2002, Milana A/S vs. County of Vestsjælland.
70. Order of the Complaints Board of 19 June 1997, Højgaard & Schultz A/S vs. Ministry of Education.
71. Judgment of the Eastern High Court of 16 August 2000, case B-1654-97, Copenhagen Business School and Ministry of Research and Information Technology vs. Højgaard & Schultz A/S.

the validity of the procedure had been called into question which constituted an objective ground for cancelling the procedure.

8.2 Irregular tenders

Sometimes the contracting authority has not received any suitable tenders that comply with the specifications at the final date for submitting tenders. In such a situation the contracting authority has no alternative, but to cancel the procedure.

Article 30, paragraph 1 (a) and Article 31, paragraph 1 (a) provide that in exceptional cases the contracting authority can make use of the negotiated procedure (with or without prior publication of a contract notice). The possibilities for negotiating with tenderers is intended to ensure that the contracting authority receives and evaluates tenders which comply with the specifications and are suitable. See also chapter 5.5.

8.3 Unacceptable tenders in terms of price

As mentioned above, the contracting authority is not, at any price, obliged to complete a commenced procedure and award a contract.

In *Dansk Transport og Logistik*[72] the waste disposal department of the local authority had submitted a tender which turned out to be the most economically advantageous tender. The local authority then chose to cancel the procedure on the ground that it could carry out the task itself at a lower price than that offered by the external tenderers. This was held to be an objective ground.

By contrast, in *Arbejdsgiverforeningen for Handel, Transport og Service*[73] the Complaints Board found that it was not an objective ground for cancelling a procedure that the price gap between the tenders submitted was too big.

8.4 Lack of competition

In *Metalmeccanica*[74] the European Court of Justice found that a contracting authority is not obliged to award a contract in a procedure where only one tenderer has submitted a tender that complies with the specifications and is

---

72. Order of the Complaints Board of 27 April 2001, Dansk Transport og Logistik vs. Nykøbing Falster Local Authority.
73. Order of the Complaints Board of 13 September 1996, Arbejdsgiverforeningen for Handel, Transport og Service vs. Tårnby Local Authority.
74. Judgment of the European Court of Justice of 16 September 1999, case C-27/98, Metalmeccanica Fracasso SpA, Leitschutz Handels- und Montage GmbH vs. Amt der Salzburger Landesregierung für den Bundesminister für wirtschaftliche Angelegenheiten.

suitable. The remaining tenderer has no right to be awarded the contract. In support thereof the European Court of Justice refers to *inter alia* the aim of the Procurement Directive to facilitate the development of effective competition and that in a procedure with only one tenderer the contracting authority cannot compare prices and other aspects if it has received only one tender. It is thus an objective ground for cancelling a procedure if only one suitable tender which complies with the specifications has been submitted.

In *Danish Council of Practising Architects*[75] the contracting authority had cancelled a procedure and launched a new procedure on the ground that only 14 of the applicants that applied for pre-qualification had submitted adequate information and documentation. The real reason was that the contracting authority wished to receive tenders from more foreign tenderers (the 14 tenderers were all Danish) as it wanted it to be an "international design contest" and that the contracting authority legitimately expected to be able to pre-qualify more foreign tenderers in a new procedure. The Complaints Board found that the wish for an "international" design contest would have constituted an objective ground for cancelling the first procedure, but at the same time condemned the contracting authority for not having informed the tenderers of this reason.

It is not an objective ground for cancelling a procedure that the evaluation of the tenders shows that the tenders are very similar and equal.[76]

8.5 Cancellation procedure

If a contracting authority wishes to cancel a commenced procedure, it must first of all make sure that there is an objective ground for the cancellation. All the undertakings which have requested pre-qualification or have submitted tenders must then be informed of the reason. Finally, pursuant to Article 43, paragraph 1 (h) of the Directive the contracting authority must draw up a report of the progress of the procedure and the reasons why it has decided to cancel it. Upon request, the report must be submitted to the Commission.

In *Kirkebjerg A/S*[77] the contracting authority had cancelled the call for tenders for a minor lot under the procedure referring to a clause in the contract documents subject to which the contracting authority had reserved the right to cancel parts of the works contract. The Complaints Board noted that a general reservation about cancellation of the whole or part of a procedure is a violation of the principle of equal treatment in accordance with which a pro-

75. Order of the Complaints Board of 12 July 2001, Danish Council of Practising Architects vs. Ministry of Culture.
76. Order of the Complaints Board of 11 October 2004, Iver C. Weilbach & Co. A/S vs., National Survey and Cadastre.
77. Order of the Complaints Board of 11 August 2000, Kirkebjerg A/S vs. County of Ribe.

cedure can only be cancelled if the contracting authority has an objective ground for doing so. To this the Complaints Board remarked the following:

"… if a contracting authority has a sound reason for deciding not to award a contract, the contracting authority must do so for the contract as a whole and cannot do it for part of the contract only, and that this would certainly have to apply to a case such as the case in hand, since tenders are made on the basis of the contract offered for tender as a whole, and since a subsequent decision not to award part of the contract shifts the competitive situation among the tenderers".

See, however, *Nybus A/S and Others*[78] in which case the Complaints Board accepted a partial cancellation of a procedure in part and a general reservation set out in the contract documents in relation thereto.

8.6 Subsequent call for tenders for the same contract

If the contracting authority still wishes to make the purchase, it must advertise a new call for tenders. For that purpose the contracting authority may organise and conduct the procedure as it pleases. Hence, the contracting authority is free to choose a new type of procedure, new award criterion etc. Nor is the contracting authority obliged to pre-qualify the same undertakings that were pre-qualified for the first procedure.

9. Duty to notify reasons for a decision

Participation in a procurement procedure may require investment of large resources (also) on the part of the undertakings, and, as a consequence, the contracting authority's decisions to award or not to award a contract must be reasoned. The reasons provide the undertakings with a basis for examining the contracting authority's decisions and possibly file a complaint against these decisions with the Complaints Board for Public Procurement.

9.1 Purpose – discourage violations and enable control

In *Kauppatalo*[79] the European Court of Justice stated that the duty to notify reasons for a decision should be understood in the light of the two-fold objective of the procurement rules of creating transparency and opening up compe-

---

78. Order of the Complaints Board of 3 July 1998, Nybus A/S and Others vs. Storstrøms Trafikselskab.
79. Judgment of the European Court of Justice of 16 October 2003, case C-244/02, Kauppatalo Hansel Oy vs. Imatran Kaupunki, paragraph 32.

tition. Against that background the European Court of Justice established that the duty to notify reasons indeed is intended to ensure a minimum level of transparency in procedures for the award of public contracts and, hence, compliance with the principle of equal treatment.

Obviously the reasons must be given by reference to the specific circumstances that brought about the contracting authority's decision. If a tenderer asks for the reasons why its tender was rejected as irregular, the specific facts that warranted the rejection must be specified, for example that the tenderer had made reservations about fundamental aspects of the contract. A tenderer's request forwarded by email satisfies the requirement that requests be made in writing.[80]

9.2 Notice of the result of the award procedure

Article 41, paragraph 1 of the Directive prescribes that contracting authorities as soon as possible must inform applicants and tenderers of the decision to award the proposed contract.

Further, pursuant to Article 41, paragraph 2 of the Directive the contracting authority must as soon as possible upon request, and within 15 days, inform all tenderers which have submitted admissible tenders of the characteristics and relative advantages of the selected tender, including the name of the successful tenderer. See also section 7.7.2 above.

Finally, the contracting authority is required to publish a "contract award notice" of the result of the procedure. The notice must be sent no later than 48 days after the conclusion of the contract, cf. Article 35, paragraph 4 of the Directive. The notice must include information on *inter alia* the body responsible for appeal (in Denmark the Complaints Board for Public Procurement) and the deadlines for lodging complaints.

9.3 Confidentiality/Access to documents

Depending on the circumstances, tender documents, and perhaps also the application for pre-qualification, usually contain information which the tenderer considers to be confidential. Article 6 of the Directive in general prohibits contracting authorities from disclosing information which the tenderers have designated as confidential. The extent of the prohibition is limited by the other provisions of the Directive regarding the duty to publish information on the award of contracts and the duty to notify candidates and tenderers of rea-

---

80. Order of the Complaints Board of 11 October 2004, Iver C. Weilbach & Co. vs. National Survey and Cadastre.

sons for decisions and to provisions of national law on *for example* access to documents.

Article 35, paragraph 4, fifth indent and Article 41, paragraph 3 of the Directive are almost identical provisions stipulating that publication of information, respectively reasons for award decisions may be withheld if the release thereof would impede "law enforcement or otherwise be contrary to the public interest, would harm the legitimate commercial interests of economic operators, public or private, or might prejudice fair competition between them".

The Directive is silent on access to documents in procurement procedures. Instead, access to documents is governed by national law. In Denmark public access to documents is governed by the Act on Public Access to Documents in Public Files[81] and the Public Administration Act.[82]

By virtue of section 4(1) of the Access to Documents Act any person who so requests may have access to documents received or issued by an administrative authority in the course of its activity. Articles 7-14 of the Access to Documents Act list information which is exempted from this general access to documents. Among this information is trade secrets which are largely exempted subject, however, to a specific assessment of whether the information is in the nature of trade secrets and whether the information is of such importance to the financial situation of the undertaking that a request for access cannot be granted, cf. section 12(1), no. 2. The undertaking cannot merely request in advance that the specific information is not disclosed. Further, the authority is under an obligation to publish those parts of a document which does not contain trade secrets – so-called duty to extract.

The right of access to the contract documents, requests for pre-qualification and tenders is thus fairly extensive. Previously an executive order exempted documents on public procurement agreements from the access to documents granted under the Access to Documents Act.[83] This order has now been repealed.[84]

---

81. Act No 572 of 19 December 1985 on Public Access to Information.
82. Act No 571 of 19 December 1985, Public Administration Act.
83. Executive Order No 4 of 4 January 1993 on documents on public procurement agreements exempted from the right of access to documents pursuant to the Act on Public Access to Information.
84. Executive Order No 331 of 24 May 2002 on documents on public procurement agreements exempted from the right of access to documents pursuant to the Act on Public Access to Information.

Pursuant to Article 15(1) of Executive Order on the Complaints Board the contracting authority is under an obligation to submit a report on the progress of the procedure and disclose the documents of the case. Further, Article 16(1) of the Executive Order prescribes that the complainant be informed of the contracting authority's report on the procedure and of all other documents submitted in the case, except where the right of access to documents is limited by other statute.

The Complaints Board for Public Procurement is part of the public administration and is thus subject to the Public Administration Act. Section 9(1) of the Public Administration Act grants any person who is party to a case access to the documents of the case. A party's right of access to documents is, however, limited by section 15(1) of the Public Administration Act to the extent that the party's interest in being able to use knowledge of documents in the matter to protect its interests gives way to the material interests of the party concerned or to other material private or public interests. It thus follows that in each case the opposite interests must be weighed against each other. In *Semco Energi A/S*[85] the Complaints Board found, having weighed the interests concerned against each other, that the need to protect the tenderers' competitive ability in future procedures carried heavier weight than the complainant's possibilities for protecting its own interests in the complaints proceedings. Consequently, the complainant was not granted access to other documents than the extract it had already received from the contracting authority.

---

85. Order of the Complaints Board of 21 September 1995, Semco Energi A/S vs. Brønderslev Local Authority.

CHAPTER 8

Enforcement

1. The Complaints Board for Public Procurement

The effective implementation of and compliance with the Procurement Directive is conditional on the existence of a speedy and relatively informal review procedure. Grounds for complaints may arise at any time during a procurement procedure and according to the circumstances the time for reaching a decision may be very short. Moreover, specific competence is required within this area of law. In Denmark the Complaints Board for Public Procurement has been charged with the responsibilities in this area.

1.1 Rules, hearing and review

The competence and duties vested in the Complaints Board for Public Procurement result from the Remedies Directive, examined below, which has been transposed into Danish law.

1.1.1 The Procurement Directive, the Act on the Complaints Board and the Executive Order

The original procurement directives, the Works Directive and the Supply Directive, date back to the 1970s. Still, it was not until 1989 that the Council adopted the Remedies Directive for Public Contracts.[1]

In the preamble the Council states that the reason for the adoption of the Remedies Directive is that the existing mechanisms at both national and Community levels for ensuring that infringements can be corrected are not adequate. The Council places particular emphasis on the fact that since pro-

---

1. Council Directive 89/665 EEC of 21 December 1989 on the coordination of the laws, regulations and administrative provisions relating to the application of review procedures to the award of public supply and public works contracts.

curement procedures are often of relatively short duration, it is necessary that effective and rapid remedies are available in order that infringements can be corrected before a contract is concluded. Furthermore, more rapid and effective review procedures are factors in ensuring that the principles of transparency and non-discrimination are complied with.

The Remedies Directive was transposed into Danish law by the Act on the Complaints Board for Public Procurement[2] establishing the Danish Complaints Board for Public Procurement. In contrast to the Procurement Directives which were transposed directly into Danish law by way of reference statute, the Remedies Directive was implemented as an Act of Parliament. Undoubtedly this method was chosen because the Remedies Directive, unlike the Procurement Directives, affords the Member States a certain scope for adjusting the review procedures to the national procedural systems. Whereas the Complaints Board Act sets out the general framework, the powers, organisation and procedures of the Complaints Board for Public Procurement are governed in detail by the Executive Order on the Complaints Board although there is considerable overlap between the Act and the Executive Order.[3]

The Complaints Board for Public Procurement is composed of a chairman, a number of vice-chairmen and a number of expert members appointed by the Danish Minister of Economic and Business Affairs for a period of four years. The chairman and vice-chairmen must be professional judges whereas the other members of the Complaints Board are persons with relevant knowledge of building and engineering, public procurement, transport, etc.

A case is heard by the chairman and/or up to two vice-chairmen and two, or exceptionally four, expert members.

1.1.2 Party autonomy and inquisitorial procedure

The Complaints Board for Public Procurement occupies a special position between the public administration, on the one hand, and the courts of law, on the other hand. The explanatory notes to the Complaints Board Act clearly specify that the Complaints Board for Public Procurement is part of the public administration and as such subject to the provisions of general administrative law, including the Public Administration Act.[4] At the same time the ex-

---

2. Act No 415 of 31 May 2000 on the Complaints Board for Public Procurement (as amended).
3. Executive Order No 602 of 26 June 2000 on the Complaints Board for Public Procurement.
4. Bill No L 243 of 30 March 2000 on the Complaints Board for Public Procurement, Official Report of Parliamentary Proceedings 1999-2000, Annex A, column 6860.

planatory notes also refer to the Complaints Board for Public Procurement as a "tribunal" within the meaning of Article 234 of the EC Treaty and as such it is competent to refer preliminary questions to the European Court of Justice.

Pursuant to the Remedies Directive it is left with the national authorities to decide whether complaints should be heard before the courts of law or before an administrative body. In Denmark it has been left with an administrative body in view of the fact that the Remedies Directive obliges the Member State to establish a review body which is competent to take interim measures and make final decisions urgently. Allegedly, the ordinary courts of law would be less suited for achieving this aim.[5]

By virtue of the special status of the Complaints Board for Public Procurement its procedure contains elements of administrative law and elements of civil law. The procedure for reviewing cases is largely similar to the hearing of civil actions. All cases are commenced with an exchange of pleadings, similar to the exchange of pleadings in civil actions, followed by oral proceedings.[6] The most significant difference compared to civil actions is without a doubt that the Complaints Board for Public Procurement applies the inquisitorial procedure and, therefore, is not limited to the parties' claims, pleas, allegations and evidence as is the case in civil actions applying the adversary procedure.

The inquisitorial procedure entails that, in theory, it is the Complaints Board for Public Procurement which is responsible for due case preparation, obtaining all necessary information and making all the required investigations before making a decision. In practice, the Complaints Board assumes the leading role in procuring evidence. In certain cases the Complaints Board is indeed very active and does not shy away from formulating, for example, new points of complaint or making observations that are not indispensable to deciding the complaint lodged by the complainant.[7]

From the point of view of the complainant the practice of the Complaints Board for Public Procurement of formulating new points of complaint can be an advantage as well as a drawback. It is to the complainant's advantage if the Complaints Board in reviewing all the

5. Bill No L 86 of 23 January 1991 on the Complaints Board for Public Procurement, Official Report of Parliamentary Proceedings 1990-91, second session, Annex A, column 1975.
6. Oral proceedings have arisen out of the Complaints Board's practice. The first Complaints Board Act provided for written proceedings, whereas the current Complaints Board Act has introduced oral proceedings as the main rule.
7. See for example order of the Complaints Board of 1 May 1997, L.R. Service ApS vs. Solrød Local Authority.

documents concerning a specific procurement procedure, which are not available to the complainant, identifies infringements that the complainant would have included in its complaint had it had access to all the documents. Conversely, where the Complaints Board for Public Procurement formulates a claim for which there is no basis for awarding subsequent damages. In the interest of saving resources the complainant would be inclined to exclude such points from the complaint, but if it is put forward by the Complaints Board, the complainant is forced to take it into account.

From the point of view of the contracting authority (the defendant) the Complaints Board's practice of formulating new points of complaint is almost always a drawback. Firstly, a new point of complaint involves another risk of an adverse decision. A point of complaint formulated by the Complaints Board for Public Procurement, and not the complainant, often leaves the defendant with the feeling that an adverse decision already has been reached on that particular point without the defendant being heard. The defendant is only heard subsequently. Secondly, also the defendant is interested in saving resources, and it goes without saying that the defendant must apply as many resources to defending points of claim formulated by the Complaints Board for Public Procurement as to defending points of claim made by the complainant.

The general assumption is that the Complaints Board has no authority to make initiative as it is indeed a review body and not a regulatory body. To this it has to be said that the authors certainly have a point in that the authority subject to which the Complaints Board for Public Procurement formulates new points of claim should be explicit. However, the practice of the Complaints Board contributes to ensuring the effective implementation of the Procurement Directive which would not be automatically achieved if the Complaints Board for Public Procurement heard complaints on the basis of the adversary procedure.

The Complaints Board for Public Procurement has been given the power to award damages to the complainant, and consideration was in that connection given to provide explicitly that the general rules of the Danish Administration of Justice Act were to apply to the hearing of the claim for damages. However, the legislator found that such a formal rule would not agree with the inquisitorial procedure applied by the Complaints Board for Public Procurement.[8] Perhaps as a compromise, it was decided on the same occasion that at least one judge should participate in the hearing of all cases before the Complaints Board for Public Procurement.

---

8.   Bill No L 243 of 30 March 2000 on the Complaints Board for Public Procurement, Official Report of Parliamentary Proceedings 1999-2000, Annex A, column 6866.

In accordance with the inquisitorial procedure the Complaints Board for Public Procurement has the authority to demand disclosure of all information required for reaching a decision in the case.

1.1.3 Reference for a preliminary ruling by the European Court of Justice

As mentioned above, the explanatory notes to the Complaints Board Act refer to the Complaints Board for Public Procurement as a "tribunal" within the meaning of Article 234 of the EC Treaty (previously Article 177) and as such it is competent to refer preliminary questions to the European Court of Justice. Whether the Complaints Board for Public Procurement actually does meet the conditions set out in Article 234 of the EC Treaty was tried by the European Court of Justice the first time in *Unitron Scandinavia A/S.*[9] On that occasion the European Court of Justice referred to point 18 of the Advocate General's opinion stating:

"On several occasions the European Court of Justice has stated that the question whether the body making the reference is a tribunal or a court within the meaning of Article 234 EC, which is a matter of Community law only, is determined by whether the body is established by statute, is a permanent establishment, is the compulsory judicial body, applies the contradictory procedure to the hearing of cases, makes decisions based on the rule of law and is independent. As the criteria which the European Court of Justice has established in case law are met by the Complaints Board, it is a "court" or a "tribunal" within the meaning of Article 234 EC."[10]

Unitron Scandinavia A/S concerned the question whether a contract for the supply of ear tags for pigs should have been put out to tender. By a ministerial order, the Ministry of Agriculture, Food and Fisheries had left the administration of the pig ear tag arrangement to Danske Slagterier (Danish Abattoirs) which is a private undertaking. The Complaints Board for Public Procurement referred two questions to the European Court of Justice concerning the interpretation of Article 2(2) in the then applicable Supply Directive.[11] According to the Directive a body other than a contracting authority which is granted special or exclusive rights to engage in public service activity must observe the principle of non-discrimination by nationality when awarding public supply contracts in the exercise of the public service activity. The European Court of Justice confirmed that the provision did *not* require that such contracts be awarded in accordance with the Supply Directive, but only that the principle of non-discrimination be observed.

---

9. Judgment of the European Court of Justice of 18 November 1999, case C-275/98, Unitron Scandinavia A/S and Others vs. Ministry of Agriculture, Food and Fisheries.
10. Opinion of 8 July 1999, case C-275/98, Unitron Scandinavia A/S and Others vs. Ministry of Agriculture, Food and Fisheries.
11. Council Directive 93/36/EEC coordinating procedures for the award of public supply contracts.

Incidentally, it is surprising that – despite the abundance of cases decided by it by now – until now the Complaints Board for Public Procurement has only once felt induced to refer preliminary questions to the European Court of Justice on the interpretation of the often very complex and highly "un-Danish" provisions of the Procurement Directives. There are probably two reasons for this reluctance. First, pursuant to the Complaints Board Act the responsibility of the Complaints Board for Public Procurement is to guarantee a rapid and effective review of complaints, also with an eye to ensuring that the contracting authority's purchase under review (if possible) can be completed as quickly and smoothly as possible. Often this overriding purpose would be wasted if the review by the Complaints Board were to be stayed pending the preliminary ruling of the European Court of Justice. Second, orders by the Complaints Board for Public Procurement can be brought before the ordinary courts of law in Denmark.[12] It follows from Article 234 of the Treaty that only the national courts of law whose decisions can*not* be appealed against are under an obligation to refer preliminary questions to the European Court of Justice. Accordingly, the Complaints Board for Public Procurement is not subject to a duty of reference no matter how complex or difficult a question is. Instead, the Complaints Board for Public Procurement can leave it to the parties to bring the case before the Danish courts of law if they do not agree with the Complaints Board's interpretation of Community law in order that the court, if necessary, can refer the question to the European Court of Justice for a preliminary ruling. In practice, hardly any of the Complaints Board's orders are brought before the courts of law. On that account it is not so surprising that, so far, Danish courts of law have only asked the European Court of Justice for a preliminary ruling in one case.[13]

Obviously, preliminary references can also be made in cases brought directly before a court of law, see section 1.3 below.

1.2 Powers of the Complaints Board for Public Procurement
The powers of the Complaints Board for Public Procurement are set out in the Complaints Board Act.

---

12. The Complaints Board Act provides that an order must be brought before the courts of law no later than 8 weeks after it was communicated to the parties.
13. Judgment of the European Court of Justice of 3 December 2001, case C-59/00, Bent Mousten Vestergaard vs. Spøttrup Boligselskab.

1.2.1 Who can lodge a complaint/has an interest in the complaint

The Remedies Directive provides that Member States must ensure that review procedures are available, as a minimum, to any person having or having
had an interest in obtaining a particular public contract and who has been or
risks being harmed by an alleged infringement. True to Danish administrative
law the Complaints Board Act instead provides that "any person having a
legal interest therein"[14] can lodge a complaint with the Complaints Board for
Public Procurement. All other things being equal, this wording is somewhat
broader than the minimum requirements of the Remedies Directive, although
the core area, of course, being persons (including undertakings) who some-
how have been passed over in the award procedure for a public contract.

In *Grosmann Air Service*[15] the European Court of Justice was asked *inter alia* whether
only a complainant that has submitted a tender for a proposed contract can establish an
interest in the complaint. To that the European Court of Justice noted that in normal circumstances that is the case, but in a situation where the undertaking concerned does not
submit a tender because there were allegedly discriminatory specifications in the contract
documents, which specifically prevented it from being in a position to provide all the
services requested, it would be entitled to seek review of those discriminatory specifications directly, even though it had not submitted a tender.

In *Miljøforeningen*[16] the Complaints Board was given the opportunity to make some
general comments on the concept of "legal interest" as set out in the Complaints Board Act.
For the purpose of a contemplated extension of Copenhagen Airport Kastrup, Københavns
Lufthavne A/S had a so-called EAS report drawn up. An environmental organisation complained to the Complaints Board for Public Procurement that the preparation of the EAS
report had not been offered for tender. The defendant argued that the environmental organisation did not have a legal interest in the complaint. To that the Complaints Board for Public
Procurement noted "that access to complain under sect. 4, subsect. 1, item 1) of the act can
only be granted to enterprises which as potential tenderers have a direct financial interest in
getting the Complaints Board's decision on whether a given assignment is to be offered or
should have been offered for tender under EEC procurement rules, and whether in a given
tender procedure these rules have been violated, as well as an interest in getting the Complaints Board's reaction to any such violation. The complaining association's more general
interest in the EAS report and its preparation did thus not give the association the right to
complain under sect. 4, subsect. 1, item 1) of the act."

---

14. Section 4(1), no 1 of the Complaints Board Act.
15. Judgment of the European Court of Justice of 12 February 2004, case C-230/02,
    Grossmann Air Service, Bedarfsluftfahrtunternehmen GmbH & Co. KG vs. Aus-
    tria.
16. Order of the Complaints Board of 15 January 1998, Miljøforeningen for bevarelse
    af miljøet omkring Københavns Lufthavn vs. Københavns Lufthavne A/S.

In *Humus/Genplast*[17] the Complaints Board for Public Procurement noted that there is no period within which a complaint must be lodged with the Complaints Board, but that it can probably be barred because of inactivity. The specific complaint had been lodged approx. nine months after the contract had been awarded which in the specific case did not amount to inactivity since the complaint was lodged "within a reasonable time of [the complainant] having become aware of the matters that resulted in the complaint". The order does not indicate the exact time that had elapsed since the complainant became aware of the matters that gave rise to the complaint.

In *Svend B. Thomsen Varde A/S*[18] the Complaints Board for Public Procurement noted in a similar vein that an undertaking that had not submitted a tender had no legal interest in a complaint despite the fact that the same undertaking had complained, properly, about a previous call for tenders which had then been cancelled.

It is the Complaints Board for Public Procurement which decides whether a person has a legal interest at the first instance. The Complaints Board's decision can be appealed against to the courts of law. Moreover, the Complaints Board for Public Procurement can allow a third party or a public authority to intervene in the case if the third party or the public authority has a substantial interest therein.

Pursuant to the Complaints Board Act the Competition Authority can submit a complaint to the Complaints Board for Public Procurement as can those organisations and public authorities which the Minister of Economic and Business Affairs so authorises. The powers of the Competition Authority in review procedures are examined below in section 1.3.

The Executive Order on the Complaints Board lists 47 organisations and authorities which have a direct right of complaint without prior establishment of a legal interest in the procedure complained about. The reason for this is that originally there was no authority which supervised the compliance with the procurement directives. Instead, several public authorities and organisations were vested with a right to complain in order that they could initiate review procedures if and when necessary concerning matters of interest to them. Since then the Competition Authority has been vested with ever more supervisory powers in the field of procurement, most recently in the field of public works contracts which previously was a matter of the Ministry of Housing and Urban Affairs. Instead, the organisations (mostly trade organisation), which have a right of complaint by virtue of the Executive Order, in-

---

17. Order of the Complaints Board of 28 September 1998, Humus/Genplast rep. by Hans Jørgen Rasmussen vs. Esbjerg Local Authority. See also order of 19 March 2003, Forlev Vognmandsforretning A/S vs. Høng Local Authority.
18. Order of the Complaints Board of 20 August 2001, Svend B. Thomsen Varde A/S vs. Blåvandshuk Local Authority.

creasingly undertake responsibility for submitting complaints on behalf of their members. For example the Danish Council of Practising Architects has conducted a number of cases on behalf of their members. Evidently, a tenderer wants to remain on good terms with the contracting authority and by letting the trade organisation submit the complaint, the tenderer can maintain anonymity, at least until a possible claim for damages is to be settled.

Organisations and authorities that are not vested with a direct right of complaint in the Executive Order can, of course, submit a complaint if they have a legal interest in the complaint.[19]

1.2.2 Complaints about contracting authorities

The Complaints Board for Public Procurement reviews complaints about contracting authorities. Reference is made to chapter 2 above concerning the definition of a contracting authority. This delimitation means that the Complaints Board cannot consider questions from contracting authorities on the interpretation of the EU procurement rules. However, in several cases the Complaints Board for Public Procurement has decided upon an allegation by a contracting authority that, for example, the tenderer submitted by the complainant was irregular.[20]

It should be noted that the Complaints Board for Public Procurement is not empowered to institute proceedings concerning infringement of the procurement rules on its own initiative. The Complaints Board for Public Procurement only reviews specific complaints submitted by a person who has an interest in the complaint.

1.2.3 Infringements of Community law, etc.

Section 1(1) of the Complaints Board Act authorises the Complaints Board for Public Procurement to review complaints about contracting authorities' infringement of Community law, including the Procurement Directives, the provisions transposing these Directives into Danish law, the Danish Tender

---

19. Order of the Complaints Board of 27 August 1997, Danmarks Automobil-Forhandlerforening (acting for several members of the Haderslev branch) vs. Haderslev Local Authority.
20. Order of the Complaints Board of 26 April 1996, E. Pihl og Søn A/S vs. I/S Avedøre Kloakværk. In this case the Complaints Board placed emphasis on the complainant's acceptance that the Complaints Board considered the contracting authority's plea. See also order of 31 October 1996, Semco Energi A/S vs. Brønderslev Local Authority.

Act[21] and any other statutory provisions in which a right of complaint to the Complaints Board for Public Procurement is laid down

1.3 Alternatives to the Complaints Board for Public Procurement

Orders by the Complaints Board for Public Procurement cannot be appealed against to another administrative authority – so-called administrative recourse. As it is clear that the Complaints Board for Public Procurement has been vested with special powers to review complaints concerning infringement of the procurement rules, it would in a sense have been logical had there been no right of complaint to other administrative authorities (other than to the Complaints Board for Public Procurement) concerning infringements of the procurement rules. This was indeed the basis on which the original Complaints Board Act was drafted.

However, by an amendment to the Executive Order on the Complaints Board in 1996 the Competition Authority was granted authority to bring cases before the Complaints Board for Public Procurement. For that purpose the Minister of Trade and Industry authorised the Competition Authority to raise cases and review complaints submitted to it concerning infringement of the procurement rules. The Competition Authority was not granted powers to issue orders or prohibition notices. Review of complaints by the Competition Authority is therefore more informal and more in the form of a dialogue than review by the Complaints Board for Public Procurement. The Competition Authority opens a dialogue with the contracting authority as early as possible in the procurement procedure and may recommend to the contracting authority that the procedure be suspended until the Competition Authority has cleared up the matter and maybe informs the contracting authority of how, in the opinion of the Competition Authority, the procedure can be lawfully continued. Usually contracting authorities comply with the Competition Authority's recommendations and it is, therefore, only exceptionally that the Competition Authority has been forced to bring a case before the Complaints Board for Public Procurement.[22] So far, only one case brought before the

---

21. Act No 338 of May 2005 on Tender Procedures for Public Work Contracts, on invitations to tender in the building and civil engineering sector.
22. Bill No L 243 of 30 March 2000 on the Complaints Board for Public Procurement, Official Report of Parliamentary Proceedings 1999-2000, Annex A, column 6861.

Complaints Board for Public Procurement by the Competition Authority has resulted in the issue of an order.[23]

In *Competition Authority vs. Tårnby Local Authority*[24] the defendant invited tenders under the restricted procedure for a contract for refuse collection. The local authority required that the proposed refuse collection essentially should correspond to the service provided so far and therefore requested a technical consultant to obtain the information necessary for the contract documents from the undertaking responsible for the service at the time, Grundejersammenslutningens Renholdningsselskab (GR). Subsequently, the local authority prequalified five undertakings, *inter alia* GR. The Competition Authority lodged a complaint with the Complaints Board for Public Procurement arguing that the assistance received by the local authority from GR was of such magnitude that GR's competitive situation had shifted and, as a consequence, the local authority should not consider the tender submitted by GR. The Competition Authority's request that the procedure be suspended was not allowed and since the local authority later concluded a contract with one of the other tenderers, the Competition Authority withdrew the complaint. At the request of the local authority the Complaints Board completed the review and issued a separate order[25] despite the Competition Authority's claim that the Complaints Board was no longer competent. The Complaints Board for Public Procurement dismissed the Competition Authority's claim in the main proceedings having found that GR had not gained such a competitive advantage from the preparation of the tender procedure that the local authority would have been entitled or obliged to exclude the tender submitted by GR.

The Competition Authority's powers in the field of procurement are such that submission of a complaint to the Competition Authority is a particularly apt alternative to lodging a complaint with the Complaints Board for Public Procurement at the early stages of a procurement procedure. By a mere request by phone to the Competition Authority a tenderer who feels that its rights are not fully respected in a procurement procedure can have its suspicion that the procurement rules have been infringed confirmed and also cause the Competition Authority to intervene in the matter. The advantages to the tenderer is that it will not have to pay the Complaints Board's fee,[26] it will not have to hire a lawyer to conduct the case before the Complaints Board and, perhaps most importantly, by letting the Competition Authority contact the contracting au-

---

23. Order of the Complaints Board of 17 March 1998, Competition Authority vs. Tårnby Local Authority.
24. Ibid.
25. Order of the Complaints Board of 25 February 1998, Competition Authority vs. Tårnby Local Authority.
26. It follows from the Executive Order on the Complaints Board that the complainant must pay a fee of DKK 4,000 which will be repaid if the complaint is dismissed or if the complainant succeeds, fully or partially, in its claim.

thority about the correct conduct of the procurement procedure, it can remain anonymous.

Incidentally, the Competition Authority is not bound by the Complaints Board Act in reviewing procedures and can therefore advise the contracting authority, too, on the correct conduct of a procurement procedure.

By virtue of Article 3, paragraph 1 of the Remedies Directive the Commission is empowered to intervene in a procurement procedure, prior to the conclusion of the contract, if it considers a clear and manifest infringement of Community law has been committed. In that capacity the Commission acts as an alternative review board to the Complaints Board for Public Procurement. Presumably, all other things being equal, this is most convenient for foreign tenderers which are not familiar with the Danish system and, perhaps on that account, find it more natural and reassuring to complain directly to the Commission. The Commission notifies the Member State and the contracting authority concerned of the reasons why it believes that the procurement rules have been infringed and requests that the infringement be corrected. The Commission has no power to order the Member State or the contracting authority to discontinue the procedure or correct the infringement, but by virtue of Article 226 of the EC Treaty the Commission can institute proceedings against the Member State before the European Court of Justice for infringement of the Treaty.

Infringement of the procurement rules is a criminal offence. The framework act[27] provides that the Executive Orders transposing the procurement rules can make infringement of the rules punishable by a fine or simple detention.[28] Under the previous and current Executive Orders transposing the Procurement Directives infringement of the Orders, and thus the Procurement Directives implemented by the Orders, is punishable by a fine. It thus follows that a disgruntled tenderer can file a report with the police against the relevant contracting authority. As far as we know, a criminal action for infringement of the procurement rules has never been brought.

Finally, a tenderer can bring a case concerning infringement of the procurement rules directly before the courts of law. If the Complaints Board for Public Procurement has already reviewed the case, an appeal against that decision must be brought no later than 8 weeks after the decision of the Complaints Board was communicated to the parties. After the expiry of the period

---

27. Consolidating Act No 600 of 30 June 1992 coordinating the procedures for awarding public works and supply contracts, etc.
28. See, however, Act No 433 of 31 May 2000 to amend various provisions for the implementation of Act on Enforcement and Execution of Penalties, etc.

allowed for appeal, the decision of the Complaints Board for Public Procurement becomes final and cannot be brought before the courts of law. Pursuant to section 225 of the Administration of Justice Act decisions by the Complaints Board for Public Procurement must be brought before the High Court as the first instance.

The Competition Authority offers assistance to economic operators which run into problems when participating in procurement procedures abroad. On the basis of a complaint from an economic operator the Competition Authority can contact the authorities in the country where the contracting authority is established, or alternatively the Commission. Before contacting the foreign authority, the Competition Authority investigates the matters that have given rise to the complaint.

In 2003 a Public Procurement Network was established comprising the 25 EU Member States, the EEA countries and Switzerland. Also the Commission participates in the Network. The objective of the Network is to establish contact between the authorities of the participating countries and exchange experience with a view to strengthening the application and enforcement of the procurement rules. First and foremost the Network is intended to provide informal solutions to public procurement problems in cross-border cases where an economic operator established in one of the participating countries finds itself in difficulties in a procurement procedure. Presumably the establishment of the Public Procurement Network has significantly improved the Competition Authority's opportunities for providing assistance in procurement cases.[29]

2. Interim measures

As mentioned above, the overriding aim of the Remedies Directive and the Complaints Board Act is to guarantee the rapid and effective review of complaints of infringements of the procurement rules. At the same time the intention is to reach a solution while the procurement procedure is still ongoing, i.e. before a contract is concluded.

---

29. Information on the assistance provided by the Competition Authority in procedures abroad and on the Public Procurement Network can be found at: http://www.ks.dk/english/procurement/network/

2.1 Suspensive effect of complaint

In view of the fact that procurement procedures typically are completed over a relatively short period of time, the Remedies Directive provides that interim measures to suspend the procedure for the award of a public contract or the implementation of any decision taken by the contracting authority until the complaint has been reviewed must be available by way of expedited procedures.

However, the Remedies Directive does not require that review procedures automatically suspend the ongoing procurement procedure. Further, the Remedies Directive provides that in considering whether interim measures should be taken, account can be had of the probable consequences of the measures for all interests at stake, as well as the "public interest" whereby is meant the adverse social consequences that may be the outcome of suspending a procurement procedure pending a review thus resulting in a delay of the supply of the products offered.[30]

In *CS Communications & Systems Austria GmbH*[31] the European Court of Justice made the following statement:

"... Article 2 of Directive 89/665 must be interpreted as meaning that it does not preclude the Member States from providing that when a body responsible for review procedures for the award of public contracts decides an application for interim measures, it is bound or authorised to take account of the prospects of success of an application for a decision of a contracting authority to be set aside on the ground that it is unlawful, so long as the national rules thus governing the adoption of those interim measures are not less favourable than those governing similar domestic actions and do not make it practically impossible or excessively difficult to exercise the rights conferred by Community law".[32]

The Complaints Board decides whether a complaint should have suspensive effect by a separate order. Orders on suspensive effect are only rarely reported by the Complaints Board for Public Procurement. It is also unusual that the Complaints Board for Public Procurement, in the order concerning the main proceedings, sheds any light on the grounds for affording or not

---

30. Similarly, the European Court of Justice weighs the interests at stake when considering whether actions brought by the Commission against Member States for infringement of the Treaties as a result of failure to comply with the Procurement Directives should act as a stay of the ongoing procurement procedure. See for example order of the European Court of Justice of 13 March 1987, case 45/87 R, Commission vs. Ireland.
31. Order of the European Court of Justice of 9 April 2003, case C-424/01, CS Communications & Systems Austria GmbH vs. Allgemeine Unfallversicherungsanstalt.
32. Ibid, paragraph 33.

affording the complaint suspensive effect. Case law shows that the Complaints Board for Public Procurement hardly ever suspends a procedure.[33]

Consequently, in practice it is often for the contracting authority to decide whether the procurement procedure should be suspended pending the outcome of the complaint. In this decision the likelihood of a subsequent claim for damages obviously carries some weight, cf. section 4 below.

2.2 Conditions for taking interim measures

The order on suspensive effect is typically made at the early stages of the review procedure. Therefore, the grounds on which an order suspending a procedure is granted must be exceptional considering the relatively serious consequences the order may have for the contracting authority, with respect to, for example, delay of contemplated projects, suspension of contracts concluded with consultants, etc.

2.2.1 A grave and clear infringement

Section 6(2) of the Complaints Board Act stipulates that a complaint can have suspensive effect only to the extent laid down in legislation or "where there are special grounds that call for such an order to be made". Accordingly, the Act prescribes that only exceptionally can a complaint have suspensive effect. In the explanatory notes to the original Bill it was stated:

When considering applications for interim measures, the Board must take account of the *gravity* of the infringement and the *consequences* of the order. In other words, all the interests at stake in the case as well as the public interest must be weighed. This is particularly important in the situations where the outcome of the order is *likely* to be a *cancellation and reopening* of the procedure after conclusion of the contract.[34] (Our emphasis).

In considering the application, the Complaints Board for Public Procurement places emphasis on the probability of the complainant succeeding in its com-

---

33. So far the following orders by the Complaints Board for Public Procurement have resulted in a suspension of the procedure: order of 26 April 1996, E. Pihl og Søn A/S vs. I/S Avedøre Kloakværk; order of 16 October 1996, Danske Vognmænd vs. Stevns Local Authority; order of 9 March, Technicomm A/S vs. Danish Railways; order of 18 March 1999, Seghers Better Technology Group vs. I/S Amagerforbrænding; order of 10 June 1999, Højgaard & Schultz A/S vs. Odder Local Authority; order of 17 December 1999, Renoflex A/S vs. Søllerød Local Authority; order of 27 June 2000, Deponering af Problem-affald ApS vs. I/S Vestforbrænding.
34. Bill No L 86 of 23 January 1991 on the Complaints Board for Public Procurement, Official Report of Parliamentary Proceedings 1990-91, second session, Annex A, column 1979.

plaint.[35] See also section 3.5 below on the significance of the contract conclusion which also has a bearing upon the suspensive effect issue.

2.2.2 Urgency

Needless to say, suspension of a procedure is only relevant where the purpose of the complaint otherwise would be defeated. However, in by far the majority of review procedures the contract for the supply in issue has already been concluded at the time when the complaint is lodged. The application for suspensive effect is therefore considered in the context of whether the alleged infringement ultimately will lead to a cancellation of the contracting authority's award decision and, in consequence, the possibility that the complainant could be awarded the contract in a possible new procedure. See section 3 below on the conditions for cancellation.

In the rare cases where the complaint is lodged before the contracting authority has awarded the contract, it makes sense that the complaint has the effect of suspending the procedure, even where the complaint is only about minor infringements of the procurement rules in that it affords the contracting authority the opportunity to correct the infringement.

2.2.3 Weighing of interests

As stated above, in considering whether a complaint is to have suspensive effect, account must be had of the interests at stake, the interests of the tenderer/complainant vs. the public interest, in completing the procurement procedure.

Another factor is whether the completion of the procurement procedure in issue is of great urgency.[36]

In *Copenhagen Business School*[37] the Eastern High Court denounced the Complaints Board for Public Procurement for having ordered a complaint to have suspensive effect despite, among other things, a tight timetable for the proposed works, and because the Complaints Board for Public Procurement, already at the time of the order, ought to have

---

35. Order of the Complaints Board of 8 March 1995, Henning Larsens Tegnestue vs. Ministry of Culture.
36. Order of the Complaints Board of 8 March 1995, Henning Larsens Tegnestue vs. Ministry of Culture.
37. Judgment of the Eastern High Court of 16 August 2000, case B-1654-97 and Others, Copenhagen Business School and Ministry of Research and Information Technology vs. Højgaard & Schultz A/S (as reported in the order of the Complaints Board of 19 June 1997 as Højgaard & Schultz vs. Ministry of Education).

foreseen the reasons which subsequently[38] led the Board not to overrule the contracting authority's decision to cancel the ongoing procedure.

Since the High Court's criticism, the Complaints Board for Public Procurement has not allowed any applications for suspension and, presumably, only in entirely exceptional circumstances would the Complaints Board for Public Procurement again order a complaint to have suspensive effect. Instead, it has largely been left with the contracting authority to decide whether the procedure should be suspended pending the decision of the Complaints Board. In this decision the risk of subsequent liability in damages is obviously a weighty factor.

The possibility for allowing a complaint to have suspensive effect is one means by which the Procurement Directive can be enforced. The suspension of a procedure before the contract is concluded may affect the contracting authority in a lesser or greater extent, but always has certain consequences. On the other hand, a decision not to suspend a procedure, prior to the conclusion of a contract, pending the outcome of a complaint, often has the effect that the most the complainant can hope for is damages. The practice in Denmark since 2000 of virtually never allowing a complaint to have suspensive effect does not seem compatible with the principle of effectiveness, cf. chapter 1.3.3. The effective implementation of the Procurement Directive and the Remedies Directive is conditional on the use of *inter alia* suspensive measures. Less reluctance to allow complaints to have suspensive effect would add to the effective implementation. Decisions by the Complaints Board for Public Procurement since 2000 reveal several cases of complaints lodged before the conclusion of a contract claiming suspension and cancellation of the procedure that were not followed by the Complaints Board for Public Procurement, even in cases where the Complaints Board subsequently found several grounds for condemning the procurement procedure and ordered that the award decision be cancelled.[39]

2.3 The effect of interim measures

Where a complaint is lodged before the procurement procedure is completed and the contract awarded and concluded, it goes without saying that the con-

---

38. Order of the Complaints Board of 19 June 1997, Højgaard & Schultz A/S vs. Ministry of Education.
39. See for example orders of the Complaints Board of 13 January 2004, E Pihl og Søn A/S vs. Hadsund Local Authority and of 20 February 2004, Miri Stål A/S vs. Esbjerg Local Authority.

tracting authority would be obliged to comply with the Complaints Board's order on interim measures, and for example suspend the procurement procedure pending the final decision of the Complaints Board for Public Procurement.

However, the effect of interim measures need not always be a complete suspension of the procurement procedure pending the outcome of the complaint. In *Technicomm*[40] the Complaints Board for Public Procurement decided that the suspensive effect of the complaint should be such that the contracting authority could not make a decision on the award of the contract, but could continue the negotiations with one of the tenderers. The specific procedure was, however, cancelled subsequently for which reason this right for the contracting authority to continue the procedure had no effect.

The question is which effect suspensive measures ordered *after* the conclusion of a contract should have. Should the performance of the contract be delayed? Suspension of a procedure must be intended as a means to correct the procurement procedure, if necessary. However, the procurement procedure ends with the award of a contract for which reason there is nothing to suspend after the award. After the award the only available measure is to set aside the award decision. In that situation an order on suspensive measures seems to serve no purpose. Nevertheless, on several occasions the Complaints Board for Public Procurement has allowed a complaint to have suspensive effect after the contract had been awarded to one of the tenderers.

In *Deponering af Problem-affald ApS*[41] the contract was already awarded when the Complaints Board on 11 January 2000 decided that the complaint should have suspensive effect. However, since 1 December 1999 the defendant had been obliged by law to provide for the disposal of electric and electronic products (the object of the contract). Following correspondence between the Complaints Board and the defendant's lawyer on the effects of the order on suspension, the defendant indicated that considering its obligation concerning disposal of electric and electronic products, it had decided that the service would be performed in accordance with the contract concluded.

However, as mentioned above, the Complaints Board for Public Procurement seems to have tightened the requirements to be met before a complaint is given suspensive effect considerably, which suggests that such effect will not

---

40. Order of the Complaints Board of 9 March 1999, Technicomm A/S vs. Danish Railways.
41. Order of the Complaints Board of 27 June 2000, Deponering af Problem-affald ApS vs. I/S Vestforbrænding.

longer be the outcome of review procedures in situations where the contract has already been awarded.

Finally, it is noted that failure to comply with a prohibition notice or an order of the Complaints Board concerning suspensive measures is punishable by a fine.

3. Setting aside decisions

By virtue of section 6(1) of the Complaints Board Act the Complaints Board for Public Procurement has the power to "dismiss a complaint or to determine it on its merits wholly or in part. In so doing it may annul unlawful decisions or order the awarding body to bring the award process into conformity with legislation".

In practice it is the power to set aside the contracting authority's decisions which is interesting. The Complaints Board for Public Procurement can, in principle, set aside any decision made by the contracting authority in the context of procurement procedures, including decisions not to put a contract out to tender under the EU procurement rules, decisions on choice of procurement directive, on pre-qualification, etc. In fact, the Complaints Board for Public Procurement has even set aside a contracting authority's decision to cancel a call for tenders.[42] Therefore, this power to set aside decisions matters a great deal in the Complaints Board's orders to correct a procedure.

In considering whether to set aside a decision, the Complaints Board for Public Procurement takes account of the following: the gravity of the contracting authority's infringement of the procurement rules; inactivity on the part of the complainant; and finally weighs the social consequences of setting aside a decision against the need to protect the complainant's interests. In practice, the decision is based on an overall assessment and it is not always clear how the Complaints Board for Public Procurement has judged each element.

3.1 Specific or general importance (gravity of the infringement)
A decision to set aside a contracting authority's award decision is a fairly drastic measure and as such it can only be used where the infringement of the procurement rules is likely to have had an effect on the award of the contract.

---

42. Order of the Complaints Board of 12 August 2002, Milana A/S vs. County of Vest-sjælland.

Hence, there must be a causal link between the infringement committed and the contracting authority's award decision. Inevitably, this assessment easily comes to resemble a relative weighing of, on the one hand, the gravity of the infringement and the actual effect thereof on the procurement procedure against, on the other hand, the consequences for the contracting authority of setting aside the decision.

A series of orders delivered by the Complaints Board for Public Procurement are examined in sections 3.1.1-6 below according to the nature of the infringement. Often more infringements are committed in the course of one procedure, and indeed in several decisions the Complaints Board for Public Procurement seems to have emphasised that it is the cumulative effect of several infringements which results in the decision to set aside an award decision.

3.1.1 Failure to call for tenders

The most serious infringement of the procurement rules occurs where a public contract is not put out to tender at all. In such a situation the principles of transparency, equal treatment and open and effective competition have all been violated, for which reason the Complaints Board for Public Procurements should set aside the decision on the award of the contract.[43] Case law has established that a complaint can be filed against a contracting authority's decision not to call for tenders.[44] The possibilities for filing a complaint are not eliminated merely because the contracting authority acknowledges that it has infringed the procurement rules.[45] Where a contracting authority has invited tenders for a contract in accordance with the Procurement Directive without being obliged to do so and in the conduct of the procedure committed mistakes, the Complaints Board for Public Procurement has established, in a specific case, that decisions could not be set aside, referring to the fact that the contracting authority could have made the purchase without a call for tenders.[46]

---

43. Order of the Complaints Board of 3 November 1994, Haulier Kenn Sonne vs. Bornholms Fælleskommunale Affaldsbortskaffelse I/S.
44. Judgment of the European Court of Justice of 11 January 2005, case C-26/03, Stadt Halle and Others vs. Arbeitsgemeinschaft Thermische Restabfall.
45. Judgment of the European Court of Justice of 3 March 2005, case C-414/03, Commission vs. Germany.
46. Order of the Complaints Board of 14 October 2004, SK Tolkeservice ApS vs. County of Copenhagen.

The defendant in *Bilhuset Randers A/S*[47] had obtained offers from four car dealers, but had not invited tenders under the EU procurement rules because it had estimated that the threshold value would not be exceeded. The local authority had based this calculation on the lowest priced car, of the make Fiat, available in the market regardless that it had stipulated other criteria than the lowest price. The Complaints Board held that the calculation of the threshold value was not objective and set aside the authority's decision to conclude a contract. Moreover, the Complaints Board ordered the authority to call for tenders under the EU procurement rules if it still wished to make the acquisition in issue.

3.1.2 Wrong Directive
In *Siemens A/S*[48] the Complaints Board for Public Procurement set aside a decision by a local authority to call for tenders under the then applicable Utilities Directive on the ground that the call for tenders should have been made under the then applicable Supplies Directive.

3.1.3 Prohibition on negotiations
In practice the prohibition on negotiations is one of the most difficult procurement law principles to comply with and violation thereof often leads to cancellation of the procedure bearing in mind that a violation, almost by definition, is capable of distorting competition.

In *Eiland Electric*[49] the Complaints Board noted that, basically, a tender must be evaluated on its content and that the contracting authority only has limited scope for asking clarifying questions of the tenderer, and in any event only concerning non-fundamental aspects. Consequently, by contacting three of the five tenderers, after the final date for submitting tenders, with questions in regard to the product specifications, which were then taken into account in the evaluation of the sub-criteria, the contracting authority had violated the prohibition on negotiations and the principle of equal treatment. Furthermore, the defendant had committed a series of other grave infringements of the procurement rules. The Complaints Board therefore decided to "… set aside the contracting authority's decision to offer the electrical wiring contract for tender in its existing form and to award the contract to one of the tenderers. Moreover, the Complaints Board instructed the contracting authority to legalise the tender procedure by offering the electrical wiring contract for tender again". The Complaints Board added that the complaint had been filed shortly after the complainant became aware of the aspects that gave rise to the complaint and that, when filing the complaint, the complainant had applied for a suspension of the procurement procedure (regardless that the Complaints Board did not grant the suspension).

47. Order of the Complaints Board of 16 December 2003, Bilhuset Randers A/S and Others vs. Sønderhald Local Authority.
48. Order of the Complaints Board of 25 October 1995, Siemens A/S vs. Esbjerg Local Authority.
49. Order of the Complaints Board of 24 October 2001, Eiland Electric A/S vs. County of Vestsjælland.

3.1.4 Principle of equal treatment

The principle of equal treatment goes to the root of procurement law. It touches upon the very principal aim of the procurement rules; to ensure equal and effective competition. Infringement of the principle of equal treatment can take a variety of forms in the course of a procurement procedure. Infringements arise in *inter alia* the following situations: personal involvement,[50] tailored contract specifications, disclosure of different information or erroneous disclosure,[51] unlawful negotiations and non-objective application of an evaluation model.

In *Aon Denmark*[52] the Complaints Board made the following statement: "In pursuance of the Service Directive, it was up to the contracting authority to ensure that all tenderers were treated equally. Consequently, the contract documents should have stated clearly that the fact that some insurance companies pay a commission to insurance brokers was to be disregarded, so that the prices tendered would have to correspond to the actual payment for the services". The defendant had failed to do so and, in consequence, awarded the contract to a tenderer which had not submitted the most economically advantageous tender. The Complaints Board set aside the defendant's award decision.

In *Brunata*[53] the Complaints Board set aside the contracting authority's award decision citing the nature of the infringements ascertained by the Complaints Board. Among the infringements was a violation of the principle of equal treatment in that one tenderer had been allowed to amend a fundamental aspect of its tender.

3.1.5 Principle of transparency

The principle of transparency is important in procurement law and is intended to ensure impartiality and objectivity in the award of public contracts. The principle of transparency is bound up with the principle of equal treatment and it is often difficult to separate the two. Needless to say, but the less transparent a procurement procedure is, the greater the risk that one of the tenderers gains, or prior to the procedure has, information giving it an unlawful competitive advantage.

As with the principle of equal treatment, there are numerous ways of infringing the principle of transparency during a procurement procedure. The

---

50. Order of the Complaints Board of 17 November 2003, Helsingør Local Authority vs. Ejendomsselskabet Stengade 56 ApS.
51. Order of the Complaints Board of 7 August 2003, KAS Transport rep. by Kim Schrøder vs. Århus Local Authority.
52. Order of the Complaints Board of 27 November 2002, Aon Denmark A/S vs. Odense Local Authority.
53. Order of the Complaints Board of 16 December 2004, Brunata A/S vs. Aalborg Boligselskab af 1956, branch 8 and Others

most serious infringement probably occurs where it is altogether unclear what the object of the proposed contract is.

In *Eiland Electric*[54] it was unclear whether the contract specifications required tenders for an electrical wiring contract to include a product specification. Various corrective statements had been sent out in the course of the procedure which had only added to the lack of clarity. The Complaints Board made the following statement: "… the mentioned lack of clarity of the contract documents had open up for random discrimination among the tenderers, which was in violation of the principle of equality, and that this lack of clarity also represented a violation of the principle of transparency, including the requirements which must be deemed to form part of EU tender regulations to the effect that an offer for tender must contain a clear and precise specification of the contract offered".

Another common violation of the principle of equal treatment is errors in the design or application of a model for evaluating the tenders submitted.

The local authority which was the defendant in *E. Pihl og Søn*[55] had during the procurement procedure found out that some evaluation models rendered inexpedient results and therefore chose not to apply these models to the evaluation of the tenders. This would have been in full compliance with the procurement rules had the authority not included the evaluation models in the contract documents. As a consequence, by not applying the models to the evaluation, it was unclear how the tenders were evaluated. The Complaints Board therefore set aside the authority's decision to award the contract to one of the tenderers regardless that the complainant did not immediately file a complaint with the Complaints Board.

3.1.6 Procedural errors

As mentioned above, the contracting authority's decision to award a contract can only be set aside if the infringement of the procurement rules was such that it may have had an effect on the outcome of the procedure.

In *Oxford Research*[56] the Complaints Board stated *ex officio* that the defendant had violated the procurement rules by pre-qualifying more tenderers than the maximum number indicated in the contract notice. However, the violation was not such that it could lead to the defendant's award decision being set aside.

---

54. Order of the Complaints Board of 24 October 2001, Eiland Electric A/S vs. County of Vestsjælland.
55. Order of the Complaints Board of 13 January 2004, E. Pihl og Søn A/S vs. Hadsund Local Authority.
56. Order of the Complaints Board of 6 August 2001, Oxford Research A/S vs. Faaborg Local Authority.

In *ISS Danmark*[57] the Complaints Board noted that the defendant had not ranked the sub-criteria to the award criterion "the most economically advantageous tender" in order of priority in the contract documents, despite an internal ranking of them, and that the defendant's evaluation model was not suitable as it would only very exceptionally produce another result than the tender of the lowest price. To this the Complaints Board stated: "[These] violations … were of a formal nature, and the violation did not constitute a case of disregarding the principle of equality or other basic principles of the tender regulations of the European Union". The Complaints Board added that the tenderers could have adapted their tenders to the evaluation model which had been forwarded to the tenderers 14 days prior to the final date for submitting tenders.

3.2 Complainant's inactivity

In considering whether a decision should be set aside, the Complaints Board for Public Procurement often places relatively great emphasis on the time elapsed since the complainant became aware of the events that brought about the complaint. The assessment seems to focus on whether, in the circumstances, it is at all practical or reasonable to cancel the procedure and also on whether the complainant's interest in a cancellation is worthy of protection considering the time elapsed.

In *AC-Trafik*[58] the Complaints Board did not allow the complainant's application for suspensive effect referring *inter alia* to the approx. five weeks that had passed since the complainant became aware of the contracting authority's decision to award the contract to the chosen tenderer.

The contracting authority in *Dansk Transport og Logistik*[59] had committed several infringements of the contract documents, *inter alia* wrongfully failed to pre-qualify four undertakings which had requested pre-qualification. However, the Complaints Board did not allow the complainant's claim for cancellation of the procedure citing that the infringements of the procurement rules were verifiable on the basis of the contract notice and the specifications and, therefore, the complainant could have requested the Complaints Board to suspend the procedure before the final date for submitting tenders. The complaint was lodged approx. three weeks after the contracting authority's award decision.

In *Uniqsoft 1998 ApS*[60] the contracting authority had *inter alia* failed to comply with the prohibition on negotiations and taken aspects into account which were not specified in the award criterion. However, the complaint was not lodged until approx. one year after the

---

57. Order of the Complaints Board of 2 April 2002, ISS Danmark A/S vs. H:S Rigshospitalet.
58. Order of the Complaints Board of 3 January 2002, AC-Trafik rep. by Anders Bødker Christiansen vs. County of Frederiksborg.
59. Order of the Complaints Board of 16 May 2000, Dansk Transport og Logistik vs. I/S Reno Syd.
60. Order of the Complaints Board of 2 May 2000, Uniqsoft 1998 ApS vs. Odense Local Authority.

award of the contract in which connection the Complaints Board made the following statement: "Regardless of the nature of the fault committed, there was thus no basis for setting aside the contracting authority's decision".

In *Brd. Thybo A/S*[61] the contracting authority had called for tenders pursuant to the Tender Act, but had not specified sub-criteria to the award criterion "the most economically advantageous tender". As a consequence, the contracting authority had in reality applied the award criterion "the lowest price" to the award of the contract. Furthermore, the contracting authority had violated the Tender Act by opening negotiations with others than the tenderer that had submitted the tender of the lowest price. The Complaints Board set aside the award decision regardless that the complaint was not lodged until approx. ten months after the award decision.

3.3 Weighing of interests

Finally, in considering whether an award decision should be set aside, the Complaints Board for Public Procurement weighs the public interests against the need to protect the interests of the complainant.

In *Visma Logistics ASA*[62] the contracting authority had awarded the contract for IT services to a tenderer whose tender was clearly irregular. To that the Complaints Board stated: "The call for tenders and the procedures used are in fundamental violation of the EU procurement rules and, therefore, not a suitable basis on which to conclude a contract. Consequently, the Complaints Board considered setting aside the contracting authority's decisions to go through with the call for tenders in the form used and to award the contract to WM-data. However considering, in particular, that the contract with WM-data, presumably, by now has been largely fulfilled and that the setting aside of the County's decision to award the contract to WM-data would lead to a waste for society which is not commensurate with Visma's [the complainant's] interest in having the decision set aside, the Complaints Board has found that the right thing to do is not to set aside those decisions."

In *Technicomm A/S*[63] the Complaints Board stated that "In the specific circumstances where the violation consisted in considering a tender from a tenderer that did not participate in the negotiations, but was precluded from the negotiations, and where the tender in issue had decisively influenced the progress of the negotiations, despite the serious consequences for the defendant, the Complaints Board for Public Procurement sees no alternative, but to cancel the procedure pursuant to section 5(1), first sentence of the Act on the Complaints Board for Public Procurement."

---

61. Order of the Complaints Board of 10 March 2004, Brd. Thybo A/S vs. Arbejdernes Andelsboligforening af 1938.
62. Order of the Complaints Board of 8 August 2000, Visma Logistics ASA vs. County of Copenhagen.
63. Order of the Complaints Board of 9 March 1999, Technicomm A/S vs. Danish Railways.

3.4 Legal effects of an order to set aside a decision

The legal effects of an order to set aside a decision are entirely dependent on whether a contract has been concluded at the time when the Complaints Board for Public Procurement makes its order. See the next section for the legal effects of a decision by the Complaints Board for Public Procurement to set aside an award decision.

In the (few) cases where review procedures are decided before the conclusion of the contract, the legal effects of an order to set aside essentially depend on which decision is set aside. If it is the contracting authority's choice of Procurement Directive, the contracting authority has no alternative, but to cancel the ongoing procedure and reopen a procedure under the correct directive. In contrast, if the decision set aside concerns, for example, the decision to use a non-objective calculation model, the contracting authority can change its decision, at least in those procedures where the calculation model is not disclosed to the tenderer prior to the final date for submitting tenders and, therefore, has not influenced the preparation of the tenders.

Incidentally, it is noted that failure to comply with a prohibition notice or an order issued by the Complaints Board for Public Procurement setting aside unlawful decisions or to correct a procurement procedure is punishable by a fine.

It is of great importance and should be emphasised that Article 2, paragraph 6 of the Remedies Directive provides that the effect of review procedures on concluded contracts should be determined by national law. The Member States can therefore provide in national law that an order to set aside a decision to award a contract also should have effects on the contract already concluded under contract law. As a consequence, in compliance with the Remedies Directive national law can provide that such a contract is invalid or that a contract is invalid if the award decision is overruled following a complaint lodged within a pre-determined time and before the award decision is advertised, etc. Such provisions are not implemented in Danish law.

3.5 Significance of contract conclusion

The explanatory notes to the current Complaints Board Act leaves no doubt as to how the legislator has interpreted the options available to the Complaints Board for Public Procurement in the cases where the complaint is not lodged with the Complaints Board until after the procurement procedure is ended and the contract concluded.

"Since the Complaints Board has no power to cancel a contract, in most cases the Complaints Board can only decide on the legality of the procurement procedure conducted. In approx. 2/3 of these cases the procurement procedure is found to have been unlawful, but seemingly, such decision has never had the effect of cancelling a contract. This is because the setting aside by the Complaints Board of an unlawful decision under administrative law on the choice of tenderer does not invalidate the contract concluded in private law."[64]

This statement is undoubtedly correct insofar as the Complaints Board for Public Procurement cannot declare a concluded contract invalid or otherwise cancel it. Consequently, the Complaints Board for Public Procurement does not cancel the contract, but only the contracting authority's decision to award/conclude the contract. Legal literature has discussed whether the contracting authority thereby is imposed an obligation to cancel/terminate the contract concluded. Failure to comply with a prohibition notice or an order issued by the Complaints Board for Public Procurement is punishable under section 12(1) of the Complaints Board Act. While the Complaints Board cannot outright invalidate concluded contracts, it should be empowered to order the contracting authority to cancel the contract concluded. Whether the contracting authority incurs liability in damages because of such cancellation is irrelevant in this respect since the Complaints Board already at an earlier stage, when weighing the "public interests", took account thereof. Incidentally, Danish law applies the principle freedom of contract for which reason the contracting authority should have allowed for the risk of a subsequent cancellation order when drawing up the contract and made provisions in the contract for its termination in the event of such order.

Following an order by the Complaints Board to set aside a contracting authority's decision to award a contract to a specific tenderer, as case law currently stands in Denmark, the contracting authority has a choice between cancelling the entire or part of the procedure and reopen a procedure in accordance with the rules of the Procurement Directive or standing by a concluded contract, despite the economic implications, such as liability in damages, legal costs, etc., involved therewith.

Finally, it is noted that since the time of the award must be distinguished from the time of the signing of the contract, the time of the conclusion of the contract is not always as clear-cut as it might seem. A procurement procedure officially ends when the contracting authority awards the contract to the successful tenderer. In theory, the award decision is to be regarded as an acceptance of the tenderer's tender and, as such, a contract is concluded at

---

64. Bill No L 243 of 30 March 2000 on the Complaints Board for Public Procurement, Official Report of Parliamentary Proceedings 1999-2000, Annex A, column 6861.

the time of the award – the signing of the contract is merely a formality. However, this presupposes that the contract to be concluded was available at the time when the tenderer submitted its tender. In many procedures a draft contract is not even included among the contract documents and in such procedures it is frequently necessary to modify the contract. In these procedures the question often arises whether the tenderer's new draft contract is to be regarded as a qualified acceptance with the effect that the contract is not concluded until the time when the parties have agreed on the contract in its entirety.

4. Damages

This section 4 deals with the contracting authority's liability in damages for infringing the Procurement Directive and the fundamental principles on equal treatment, etc. in the course of a procurement procedure.

4.1 Legal basis for liability in damages

If in the course of a procurement procedure the contracting authority infringes the provisions of the Procurement Directive or the principles of equal treatment, transparency, non-discrimination, proportionality and mutual recognition, it may of course incur liability in damages for loss suffered. This liability is not conditional on separate authority, but follows from the general rules of Danish law. It is the contracting authority which is bound by the Procurement Directive and which must comply with the rules set out therein. The parties harmed are typically tenderers and undertakings that have requested pre-qualification, but sometimes also undertakings which could have submitted tenders or requested pre-qualification, but omitted to do so.[65]

Contracting authorities can also incur liability in damages for breach of the concluded contract on the basis of the award procedure. Such cases are considered under the general contract law and the effects of procurement law are negligible. The same is true of breach of the concluded contract committed by the selected supplier. It is also true even despite that infringements of the Procurement Directive are mirrored in the provisions of the contract.[66]

Tenderers and undertakings requesting pre-qualification can, depending on the circumstances, incur liability in damages to the contracting authority on account of their conduct during the procedure. However, such liability

---

65. Order of the Complaints Board of 22 November 2001, Forlaget Magnus A/S vs. Customs and Tax Authority.
66. Order of the Complaints Board of 9 March 2004, Georg Berg A/S vs. Køge Local Authority.

does not derive from infringements of the Procurement Directive and, therefore, falls outside the scope of this section 4.

4.1.1 Liability in damages for infringement of the Procurement Directive
Member States are obliged to implement the Procurement Directive into national law, cf. Article 249 of the EC Treaty. The rules must be fully and effectively implemented and applied in accordance with EU case law.[67] The possibility for being awarded full damages for loss suffered because of the contracting authority's infringement of the Procurement Directive is an indispensable precondition of effective implementation. Therefore, national law cannot exclude the possibility of being awarded damages for the contracting authority's infringement of certain provisions of the Procurement Directive. The liability incurred by the contracting authority as a result of infringement of the Procurement Directive should be assessed in the light of and subject to the obligations imposed by EU law. The Procurement Directive is supplemented by the Remedies Directive,[68] cf. section 1 above, which is examined further in section 4.1.2 below.

There is an abundance of decided cases concerning liability in damages for violation of the now repealed Tender Invitation Act. However, these decisions are only of limited relevance as precedents in cases concerning infringement of the Procurement Directive. Firstly, because the now repealed Tender Invitation Act did not originate in EU provisions, let alone the Procurement Directive, and secondly, because under the Tender Invitation Act the contracting authority was entitled to reject all tenders submitted to a call for competition.[69] By contrast, pursuant to the Procurement Directive a contracting authority can only cancel a procedure on objective grounds; hence, a discretionary rejection of all tenders would be a manifest infringement of the Procurement Directive. Thus, under the EU procurement rules as set out in the Procurement Directive there is an implied obligation to contract, cf. chapter 7.8.

The comments above concerning the limited relevance of cases decided pursuant to the Tender Invitation Act for establishing liability for the contracting authority's infringement of the Procurement Directive are also true of cases

---

67. Judgment of the European Court of Justice of 9 March 1978, case 106/77, Italian Ministry of Finance vs. S.P.A. Simmenthal.
70. Council Directive 89/665 EEC of 21 December 1989 on the coordination of the laws, regulations and administrative provisions relating to the application of review procedures to the award of public supply and public works contracts.
69. Act No 216 of 18 June 1966, the Tender Invitation Act, Section (3)(2).

decided pursuant to the Tender Act.[70] Neither the Tender Act originates in EU Law.

4.1.2 The Remedies Directive

Council Directive 89/665/EEC of 21 December 1989 provided that procedures be established for reviewing tender procedures conducted under the now repealed Supply, Service and Works Directives. In the preamble to the Remedies Directive it is pointed out that the then applicable Directives, like the Procurement Directive, did not contain any specific provisions ensuring their effective application. For that reason it was considered important to ensure that adequate procedures were implemented in all Member States to permit the setting aside of decisions taken unlawfully by contracting authorities in the course of procurement procedures and the award of damages to undertakings harmed by an infringement.

Against that background Member States were imposed obligations to take the measures necessary to ensure that complaints alleging infringement of the procurement rules could be reviewed effectively and, in particular, as rapidly as possible, cf. Article 1, paragraph 1 of the Remedies Directive.

In Article 1, paragraph 2 of the Remedies Directive it is emphasised that Member States are under a particular obligation to ensure that undertakings claiming damages for infringement of the EU procurement rules are not discriminated against compared to undertakings claiming damages under other national rules.

By virtue of Article 2 of the Remedies Directive Member States must ensure that the review procedures *inter alia* include provision for the power to award damages to undertakings harmed by an infringement. Member States must not make the award of damages subject to proof by the undertaking claiming damages that the contracting authority acted culpably or maliciously, since such a precondition would render it considerably more difficult or indeed impossible for undertakings to be awarded damages which would undermine the principle of effectiveness.[71]

The Act on the Complaints Board for Public Procurement transposes the Remedies Directive into Danish law, cf. section 1 above.

---

70. Act on Tendering Procedures for Works Contracts – Act No 338 of May 2005 on Tender Procedures for Public Work Contracts.
71. Judgment of the European Court of Justice of 14 October 2004, case C-275/03, Commission vs. Portugal.

4.1.3 The Complaints Board Act

The Remedies Directive was implemented into Danish law by the Complaints Board Act. Pursuant to Section 6(3) of the Complaints Board Act the Complaints Board for Public Procurement is empowered to award damages to a complainant which has suffered a loss in consequence of an infringement of the Directive.

Damages are only awarded if a claim for damages is brought forth in the complaint. It thus follows that damages are not awarded *ex officio.*

Claims for damages need not be brought before the Complaints Board. They can be brought before the ordinary courts of law directly. However, for various reasons it is in practice preferable to have the question of damages settled by the Complaints Board first. These reasons can be found in the expertise of the Complaints Board, the relative speed with which it settles cases, at least in comparison with the courts of law, and not least that consideration of claims for damages by the Complaints Board is not conditional on the payment of a fee under the Act on Payment of Court Fees, but is covered by the fee paid when a complaint is lodged with the Complaints Board. The unbalanced provision on costs contained in Section 7 of the Complaints Board Act is another reason for having the Complaints Board decide the claim for damages, cf. section 4.5.

In practice, the Complaints Board usually starts its review by considering whether the alleged infringement has been committed, and if it finds that it has, it then decides on the claim for damages. This practice serves to ensure that the review of whether an infringement has occurred is not delayed by possibly unnecessary measures and documentation requirements in respect of the liability in damages and loss assessment.

4.1.4 Liability in damages in public and private law

From a public law perspective the risk of incurring liability in damages in combination with the particularly lax rules for claiming damages serves to ensure that contracting authorities comply with the provisions of the Procurement Directive. The risk of incurring liability in damages has a preventive effect, albeit depending on the amount of damages awarded by the Complaints Board and the courts of law. The sheer possibility of being awarded damages provides an incentive for lodging complaints with the Complaints Board and is therefore a means in ensuring greater control over compliance with the provisions of the Procurement Directive. While an order whereby a complainant succeeds in a complaint is not of much value to the complainant if it leads to nothing more than verification of an infringement, the possibility of being awarded damages justifies the lodging of a complaint, also from a business point of view.

From a private law perspective the possibility of claiming damages serves to remedy the situation of an undertaking harmed by an infringement of the Procurement Directive in the course of a procurement procedure. Accordingly, where an undertaking has submitted a tender in reply to a call for competition to no avail because the contracting authority infringed the Procurement Directive, the undertaking may be awarded damages for the costs incurred to prepare the tender. And if the undertaking was wrongfully passed over for the award of the contract, damages may be awarded for loss of profit. Undoubtedly, the Complaints Board's power to award damages in review procedures has the effect that the number of complaints lodged is higher than it would have been had it not had this power, regardless that the award of damages is secondary to the award of the contract. To the complainant award of damages is usually of secondary importance when compared to the redress achievable if infringements committed could be corrected to the effect that the complainant, depending on the competitiveness of its tender, would be afforded the opportunity to perform the contract, be entitled to the resulting profit and enjoy the benefits of using the contract as a reference, etc. However, if the contracting authority has announced that a contract has been concluded with the supplier to which the contract was awarded, the possibility for being awarded damages is the primary interest of the complainant.

4.1.5 Nature of the liability in damages

The contracting authority may incur liability in damages for infringement of the Procurement Directive in the course of a procurement procedure. Undertakings which have submitted tenders or requested pre-qualification or which could have submitted tenders or requested pre-qualification can claim damages, cf. section 4.1.1. Since there is no contract, strictly speaking, it is not liability in contract. Rather, the liability incurred by the contracting authority for infringement of the Procurement Directive is in the nature of a pre-contractual liability arising from the publication of the contract notice, the invitation to submit tenders and the content of the contract documents. The liability in damages, which the contracting authority may incur for infringement of the Procurement Directive, can be seen as the result of a special duty of good faith which the contracting authority has towards those undertakings that are eligible for participation in a procurement procedure advertised by the contracting authority. Such liability is not unprecedented in Danish law.[72]

The liability in damages is not an actual penalty provision, but in view of the particular nature of the procurement rules and considering the situations from which the liability in damages can arise, the liability may at times be perceived, with some legitimacy, as being of a punitive nature. In particular the situation where the contracting authority is ordered to pay expectation damages to a tenderer which was wrongfully passed over is likely to be perceived as a punishment.

The liability in damages derives from public law as well as private law. The liability has roots in public law in that the possibility for being awarded damages is authorised in the Complaints Board Act and is, moreover, an indispensable precondition of the effective implementation of the Procurement Directive and the Remedies Directive. With respect to the principle of effectiveness reference is made to chapter 1.3.3. The elements of private law stem from the fact that the claim is set up by one or more undertakings which have participated in a procedure in which the provisions of the Procurement Directive were not complied with. In terms of the measure of damages private law dictates that damages must be awarded in full, cf. section 4.4.2.

4.1.6 Generally about the liability

According to the legislative history of the Complaints Board Act[73] claims for damages for infringement of the Procurement Directive must be settled in accordance with Danish general law of damages, also with respect to the measure of damages. This means that in order to be awarded damages, a basis of liability must be established and there must be a causal link to the loss which must also have been foreseeable. Also matters such as contributory negligence, assumption of risk and inactivity may be of relevance. However compared to Danish general law of damages, the liability in damages in the context of procurement has been extended by virtue of the pre-contractual origins of the liability and, in particular, the requirements of EU law for effective implementation, compliance with and enforcement of the Procurement Directive.

Contracting authorities covered by the Utilities Directive are subject to extended liability in damages.[74] The preamble and the wording of the Reme-

---

72. See for example Section 15 of the Marketing Practices Act.
73. Bill No L 243 of 30 March 2000 on the Complaints Board for Public Procurement, Official Report of Parliamentary Proceedings 1999/2000, Annex A, column 6856 ff.
74. Council Directive 2004/17/EC of 31 March 2004.

dies Directive for Utilities[75] are more elaborate with respect to liability in damages than the Remedies Directive for Public Contracts. Article 2, paragraph 7 of the Remedies Directive for Utilities stipulates that where an undertaking makes a claim for damages representing the costs of preparing a tender or of participating in an award procedure, it is only required to prove an infringement of Community law in the field of procurement or national rules implementing that law and that it would have had a real chance of winning the contract and, as a consequence of the infringement, that this chance was adversely affected. It is emphasised in the preamble that where an undertaking makes a claim for reliance damages – the costs of preparing a tender and of participating in an award procedure – it cannot be required, in order to obtain the damages, to prove that the contract would have been awarded to it in the absence of such infringement. The more elaborate provisions of the Remedies Directive for Utilities largely extend to the liability in damages incurred by a contracting authority for infringement of the Procurement Directive for which reason there is a certain spillover effect on the liability of contracting authorities covered by the Procurement Directive.

4.1.7 Danish general law of damages

As a general rule, loss caused by harm remains with the person harmed. The law of damages lays down the conditions to be satisfied in order for somebody to be liable for harm and on the basis of which the person harmed can claim damages from the tortfeasor. The general law of damages applies to contractual liability and to liability in tort, but where a contract exists, these general provisions are often relaxed or aggravated by the agreement governing the parties' relationship. This is because the agreement often contains provisions on the liability in damages and also grants the parties other remedies for breach than damages.

In order for a tortfeasor to be liable in damages three fundamental conditions must be satisfied: the existence of a basis of liability; the person harmed must have suffered a loss; and the existence of a causal link between the action giving rise to liability and the harm suffered. The principle of fault is the general rule of liability meaning that a person is liable for harm caused by malicious or negligent actions. As a main rule, a person is only liable for

---

75. Council Directive 92/13/EEC of 25 February 1992.

culpable conduct and not for omissions, but this main rule may be derogated from in the event of, for example, failure to take measures to avert danger. The principle of fault is in the nature of a minimum rule since its application is not conditional on statutory authority and, as such, it can be relied upon in the event of harm which is not governed by other specific rules. By contrast, a person can only fall subject to stricter liability if provided by law; strict liability, for example, subject to which liability is incurred for harm that is not caused by malicious or negligent actions (accidental harm). The doctrine of presumption of negligence is another type of stricter liability subject to which the tortfeasor is presumed to be at fault.

If the tortious action or omission causes harm, for example damage to property or bodily injury, the person harmed is entitled to recover his loss. The governing principle is that the financial situation of the person harmed must be restored ruling out any form of enrichment. On the other hand, the person harmed is always obliged to mitigate his loss.

The claim for damages is a pecuniary claim, and the loss is the result of a conversion of the harm into money by application of an objective measure, for example loss of earnings because of incapacity for work. The Act on Liability for Damages applies in the event of bodily injury or loss of dependency, and the loss is measured in accordance with the relevant provisions in the Act.

Finally, whether damages can be claimed of the tortfeasor depends on whether the tortious action or omission brought about the harm and the resulting loss – the requirement of causal link. In this context it must also be assessed whether the existence of a causal link was foreseeable meaning that the risk that the harm in issue would occur was enhanced by the action or omission. It thus follows that considerations of foreseeability contribute to limiting the liability.

It is essentially for the person harmed to prove the existence of the conditions subject to which liability can be incurred, the extent of the harm and the existence of a causal link. However, in the event that the presumption of negligence doctrine can be relied upon, the burden of proof shifts and it is for the tortfeasor to prove that the conditions for incurring liability are not satisfied.

In addition to the three fundamental conditions it must always be taken into account whether the person harmed showed contributory negligence, assumed a risk or perhaps consented to the harm; all matters which are capable of mitigating the liability or extinguishing it completely. Also, the general mitigation rule contained in Section 24 of the Act on Liability for Damages may mitigate or extinguish the liability in damages either if it would be unreasonably onerous to the person liable in damages or where exceptional circumstances make it reasonable to do so.

Furthermore, the claim may be covered under an insurance if the tortfeasor or the person harmed has entered into an agreement in that respect with an insurance company. In certain circumstances a claim for damages cannot be made against the tortfeasor under Danish law. The claim for damages usually arises after the tortious action or omission has occurred and pursuant to Act No 274 of 22 December 1908, Section 1(1), no. 5, claims for liability in tort become statute-barred five years after the tortious action or omission occurred. To this it should be noted that the effect of protracted inactivity on the part of the person harmed can be that the claim is forfeited before it becomes statute barred, mainly because the proof available to the person harmed is likely to have weakened.

4.2 Basis of liability

Liability may arise if the contracting authority infringes the provisions of the Procurement Directive in the course of a procurement procedure. Liability may also arise if the contracting authority in the course of a procurement procedure infringes the principles of equal treatment, non-discrimination, mutual recognition, proportionality and transparency.[76] Liability is established on an objective basis without regard to whether the contracting authority knew or ought to have known that the Procurement Directive or the principles were not complied with.

4.2.1.1 Generally

Infringements of the Procurement Directive and/or the principle of equal treatment, etc. are the basis on which liability arises. If the contracting authority does not commit any infringements, it is not liable in damages towards

---

76. Judgment of the Eastern High Court of 30 May 1996, Kampsax Bridge Consortium and Others vs. A/S Storebæltsforbindelsen; order of the Complaints Board of 22 November 2001, Forlaget Magnus A/S vs. Customs and Tax Authority; order of the Complaints Board of 3 July 2002/judgment of the Western High Court of 16 March 2004, Judex A/S vs. County of Århus.

tenderers or undertakings that have requested pre-qualification. Undertakings participating in procedures where no infringements are committed are not entitled to damages merely because they are not awarded the contract.

Liability can arise on the basis of actions as well as omissions pertaining to the obligations imposed by the Procurement Directive or the principles. It may, for example, be an infringement of the principle of equal treatment if one pre-qualified undertaking receives the contract documents before all other pre-qualified undertakings, or if an undertaking is rejected regardless that it complies with the selection criteria and does not fall subject to any of the grounds for exclusion. Infringements typically contain both actions as well as omissions.

4.2.1.2 Own tender is irregular

In many cases where an undertaking claiming damages succeeds in its complaint that the contracting authority infringed the Procurement Directive, the principle of equal treatment, etc., it is also established that its own tender, as submitted, was irregular. Case law seems to be somewhat inconsistent with respect to whether this irregularity should be assessed against the contracting authority's liability or on the basis of whether there is a causal link. It goes without saying that such a claimant cannot be awarded expectation damages, but it may very well be entitled to reliance damages regardless that its own tender was irregular. Whether the claimant is awarded damages, therefore, depends on the existence of a causal link, cf. chapter 4.3.[77] The view that the award of damages in actions where the claimant's tender was irregular depends on the existence of a causal link finds support in the fact that damages can be awarded even to a claimant that has not submitted a tender.[78] On that account, it is evident that irregularity of a claimant's own tender does not prevent it from claiming damages, albeit only measured as reliance damages.

---

77. Order of the Complaints Board of 24 March 2003, Restaurant owner Willy Antonsen vs. Års Local Authority; order of the Complaints Board of 3 July 2002, Judex A/S vs. County of Århus (This order must be constructed so as to mean that the reason why there was no liability to pay damages arising out of the original tender was the absence of a causal link; the same is true of the judgment by the Western High Court of 6 March 2004 in the same case).
78. Order of the Complaints Board of 22 November 2001, Forlaget Magnus A/S vs. Customs and Tax Authority.

4.2.1.3 Is the award of damages conditional on decisions being set aside?

Another key question is whether it is a precondition of the award of damages that decisions made by the contracting authority have been set aside on grounds that they infringed the Procurement Directive and/or the principle of equal treatment, etc. As mentioned above in section 4.1.3, in many cases the Complaints Board first reviews whether an infringement has been committed, and only if that is the case, does it consider the claim for damages. In such cases there is no doubt as to whether the Complaints Board, before considering the claim for damages, has set aside decisions made by the contracting authority. However, it is a fact that it is not a condition for being awarded damages in cases before the Complaints Board for Public Procurement that the Complaints Board has set aside decisions made by the contracting authority. An order by the Complaints Board to set aside a decision made by the contracting authority is based on the Complaints Board's overall assessment of the nature of the infringement or infringements in which assessment also the defendant's interests are taken into account; hence, such an order is based on other considerations than those which are relevant in deciding the claim for damages. To this should be added that in actions for damages before the courts of law the award of damages is clearly not conditional on the setting aside of one or more decisions made by the defendant, and often the claims concerning infringements put forward before the Complaints Board for Public Procurement are submitted as allegations in cases before the courts of law.

4.2.1.4 Contracting authority's liability for cancelling a call for tenders?

A contracting authority can cancel a call for tenders provided that it does this on objective grounds. Nevertheless, even where a call for tenders is lawfully cancelled on objective grounds, the question arises whether the undertakings which participated in the procedure can claim damages (in the form of reliance damages; award of expectation damages is precluded for the mere reason that the procedure was cancelled on objective grounds[79]). The main rule is that a contracting authority is not liable in damages if the cancellation of the call for tenders was founded on objective grounds, for example where the price of the submitted tenders is far greater than the budgetary framework fixed by the contracting authority on grounds of fact. The situation may be different where the cancellation is due to the contracting authority having prepared erroneous or insufficient contract documents or to the contracting

---

79. Order of the Complaints Board of 20 February 2004, Miri Stål A/S vs. Esbjerg Local Authority.

authority's conduct in the course of the procedure. The ground for cancelling the procedure may be objective, but the tenderer has participated in vain and to that end incurred costs which it seems justified to claim compensated by the contracting authority. Cancellation by a contracting authority upon realising that mistakes have been made followed by a new and correct invitation to tender does not rule out the possibility for claiming damages.[80]

Where the contracting authority ascertains that only one undertaking complies with the pre-qualification criteria – exclusion and selection criteria – and, on that account, lawfully cancels the procedure,[81] the undertaking that complied with the pre-qualification criteria cannot claim damages from the contracting authority.

4.2.2 Specifically about particular infringements

It is not possible to give an exhaustive account of whether every single conceivable infringement is capable of giving rise to liability for the contracting authority. The number of possible infringements is simply too great quite apart from the varying degrees of gravity of each infringement.

Instead, a number of specific infringements can be examined to establish whether they are capable of giving rise to liability.

In procedures where mistakes or infringements have been committed, but where they *did not affect*, in particular, the compliance with the Procurement Directive and the principle of equal treatment, there is no basis of liability. Therefore, if the contracting authority, from mere habit, reserves the right to reject all tenders, but does not do so, there is obviously no basis of liability. Likewise, where a contracting authority, in the contract documents, has stipulated that it will submit the tenders to a test to evaluate a sub-criterion such as quality, for example, but omits to do so. If the contracting authority in another manner has evaluated the sub-criterion on a sufficient and objective basis, there is no basis of liability.[82]

---

80. Order of the Complaints Board of 12 October 2004, Køster Entreprise A/S vs. Morsø Local Authority, the contracting authority admitted having made a number of mistakes, but contended that an action for damages was not possible as there was no cause for action considering the possibility for submitting a tender in reply to the new call for tenders.
81. Judgment of the European Court of Justice of 16 September 1999, case C-27/98, Metalmecanica SpA and Others.
82. Order of the Complaints Board of 28 May 2003, Bilhuset Ringsted ApS and Others vs. Ringsted Local Authority and judgment of the Eastern High Court of 6 November 2000, Skjortegrossisten A/S and Post Danmark A/S, upheld by the Supreme Court; Danish weekly law reports 2004.1294H.

Infringements pertaining to the application and evaluation of *exclusion and selection criteria* are, depending on the circumstances, capable of giving rise to liability. Accordingly, a contracting authority's unfair rejection of an undertaking that has submitted a tender or requested pre-qualification would give rise to liability. The same is true of the situation where the contracting authority wrongly omits to apply an exclusion criterion, for example. Although, the liability is probably conditional on the undertaking that was unjustly admitted to the competition either being awarded the contract or its participation adversely affecting the other tenderers' chances of being awarded the contract. In the first case mentioned above, the contracting authority may be liable towards the wrongly rejected undertaking, whereas, in the last mentioned case, it may be liable towards those other undertaking(s) participating in the procedure which were affected by the infringement.

Infringement of the *principle of equal treatment* almost always gives rise to liability. Such an infringement is committed, for example, where the contracting authority first uses an undertaking as adviser in the preparation of the contract documents and then accepts a tender submitted by that undertaking, instead of rightly excluding that undertaking from the competition, cf. chapter 6.4. If this undertaking subsequently is awarded the contract or if its participation in the procedure affects the other tenderers' chances, the contracting authority has undoubtedly incurred liability. The same would be the case where a contracting authority admits a tenderer to a procedure regardless that, in the procedure, it is assisted by the same advisers as the contracting authority.[83]

Also infringements of the *principle of transparency* are likely to give rise to liability. If the description of the proposed service, product or works or the procedures or requirements determined by the contracting authority is not transparent, tenderers do not genuinely compete on equal terms notwithstanding that this is exactly what the contracting authority is obliged to ensure. As a consequence, if the contracting authority has not thought over and specified which reservations it will accept, but merely stated that reservations can be made about all aspects of the contract documents, the competition is not genuine and effective.[84]

---

83. Judgment of the Eastern High Court of 16 September 2002, European Metro Group vs. Ørestadsselskabet. The judgment was upheld by the Supreme Court by judgment of 31 March 2005.
84. Order of the Complaints Board of 22 November 2001, Forlaget Magnus A/S vs. Customs and Tax Authority.

Infringements of the *principle of non-discrimination* are also capable of giving rise to liability. Such an infringement is committed where the contract documents require that Danish materials or Danish labour be used.[85]

A contracting authority which conducts a *sham procedure* obviously incurs liability in damages. Consequently, if a contracting authority has selected its supplier already before the procedure is commenced, the other undertakings that participated in the procedure are certainly entitled to recover their costs of preparing tenders, and an undertaking, which evaluated on the formal contract documents, should have been awarded the contract, can probably also obtain expectation damages.[86]

Late tenders must be rejected. If the contracting authority fails to reject a tender which is submitted late, it can be liable for any loss suffered on that account.[87]

Mistreatment of reservations also gives rise to liability. A contracting authority which fails to reject tenders containing reservations about fundamental specifications or fails to price reservations objectively incurs liability.[88]

Where a contracting authority, despite the prohibition on negotiations, in the open procedure and the restricted procedure opens negotiations, it incurs liability. Likewise, where a contracting authority in the competitive dialogue procedure does not open a dialogue or in the negotiated procedure does not enter into negotiations.

Infringements committed in connection with the *evaluation of the selection criteria*, whether because of a wrong application of lawful criteria or because unlawful criteria were applied, almost always give rise to liability.

Finally, it should be mentioned that a contracting authority which wrongly *cancels* a call for tenders may incur liability in damages.

4.3 Causal link and foreseeability

Pursuant to the general rules of Danish law, to which reference is made in the legislative history of the Complaints Board Act, there must be a causal link between the infringement (violation) and the loss which is claimed compen-

---

85. Judgment of the Eastern High Court of 30 May 1996, Kampsax Bridge Consortium and Others vs. A/S Storebæltsforbindelsen; order of the Complaints Board of 24 March 2003, Restaurant owner Willy Antonsen vs. Års Local Authority.
86. Judgment of the Supreme Court of 12 March 2002 – Danish weekly law reports 2002.1180H, Fredericia Local Authority vs. KKS Entreprise A/S in liquidation.
87. Danish weekly law reports 2000.1425V, IBF Nord A/S and Frejlev Cementstøberi A/S vs. Aalborg Local Authority.
88. Judgment of the Eastern High Court of 30 May 1996 Kampsax Bridge Consortium and Others vs. A/S Storebæltsforbindelsen.

sated. Also, the loss must have been foreseeable in that it must have been a foreseeable consequence of the infringement.

It is the contracting authority which is bound by the Procurement Directive, the principle of equal treatment, the principle of transparency, etc. Therefore, the condition of foreseeability is almost always complied with to the effect that it only has a bearing on the loss assessment.

The general rules on causality of Danish law are somewhat modified when applied to damages for infringement of the procurement rules. This is due to the special nature of the liability in question. If the procedure is conducted in accordance with the rules, the contract is awarded to the tenderer which on objective grounds wins the competition. The other tenderers gain nothing and must bear the costs of participating in the procedure themselves. Evidently, any undertaking participating in a procurement procedure runs the risk of not being awarded the contract and, consequently, finding itself in the above situation. If the causality rule were not modified in this context, it would mean that only tenderers that are able to prove that they should have been awarded the contract could be awarded damages. The modification is thus in the nature of a relaxation. In the Great Belt case the Eastern High Court expressed the modification as follows: In the light of the nature of the basis of liability, the causal link between the defendant's conduct and the harm has been established on a balance of probabilities to the satisfaction of the court.[89] The state of the law on causality, also in the context of infringements of the Procurement Directive, is best described in the Remedies Directive for Utilities[90] stipulating that where a claim is made for damages, the claimant is only required to prove an infringement and that the infringement adversely affected its real chance of being awarded the contract. In the preamble to the Remedies Directive for Utilities it is further stipulated that where a claim is made for damages representing the costs of preparing a tender or of participating in an award procedure, the claimant is not required to prove that it would have been awarded the contract in the absence of such infringement.

The causality rule means that in order for a claimant, having participated in an open procedure or a restricted procedure, to be awarded expectation damages, it must prove that it should have been awarded the contract[91] (in

---

89. Judgment of the Eastern High Court of 30 May 1996, Kampsax Bridge Consortium and Others vs. A/S Storebæltsforbindelsen.
90. Article 2, paragraph 7 of Council Directive 92/13/EEC.
91. Judgment of the Court of First Instance of 28 November 2002, case T-40/01 Scan Office Design SA vs. Commission. See also order of the Complaints Board of 2

practice, this is rather more difficult where the contract is awarded to the most economically advantageous tender based on a number of sub-criteria than to the tender of the lowest price, see for example Skjortegrossisten A/S vs. Post Danmark A/S and European Metro Group vs. Ørestadsselskabet I/S [92]). This is also true where the contract is awarded subject to the negotiated procedure, although the rule is probably further modified. The essential feature of the negotiated procedure is that both the price and content of the tenders are subject to negotiations and tenderers often submit more tenders. Therefore, if a contracting authority infringes, for example, the principle of equal treatment in the course of the negotiations and, as a consequence of that infringement, a tenderer is not invited to submit its best tender, it is very often impossible for that tenderer to prove that it should have been awarded the contract. In such a situation the burden of proving the existence of a causal link should be shifted, *inter alia* as a deterrent, to the effect that it is for the contracting authority to establish that the infringements committed did not adversely affect the tenderer's chances of being awarded the proposed contract.[93]

As to the possibility for being awarded reliance damages, usually representing the costs of having participated in the procedure in vain, application of the modified causality rule means that damages are awarded where an infringement has affected the claimant's chances of being awarded the proposed contract and that the claimant is not required to prove that it would have been awarded the contract had the infringement not been committed.

The modified causality rule, as described above, is necessary in order for the EU Member States to fulfil the obligation to ensure the effective and full implementation of the Procurement Directive, cf. Article 249 and Article 10

December 2004, Banverket vs. Nordjyske Jernbaner A/S, in which the Complaints Board found that liability in damages had been incurred, but that the infringements ascertained had not affected the tenders submitted by the undertakings claiming damages. Se also order of the Complaints Board of 3 February 2005, Sammenslutningen af Glatførerbekæmpende Vognmænd i Nordjyllands Amt ApS vs. County of Nordjylland.

92. Danish weekly law reports 2004.1294H, Skjortegrossisten A/S vs. Post Danmark A/S; judgment of the Supreme Court of 31 March 2005, European Metro Group vs. Ørestadsselskabet I/S.

93. Order of the Complaints Board of 3 July 2002, Judex A/S vs. County of Århus (although overturned on this point by judgment of the Western High Court of 16 March 2004 without specifying the grounds). In judgment of the Supreme Court of 31 March 2005, European Metro Group vs. Ørestadsselskabet I/S, the Supreme Court did not decide on this issue as it agreed with the Complaints Board and the Eastern High Court that no relevant infringements had been committed in the course of the negotiations.

of the EC Treaty. The possibility of being awarded damages would be only illusory if the causality rule was not modified. The requirement for effective implementation embraces the above requirement of full implementation and the requirement that the sanctions for infringement must act as a deterrent, to which end the risk of incurring liability is appropriate.[94] Reference is made to chapter 1.3.3.

In certain actions for damages the circumstances of the undertaking claiming damages are thoroughly examined, *inter alia* to establish whether the claimant's own tender complied with the specifications. In other cases it is sought established whether the claimant was at all capable of submitting a successful tender.[95] Such an assessment appears to be reasonable where it is manifest that the claimant could not have been awarded the contract, for example because of lack of capacity or inadequate distribution facilities. However, the ruling out of the possibility for awarding damages in all cases where the ability of the claimant to perform the contract is uncertain would be too excessive. Besides, the claimant can always legitimately refer to the use of subcontractors.

4.4 Financial loss

In the light of the particular nature of the basis on which liability arises in procurement law the loss assessment, which is the measure of the damages to be awarded, requires special consideration, in particular in terms of whether it should be assessed as expectation damages or reliance damages.

4.4.1 Documentation – burden of proof

The reference in the legislative history of the Complaints Board Act that the measure of damages be determined by application of Danish general law of damages means that, as a rule, the person claiming damages must be restored to the position it would have been in had proper performance taken place. In the field of procurement law this means that the claimant must be restored to a financial position which redresses the infringement that gave rise to the liability.

It is for the claimant to assess and document its loss.

---

94. Enforcement of the E.C. procurement rules; The Standards Required of National Review Systems under E.C. Law in the Context of the principle of Effectiveness, Despina Pachnou, Public Procurement Law Review 2000, no. 2, p. 55ff.
95. Order of the Complaints Board of 24 March 2003, Restaurant owner Willy Antonsen vs. Års Local Authority.

If the claim is for expectation damages, the claimant must usually produce evidence of its anticipated earnings in the form of estimates based on the tender submitted substantiated by information on normal earnings in the particular industry and/or the undertaking's normal earnings from similar sales. Where damages are assessed as expectation damages, the claimant's costs of participating in the procedure can obviously not be recovered since the claimant would also have incurred these costs had the procedure been conducted according to the rules. Case law shows that the courts of law and the Complaints Board for Public Procurement are suspicious of the correctness of loss assessments, and it seems to be the rule that expectation damages are awarded in a lower amount than that claimed and assessed by the claimant.

Claims for reliance damages usually comprise the claimant's external and internal costs of submitting the tender.[96] Whereas invoices from advisers, etc. are evidence of external costs, more often than not there is no documentary evidence of the use of own resources, for which reason internal costs are usually in the nature of estimates. Another typical problem involved with the valuation of own resources is that the people who prepared the tender and participated in the procurement procedure on behalf of the undertaking usually do not provide services to an hourly rate. It is, though, possible to determine a cost price for this or these employee(s) corresponding to their pay per hour plus all other usual employee benefits, such as holiday pay.

The duty to mitigate damages is often relevant in the context of the loss assessment, in particular where damages are measured as expectation damages. However, the duty to mitigate damages can also be of relevance where the damages are assessed as reliance damages, especially where excessive resources have been used to submit a tender because the contract documents were not transparent.[97]

4.4.2 Principles for measuring damages

For the purpose of measuring damages the general rules of Danish law and relevant case law apply. The main rule is that full damages are awarded, measured as either expectation damages or reliance damages.

In measuring expectation damages account should be had of any options to a proposed contract, either in the form of quantitative additions or in the form of renewals. If the contracting authority, besides its reluctance to pay

---

96. Order of the Complaints Board of 22 November 2001, Forlaget Magnus A/S vs. Customs and Tax Authority.
97. Order of the Complaints Board of 22 November 2001, Forlaget Magnus A/S vs. Customs and Tax Authority.

higher damages, succeeds in proving that the option would not have been exercised, it is unlikely that the option will be taken into account. In practice, the question is largely determined by whether or not options to a perhaps already concluded contract with another tenderer have been exercised.

Where the infringements of the Procurement Directive and/or the principle of equal treatment, etc. committed by the contracting authority are serious in nature, the standard required for proving the amount of the loss is lowered.

Regardless that the principle that damages be measured in full entails that damages are also awarded for injurious consequences, it is only exceptionally that such damages are awarded. However, also damages for indirect loss may, depending on the circumstances, be awarded. For example, where a contracting authority wrongfully fails to award the contract to the tenderer which has submitted the tender that best satisfies the chosen award criterion and where the procedure was accelerated to the effect that the tenderer was forced to adjust, on a considerable scale, its business capacity and delivery capabilities so that it would be able to perform the contract.

4.4.3 Specifically about costs (reliance damages)

Reliance damages are usually measured as external and internal costs, costs of submitting a tender and participation in the procedure. Depending on the magnitude and complexity of the contract documents and on the procedures chosen by the contracting authority, vast resources may be required to submit a tender. For example where hundreds of pages of technical specifications have to be reviewed, drawings prepared and quotations obtained from sub-suppliers, costs may run into considerable amounts.[98]

Damages are awarded as reliance damages where the contract documents suffer from such a lack of clarity that it makes it impossible to submit tenders, even where potential tenderers apply considerable external and internal resources thereto.[99] Other examples of infringements for which reliance damages are awarded are where the contracting authority fails to reject an irregular tender and that irregular tender either turns out to be the successful tender or edges out the claimant's tender from the competition; infringements of the principle of equal treatment by conducting negotiations in contravention of

---

98. Judgment of the Supreme Court of 31 March 2005, European Metro Group vs. Ørestadsselskabet – costs of tender some DKK 25m; judgment of the Supreme Court of 12 March 2002, Danish weekly law reports 2002. 1180H, Fredericia Local Authority vs. KKS Entreprise A/S in liquidation – costs of tender approx. DKK 1m.
99. Order of the Complaints Board of 22 November 2001, Forlaget Magnus A/S vs. Customs and Tax Authority.

the prohibition on negotiations to the effect that the undertaking(s) with which negotiations were conducted is/are awarded the contract, or the negotiations otherwise eliminate or adversely affect the claimant's chances; and, finally, where the principle of equal treatment is otherwise infringed, which infringement adversely affects, directly or indirectly, the claimant's chances of being awarded the contract. The standard of proof to be met is determined by the requirement under EU law for effective implementation and the pre-contractual nature of the liability in damages.

As mentioned, infringements of the principle of equal treatment may give rise to liability to pay damages measured as reliance damages seeing that the tenderers did not compete on fair and equal terms. On that account, it may have been a waste of costs to submit the tender.[100] Similarly, it is a waste of resources to submit a tender in reply to a sham call for tenders.[101] Where the contracting authority has infringed the principle of non-discrimination, damages are also measured as reliance damages. The classic example is "the Danish content clause" in the procedures pertaining to the Great Belt link.[102]

A contracting authority which unjustly rejects an undertaking requesting pre-qualification may also incur liability to pay reliance damages. The same is true where a tender is unjustly rejected.

Where a contracting authority conducts a procurement procedure in a manner which does not allow the tenderer to submit a comparable tender, it infringes the principle of equal treatment and, consequently, incurs liability to pay reliance damages.[103] Where a contracting authority requires compliance with certain standards that are irrelevant to the supplies or services proposed, it can give rise to a claim for reliance damages.[104]

---

100. Judgment of the Western High Court of 16 March 2004, Judex vs. County of Århus (+ reliance damages); Danish weekly law reports 2004.1294H, Skjortegrossisten A/S vs. Post Danmark A/S (÷ reliance damages). See also judgment of the Court of First Instance of 17 March 2005, case T-160/03, AFCon Management Consultance vs. Ireland, in which the CFI found that the Commission had infringed Community law due to an ascertained conflict of interest, a member of the evaluation committee had previously been employed with the undertaking that was awarded the contract, and the CFI ordered that the claimant should be awarded reliance damages representing the costs of participation in the procedure.
101. Judgment of the Supreme Court of 12 March 2002, Danish weekly law reports 2002.1180H, Fredericia Local Authority vs. KKS Entreprise A/S in liquidation.
102. Judgment of the Eastern High Court of 30 May 1996, Kampsax Bridge Consortium and Others vs. A/S Storebæltsforbindelsen.
103. Judgment of the Western High Court of 16 March 2004, Judex vs. County of Århus.
104. Order of the Complaints Board of 1 March 2005, BN Produkter Danmark A/S vs. Odense Renovationsselskab.

In conclusion, damages are measured as reliance damages where infringements of the Procurement Directive or the principle of equal treatment, etc. committed by the contracting authority have had the effect that the undertaking claiming damages was not allowed the opportunity to participate in the competition on fair and equal terms. Essentially, it is for the undertaking claiming damages to establish that the infringements had such effect, but in cases of doubt, the burden of proof rests with the contracting authority that committed the infringement. Especially in the more complex procedures, such as "the negotiated procedure", the burden of proving that an infringement did not adversely affect the claimant's chances of being awarded the contract should, as a main rule, rest with the contracting authority.[105]

According to case law in Denmark the award of reliance damages is conditional on that the undertaking claiming damages would not have submitted a tender, had it known that infringements were committed in the course of the procedure.[106]

Finally, it is noted that the award of reliance damages is possible where the conditions for being awarded expectation damages are met.[107]

4.4.4 Specifically about profit (expectation damages)

Where the award of damages is measured as expectation damages, the claimant is awarded compensation for loss of net profit suffered as a result of not having obtained and performed the order. It is not possible to claim compensation for loss of gross profit (contribution margin 1); compensation will only

---

105. Judgment of the Supreme Court of 31 March 2005, European Metro Group vs. Ørestadsselskabet; judgment of the Western High Court of 16 March 2004, Judex vs. County of Århus.

106. Danish weekly law reports 2004.1294H, Skjortegrossisten A/S vs. Post Danmark A/S. The order of the Complaints Board for Public Procurement of 28 December 1999 was based on the assumption that Post Danmark A/S had violated the procurement rules by *inter alia* having mixed up selection and award criteria. The Complaints Board had stated that sub-criteria that had not been advertised had been applied to identify the most economically advantageous tender, whereas in reality the sub-criteria had been advertised. The Complaints Board had not considered the legality of using *inter alia* "an overall evaluation" as a sub-criterion. As a consequence, the High Court and the Supreme Court presumed that "an overall evaluation" is a lawful sub-criterion which it is not, cf. chapter 7 and the case law cited in that chapter.

107. Judgment of the Eastern High Court of 30 May 1996, Kampsax Bridge Consortium and Others vs. A/S Storebæltsforbindelsen – although held that Bouygues could not have claimed that the contract be transferred to it.

be awarded for loss of net profit (contribution margin 2).[108] Consequently, the claimant will not be awarded damages measured as if the performance of the contract would have been a marginal task for the claimant. Only damages representing the net profit can be claimed and measured.[109]

In the context of framework agreements for the delivery of a product in an estimated quantity within a specific period of time, expectation damages are assessed either on the basis of the estimated quantity or, if this is known at the time when the damages are awarded, the actual quantity purchased by the contracting authority provided that the product has not been sold in artificially small quantities in preparation for a claim for damages. If a framework agreement has been concluded with others concerning the same products, expectation damages can be assessed on the basis of the actual purchases made.[110]

A tenderer claiming damages must be awarded expectation damages where it was the only tenderer that could lawfully have been awarded the contract on the basis of the specific contract documents had the procedure been conducted in accordance with the rules.[111] Of importance in this context

---

108. Order of the Complaints Board of 20 August 2004, Miri Stål A/S vs. Esbjerg Local Authority.
109. Order of the Complaints Board of 3 July 2002, Judex A/S vs. County of Århus (reversed by judgment of the Western High Court of 16 March 2004 to reliance damages).
110. Order of the Complaints Board of 20 August 2004, Miri Stål A/S vs. Esbjerg Local Authority.
111. Expectation damages for infringement of the procurement rules have been awarded in several cases: judgment of the Western High Court of 14 March 2000, IBF Nord A/S and Frejlev Cementstøberi A/S vs. Aalborg Local Authority (DKK 1.1m); order of the Complaints Board of 20 August 2004, Miri Stål A/S vs. Esbjerg Local Authority; order of the Complaints Board of 3 July 2002, Judex A/S vs. County of Århus (reversed to reliance damages, assessed discretionarily, by judgment of the Western High Court of 16 March 2004); and order of the Complaints Board of 8 March 2005, Per Aarsleff A/S vs. Amager Strandpark I/S (damages of DKK 5m for loss of contribution margin). In Norway expectation damages are awarded for infringement of provisions similar to those of the Directive, see judgment of the Norwegian Supreme Court of 30 May 2001, Møve and Romsdal Fylges Local Authority vs. Andreassen Arkitektkontor A/S and Others. As to violations of the Tender Invitation Act, reference is made to judgment of the Supreme Court of 17 April 2000, Jøni Container- og Vognfabrik ApS vs. Fårup Sommerland, Amusement Park; judgment of the Supreme Court of 1 July 1997, Investeringsselskabet af 11.02.1993 A/S vs. Gl. Skanderborg Ejendom; judgment of the Eastern High Court of 18 December 1991, Thyges VVS, rep. by Thyge Andersen vs. Boligselskabet Fjordparken, branch 8, rep. by KAB s.m.b.a.; and judgment of the Supreme Court of 30 April 1985, Bredkjær Industri A/S vs. Hals Local Authority. For violation of

is that the Procurement Directive prescribes that a contracting authority cannot reserve the right to reject all tenders thereby stipulating an implicit obligation to contract. A contracting authority can only cancel a call for tenders on objective grounds, cf. chapter 7.8.

Where a contracting authority has infringed the Procurement Directive and/or the principle of equal treatment, etc. and, as a consequence, awarded the contract to the wrong tenderer, and where the tenderer which, evaluated on the basis of the chosen award criterion, should have been awarded the contract, had the infringement not been committed, makes a claim for expectation damages, it is commonly alleged by the contracting authority, in the action for damages, that had it been aware that its conduct would constitute an infringement, it would have cancelled the procedure, for which reason the undertaking claiming damages could not have expected to be awarded the contract. However, where the contracting authority could have cancelled the tender, but failed to do so, it cannot allege, in a subsequent action for damages, that damages be measured as if the procedure had actually been cancelled.[112]

The claimant's chances of establishing that it should have been awarded the contract are best in the open procedure and the restricted procedure and where the award criterion is the lowest price. In these procedures all tenderers submit one tender each which cannot be negotiated and the only measure for finding the successful tender is price. Nevertheless, there may be situations, also in these procedures, where it is not altogether clear which is the best tender; for example, where it is necessary to price reservations.

Has the open procedure or the restricted procedure been chosen, but the award criterion is the most economically advantageous tender evaluated on a number of sub-criteria it may be somewhat more difficult to establish, in practice, whether the claimant did indeed submit the best tender and, therefore, should have been awarded the contract.[113] The special expertise of the Complaints Board for Public Procurement is essential to whether it is at all feasible to reach a decision. Although, there may always be cases where it is

---

the Tender Act expectation damages have been awarded by the Complaints Board by the orders of 14 April 2004, Nibe Entreprenør of Transport ApS vs. Støvring Local Authority and 13 September 2004, Brd. Thybo A/S vs. Andelsforeningen af 1938.

112. Order of the Complaints Board of 20 August 2004, Miri Stål A/S vs. Esbjerg Local Authority.

113. See for example Danish weekly law reports 2004.1294H, Skjortegrossisten A/S vs. Post Danmark A/S. For more about this judgment see note 104.

practically impossible to establish that the claimant should have been award-ed the contract.

The above also applies to "the negotiated procedure" whether the award criterion is the lowest price or the most economically advantageous tender in so far as the negotiations have been ended and the final tenders are capable of being compared. However, infringements committed by the contracting au-thority in a negotiated procedure may have had the effect that the tenderer claiming damages was not given the opportunity to submit its best tender or indeed to submit a final tender because it was wrongly deselected in the course of the negotiations. In such a situation the tenderer can legitimately claim that it would, in a negotiated procedure, have been capable of submit-ting a better and successful tender even though the tender that it did submit was not the best in comparison to the successful tender.

4.4.5 Burden of proof particularly for the award of expectation damages
Apart from the cases in which it seems obvious that the claimant could not have submitted the successful tender it is all important where the burden of proof lies and which standard of proof is required. In these cases it seems most reasonable that the burden of proving that the tenderer claiming dam-ages would not have been capable of submitting the successful tender lies with the contracting authority seeing that the contracting authority, first of all, chose "the negotiated procedure" and, second, committed the infringements of the Procurement Directive and/or the principle of equal treatment, etc. This seems to be best in keeping with general rules on burden of proof and is also the principle applied by the Complaints Board for Public Procurement.[114]

In the above-mentioned negotiated procedures where the claimant was not allowed the opportunity to submit its final or best tender and in the cases, in the open procedure and the restricted procedure, where it is difficult to deter-mine conclusively whether the claimant had submitted the successful tender

---

114. Order of the Complaints Board of 3 July 2002, Judex A/S vs. County of Århus. The order was reversed by judgment of the Western High Court of 16 March 2004 in which the High Court does not cite the ground relied upon by the Complaints Board that it did not seem possible to assess the real chances of Judex A/S having been awarded the order had the County not infringed the EU procurement rules which should be counted as evidence against the County. The High Court does not give specific reasons for its ruling on this point. If the claimant unilaterally is charged with the burden of proof, although modified to a certain extent, which it fails to establish because of mistakes committed by the contracting authority, a burden of proof lying exclusively on the claimant is probably not in compliance with the principle of effectiveness under EU law, cf. chapter 1.

(for example because the pricing of reservations is not clear or because of difficulties in evaluating the specified sub-criteria), decisions by the Complaints Board for Public Procurement and the courts of law with respect to whether the claimant is entitled to expectation damages in reality depend on whether the contracting authority or the claimant bears the burden of proof.[115] If the infringements committed are serious, the standard of proof required of the claimant is reduced. However, the scope available to the Complaints Board and the courts of law for determining who bears the burden of proof is probably limited. In addition, the effective implementation of the Procurement Directive requires that full compensation be awarded in such cases. Indeed by virtue of the requirement for effective implementation, it seems inevitable that the contracting authority bears the burden of proof. A conventional evaluation of the existence of a causal link for the purpose of determining the amount of the loss suffered cannot be applied, since that would constitute a limitation imposed by national law of the opportunities for being awarded damages.

Reference is in this connection made to judgment by the European Court of Justice of 2 August 1993, case C-271/91 – M.H. Marshall vs. Southampton and Southwest Hampshire Area Health Authority. The case concerned Directive 76/207 of 9 February 1976 on equal treatment for men and women and whether English law was compatible with that Directive. Article 6 of the Directive stipulates that the Member States must introduce into their national legal systems such measures as are necessary to enable all persons who consider themselves wronged by discrimination to pursue their claims by judicial process. Like the Procurement Directive, Article 6 of the Directive 76/207 of 9 February 1976 does not specify the effect thereof on the award of damages. An upper limit on the amount that could be awarded as damages had been introduced in English law which in this case meant that the claimant, M.H. Marshal, could not be awarded damages measured as expectation damages regardless that the defendant had admitted infringements of the Directive. In paragraph 17 the European Court of Justice held that the Member States to which the Directive is addressed are required to adopt, in their national legal systems, all the measures necessary to ensure that the provisions of the Directive are fully effective, in accordance with the objective pursued by it. In paragraph 19 the ECJ points out that the purpose of Directive 76/207 of 9 February 1976 is to put into effect in the Member States the principle of equal treatment for men and women, including the conditions governing dismissal. Further, in paragraph 22 it is established that the Member States are under a duty to take the necessary measures to enable all persons who consider themselves wronged by discrimination to pursue their claims by judicial process. Such obligation implies that the measures in question should be sufficiently effective to achieve the objective of the Direc-

---

115. Danish weekly law reports 2000.521H; judgment of the Western High Court of 16 March 2004, Judex A/S vs. County of Århus; judgment of the Eastern High Court of 30 May 1996, Kampsax Bridge Consortium and Others A/S Storebæltsforbindelsen.

tive. Next in paragraph 24 the ECJ states that the objective is to arrive at real equality of opportunity and that this cannot be attained in the absence of measures appropriate to restore such equality when it has not been observed. Finally, in paragraph 26 the ECJ establishes that where financial compensation is the measure adopted in order to achieve the objective indicated above, it must be adequate, in that it must enable the loss and damage actually sustained as a result of the discriminatory dismissal to be made good. Against that background the European Court of Justice concluded that the national provisions of English law stipulating an upper limit on the amount of compensation that can be awarded to a person harmed by discrimination contravened Article 6 of Directive 76/207. M.H. Marshal was therefore entitled to full compensation plus interest.

Professor Sue Arrowsmith has commented upon this judgment by the European Court of Justice in Public Procurement Law Review 1993, no. 6, in the article "The implications of the Court of Justice's decision in Marshall for damages in the field of public procurement". Professor Arrowsmith argues that the judgment in Marshall can be applied to infringements of the Procurement Directive which in a similar manner must be effectively implemented into national law. Where a tenderer which has been wrongly passed over and where, because of precedents in national law concerning damages and amount of damages, the tenderer is not awarded full compensation equivalent of expectation damages, it contravenes the principle of effective implementation of directives into the national legal systems of the Member States.

As a consequence of the above reasoning, in procurement procedures, in the negotiated procedure – and perhaps in the above-mentioned open procedures and restricted procedures where it is particularly difficult to determine whether the undertaking claiming damages would have submitted the successful tenderers – the contracting authority risks having to pay expectation damages to not only one, but potentially several tenderers that were passed over.

An alternative to making the decisions hinge exclusively on who bears the burden of proof is to assess the chance of award and on that basis award the claimant damages corresponding to a proportion of the net profit lost. Accordingly, where it is uncertain whether the claimant or the successful tender submitted the best tender evaluated on the chosen award criterion, and obviously provided that the contracting authority has infringed the Procurement Directive and/or the principle of equal treatment, etc., the claimant could be awarded 50% of the net profit lost. This is in fine keeping with, in particular, the wording of the Remedies Directive for Utilities that it is appropriate to assess the tenderer's and claimant's opportunities for being awarded the contract, which is thus more in the nature of an assessment of the chance of award. This principle of application of a chance-of-award measure is *inter alia* known in English law ("Rule in Chaplin V. Hicks") and is referred to in the above-mentioned article by Professor Arrowsmith. To this can be added that the European Court of Justice in judgment of 15 June 2000, case C-13/99P, Team Srl vs. Commission in paragraph 54 stated "… it is an established principle in matters of public procurement that, in the event of irregularity in a tendering procedure, a tenderer who has complied with the detailed rules governing participation in that procedure may claim compensation for the damage suffered as a result both of the loss of chance of award of the contract and of his incurring the costs and expenses in participating in that procedure".

If the undertaking claiming damages has submitted an irregular tender, it is, for that reason, precluded from being awarded expectation damages.[116]

Almost certainly a contracting authority cannot eliminate the risk of incurring liability to pay expectation damages by stipulating provisions to that effect in the contract documents. The requirement for effective implementation of the procurement directives prevents that.

4.4.6 Contributory negligence and assumption of risk

If a basis of liability is established, it is examined whether the tenderer or undertaking that requested pre-qualification and which is claiming damages showed contributory negligence. The obligation to comply with the Procurement Directive rests solely on the contracting authority, but also the tenderers are required to act professionally. Where a contracting authority has committed infringements by providing a tenderer with incorrect information orally and by informal means, the tenderer cannot claim damages on that account, since the tenderer, too, is obliged to obtain the necessary information in a professional manner.[117]

4.4.7 Inactivity

It goes without saying that an otherwise legitimate claim for damages can be forfeited because of inactivity (or statute-barring).

This raises the question whether undertakings participating in a procurement procedure forfeit the right to claim damages if they do not raise objections if and when an infringement is ascertained. Forfeiture of the right to raise objections and claim damages because of inactivity obviously and fundamentally requires that the undertaking potentially entitled to damages was aware of the particular infringement.

It seems very unlikely indeed that undertakings participating in a procurement procedure should be under an obligation to raise objections in the course of that procedure, nor does the contracting authority's conduct become any less incorrect in the absence of objections. Considering that a purchase is about to be made, potential suppliers will show a natural reluctance to object to mistakes made by a possible future customer, in particular where the contract is awarded

---

116. Judgment of the Supreme Court of 12 March 2002, Danish weekly law reports 2002.1180H, Fredericia Local Authority vs. KKS Entreprise A/S in liquidation and section 4.2.1.
117. Order of the Complaints Board of 29 April 2004, KAS Transport rep. by Kim Schrøder vs. Århus Local Authority.

to the most economically advantageous tender based on a number of sub-criteria, the evaluation of which leaves some room for discretion.

Furthermore, it would be almost grotesque if it were held that a tenderer upon becoming aware of a mistake committed by the contracting authority should omit to submit a tender. Had that tenderer ended its participation in the procedure, regardless of the chances of winning the contract, it would in effect have precluded itself from being awarded the proposed contract or obtaining expectation damages.

In the light of the provisions of the Remedies Directive and the principle of effectiveness, it seems that inactivity can only be relied upon in exceptional circumstances.[118]

4.4.8 Duty to mitigate damage

Danish general law of damages applies, which *inter alia* means that the person claiming damages is subject to a duty of mitigation. In the context of reliance damages this duty concerns, in particular, whether the costs incurred to submit a tender (or to understand the contract documents) are reasonable.[119]

In the context of claims for expectation damages the duty of mitigation is often purely theoretical. The contracting authority may argue that the tenderer claiming damages could have applied its resources to perform other services, but will only exceptionally be able to substantiate that this was actually possible or that they indeed were. Further, the contracting authority is usually, and rightly so, countered by the argument that if the claimant were also awarded many other and new contracts, the capacity already available to it, or the use of sub-contractors, would have allowed it to perform these contracts. Consequently, in these situations the only point in dispute is the amount of the net profit.

---

118. The question of inactivity was considered by the Supreme Court in its judgment of 31 March 2005, European Metro Group vs. Ørestadsselskabet I/S. Both the Eastern High Court, in its judgment of 16 September 2002, and the Supreme Court found that the contracting authority had infringed the principle of equal treatment. Whereas the High Court with reference to inactivity ruled out liability in damages on that account, presumably on the grounds that the claimant knew of the circumstances that constituted the infringement of the principle of equal treatment, the Supreme Court dismissed inactivity as a ground for dismissing liability in damages in the case.
119. Order of the Complaints Board of 22 November 2001, Forlaget Magnus A/S vs. Customs and Tax Authority.

4.5 Legal costs

An unbalanced provision on legal costs is applied in cases before the Complaints Board for Public Procurement. According to Section 7 of the Complaints Board Act, the Complaints Board can order a losing contracting authority complained against to reimburse the complainant of its legal costs. By contrast, if the complaint is dismissed by the Complaints Board, the complainant cannot be ordered to pay the legal costs of the contracting authority.

In cases before the courts of law orders on legal costs follow the normal practice of the courts.

Bibliography

Arrowsmith, Sue, The law of Public and Utilities Procurement, Sweet & Maxwell 1996

Barnard, Catherine, The Substantive Law of the Eu: The Four Freedoms, Oxford University Press, 2004

Commission, Green Paper – Public Procurement in the European Union: Exploring the way forward represented by the Commission, COM/1996/583

Commission, Green Paper – Defence Procurement presented by the Commission, COM/2004/608

Commission, Green Paper on public-private partnerships and Community law on public contracts and concessions presented by the Commission, COM/2004/327

Commission, 23rd Competition Report for 1993

Commission, Interpretative communication of the Commission on the Community law applicable to public procurement and the possibilities for integrating social considerations into public procurement, COM/2001/566

Commission, Commission interpretative communication on the Community law applicable to public procurement and the possibilities for integrating environmental considerations into public procurement, COM/2001/274

Commission, Commission Communication on State aid elements in sales of land and buildings by public authorities, Official Journal C 209 10/07/1997 pp 3-5

Commission, Commissions Guidelines of 20 January 1993, entitled: "Policy Guidelines on Contracts awarded by Separate Units of a Contracting Entity under Directive 90/531/EEC ("Utilities")", document CC/92/87

Commission: Commission Staff Working Paper of 18 August 2004: Buying Green – A handbook on environmental public procurement, SEC/2004/ 1050

Danish Competition Authority: Guidelines from the Competition Authority: Social considerations in public procurement – guidelines into the possibilities for including social considerations in procurement procedures, 2004

Danish Competition Authority and the Environmental Protection Agency, Guidelines from the Competition Authority and the Environmental Protection Agency: Green Procurement – guidelines into the possibilities of taking environmental considerations into account in procurement procedures, 2002

Articles

Arnould, Joël, Secondary Policies in Public Procurement: The Innovations of the new Directives, 13 Public Procurement Law Review, issue 4, 2004, pp. 187ff.

Arrowsmith, Sue, The implications of the Court of Justice's decision in Marshall for damages in the field of public procurement. Public Procurement Law Review, issue 6, 1993.

Bibliography

Braun, Peter, A matter of Principle(S) – The Treatment of Contracts Falling Outside the Scope of the European. Public Procurement Directives, 9 Public Procurement Law Review, issue 1, 2000 pp. 39ff.

Brown, Adian, The impact of the new Procurement Directive on Large Public Infrastructure Projects: Competitive Dialogue or Better the Devil you know? 13 Public Procurement Law Review, issue 4, 2004 pp. 160ff.

Krüger, Kai, Ban-On-Negotiation in Tender Procedures: Undermining Best Value for Money? 13 Public Procurement, issue 4, 2004, pp. 397ff.

Pachnou, Despina, The Standards Required of National Review Systems under E.C. Law in the Context of the principle of Effectiveness. Public Procurement Law Review, issue 2, 2000, pp. 55 ff.

Treumer, Steen, Competitive dialogue. 13 Public Procurement Law Review, issue 4, 2004, pp. 178ff.

Table of Legislation

EU regulation:

EC Treaty, Treaty establishing the European Community

2004/17, Directive 2004/17/EC of the European Parliament and of the Council of 31 March 2004 coordinating the procurement procedures of entities operating in the water, energy, transport and postal services sectors

2004/18, Directive 2004/18/EC of the European Parliament and of the Council of 31 March 2004 on the coordination of procedures for the award of public works contracts, public supply contracts and public service contracts

76/207, Council Directive 76/207/EEC of 9 February 1976 on the implementation of the principle of equal treatment for men and women as regards access to employment, vocational training and promotion, and working conditions

77/62, Council Directive 77/62/EEC of 21 December 1976 coordinating procedures for the award of public supply contracts

89/665, Council Directive 89/665/EEC of 21 December 1989 on the coordination of the laws, regulations and administrative provisions relating to the application of review procedures to the award of public supply and public works contracts

92/13, Council Directive 92/13/EEC of 25 February 1992 coordinating the laws, regulations and administrative provisions relating to the application of Community rules on the procurement procedures of entities operating in the water, energy, transport and telecommunications sectors

92/50, Council Directive 92/50/EEC of 18 June 1992 relating to the coordination of procedures for the award of public service contracts

93/36, Council Directive 93/36/EEC of 14 June 1993 coordinating procedures for the award of public supply contracts

98/34, Directive 98/34/EC of the European Parliament and of the Council of 22 June 1998 laying down a procedure for the provision of information in the field of technical standards and regulations

2151/2003, Commission Regulation (EC) No 2151/2003 of 16 December 2003 amending Regulation (EC) No 2195/2002 of the European Parliament and of the Council of 5 November 2002 on the Common Procurement Vocabulary (CPV)

139/2004, Council Regulation (EC) No 139/2004 of 20 January 2004 on the control of concentrations between undertakings (the EC Merger Regulation)

Danish regulation:

Act No 274 of 22 December 1908 on claims for liability in tort

The constitutional act of Denmark of 5 June 1953

Act No 216 of 18 June 1966, the Tender Invitation Act

Act No 571 of 19 December 1985, Public administration act

Act No 572 of 19 December 1985 on Public Access to Information

Act No 378 of 14 June 1995 on local authorities and county authorities' performance of assignments for other public authorities

Consolidating act No 336 of 13 May 1997 on limiting debtors' possibilities of participating in public procurement   procedures

Act No 415 of 31 May 2000 on the Complaints Board for Public Procurement (as amended)

Act No 433 of 31 May 2000 to amend various provisions for the implementation of Act on Enforcement and Execution of Penalties, etc.

Act No 968 of 2 December 2003 as amended by Act No 439 of 9 June 2004 on the government of local authorities

Act No 338 of May 2005 on Tender Procedures for Public Work Contracts. It entered into force on September 2005 and replaces law number 450 of 7 June 2001 on tendering procedures for work contracts and governmental order number 595 of 9 July 2002.

Act No 1187 of 7 December 2005 on social service

Executive Order No 472 of 20 June 1991 on public procurement for sale of local authority real properties

Executive Order No 4 of 4 January 1993 on documents on public procurement agreements exempted from the right of access to documents pursuant to the Act on Public Access to Information

Executive Order No 602 of 26 June 2000 on the Complaints Board for Public Procurement

Executive Order No 331 of 24 May 2002 on documents on public procurement agreements exempted from the right of access to documents pursuant to the Act on Public Access to Information

Executive Order No 595 of 9 July 2002 on tender procedures for public work contracts

Executive Order No 649 of 30 July 2002 on the procedures for the award of public work contracts in the European Union

Executive Order No 650 of 30 July 2002 on the procedures for public supply in the European Union

Executive Order No 651 of 30 July 2002 on the procedures for the award of public service contracts in the European Union

Executive Order No 652 of 30 July 2002 on procurement of supply of water, energy, transport and telecommunication in the European Union

Executive Order No 937 of 16 September 2004 concerning the procedures for the award of public works contracts, public supply contracts and public service contracts

Danish Guidelines and Circulars:

Circular No 12011 of 22 December 1986 on sale of real property administered by the parochial church council

Circular No 158 of 13 December 2002 on sale of the states real properties

Circular No 159 of 17 December 2002 from the Ministry of Finance on the invitation to tender for Government works

Guideline No 9020 of 17 February 2003: Guidance on circular writing

Guideline No 60 of 28 June 2004 on public procurement for sale of local authority real properties

Table of Cases

Judgments of other Courts

Møve and Romsdal Fylges Local Authority vs. Andreassen Arkitektkontor A/S and Others. Judgment of the Norwegian Supreme Court of 30 May 2001. *411*

Judgments of the Danish Courts
(chronological according to the date of the judgment)

Judgment of the Supreme Court of 30 April 1985, Bredkjær Industri A/S vs. Hals Local Authority *411*

Judgment of the Eastern High Court of 18 December 1991, Thyges VVS represented by Thyge Andersen vs. Boligselskabet Fjordparken, branch 8, represented by KAB s.m.b.a. *411*

Judgment of the Eastern High Court of 30 May 1996, Kampsax Bridge Consortium and Others vs. A/S Storebæltsforbindelsen *398, 403, 404, 409, 410, 414*

Judgment of the Supreme Court of 1 July 1997, Investeringsselskabet af 11.02.1993 A/D vs. Gl. Skanderborg Ejendom *411*

Judgment of the Supreme Court of 17 April 2000, Jøni Container- og Vognfabrik ApS vs. Fårup Sommerland, Amusement Park *411*

Judgment of the Eastern High Court of 16 August 2000 (5th div) in Case B-1654-97 and others, Copenhagen Business School and Ministry of Research vs. Højgaard & Schultz A/S *355, 378*

Danish weekly law reports 2000.521H Dan Skoubo vs. Revisionsfirmaet Teddie Thulstrup A/S *414*

Danish weekly law reports 2000.1425V IBF Nord A/S og Frejlev Cementstøberi A/S vs. Aalborg Local Authority (Judgment of the Western High Court of 14 March 2000 in Case B-2766-96, IBF Nord A/S vs. Aalborg Local Authority) *39, 403, 411*

Judgment of the Western High Court of 3 May 2001 in Case B-1447-99, Humus/Genplast ApS vs. Den Selvejende Virksomhed Århus Renholdningsselskab *260*

Judgment of the Eastern High Court of 16 September 2002 (3rd div) in Case B-104-97, European Metro Group vs. Ørestadsselskabet Development Corporation *203, 262, 316, 402, 417*

Danish weekly law reports 2002.1180H Fredericia Local Authority vs. KKS Enterprise A/S in liquidation *403, 408, 409, 416*

Danish weekly law reports 2002.1297V Bent Mousten Vestergaard vs. Spøttrup Housing Boligselskab *61*

Judgment of the Western High Court of 16 March 2004 in the Cases B-2567-01 and B-1979-02, County of Århus vs. Judex A/S *398, 399, 405, 409, 411, 413*

Judgment of the Eastern High Court of 7 December 2004 (8th div) in Case B-156803, Lindpro A/S vs. Jørgen Mortensen & Sønner ApS *345*

Danish weekly law reports 2004.1294H Skjortegrossisten A/S vs. Post Danmark A/S *401, 405, 409, 410, 412*

Danish weekly law reports 2005.1799H, Judgment of the Supreme Court of 31 March 2005 (2nd div) in Case 428, European Metro Group vs. Ørestadsselskabet *316, 402, 405, 408, 410, 417*

Judgments of other Courts:

Orders of the Complaints Board for Public Procurement (alphabetical)

Orders of the Complaints Board for Public Procurement
(chronological according to the date of the order)

Table of Cases

Orders by the European Court of Justice and by the Court of First Instance (alphabetical)

Orders by the European Court of Justice and by the Court of First Instance (chronological, according to the case number)

Index

.